# CRIME AND PUNISHMENT

## THE COULSON TRANSLATION
## BACKGROUNDS AND SOURCES
## ESSAYS IN CRITICISM

⟶≫≪⟵

### THIRD EDITION

≫ A NORTON CRITICAL EDITION ≪

# FEODOR DOSTOEVSKY

# CRIME AND PUNISHMENT

### THIRD EDITION

## THE COULSON TRANSLATION
## BACKGROUNDS AND SOURCES
## ESSAYS IN CRITICISM

≫≪

*Edited by*

## GEORGE GIBIAN

CORNELL UNIVERSITY

≫ ≪

W · W · NORTON & COMPANY
NEW YORK · LONDON

Library of Congress Cataloging in Publication Data
Dostoyevsky, Fyodor, 1821–1881.
Crime and punishment.
(A Norton critical edition)
Translation of: Prestuplenie i nakazanie.
Bibliography: p. 693
I. Coulson, Jessie Senior, 1903–    . II. Gibian,
George. III. Title.
PG3326.P7   1989        891.73′3        88-25502

ISBN 0-393-95623-7

W. W. Norton & Company, Inc., 500 Fifth Avenue, New York, N.Y. 10110
W. W. Norton & Company Ltd., 10 Coptic Street, London, WC1A 1PU

*3 4 5 6 7 8 9 0*

# Contents

Preface to the Third Edition      vii

The Text of *Crime and Punishment*      1
  The Names of the Principal Characters      466

Backgrounds and Sources      467
  Map: The St. Petersburg of *Crime and Punishment*      468
  From Dostoevsky's Notebooks      470
  From Dostoevsky's Letters      476
    To A. A. Kraevsky (June 8, 1865)      476
    Draft, to M. N. Katkov (Sept., 1865)      476
    To A. E. Vrangel (Feb. 18, 1866)      478
    To M. N. Katkov (April 25, 1866)      478
    To A. V. Korvin-Krukovskaya (June 17, 1866)      479
  A Passage from an Early Draft      480

Essays in Criticism      483
  N. Strakhov · [The Nihilists and Raskolnikov's New Idea]      485
  Leo Tolstoy · [How Minute Changes of Consciousness
    Caused Raskolnikov to Commit Murder]      487
  Sergei V. Belov · The History of the Writing of the Novel      488
  Georgy Chulkov · [Dostoevsky's Technique of Writing]      494
  K. Mochulsky · [The Five Acts of *Crime and Punishment*]      500
  José Ortega y Gasset · [Why Dostoevsky Lives in the
    Twentieth Century]      512
  Ernest J. Simmons · The Art of *Crime and Punishment*      516
  George Gibian · Traditional Symbolism in *Crime
    and Punishment*      526
  Philip Rahv · Dostoevsky in *Crime and Punishment*      543
  Joseph Frank · The World of Raskolnikov      567
  Nicholas Berdyaev · [Dostoevsky, the Nature of Man,
    and Evil]      578
  Vyacheslav Ivanov · The Revolt Against Mother Earth      584
  Maurice Beebe · The Three Motives of Raskolnikov:
    A Reinterpretation of *Crime and Punishment*      592
  Karen Horney · [Raskolnikov's Self-Destructive "Should"]      603

Ralph E. Matlaw · Recurrent Imagery in *Crime
  and Punishment*                                                606
A. Bem · [The Problem of Guilt in Dostoevsky's Fiction]         609
Simon Karlinsky · Dostoevsky as Rorschach Test                 612
Alberto Moravia · The Marx-Dostoevsky Duel                     619
V. Pereverzev · [A Marxist Summing-Up of Dostoevsky]           623
U.S.S.R. Ministry of Culture · [The 1953 Outline for
  the Study of Dostoevsky in Soviet Universities]              624
U.S.S.R. Ministry of Culture · [The 1955 Outline for
  the Study of Dostoevsky in Soviet Universities]              626
U.S.S.R. Ministry of Culture · [The 1984 Outline for the
  Study of Dostoevsky in Soviet Universities]                  627
Leonid P. Grossman · [The Construction of the Novel]           628
Leonid P. Grossman · [Dostoevsky's Descriptions: The
  Characters and the City]                                     631
F. I. Evnin · [Plot Structure and Raskolnikov's
  Oscillations]                                                635
Mikhail Bakhtin · From Problems of Dostoevsky's Poetics        643
Michael Holquist · Puzzle and Mystery, the Narrative
  Poles of Knowing: *Crime and Punishment*                     656
Czeslaw Milosz · Dostoevsky and Western Intellectuals          670
Richard Weisberg · The Brilliant Reactor: The Inquisitor
  in *Crime and Punishment*                                    682
Michael T. Kaufman · Polish Director Finds Haunting
  Relevance in Dostoevsky                                      688

A Chronology of Dostoevsky's Life                              691

Selected Bibliography                                          693

# Preface to the Third Edition

The original Norton Critical Edition of *Crime and Punishment* (1964) and the Second Edition of 1975 were well received by readers and students. The editor and the translators are most grateful to the users of these editions over the past two decades. Since the last revision, however, important new critical and scholarly works have been published about Dostoevsky. Stimulating reinterpretations have made his works more relevant to the readers of the present time, and fresh scholarly discoveries have been made. The time has come to incorporate some of the work done in recent years in another, new edition.

The new articles included in this expanded edition are by authors from several countries. Outstanding among them, for example, is an essay by the Polish Nobel Prize winner, poet, scholar, and novelist Czeslaw Milosz, whose discussion of Dostoevsky contrasts American and European approaches to his works.

The writings of Mikhail Bakhtin, the Russian theoretician of culture, semiotician, and literary scholar, have become highly admired and very influential in the literary circles of Europe and the United States and have led to reevaluations of various classical authors. The present edition includes passages from Bakhtin's writings on Dostoevsky, in the new, excellent translation by Caryl Emerson. It also contains a section taken from an essay by Dostoevsky's great Russian contemporary, the novelist Leo Tolstoy. In 1890, Tolstoy wrote an introduction to a book on drunkenness by another Russian, P. S. Alexeev, a piece of truly vintage Tolstoy writing, which contains acute and very characteristic pages on *Crime and Punishment*. It illustrates at its most fascinating Tolstoy's approach to literature as a repository of moral and psychological lessons. Tolstoy's essay deserves to be far more widely known than it is in the English-speaking world.

The relevance of *Crime and Punishment* to modern men and women is discussed by Andrzej Wajda, the internationally known Polish film and theater director, as reported in the article by Michael T. Kaufman in the *New York Times*. Michael Holquist's provocative discussion of time and space in the narrative structure of *Crime and Punishment*, from his book *Dostoevsky and the Novel*, is also included. Richard Weisberg throws light on a little-known subject, the legal aspects of the action in *Crime and Punishment*, and on the actual methods of police criminal investigations in Tsarist Russia.

The critical essays, taken as a whole, are a selection of Russian (nineteenth-century, Soviet, emigré), American, Italian, Spanish,

Polish, and German criticism. A few are illustrative and representative (the syllabi from Moscow University courses showing the Soviet
attitude towards Dostoevsky in 1953 and 1955, and the Marxist
approach shown in Pereverzev's encyclopedia article), but the majority are chosen because they make outstanding contributions to the
interpretation, study, understanding, and appreciation of Dostoevsky's work. Many of the critical selections had never been translated
before their publication in the Norton Critical Edition.

The section of background materials offers aids to a twentieth-
century reader's understanding of the novel. Relevant extracts from
Dostoevsky's letters and notebooks from the period of composition
of *Crime and Punishment*, as well as a list of names of characters
with indications of stress and pronunciation, are included. Dostoevsky had the local geography firmly in mind; a map of Petersburg
enables one to follow Raskolnikov's and other characters' movements
in the city. Soviet sources and information supplied by Dostoevsky's
grandson, who lived in Leningrad and made a specialty of studying
Dostoevskian landmarks, have been used in preparing the map.

The translation of the novel by Jessie Coulson represents accurately, in contemporary English, Dostoevsky's nineteenth-century
Russian original. It distorts neither through modernization nor
through Victorianisms, and it is readable in its own right, instead
of sounding like a translation.

Some footnotes have been added to the text of the novel, based
on material in the handbook published in 1985 in Moscow by a
Soviet scholar who has devoted his life to tracking down the factual
background of Dostoevsky's life and work: S. V. Belov's *Roman F.
M. Dostoevskogo "Prestuplenie i Nakazanie": Kommentariy (Dostoevsky's Novel* Crime and Punishment: *A Commentary*). A passage
has also been included in the Criticism section of the present volume,
from the same book by Belov, in which he draws on perhaps the
most exciting contemporary Soviet Russian writer on Dostoevsky,
Yu. F. Karyakin. Belov, following the lead of Karyakin, stresses
themes in *Crime and Punishment* that may surprise Western readers
in a Soviet critic: spiritual and religious aspects.

The volume of Dostoevskian scholarship and criticism is vast. It
is difficult to find one's way within it; one looks for valuable studies
amidst the mass of derivative or mediocre writing. Some of the most
excellent articles and books, moreover, are to be found only in one
or two libraries in the United States. The language barrier excludes
many English-speaking readers from some of the European sources.
It is our hope that this translation and the critical studies and other
aids accompanying it will, for a wide range of readers interested in
Dostoevsky, open the door to various interpretations that scholars of
several countries have made of *Crime and Punishment* and lead them
to renewed consideration of Dostoevsky's classic.

GEORGE GIBIAN

# The Text of
# Crime and Punishment[†]

## Translated by Jessie Coulson

† This text is reprinted by permission of Oxford University Press.

A map of St. Petersburg in Dostoevsky's time, showing locations important in *Crime and Punishment*, will be found on pages 468–69.

# Part One

## CHAPTER I

TOWARDS the end of a sultry afternoon early in July a young man came out of his little room in Stolyarny Lane and turned slowly and somewhat irresolutely in the direction of Kamenny Bridge.[1]

He had been lucky enough to escape an encounter with his landlady on the stairs. His little room, more like a cupboard than a place to live in, was tucked away under the roof of the high five-storied building. The landlady, who let him the room and provided him with dinners and service, occupied a flat on the floor below, and every time he went out he was forced to pass the door of her kitchen, which nearly always stood wide open. He went past each time with an uneasy, almost frightened, feeling that made him frown with shame. He was heavily in debt to his landlady and shrank from meeting her.

It was not that he was a cowed or naturally timorous person, far from it; but he had been for some time in an almost morbid state of irritability and tension. He had cut himself off from everybody and withdrawn so completely into himself that he now shrank from every kind of contact. He was crushingly poor, but he no longer felt the oppression of his poverty. For some time he had ceased to concern himself with everyday affairs. He was not really afraid of any landlady, whatever plots he might think she was hatching against him, but to have to stop on the stairs and listen to all her chatter about trivialities in which he refused to take any interest, all her complaints, threats, and insistent demands for payment, and then to have to extricate himself, lying and making excuses—no, better to creep downstairs as softly as a cat and slip out unnoticed.

This time, however, he reached the street feeling astonished at the intensity of his fear of his landlady.

'To think that I can contemplate such a terrible act and yet be afraid of such trifles,' he thought, and he smiled strangely. 'Hm . . . yes . . . a man holds the fate of the world in his two hands, and yet, simply because he is afraid, he just lets things

1. For this and other locations, see the map of St. Petersburg. Raskolnikov lives in the slums, in a poor section of Petersburg near the Haymarket.

drift—that is a truism . . . I wonder what men are most afraid of . . . Any new departure, and especially a *new word*—that is what they fear most of all . . . But I am talking too much. That's why I don't act, because I am always talking. Or perhaps I talk so much just because I can't act. I have got into a habit of babbling to myself during this last month, while I have been lying in a corner for days on end, thinking . . . fantastic nonsense. And why have I come out now? Can I really be capable of *that*? Am I really serious? No, of course I'm not serious. So I am just amusing myself with fancies, children's games? Yes, perhaps I am only playing a game.'

The heat in the streets was stifling. The stuffiness, the jostling crowds, the bricks and mortar, scaffolding and dust everywhere, and that peculiar summer stench so familiar to everyone who cannot get away from St. Petersburg into the country, all combined to aggravate the disturbance of the young man's nerves. The intolerable reek from the public houses, so numerous in that part of the city, and the sight of the drunken men encountered at every turn, even though this was not a holiday, completed the mournfully repellent picture. An expression of the deepest loathing passed across the young man's delicate features. (He was, by the way, a strikingly handsome young man, with fine dark eyes, brown hair, and a slender well-knit figure, taller than the average.) Soon, however, he relapsed again into profound thought, or rather into a sort of abstraction, and continued on his way in complete and wilful unconsciousness of his surroundings. Once or twice he muttered something to himself in a manner that, as he had just confessed, had grown habitual with him. He himself realized that at times his thoughts were confused and that he was very weak; he had eaten practically nothing for two days.

He was so wretchedly dressed that anybody else, however used to them, might have hesitated to go out in daylight in such rags. It is true that it would have been difficult to attract attention by one's dress in this part of central St. Petersburg. In these streets and alleys near the Haymarket, with their numerous houses of ill fame and their swarming population of artisans and labourers, such queer figures sometimes appeared on the scene that even the oddest of them could hardly arouse any surprise. Besides, the young man's heart was so full of bitter scorn that, in spite of his often very youthful sensitiveness, wearing his rags in the street caused him no embarrassment. It would have been different had he come across any of his acquaintances or former friends, whom he wished in any case to avoid . . . All the same, when a drunken man, who was being carted off somewhere in an enormous dray drawn by an equally enormous cart-horse, suddenly yelled as he went by

'Hi, you in the German hat!'[2] and went on pointing at him and bawling at the top of his voice, the young man stopped dead and clutched feverishly at his hat. It was a high, round hat, which had come from Zimmermann's famous hat-shop,[3] but was now all rubbed and rusty with age, stained and full of slits; what remained of its battered brim was cocked up grotesquely at one side. But it was not shame but an entirely different emotion, more like terror, that had seized him.

'I knew it!' he muttered in confusion. 'I foresaw something like this, but this is worse than anything I thought of. A piece of stupidity like this, an insignificant trifle, might wreck the whole affair. Yes, the hat is too noticeable. It is ridiculous, and that means that it attracts attention. I must get a cap, any sort of old cap, to go with my rags, not this monstrosity. Nobody wears this sort of thing. It would be noticed a mile off, and remembered . . . that's the point: it would be remembered afterwards, and it would be evidence . . . I must be as inconspicuous as possible . . . Trifles are important! . . . Trifles like this can bring disaster.'

He had not far to go; he even knew how many paces it was from his own door—exactly seven hundred and thirty.[4] He had counted them once, when he had first begun to give his imagination free rein. At that time he did not believe in the reality of his imaginings, and their audacity, which both repelled and fascinated him at the same time, was merely irritating. Now, a month later, he saw them in a different light, and had somehow grown used to regarding the 'ugly' dream as a real project, although he still did not trust himself to carry it out, and reproached himself for his own weakness and lack of resolution. He was now engaged in *rehearsing* his project, and his agitation increased with every step he took.

With a fainting heart and shuddering nerves he approached an enormous building which fronted the canal on one side, and Sadovaya Street on the other. The building was split up into small tenements, which housed all kinds of tradespeople—tailors, locksmiths, cooks, various German craftsmen, prostitutes, clerks, and so on. People were hurrying in and out of its two gates and across its two courtyards. The building had three or four porters, and the young man thought himself lucky not to meet any of them as he slipped from the gate to the first staircase on the right. It was narrow and dark, but he already knew that, and the circumstance pleased him; in such ob-

2. All Western (i.e., not of native Russian style) clothes were popularly called German.

3. Zimmermann was an actual—and expensive—Petersburg hatmaker.

4. In most of his references to Petersburg streets and landmarks, Dostoevsky uses real names. The distance between the actually existing buildings which he had in mind, from Raskolnikov's room to the pawnbroker's, was indeed about 730 paces.

scurity there was no danger from prying eyes. 'If I feel so afraid at this moment, what would it be like if I had really brought myself to the point of doing *the thing itself*?' he thought involuntarily, as he came up to the fourth floor. Here his way was blocked by two porters, old soldiers, who were removing furniture from one of the flats. He knew that a German clerk lived here with his family. 'The German must be removing, and that means that the old woman's will be the only flat occupied on the fourth floor on this staircase, at any rate for some time. That's fine . . . in case I . . .' he thought, as he rang the old woman's bell. The bell tinkled feebly, as though it were made of tin, not copper. Small flats in that kind of house nearly all have such bells, but he had forgotten what it sounded like and its peculiar tinkle seemed to startle him, as if it brought back something to his memory with great clearness . . . He shuddered; evidently his nerves were too weak *this time*. After a short interval the door opened the merest crack, and a woman peered suspiciously out at her visitor; only her glittering little eyes were visible in the gloom. She seemed reassured, however, when she saw that there were several people on the landing, and opened the door wider. The young man stepped across the threshold into a dark hall divided by a partition from the tiny kitchen. The old woman stood silently before him, looking at him with a question in her eyes. She was a tiny dried-up scrap of a creature, about sixty years old, with sharp, malicious little eyes and a small sharp nose. She was bare-headed and her fair hair, just beginning to go grey, was thick with grease. A strip of flannel was twisted round her long thin neck, which was wrinkled and yellow like a hen's legs, and in spite of the heat a short jacket of worn fur, yellow with age, hung from her shoulders. She coughed and groaned continually. The young man must have been looking at her rather oddly, for distrust flashed into her eyes again.

Reminding himself that he must be as polite as possible, the young man made a hurried half-bow and muttered: 'Raskolnikov, a student. I was here a month ago.'

'I remember you were, my friend, I remember very well,' the old woman answered drily, still without taking her eyes from his face.

'Well . . . I've come again on the same business,' continued Raskolnikov, rather disconcerted by her suspicion. 'Perhaps, though,' he thought uneasily, 'she was always like this, only I didn't notice it before.'

The old woman remained silent, apparently still doubtful, and then stood aside and pointed to a door, saying, as she let her visitor pass: 'Go in, my friend.'

The little room the young man entered, with its faded wall-paper, geraniums, and muslin window-curtains, was bright with the rays of the setting sun. The unexpected thought crossed his mind: 'The sun will be shining *then*, too, just as it does now!' He glanced rapidly round the room, trying to fix its appearance as firmly in his mind as possible. There was nothing special about it. The old furniture, all of painted yellow wood, consisted of a sofa with a high curved wooden back, an oval table in front of it, a toilet-table with a small mirror between the windows, some chairs against the wall, and two or three cheap pictures in yellow frames, representing German young ladies with birds in their hands: that was all. In a corner a lamp was burning before a small icon. Everything was very clean; both furniture and floor were highly polished, and everything shone. 'Lizaveta's work,' thought the young man. There was not a speck of dust anywhere in the flat. 'How do nasty old widows contrive to have everything so clean?' he continued to himself, with his curious glance fixed on the print curtain hanging over the door into another tiny room. In this stood the old woman's bed and chest of drawers, and he had never contrived to see into it. The flat contained only these two rooms.

'What can I do for you?' inquired the old woman in a forbidding tone. She had followed him in and planted herself squarely in front of him, and was looking him in the face as before.

'I have brought something to pawn. Here,' and he drew from his pocket an old flat silver watch, with a globe engraved on the back and a steel guard.

'But it is time you redeemed your other pledge. The month was up two days ago.'

'I will pay you another month's interest. Please be patient.'

'I shall please myself, my friend, whether I am patient or sell your property now.'

'How much for the watch, Alëna Ivanovna?'

'It is not really worth anything; you bring me nothing but trash, my friend. Last time I lent you two roubles on a ring you could buy from a jeweller for a rouble and a half.'

'Let me have four roubles. I will redeem it; it was my father's. I am expecting some money soon.'

'A rouble and a half, interest in advance. Take it or leave it.'

'One and a half roubles!' exclaimed the young man.

'Just as you like.' And the old woman held out the watch to him. The young man took it, so angry that he was on the point of leaving at once; but he changed his mind, remembering that he had nowhere else to turn, and that he had had another object in coming.

'All right,' he said roughly.

The old woman felt in her pocket for her keys and went into the other room, behind the curtain. The young man, left alone, strained his ears and followed her movements in imagination.

He could hear her opening the chest of drawers. 'That will be the top drawer,' he fancied. 'I know she keeps the keys in her right-hand pocket . . . They are all in one bunch, on a steel ring . . . There is one with toothed wards, three times as big as the others; that can't belong to the drawer, of course. There must be something else, a chest or a trunk . . . I wonder if there is. Those big wooden trunks always have that kind of key . . . All the same, how sickening all this is! . . .'

The old woman returned.

'Now, my friend, ten copecks per rouble per month makes fifteen copecks from you for a rouble and a half for one month, in advance. Then there are twenty copecks due for the two roubles I lent you before at the same rate. Thirty-five altogether. That makes one rouble fifteen copecks for the watch. Here you are.'

'What? So now it's one rouble fifteen copecks?'

'Quite correct.'

The young man did not argue but took the money. He was in no hurry to leave and stood there looking at the old woman as if he wanted to say or do something more, but did not know exactly what.

'Perhaps, Alëna Ivanovna, I will bring you something else in a day or two . . . It's silver . . . valuable . . . a cigarette-case . . . I have to get it back from a friend . . .' He faltered and stopped.

'Time enough to talk about it then, my friend.'

'Good night. . . . You always seem to be alone in the place; isn't your sister here?' he asked as carelessly as he could, as he went into the hall.

'And what do you want with her, my friend?'

'Nothing in particular. I only asked. But you . . . Good-bye, Alëna Ivanovna.'

Raskolnikov went out in great confusion. The confusion grew and grew, and on his way downstairs he stopped more than once as if suddenly struck by something or other. When at last he reached the street, he broke out:

'Oh God, how repulsive! Can I possibly, can I possibly . . . no, that's nonsense, it's ridiculous!' he broke off decisively. 'How could such a horrible idea enter my mind? What vileness my heart seems capable of! The point is, that it is vile, filthy, horrible, horrible! . . . And for a whole month I have . . .'

But words and exclamations were not a sufficient outlet for his agitation. The feeling of infinite loathing that had begun to burden and torment him while he was on his way to the old woman's had now reached such a pitch that he did not know what to do with himself in his anguish. He walked along the pavement like a drunken man, not seeing the passers by and sometimes bumping into them. He had left that street behind before he succeeded in collecting his wits. He looked round and saw that he was standing outside a public house, whose entrance led down several steps from the street into a basement. Two tipsy men were at that moment emerging, supporting each other and swearing as they staggered up into the street. Raskolnikov hesitated only for a moment and then went down the steps. He had never set foot in such a place before, but now his head was swimming and his throat was parched. He felt a need for cold beer, especially as he now attributed his sudden weakness to having had nothing to eat. He sat down in a dark and dirty corner behind a small sticky table, ordered his beer, and drank the first glass thirstily. He began to feel better at once, and his thoughts grew clearer. 'This is all nonsense,' he said to himself hopefully, 'and there was no need to get so agitated. It was simply physical weakness. One glass of beer and a rusk and my mind grows keen, my thoughts clear, my resolution firm. Bah, how paltry it all is!' But in spite of the scorn with which he spat out these words, his outlook had grown cheerful, as if he had been suddenly freed from a terrible burden, and he cast friendly glances at the other people in the room. Even at this moment he dimly perceived, however, that there was something morbid in his sudden recovery of spirits.

Few people now remained in the place. Besides the two tipsy men he had met on the stairs, a party of four or five men and a woman, with an accordion, had also gone out. After they left the place seemed quiet and empty. There remained a man who looked like a small tradesman, drunk, but not very, sitting over his beer; his companion, a huge fat man with a grey beard, wearing a long Siberian tunic, was very drunk and sat dozing on a bench. Every now and then, half waking up, he would suddenly begin to snap his fingers, throw his arms wide and jerk the top part of his body about, without getting up from his bench. Meanwhile he would drone out the half-forgotten words of some rubbishy song, something like:

> For a whole year I loved my wife,
> For a who-o-ole yea-ear I lo-o-oved my wife . . .

or:

> As I was walking down the street
> My old lost love I chanced to meet . . .

But there was nobody to share his jollity. His friend watched all these outbursts silently and with a hostile and suspicious expression.

There was one other man, who looked like a retired Government clerk, sitting apart with his bottle of vodka, taking a drink from time to time, and gazing round. He, too, seemed to be in rather a disturbed state of mind.

## CHAPTER II

RASKOLNIKOV was not used to crowds and, as we have said, had lately avoided all social contacts, but now he suddenly felt drawn to people. Something as it were new had been accomplished in his soul, and with it had come a thirst for society. He was so weary after a whole month of concentrated misery and gloomy agitation that he longed to breathe, if only for a moment, the air of some other world, and so, in spite of the filthy surroundings, he took pleasure in this visit to the public house.

The master of the establishment was in another room, but he often came into the main room by way of a flight of steps, so that the first parts of him to appear were his smart well-greased boots with their wide red tops. He wore a long Russian tunic, a black satin waistcoat horribly smeared with grease, and no neck-cloth; his face looked as if it had been smeared all over with grease, like an iron lock. There was a lad of about fourteen behind the bar and another, younger, who waited on the customers. On the bar were sliced cucumbers, rusks of black bread, and fish cut into small pieces, all very evil-smelling. The atmosphere was unbearably stuffy and so saturated with alcohol that it almost seemed that five minutes in it would be enough to make one drunk.

It sometimes happens that we find ourselves interested from the first glance in complete strangers, even before we have spoken to them. The customer who was sitting apart, and who looked like a retired clerk, made just such an impression on Raskolnikov. Later the young man more than once recalled this first impression and put it down to a prophetic insight. He kept his eyes fixed on the man, partly because the stranger gazed at him equally steadily and plainly wished to enter into conversation with him. The others present, including the landlord, he regarded with the boredom of long habit and with a shade of lofty disdain, as if he considered them too much his inferiors in rank and education to speak to. He was a man of over fifty, of middle height and corpulent build, with grizzled hair and a large bald patch. His face was bloated with continual drinking and his complexion was yellow, even greenish. From between his swollen eyelids his little reddish slits of eyes glittered with animation. But there was something very strange about him; his eyes had an almost rapturous shine, they seemed to hold both intelligence and good sense, but gleams of something like madness showed in them as well. His old black frock-coat was terribly frayed and had lost all but one button, but this, with evident regard for the proprieties, he kept carefully fastened. A crumpled, stained, and dirty shirt-front protruded from under his nankeen waistcoat. The thick grey stubble on his cheeks and chin, once clean-shaven in civil-service style, revealed that it was some time since they had known a razor. His bearing, too, was solidly official. But he seemed disturbed, his hair was ruffled, and from time to time, propping his ragged elbows on the stained and sticky table, he leaned his head on his hands in utter dejection. At length he looked straight at Raskolnikov and addressed him in a loud and decided tone:

'My dear sir, will you allow me to address some words of seemly conversation to you? For, although you bear no outward evidence of distinction, my experience discerns in you a man of education and one unaccustomed to potations. I have always held education, coupled with sincerity of feeling, in the highest respect, and indeed I am myself a Titular Councillor.[5] Marmeladov is my name, sir, Titular Councillor. May I take the liberty of asking if you are in the Service?'

'No, I am studying . . .' replied the young man, surprised partly at being so directly addressed and partly by the other's peculiarly florid manner of speech. In spite of his recent momentary wish for contact, of whatever kind, with other people, no sooner was a word actually spoken to him than he experienced the old unpleasant feeling of exasperated dislike for any person who violated, or even seemed desirous of disturbing, his privacy.

'A student, then, or a former student,' cried the clerk; 'I thought so! Experience, my dear sir, experience!' and he laid his finger to his forehead in self-congratulation. 'You have been a student, or you have moved in academic circles! But permit me . . .' He rose, wavering a little, took his bottle and glass and sat down close to the young man and a little to one side. Although he was drunk, he spoke glibly and fluently, only occasionally hesitating and losing the thread. The avidity with which he seized upon Raskolnikov was such that it almost seemed as though he too had spoken to nobody for a month.

'My dear sir,' he began almost portentously, 'it is a true saying that poverty is no crime. And even less, as I well know, is drunkenness a virtue. But beggary, my dear sir, beggary is a vice. In poverty, the inborn honourable sentiments may still be preserved, but never in beggary—not by anybody. In beggary, a man is not driven forth from human society with a cudgel, but, to make his condition more humiliating, is swept away with a broom—and with justice, for as a beggar I am

5. In the Russian Civil Service, a "Table of Ranks" governed the titles, uniforms, and ranks. "Titular Councillor" is a rather low rank—the ninth of fourteen, corresponding to that of a captain in the army.

the first to humiliate myself; hence the public house. My dear sir, a month ago Mr. Lebezyatnikov gave my wife a terrible beating, and my wife, you must understand, is not at all the same thing as myself. May I be allowed to ask you, even though it has the appearance of simple curiosity, whether you have ever passed the night on a hay barge on the Neva?'

'No, as it happens, I haven't,' answered Raskolnikov. 'Why do you ask?'

'Well, sir, I come from spending five nights there . . .'

He filled his glass, drank it off, and sat deep in thought. There were, in fact, wisps of hay clinging to his clothing and even in his hair. It was easy to believe that he had neither undressed nor washed for five days. His greasy red hands were particularly dirty, with black-rimmed nails.

His talk seemed to have attracted general, though languid, interest. The lads behind the bar began to snigger. The landlord seemed to have come down from the upper room on purpose to listen to the 'comic turn', and sat in dignified aloofness, yawning lazily. It was plain that Marmeladov was well known in this place. Even his florid way of speaking appeared to derive from his constant habit of talking to strangers of all kinds in public houses. This habit becomes a necessity to some drunkards, especially if they are harshly used and domineered over at home. Then in the company of other drinkers they strive to justify themselves and even, if they can, to inspire respect.

'A regular comic!' said the host loudly. 'Why don't you do some work? If you are in the civil service, why don't you perform your duties?'

'Why don't I perform my duties, my dear sir?' retorted Marmeladov, addressing himself exclusively to Raskolnikov, as if it were he who had put the question, '—why don't I perform my duties? Does not my heart bleed because I am an abject and useless creature? Did I not suffer when, a month ago, Mr. Lebezyatnikov beat my wife with his own hands while I lay fuddled with drink? Allow me to ask, young man, if you have known what it is to . . . hm . . . well, to plead without hope for a loan?'

'Yes, I have . . . but what do you mean by "without hope"?'

'I mean utterly without hope, sir, knowing beforehand that nothing will come of it. For instance, you know quite definitely, beforehand, that this person, this most right-minded and useful citizen, will not in any circumstances give you the money. And why, indeed, I ask, should he give me it, when he knows that I shall not repay it? Out of compassion? But recently

Mr. Lebezyatnikov, who is a follower of the latest ideas,[6] was explaining that in this age the sentiment of compassion is actually prohibited by science, and that that is how they order things in England, where they have political economy. Why, then, I ask, should he give you it? Nevertheless, knowing in advance that he will give you nothing, you turn your steps towards him and . . .'

'But then why go?' put in Raskolnikov.

'But if you have nobody else, no other place, to turn to! Every man must needs have somewhere to turn to. For there comes a time when it is absolutely essential to turn somewhere. The first time my only daughter went on the streets I too went . . . (for my daughter is a street-walker, sir),' he added parenthetically, regarding the young man somewhat uneasily. 'It is nothing, my dear sir, it doesn't matter,' he hastily, but with apparent tranquillity, declared, when the two lads at the bar burst out laughing and even the host himself smiled. 'It matters nothing, sir. This wagging of heads does not discountenance me, for all these things are already known to everybody and all secrets are revealed; and I bear myself in this matter with humility, not with scorn. Suffer them, suffer them! "Behold the man!" Allow me to ask, young man, can you . . .? Or no, let me express it with greater force and exactness: not *can* you, but *dare* you, looking upon me at this moment, say with conviction that I am not a swine?'

The young man made no answer.

'Well, sir,' continued the orator sedately and with even greater dignity waiting for the sniggering to die down again, 'well sir, grant that I am a swine, but she is a lady! I have the form of a beast, but Katerina Ivanovna, the partner of my life, is an educated person and by birth the daughter of a staff officer. Grant that I am an infamous wretch, but she is a creature of lofty mind, filled with sentiments ennobled by education. And yet . . . oh, if only she showed some sympathy for me! My dear sir, my dear sir, it is necessary for every man to have one place, if only one, where he can find sympathy. But Katerina Ivanovna, although she is a great-souled lady, is unjust . . . And although I fully understand that when she pulls me by the hair it is only out of compassion (for, I repeat without embarrassment, she does pull me by the hair, young man),' he affirmed with enhanced dignity, when he heard the sniggers break out again, 'but, Oh God, if she would only, just once . . . But no, no! it is all in vain, it is useless to talk! Useless to talk!

6. In this passage and in other places, ideas attributed to Lebezyatnikov (and Luzhin) are paraphrases, and sometimes oversimplifications and exaggerations, of English Utilitarian and Positivist views. John Stuart Mill's *Principles of Political Economy* were published in Petersburg in translation in 1865.

. . . for, more than once before, my wish has been granted, and more than once she has taken pity on me, but . . . but— such is my character, I am a beast by nature!'

'I should think so!' yawned the landlord.

Marmeladov emphatically banged his fist on the table.

'Yes, such is my character! Do you know, do you know, sir, that I have drunk her very stockings? Not her shoes, for that might have some small resemblance to a natural action, but her stockings, I have drunk even her stockings, sir! And I have drunk her mohair shawl as well, and it was her own, a gift made to her in the old days, not mine; and the room where we live is cold, and this winter she caught a chill and began to cough and even to spit blood. We have three small children and Katerina Ivanovna is working from morning till night, scrubbing and washing and bathing the children, for she has been accustomed to cleanliness from a child; but her chest is weak and she has a consumptive tendency, and I feel it. Could I fail to feel it? The more I drink, the more deeply I feel it. That indeed is why I drink, to find compassion and feeling in drink . . . I drink because I wish to multiply my sufferings!' And in apparent despair he laid his head on the table.

'Young man,' he continued, raising himself again, 'I read a certain affliction in your features. I saw it as soon as you entered, and for that reason I addressed myself to you. For when I confide the story of my life to you, it is not in order to expose my shame to these idlers here, who know it already, but because I seek the company of a man of feeling and education. You must know that my wife was educated in a provincial Imperial Academy for the daughters of gentlemen; on leaving she performed a shawl dance[7] before the Governor and other distinguished persons, for which she was presented with a gold medal and a certificate of merit. The medal . . . well, the medal was sold long ago . . . hm, but she has the certificate in her trunk to this day, and she was displaying it to our landlady quite recently. Although there is the most unremitting hostility between the landlady and herself, she needed somebody to show off to a little, and to tell of the vanished happy days. And I do not judge her, I do not judge her, for these things are cherished in her memory, and everything besides is gone with the wind! Yes, yes, she is a lady of passionate, proud, and inflexible character. She washes the floor with her own hands, she eats the bread of affliction, but she will not brook disrespect. For that reason she refused to tolerate Mr. Lebezyatnikov's incivility, and when Mr. Lebezyatnikov beat her for it and she took to her bed, it was not so much from her physical injuries as from wounded feelings. She was a widow when I

7. The shawl dance was associated with upper class young ladies, especially those educated in socially desirable finishing schools.

married her, with three children—small, smaller, and smallest. She married her first husband, an infantry officer, for love, and she ran away from home with him. She loved him immoderately, but he fell into gambling habits, was brought into court, and died of it. He began to beat her towards the end, and although, as I know for a fact, from written evidence, she repaid him in kind, yet she remembers him to this day with tears, and uses him to reproach me with—and I am glad, I am glad, for even if it is only her imagination, she thinks of herself as having been happy once . . . And she was left with three young children in a wild and remote part of the provinces, where I happened to be at the time. She was left in such hopeless destitution that, with all my wide and varied experience, I lack words to describe it. All her family had renounced her. Besides, she was proud, proud to excess . . . And it was then, my dear sir, then that I, who was myself a widower with a fourteen-year-old daughter, offered her my hand, for I could not bear to see such suffering. And from the fact that she, an educated and well-bred person bearing a well-known name, consented to marry me, you may judge the extent of her affliction. But she did marry me! Weeping and sobbing and wringing her hands, she married me! For she had nobody to turn to! Do you understand, young man, do you understand what it means to have nowhere left to turn to? No, you do not understand that yet . . . And for a whole year I religiously fulfilled my sacred obligations and never touched this' (he poked at the bottle with his finger), 'for I am not without feeling. But I could not please her, even by that; and then I lost my situation, not through any fault of mine but through reorganization in the Service, and then I did touch it! . . . It must be a year and a half since, after all our wanderings and numerous disasters, we finally found ourselves in this magnificent capital city, adorned with so many monuments. And here I found a situation . . . Found it, and lost it again. Do you understand, sir? Here it was by my own fault that I lost it, for my characteristic failing had reasserted itself . . . Now we are living in a corner at Amalia Fëdorovna Lippewechsel's, though what we live on and how we pay the rent I do not know. There are many other people living there besides ourselves . . . It is an absolute bear-garden, sir, most disgraceful . . . hm . . . yes . . . And meanwhile my little daughter by my first wife has grown up, and what she has borne, poor child, from her stepmother while she was growing up I will not speak of. For although Katerina Ivanovna is full of generous sentiments, she is a hasty, irritable, and sharp-tongued lady . . . Yes, sir. Well, it does no good to talk of that! Sonya, as you may well imagine, has had no education. About four years ago I tried to study geography and the history of the world with her, but as my own knowledge was limited and we had no suitable textbooks, while the few poor books we did possess . . . hm . . . well, we no longer have even them now, and so that was the end of our studies. We stopped at Cyrus the Persian.[8] Later, after she grew up, she read a few novels, and not long since, through the kindness of Mr. Lebezyatnikov she read with great interest a little book, Lewes's *Physiology*[9]—perhaps you know it, sir?—, and even read parts of it aloud to us; and that is the sum total of her education. And now, my very dear sir, I wish to put to you a confidential question on my own account: do you think that a poor but honourable girl can earn much by honest labour? . . . She cannot earn fifteen copecks a day, sir, if she is honest and without special talents, even though her hands are never still for a moment. And even so, State Councillor Ivan Ivanovich Klopstock—perhaps you may have heard of him?—not only has not paid her to this day for making half a dozen fine linen shirts, but even shouted at her and drove her from the house, stamping and calling her abusive names, on the pretext that the collars were the wrong size and set in crooked. And here were the children hungry. . . . And here was Katerina Ivanovna walking up and down the room, wringing her hands, with a red flush in her cheeks, as there always is in her disease: "Here you are," she says, "living with us, eating and drinking and keeping warm, you lazy good-for-nothing"— though what is there to eat and drink when even the little ones haven't seen a crust for three days? . . . At the time I was lying . . . well, why make any bones about it? . . . I was tipsy, and I heard my Sonya saying (she is meek and her voice is so soft and gentle . . . she is fair, and her little face is always thin and pale)—saying: "Oh, Katerina Ivanovna, must I really come to that?" I must tell you that Darya Franzovna, a woman well known to the police, had tried two or three times to approach her through the landlady, with evil intentions. "Why not?" answered Katerina Ivanovna mockingly; "what is there to preserve so carefully? What a treasure!" But don't blame her, don't blame her, my dear sir, don't blame her! It was said in distraction, when she was ill and wrought up, and the children were crying with hunger, and besides it was said more to hurt her feelings than with any exact intention . . . For Katerina Ivanovna's disposition is like that, and if the children cry, even if it is with hunger, she lashes out at them at once. And towards six o'clock I saw my little Sonya get up and put on her kerchief and her pelisse and go out, and at some time after eight she

---

8. Cyrus, a Persian ruler in the sixth century B.C., would naturally be studied very early in a world history course, at the beginnings of ancient history.
9. George Lewes (1817–78), an English author, wrote *The Physiology of Everyday Life* (translated into Russian in 1861), which was very popular with progressives in Russia. He was influenced by the French positivist Auguste Comte.

came back. She came in and went straight to Katerina Ivanovna and laid thirty silver roubles on the table in front of her without a word. She looked at her, but she did not utter a single word, only took our big green woollen shawl (we have one which serves for all of us), wrapped it round her head and face and lay down on the bed, with her face to the wall, and her little shoulders and her whole body were trembling . . . And I was still lying there, in the same state . . . And then, young man, then I saw Katerina Ivanovna, also without a word, go to my little Sonya's bed-side, and she stayed there on her knees all the evening, kissing her feet, and would not get up, and then they both fell asleep with their arms round one another . . . both of them . . . both of them . . . yes, sir, and I . . . lay there tipsy.'

Marmeladov was silent, as though his voice failed him. Then he hastily filled his glass, drank it, and cleared his throat.

'From that time, sir,' he continued after a short silence, 'from that time, because of one unfortunate happening and because of information laid by persons of ill will (among whom Darya Franzovna was the most prominent, apparently because she thought she had not been treated with proper consideration), from that time my daughter, Sonya Semënovna, has had to carry a prostitute's yellow card,¹ and for that reason could not go on living with us. For the landlady, Amalia Fëdorovna, would not allow it (although, before, she herself had abetted Darya Franzovna), and besides, Mr. Lebezyatnikov . . . hm . . . Indeed, it was on Sonya's account that there was all that trouble between him and Katerina Ivanovna. At first he had tried to win my little Sonya's favours himself, and then suddenly he got up on his high horse: "What?" says he, "am I, a man of culture, to live in the same flat with a creature of that kind?" Katerina Ivanovna would not allow this and intervened . . . and it developed into . . . And now when Sonya comes to see us it is usually after dark; she comforts Katerina Ivanovna and brings what money she can . . . She is living now in the flat of Kapernaumov, the tailor; she rents a room from them. Kapernaumov is lame and has an impediment in his speech, and all his many children have the same impediment. So has his wife . . . They all live in one room, but Sonya's is partitioned off . . . Hm . . . yes . . . They are very poor people, and they all stammer . . . yes . . . Well, then I got up in the morning, sir, and put on my rags; I raised my hands to heaven and went to His Excellency Ivan Afanasyevich. Do you know His Excellency Ivan Afanasyevich? No? Then you do not know one of God's saints. He is—wax . . . wax before the face of the Lord; melting as wax! . . . There were even tears in his eyes, when he had kindly listened to all my story. "Well,

1. Prostitutes in Russia were registered with the police and required to carry yellow identity cards.

Marmeladov," he said, "you disappointed my expectations once before . . . I will take you once more on my own personal responsibility," that's what he said; "remember that," says he, "and now go!" I kissed the dust at his feet—in thought, for he would not have allowed it in fact, being a high official, an enlightened man, and a believer in advanced political ideas; I returned home and when I announced that I was again a member of the Service, and should receive a salary, what excitement there was! . . .'

Marmeladov stopped again in violent agitation. At this moment a whole party of merry-makers, who had already had too much to drink, came in and from near the door came the sound of a barrel-organ and the cracked childish voice of a seven-year-old singing *The Little Hut*.[2] There was a lot of noise. The landlord and his assistants were busy with the new-comers. Marmeladov resumed his story without paying any attention to them. He was apparently very much 'under the influence', but the drunker he got, the more voluble he became. The recollection of his recent successful application for re-instatement had restored his spirits and the reflection of his satisfaction shone in his face. Raskolnikov was listening attentively.

'This, sir, happened five weeks ago. Yes . . . As soon as they, Katerina Ivanovna and my little Sonya, heard of it, Lord! it was like being transported to Heaven. Before, it was nothing but abuse: lie there like a pig! But now, they walked on tiptoe, hushed the children: "Semën Zakharovich has been working and is tired; now he is resting. Sh!" They brought me coffee with scalded cream in it, before I went to work. We began to have real cream, think of that! And how they scraped together the money for a decent outfit, eleven and a half roubles, I can't imagine. Boots, calico shirt-fronts, the most magnificent uniform,[3] all got up in capital style, for eleven roubles and a half. I came home from work the first day and found that Katerina Ivanovna had made a two-course dinner,—soup and salt beef with horse-radish—a thing we had never even dreamed of before. She didn't possess any dresses, not one, sir, yet she looked as if she were dressed for a party, and it wasn't as if she had had anything to do it with, but she had managed it out of nothing: she had done her hair, found a clean collar of some sort, and cuffs, and she looked quite a different person, alto-gether younger and prettier. My little Sonya, my darling, had only helped with money, "but," she said, "for the time being it is better for me not to come and see you too often myself. Perhaps after dark, so that nobody will see me." Do you hear that, do you hear it? After dinner I took a nap, and what do

2. A popular song, to lyrics by the poet A. V. Koltsov.    3. Russian civil servants wore uniforms, with distinguishing signs of their rank.

you think? Katerina Ivanovna had broken off completely with our landlady, Amalia Fëdorovna, a week before, they had had a terrible quarrel, and yet now she invited her in for coffee. They sat whispering together for two hours. "Semën Zakharovich is in the Service now," says she, "and drawing a salary. He went out to see His Excellency, and His Excellency himself came out to see him, told all the others to wait, took Semën Zakharovich by the hand, and led him past them all into his study." Do you hear that, do you hear? "Of course, Semën Zakharovich," he said, "remembering your services, and although you are given to that irresponsible weakness, yet since you now give me your promise, and especially since things have gone badly here without you" (listen, listen!), "I put my trust now," he said, "in your honourable word." And I tell you, she had just that moment made it up, not out of flightiness or for the sake of boasting. No, sir, I swear she believed it all herself; it was all her own imagination, but she gloried in it. And I do not condemn her; no, I do not condemn her for that. . . . Six days ago, when I took home my first salary, twenty-three roubles and forty copecks, she called me her poppet: "What a poppet you are!" she said. This was in private, you understand. Well, I suppose I'm not remarkable for beauty, and I'm a poor sort of a husband. But she pinched my cheek: "What a poppet you are!" she said.'

Marmeladov stopped and tried to smile, but his chin began to quiver. He controlled himself, however. This tavern, his look of debauchery, the five nights spent in a hay-barge, the bottle, combined with his painful affection for his wife and family, bewildered his hearer. Raskolnikov was listening with close attention, yet with a feeling of discomfort. He felt vexed that he had come here.

'Oh, dear sir, dear sir!' exclaimed Marmeladov, recovering himself, 'oh, dear sir, perhaps all this seems ludicrous to you, as it does to these others, perhaps I am only worrying you with all these stupid and pitiful details of my domestic life, but it is not ludicrous to me! For I am capable of feeling it all . . . I spent the remainder of that heavenly afternoon, and all the evening, in fleeting dreams, of how I would reconstruct our life, get clothes for the children, give her tranquillity and restore my only daughter from dishonour to the bosom of her family . . . And many, many things besides. It was pardonable, sir. Well, my dear sir' (here Marmeladov gave a sort of shudder, raised his head, and gazed steadily at his hearer), 'well, sir, the very next day after all this dreaming (that is, exactly five days ago), in the evening, by a cunning trick, I stole the key of her box from Katerina Ivanovna and took out all that was left of the money I had brought her, how much I don't remember exactly, and now look at me, all of you! This is my fifth day away from home, and they are looking for me there, my employment is gone, and my uniform is in a pot-house near the Egyptian Bridge, where I exchanged it for these clothes . . . all is over!'

Marmeladov struck his forehead with his fist, clenched his teeth, closed his eyes and leant his elbow heavily on the table. But after a minute his face changed suddenly, and he looked at Raskolnikov with an assumption of slyness and artificial bravado, laughed, and went on: 'I went to see Sonya this morning and asked her for money to get something for my thick head. He-he-he!'

'She didn't give it you, did she?' shouted one of the new-comers, and roared with laughter.

'This very bottle, sir, was bought with her money,' announced Marmeladov, still addressing himself exclusively to Raskolnikov. 'Thirty copecks she gave me with her own hands, her last, all she had, as I saw for myself . . . She said nothing, she only looked at me in silence . . . A look like that does not belong to this world, but there . . . where they grieve over mankind, they weep for them, but they do not reproach them, they do not reproach! . . . but it hurts more, when there are no reproaches! . . . Thirty copecks, yes, sir. And surely she needs them herself now, eh? What do you think, my dear sir? Now she must take care to be always neat and clean. And that neatness, that special cleanness, costs money, you understand. Do you understand? Then she must buy rouge as well, it's absolutely essential; starched petticoats, coquettish little boots to set off her little foot when she has to step across a puddle. Do you understand, do you understand, sir, what that smartness means? Well, sir, and I, her own father, took those thirty copecks of hers for drink! And I am drinking it, sir! I have already drunk it all! . . . Now, who could be sorry for a wretch like me, eh? Are you sorry for me now, sir, or not? Tell me, sir, are you sorry or aren't you? He-he-he-he!'

He tried to pour himself another drink, but there was no more. The bottle was empty.

'Why should anyone be sorry for you?' cried the landlord, who happened to be near them again.

There was an outburst of laughter, and some cursing. It came partly from those who had been listening, and the others, who had not listened, laughed and cursed at the mere sight of the dismissed clerk.

'Sorry! Why be sorry for me?' exclaimed Marmeladov, positively inspired, as if he had been waiting for just those words, and rising to his feet with outstretched arms, 'Why be sorry, you say? No, there is no need to be sorry for me! I ought to be crucified, crucified, not pitied! Crucify, oh judge, crucify me, but pity your victim! Then I will come to you to be crucified, for I thirst for affliction and weeping, not for merriment! . . . Do you think, you who sold it, that this bottle of yours has been sweet to me? Affliction, I sought affliction at the bottom of it, tears and affliction, and I found them, I tasted them. But He will pity us, He who pitied all men and understood all men and all things, He alone is the judge. In that day He shall come and ask: "Where is the daughter who gave herself for a harsh and consumptive stepmother and the little children of another? Where is the daughter who showed compassion to that filthy drunkard, her earthly father, and did not shrink from his beastliness?" And He will say: "Come unto Me! I have already forgiven thee . . . I have forgiven thee . . . Thy sins, which are many, are forgiven, for thou didst love much . . ." And He will forgive my Sonya, He will forgive her; I know that He will forgive . . . When I was with her, a short time ago, I felt it in my heart . . . And He shall judge all men, and forgive them, the good and the evil, the wise and the humble . . . And when He has done with all men, then shall he summon us also: "Come forth," He will say "ye also, ye drunkards, ye weaklings, ye infamous, come forth!" And we shall come forth without shame and stand before Him. And He will say: "Ye are swine! ye are made in the image of the beast and bear his mark; yet come ye also unto Me!" And the wise and learned shall say: "Lord, why dost Thou receive these?" And He shall say: "I receive them, oh ye wise men, I receive them, oh ye learned ones, inasmuch as not one of these has deemed himself worthy . . ." And He will stretch out His arms to us, and we shall fall at His feet and weep, and we shall understand all things. Then we shall understand . . . and all shall understand . . . and Katerina Ivanovna, she shall understand also . . . Lord, Thy kingdom come!'

And he sank back on the bench, weak and exhausted, not looking at anyone, as though he were plunged in thought and had forgotten his surroundings. His words had made some impression; silence reigned for a short time, and then laughter and curses broke out again.

'There spoke the great intellect!'

'A lot of rubbish!'

'There's a civil servant for you!'—and so on, and so on.

'Let us go, sir,' said Marmeladov suddenly raising his head and turning to Raskolnikov, 'take me home . . . Kozel's house, at the back. It is time I went . . . to Katerina Ivanovna.'

Raskolnikov had long wished to leave, and had already made up his mind to help him. Marmeladov proved to be much more affected in his legs than in his speech, and leaned heavily on the young man. They had some two or three hundred yards to go. The drunkard's agitation and apprehension grew steadily greater as they neared the house.

'I am not afraid of Katerina Ivanovna now,' he muttered anxiously, 'nor of her pulling me by the hair. What does my hair matter?—my hair is nothing! That is what I say. It will be better, indeed, if she does pull my hair, I am not afraid of that . . . I . . . it is her eyes I am afraid of . . . yes . . . her eyes. I am afraid of the red patches on her cheeks, . . . and her breathing. Have you seen how people with her disease breathe . . . when they are upset? I am afraid of the children's crying, too . . . Because, unless Sonya has given them food, then . . . I don't know what, I don't know! But I am not afraid of blows . . . You must know, sir, that such blows not only do not distress me, but they give me pleasure . . . For I cannot do without them. It is better to have them. Let her beat me, it will relieve her feelings . . . it is better so . . . But here is the house, the house of Kozel the locksmith, the German, the rich man . . . Take me in!'

They entered from the yard and went up to the fourth floor. The higher they went, the darker grew the staircase. It was nearly eleven o'clock, and although it is never really night in St. Petersburg at that season, it was very dark at the top of the stairs.

The grimy little door at the head of the stairs stood open. A candle-end lighted up a poverty-stricken room about ten paces long; all of it could be seen from the landing. It was disordered and untidily strewn with various tattered children's garments. A torn sheet was stretched across the corner at the back of the room. The bed was probably behind it. There was nothing in the room but two chairs and a sofa covered with ragged oilcloth, with an old deal kitchen table, unpainted and uncovered, standing before it. On the edge of the table stood the stump of a tallow candle in an iron candlestick. It appeared that Marmeladov had a room, not only a corner of one, but the room was no more than a passage. At the farther end the door leading to the other rooms, or rabbit-hutches, into which Amalia Lippewechsel's flat was divided, stood ajar. From beyond it came a great deal of noisy talk and laughter. People seemed to be playing cards and drinking tea. Occasionally the most indecorous words came flying out of the door.

Raskolnikov knew Katerina Ivanovna at once. She was terribly wasted, a fairly tall, slender, shapely woman with still beautiful dark-brown hair and cheeks flushed with hectic red. She was walking up and down the little room with her hands pressed to her breast. Her lips looked parched and her breathing was harsh and uneven. Her eyes had a feverish glitter, but their gaze was hard and fixed. The consumptive and agitated creature was a painful spectacle, with the last light of the guttering candle flickering on her face. She appeared to Raskolnikov to be about thirty years old, and she and Marmeladov were certainly ill-matched . . . She did not hear or notice them as they entered; she seemed to be in a sort of stupor, deaf and blind to everything. The room was stuffy, but she had not opened the window; a foul smell came from the stairs, but the door to the landing was not shut; clouds of tobacco-smoke blew in from the other rooms through the half-open door, and she coughed but did not close it. The smallest child, a little girl of about six, was asleep on the floor, sitting hunched up with her head resting against the sofa. A boy about a year older stood crying and shaking in a corner; he had evidently just had a whipping. The eldest child was standing by her brother with her arm, as thin as a matchstick, about his neck. She was a tall and painfully thin little girl about nine years old, and her only garment was a worn and tattered chemise; round her bare shoulders was thrown an old woollen pelisse which might have fitted her two years earlier but now came down only to her knees. She was whispering to the boy to soothe him and doing her best to prevent a fresh outburst of sobs, while her enormous, frightened dark eyes, which looked still larger in her pinched and terrified little face, followed her mother's movements. Marmeladov did not go right into the room, but gave Raskolnikov a push which sent him forward, and himself fell on his knees at the door. At the sight of the stranger the distracted woman paused for a moment before him, evidently pulling herself together and wondering why he had come, but then it seemed to occur to her that he must be going to one of the other rooms, to which theirs served as a passage. Having come to this conclusion she paid him no further attention, but turned towards the entrance to shut the door, and suddenly cried out at the sight of her husband on his knees on the threshold.

'Ah!' she shrieked in a frenzy, 'so you've come back! Gaol-bird! Monster! . . . Where's the money? What have you got in your pockets?—show me! But those aren't your clothes! Where are yours? Where's the money? Say something! . . .'

And she threw herself forward and began to ransack his pockets. Marmeladov at once raised his arms, in a humble and submissive gesture, to make the search easier. There was not a single copeck.

'Where is the money, then?' she cried. 'Oh God, he can't have drunk it all! There were twelve silver roubles left in my box! . . .' Then, beside herself, she clutched his hair with a sudden swift movement and dragged him into the room. Marmeladov himself helped, shuffling meekly on his knees after her.

'This is a sweet satisfaction to me! This gives me not pain but plea-ea-sure, my-y-y dear sir!' he exclaimed, while he was shaken by the hair and once even had his forehead bumped on the floor. The child asleep on the floor woke up and began to cry. The boy in the corner could bear it no longer, but in a paroxysm of terror flung himself crying and shivering into his sister's arms. She was trembling like a leaf.

'You've drunk it all, drunk all of it!' wailed the poor woman in despair, 'and those clothes aren't yours! Hungry, they are hungry!' (she pointed to the children and wrung her hands). 'Oh, accursed, wretched life! And you, aren't you ashamed,' she turned suddenly on Raskolnikov, 'coming here from the public house? Have you been drinking with him? Get out!'

The young man left hurriedly without a word. Meanwhile the inner door had been pushed wide open and impudent laughing faces, adorned with pipes or cigarettes, or topped with skull-caps, were peering out inquisitively. There were figures in dressing-gowns left quite unfastened, others so scantily dressed as to be indecent; some of them held cards in their hands. They laughed with special glee when Marmeladov, dragged about by the hair, cried out that he enjoyed it. Some of them even began crowding into the room. Finally there came an ominous piercing yell from Amalia Lippewechsel herself, who came pushing to the front to restore order in her own fashion and to frighten the poor woman by ordering her for the hundredth time, with a string of oaths, to quit the flat the very next day. As he went out, Raskolnikov, thrusting his hand into his pocket and scraping together the coppers remaining from the rouble he had changed in the tavern, managed to put them unobserved on the window-sill. Afterwards, on his way downstairs, he repented of his action and almost turned back.

'What a stupid thing to do,' he thought, 'since after all they have Sonya and I need it myself.' But reflecting that it was no longer possible to take back the money and that in any case he would not have done so, he shrugged his shoulders and turned homewards. 'Besides, of course Sonya needs rouge,' he went on with a sarcastic laugh, as he walked along, 'and such smartness costs money . . . Hm! And perhaps Sonya will be empty-handed herself to-day, for there is always that risk, when one is hunting . . . or prospecting for gold . . . and that means they would all be in a bad way tomorrow, without that money of mine . . . Poor Sonya! What a little gold-mine they've managed to get hold of there!—and profit from! Oh yes, they draw their profits from it! And they've got used to it. They wept at first, but now they are used to it. Men are scoundrels; they can get used to anything!'

He pondered.

'Well, and if I am wrong,' he burst out suddenly, 'if men are not really scoundrels, men in general, the whole human race, I mean,—then all the rest is just prejudice, imaginary fears, and there are no real barriers, and that is as it should be!'

## CHAPTER III

THE next day Raskolnikov awoke late from an uneasy and unrefreshing sleep. He woke feeling bilious, peevish, and irritable, and gazed round his little room with loathing. It was a tiny little cubby-hole of a place, no more than six paces long, and so low that anybody of even a little more than average height felt uncomfortable in it, fearful that at any moment he might bump his head against the ceiling. The yellowish dusty wall-paper peeling off the walls gave it a wretchedly shabby appearance, and the furniture was in keeping; there were three rickety old chairs and a stained deal table in a corner, holding a few books and papers so covered with dust that it was plain that they had not been touched for a long time; and lastly there was a large and clumsy sofa, taking up almost the whole of one wall and half the width of the room, and with a print cover now old and worn into holes. This served Raskolnikov as a bed. He often slept on it just as he was, without undressing, without sheets, covered with his old worn-out student's overcoat, his head resting on a little cushion with his whole stock of linen, clean and dirty, bundled together under it for a bolster. Before this sofa stood a small table.

A more slovenly and degraded manner of life could hardly have been imagined, but it suited Raskolnikov's present mood. He had resolutely withdrawn from all human contacts, like a tortoise retreating into its shell, until the sight even of the face of the servant-girl who was supposed to look after him, and who looked in on him from time to time, made him shudder with revulsion. Such behaviour is found among monomaniacs when they have concentrated all their energies on one point. His landlady had stopped supplying him with food two weeks earlier and it had not yet occurred to him to go down and have things out with her, although he had been left without dinner. The cook, Nastasya, the landlady's only servant, was inclined to welcome the lodger's mood and had quite stopped cleaning and tidying his room, though she might pick up a broom once a week or so. It was she who had waked him now.

'Get up!—why are you still asleep?' she exclaimed, standing over him; 'it's past nine o'clock. I've brought you some tea; wouldn't you like some? You'll be wasting away!'

Raskolnikov opened his eyes with a start and recognized Nastasya.

'Did the landlady send up the tea?' he asked, slowly and painfully raising himself on the sofa.

'Likely, isn't it?'

She put down before him her own cracked teapot with some tea still remaining in it, and laid beside it two yellowed pieces of sugar.

'Here, Nastasya, take this, please,' he said, groping in his pocket (he had slept in his clothes) and taking out a small handful of coppers, 'and go and buy me a loaf. And go to the provision-shop and get me a bit of sausage, the cheapest kind.'

'I'll bring you the loaf this minute, but instead of the sausage wouldn't you like some cabbage soup? It's good soup, yesterday's. I saved it for you yesterday, but you came in too late. It's good soup.'

When the cabbage soup had been brought and Raskolnikov had begun to eat it, Nastasya sat down beside him on the sofa and began to chatter. She was a peasant, not a townswoman, and very talkative.

'That Praskovya Pavlovna's going to go to the police about you,' she said.

He scowled.

'To the police? What does she want?'

'You won't pay her her money, and you won't get out. It's plain enough what she wants.'

'The devil! It only needed that!' he muttered, grinding his teeth. 'No! Just now that's ... not convenient for me ... She's a fool,' he added aloud. 'I'll go and talk to her tomorrow.'

'Of course she's a fool, and so am I, and you're very clever—but in that case, why do you lie here like an old sack, with nothing to show for your cleverness? You say you used to go and teach children; why do you do nothing now?'

'I am doing ...' began Raskolnikov grimly and reluctantly.

'What?'

'Work ...'

'What sort of work?'

'Thinking,' he replied seriously, after a moment's pause.

Nastasya fairly shook with laughter. She laughed easily and often, and when anything amused her, her whole body shook and quivered with noiseless mirth until she almost choked.

'Well, and have you thought up how to get a lot of money?' she inquired when at last she was able to speak.

'I can't teach children when I have no boots. Besides, I despise the whole business.'

'It's no good quarrelling with your bread and butter.'

'Teaching children is very badly paid. What can you do with a few copecks?' he went on reluctantly, as if in answer to his own thoughts.

'I suppose you want a fortune straight off?'

He looked at her strangely and paused for a moment.

'Yes, I do,' he answered firmly.

'Well, you'd better go slow, or you'll frighten me; in fact

I'm frightened already. Am I to go for the loaf or not?'

'If you like.'

'Oh, I forgot! A letter came for you yesterday while you were out.'

'A letter? For me? Who from?'

'I don't know. I gave the postman three copecks. Will you pay me back?'

'Well, bring it here then, for God's sake!' cried Raskolnikov in great excitement. 'Good heavens!'

A minute later the letter appeared. As he thought, it was from his mother in the province of ——. He turned pale as he took it. It was a long time since he had received a letter, but it was something else that suddenly oppressed his spirit.

'Nastasya, please go away; here are your three copecks, only please go quickly!'

The letter trembled in his hands; he did not wish to open it in her presence, he wanted to be alone with it. When Nastasya went out, he lifted it quickly to his lips and kissed it, then for a long time he sat studying the small sloping writing on the envelope, the dear familiar handwriting of the mother who had long ago taught him to read and write. He hesitated, almost as though he were afraid of something. At last he opened the thick heavy packet; the letter was a long one, two large sheets of paper covered with small close writing.

'My dear Rodya,' wrote his mother,

'It is now more than two months since I last talked to you by letter, and I am very distressed about this, so much so that sometimes I cannot sleep at night for thinking of it. But I am sure you will forgive my silence; it has not been my own choice. You know how much I love you; you are all we have, Dunya and I, you are everything to us, our only hope and trust. How deeply it grieved me to learn that you had left the university several months ago because you could not afford to keep yourself there, and that your teaching and other sources of income had come to an end. What could I do to help you with my hundred and twenty roubles of pension? The fifteen roubles I sent you four months ago I borrowed, as you know, on the security of my pension from one of the merchants here, Vassily Ivanovich Vakhrushin. He is a good, kind man, and used to be a friend of your father's. But as I had made over to him the right to draw my pension I had to wait until the debt was paid off; that has only just been done, so I haven't been able to send you anything all this time. But now, thank God, I think I shall be able to send you a little more. Indeed, we can now congratulate ourselves that our fortunes in general have taken a turn for the better, and I hasten to tell you about it.

'To begin with, dear Rodya, you will hardly guess—your sister has been with me for the last six weeks, and we shall never have to part again in future. Thank God, her torments are over. I must tell you everything from the beginning, so that you shall know how it all happened, and all the things we have been keeping from you till now. Two months ago, when you wrote that you had heard from somebody that Dunya had a great deal of unkindness and rudeness to put up with at the Svidrigaylovs', and asked me for full particulars, what answer could I give you? If I had told you the whole truth, you would perhaps have thrown everything up and come home to us, even if you had had to walk all the way, for I know your character and your feelings, and you would not have allowed your sister to be insulted. I was desperate myself, but what could I do? And even I didn't know the whole truth then. The chief difficulty was that when Dunechka went to them as governess last year, she drew a whole hundred roubles in advance, to be repaid monthly out of her salary, and that meant that she could not leave until the debt was settled. She took this money (I can tell you all this now, dearest Rodya) principally so that she could send you the sixty roubles you needed so badly just then, which you had from us last year. We deceived you at the time, writing to you that it was money that Dunechka had saved before, but that was not true, and now I am telling you the whole truth because everything has suddenly changed for the better, by God's will, and because I want you to know how much Dunya loves you, and what a priceless treasure her heart is. Mr. Svidrigaylov really behaved very rudely to her at first, and made sarcastic and discourteous remarks to her at table . . . But I don't want to go into all the unpleasant details, I want to spare you unnecessary distress and it is all over now. In short, although Marfa Petrovna, Mr. Svidrigaylov's wife, and the rest of the household, treated her kindly and generously, things were very difficult for Dunechka, especially when Mr. Svidrigaylov, who had acquired the habit in his old regimental days, was under the influence of Bacchus.

'But worse was to come. Can you believe that he had long since conceived an extravagant passion for Dunya and that all his rudeness and contempt was simply assumed to hide it? Perhaps he was ashamed and frightened when he found himself, well on in years and the father of a family, cherishing such irresponsible hopes, and for that reason felt involuntary hostility to Dunya. Or perhaps he simply wanted to hide the true state of affairs from other people by behaving rudely and jeering at her. But at last he lost all control, and had the effrontery to make dishonest proposals quite openly to Dunya, promising her all sorts of things in return. He was even prepared to throw up everything and run away with her to some other estate, or perhaps abroad. You may imagine how Dunya suffered! It was impossible to leave her position at once, not only because of her debt, but also out of consideration for Marfa Petrovna, whose suspicions might have been aroused, which would have bred discord in the family. Besides Dunya herself could not have avoided disgrace and scandal. So there were several different reasons why she could not bring herself to escape from that horrible house until six weeks ago. Of course you know Dunya, with her wise head and her resolute character. Dunechka is capable of bearing a great deal, and even in the worst straits would still retain the nobility and firmness of her character. Even to me she didn't tell everything, for fear of upsetting me, although we often wrote to one another.

'The *dénouement* came unexpectedly. Marfa Petrovna happened to overhear her husband pleading with Dunechka in the garden and, completely misunderstanding everything, accused her of being the cause of the whole thing. There was a dreadful scene there in the garden; Marfa Petrovna even struck Dunya, and wouldn't listen to a word from her, but went on raving at her for a whole hour. Finally, she ordered Dunya to be sent back to me at once in a common peasant's cart, into which all her things were thrown pell-mell, without packing or anything. It began to pour with rain and Dunya, insulted and humiliated, had to travel the whole seventeen versts with a peasant in an open cart.

'Now think, what could I possibly have said in answer to your letter of two months ago, what could I have written about? I felt desperate; I dared not tell you the truth, because that would only have made you unhappy, anxious, and angry, and what could you have done, except perhaps ruin your own life? —and besides Dunya would not let me; yet I could not fill a letter with trifles and everyday affairs when my heart was so heavy. The whole town talked of the scandal for weeks, and things got to such a pitch that Dunya and I could not go to church because of the contemptuous looks we got, and the whispering, and even remarks made aloud in our presence. None of our acquaintances would have anything to do with us, they even cut us in the street, and I learned for a fact that some shop assistants and junior clerks planned to insult us in the basest manner by smearing the gates of the house with tar, so that the landlord began to press us to leave the flat. The cause of all this was Marfa Petrovna, who had managed to carry her accusations and her attacks on Dunya's good name into every house in the town. She knows everybody here, and she spent all that month running about the town. As she is rather garrulous and likes to talk about her domestic affairs and complain about her husband to all and sundry, she soon spread the story all over the district as well as in the town itself. It made me ill, but Dunya is made of sterner stuff; I wish you could have seen how well she bore it all, and comforted and sustained me at the same time. She is an angel.

'Mercifully, our sufferings were quickly brought to an end; Mr. Svidrigaylov had a change of heart and repented. He was apparently seized with pity for Dunya, for he gave Marfa Petrovna full documentary proof of her innocence, in the form of a letter which Dunya had found herself obliged to write and give to him, declining the private explanations and secret interviews he was trying to insist on. This letter, which remained in his possession after Dunya's departure, fervently and indignantly reproached him with the unworthiness of his conduct towards Marfa Petrovna and reminded him that he was a husband and father, and that it was base of him to torment and make miserable a defenceless girl who was unhappy enough already. In a word, dear Rodya, it was so noble and touching a letter that I sobbed as I read it, and even now I cannot read it without tears. Besides this, there now came out at last the evidence of the servants, who, as is always the case, had seen and known a good deal more than Mr. Svidrigaylov supposed, and who also exonerated Dunya.

'Marfa Petrovna was thunder-struck and "completely overwhelmed", as she herself confessed to us. She was, however, fully convinced of Dunya's innocence, and the very next day, Sunday, she went straight to the cathedral and on her knees prayed with tears to Our Lady to give her strength to bear this new trial and perform her duty. Then she came straight to us from the cathedral and told us everything, and, full of remorse and weeping bitterly, embraced Dunya and begged her forgiveness. The same morning, without losing any time, she went straight from us to every house in the town and everywhere, in the most flattering terms, proclaimed with tears Dunya's innocence and the nobility of her feelings and conduct. What is more, she showed everybody Dunya's letter to Mr. Svidrigaylov, read it aloud, and even allowed people to copy it (which seems to me to be going too far). She spent several days in going the rounds in this way, and some people began to complain that preference had been shown to others, and so turns were arranged, so that people were already waiting for her in each house, and everybody knew that on such-and-such a day she would be in such-and-such a place to read the letter. To every reading people came who had already heard it both in their own homes and in other people's as well. It is my opinion that a great deal, a very great deal, of all this was unnecessary, but Marfa Petrovna is like that. At all events she fully re-established Dunechka's reputation, and such indelible shame for his ignoble conduct has come to her husband as the principal offender that I am sorry even for him; his folly has been too severely punished. Dunya was invited to give lessons in various houses, but she refused. The general attitude towards her has suddenly changed to one of marked respect.

'All this helped considerably to make possible the event which, I may venture to say, has completely changed our destiny. You must know, dear Rodya, that a suitor has presented himself for Dunya, and that she has found it possible to accept him. Now I want to take this first opportunity of telling you all about it. And although matters have been arranged without consulting you, you will not nurse any grievance against either your sister or me, for you will see, when I have told you about it, that it would have been impossible to postpone the decision and wait until we had had an answer from you. Besides, you could not have formed an accurate judgement without being here. This is how it happened: Peter Petrovich Luzhin, who has already attained the rank of Civil Councillor, is a distant connexion of Marfa Petrovna's, who has done a great deal to assist him in this. It all began with his expressing through her a wish to meet us; he was received in a fitting manner and took coffee with us, and the very next day sent us a letter in which he expressed his proposal very civilly and asked for a speedy decision. He is a practical man and very busy, and he had to go to St. Petersburg in a hurry, so every minute counted. Of course, we were taken aback at first; it all happened too quickly and unexpectedly. We spent the whole day weighing and considering the question. He is a dependable person, in a secure position, and already has some capital of his own; he has two different situations. It is true that he is forty-five years old, but his appearance is quite pleasant and may still be attractive to women; altogether, he is a solid and worthy man, if rather overbearing and harsh in manner. But this, perhaps, is only one's first impression.

'I warn you, dear Rodya, not to judge him too rashly and hastily, as you are inclined to do, if, when you meet him in St. Petersburg (as you will very shortly), there seems to you at first glance to be something lacking in him. I say this just in case, although I am certain that he will make a favourable impression on you. Besides, if you want to know a person thoroughly, you must go slowly and carefully, so as to avoid mistakes and prejudices, which are always difficult to correct or eradicate afterwards. And Peter Petrovich is, at heart, in many ways a man to be respected. On his first visit he explained to us that he was a man of settled opinions, but in many things shared, as he put it, "the convictions of the younger generation" and was an enemy of all prejudice. He said a great many other things, for he is a little vain and likes to have an audience, but that is a small fault. Of course, I didn't understand much of it, but Dunya explained to me that, although not very highly educated, he is intelligent and seems good and kind. You know your sister's character, Rodya. She is steadfast, sensible, patient, generous, even if she is impetuous too, as I have good cause to know. Of course, there is no particular love either on her side or on his, but Dunya, besides being a sensible girl, is a noble creature too, like an angel, and would make it her duty to ensure her husband's happiness if he, for his part, concerned himself with hers. On this score we have little cause for doubt, although, I confess, the thing has been done rather quickly. Besides, he is a very prudent man, and will certainly see for himself that the happier Dunya is, married to him, the more certain his own married life is to be happy. As for some dissimilarities in temperament, some confirmed old habits, even some incompatibility in opinion that may exist (and that cannot be avoided even in the happiest unions), Dunechka has told me that she can rely on herself, and that there is no reason for uneasiness on that account, since she can put up with a good deal provided that their further relationship is on an honest and honourable footing. For instance, he seemed to me at first rather brusque, but that may be—it must be—only because he is outspoken; he is certainly that. On his second visit, for example, after he had been accepted, he told us in the course of conversation that even before he knew Dunya he had intended to take as his wife an honest girl without a dowry, who must have known poverty, because, as he explained, a husband ought not to be under any sort of obligation to his wife, and it was much better if she looked upon him as her benefactor. I must add that he expressed himself rather less crudely and harshly than this, because I have forgotten his actual words and remember only the sense of them; and besides, he really did not intend to say them at all, but evidently let them slip in the heat of the conversation, and afterwards he tried to correct himself and tone down what he had said; all the same it seemed just a little crude to me, and I told Dunya so afterwards. But Dunya was quite angry and answered rather sharply that "words are not deeds", and of course that is true.

'The night before she came to her decision, Dunya did not sleep at all, but when she thought I was asleep got out of bed and walked about the room all night; finally she knelt down before the icon and prayed fervently; and in the morning she told me that she had decided.

'I have already mentioned that Peter Petrovich is now on his way to St. Petersburg. He has important business to do, and he hopes to open a law office there. He has been engaged for some time in the conduct of various actions and lawsuits and only recently he won an important case in the Senate. Now he has important business to deal with in the Senate, so it is essential for him to go to St. Petersburg. So, dear Rodya, he will be able to be very helpful to you in every way, and Dunya and I expect that from this very day you can make a definite start on your future career and see your destiny taking clear shape. Oh, if only our expectations are realized! It would be such a blessing that we could only ascribe it to the direct intervention of Providence. Dunya dreams of nothing else. We have even ventured to say a few words on the subject to Peter Petrovich. His answer was expressed cautiously; he said that a secretary was certainly necessary to him and that it was obviously better to pay a salary to a relative than to a stranger, provided he is capable of fulfilling his duties (as if you could possibly not be capable!), but he expressed some doubt whether your university studies would leave you time for his office. That was the end of the matter for the moment, but now Dunya can think of nothing else. She has been in a fever of excitement for several days and has thought up a complete plan for you to become Peter Petrovich's colleague and even partner in his law business, especially as you are studying in the Faculty of Law yourself. I fully agree with her, Rodya, and share all her plans and hopes, which I think very likely to be fulfilled; and in spite of Peter Petrovich's easily explainable evasiveness (after all, he doesn't know you yet), Dunya is firmly convinced that she will accomplish it all by her good influence over her future husband. Of course, we have taken care not to say anything to Peter Petrovich about these more distant dreams of ours, especially about your being his partner. He is a very sober-minded man, and what would seem to him to be the wildest day-dreams might get a cold reception from him. Equally, neither Dunya nor I have breathed a word to him of our profound hope that he will help us to assist you with money while you remain at the University, because, in the first place, it will come of itself later on, and he himself will probably make the offer without being urged (would he be likely to refuse Dunya such a thing?), the more readily as you may become his right-hand man in the office and receive the help not as a benefaction but as well-earned salary. That is how Dunya wants it to be, and I agree with her. In the second place, we have not spoken of it because we particularly want you to meet as equals when, very soon now, you make his acquaintance. When Dunya talked enthusiastically to him about you, he replied that he found it necessary to make a close personal study of any person in order to form an opinion of him, and that he would rely on his own judgement when he came to know you.

'Do you know, my dearest Rodya, I think (without the

slightest reference to Peter Petrovich or to anything but my own personal whims, those perhaps of a silly old woman)— I think that I should perhaps do better to go on, after their marriage, living by myself, as I do now, rather than with them. I am quite sure that he will have the delicacy and consideration to invite me to live with them, and not to part again from my daughter, and if he has not already done so, it is because it is taken for granted; but I shall refuse. More than once in my life I have noticed that husbands have no great liking for their mothers-in-law, and I not only don't want to be in the slightest degree a burden to anybody, but I also want to be completely free myself, so long as I have a crust of bread, and two such children as you and Dunechka. If possible, I shall settle somewhere near both of you.

'For you must know, Rodya, that I have saved the best news till the end; it is that we shall perhaps all three be together again in a very short time, my dear, and be able to embrace one another again after nearly three years of separation. It has been *definitely* decided that Dunya and I are to move to St. Petersburg. I don't know exactly when, but very, very soon in any case, perhaps even next week. It all depends on Peter Petrovich's arrangements, and as soon as he has had time to look round in St. Petersburg he will let us know. For various reasons he wants the wedding to take place very soon, even before the next fast, if possible, and if the time is too short, then immediately after the Assumption.[4] Oh, what happiness it will be to press you to my heart! Dunya is full of joy at the thought of seeing you again and once she said, in jest, that she would have married Peter Petrovich if only for that. She is an angel! She is not writing to you now, but she told me to tell you that she has a lot to say to you, so much that she won't put a finger to her pen at the moment, because writing a few lines doesn't get anything said and only upsets one. She told me to send you her love and any number of kisses.

'Although we are perhaps to see each other face to face so soon, all the same I will send you some money in a few days, as much as I can. Now that everybody knows that Dunya is going to marry Peter Petrovich my credit has suddenly improved, and I am quite sure that Afanasy Ivanovich will advance me up to seventy-five roubles on the security of my pension, so that I shall be able to send you perhaps twenty-five or even thirty. I should send more except that I am afraid of our travelling expenses; although Peter Petrovich has been good enough to take on himself part of the cost of our journey to the capital, offering to make himself responsible for the conveyance of the big trunk and our other luggage, through

4. The Assumption Fast, one of the four fasts of the Russian Orthodox calendar, is from August 1 to August 15.

the good offices of some acquaintances of his up there, all the same we have to think of our arrival in St. Petersburg, where we couldn't turn up without a farthing, even for the first day or two. However, Dunya and I have already gone into all the details, and we find that the actual journey will not be very expensive. It is only ninety versts from here to the railway, and we have already made arrangements with a peasant we know, who is a carrier; then we shall be quite happy travelling on from there third class. So perhaps it will be not twenty-five, but more likely thirty roubles that I shall contrive to send you.

And now, my darling Rodya, until our speedy reunion, all my love and a mother's blessing. You must love your sister Dunya, Rodya, love her as she loves you—and her love for you is boundless; she loves you more than herself. She is an angel, Rodya, and you—you are everything to us; all our hope and trust is in you. If only you are happy, we shall be happy too. Do you pray to God, Rodya, as you used to do, and do you believe in the mercy of our Creator and Redeemer? I am afraid, in my heart, that you too may have been affected by the fashionable modern unbelief. If that is so, I will pray for you. Remember, my dear, how, when you were a child and your father was still alive, you lisped your prayers at my knee, and remember how happy we all were then! Good-bye—or rather, *au revoir*. I send you all my love, and many, many kisses.

Your devoted mother,
Pulkheria Raskolnikova.'

Almost all the time that Raskolnikov was reading this letter his face was wet with tears, but when he came to the end it was pale and convulsively distorted and a bitter angry smile played over his lips. He put his head down on his thin, crumpled pillow and lay there for a long time, thinking. His heart was beating fiercely and his thoughts were wildly agitated. At last it began to seem close and stuffy in the shabby little room, so like a box or a cupboard. His eyes and his thoughts both craved more space. He seized his hat and went out, this time without fearing to meet anybody on the stairs; he had forgotten all about that. He turned his steps in the direction of Vasilyevsky Island, along the Voznesensky Prospect, hurrying as though he had business there, but, as usual, he walked without noticing where he was going, whispering and sometimes even talking aloud to himself, to the surprise of the passers-by. Many of them supposed him to be drunk.

## CHAPTER IV

His mother's letter had tortured him. On the most important, the fundamental, point, he had not a moment's doubt, even while he was reading the letter. The most essential question was decided in his mind, and decided with finality. 'This marriage shall never take place while I live, and Mr. Luzhin may go to the devil!'

'Because the thing is obvious,' he muttered to himself, smiling with malicious enjoyment at the anticipated triumph of his decision. 'No, mama, no, Dunya, you cannot deceive me! . . . And yet they make excuses for not asking my advice and for coming to their decision without me. Of course! they think it's impossible to break it off now, but we shall see whether it is impossible or not. And what marvellously flimsy excuses they find: "Peter Petrovich is such a busy man," say they, "so busy that he can't even get married except post-haste; everything must be done at express speed." No, Dunechka, I see it all, and I know what it is you have such a lot to say about to me; I know, too, what you were thinking of, while you paced the room all night, and what you prayed for, kneeling before the icon of Our Lady of Kazan[5] in mama's room. The way to Golgotha is hard. Hm . . . So it's all decided and settled; you, Avdotya Romanovna, are graciously pleased to marry a practical, a rational man, who has some capital of his own (*already* has some capital, that makes it sound solider and more imposing), a man who has two situations and shares the convictions of the younger generation (as mama says) and who seems good and kind, as Dunechka herself remarks. That *seems* is magnificent!—and Dunechka is going to marry that *seems*! . . . Magnificent, magnificent!

'I wonder, though, why mama wrote that to me about the "younger generation." Simply because it is characteristic of the man, or with the ulterior object of influencing me in Mr. Luzhin's favour? What diplomacy! I should like one thing made clear, though; how open were they with each other, that day and that night, and later? Were their real thoughts put into actual words, or did each of them tacitly understand that the same thing was in the hearts and minds of both of them, so that there was no need to name it aloud or to waste words in discussing it? Probably that was it, at least partly; but you can tell from the letter that when mama found him crude, *just a little*, she was naïve enough to go to Dunya with her observations. *She*, of course, was angry and "answered rather sharply." Naturally! it would have irritated anybody, when the thing was understood, without naïve questions, and when it had been settled that there was no need to put anything into words. And why does she write to me: "Love Dunya, Rodya; she loves you more than she loves herself"?; isn't it because her conscience torments her with remorse at having consented

5. This famous Russian painting of the Virgin was kept in the Kazan Cathedral in Petersburg. Among all the cults of various Russian icons, it was one of the most popular.

to sacrifice her daughter for the sake of her son? "You are everything to us, our only hope and trust." Oh, mama! . . .' Resentment welled up in him, more and more bitter, and if he had chanced to meet Mr. Luzhin at that moment, he would have felt like murdering him.

'Hm, it is true,' he continued, trying to follow the whirlwind of thoughts spinning in his brain, 'it is true that one must "go slowly and carefully" with a man if one wants to study him thoroughly; but Mr. Luzhin is transparent. The main thing is that he's "a practical man and *seems* good and kind": is it a small thing that he has undertaken responsibility for the luggage, and will himself see that the big trunk is safely conveyed here? Of course he's good and kind! Meanwhile, the two of them, the *bride* and her mother, bespeak a peasant's cart covered with matting (I've travelled in it myself)! It's nothing, it's only ninety versts; "then we shall be quite happy travelling third class" another thousand versts. And very sensible too; one must cut one's coat according to one's cloth; but you, Mr. Luzhin, what do you think of it? After all, she is your bride . . . And how could you avoid knowing that her mother must borrow money on her pension for the journey? Of course, here you have a common commercial transaction, an undertaking for mutual profit, with equal shares, and that means expenses shared equally too; bread and salt in common, but supply your own tobacco, as the proverb says. And the practical man has indulged in a little sharp practice here; the luggage costs less than their journey and perhaps he will even get it brought for nothing. Why don't they see what all this means, or are they turning a blind eye on purpose? And they are content, content! When one thinks that this is only the blossom, and the real fruit is yet to come! What is significant here is not the meanness, not the stinginess, but the *tone* of everything. It foreshadows the tone of their relationship after the marriage . . . yes, and mama, what is she so pleased about? What is she going to appear in St. Petersburg with? Three silver roubles, or "a couple of rouble-bills", as that . . . old woman . . . called them . . . Hm . . . What does she hope to live on in St. Petersburg afterwards? She has surely had some cause already to surmise that it will be *impossible* for her and Dunya to live together after the wedding, even at first? The dear man has evidently *let it slip*, quite by chance of course, and made himself very clear, although mama waves any such idea away with both hands: "*I*," she says, "shall refuse." What is she thinking of, what can she rely on? On her hundred and twenty roubles of pension, less deductions for the debt to Afanasy Ivanovich? She ruins her old eyes knitting winter shawls and embroidering cuffs, and I know that all of it doesn't add more than twenty roubles a year to her hundred and twenty. That means that in spite of everything she still relies on Mr. Luzhin's generosity of spirit. "He will invite me himself to live with them," says she, "he will urge me to." Yes, that's likely! These Schilleresque beautiful souls are always the same; up to the very last moment they see people through rose-coloured spectacles; up to the very last moment they hope for good and not evil; and even if they have some misgivings that there is a reverse side to the medal, they refuse to admit them even to themselves; they shrink from the very notion; they wave the truth away with both hands until the very moment when the over-idealized person appears in his true colours and cocks a snook at them.

'I wonder if Mr. Luzhin has any decorations; I'm willing to bet he has an order of St. Anna[6] for his button-hole and wears it at contractors' and merchants' dinners. Perhaps he'll even wear it at his wedding. However, he can go to the devil! . . .

'Well, but let mama take that line—she can't help it, bless her, it's the way she's made—but Dunya? Dunechka, my dear, I know you! You were nineteen when last we saw each other; and I already understood your nature. Mama writes that "Dunechka is capable of bearing a great deal". I know that. I knew it two and a half years ago, and I have kept thinking of it during that two and a half years, of the fact that "Dunechka is capable of bearing a great deal". And now she and mama together have conceived the idea that she can bear even Mr. Luzhin's expounding his theory that wives ought to be rescued from beggary and loaded with benefactions by their husbands, and expounding it almost the first time he saw them. Even if we assume that "he only let it slip" (although he is a rational man and that means that perhaps the slip was intentional, so as to make his position clear from the outset)—but Dunya, what of Dunya? Surely she must see what the man is; and to live with him! She would certainly eat only black bread and drink only water rather than sell her soul, and she would not surrender her moral freedom in return for comfort; she wouldn't surrender it for all Schleswig-Holstein,[7] let alone for Mr. Luzhin! No, Dunya, as I knew her, was not like that and . . . of course, she hasn't changed now! . . .

'Oh, it's all quite clear! The Svidrigaylovs are not easy. It is not easy to spend one's life trailing round the provinces as a governess at two hundred roubles, but all the same I know she would sooner go to the plantations as a negro slave, or live like a Latvian serf in some Baltic German household, than degrade her spirit and her moral feelings by a union with a man whom she does not respect and with whom she has nothing in common—for ever, just for her own personal advantage. And, even if Mr. Luzhin were made of the purest gold, if he were

6. One of the chief Russian decorations, awarded for civilian service to the government.

7. Denmark, Austria, and Prussia were fighting a war over Schleswig-Holstein in 1864.

nothing but one large diamond, even then she would never consent to become his legal concubine. Then why does she consent now? What is the reason? What is the key to the riddle? It is quite clear; for herself, for her own comfort, even to save herself from death, she would not sell herself, but for another she would! For a dear one, for someone she adores, she would! That is the key to the riddle: for her brother, for her mother, she would!—she would sell everything! Ah, in such circumstances we throw our moral feelings into the bargain as well; we carry our freedom, our peace of mind, even our consciences, everything, everything, to Rag Fair. Let our lives go, if only these beloved creatures of ours are happy! Nay more, we invent casuistical arguments for ourselves, we take a lesson from the Jesuits, and, for a time, contrive to allay our own doubts and convince ourselves that what we are doing is necessary, absolutely necessary, in a good cause. That is the way we are made; it is all as clear as daylight. It is clear that nobody but Rodion Romanovich Raskolnikov is in question here, he occupies all the foreground. Well, his happiness may be secured, he may be kept at the University, made a partner in the office, his future provided for; perhaps later on he may be rich, respected, honoured, he may even die famous! And my mother? But this is a question of Rodya, precious Rodya, the first-born! Why hesitate to sacrifice even such a daughter for the sake of such a first-born? Oh loving hearts, without any notion of justice! Why, perhaps we would not refuse even Sonechka's fate. Sonechka, Sonechka Marmeladova, Sonechka the eternal, while the world lasts! But this sacrifice, have you plumbed the full depths of this sacrifice? Really? Is your strength great enough? Will it really bring such great benefits? Is it really sensible and wise? Do you know, Dunechka, that Sonechka's fate is no whit worse than yours with Mr. Luzhin? "There can be no particular love here," writes mama. But what if, besides there being no particular love or respect, there is already abhorrence, scorn, loathing, what then? Then it follows, once more, that "one must preserve one's cleanness and purity". It is so, isn't it? Do you understand, do you understand, what that cleanness means? Do you understand that a Mrs. Luzhin's cleanness is exactly the same thing as Sonechka's, or perhaps even worse, fouler, more despicable, because you, Dunechka, can after all reckon on comforts into the bargain, and with the other it is a question simply of dying of hunger. "That purity and cleanness costs dear, dear, Dunechka!" Well, and what if your strength is not equal to it, and you repent? How much grief, how many laments, how many curses, how many tears hidden from all the world, hidden because you, after all, are not Marfa Petrovna! And what of your mother then? She is uneasy and worried even now;

what then, when everything is clearly revealed? And what of me? . . . How indeed have they been thinking of me? I will not have your sacrifice, Dunechka, I will not have it, mama! It shall not be, while I live, it shall not, it shall not! I will not accept it!'

Suddenly he recollected himself, and stopped. 'It shall not be? What are you going to do to prevent it? Will you forbid it? But what right have you to do so? What can you offer that will give you the right? To consecrate your destiny, your whole future, to them, *when you have finished your studies and obtained a situation*? We've heard all that before, and it's all right for the *future*; but what about now? Something must certainly be done now, do you understand that? And what are you doing now? You are fleecing them. And they get the money for you on the security of a hundred-rouble pension or as an advance from the Svidrigaylovs. And how will you protect them from the Svidrigaylovs or from Afanasy Ivanovich Vakhrushin, you future millionaire, disposing of their fates as though you were Zeus himself? Do you need ten years? In that ten years your mother will have time to go blind with knitting, and perhaps with tears; she will waste away with fasting; and your sister? Well, think what would become of her after those ten years, or during them. Have you thought?'

Thus he teased and tormented himself with his problems, and even found a kind of pleasure in doing so. The problems were not new, however; they did not confront him unexpectedly, but were an old and painful story. It was a long time since they had begun to lacerate his feelings. Long, long ago his present anguish had first stirred within him, and it had grown and accumulated until of late it had come to a head and concentrated itself into the form of a wild, fantastic and terrible question, that tortured his emotions and his reason with its irresistible demands to be answered. Now his mother's letter had struck him like a thunderbolt. It was clear that now the time had come, not to languish in passive suffering, arguing that his problems were insoluble, but to act, to act at once and with speed. He must decide on something or other, come what might, or . . .

'Or renounce life altogether!' he exclaimed suddenly, as if inspired, 'submit obediently, once for all, to destiny, as it is, and stifle everything within oneself, renouncing every right to act, to live, or to love!'

Suddenly Marmeladov's question of the previous day came back to him: 'Do you understand, my dear sir, do you understand what it means to have nowhere left to turn to? for every man must needs have somewhere to turn to . . .'

Suddenly he gave a shudder; another thought, also from

yesterday, had come into his head again. But the shudder was not because the thought had returned. Indeed, he had known, he had *foreseen*, that it would return, and he had been expecting it; but this thought was not quite the same as yesterday's. The difference was that a month earlier, and even yesterday, it had been no more than a bad dream, but now . . . it was revealed as no dream, but in a new, unfamiliar, and terrible form; and he had suddenly become conscious of this fact . . . His head throbbed and things went dark before his eyes.

He glanced hastily round, looking for something. He needed to sit down, and he was looking for a bench. He was walking along Konnogvardeysky Boulevard, and he could see a bench about a hundred yards away, in front. He began to walk as quickly as he could, but on the way a small incident absorbed all his attention for a few minutes.

As he looked at the bench he saw a woman walking some twenty paces in front of him, but at first he paid her no more attention than he had given before to all the other objects which had passed before his eyes. He had grown used, for example, to arriving at home, as he often did, without having any idea of how he had come there. But there was something so strange and striking, even at the first glance, about this woman walking along, that little by little his attention became fixed on her, at first unwillingly and almost with some vexation, and then with more and more concentration. Suddenly he felt a desire to know just what it was that was strange about her. To begin with, she seemed to be very young, no more than a girl, and she was walking through the blazing heat bare-headed and without gloves or parasol, waving her arms about queerly. Her dress was of a thin silken material, but it also looked rather odd; it was not properly fastened, and near the waist at the back, at the top of the skirt, there was a tear, and a great piece of material was hanging loose. A shawl had been flung round her bare neck and hung crooked and lop-sided. To crown everything, the girl's gait was unsteady and she stumbled and even staggered from side to side. The encounter had by now fully engaged Raskolnikov's attention. He came up with her close to the bench; she went up to it and let herself fall into a corner of it, resting her head against the back and closing her eyes as if overcome with weariness. Looking closely at her, Raskolnikov realized at once that she was quite drunk. It was a strange, sad sight; he even thought he must be mistaken. Before him he saw the small face of a very young girl, of sixteen, or perhaps only fifteen or so, small, pretty, fair-haired; but the face looked swollen and inflamed. The girl seemed to have little understanding of her surroundings; she crossed one leg over the other, displaying more of it than was seemly, and to all appearances hardly realized that she was in the street.

Raskolnikov did not sit down, but stood irresolutely in front of her, not wanting to go away. This boulevard is always rather deserted, but now at one o'clock, and in such heat, it was almost empty. Fifteen paces away, however, a gentleman had stopped at the edge of the boulevard, a little to one side, and it was plain that he was desirous of approaching the girl for some purpose. He too had probably seen her from a distance and followed her, but Raskolnikov's presence hampered him. He cast bad-tempered glances at him, yet tried not to be observed doing so, and impatiently awaited his opportunity when the vexatious intrusion of this ragamuffin should cease. He was a man of about thirty, thick-set and plump, with a pink-and-white complexion and red lips; he wore a small moustache and was foppishly dressed. Raskolnikov grew furiously angry and was seized with a desire to make himself offensive to the fat dandy. He left the girl for a moment and went up to the gentleman.

'Hey, you Svidrigaylov, what do you want here?' he exclaimed, clenching his fists and grinning with lips that foamed with rage.

'What does this mean?' asked the gentleman sternly, frowning with haughty astonishment.

'Clear off! That's what it means.'

'How dare you, *canaille*?'

He flourished his cane. Raskolnikov threw himself upon him with both fists, without stopping to consider that the stout gentleman was capable of dealing with two of him. But at that moment he was firmly seized from behind; a policeman stood between them.

'That's enough, gentlemen! No brawling in the public streets, if you please! What do you want? Who are you?' he turned to Raskolnikov, sternly surveying his rags.

Raskolnikov looked at him attentively. He had a manly, soldier's face, with grey moustache and whiskers and a sensible expression.

'What do I want? I want you!' he exclaimed, seizing his arm. 'I am a former student, Raskolnikov . . . *You* may as well know, too,' he added turning to the gentleman. 'But come along here, I have something to show you.'

And he pulled the policeman by the arm towards the bench.

'There, look, she's quite drunk; she has just come along the boulevard; Heaven knows who she is, but she can hardly be a professional. More likely somebody made her drunk and abused her . . . do you understand me? . . . for the first time . . . and then turned her out into the street like this. Look, her dress is torn; look how it is put on; clearly she didn't dress herself, she was dressed by somebody else, and dressed by unskilful hands, masculine hands. That is plain. And now look over here; that overdressed scoundrel that I was trying to fight is a stranger to me, this is the first time I have seen him, but he saw her as well, just now, this drunken girl, in no condition to take care of herself, and now he is aching to come and get hold of her—since she is in such a state—and take her off somewhere. It really is so; believe me, I am not mistaken. I saw him watching her and following her, but I was in his way, and now he is simply waiting for me to go. Look, now he's moved a bit farther away, and stopped as if he wanted to roll a cigarette . . .[8] How are we to keep her out of his hands? How can we get her home?—try to think!'

The policeman had understood at once, and now he was considering. The stout gentleman's position was, of course, clear; there remained the girl. He stooped down to look at her more closely, and sincere compassion showed in his face.

'Ah, it's a great pity!' he said, shaking his head, 'she's no more than a child. She's been led astray, that's right enough. Listen, miss,' he went on to her, 'where do you live?' The girl opened her tired, bleary eyes, looked dully at her questioners, and waved them away with her hand.

'Listen,' said Raskolnikov, rummaging in his pocket and taking out twenty copecks that he found there, 'look, take a cab and tell him to drive to her address. Only we must get to know the address.'

'Young lady, young lady!' began the policeman again, accepting the money, 'I'll get a cab for you right away, and I'll take you home myself. But where to, eh? Where do you live?'

'Pshaw! . . . pestering me . . .' muttered the girl with another wave of the hand.

'Dear, dear, it's a bad business! Oh, how shameful this is, young lady, what a disgrace!' He began to shake his head with a mixture of pity and indignation. 'You know, this is a bit of a problem,' he added, turning to Raskolnikov and again enveloping him from head to foot with a quick glance. Probably he seemed more than a little strange too, giving away money and wearing such rags.

'Was she far from here when you found her?' asked the policeman.

'I tell you she was reeling along the boulevard just here, in front of me. When she came to the bench she just slumped down on it.'

'Oh, what shameful things there are in the world now, sir!

8. Smoking on the streets, which had previously been forbidden by law, was permitted after July 4, 1865.

Such a simple young thing, and drunk already! She's been betrayed, that's what it is; look how her dress is torn . . . What wickedness there is nowadays! . . . Maybe she belongs to decent people, poor ones, perhaps . . . Lots of things like this happen nowadays. She looks as if she had been quite nicely brought up, almost like a real young lady,' and he stooped over her again.

Perhaps he had daughters like her himself, who were 'nicely brought up, like young ladies', had good manners and copied all the new fashions.

'The main thing,' said Raskolnikov anxiously, 'is to keep her out of that scoundrel's hands. He would only dishonour her again. It's quite plain what he wants; look, he's not going away, the wretch.'

Raskolnikov spoke loudly and pointed straight at him. The man heard him and seemed on the point of losing his temper again, but thought better of it and contented himself with a scornful glance. Then he slowly moved away another ten paces, and stopped again.

'Well, that can be managed, sir,' answered the police officer, but with some hesitancy. 'If she would only tell us where to take her—otherwise . . . Young lady, young lady!' and he stooped down again.

Suddenly the girl opened her eyes wide, with an attentive expression, as though she had just grasped something. She got up from the bench and started back in the direction she had come from. 'Pah! They have no shame, they keep on pestering me,' she said, with another wave of her hand. She walked quickly, staggering as she had before. Keeping his eyes fixed on her, the dandified gentleman followed, but along the other pavement.

'Be easy, I will not let him!' said the policeman resolutely, turning to follow them.

'Eh, what wickedness there is nowadays!' he repeated aloud, with a sigh.

At this moment an instantaneous revulsion of feeling seemed as it were to sting Raskolnikov.

'No, listen!' he cried after the moustached policeman.

He turned round.

'Stop! What is it to you? Drop it! Let him amuse himself!' (he pointed at the gentleman). 'What business is it of yours?'

The policeman stared uncomprehendingly. Raskolnikov laughed.

'Eh!' said the officer, and with a gesture of his hand followed the girl and the man, evidently taking Raskolnikov for a lunatic or worse.

'He's gone off with my twenty copecks,' said Raskolnikov bitterly, when he was alone. 'Now he can take something from the other as well, and let the girl go with him, and that will be the end of it . . . Why did I take it on myself to interfere? Was it for me to try to help? Have I any right to help? Let them eat one another alive—what is it to me? And how dared I give away those twenty copecks? Were they mine to give?'

In spite of these strange words, he felt depressed. He sat down on the now empty bench. His thoughts were disconnected, and indeed, he felt too weary at that moment to think at all, on whatever subject. He would have liked to forget himself, to forget everything in sleep, and then to wake up and make a fresh start.

'Poor girl!' he said, looking at the empty corner of the bench . . . 'When she comes to herself, there will be tears, and then her mother will get to know . . . First she will get a thrashing, then she will be beaten with a whip, painfully and shamefully, and perhaps she will even be driven out . . . And even if she isn't, the Darya Franzovnas will get wind of her, and she will be hunted this way and that . . . Then will come the hospital (that's always the way with these girls when they live with very respectable mothers and have to take their fun on the sly), well, and then . . . and then the hospital again . . . vodka . . . dram-shops . . . the hospital once more . . . a wreck in two or three years, her life finished at no more than eighteen or nineteen years old . . . Haven't I seen others like her? And what became of them? That's what became of them . . . Pah! Let it go! They say it must be so. Such and such a percentage they say, must go every year . . . somewhere or other . . . to the devil, I suppose, so that the rest may be left in peace and quiet. A percentage![9] They have some capital words: they are so soothing and scientific. Once you've said "a percentage" there is no need to worry any more. If you used a different word, why then perhaps . . . it might be disturbing . . . And what if Dunechka is included in the percentage? . . . If not in one, then in another? . . .'

'But where am I going?' he thought suddenly. 'It's strange. I must have come for some reason. I came as soon as I had read that letter . . . I was going to Vasilyevsky Island, to Razumikhin's, . . . I remember now. But why? How did the idea of going to see Razumikhin come to enter my head just at this moment? It's very odd!'

He wondered at himself. Razumikhin was one of his old university friends. It should be noted that Raskolnikov had had scarcely any friends at the university. He held himself aloof, never went to see anyone and did not welcome visitors. Very soon, however, he found himself left severely alone. He took no part in the usual assemblies, discussions, or amusements. He worked strenuously, not sparing himself, and for this he was

9. A reference to positivistic and scientific utilitarian ethics; see footnote to p. 11.

respected, but he was not liked. He was very poor and super-
ciliously proud and reserved. It seemed to some of his fellow
students that he looked down on them all as children, as if he
had outdistanced them in knowledge, development, and ideas,
and that he considered their interests and convictions beneath
him.

With Razumikhin, though, he did make friends, or rather,
he did not exactly make friends, but he was more open and
communicative with him than with others. With Razumikhin,
indeed, it was impossible to be otherwise. He was an unusually
lively and talkative fellow, so goodhearted as to seem almost
simple. But the simplicity concealed both depth and considerable merit. The best of his fellow students understood this and
they all loved him. He was far from stupid, although he was
sometimes really rather naïve. In appearance he was striking,
tall and thin, with black hair, and always badly shaved. He
was subject to violent fits of rage, and had a reputation for great
physical strength. On one occasion, out at night with a band
of boon companions, he felled with one blow an enormous
policeman well over six feet tall. He could indulge in endless
drinking bouts, or refrain from drinking altogether; sometimes
the pranks he played were carried much too far, but he was
also capable of being completely serious. Razumikhin was
remarkable also in that failure never disconcerted him and
adverse circumstances seemed powerless to subdue him. He
could have lived on a roof and suffered the severest extremes of
hunger and cold. He was very poor, with absolutely no other
resources than the money he obtained by doing all sorts of odd
jobs. He knew a thousand and one ways of earning money.
Once he went a whole winter without any heat at all in his
room, affirming that he preferred it, because one sleeps better
in the cold. At the present moment he also had been obliged
to leave the university, but only for a short time, and he was
straining every nerve to improve his circumstances in order to
continue his studies. Raskolnikov had not been to see him for
the past four months, and he did not even know Raskolnikov's
address. Two months or so previously, they had on one occasion
nearly come face to face in the street, but Raskolnikov turned
aside and crossed to the other side to avoid being seen, and
Razumikhin, although he had in fact seen him, walked past,
not wanting to worry his friend.

## CHAPTER V

'YES, I did think not so long ago of going to Razumikhin again
to ask him to get me some work, lessons or something,' . . .
Raskolnikov began to remember, 'but how can he help me
now? Suppose he gets me some lessons, suppose he shares his

last copeck with me, if he has such a thing, so that I can buy boots and make my clothes decent enough to go out in to give the lessons . . . hm. What then? What can I do with a few coppers? They will hardly meet my needs now. Really, it is almost comic that I was on my way to see Razumikhin . . .'

The question of why he had been going to see Razumikhin troubled him more than he himself recognized; he looked uneasily for some sinister meaning in this, it would seem, quite natural step.

'Why, did I really think I could settle everything with no more than some help from Razumikhin; did I think I had found a way out of all my difficulties?' he asked himself in some astonishment.

He went on thinking and rubbing his forehead and then, after a long time, unexpectedly and almost of its own accord, an extremely strange idea came into his head.

'Hm . . . I will go,' he said suddenly and composedly, as if he had reached a definite decision. 'I will go to see Razumikhin, of course . . . but—not now. I will go to him the day after, when *that* is over and done with and everything is different . . .'

Then he realized what he had said.

'After?' he cried, jumping up from the bench; 'but is *it* going to happen? Can it really be going to happen?'

He left the bench almost running; he had meant to turn back, but now the idea of going home seemed suddenly unbearable: it was there, in that dreadful little cupboard of a place that the thought of *it* had been maturing in his mind for more than a month. He walked on, without heeding where he went.

His nervous shudderings seemed to have turned into a fever; he even felt chilly; in that terrible heat he was cold. Driven by an inner compulsion, he tried to make himself be interested in everything and everybody he met, but with little success. He kept relapsing into abstraction, and when he again raised his head with a start and looked around, he could remember neither what he had just been thinking of nor which way he had come. In this fashion he walked right across Vasilyevsky Island, came out on the Little Neva, crossed the bridge, and turned on to the Islands. At first the greenery and freshness pleased his tired eyes, accustomed to the dust and lime of the town, and its tall buildings crowding oppressively together. Here there was no stuffiness, no evil smells, no public houses. But these pleasant new sensations soon gave place to painful and irritating ones. Occasionally he would stop before some picturesque *dacha* in its green setting, look through the fence and see in the distance gaily-dressed ladies on balconies or terraces, and children running about the gardens. He took a particular interest in the flowers and looked at them longest of all. Splendid carriages, and ladies and gentlemen on horseback, passed him, and he gazed after them with curious eyes and forgot them before they were out of sight. Once he stopped and counted his money; he found that he had about thirty copecks. 'Twenty to the policeman, three to Nastasya for the letter—that means I gave forty-seven or fifty to the Marmeladovs yesterday,' he calculated, but soon he forgot even why he had taken his money out of his pocket. He thought of it again as he passed a sort of tavern or eating-house, and realized that he was hungry. He went in, drank a glass of vodka and bought a pasty, which he finished eating as he walked along. It was a very long time since he had tasted vodka, and although he had drunk only one glass it began to affect him almost at once. His legs seemed suddenly heavy and he began to feel very sleepy. He turned homewards, but by the time he reached Petrovsky Island he was too exhausted to go on, and he turned aside from the road into some bushes, let himself fall to the ground, and was asleep at once.

A sick man's dreams are often extraordinarily distinct and vivid and extremely life-like. A scene may be composed of the most unnatural and incongruous elements, but the setting and presentation are so plausible, the details so subtle, so unexpected, so artistically in harmony with the whole picture, that the dreamer could not invent them for himself in his waking state, even if he were an artist like Pushkin or Turgenev. Such morbid dreams always make a strong impression on the dreamer's already disturbed and excited nerves, and are remembered for a long time.

Raskolnikov dreamed a terrible dream. He dreamt that he was a child again, back in the little town they used to live in. He was a boy of seven, walking one holiday with his father outside the town. The afternoon was grey and sultry, the place just as he remembered it, except that the dream was more vivid than his recollection. He saw the little town as clearly as though he held it in his hand; there was not a single tree anywhere, except for a little wood very far away, dark against the horizon. A few paces beyond the last gardens of the town stood a large tavern, which always made an unpleasant impression on him, even frightened him, whenever he and his father passed it on their walks. There was always such a crowd there, so much shouting, laughter, and cursing, such hoarse bawling of songs, such frequent brawls, and so many people lounging about outside, drunk, with horrible distorted faces. If ever they met any of these, he would press close to his father, shivering. The unmade road winding past the tavern was always dusty, and the dust just here was always black. Some three hundred yards farther on it curved to the right round the cemetery. In the cemetery was a stone church with a green cupola, where he came once or twice a year with his father and mother to a requiem in memory of the dead grandmother whom he had never seen. On these occasions they always took with them, wrapped in a napkin, a white dish of rice boiled with sugar and raisins, with a cross of raisins on the top. He loved this church with its ancient icons, most of them without frames, and the old priest with his trembling head. Near his grandmother's grave, which was marked by a stone, was the little grave of his younger brother, who had died at six months old and whom he could not remember. He had been told about his little brother and every time they visited the cemetery he devoutly and reverently crossed himself before the little grave and bowed down and kissed it.

Now he dreamt that he and his father were passing the tavern on their way to the cemetery; he was holding his father's hand and looking fearfully over his shoulder at the tavern. There seemed to be some special festivity going on, which attracted his attention; there was a crowd of townsfolk and peasants and all kinds of rabble, all in their best clothes, and all drunk and bawling out songs. Near the entrance stood a cart, not an ordinary peasant's cart, but one of the huge drays drawn by great cart-horses, which are used for carrying bales of goods or barrels of liquor. He always loved to watch those massive dray-horses with their long manes and thick legs, plodding along at a steady pace and effortlessly pulling mountainous loads behind them, almost as if they found it easier than drawing an empty cart. The strange thing about this one was that a peasant's small, lean, decrepit old dun-coloured horse was harnessed to it, one such as he had often seen straining under a high-piled load of hay or firewood, especially when the cart was stuck in a rut or in the mire, while the peasant lashed it mercilessly with his whip, sometimes even beating it about the head and eyes. He would be so sorry, so sorry for the poor horse that he almost cried, and mama always used to take him away from the window.

Suddenly there was a din of shouting and singing, and the strumming of balalaikas, as a number of peasants, big men in red and blue shirts, with their coats slung over their shoulders, came out of the tavern roaring drunk. 'Get in, everybody get in!' shouted one, a young man with a thick neck and fleshy face as red as a beetroot, 'I'll take the lot of you. Get in!' There was a burst of laughter and shouting.

'What, with that broken-down old nag?'

'You must be out of your wits, Mikolka, to put that little old mare to that cart!'

'The poor old beast must be twenty years old if she's a day, lads!'

'Get in! I'll take all of you,' shouted Mikolka again, jumping in first himself. He gathered up the reins and stood upright at the front of the cart. 'Matvey has taken the bay,' he shouted from the cart, 'and as for this old mare, lads, she's just breaking my heart. It can kill her for aught I care; she's only eating her head off. Get in, I tell you! I'll make her gallop! She'll gallop, all right!' and he took up the whip, enjoying the thought of beating the old nag.

'Well, get in, then!' laughed the crowd. 'You heard him say he'd get a gallop out of her! She can't have galloped for ten years, I dare say.'

'She's going to now!'

'Come on, lads, all bring your whips. No being sorry for her!'

'That's it; let her have it!'

They all clambered into Mikolka's wagon, with witticisms and roars of laughter. There were six of them, and there was still room for more. They took up with them a fat red-faced peasant-woman in red cotton, with a head-dress trimmed with beads, and clogs on her feet. She was cracking nuts and laughing. The crowd round about was laughing too, and indeed, who could help laughing at the idea that such a sorry beast was going to pull such a load, and at a gallop? Two of the lads in the cart picked up their whips to help Mikolka. There was a roar of "Gee up!" and the wretched old nag tugged with all her might, but far from galloping she could barely stir at all, but simply scraped with her feet, grunting and flinching under the blows showering on her like hail from the three whips. The laughter in the cart and among the crowd redoubled, but Mikolka lost his temper and began raining blows on the little mare in a passion of anger, as if he really expected her to gallop.

'Let me come as well, lads,' shouted a fellow from the crowd, attracted by the sport.

'Get in, everybody get in,' yelled Mikolka, 'she'll pull you all. I'll give it her!' and he lashed away, so furious that he hardly knew what he was doing.

'Papa, papa,' cried the child, 'look what they are doing, papa! They are beating the poor horse!'

'Come away,' said his father. 'They are drunk and playing the fool, the brutes. Come away; don't look!' and he tried to draw the boy away. But he tore himself from his father's grasp and ran heedlessly towards the horse. The poor creature was in a sad state. She was panting and kept stopping and then beginning to tug again, almost ready to drop.

'Beat her to death!' howled Mikolka, 'that's what it's come to. I'll give it her!'

'You're more like a brute beast than a proper Christian!' called an old man in the crowd.

'The very idea of such a horse pulling a load like that!' added another.

'You'll founder the poor old thing,' shouted a third.

'You keep out of this! She's mine, isn't she? I can do what I like with my own. Get in, some more of you! Everybody get in! She's damn well going to gallop!....'

Suddenly there was a great explosion of laughter that drowned everything else: the old mare had rebelled against the hail of blows and was lashing out feebly with her hoofs. Even the old man could not help laughing. Indeed, it was ludicrous that such a decrepit old mare should still have a kick left in her.

Two men in the crowd got whips, ran to the horse, one on each side, and began to lash at her ribs.

'Hit her on the nose and across the eyes, beat her across the eyes!' yelled Mikolka.

'Let's have a song, lads!' someone called from the wagon, and the others joined in. Somebody struck up a coarse song, a tambourine rattled, somebody else whistled the chorus. The fat young woman went on cracking nuts and giggling.

. . . The boy ran towards the horse, then round in front, and saw them lashing her across the eyes, and actually striking her very eyeballs. He was weeping. His heart seemed to rise into his throat, and tears rained from his eyes. One of the whips stung his face, but he did not feel it; he was wringing his hands and crying aloud. He ran to a grey-haired, grey-bearded old man, who was shaking his head in reproof. A peasant-woman took him by the hand and tried to lead him away, but he tore himself loose and ran back to the mare. She was almost at her last gasp, but she began kicking again.

'The devil fly away with you!' shrieked Mikolka in a fury.

He flung away his whip, stooped down and dragged up from the floor of the cart a long thick wooden shaft, grasped one end with both hands, and swung it with an effort over the wretched animal.

Cries arose: 'He'll crush her!' 'He'll kill her!'

'She's my property,' yelled Mikolka, and with a mighty swing let the shaft fall. There was a heavy thud.

'Lash her, lash her! Why are you stopping?' shouted voices in the crowd.

Mikolka flourished the heavy bar again and brought it down with another great swing on the back of the wretched creature. Her back legs gave way under her, but she staggered up, tugging and jerking one way and the other to get away; six whips rained blows on her from every side, and the shaft rose and fell a third time, and then a fourth, with a rhythmical swing. Mikolka was frenzied with rage at not having killed her with one blow.

'She's tough!' yelled one of the crowd.

'This time she'll go down, for certain, lads. She's finished,' shouted another.

'Take an axe to her! Finish her off at one go!' cried a third.

'Oh, may you be bitten to death by mosquitoes!' shrieked Mikolka furiously, dropping the shaft and stooping down again to drag out an iron crowbar. 'Look out!' he yelled, and crashed it down with all his strength on the poor old mare. The blow was a crushing one; the mare staggered, sank down, and then made another effort to get up, but the crowbar struck another swinging blow on her back, and she fell as if her legs had been cut from under her.

'Finish her!' shouted Mikolka, and jumped down, quite beside himself, from the cart. A few of the young men, as drunk and red in the face as he, snatched up whatever came to hand—whips, sticks, the shaft—and ran to the dying mare. Mikolka stationed himself at the side and belaboured her back at random with the crowbar. The wretched animal stretched out her muzzle, drew a deep, labouring breath, and died.

The crowd was still shouting.

'He's done for her!'

'All the same, she didn't gallop!'

'My own property!' cried Mikolka, who, with bloodshot eyes, was standing with the crowbar in his hands and looking sorry that there was no longer anything to beat.

Many voices in the crowd were now calling, 'Shame! You're no better than a heathen!'

The poor little boy was quite beside himself. He pushed his way, shrieking, through the crowd to the mare, put his arms round the dead muzzle dabbled with blood and kissed the poor eyes and mouth . . . Then he sprang up and rushed furiously at Mikolka with his fists clenched. At that moment his father, who had been looking for him for a long time, caught him up and carried him out of the crowd.

'Come along, come along!' he said. 'Let us go home.'

'Papa, why did they . . . kill . . . the poor horse?' the boy sobbed, catching his breath. The words forced themselves out of his choking throat in a scream.

'They are drunk, they are playing the fool. It is none of our business. Let us go.' He put his arm round his father, but his breast was convulsed with sobs. He struggled for breath, tried to cry out, and awoke.

He woke panting and sweating, his hair damp with perspiration, and sprang up in alarm.

'Thank God, it was only a dream,' he said, sitting down under a tree and drawing long breaths. 'But why did I dream it? Can I be starting some sort of fever? It was such a horrible dream.'

His whole body felt bruised, and his mind dark and confused. He put his elbows on his knees and propped his head in his hands.

'God!' he exclaimed, 'is it possible, is it possible, that I really shall take an axe and strike her on the head, smash open her skull . . . that my feet will slip in warm, sticky blood, and that I shall break the lock, and steal, and tremble, and hide, all covered in blood . . . with the axe . . .? God, is it possible?'

He was shaking like a leaf.

'But why am I saying this?' he went on, leaning back again as if amazed at himself. 'I must have realized that I should never carry it out, so why have I gone on tormenting myself until now? Yesterday again, yesterday, when I went for that . . . *rehearsal*, I must certainly have been quite sure yesterday that I should never do it . . . Then why am I talking about it now? Why do I still go on harbouring doubts? Yesterday, as I came downstairs, didn't I tell myself that it was vile, disgusting, base, base . . . didn't I turn sick at the very thought of it, *when I was not dreaming*, and run away in terror . . .?'

'No, I shall not do it, I will not do it! Grant that there is no element of doubt in all those calculations of mine, grant that all the conclusions I have come to during the past month are as clear as daylight, as straightforward as arithmetic, all the same I shall never summon up enough resolution to do it. Of course I shall not carry it out, I shall not! . . . Then why, why, am I still . . .?'

He stood up, looked round as if wondering how he came to be there, and walked away to the Tuchkov Bridge. He was pale, his eyes glittered, exhaustion filled every limb, but he had suddenly begun to breathe more easily. He felt that he had thrown off the terrible burden that had weighed him down for so long, and his heart was light and tranquil. 'Lord!' he prayed, 'show me the way, that I may renounce this accursed . . . fantasy of mine!'

As he crossed the bridge he gazed with quiet tranquillity at the river Neva and the clear red sunset. Although he was so weak, he was not conscious even of being tired. It was as though the sore that had festered in his heart for a month had burst at last. Freedom! He was free now from the evil spells, from the sorcery and fascination, from the temptation.

When, later, he recalled this time and everything that happened in these few days, minute by minute, point by point, feature by feature, he was always struck with superstitious awe by one circumstance, which, though not really very out of the ordinary, seemed to him afterwards to have determined his fate. He could never understand or explain to himself why, tired and harassed though he was, he went out of his way to cross the Haymarket instead of returning home by the quickest and most direct route. The detour was not a great deal farther, but it was obviously quite unnecessary. Scores of times before, of course, he had gone home without being able to remember which streets he had passed through. But why, he used to ask himself, did such an important and fateful encounter for him take place in the Haymarket (through which he had no reason to go) just at this time, just at this moment of his life, when his mood and the circumstances were exactly those in which the meeting could have so fateful and decisive an influence on his destiny? It was almost as if fate had laid an ambush for him.

It was about nine o'clock when he crossed the market-place. All the dealers were locking up their shops and booths or putting away the wares from their stalls and trays, and going home, and so were the shoppers. Numbers of dealers and rag-and-bone men of every kind thronged in the basement cook-shops, the dirty and stinking courtyards of the houses, and especially the public houses in the market-square. Raskolnikov preferred these places and all the neighbouring back-streets and alleys when he went wandering aimlessly about. Here his rags drew no supercilious glances, and he could look as disreputable as he liked without scandalizing anybody. At the corner of Konny Street a dealer in thread, tapes, cotton handkerchiefs, and similar things displayed his wares on two trestle tables. He and his wife, who was a countrywoman, were also preparing to go home, but had lingered to talk to an acquaintance. This was Lizaveta Ivanovna, known to everybody simply as Lizaveta, the younger sister of that same old woman, Alëna Ivanovna, the moneylender, whom Raskolnikov had gone to see the day before, to pawn his watch and conduct his *rehearsal*. He had known all about Lizaveta for a long time, and she knew him slightly. She was tall and clumsily made, timid, submissive, and almost feeble-minded; she was about thirty-five years old and unmarried, and she was an absolute slave to her sister, working for her day and night, trembling before her and even submitting to blows from her. Now she was standing irresolutely with the dealer and his wife, holding a bundle and listening to them attentively. They were heatedly explaining something to her. When Raskolnikov caught sight of her he was filled with a strange feeling of utter astonishment, although there was nothing surprising about such a meeting.

'You ought to decide for yourself, Lizaveta Ivanovna,' said the man. 'Come tomorrow, some time before seven. They will be here too.'

'Tomorrow?' drawled Lizaveta doubtfully, as if she could not make up her mind.

'Eh, that Alëna Ivanovna has got you really scared,' babbled the dealer's brisk little wife. 'To look at you, anyone might think you were a little child. And she's not even your real sister, only a half-sister, and look how she's got you under her thumb!'

'This time, don't say anything to Alëna Ivanovna about it,' broke in her husband; 'that's my advice; you come without asking her. It's a paying proposition; afterwards even your sister might have to own that.'

'Shall I?'

'You come tomorrow, after six. Some of them will be here; you can decide for yourself.'

'And we'll have a drop of tea,' added his wife.

'All right, I'll come,' said Lizaveta, still rather doubtful, and moved slowly away.

Raskolnikov had already passed on and heard no more. He had gone past them unnoticed, walking quietly and trying not to lose a word. His first astonishment changed gradually into something like terror and a cold shiver ran up his spine. He had learnt, suddenly and quite unexpectedly, that at seven o'clock the next day Lizaveta, the old woman's sister and only companion, would be out, and that meant that at seven o'clock in the evening the old woman *would be at home alone*.

It was only a few steps farther to his lodging. He went in like a man condemned to death. He did not reason about anything, he was quite incapable of reasoning, but he felt with his whole being that his mind and will were no longer free, and that everything was settled, quite finally.

It was clear that even if he waited years for a favourable opportunity to execute his design, it would be impossible to count on so likely a chance of success as had suddenly presented itself at this moment. In any case, he could hardly expect to learn the day before, with greater exactness or less risk, without any dangerous questioning or investigation on his part, that on the next day at a certain time the old woman on whom the attempt was to be made would be at home alone, quite alone.

## CHAPTER VI

LATER Raskolnikov learnt, by some chance, why the dealer and his wife had asked Lizaveta to come and see them. It was a perfectly usual transaction, with nothing out of the ordinary about it. An impoverished family, lately come to St. Petersburg, wished to dispose of some articles of women's clothing and similar things. It would not have paid them to sell in the market and so they were looking for a dealer. Lizaveta undertook such transactions, selling on commission, and going round arranging business deals, and she had a large clientele because she was honest and never haggled, but named her price and stuck to it. She did not talk much and, as we have said, was timid and meek . . .

Raskolnikov had recently become superstitious. Traces of this superstition remained in him long afterwards, almost ineradicable. And in after years he was always inclined to see something strange and mysterious in all the happenings of this time, as if special coincidences and influences were at work. As long before as the previous winter a fellow student, Pokorev, who was leaving for Kharkov, had mentioned Alëna Ivanovna's address to him in conversation, in case he ever needed to pawn anything. For a long time he did not go near her, since he had his lessons and was managing to get along somehow, but six weeks earlier he had remembered the address. He had two things suitable for pawning: his father's old silver watch and a gold ring set with three little red stones, given to him as a keepsake by his sister when they parted. He decided to take the ring, and sought out the old woman; at first sight, before he knew anything about her, he felt an irresistible dislike of her. He took her two rouble notes and on his way home stopped at a miserable little tavern and asked for tea. He sat down, deep in thought; a strange idea seemed to be pecking away in his head, like a chicken emerging from the shell, and all his attention was fixed on it.

At another table near by, a student, who was unknown to him and whom he did not remember ever seeing, was sitting with a young officer. They had been playing billiards and were drinking tea. Suddenly he heard the student talking about the moneylender Alëna Ivanovna, giving the officer her address. This struck Raskolnikov as rather odd: he had just left her, and here they were talking about her. Of course, it was the merest chance, but exactly when he was finding it impossible to rid himself of an extraordinary impression, here was somebody reinforcing it, for the student was beginning to tell his friend some details about this Alëna Ivanovna.

'She's quite famous,' he said; 'she always has money to lay out. She's as rich as a Jew, she can put her hands on five thousand roubles at once, and yet she doesn't turn up her nose at the interest on a rouble. A lot of our fellows have been to her. But she's an old bitch . . .'

And he began to recount how spiteful and cranky she was, and how, if payment was only one day overdue, the pledge would be lost. She would lend only a quarter as much as things were worth, she would demand five or even seven per cent. a month, and so on. The student's tongue had run away with him, and, among other things, he informed his hearer that the old woman had a sister, Lizaveta, whom the vicious little thing was always beating and whom she kept in complete subjection and treated as if she were a child, although Lizaveta stood at least five foot ten . . .

'She's another extraordinary creature, you know!' cried the student, and burst out laughing.

They began to talk about Lizaveta. The student seemed greatly to enjoy this and kept on laughing, and the officer listened with great interest and asked the student to send this Lizaveta to do his mending. Raskolnikov also learned all about her, not missing one word. Lizaveta was the old woman's younger step-sister (they had different mothers) and was about thirty-five. She worked for her sister day in and day out, did all the cooking and washing in the house, and in addition took in sewing and even went out scrubbing floors, and everything she earned she handed over to her sister. She dared not accept any orders or undertake any work without the old woman's permission. As Lizaveta knew, the old woman had already made her will, leaving to the younger sister only furniture and other chattels, while all the money went to a monastery in N—— Province for masses for the eternal repose of her soul. Lizaveta was a woman of the working-class, not educated, and unmarried; she was remarkably tall and extremely ungainly, with big, long, splay feet, shod with down-at-heel goat-skin shoes, and she always kept herself very clean. But what the student found the most surprising and amusing was that Lizaveta was pregnant . . .

'But I thought you said she was monstrously ugly,' remarked the officer.

'Well, she's very dark-skinned, and looks like a guardsman in disguise, but, you know, she's no monster. She has a nice kind face and eyes—she's even very attractive. The proof is, a lot of people like her. She is so quiet and gentle and mild, and will consent to anything. And she's really got a very nice smile.'

'You like her yourself, don't you?' laughed the officer.

'Because she's an oddity. But I'll tell you what: I swear I could kill that damned old woman and rob her, without a single twinge of conscience,' exclaimed the student hotly.

The officer laughed again, but Raskolnikov found this so strange that he shuddered.

'Let me ask you a serious question,' went on the student, even more heatedly. 'I was joking just now, of course, but look here: on the one hand you have a stupid, silly, utterly unimportant, vicious, sickly old woman, no good to anybody, but in fact quite the opposite, who doesn't know herself why she goes on living, and will probably die tomorrow without any assistance. Do you understand what I am saying?'

'Oh, I follow you,' answered the officer, earnestly studying his companion's vehemence.

'Listen, then. On the other hand you have new, young forces running to waste for want of backing, and there are thousands of them, all over the place. A hundred, a thousand, good actions and promising beginnings might be forwarded and directed aright by the money that old woman destines for a monastery; hundreds, perhaps thousands, of existences might be set on the right path, scores of families saved from beggary, from decay, from ruin and corruption, from the lock hospitals —and all with her money! Kill her, take her money, on condition that you dedicate yourself with its help to the service of humanity and the common good: don't you think that thousands of good deeds will wipe out one little, insignificant transgression? For one life taken, thousands saved from corruption and decay! One death, and a hundred lives in exchange— why, it's simple arithmetic![1] What is the life of that stupid, spiteful, consumptive old woman weighed against the common good? No more than the life of a louse or a cockroach— less, indeed, because she is actively harmful. She battens on other people's lives, she is evil; not long since she bit Lizaveta's finger, out of sheer malice, and it almost had to be amputated!'

'She doesn't deserve to live, certainly,' remarked the officer, 'but there you are, that's nature.'

'But don't you see, man, nature must be guided and corrected, or else we should all be swamped with prejudices. Otherwise there could never be one great man. They talk of "duty, conscience"—I've got nothing to say against duty and conscience—but what are we to understand by them? Stop, I will put another question to you. Listen!'

'No, you stop; I will ask you a question. Listen!'

'Well?'

'Here you've been holding forth and making a regular speech, but tell me this: would you kill the old woman with your own hands, or not?'[2]

'Of course not! For the sake of justice, I . . . This is not a question of me at all!'

'Well, if you ask me, so long as you won't, justice doesn't come into it. Let's have another game!'

Raskolnikov was deeply disturbed. No doubt there was nothing in all this but the most usual and ordinary youthful talk and ideas, such as he had heard often enough in other forms and about other subjects. But why must he listen at this particular moment to that particular talk and those particular ideas when there had just been born in his own brain *exactly the same ideas*? And why, at the very moment when he was

1. See note to p. 11.
2. This is a paraphrase of the conversation of Rastignac and a student in Balzac's novel *Father Goriot*.

carrying away from the old woman's flat the germ of his idea, should he chance upon a conversation about that same old woman? . . . . This always seemed to him a strange coincidence. This casual public-house conversation had an extraordinary influence on the subsequent development of the matter, as if there were indeed something fateful and fore-ordained about it.

When he returned home from the Haymarket he threw himself on the sofa and sat there without moving for an hour. It grew dark, and he had no candles, not that it would have entered his head to light one if he had. Afterwards he was never able to remember whether he had been thinking of anything definite during that hour. At length he felt his recent chills and fever return, and realized with pleasure that he could lie down where he was. Soon a heavy leaden sleep weighed him down.

He slept unusually long and dreamlessly. Nastasya, coming into his room next morning at ten o'clock, could hardly shake him awake. She had brought him some tea and bread. The tea was once again what remained in her own teapot.

'Goodness, he's still asleep!' she exclaimed indignantly, 'he's always asleep!'

He raised himself with an effort. His head ached; he stood up, took a few steps, and fell back on the sofa again.

'Are you going to sleep again?' exclaimed Nastasya. 'Are you ill, or what?'

He did not answer.

'Do you want any tea?'

'Afterwards,' he said with an effort, closing his eyes again and turning to the wall. Nastasya stood over him.

'Perhaps he really *is* ill,' she said, turned on her heel and went out.

She came back at two o'clock with some soup. He was lying there as before. The tea was untouched. Nastasya was quite offended and began to shake him roughly.

'Whyever do you still go on sleeping?' she exclaimed, looking at him with positive dislike. He sat up and remained gazing at the floor without a word to her.

'Are you ill or aren't you?' asked Nastasya, and again received no answer.

'You want to go out for a bit,' she said, after a short silence, 'and get a bit of a blow. Are you going to have anything to eat, eh?'

'Later,' he said feebly. 'Clear out!' He waved her away.

She stood there a little longer, looking at him pityingly, and then went out.

After a few minutes he raised his eyes and stared at the tea and soup. Then he took up some bread and a spoon and began to eat.

He ate a little—two or three spoonfuls—but without appetite, and quite mechanically. His head no longer ached so much. When he had eaten, he stretched out once more on the sofa, but he could not go to sleep again and lay without stirring, face downwards, with his head buried in the pillow. He lost himself in a maze of waking dreams, and very strange ones they were; in the one that recurred most often he was in Africa, in Egypt, at some oasis. A caravan was resting, the camels lying peacefully and the men eating their evening meal; all around, the palms stood in a great circle. He was drinking the water from a stream which flowed babbling beside him, clear and cool, running marvellously bright and blue over the coloured stones and the clean sand with its gleams of gold . . . All at once he distinctly heard a clock strike. He roused himself with a start, raised his head and looked at the window, trying to estimate the time, and then, suddenly wide awake, sprang up as if he had been catapulted from the sofa. He crept to the door on tiptoe, quietly eased it open, and stood listening for sounds from the staircase. His heart was beating wildly. But the staircase was quiet, as though everyone were asleep . . . It seemed to him incredibly strange that he could have gone on sleeping in such utter forgetfulness ever since the previous night, without having made the least preparation . . . And it might have been six o'clock that struck just now . . . An extraordinarily confused and feverish bustle had now replaced his sleepy torpor. He had not many preparations to make. He was straining every nerve to take everything into consideration and let nothing slip his memory, and his heart thumped so heavily that he could scarcely breathe. First of all he must make a loop and sew it into his overcoat, the work of a moment. He groped under his pillow and drew out from among the linen stuffed under it an old unwashed shirt that was falling to pieces. From among its tatters he ripped out a strip about an inch and a half wide and twelve long. He folded this strip in two, took off his only outer garment, a loose summer overcoat of thick stout cotton material, and sewed the two ends of the strip together to the inside, under the left armhole. His hands shook as he sewed, but he controlled them, and when he put the coat on again nothing showed from outside. He had got the needle and thread ready long before, and had kept them on the little table, pinned into a piece of paper. As for the loop, that was an ingenious device of his own; it was meant to hold the axe. He could hardly carry an axe in his hands through the streets. And even if he had hidden it under his coat, he would still have had to support it with his hand, which would be noticeable. But now he need only lay the axe-head in the loop and it would hang peacefully under his arm all the way. With his hand in his pocket he could support the end of the shaft so that it would not swing; and as the coat was very wide and hung like a sack, nobody could possibly notice that he was holding something through the pocket. He had thought of this loop at least two weeks before.

Having finished this task, he thrust his fingers into the narrow crevice between the bottom of his 'Turkish' divan and the floor, groping under the left-hand corner for the *pledge* he had prepared and hidden there. It was not really a pledge at all, however, but simply a piece of smoothly-planed board, about the size and thickness of a silver cigarette-case. He had found it by chance, on one of his walks, in a yard where there was some sort of workshop in an out-building. On the same occasion he picked up in the street, a little later, a smooth thin iron plate, rather smaller than the wood, apparently broken off something. Laying the two together, he had tied them securely with thread and then wrapped them neatly and carefully in clean white paper and made them into a parcel with thin string tied in a complicated knot that would need a great deal of skill to undo. This was done in order to distract the old woman's attention for a time while she dealt with the knot, and thus enable him to choose his moment. The iron plate had been added to increase the weight, so that she should not immediately recognize that the 'pledge' was made of wood. He had hidden the whole thing under the sofa until he needed it. He had just got it out when he heard someone shouting in the courtyard.

'It went six ages ago.'

'Ages ago! Oh God!'

He flung himself towards the door, listened, seized his hat, and crept as stealthily as a cat down his thirteen stairs. The most important step still lay before him—stealing an axe from the kitchen. He had long since come to the conclusion that he needed an axe to accomplish his purpose. He did possess a folding garden-knife, but he could not rely on a knife, or on his own strength in wielding it, and therefore finally settled on an axe. One noticeable peculiarity characterized all the final decisions he arrived at in this affair: the more settled they were, the more hideous and absurd they appeared in his eyes. In spite of his agonizing internal struggles he could never throughout the whole time believe for one instant in the practicability of his schemes.

If it had somehow come about that the whole project had been analysed and finally decided down to the last detail, and no further doubts remained, he would very likely have renounced the whole idea for its absurdity, enormity, and impossibility. But there were in fact innumerable doubts and unsettled details. As for where he would obtain the axe, this trifle did not disturb him in the slightest, for nothing could be easier. The fact was that Nastasya was often out of the house, especially in the evening; she was always calling on the neighbours or running out to the shops, and the door was always left wide open; this was the landlady's only quarrel with her. Thus it would only be necessary to slip quietly into the kitchen, when the time came, take the axe, and then an hour later (when *it* was all over), put it back again. One doubt still remained, however: suppose he came back after an hour to return the axe, and found Nastasya back at home? It would, of course, be necessary to go straight past and wait until she went out again, but what if meanwhile she remembered the axe and looked for it, and raised an outcry? That would create suspicion, or at least give grounds for it.

But all these were trifles, about which he had not even begun to think, and there was no time for them now. He had thought about the main point, but he had put the details aside until *he had convinced himself.* This last, however, appeared definitely unrealizable. So at least it seemed to him. He could not, for example, picture himself ceasing at a given moment to think about it, getting up and—simply going there . . . Even his recent *rehearsal* (that is, his visit for a final survey of the scene) had been no more than a *test*, and far from a serious one, as though he had said to himself: 'Very well, let us go and try whether it's just an idle fancy!'—and then immediately failed in the test, spat, and run away, exasperated with himself. And yet it would seem that his analysis, in the sense of a moral solution of the question, was concluded; his casuistry had the cutting edge of a razor, and he could no longer find any conscious objections in his own mind. But in the last resort he simply did not believe himself and obstinately, slavishly groped for objections on all sides, as if he were driven by some compulsion. His reactions during this last day, which had come upon him so unexpectedly and settled everything at one stroke, were almost completely mechanical, as though someone had taken his hand and pulled him along irresistibly, blindly, with supernatural strength and without objection. It was as if a part of his clothing had been caught in the wheel of a machine and he was being dragged into it.

The first question he had been concerned with—a long time ago now—was why most crimes were so easily discovered and solved, and why nearly every criminal left so clear a trail. He arrived by degrees at a variety of curious conclusions, and, in his opinion, the chief cause lay not so much in the material impossibility of concealing the crime as in the criminal himself; nearly every criminal, at the moment of the crime, was subject to a collapse of will-power and reason, exchanging them for an extraordinarily childish heedlessness, and that just at the moment when judgement and caution were most indispensable. He was convinced that this eclipse of reason and failure of will attacked a man like an illness, developed gradually and reached their height shortly before the commission of the crime, continuing unchanged at the moment of commission and for some time, varying with the individual, afterwards; their subsequent course was that of any other disease. The further question whether the disease engenders the crime, or whether the nature of crime somehow results in its always being accompanied by some manifestation of disease, he did not feel competent to answer.

Having arrived at this conclusion, he decided that he personally would not be subject to any such morbid subversion, that his judgement and will would remain steadfast throughout the fulfilment of his plans, for the simple reason that what he contemplated was 'no crime' . . . We omit the course of reasoning by which he arrived at this latter verdict, since we have already run too far ahead . . . We shall add only that the practical, material difficulties played only a very secondary role in his thinking. 'It will suffice to concentrate my will and my judgement on them, and they will all be overcome, when the time comes, when I have to come to grips with all the details of the affair, down to the most minute . . .' But he made no progress towards action. He continued to have less and less faith in his final decisions, and when the hour struck, everything seemed to go awry, in a haphazard and almost completely unexpected way.

One small circumstance nonplussed him even before he reached the foot of the stairs. As he drew level with his landlady's kitchen door, which stood open as usual, he peered carefully round it to make sure beforehand that the landlady herself was not there in Nastasya's absence, and if she was not, that her door was firmly closed so that she would not happen to look out and see him when he went in for the axe. But what was his consternation at seeing that Nastasya was at home in her kitchen on this occasion, and busy taking linen from a basket and hanging it on a line. When she caught sight of him she ceased her occupation and turned towards him, watching him as he went past. He turned his eyes away and walked on as if he had not noticed her. But it was all over: he had no axe! It was a terrible blow.

'Where did I get the idea,' he thought, going out through the gate, 'where did I get the idea that she was certain to be out now? Why, why, why, was I so convinced of it?' He felt crushed, even humiliated, and ready to laugh spitefully at himself . . . He was seething with dull, brutal rage.

He had stopped uncertainly in the gateway. To go out now

and walk about the streets for form's sake, and to return to his room, were both equally repugnant to him. 'What an opportunity is lost for ever!' he muttered, standing aimlessly in the gateway, just opposite the porter's dark little room, which also stood open. Suddenly he started. Inside the little room, not two paces away, under a bench on the right-hand side, something shining caught his eye . . . He looked all round—nobody! On tiptoe he approached the porter's lodge, went down the two steps, and called the porter in a feeble voice. 'Yes, he's out! but he must be somewhere near, in the courtyard, since the door is open.' He threw himself headlong on the axe (it was an axe), drew it out from where it lay between two logs under the bench, hung it in the loop on the spot, thrust both hands into his pockets and went out. He had not been seen. 'It was not my planning, but the devil, that accomplished that!' he thought, and laughed strangely, extraordinarily heartened by this stroke of luck.

He walked quietly and sedately, without hurrying, so as not to arouse suspicion. He paid little attention to the passers-by, and carefully avoided looking at their faces, trying to be unnoticed himself. Suddenly he remembered his hat. 'My God! I had the money two days ago, and hadn't the sense to spend it on a cap!' and he cursed himself from the bottom of his heart.

Glancing casually into a shop, he saw from the clock that hung on the wall that it was already ten minutes past seven. He would have to hurry; he wanted to go round about, so as to approach the house from the other side.

Earlier, when he had tried to imagine what all this would be like, he had thought he would be very frightened. But he was not; indeed he was not frightened at all. His mind was even occupied, though not for long together, with irrelevant thoughts.

Passing the Yusupov Gardens, he began to consider the construction of tall fountains in all the squares, and how they would freshen the air. Following this train of thought he came to the conclusion that if the Summer Gardens could be extended right across the Champ de Mars and joined to those of the Mikhaylovsky Palace, it would add greatly to the beauty and amenities of the city. Then he suddenly began to wonder why, in big towns, people chose of their own free will to live where there were neither parks nor gardens, but only filth and squalor and evil smells. This reminded him of his own walks in the neighbourhood of the Haymarket, and brought him back to himself. 'What rubbish!' he thought. 'It would be better not to think at all!'

'So it is true that men going to execution are passionately interested in any object they chance to see on the way.' The thought passed through his mind as briefly as a flash of lightning, for he suppressed it at once . . . But he had arrived; here was the house and the gate. Somewhere a clock struck once. 'What, can it possibly be half-past seven? Surely not; time is really flying!'

Luck was again with him as he turned in at the gate. At that very moment, as if by design, a huge load of hay also turned in, just in front of him, and completely screened him while he was passing through the archway. As soon as it had cleared the gateway and was in the courtyard, he slipped past it to the right. On the other side of the cart he could hear several voices shouting and quarrelling, but nobody noticed him and nobody passed him. Many of the windows opening on to the great courtyard stood open, but he could not find the strength to raise his head. The old woman's staircase was near, immediately to the right of the gate. Already he was on the stairs.

Drawing a deep breath and pressing his hand above his wildly beating heart, he once more felt for the axe and settled it in its loop, then began to mount the stairs carefully and quietly, listening at every step. But the staircase was empty at this hour; all the doors were closed and nobody was to be seen. On the second floor, it is true, the door of an empty flat was open, and painters were at work inside, but they did not even look up. He stopped for a moment, considering, and then went on. 'Of course, it would be better if they were not there, but . . . there are two floors above them.'

But here was the fourth floor, here was the door, here was the empty flat opposite. On the third floor the flat immediately below the old woman's also showed every sign of being empty: the visiting-card tacked to the door had been removed—they had left . . . He was out of breath. For a moment the thought stirred in his mind: 'There is still time to go away.' But he ignored it and began to listen at the old woman's door—dead silence! Then once more he listened down the stairs, long and attentively . . . Then he looked round for the last time, crept close to the door, straightened his clothes, and once again tried the axe in its loop. 'I wonder if I look too pale,' he thought, 'and too agitated. She is mistrustful . . . Wouldn't it be better if I waited a little longer . . . until my heart stops thumping so? . . .'

But his heart did not stop. On the contrary, its throbbing grew more and more violent . . . He could stand it no longer, but stretched his hand slowly towards the bell, and rang it. After a few moments he rang again, louder.

There was no answer. There was no point in going on ringing in vain, and he was not in the mood to do so. The old woman was certainly at home, but she was suspicious and she was alone. He knew something of her habits . . . and he applied his ear to the door again. Either his hearing had grown strangely acute (which did not seem likely) or the sound was really distinctly audible, but at any rate he suddenly heard the careful placing of a hand on the handle of a lock and the rustle of clothing close to the door. Someone was standing silently just inside the door and listening, just as he was doing outside it, holding her breath and probably also with her ear to the door . . .

He purposely shifted his position and audibly muttered something, so as not to give the impression that he was being furtive; then he rang a third time, but quietly and firmly, without betraying any impatience. When he was afterwards able to recall everything clearly and plainly, that minute seemed stamped into his memory for ever; he could not understand whence he had acquired so much cunning, especially as his mind seemed momentarily to cloud over, and he lost all consciousness of his own body . . . A moment later, he heard the bolt being lifted.

# CHAPTER VII

As before, the door opened the merest crack, and again two sharp and mistrustful eyes peered at him from the darkness. Then Raskolnikov lost his head and made what might have been a serious mistake.

Apprehensive that the old woman might be alarmed at their being alone, and without any hope that his appearance would reassure her, he took hold of the door and pulled it towards him, so that she should not be tempted to lock herself in again. Although she did not pull the door shut again at this, she did not relinquish the handle, so that he almost pulled her out on the stairs. When he saw that she was standing across the doorway in such a way that he could not pass, he advanced straight upon her, and she stood aside startled. She seemed to be trying to say something but finding it impossible, and she kept her eyes fixed on him.

'Good evening, Alëna Ivanovna,' he began, as easily as possible, but his voice refused to obey him, and was broken and trembling, 'I have . . . brought you . . . something . . . but hadn't we better come in here . . . to the light? . . .' And without waiting for an invitation, he passed her and went into the room. The old woman hastened after him; her tongue seemed to have been loosened.

'Good Lord! What are you doing? . . . Who are you? What do you want?'

'Excuse me, Alëna Ivanovna . . . You know me . . . Raskolnikov . . . See, I have brought the pledge I promised the other day,' and he held it out to her.

The old woman threw a glance at it, but then immediately fixed her eyes on those of her uninvited guest. She looked at him attentively, ill-naturedly, and mistrustfully. A minute or so went by; he even thought he could see a glint of derision in her eyes, as if she had guessed everything. He felt that he was losing his nerve and was frightened, so frightened that he thought if she went on looking at him like that, without a word, for even half a minute longer, he would turn tail and run away.

'Why are you looking at me like that, as though you didn't recognize me?' he burst out angrily. 'Do you want it, or don't you? I can take it somewhere else; it makes no difference to me.'

He had not intended to say this, but it seemed to come of its own accord.

The old woman collected herself, and her visitor's resolute tone seemed to lull her mistrust.

'Why be so hasty, my friend? . . . What is it?' she asked, looking at the packet.

'A silver cigarette case; surely I told you that last time?'

She stretched out her hand.

'But what makes you so pale? And your hands are trembling. Are you ill or something?'

'Fever,' he answered abruptly. 'You can't help being pale . . . when you haven't anything to eat,' he added, hardly able to articulate his words. His strength was failing again. But apparently the answer was plausible enough; the old woman took the packet.

'What is it?' she asked, weighing it in her hand and once again fixing her eyes on Raskolnikov.

'A thing . . . a cigarette-case . . . silver . . . look at it.'

'It doesn't feel like silver. Lord, what a knot!' Trying to undo the string she turned for light towards the window (all her windows were closed, in spite of the oppressive heat), moved away from him and stood with her back to him. He unbuttoned his coat and freed the axe from the loop, but still kept it concealed, supporting it with his right hand under the garment. His arms seemed to have no strength in them; he felt them growing more and more numb and stiff with every moment. He was afraid of letting the axe slip and fall . . . His head was whirling.

'Why is it all wrapped up like this?' exclaimed the woman sharply, and turned towards him.

There was not a moment to lose. He pulled the axe out, swung it up with both hands, hardly conscious of what he was doing, and almost mechanically, without putting any force behind it, let the butt-end fall on her head. His strength seemed to have deserted him, but as soon as the axe descended it all returned to him.

The old woman was, as usual, bare-headed. Her thin fair hair, just turning grey, and thick with grease, was plaited into a rat's tail and fastened into a knot above her nape with a fragment of horn comb. Because she was so short the axe struck her full on the crown of the head. She cried out, but very feebly, and sank in a heap to the floor, still with enough strength left to raise both hands to her head. One of them still held the 'pledge'. Then he struck her again and yet again, with all his strength, always with the blunt side of the axe, and always on the crown of the head. Blood poured out as if from an overturned glass and the body toppled over on its back. He stepped away as it fell, and then stooped to see the face: she was dead. Her wide-open eyes looked ready to start out of their sockets, her forehead was wrinkled and her whole face convulsively distorted.

He laid the axe on the floor near the body and, taking care not to smear himself with the blood, felt in her pocket, the right-hand pocket, from which she had taken her keys last time. He was quite collected, his faculties were no longer clouded nor his head swimming, but his hands still shook. Later he remembered that he had been very painstakingly careful not to get bedaubed . . . He pulled out the keys; they were all together, as he remembered them, on a steel ring. He hurried straight into the bedroom with them. It was a very small room; on one wall was an enormous case of icons, and another was occupied by the big bed, very clean, covered with a silk patchwork quilt. The chest of drawers stood against the third wall. It was strange, but as soon as he began to try the keys in it, and heard their jingling, a convulsive shudder shook him; he longed suddenly to abandon the whole affair and go away. But this lasted only for a moment; it was too late now to retreat. He was even laughing at himself when another, most alarming, idea flashed into his mind, the idea that perhaps the old woman was still alive and might yet recover consciousness. He left the keys and the chest and ran back to the body, seized the axe and brandished it over the old woman again, but did not bring it down. There could be no doubt that she was dead. Stooping down again to examine the body more closely, he saw clearly that the skull was shattered. He stretched out his hand to touch her, but drew it back again; he could see plainly enough without that. By this time the blood had formed a pool on the floor. Then he noticed a cord round the old woman's neck and tugged at it, but it was too strong to snap, and besides, it was slippery with blood. He tried to draw it out from the bosom of her dress, but it seemed to be caught on something and would not come. Impatiently he raised the axe again, to sever the cord with a blow as it lay on the body, but he could not bring himself to do this, and finally, after struggling with it for two minutes, and getting the axe and his hands smeared with blood, he managed with some difficulty to cut the cord without touching the body with the axe; he took it off, and found, as he expected, a purse hanging there. There were two crosses on the cord, one of cypress-wood and the other of brass, as well as an enamelled religious medal, and beside them hung a small, soiled, chamois-leather purse, with a steel frame and clasp. It was crammed full; Raskolnikov thrust it into his pocket without examining it and threw the crosses down on the old woman's breast; then, this time taking the axe with him, he hurried back into the bedroom.

With dreadful urgency he seized the keys and began to struggle with them once more. But all his efforts failed to force them into the locks, not so much because his hands were trembling as because his energy was misdirected; he would see, for example, that a key was the wrong one and would not fit, and yet go on thrusting at the lock with it. He pulled himself together and remembered that the big key with toothed wards, hanging with the other smaller ones, could not possibly belong to the chest of drawers, but must be for some trunk or other (as he had thought on the previous occasion), and that perhaps it was there that everything was hidden. He left the chest and looked first of all under the bed, knowing that old women usually keep their trunks there. He was right; there stood an important-looking steel-studded trunk of red leather, about thirty inches long, with a rounded lid. The toothed key fitted the lock and opened the trunk. On top, under a white sheet, lay a hare-skin coat with a red lining; under this were a silk dress, then a shawl, and then, at the bottom, what looked like a heap of rags. His first impulse was to wipe his bloody hands on the red lining of the fur coat. 'It is red, so blood will not show on it,' he reasoned, and then suddenly realized what he was doing and thought, with fear in his heart, 'Good God, am I going out of my mind?'

But no sooner had he disturbed the rags than a gold watch slid out from under the coat. Hastily he began turning everything over, and found a number of gold articles thrust in among the rags, bracelets, chains, earrings, pins, and so forth, probably pledges, some of them perhaps unredeemed. Some were in cases, some simply wrapped in newspaper, but neatly and carefully, with the paper tidily folded and the packets tied with tape. He began to cram them hastily into the pockets of his overcoat and trousers, without opening the cases or undoing the parcels, but he did not manage to collect very many . . .

A footstep sounded in the room where the old woman lay. He stopped and remained motionless as the dead. But all was still; he must have imagined it. Then he distinctly heard a faint cry, or perhaps rather a feeble interrupted groaning, then dead silence again for a minute or two. He waited, crouching by the trunk, hardly daring to breathe; then he sprang up, seized the axe, and ran out of the room.

There in the middle of the floor, with a big bundle in her arms, stood Lizaveta, as white as a sheet, gazing in frozen horror at her murdered sister and apparently without the strength to cry out. When she saw him run in, she trembled like a leaf and her face twitched spasmodically; she raised her hand as if to cover her mouth, but no scream came and she backed slowly away from him towards the corner, with her eyes on him in a fixed stare, but still without a sound, as though she had no breath left to cry out. He flung himself forward with the axe; her lips writhed pitifully, like those of a young child when it is just beginning to be frightened and stands ready to scream, with its eyes fixed on the object of its fear. The wretched Lizaveta was so simple, brow-beaten, and utterly terrified that she did not even put up her arms to protect her face, natural and almost inevitable as the gesture would have been at this moment when the axe was brandished immediately above it. She only raised her free left hand a little and slowly stretched it out towards him as though she were trying to push him away. The blow fell on her skull, splitting it open from the top of the forehead almost to the crown of the head, and felling her instantly. Raskolnikov, completely beside himself, snatched up her bundle, threw it down again, and ran to the entrance.

The terror that possessed him had been growing greater and greater, especially after this second, unpremeditated murder. He wanted to get away as quickly as possible. If he had been in a condition to exercise a soberer judgement and see things more clearly, if he could only have recognized all the difficulty of his position and how desperate, hideous, and absurd it was, if he could have understood how many obstacles to surmount, perhaps even crimes to commit, still lay before him, before he could escape from the house and reach home—very probably he would have abandoned everything and given himself up, not out of fear for himself so much as from horror and repulsion for what he had done. Repulsion, indeed, was growing in his heart with every moment. Not for anything in the world would he have returned to the trunk, or even to the room.

But a growing distraction, that almost amounted to absent-mindedness, had taken possession of him; at times he seemed to forget what he was doing, or rather to forget the important things and cling to trivialities. However, when he glanced into the kitchen and saw a pail half full of water on a bench, it gave him the idea of washing his hands and the axe. His hands were sticky with blood. He put the head of the axe in the water, then took a piece of soap that lay in a broken saucer on the window-sill, and began to wash his hands in the pail. When he had washed them he drew out the axe and washed the blade and then spent some three minutes trying to clean the part of the handle that was blood-stained, using soap to get the blood out. After this he wiped it with a cloth which was drying on a line stretched across the kitchen, and then spent a long time examining it carefully at the window. There were no stains left, but the handle was still damp. With great care he laid the axe in the loop under his coat. Then, as well as the dim light in the kitchen allowed, he examined his overcoat, trousers, and boots. At first glance there was nothing to give him away, except for some stains on his boots. He wiped them with a damp rag. He knew, however, that he had not been able to see very well, and might have failed to notice something quite conspicuous. He stood hesitating in the middle of the room. A dark and tormenting idea was beginning to rear its head, the idea that he was going out of his mind and that he was not capable of reasoning or of protecting himself. Perhaps what he was doing was not at all what ought to be done . . . 'My God, I must run, I must run!' he muttered and hurried back to the entrance. Here there awaited him a more extreme terror than any he had yet experienced.

He stood still, staring, unable to believe his eyes; the door, the outer door leading to the staircase, the door at which he had rung a short time ago, and by which he had entered, was at least a hand's-breadth open; all this time it had been like that, neither locked nor bolted, all the time! The old woman had not locked it behind him, perhaps by way of precaution. But, good God, he had seen Lizaveta after that! And how could he have failed to realize that she had come from outside, and could certainly not have come through the wall?

He flung himself at the door and put up the bolt.

'But no, that's not right either! I must go, I must go . . .'

He lifted the bolt clear, opened the door, and stood listening on the landing.

He stood there a long time. Somewhere far below, probably under the gateway, two voices were raised loudly and shrilly in argument. 'What are they doing?' He waited patiently. At last the voices fell silent, as though they had been cut off; 'they' had gone away. He was preparing to descend when suddenly a door on the floor below opened noisily and somebody started down the stairs, humming a tune. 'Why are they making so much noise?' he wondered for a moment. He closed the door again behind him and waited. At last all was quiet; there was not a sound. He was already setting his foot on the stairs when once more he heard footsteps.

When he first heard them, the steps were far away, at the very bottom of the staircase, but he afterwards remembered clearly and distinctly that from the very first sound he guessed that they were certainly coming *here*, to the fourth floor, to the old woman's flat. Why? Was there something special, something significant, about them? The steps were heavy, regular, unhurrying. Already they had reached the first floor, they were coming on, their sound was clearer and clearer. He could hear the newcomer's heavy breathing. Already the steps had passed the second floor . . . They were coming here! Suddenly he felt as if he had turned to stone, like a sleeper who dreams that he is being hotly pursued and threatened with death, and finds himself rooted to the spot, unable to stir a finger.

At length, when the footsteps had begun the last flight, he started to life, and just managed to slip swiftly and dextrously back from the landing into the flat and close the door behind him. Then he grasped the bolt and slid it gently, without a sound, into its socket. Instinct had come to his aid. When he had done, he stayed quiet, holding his breath, close to the door. The unknown visitor was also at the door. They were standing now, opposite one another, as he and the old woman had stood, with the door dividing them, when he had listened there a short time ago.

The visitor drew several heavy breaths. 'He must be a big stout man,' thought Raskolnikov, grasping the axe tightly. Everything seemed to be happening in a dream. The visitor seized the bell and rang it loudly.

As soon as its tinny sound had died, Raskolnikov imagined he heard movement inside the room, and for some seconds he listened as seriously as though it were possible. The unknown rang again, waited a little longer and then suddenly began to tug impatiently at the door-handle with all his might. Terrified, Raskolnikov watched the bolt rattling in its socket and waited in numb fear for it to jump clean out. This seemed likely to happen at any moment, so violently was the door shaken. He would have held the bar with his hand, except that *he* might discern it. His head was beginning to spin again. 'I am going to faint!' he thought, but the unknown began to speak and he recovered himself immediately.

'Are they fast asleep in there, or dead, or what, confound them?' the visitor boomed in a resounding voice. 'Hey! Alëna Ivanovna, you old witch! Lizaveta Ivanovna, my peerless beauty! Open the door! Oh, confound it all, they must be asleep or something!'

Thoroughly annoyed, he tugged at the bell again with all his might, a dozen times in succession. He was plainly a person of imperious temper and familiar with the place.

At this moment light, hurrying footsteps sounded not very

far down the stairs. Somebody else was approaching, whom Raskolnikov had not heard at first.

'Isn't anybody in?' cried the new arrival in loud and cheerful tones to the first visitor, who was still tugging at the bell. 'How are you, Koch?'

'Judging by his voice, he must be very young,' thought Raskolnikov.

'God only knows! I've nearly broken the door down,' answered Koch. 'But how is it that you know me?'

'Surely you remember? The day before yesterday, at Gambrinus's, I beat you three times running at billiards.'

'O-o-oh . . .'

'Aren't they here then? That's strange. In fact, it's quite absurd. The old woman's got nowhere to go to. And I am here on business.'

'So am I, old man.'

'Well, what are we to do? Go back, I suppose. And I was expecting to get some money!' exclaimed the young man.

'Of course we must go back, but why make an appointment? The old witch fixed a time with me herself. It's a long way for me to come here, too. And where the devil she can have got to, I don't know. She sits here, day in and day out, the old witch, with her bad legs, and never lifts a finger, and now all at once she goes gallivanting off!'

'Hadn't we better ask the porter?'

'Ask him what?'

'Where she's gone and when she's coming back.'

'Hm . . . the devil! . . . ask him . . . But she never goes anywhere . . .' and he pulled at the handle again. 'The devil! There's nothing for it; we must go.'

'Stop!' exclaimed the young man. 'Look! Do you see how the door resists when you pull it?'

'Well?'

'That means it's bolted, not locked! Can you hear the bar rattling?'

'Well?'

'Don't you understand? That means one of them is at home. If everybody were out, they would have locked the door from outside, not bolted it from inside. But now—do you hear the bolt rattle? But to bolt the door from inside, somebody must be at home. Do you understand? They must be in, but they aren't opening the door.'

'Tck! That's quite right!' exclaimed Koch, surprised. 'Then what on earth are they doing?' And he shook the door again, in a rage.

'Stop!' cried the young man again, 'leave the door alone! There's something very wrong here . . . After all, you rang, and shook the door, and they haven't opened it; so either they've both fainted, or . . .'

'What?'

'I'll tell you what; let's go to the porter and get him to rouse them.'

'Done!' Both started downstairs.

'Stop! Why don't you stay here while I run down for the porter?'

'Why?'

'Well, one never knows!'

'All right . . .'

'You see, I am studying to be an examining magistrate. There is plainly, plai-ainly something wrong here!' cried the young man excitedly, as he ran down the stairs.

Koch, left alone, touched the bell again, so softly that it made only one tinkle; then, as though he were considering the matter and making tests to convince himself once more that the door was held only by the bolt, he began to move the handle, pulling it towards him and letting it go again. Then he stooped down, puffing, and looked through the keyhole, but the key was in it on the inside and consequently nothing could be seen.

Raskolnikov stood clutching his axe, in a sort of delirium. He was even prepared to fight them when they came in. While they were knocking at the door and arranging what they would do, he was more than once tempted to put an end to it all at once by calling out to them from behind the door. Several times he felt like railing and jeering at them, while the door remained closed. 'If only they would be quick!' he thought.

'What the devil? . . .'

The time was passing—one minute, two minutes, and nobody came. Koch was getting restless.

'Oh, the devil! . . .' he exclaimed impatiently, abandoning his watch and starting to hurry downstairs, with his boots clattering on the steps. The sounds died away.

'Oh, God, what am I to do?'

Raskolnikov took off the bolt and opened the door a little. Since he could hear nothing, he walked out without stopping to consider, closed the door behind him as well as he could, and went downstairs.

He had gone down three flights when a great commotion broke out below him. Where could he go? There was nowhere to hide. He was on the point of running back to the flat.

'Hi, stop! You devil! Just wait!'

Down below someone tore out of a flat shouting and did not so much run as tumble down the stairs, yelling at the top of his voice:

'Mitka! Mitka! Mitka! Mitka! Blast your eyes!'

The shout rose to a shriek; its last echoes resounded from the courtyard; it died away. At the same instant several persons talking loudly and rapidly started noisily up the stairs. There were three or four of them. He could distinguish the young man's voice. 'It's them!'

In complete desperation he went straight towards them: let come what might! If they stopped him, all was lost; if they let him pass, all was still lost: they would remember him. They were already close; only one flight still lay between them —and suddenly, salvation! A few steps below him on the right, the door of an empty flat was wide open; it was the second-floor flat in which painters had been working, but now, most opportunely, they had gone. Probably it was they who had run out so noisily a few minutes before. The floors had just been painted, and in the middle of the room stood a tub and an earthenware crock of paint with a brush in it. In a trice he had slipped through the open door and hidden himself against the wall. It was none too soon; *they* had already reached the landing. They turned up the stairs and went on to the fourth floor, talking loudly. He waited a little, tiptoed out and ran downstairs.

There was nobody on the stairs, nobody in the gateway. He walked through quickly and turned to the left along the street.

He knew very well, he was terribly aware, that at this moment they were inside the flat, that they had been astonished to find the door unfastened when it had been closed against them so recently, that they had already seen the bodies and that no more than a minute would pass before they would begin to suspect, and then realize fully, that the murderer had only just left, and had managed to conceal himself somewhere, slip past them, and make his escape; perhaps they would even guess that he had been in the empty flat when they passed it on their way upstairs. All the same, he simply dared not increase his pace, even though it was still nearly a hundred yards to the first turning. 'Hadn't I better slip into some gateway and wait on a staircase? No, that would be disastrous! Oughtn't I to get rid of the axe? What about taking a cab? . . . A fatal blunder!'

At last he reached a side-street and, half dead, turned into it; now he knew that he was already half-way to safety; his presence here was less suspicious, and besides there were very many people about and he could lose himself among them like one grain of sand on the sea-shore. But his racking anxieties had taken so much out of him that he could hardly move. Sweat poured out of him; his neck was quite wet. 'You've had a drop too much!' someone called after him as he came out on the canal.

He no longer knew quite what he was doing, and the farther he went the worse his condition became. Afterwards he remembered, however, that he had been afraid, coming to the canal bank, because there were fewer people about, which made him more conspicuous, and he nearly turned back into the street he had just left. Although he could hardly stand he took a roundabout way and arrived home from an entirely different direction.

Even when he entered his own gateway he had hardly recovered control of himself; at least, he was already on the stairs before he remembered the axe. Now he had to face a very important task—returning it without being seen. He was certainly in no condition to realize that perhaps it would be much better if he did not restore the axe to its former place but threw it away, perhaps later, in some other courtyard.

Everything, however, went without a hitch. The porter's door was closed but not locked, which meant that he was probably at home. But Raskolnikov had so completely lost his powers of reasoning that he went straight to the door of the lodge and opened it. If the porter had asked him what he wanted, he might quite possibly have simply handed him the axe. But the porter was again out and he put the axe in its former place under the bench; he even partly covered it with logs as before. Afterwards, on his way to his room, he met no one, not a soul; even the landlady's door was closed. He went in and flung himself down on the sofa just as he was. He did not sleep, but lay there in a stupor. If anybody had entered the room he would have sprung up at once with a cry. Disjointed scraps and fragments of ideas floated through his mind, but he could not seize one of them, or dwell upon any, in spite of all his efforts . . .

# Part Two

## CHAPTER I

HE lay there a long time. Occasionally he would rouse, and at such moments he would notice that the night was far spent, but it did not enter his head to get up. Finally he saw that it was daylight. He was lying on his back, still in a half-stunned condition. Terrible despairing wails rose shrilly to his ears from the street below; they were, however, only what he was used to hearing below his window between two and three o'clock in the morning. They were what had roused him now. 'Ah, the drunks are being turned out of the pubs,' he thought, 'it must be after two;' and suddenly he leapt from the sofa in one bound. 'What, past two already?' He sat down again and it all came back to him; everything came back in one flash.

In the first few moments he thought he must be going mad. A dreadful chill enveloped him, but this was partly the result of the feverishness that for many weeks had always accompanied his sleep. Now, however, he was seized with such a violent fit of shivering that his teeth chattered uncontrollably, and every limb shook. He opened the door and listened; the whole house was asleep. He looked at himself and at everything in the room with consternation, unable to understand how he could have omitted to fasten his door when he came in the evening before, and have thrown himself down not only without undressing, but even without taking off his hat; it had fallen off and lay on the floor near his pillow. 'If somebody had come in, what would they have thought? That I was drunk? But . . .' He hurried to the window. There was enough light to see by, and he began to examine himself from head to foot, and all his clothes; were there no traces? But he could not tell like this, and so, shivering with cold, he undressed completely and examined his clothes again. He scrutinized them minutely, down to the last thread, turning them over and over, and, unable to trust himself, repeated the process three times. But there seemed to be nothing, not a trace, except that the ragged fringes at the bottom of his trouser-legs were stiff and clotted with dried blood. He took out his big clasp-knife and cut off the fringes. He could find nothing more. Suddenly he remembered that the purse and all the things he had stolen from the old woman's trunk were still in his pockets. Till that moment it had not even occurred to him to take them out and hide them. He had not remembered them even while he was inspecting his clothes. How could that be? He hurriedly began to pull them out and throw them on the table. When he had emptied his pockets and even turned them inside out to satisfy himself that there was nothing left in them, he carried the whole heap into a corner. There, near the floor, the wall-paper was torn where it had come loose from the wall; hastily he crammed everything under the paper, into this hole; it all went in. 'It's all out of sight, even the purse!' he thought joyfully, standing and staring stupidly at the place where the torn paper bulged more than ever. Suddenly he shivered with terror: 'My God!' he whispered in despair, 'what is the matter with me? Can I call that hidden? Is that the way to hide anything?'

The truth was that he had not counted on there being any things of that kind, he had thought only of money, and therefore had not prepared any place to hide things in. 'But now, why on earth am I so pleased now?' he thought. 'Is that the way to hide anything? I really must be losing my reason.' He sat down exhausted on the sofa, and at once an unbearably violent shivering shook him again. Mechanically he took up from where it lay on the chair beside him the old winter overcoat he had worn as a student, which was warm even if ragged, covered himself with it and surrendered himself once more to mingled sleep and delirium.

Not more than five minutes later he sprang up again and rushed back to his clothes. 'How could I fall asleep, with nothing done? I was right, I was right: I haven't taken out that loop yet. I forgot it, but how could I forget such a thing, a clue like that?' He tore out the loop and quickly reduced it to scraps, which he thrust among the linen under his pillow. 'Torn-up pieces of linen will never by any chance arouse suspicion, I think; no, I think not,' he repeated, standing in the middle of the room and with painfully strained attention he began to look all round, on the floor and everywhere else, to see whether he had not forgotten something else. The conviction that everything, even memory, even the simple power of reflection, was deserting him, had begun to torment him unbearably. 'What if it is beginning already? Can this really be the beginning of my punishment? Look, over there!—I thought so!' Indeed, the frayed scraps of fringe he had cut off his trousers lay scattered on the floor in the middle of the room for everyone to see. 'But what can be the matter with me?' he wailed again like a lost soul.

Now a strange idea entered his head: perhaps all his clothes were soaked and stained with blood and he could not see it

because his mental powers were failing and crumbling away
. . . his mind was clouded . . . He remembered suddenly that
there had been blood on the purse. 'Ha, so of course there must
be blood on my pocket too, because when I pushed the purse
in it was still all wet!' He turned his pocket inside out and he
was right—there were stains on the lining. 'So I can't have
gone completely out of my mind yet, I must still have some
understanding and memory left, since I remembered and
realized this for myself,' he thought triumphantly, filling his
lungs with a deep breath of relief; 'it was only the weakness of
fever, a momentary delirium.' He tore the lining out of his
left-hand trouser-pocket. As he did this a ray of sunlight lit
up his left boot. There on the sock, which projected from a
hole in the boot—were there marks? He dragged his boot off:
'Yes, there are certainly marks; the whole toe of the sock is
soaked with blood;' he must have stepped carelessly into that
pool . . . 'But what am I to do with these things? Where
can I put the sock and the frayed trouser-ends, and the
pocket?'

He gathered them all into his hands and stood in the middle
of the room. 'Shall I put them in the stove? But they nearly
always begin by rummaging in the stove. Burn them? But
what with? I haven't even any matches. No, the best thing is
to go out somewhere and throw them all away. Yes, I'll throw
them away!' he repeated, sitting down again on the sofa, 'and
this minute, without a moment's delay! . . .' But instead, his
head declined once more towards his pillow; once more a
sudden chill congealed his blood; once more he drew his
greatcoat over him. For several hours, as he lay there, the
thought kept flickering through his brain: 'I must go now,
I mustn't put it off; I'll go somewhere and throw them all
away, get them out of sight, but quickly, quickly!' Several
times he tried to tear himself from his couch and get up, but
he could not do it. Finally he was awakened by a loud knocking
on his door.

'Open the door! You're not dead, are you? He's always
fast asleep!' cried Nastasya, beating on the door with her fist.
'Lying there fast asleep all day like a dog! A dog, that's what he
is! Open the door, can't you? It's past ten o'clock.'

'Perhaps he's not at home,' said a man's voice.

'Ah! that's the porter . . . What does he want?'

He sprang up and sat on the edge of the sofa. His heart
thumped so heavily that it was painful.

'Who's fastened the door then? See, he's taken to locking
his door now! Does he think someone's going to run off with
him? Open the door, my lad; wake up!'

'What do they want? Why is the porter here? They must
have found out. Shall I resist, or shall I open the door? Better

open it! Damnation!...'

He half rose, stretched forward, and undid the hook. The room was so small that it was possible to do this without leaving his bed.

He was right; the porter was there with Nastasya.

Nastasya looked at him rather oddly. He was gazing with an imploring and despairing expression at the porter, who silently held out a grey paper folded in two and sealed with wax.

'A summons, from the office,' he said as he handed over the paper.

'What office?...'

'I mean the police want to see you; you've to go to their office. Everyone knows what office.'

'The police!... Why?'

'How should I know? You've been summoned, so go.' He looked closely at him, glanced round the room, and turned to go out.

'You seem really ill,' remarked Nastasya, who had not taken her eyes off him. The porter also turned his head for a moment. 'You've had a temperature since yesterday,' she added.

He did not answer, but sat holding the unopened paper.

'Don't you get up,' went on Nastasya, feeling sorry for him, as she saw him lowering his feet to the floor. 'You are ill, so don't go; there's no hurry. What's that in your hand?'

He looked down; in his right hand he was still holding the fringe he had cut off, the sock, and the torn pieces of his pocket. He had slept with them like that. Afterwards, thinking about it, he remembered that when he half woke in his fevered state, he had clutched them tightly in his fingers and so fallen asleep again.

'Look, he's collected a handful of rags and taken them to bed with him as if they were something precious...' And Nastasya broke into one of her painfully violent fits of laughter. He whisked everything under the greatcoat and stared fixedly at her. Although he was hardly capable at that moment of making much sense of anything, he felt he would not be treated like this if he were on the point of being arrested... 'But—the police?'

'Could you drink some tea? Would you like some? I'll bring it; there's some left...'

'No... I'm going; I'll go now,' he muttered, struggling to his feet.

'Going? But you won't even be able to get downstairs!'

'I'm going...'

'Oh, all right.'

She followed the porter out. He hurried at once to the window to examine the sock and the scraps of frayed cloth:

'There are marks, but they are not very conspicuous, everything is so dirty and rubbed and discoloured. Nobody would notice anything if they didn't know beforehand. So Nastasya can't have seen anything from where she was, thank God!' Then with a shiver of alarm he opened the paper and read it; he had to spend a long time studying it, but at last he understood. It was the usual summons from the local police headquarters to appear there that same day at half past nine.

'But this is unheard of! I have never had anything to do with the police! And why should it happen just to-day?' he thought, tormented with indecision. 'Oh, Lord, at least let it be over soon!' He could almost have knelt down and prayed, but he laughed at his own impulse; he must put his trust in himself, not in prayer. He began to dress hurriedly. 'If I'm done for, I'm done for! It's all one . . . I'll put the sock on!' he thought suddenly, 'it will get more dirt rubbed into it and all the stains will disappear.' But no sooner had he put it on than he dragged it off with horror and loathing. Then, realizing that he had no other, he took it and put it on again—and again he laughed. 'This is all conditional, all relative, all merely forms,' flashed into one corner of his mind, while his whole body trembled. 'I did put it on, after all. It all ended with my putting it on!' The laughter gave place immediately to despondency. 'No, I'm not strong enough . . .' he thought. His legs were shaking. 'With fear,' he muttered to himself. He felt dizzy and the fever had given him a headache. 'This is a trap. They want to entice me into a trap and then spring it,' he went on to himself, as he went out on to the landing. 'The trouble is that I am almost delirious . . . I might get caught in some stupid lie . . .'

On the way downstairs he remembered that he had left all the things behind the wallpaper, and thought that perhaps he was being got out of the way on purpose for a search to be made, and he stopped. But overwhelming despair and what might perhaps be called a cynical view of disaster made him shrug his shoulders and walk on.

'Only let it be over quickly!'

The heat outside was again overpowering; not so much as a drop of rain had fallen all this time. Again the same dust and bricks and mortar, the stinking shops and public houses, the drunkards everywhere, the Finnish hawkers, the broken-down old cabs. The blazing sun shone full in his eyes and made them ache and his head was spinning, as it might be expected to do when he, in his feverish state, emerged suddenly into the bright sunny day.

When he came to the turning into *yesterday's* street, he looked down it, at *that* house, with tormented anxiety . . . and turned his eyes away at once.

'If they ask me, I shall probably tell them,' he thought as he drew near the office.

The police office was not far from where he lived, about a quarter of a verst. It had just moved into new quarters on the fourth floor of a new building. He had been in the old office once, a long time ago. As he passed under the gateway he saw a staircase on the right and a peasant coming down it with a book in his hand: 'That must be the porter; so the office must be there,' and he started up, acting on his guess, since he did not want to ask any questions.

'I shall go in, fall on my knees, and tell the whole story,' he thought as he came to the fourth floor.

The staircase was steep and narrow and smelt of dishwater. All the kitchens of all the flats on all four floors opened on to the staircase, and as all the doors stood open almost the whole day, it was terribly stuffy. Up and down these stairs moved porters with books under their arms, messengers, and various visitors of both sexes. The door into the office also stood wide open. He went in and stopped in the ante-room. Several peasants were always standing there waiting. Here also it was extremely stuffy and in addition the nostrils were assailed by the sickly odour of new paint which had been mixed with rancid oil. He waited a little and then decided to move forward into the next room. All the rooms were very small and low-ceilinged. A terrible impatience drove him farther and farther. Nobody took any notice of him. In the second room some clerks were sitting writing; they were perhaps a little better dressed than he was, but they were odd-looking figures enough. He went up to one of them.

'What do you want?'

He showed his summons.

'You are a student?' asked the other, glancing at the notice.

'A former student.'

The clerk looked at him, but without any curiosity. He was a man with wildly tousled hair and a preoccupied look.

'You won't find out anything from him, because he isn't interested in anything,' thought Raskolnikov.

'Go in there, to the chief clerk,' said the clerk, and pointed to the inmost room.

He went into this room (the fourth from the ante-room), which was very small and crammed full of people, who looked a little neater and cleaner than those in the other room. Among them were two ladies. One of these, poorly dressed in mourning, was sitting at a table opposite the chief clerk and writing to his dictation. The other, a very stout, showy woman, with a blotchy red complexion, rather ostentatiously dressed, with a brooch on her bosom as big as a saucer, was standing and waiting. Raskolnikov put his summons under the eyes of the chief clerk, who glanced at it, said 'Please wait,' and went on with what he was doing.

Raskolnikov breathed more freely. 'It can't be that!' Little by little his resolution was returning, and he earnestly exhorted himself to pluck up his courage and control his nerves.

'It's only about some silly formality, or perhaps some trifling indiscretion, and I might have given myself away completely! Hm . . . it's a pity there's no air here . . .' he went on, 'it's stuffy . . . My head seems to be spinning worse than ever, and my thoughts with it . . .'

He was conscious of a terrible inner confusion. He was afraid of losing command of himself. He tried to fix his attention, to think of something quite outside himself, but he could not do it. The chief clerk, however, interested him deeply; he wished he could read his face and guess what he was thinking. He saw a very young man of about twenty-two, with a dark and mobile countenance, who seemed older than his years. His dress was modish and elegant, his pomaded hair was brushed forward from a back-parting, and he wore a number of rings on his white well-cared-for hands and a gold chain on his waistcoat. He even exchanged a few words of very passable French with a foreigner who was present.

'Louisa Ivanovna, pray be seated,' he said in passing to the overdressed lady with the red face, who was still standing as if she dared not take it on herself to sit down, although there was a chair at her side.

'Ich danke,' said she, and sat down quietly, with a rustle of silk. Her light-blue dress with its white lace trimming ballooned out round her chair and filled almost half the room. A wave of perfume was wafted from her. But the lady seemed abashed at filling the room with her skirts and her scent, and her uneasy smile mingled timidity and boldness.

The lady in mourning finished her business at last and was getting up to go when an officer entered the room somewhat noisily, with a very dashing and characteristic swagger, threw his cockaded cap on the table and sat down in an armchair. The showily dressed lady jumped up instantly and swept him a curtsy as though she was delighted to see him, but the officer paid not the slightest attention to her, and she did not venture to sit down again in his presence. He was a lieutenant, the police-captain's assistant. The points of his sandy moustaches stood out horizontally; he had remarkably small features, which expressed nothing but a certain insolence. He looked askance and with some displeasure at Raskolnikov; his dress was really too disgraceful and yet his bearing, in spite of its humility, was not in harmony with it. Raskolnikov imprudently returned his gaze with such directness and steadiness that he took offence.

'What do you want?' he cried, apparently astonished that such a ragamuffin was not struck down by the lightning that flashed from his eyes.

'I was ordered ... by a summons ...' Raskolnikov managed to bring out.

'It concerns the recovery of money from him, from this student,' put in the chief clerk hastily, tearing himself away from his papers. 'Here you are, sir,' and he pointed out a place in a notebook and then tossed it across to Raskolnikov. 'Read it!'

'Money? What money?' thought Raskolnikov. 'But ... then it really can't be *that*!' He trembled with joy; his heart was suddenly, inexpressibly light. A burden had rolled from his shoulders.

'At what hour, my good sir, were you instructed to come here?' cried the lieutenant, growing for some unknown reason more and more outraged. 'You were told nine o'clock and it is now twelve!'

'It was handed to me only a quarter of an hour ago,' Raskolnikov threw over his shoulder in a loud voice. He also felt suddenly and unexpectedly irritated, and was even enjoying the sensation. 'And it should be enough that I came at all, in my state of illness!'

'Kindly do not shout!'

'I am not shouting; I am speaking quite calmly. It is you who are shouting at me, and I am a student and will not allow anyone to shout at me.'

The officer flared up so violently that for a moment he was unable to speak at all, but only spluttered. He leapt up from his seat.

'Be good enough to ho-o-old your tongue! Remember where you are! Do not be impertinent, sir!'

'Remember where you are yourself!' yelled Raskolnikov. 'Not only are you shouting, you are smoking a cigarette as well, and that is showing disrespect to everybody here.' This speech gave him inexpressible pleasure.

The chief clerk was looking at them with a smile. The fiery lieutenant was evidently taken aback.

'That, sir, is no affair of yours!' he exclaimed at last in a voice of unnatural loudness. 'Be kind enough to make the declaration required of you. Show him, Alexander Grigoryevich. A complaint has been lodged against you! You will not pay your debts! A fine young spark you are!'

Raskolnikov was no longer listening to him, but had seized avidly on the paper and was trying to find in it the answer to the riddle. He read it through once and then again, but he could not understand it.

'What is this?' he asked the chief clerk.

'It is a demand for the recovery of money on a bill. Either you must repay it together with all arrears, penalties, etcetera, or you must sign an undertaking to pay at a given date, with an obligation not to leave the capital before repayment is made, nor to sell your property or conceal your assets. The creditor is entitled to sell your goods or institute judicial proceedings against you.'

'But I . . . don't owe anybody anything!'

'That is not our affair. An application has been made to us for the recovery of one hundred and fifteen roubles on an overdue and legally protested note of hand given nine months ago to the widow of Collegiate Assessor Zarnitsyn, and assigned by the widow Zarnitsyna to Civil Councillor Chebarov. You are accordingly invited to enter your reply.'

'But she's my landlady!'

'What if she is?'

The clerk looked at him with a smile of condescending pity but also with a certain air of triumph, as if he were an old hand watching a new recruit coming under fire for the first time and ready to ask 'Well, how are you feeling now?'

But what did I.O.U.'s or the recovery of debts matter to him now? Did they merit the slightest concern, or even attention? He stood there reading, listening, answering, even asking questions himself, but all quite mechanically. Triumphant satisfaction in his safety, his escape from imminent looming danger, filled for the time his whole being, to the exclusion of all forebodings, all doubts and questions, all critical analysis, all riddles about the future. It was a moment of full, spontaneous, and purely animal rejoicing. The same moment saw something like the outbreak of a thunderstorm in the office. The lieutenant, still outraged by the want of respect he had met with, blazing with anger and determined to soothe his smarting vanity, had brought all his guns to bear on the unhappy 'elegant lady', who had been smiling at him with the most complete fatuity ever since he came in.

'And you, you so-and-so,' he shouted at the top of his voice (the lady in mourning had already left). 'What happened at your house last night? You are bringing shame and disgrace on the whole street again. Fighting and drunkenness! You are simply asking for quod! You know perfectly well you've been told, I've warned you myself a dozen times, that you wouldn't get off another time! And yet you go on and on, you ——!'

The paper slipped from Raskolnikov's grasp and he stared wildly to hear the stylish lady so unceremoniously abused; however, he soon grasped what it was all about and began to find considerable amusement in the whole affair. He listened with great enjoyment, feeling tempted to laugh and laugh and laugh . . . All his nerves were quivering with tension.

'Ilya Petrovich,' began the clerk, but stopped at once and bided his time, knowing from experience that once the lieutenant had taken the bit between his teeth he must be allowed to run his course.

As for the elegant lady, at first she cowered before the storm unleashed on her head, but, strangely enough, the more numerous and outrageous the abuses heaped on her, the more amiable became her look, and the more charming the smile she turned on the thundering lieutenant. She curtsied incessantly and tapped the ground with her foot, waiting impatiently until at last she could get a word in.

Words tumbled out of her mouth like peas rattling on a drum; her Russian was glib, but she had a marked German accent.

'Disturbance and brawling in my house has not been, *Herr Kapitän*, and not any kind of *skandal*, but they are coming drunk, and I will tell you everything, *Herr Kapitän*, I am not being to blame . . . Mine house is respectable, *Herr Kapitän*, and respectable behaviour, *Herr Kapitän*, and never, never, would I any *skandal* . . . But they are coming quite drunk and after as well they are calling for three bottles, and then one is lifting up his feets and is playing the piano with his feets and that is not good in a respectable house and he has the piano *ganz* broken and that is altogether not manners and I am telling him. And he was taking a bottle and pushing all peoples behind with a bottle. Then I am calling the porter and Karl is coming and he is taking Karl and in the eye hitting and Henrietta also is he in the eye hitting, and mine cheek five times he is hitting. And that is in a respectable house indelicate, *Herr Kapitän*, and I am screaming. And he has the window on the canal opened and is in the window standing and squealing like a little *schwein*, it is shameful. How is it possible to stand in the window and squeal into the street like a little *schwein*? Wee-wee-wee! And Karl behind him is pulling him out of the window by the coat and here, it is true, *Herr Kapitän*, he has *sein* coat behind torn. And then he is shouting, that *man muss* him fifteen roubles to pay. And, *Herr Kapitän*, I myself am paying him *sein* coat five roubles. This is not a respectable guest, *Herr Kapitän*, and he is making a big *skandal*! He is saying to me, I will a big satire over you to print, because in all the newspapers I will all about you write.'

'Do you mean that he is an author?'

'Yes, *Herr Kapitän*, and he is not a respectable guest, *Herr Kapitän*, when in a respectable house . . .'

'Now, that's enough! I've told you again and again, I've told you . . .'

'Ilya Petrovich!' said the clerk again, significantly. The lieutenant hastily glanced at him; the clerk gave a slight shake of the head.

'. . . So, my dear *respectable* Louisa Ivanovna, this is my last word to you, I am telling you for the last time,' continued the lieutenant, 'if such a scandalous scene occurs in your respectable house only once more, you'll find yourself in the jug, as they say in the highest circles. Do you hear? . . . So a man of letters, a writer, got five roubles for his coat-tails in a "respectable house"! These writers are all alike!' and he threw a contemptuous glance at Raskolnikov. 'There was another scene in a public house the day before yesterday; someone who had dined refused to pay, and, says he, "I'll put you in a satire for this!" Another one, last week, grossly insulted the respectable wife and daughter of a State Councillor on a steam-ship. Not long ago one of them had to be turned out of a pastrycook's. That's the sort they are, authors, men of letters, students, town-criers . . . pshaw! Now get out! I shall keep an eye on you . . . so take care! Do you hear?'

Louisa Ivanovna with hasty civility curtsied all round and then, still curtsying, backed towards the door. In the doorway she bumped into a handsome officer with a fresh open countenance and magnificent fair bushy whiskers. This was Nikodim Fomich, chief of police of the district. Louisa Ivanovna curtsied almost to the ground and skipped from the office with little mincing steps.

'Thunderstorms, tornadoes, waterspouts, and hurricanes again!' said Nikodim Fomich in an amiable and friendly tone to Ilya Petrovich. 'You've got upset again and lost your temper; I could hear you from the stairs.'

'Well, look heah,' answered Ilya Petrovich, with well-bred negligence as he took a handful of papers over to another table with his picturesque swagger, 'look at this, sir; this gentleman, an author, I mean a student, or rather an ex-student, won't pay up, his note of hand is overdue, he won't give up his flat, there are constant complaints about him, and he wanted to make a grievance of my smoking in his p-p-presence! His own conduct is disgraceful, and then, sir, just look at him; there he is, a most attractive spectacle, sir!'

'Poverty is no crime, my dear chap; and besides, everybody knows that you are like gunpowder, always ready to explode. I expect you felt he had affronted you in some way,' went on Nikodim Fomich, turning with a friendly air to Raskolnikov, 'and so you let fly yourself. But you were wrong; he is a dee*light*ful, a no-o-oble fellow, I assure you, but gunpowder, gunpowder!—he flares up, goes off with a flash and a bang, and it's all over! When it comes to the point, he has a heart of solid gold! His nickname in the regiment was "the Squib" . . .'

'And w-w-what a regim̃ent it was!' exclaimed Ilya Petrovich, mollified by being so pleasantly teased, but still a little sulky.

Raskolnikov felt a sudden desire to say something particularly amiable to all of them.

'Excuse me, captain,' he began easily, turning to Nikodim Fomich, 'put yourself in my place . . . I am ready to beg his pardon if I have been remiss. I am a poor student, ill, and crushed' (he used the word 'crushed') 'by poverty. I have had to give up my studies, because I cannot maintain myself, but I receive some money . . . I have a mother and sister in R—— Province . . . They send it to me and I . . . will pay. My landlady is good, but she is so annoyed with me for having lost my lessons and not paying the rent for three months that she does not even send up my dinner . . . I don't understand all this about a bill of exchange! Now she is claiming repayment on this I.O.U., but why should I pay, I ask you? . . .'

'But you know that has nothing to do with us . . .' the clerk was beginning again.

'Allow me, allow me, I quite agree with you, but allow me to explain,' interrupted Raskolnikov, still addressing not the chief clerk but Nikodim Fomich, and trying with all his might to draw in Ilya Petrovich as well, although the latter was obstinately pretending to rummage through his papers and to have no attention to spare for such a contemptible person; 'allow me for my part to explain that I have been living in her house for about three years, ever since I arrived here from the provinces, and formerly . . . formerly . . . well, why shouldn't I confess it? At the very beginning I gave my promise to marry her daughter, a verbal promise, only verbal . . . She was a young girl, and I liked her . . . although I wasn't in love with her . . . in a word, it was youth . . . and at that time my land-lady gave me a good deal of credit, and I led a life which . . . I was very irresponsible . . .'

'These intimate details are not required of you at all, my good sir, and there is no time for them,' Ilya Petrovich was breaking in, roughly and overbearingly, but Raskolnikov stopped him and continued hotly, although he was suddenly finding it difficult to speak.

'But allow me, do allow me to tell you everything . . . how things were and . . . in my turn . . . even though it is unneces-sary, I quite agree with you—but a year ago this girl died of typhus, but I stayed on as a lodger, and when my landlady moved into her present flat she told me . . . in a very friendly way . . . that she trusted me completely and everything . . . but would I like to give her a bill for a hundred and fifteen roubles, the total sum she reckoned I owed her? Allow me, sir: she told me explicitly that as soon as I gave her this paper, she would give me as much more credit as I wanted, and that never, never, for her part—these are her very words—would she make any use of the paper, until I paid of my own accord . . . But now, when I have lost my pupils and have nothing, she presents it for repayment . . . What can I say now?'

'All these sentimental details, my good sir, do not concern us,' interrupted Ilya Petrovich. 'You have to enter a reply and undertake an obligation, and whether you were pleased to be in love or not, and all these tragic bits, have absolutely nothing to do with us.'

'Well, you are rather . . . harsh . . .' murmured Nikodim Fomich, sitting down at a table and beginning to sign papers. He seemed rather uncomfortable.

'Please write,' said the chief clerk to Raskolnikov.

'Write what?' asked he roughly.

'I will dictate to you.'

It seemed to Raskolnikov that the chief clerk's manner to him had become more off-hand and contemptuous since he had made his confession, but strangely enough he had become completely indifferent to anybody's opinion of him, and this change had taken place all in a moment. If he had cared to stop and consider it, he would no doubt have wondered how, a few minutes ago, he could have talked to them as he did and even made a parade of his emotions, and wondered too where those emotions had come from. Now, if the room had suddenly been filled not with police officers but with his closest friends, he could not, he thought, have found a single word to say to them, so empty had his heart become. In his soul he was tormentingly conscious of a dreary feeling of eternal loneliness and estrangement. It was not the abjectness of his outpourings of emotion in front of Ilya Petrovich, nor the lieutenant's triumph over him, that had produced this revulsion. What concern of his were now his own baseness, other people's ambitions, lieutenants, German woman, proceedings for the recovery of debts, police officers, and all the rest of it? If he had heard himself condemned to be burnt at this moment he would hardly have stirred, indeed it is doubtful if he would have paid the slightest attention. Something new and unexpected, something hitherto unknown and undreamt of, had taken place in him. He did not so much understand with his mind as feel instinctively with the full force of his emotions that he could never again communicate with these people in a great gush of feeling, as he had just now, or in any way whatever. Even if they had been his own brothers and sisters, instead of police officers, it would still have been impossible for him to turn to them for any reason or in any circumstances. He had never in his life before experienced so strange and desolating a feeling, and the most painful thing about it was that it *was* a feeling, an immediate sensation, and not knowledge or intellectual understanding.

The chief clerk began to dictate to him the usual form of declaration in such cases, that is: 'I cannot pay, I undertake to do so at a certain date, I will not leave the city, I will not sell or give away any of my property,' and so on.

'But you cannot write properly, you can hardly hold the pen,' the clerk remarked, looking at Raskolnikov with curiosity. 'Are you ill?'

'Yes . . . my head is going round . . . Go on!'

'That is all; sign it.'

The clerk took the document, and busied himself with something else.

Raskolnikov gave back the pen, but instead of getting up to go put both elbows on the table and pressed his hands to his head. He felt as if a nail had been driven into his temples. A strange idea flashed into his mind: he would get up, go over to Nikodim Fomich and tell him all that had happened the day before, down to the last detail, and then go back with them to his room and show them the things in the corner, under the wall-paper. The impulse was so strong that he stood up to carry it out. 'Hadn't I better think it over for a minute?' passed through his mind. 'No, better do it without thinking, and be done with it.' Then he stopped, rooted to the ground: Nikodim Fomich was warmly discussing something with Ilya Petrovich, and the words reached his ears.

'It's quite impossible; we shall have to let them both go. To begin with, everything is against it: why should they call the porter, if they had done it? To call attention to themselves? Or out of cunning? No, that would be altogether too cunning! Finally, both porters and the workman saw the student Pestryakov at the gate when he went in; he had three friends with him, and he stopped at the gate to ask the porter about the people living in the house, still in the presence of his friends. Now, would he have asked about them like that if he had come with any such intention? As for Koch, he had been sitting in the silversmith's downstairs for half an hour before he went up to the old woman's, and he left him at exactly a quarter to eight to go upstairs. Now, consider . . .'

'Excuse me, look at the contradictions in their statements. They assert that they knocked and that the door was fastened, but three minutes later, when they had the porter with them, it was open.'

'That is just the point, the murderer must have been inside, with the bolt up, and they would certainly have found him there if Koch hadn't been fool enough to go for the porter himself. During that interval *he* managed to get downstairs and somehow give them the slip. Koch says "If I had stayed he would have sprung out on me with the axe and killed me too!" and he crosses himself with both hands. He'd like to hold public thanksgiving services, no doubt! Ha-ha-ha!'

'And nobody saw the murderer?'

'How could they? The house is a regular Noah's Ark,' put in

the chief clerk, listening from his place.

'It's quite clear, quite clear,' repeated Nikodim Fomich warmly.

'No, it's not at all clear,' insisted Ilya Petrovich.

Raskolnikov picked up his hat and went to the door. But he did not reach it . . .

When he came round he saw that he was sitting in a chair, supported by some person on his right, with somebody else on his left holding a dirty tumbler filled with yellowish water,[3] and that Nikodim Fomich was standing in front of him looking at him attentively. He stood up.

'What is it? Are you ill?' asked Nikodim Fomich rather sharply.

'When he was signing his name he could hardly guide the pen,' remarked the chief clerk, sitting down and turning back to his papers.

'Have you been ill long?' cried Ilya Petrovich from his place, where he also was shuffling papers. He also had certainly been over to look at the patient while he was in the faint, but had left him as soon as he recovered consciousness.

'Since yesterday . . .' muttered Raskolnikov in reply.

'Did you go out yesterday?'

'Yes.'

'When you were ill?'

'Yes.'

'At what time?'

'Eight o'clock in the evening.'

'Where, may I ask?'

'Along the street.'

'Short and plain.'

Raskolnikov had answered sharply and jerkily. He was as white as a handkerchief, but he did not drop his dark, inflamed-looking eyes before Ilya Petrovich's glance.

'He can hardly stand, and you . . .' began Nikodim Fomich.

'All right!' said Ilya Petrovich in a peculiar tone. Nikodim Fomich seemed to want to say something more, but, glancing at the chief clerk, who was looking at him fixedly, he was silent. A sudden strange silence fell on them all.

'Well, all right,' concluded Ilya Petrovich. 'We will not detain you any longer.'

Raskolnikov went out. As he did so, he heard animated talk break out behind him, with Nikodim Fomich's inquiring tones rising above the rest . . . When he reached the street he had quite recovered.

'Search, search, they are going to search at once!' he repeated to himself, hurrying along; 'the scoundrels, they are suspicious!' His former fear enveloped him once again from head to foot.

3. Petersburg at that time had no municipal water supply. Water was taken out of rivers and canals; there were few wells.

## CHAPTER II

'WHAT if they have searched already? What if I find them in my room now?'

Here was his room. Nobody; nothing; nobody had been in. Even Nastasya had touched nothing. But good God! how could he have left all those things in the hole?

He flung himself across the room, thrust his hand under the paper, and began pulling out the things and cramming them into his pockets. There were eight articles altogether: two small boxes with earrings or something of the kind in them (he did not examine them closely), then four small morocco cases, a chain wrapped in newspaper and something else, perhaps a decoration, also in newspaper . . .

He distributed them among the pockets of his overcoat and the remaining right-hand pocket of his trousers, trying to make them inconspicuous. He put the purse in with them as well. Then he went out of the room, this time leaving the door wide open.

He walked quickly and resolutely, and although he felt broken with fatigue, his senses were alert. He was afraid of pursuit, afraid that in half an hour, or a quarter, instructions would be issued to follow him; that meant that come what might he must cover up his tracks before then. He must manage to do it, also, while a little strength and power of reasoning still remained to him . . . But where should he go?

He had long since decided to 'throw everything into the canal, so that all traces will vanish and the affair be done with.' He had reached the decision during the night, in his delirium, at a time, he remembered, when he had more than once tried to get up and go 'quickly, quickly and get rid of it all.' But it was not so easy.

He had wandered along the embankment of the Ekaterininsky canal for half an hour or perhaps longer, looking at the ways down to the water as he came across them. But he could not even dream of fulfilling his purpose here: either there were rafts at the foot of the stairs with women washing linen on them, or boats were moored there, and everywhere there were swarms of people, and besides, he could be overlooked everywhere from the embankment and it would look suspicious for someone to go down on purpose to throw something into the water. Again, what if the cases did not sink, but floated? Indeed, they were sure to. Everyone would see. Even as it was everybody he met looked at him as if they had some business with him. 'Why is that, or am I just imagining it?' he thought.

Finally it occurred to him that it might be better to go

somewhere along the Neva. There were fewer people there and he would be less noticeable; besides, it would be more convenient there, and, most important of all, it was farther away. He felt surprised that he had been wandering for at least half an hour in anguished worry, in dangerous places, before he thought of this. And he had wasted that half-hour in an ill-judged project simply because he had come to a decision in his sleep or in delirium! He was becoming extraordinarily absent-minded and forgetful, and he realized it. Decidedly, he must hurry.

He walked along the Voznesensky Prospect towards the Neva, but another idea came to him on the way: 'Why in the Neva? Why in the water at all? Would it not be better to go somewhere a long way off, perhaps as far as the Islands again, and, in a solitary place in a wood, bury everything under a bush, and perhaps mark the spot?' He could find no fault with this idea, although he felt that he was not at this moment capable of judging clearly and soundly.

He was not destined, however, to reach the Islands, either: emerging from the Voznesensky Prospect into a square, he caught sight on his left of the entrance to a courtyard entirely surrounded by blank walls. Immediately to the right of the gate stretched the long windowless side of a neighbouring four-storied building. To the left, parallel with this wall and also from close by the gate, a wooden hoarding ran in for about twenty paces and then bent round to the left. It was a piece of fenced-off waste land, strewn with various rubbish. Farther in, in the far depths of the yard, the corner of a low, sooty, stone shed, evidently part of some workshop, showed behind the fence.

Apparently there was some carriage-maker's or carpenter's shop here, or something of the kind; there was a good deal of coal-dust everywhere, nearly down to the gates. 'This would be a place to throw the things and get away,' he thought at once. Seeing nobody in the yard he stepped into the gateway, and immediately saw, just inside by the hoarding, a trench or channel such as is often constructed where there are many factory-hands, handicraftsmen, cab-drivers, and so on, in a building, and above it, on the hoarding, was written in chalk the usual witticism: 'Rubbitch must not be shot hear.' This was good, because it would not look suspicious if he went in and stopped. 'This is just the place to throw everything down in a heap and leave it!'

He looked round once more and had already thrust his hand into a pocket when he saw, close against the outer wall, in a space between the gate and the trench not more than thirty inches across, a great unhewn block of stone, which must have weighed sixty pounds. Beyond the wall was the street, and the sound of passers-by hurrying along the pavement could be heard quite often, but he could not be seen there behind the gate unless someone came right in from the street. This, however, was quite possible and the thought prompted him to make haste.

He bent over the stone, seized it firmly near the top with both hands, exerted all his strength, and turned it over. There was a small hollow under the stone and he threw into it all the things from his pockets. The purse went on top of the other things, and the little hollow did not seem too full. Then he seized the stone and rolled it back again; it settled into its old position, except that it was barely perceptibly higher. He scraped up a little earth and pressed it against the edges of the stone with his foot. No appearance of disturbance remained.

He left the yard and turned towards the square. A violent, almost unbearable rejoicing filled him for a moment as it had done before in the police office. 'My tracks are covered! And who would ever dream of searching under that stone? It may have been there ever since the house was built, and perhaps it will be there for as long again. And even if they found the things, who would think of me? It's all over; there's no evidence,' and he laughed. Yes, afterwards he remembered that he laughed a long, nervous, shallow, noiseless laugh, and went on laughing all the time he was crossing the square. But the laughter ceased as he turned on to Konnogvardeysky Boulevard, where two days before he had encountered the young girl. Other ideas had come into his mind. He felt a sudden violent repugnance to passing the bench on which he had sat and thought after the girl left, and it seemed to him also that it would be terrible to meet again the moustached policeman to whom he had given the twenty copecks. 'Devil take him!'

As he walked, he looked about him with an air of irritated distraction. All his thoughts were now centred round one most important point, whose importance he fully recognized, and he felt that now he had come face to face with it, for the first time, after these two months.

'Oh, the devil take it all!' he thought in a sudden access of ungovernable irritation. 'If it's begun, it's begun, and to the devil with her, and with the new life! Oh God, how stupid it all is! . . . How much lying and cringing I did today! How loathsomely I fawned on that filthy Ilya Petrovich and played up to him! However, that's rot too! I ought to spit on all of them, and on my own behaviour! It's all wrong! It's all wrong! . . .'

Suddenly he stopped, baffled and bitterly disconcerted by a new and entirely unexpected but extraordinarily simple question: 'If you really knew what you were doing, and weren't just blundering along, if you really had a definite and constant objective, how is it that you have never even looked into the purse, and have no idea what you gained, or for what you underwent all those torments and consciously performed such base, vile, and ignoble actions? Indeed, you only wanted to throw the purse into the water, together with the other things, without looking at them either . . . Why is that?'

Yes, it was true, it was all true. He had, however, known it before, and the problem was not new; and when he had made his decision in the night, to throw everything into the water, he had made it without hesitation or reconsideration, but as if it had to be, as if it could not be otherwise . . . Yes, he knew it all, and he remembered everything; indeed, it was all but decided yesterday, in that moment when he crouched above the trunk, and dragged the cases out of it . . . It was indeed so! . . .

'It's because I am very ill,' he morosely decided at last; 'I have been tormenting and torturing myself, and I hardly know what I am doing . . . Yesterday, and the day before, and all this time, I have been tormenting myself . . . When I am well . . . I shall not torture myself like this . . . But what if I never get quite well again? Oh God, how sick I am of it all! . . .' He went on walking. He longed to find some distraction, but he did not know what to do or how to begin. A new and irresistible sensation of boundless, almost physical repulsion for everything round him, an obstinate, hateful, malicious sensation, was growing stronger and stronger with every minute. He loathed everyone he met—their faces, their walk, their gestures. He thought that if anybody were to speak to him, he would spit and snarl at them like an animal . . .

When he came out on to the embankment of the Little Neva, on Vasilyevsky Island near the bridge, he stopped. 'Why, he lives there, in that house,' he thought. 'How does it come about that I have somehow arrived at Razumikhin's? It's just like the way it happened before . . . I wonder, though, whether I really meant to come here, or simply walked along and came out here by chance? It makes no difference; . . . the day before yesterday . . . I said I should come here on the day after *that*, and here I am! As if I could possibly not come!'

He went up to the fifth floor, where Razumikhin lived, and found him at home, busy writing in his little room. They had not seen each other for four months. Razumikhin opened the door; he was wearing a dressing-gown worn to tatters, and slippers on his bare feet, and he was unkempt, unshaven, and unwashed. He looked astonished.

'What brings you here?' he exclaimed, eyeing his friend from head to foot; then he stopped and whistled.

'Are things as bad as that? And you, my dear chap, used to

be the smartest of us all,' he added, glancing at Raskolnikov's rags. 'But sit down; you must be tired.' When his visitor sank on to an oilcloth-covered sofa, in even worse condition than his own, Razumikhin realized that he was ill.

'You are seriously ill, do you know that?' He tried to feel his pulse, but Raskolnikov snatched his hand away. 'Don't! . . .' he said. 'I have come . . . it is like this: I haven't any pupils . . . I should like . . . however, I don't want any pupils . . .'

'Do you know, you are delirious,' remarked Razumikhin, who was watching him closely.

'No, I'm not . . .' Raskolnikov got up. When he came up to Razumikhin's room he had somehow not thought of how he would have to come face to face with him. Now it had taken him only a moment's trial to realize that he was less inclined than ever to enter into personal relations with anybody on the face of the earth. Gall welled up in him. He felt choked with rage at himself as soon as he crossed Razumikhin's threshold.

'Good-bye!' he said abruptly, and made for the door.

'Since you're here, stay a little. Don't be so freakish!'

'Don't! . . .' repeated Raskolnikov, again snatching his hand away.

'What the deuce did you come for, then? Have you gone clean off your head? You know, this is . . . almost an insult. I won't put up with it.'

'Well, listen: I came to you because I didn't know anyone else who might help me . . . to begin . . . because you're the nicest of the lot, I mean the most sensible, and can judge . . . But now I see that I don't want anything, do you hear, anything at all . . . I want nobody's help or pity . . . I myself . . . alone . . . Oh, that's enough! Leave me in peace!'

'Stop a minute, chimney-sweep! You're quite mad! Do as you like, as far as I'm concerned. Look: I haven't any pupils myself, and much I care; but there's a bookseller, Kheruvimov, in the Rag Market, and he's as good as lessons any day. I wouldn't exchange him for the chance of teaching in five rich merchants' houses. He does a bit of publishing, and is bringing out some little books on the natural sciences—and how they sell! The titles alone are worth I don't know what! You've always maintained that I was stupid: let me tell you, my dear fellow, there are some people even stupider than I! Now he's sneaked into the Movement; he himself doesn't understand the first thing, but needless to say I urge him on. Here are two sheets and a bit of German text—in my opinion it is the silliest sort of charlatanism: the question discussed, in one word, is whether a woman is a human being or not, and, of course, it is triumphantly proved that she is. Kheruvimov is bringing it out as a contribution to the Woman question; I am doing the translation; he will stretch the two and a half sheets to about six, we shall add half a page of grandiloquent titles, and issue it at half a rouble. It will pass! I get six roubles a sheet for the translation, that means fifteen for the whole thing, and I have had six roubles in advance. When we have finished this, we shall begin on another about whales, and afterwards there are some very boring pieces of gossip marked out in the second part of the *Confessions*,[4] and we will translate them; someone or other has told Kheruvimov that Rousseau is in his way a sort of Radishchev.[5] Of course, I don't contradict him; he can go to the devil! Well, would you like to translate the second sheet of *Woman: Is she a Human Being?* If you would, take the text now, and pens and paper—they are all supplied— and take three roubles, because I had an advance on the whole thing, both the first and the second sheet, and that means three roubles are due as your share. When you have finished, you get three roubles more. And there's one other thing, please don't think I am only trying to do you a good turn. On the contrary, as soon as you came in I began to see how useful you could be to me. To begin with, my spelling is bad, and in the second place, my German is sometimes very weak, so that I am reduced to making up most of it myself, comforting myself with the idea that it is probably an improvement. But who knows, perhaps I'm not improving it, but spoiling it . . . Are you going to take it or not?'

Without a word Raskolnikov picked up the sheets of German text and the three roubles, and went out. Razumikhin looked after him in surprise. Raskolnikov had already reached the First Line when he turned abruptly on his heel, climbed once more to Razumikhin's room, laid the papers and the money on the table, still without a word, and was gone.

'You must be raving mad or something,' roared Razumikhin, losing his temper at last. 'What sort of game do you think you are playing? You baffle even me ... What the devil did you come for, anyhow?'

'I don't want . . . translations . . .' muttered Raskolnikov, already half-way downstairs.

'Then what the deuce do you want?' cried Razumikhin from above. Raskolnikov went on down in silence.

'Hi, you! Where do you live?'

There was no answer.

'Well then, be damned to you! . . .'

But Raskolnikov had already reached the street. He was on the Nikolaevsky Bridge before he came to himself again, as

4. Jean-Jacques Rousseau's *Confessions* (1781–88), one of the most famous and candid of all autobiographies. A Russian translation was published in 1865.
5. Alexander Radishchev (1749–1802), a leading liberal Russian writer who inveighed against abuses of serfdom and the judicial system in his *Journey from Peters-* *burg to Moscow*, a work for which he was exiled to Siberia by Catherine the Great. Two radical literary critics and journalists, N. G. Chernyshevsky and D. I. Pisarev, compared Rousseau and Radishchev in articles published in 1860 and 1866 respectively.

a consequence of a very unpleasant incident. The driver of a carriage laid his whip heavily across his back, because he had almost fallen under the horses' feet, in spite of the coachman's repeated cries. The blow so enraged him that, leaping for the parapet (for some unknown reason he had been walking in the middle of the roadway), he ground his teeth viciously with a clicking noise. Of course, there was laughter and comment from the passers-by.

'Serve him right!'

'An unmitigated scoundrel!'

'It's a well-known trick; they pretend to be drunk and get under the wheels on purpose; and you are responsible.'

'That's the way they make a living, my dear sir . . .' Just then, as he stood by the parapet gazing uselessly and angrily after the retreating carriage and rubbing his back, he felt some money being thrust into his hand. He looked and saw an elderly woman of the merchant class, in a Russian head-dress and goat-skin shoes, and a young girl, who seemed to be her daughter, wearing a hat and carrying a green parasol. 'Take it, in the name of Christ!' He took the money—it was a twenty-copeck piece—and they passed on. His dress and appearance might well have induced them to take him for a beggar, someone who picked up farthings in the streets, but for the gift of so much as twenty copecks he was probably indebted to the pity aroused by the blow from the whip.

He clasped the money in his hand, walked a few steps, and turned his face towards the Neva, looking towards the Palace. There was not a cloud in the sky and the water, unusually for the Neva, looked almost blue. The dome of the cathedral, which is seen at its best from this point, not more than twenty paces towards the chapel from the centre of the bridge, shone through the clear air, and every detail of its ornament was distinct. The sting of the lash had abated, and Raskolnikov forgot the blow; a disquieting but vague idea occupied his whole mind. He stood for a long time gazing steadily into the distance; this spot was particularly familiar to him. A hundred times, while he was at the university, had he stopped at this very place, usually on his way home, to fix his eyes on the truly magnificent view and wonder each time at the confused and indescribable sensation it woke in him. An inexplicable chill always breathed on him from that superb panorama, for him a deaf and voiceless spirit filled the splendid picture . . . Each time he marvelled at his gloomy and mysterious impression, and then, mistrustful of himself, deferred consideration of the riddle to some future time. Now he was sharply reminded of his former questionings and perplexities, and it seemed to him that the recollection did not come by chance. It appeared to him strange and marvellous that he should have stopped in the very same place as he used to do, as if he really imagined he could think the same thoughts now as then, and be interested in the same ideas and images as had interested him once . . . not long ago. This was almost laughable, and yet his heart was constricted with pain. In some gulf far below him, almost out of sight beneath his feet, lay all his past, all his old ideas, and problems, and thoughts, and sensations, and this great panorama, and his own self, and everything, everything . . . He felt as if he had soared upwards and everything vanished from his sight . . . He made an involuntary gesture with his hand, and became aware of the twenty-copeck piece squeezed in his fist. He unclasped his hand and stared at the money, then flung it into the water with a sweep of his arm; then he turned away and walked homewards. He felt that he had in that moment cut himself from everybody and everything, as if with a knife.

It was evening when he reached home, so that he must have been walking for about six hours. How and by what route he went back he could never afterwards remember. He undressed and lay down, shuddering like an overdriven horse, pulled his winter overcoat over him, and fell instantly asleep.

It was dusk when he was startled awake by a terrible cry. God, what was that shriek? He had never before heard such a babble of unnatural noises, such howling and wailing, grinding of teeth, tears, blows, and curses. He could never even have imagined such ferocity and frenzy. He raised himself in a panic, and sat on his bed in a torment of fear. The sounds of struggling, wailing, and cursing grew louder and louder. Suddenly, to his utter amazement, he recognized his landlady's voice. She was howling, shrieking, and wailing, the words tumbling out of her mouth in an indistinguishable spate; she seemed to be imploring someone to stop, for she was being unmercifully beaten, out there on the stairs. Her assailant, hoarse with rage and fury, was also pouring out a stream of unrecognizable words, stuttering with haste. Raskolnikov began to tremble like a leaf; he knew that voice, it was the voice of Ilya Petrovich. Ilya Petrovich here, and beating his landlady! He was kicking her, thumping her head on the stairs—that was clear, the noises, the howls, the blows, revealed it. What was it? Had the world come to an end? He could hear a crowd gathering on the landings and all up the stairs; there were voices, outcries, footsteps running up and down the stairs, raps, doors slamming. 'But what is it for? What is it all about? How could it possibly be happening?' he repeated to himself, seriously wondering if he had gone mad. But no, he could hear it too plainly for that. But then, if he were not mad, they must be coming here, this moment, 'because . . . it must be all on account of . . . yesterday . . . Oh God!' He thought of fastening his door, but he could not raise his arm . . . and besides it would be no use! Fear crept like ice round his heart, tortured his nerves, numbed his spirit . . . The uproar, which had probably lasted for ten minutes, died down gradually; his landlady groaned and lamented still; Ilya Petrovich went on cursing and threatening . . . At last he too seemed quiet; no more was heard of him; 'Good Heavens! Can he possibly have gone away?' Yes, the landlady was going too, still groaning and weeping . . . that was her door slamming . . . The crowd was melting away into the different flats—exclaiming, arguing, calling to one another in voices that now rose to a scream, now sank to a whisper. There must have been very many of them; practically everybody in the house had come running. 'But, good God, how can all this have really happened? And why, why, did he come here?'

Raskolnikov fell back exhausted on his sofa, but he could not close his eyes again; he lay there for half an hour, in the grip of such anguish, such an intolerable feeling of limitless terror, as he had never before experienced. Suddenly a bright light illuminated the room; Nastasya had come in with a candle and a plate of soup. She looked at him and, seeing that he was not asleep, put the candle on the table and began to set out the things she had brought, bread, salt, a spoon, and the plate.

'I suppose you've had nothing to eat since yesterday. You've been wandering about all day, and you've got a fever.'

'Nastasya . . . why were they beating the landlady?'

She stared at him.

'Who was?'

'Just now . . . half an hour ago, Ilya Petrovich, the chief police officer's assistant, on the staircase . . . Why was he beating her like that? And . . . why did he come?'

Nastasya studied him silently for a long time, frowning. He found her scrutiny very unpleasant, even frightening.

'Nastasya, why don't you say something?' he asked at last hesitantly, in a weak voice.

'It's the blood,' she answered at last quietly, as if she were talking to herself.

'Blood! . . . What blood? . . .' he mumbled. He had turned pale, and moved closer to the wall. Nastasya went on looking at him in silence.

'Nobody was beating the landlady,' she said again in a severe, decided voice. He looked at her, hardly breathing.

'I heard it myself . . . I wasn't asleep . . . I was sitting here . . .' he said, even more hesitantly. 'I listened for a long time . . . The assistant chief of police came . . . Everybody came on to the stairs, out of all the flats . . .'

'Nobody came. It's your blood that makes a noise. It's

when it hasn't got any outlet, and it begins to get all clotted, and then you begin to get visions . . . Are you going to have something to eat, eh?'

He did not answer. Nastasya still stood near him, with her eyes fixed on him.

'Give me a drink . . . dear Nastasya.'

She went downstairs and returned in a minute with water in a white earthenware mug; but he hardly knew what happened next. He only remembered swallowing a few drops of cold water and spilling some on his chest. Then came complete unconsciousness.

## CHAPTER III

He was not entirely unconscious throughout the whole time of his illness; he lay in a fever, delirious and sometimes half-conscious. Afterwards he could remember a good deal about it. At one time it seemed to him that he was surrounded by many people, who wanted to carry him away somewhere, and that they were wrangling and quarrelling over him. Then suddenly he was alone in the room; everybody had gone out, they were afraid of him, and only occasionally opened the door a crack to look in at him. They would threaten him, hatch out plots among themselves, laugh and jeer at him. He remembered Nastasya's being with him often; he could also distinguish a man, who seemed very well known to him, but who it was he could not think, and he worried and even wept over this. Once it would seem to him that he had lain there for a month; another time, that it was still the same day as he fell ill. About *that*—about *that* he had quite forgotten; but he was conscious all the time that he had forgotten something that he ought not to forget, and he tortured himself, racked his brains to remember, groaned, fell into mad rages or into the grip of terrible, unbearable fear. Then he tried to drag himself up, to run, but somebody always restrained him by force, and he would fall back into helplessness and oblivion. At last he came completely to himself.

This was one morning at ten o'clock. At this hour, when the weather was clear, the sunlight always fell in a long streak across the right-hand wall of his room and lit up the corner near the door. Near his bed stood Nastasya with somebody else, quite unknown to him, who was watching him with great curiosity. This was a bearded young man in a caftan, who looked like a superior workman. The landlady was peering round the half-open door. Raskolnikov raised himself.

'Who is this, Nastasya?' he asked, pointing to the man.

'Look, he's come round!' said she.

'He's come round,' echoed the visitor. Realizing that he was conscious, the landlady, who had been looking round the door, concealed herself by closing it. She was always very shy, and avoided conversations and explanations. She was about forty, stout and heavy, and quite good-looking, with black eyes and hair; she had the good nature of the fat and lazy, but her shyness was altogether excessive.

'Who are . . . you?' Raskolnikov went on, turning to the man himself. At this moment, however, the door was opened wide again, and Razumikhin, stooping a little because of his height, came in.

'This place is no better than a ship's cabin,' he exclaimed as he came in; 'I always bump my head. And they call it a lodging! Well, my dear fellow, you've come round, have you? I've just heard it from Pashenka.'

'He's just this minute come to,' said Nastasya.

'Just this minute come to,' assented the strange man, with a slight smile.

'And who might you be, sir?' asked Razumikhin, turning to him. 'Allow me to present myself, Vrazumikhin, not Razumikhin as I am usually called, but Vrazumikhin, a student and a gentleman, and this is my friend. Well, sir, and who are you?'

'I am the foreman-clerk in the merchant Shelopaev's counting-house, sir, and I am here on business, sir.'

'Be good enough to sit down here,' and Razumikhin sat down himself on the other side of the little table. 'I'm glad you've come to yourself, my dear chap,' he went on, addressing Raskolnikov. 'You've hardly eaten or drunk anything for three days. It's true they did give you tea in a spoon. I brought Zosimov to see you twice. Do you remember him? He examined you carefully, and said at once that it was nothing much—you've just been a bit queer in the head. Some sort of nonsensical nervous trouble, and the wrong sort of food, he says, not enough beer and horse-radish; that made you ill, but it's nothing—it will pass, and you'll be all right again. He's a clever chap, Zosimov. His treatment was capital.' He turned to the workman again. 'Well, I don't want to detain you; would you care to explain your business? Observe, Rodya, this is the second time someone has been here from their office, only before it was not this man but somebody else, and I had a talk with him. Who was it who came here before?'

'Let's see: that would be the day before yesterday. Yes. It were Alexey Semënovich; he belongs to our office, too.'

'I suppose he is a bit more competent than you; don't you think so?'

'Yes, sir; he be just that, a bit sounder, like.'

'Admirable! Well, go on.'

'Well, through Afanasy Ivanovich Vakhrushin, who I don't doubt you've heard of, more than once, and by request from your mama, sir, there is money coming to you through our office, sir,' began the workman, addressing Raskolnikov direct. 'In case you was to have come to yourself, sir, by now—thirty-five roubles is what I have to hand over, sir, Semën Semënovich having been notified to that effect by Afanasy Ivanovich by request of your mama as aforesaid. Are you informed of it, sir?'

'Yes, . . . I remember . . . Vakhrushin,' said Raskolnikov thoughtfully.

'You hear: he knows the merchant Vakhrushin,' exclaimed Razumikhin. 'Who says he's not come to himself? By the way, I observe that you are also a very competent man. Well, it does one good to hear such wise and intelligent speeches.'

'That's the very man, sir, Vakhrushin, Afanasy Ivanovich, and by request of your mama, who in the manner aforesaid has already once remitted money through him, he did not refuse this time, sir, and notified Semën Semënovich as of that date to transfer to you thirty-five roubles, sir, in anticipation of better, sir.'

'Well, "in anticipation of better" is the best thing you have said yet; although that about "your mama" isn't bad, either. Well, what is your opinion: is he or isn't he in full possession of his faculties, eh?'

'It isn't my opinion that matters but only on account of the receipt he would have to be, sir.'

'He'll manage to scribble it somehow. What's that you've got, a receipt-book?'

'Yes, sir, here it is, sir.'

'Give it here. Now, Rodya, raise yourself up a little. I'll help you. Just sign "Raskolnikov" for him. Come, take the pen; money is sweeter to us just now, brother, than honey.'

'I don't want it,' said Raskolnikov, pushing away the pen.

'You don't want what?'

'I am not going to sign.'

'What the devil?—A receipt is absolutely necessary.'

'I don't want . . . the money . . .'

'Oh, it's the money you don't want, is it? Now there, my dear fellow, you lie, as I can bear witness!—Don't worry, please, this is only because he . . . is wandering again. He is quite capable of that even when he is wide awake . . . You are a man of discernment; we will guide his hand and he will sign. Let us set about it . . .'

'Oh, I can come another time, after all, sir.'

'No, no: why should we trouble you? You are a man of sense and judgement . . . Well, Rodya, don't detain your visitor . . . you can see he is waiting,' and he prepared in all seriousness to guide Raskolnikov's hand.

'No, don't, I'll do it myself . . .' said he, and he took the pen and wrote his signature in the book. The man laid the money on the table and departed.

'Bravo! And now, my dear fellow, do you want something to eat?'

'Yes, I do,' answered Raskolnikov.

'Have you got any soup?'

'Yesterday's,' answered Nastasya, who had been standing there all the time.

'Made with potatoes and rice?'

'Yes, potatoes and rice.'

'I know it by heart. Sling it in, and bring tea as well.'

'Very well.'

Raskolnikov watched everything with deep astonishment and dull, unreasoning fear. He made up his mind to say nothing, but wait to see what came next. 'I don't think I'm delirious,' he thought; 'it seems real enough . . .'

Two minutes later Nastasya returned with the soup, and explained that the tea would not be long. With the soup appeared two spoons, two plates, and a complete set of condiments: salt, pepper, mustard for the beef, and other things that had not been seen on his table, in such neat order, for a long time past. The tablecloth was clean.

'It wouldn't be a bad idea, Nastasyushka, if Praskovya Pavlovna were to order a couple of bottles of beer. We could do with them.'

'Well, that's cool!' grumbled Nastasya, as she went to do his bidding.

Raskolnikov still watched with close attention. Meanwhile Razumikhin sat down beside him on the sofa, as clumsy as a bear, encircled his friend's head with his left arm (although he could quite well have raised himself) and with his right carried a spoonful of soup to his mouth, first blowing on it once or twice so that it should not be too hot. The soup was in fact only luke-warm. Raskolnikov eagerly swallowed a spoonful, then a second and a third. After a few more mouthfuls, Razumikhin stopped, explaining that he must consult Zosimov about any more.

Nastasya came in, carrying two bottles of beer.

'Would you like some tea?'

'Yes, I should.'

'Roll up some tea as well, Nastasya; I think he can have tea without waiting for the doctor's permission. But here's the beer!' He moved across to his chair, drew soup and beef towards him and began to eat with as much appetite as though he had not broken his fast for three days.

'I have been having dinner here at your place every day, Rodya, my dear fellow,' he muttered as clearly as a mouth

stuffed with beef would allow, 'and Pashenka, your nice little
landlady, has provided it; she delights to feed me. I, of course,
do not demand it; but I don't, as a matter of fact, raise any
objections either. But here is Nastasya with the tea. How
quick she can be! Nastenka, would you like some beer?'

'Get away with you!'

'A drop of tea, then?'

'I don't mind.'

'Pour it out. Wait, I will pour it for you myself. You sit
down.'

He took command of the teapot and poured out a cup,
and then another. Then he abandoned his luncheon and
crossed again to the sofa. As before, he put his left arm round
the sick man's head, raised him, and began to feed him tea-
spoonfuls of tea, again blowing on them fervently and incessantly, as if this process of blowing were the most important
and salutary part of the treatment. Raskolnikov remained
silent, making no protest, although he felt that he was quite
strong enough to sit up without any outside assistance, and
that he had sufficient command of his limbs not only to hold
a spoon or cup but even, perhaps, to walk. But a strange, all
but feral cunning prompted him to conceal how strong he was,
to lie low, even to pretend, if it proved necessary, that he had
not completely recovered his understanding, and meanwhile
to listen and try to find out what was going on. He could not,
however, quite master his repugnance; when he had swallowed
a dozen spoonfuls of tea, he jerked his head free, pettishly
pushed away the spoon, and lay back again on his pillow.
A real pillow, filled with down and covered with a clean
pillowcase, now lay under his head; he noticed this as one
more of the things he must try to understand.

'Pashenka must send up some raspberry jam today, to make
a drink for him,' said Razumikhin, sitting down at the table
and applying himself again to the soup and beer.

'And where is she supposed to get raspberries?' asked
Nastasya, balancing her saucer on the tips of her outstretched
fingers and drinking her tea 'through a piece of sugar'.

'She will get them, my dear girl, from the shop. You see,
Rodya, a great many things have been happening here that
you don't know about. When you ran away in such a scoun-
drelly fashion and wouldn't tell me your address, I got so
furious that I decided to seek you out and punish you. I set
about it the very same day. I walked all over the place, and
made inquiries everywhere. I couldn't remember your present
address, which is not surprising, since I never knew it. About
your last lodgings I could recollect only that they were near
Five Corners, in Kharlamov's house—and then afterwards it
turned out not to be Kharlamov's at all, but Buch's—what

mistaken ideas about sounds we get sometimes! Well, I got very annoyed. I got annoyed, and so, next day, I thought I might as well try the Register of Addresses, and just imagine: they found you for me inside two minutes. They've got you down there.'

'Me!'

'Of course; and yet while I was there they simply couldn't find General Kobelev. Well, to cut a long story short, as soon as I stumbled on this place, I got to know all your affairs; all of them, brother, all of them. Nastasya here knows that; I made the acquaintance of Nikodim Fomich, of the porter, and of Mr. Zametov, Alexander Grigoryevich, the chief clerk at the police office here, and had Ilya Petrovich pointed out to me; lastly I got to know Pashenka, and that was the crowning point; Nastasya here knows . . .'

'You got round her,' murmured Nastasya, with a mischievous smile.

'You ought to put that sugar in your tea, Nastasya Nikiforovna.'

'Go on with you, you dog!' cried Nastasya, bursting out laughing. 'Besides, I'm Petrovna, not Nikiforovna,' she added as soon as she could for laughing.

'We appreciate your confidence. Well, my dear chap, not to waste words, I wanted to get rid at one sweep of all the cobwebs of prejudice here, to galvanize everybody, as it were, but Pashenka was too much for me. I didn't expect that she would be so . . . sweet and charming . . . eh, brother? What do you think?'

Raskolnikov did not answer, but he kept his anxious eyes fixed on his friend, as they had been throughout. Not in the least disconcerted by his silence, Razumikhin went on, exactly as if he had received a reply and were expressing his agreement with it: 'Yes, she is indeed a very nice, good creature, in all respects.'

'Well, you are a one!' exclaimed Nastasya, who seemed to derive inexplicable enjoyment from this conversation.

'It's a pity, my dear fellow, that you didn't understand how to deal with the situation at the very beginning. The way you handled her was wrong. You know, she is, shall I say, a most unexpected character. But we can talk of that later . . . Only how on earth did things reach such a pass that she dared to stop sending up your dinner? And that bill of exchange? You must surely have been out of your mind, to sign a thing like that. And then that proposed marriage, when her daughter, Natalya Egorovna, was still alive . . . I know everything! But I see that I have touched a sensitive spot—I am an ass. You must forgive me. But talking of stupidity—don't you think Praskovya Pavlovna is not nearly as stupid as she might appear at first sight, eh, brother?'

'Yes . . .' Raskolnikov let fall, looking away, but conscious that the conversation had better be kept going.

'That's true, isn't it?' exclaimed Razumikhin, visibly pleased to have received an answer, 'but she's not clever either, is she? She's a quite, quite unexpected character. I tell you, my dear fellow, I have lost my head a little . . . She must be forty. She admits to thirty-six, and she's certainly not over-stating it. However, I swear my relations with her are purely platonic, though more complicated than any of your algebraic formulas could ever be—completely incomprehensible, in fact. But this is all beside the point; the fact is, that when she realized you were no longer a student, had lost your pupils, and had no decent clothes, and that since her daughter's death you could no longer be looked on as a member of the family, she took fright, and when you for your part skulked in a corner, and would take up none of the threads of your former life, she decided she must get rid of you. She had nourished this intention a long time but she didn't want to say good-bye to that bill of exchange. Besides, you had assured her that your mama would pay it . . .'

'It was very wrong of me to say that . . . My mama has barely enough money to keep her from having to accept charity . . . and I lied so that I should be allowed to remain here and . . . get my food,' said Raskolnikov loudly and distinctly.

'Yes, that was very sensible of you. Only the snag is, that this Mr. Chebarov, a man of business and a Civil Councillor, turned up. Without him, Pashenka would have been altogether too bashful to do anything; but men of business are not shame-faced, and of course his first question was: "Is there any hope of realizing on the bill?" Answer: "Yes, because there is a mama who will come to Rodenka's rescue with her pension of a hundred and twenty-five roubles, if it means going without enough to eat herself, and a sister who would sell herself into slavery for him." That was enough for him . . . Now, don't get restless! My dear fellow, I've ferreted out all your secrets now; you did right to open your heart to Pashenka, when you were practically one of the family, and what I am saying now is in pure affection . . . This is what happens: the sensitive and honest man opens his heart, and the business man listens and takes it all in, so that he can swallow up the honest fellow. Well, she hands over this bill of yours in payment for something to this Chebarov and he makes a formal claim on it and is not to be put off. When I learnt all this, I would have liked to give him a piece of my mind, simply to relieve my feelings, but at that time Pashenka and I were on very harmonious terms, and I got the business stopped, at its source, by undertaking that you would pay. You understand, my dear fellow, I vouched for you. Chebarov was summoned and paid ten roubles on the nail, and we got the paper back; I have the honour to present it to you;—now they rely on your word alone. Here it is—take it! Now it has no force.'

Razumikhin laid the note of hand on the table; Raskolnikov glanced at it and, without saying a word, turned to the wall. The gesture jarred even on Razumikhin.

'I see, brother,' he went on after a moment's pause, 'that I have made a fool of myself again. I wanted to entertain you and amuse you with my chatter, but it seems I've only annoyed you!'

'Was it you that I didn't recognize in my delirium?' asked Raskolnikov after another short silence, without turning his head.

'Yes, it was, and you got very excited about it, especially once when I brought Zametov with me.'

'Zametov? . . . The chief clerk? . . . What for?' Raskolnikov swung round and fixed his eyes on Razumikhin.

'What makes you . . .? Why are you so alarmed? He wanted to get to know you; it was his own wish, because we had talked so much about you . . . Who else do you suppose I could have learned so much from? He's a good chap, a fine fellow . . . in his own way of course. We are friends now, we see each other nearly every day. I've moved into this district, you know. Didn't you know? I've only just removed. I've been at Louisa's a couple of times with him, too. You remember Louisa, don't you—Louisa Ivanovna?'

'Did I say anything when I was delirious?'

'Of course you did. You were out of your mind.'

'What did I say?'

'Good heavens! What did you say? What anyone says when they're raving . . . Well, my dear fellow, don't let's lose any more time—to business!'

He got up and seized his cap.

'What did I say?'

'You're repeating yourself, you know. Are you worrying about some secret or other? Don't be afraid; the Countess was never mentioned. But you talked about some bulldog, and about ear-rings, and a chain, and Krestovsky Island, and some porter, and Nikodim Fomich, and a lot about Ilya Petrovich, the assistant chief of police. Besides that, you were very interested in your own sock, very. You were whining: "Give it me, that's all I want." Zametov himself looked for your socks everywhere, and handed you that rubbish with his own fair hands, washed in scent and covered with rings. Only then did you calm down, and you held the rubbish in your hand for days together; we couldn't get it away from you. It must still be there somewhere under your blankets. And then again you asked for the fringe from your trousers, and so tearfully! We questioned you about it: what sort of fringe did you mean? But we couldn't make anything out . . . Well, now to business. Here are the thirty-five roubles; I am taking ten of them, and I'll render you an account in an hour or two. At the same time, I'll let Zosimov know, though he ought to have been here long ago anyhow; it's twelve o'clock. And you, Nastenka, while I'm out you must come and inquire frequently whether he wants something to drink or anything like that . . . And I'll tell Pashenka myself what is wanted. Good-bye!'

'He calls her Pashenka! Sly rogue!' said Nastasya after him. She opened the door and listened, but soon grew tired of this and ran downstairs herself. She seemed very anxious to find out what he was saying to the landlady, and it was evident that she herself was quite charmed with Razumikhin.

The door had hardly closed behind her when the sick man flung off the bedclothes and jumped up like one possessed. He had been waiting with feverish, burning impatience for them to go, so that as soon as they were out of the way he could apply himself to what he had to do. But what?—what had he to do? He seemed to have clean forgotten. 'Oh Lord, tell me just one thing; do they know everything or not? What if they know it all already and were only pretending, mocking me while I lay here, and what if they come in now and say that they have known everything for a long time, and they were only . . .? What shall I do now? I've forgotten! I knew a moment ago, but now it's gone! . . .'

He stood in the middle of the room and looked round in an agony of indecision; he went to the door, opened it, and listened, but that was not it. Suddenly, as if he had remembered, he rushed to the corner where the wallpaper was torn, looked it over carefully, thrust his hand into the hole and rummaged there, but that was not it either. He went to the stove, opened it, and sought among the ashes; the bits of fringe from his trousers and the pieces of his torn pocket still lay there as he had thrown them; so nobody had looked there! Then he remembered the sock that Razumikhin had been talking about. Yes, here it was on the sofa, under the blanket, but it was so much more rubbed and dirty since that time that Zametov could certainly not have noticed anything.

'Ah, Zametov! . . . the office! . . . Why have I been summoned to the office? And where is the summons? Bah! . . . I am getting confused, that was before! I examined the sock then, as well, and now . . . now I have been ill. But why did Zametov come here? Why did Razumikhin bring him? . . .' he murmured weakly, sitting on his sofa again. 'But what is this? Am I still delirious, or is all this real? It seems real enough . . . Ah, I remember: I must run away, run away at once; I must, I

absolutely must, fly. But . . . where? And where are my clothes?
My boots are not here! They've been taken away! Someone
has hidden them—now I understand! Ah, here is my coat—
they overlooked that! And here is the money on the table,
thank God, and the I.O.U. . . . I will take the money and go
away, and take other lodgings, where I shall not be found! . . .
Yes, but the Register of Addresses? They'll find me! Razumikhin will find me. It would be better to run away altogether
. . . a long way . . . to America, and be damned to them! I
must take the bill as well . . . it will come in useful there. What
else? They think I'm ill! They don't even know that I can
walk, he-he-he! . . . I could tell by their eyes that they knew
everything! If only I can get downstairs! But what if they have
someone watching there, a police guard? What is this, tea? Ah,
there's some beer left too, half a bottle, and cold!'

He seized the bottle, in which there still remained a whole
glassful of beer, and drank it off in one gulp, as if he were
trying to extinguish the fire in his breast. Before a minute had
passed, the beer had gone to his head, and a slight and somehow pleasurable shudder ran up his spine. He lay down and
drew the blankets over him. His thoughts, disjointed and feverish enough before, now grew more and more confused, and
soon a light and pleasant sleep enveloped him. Enjoying his
new comfort, he found a place for his head on the pillow,
wrapped himself closer in the thick soft quilt that covered him
now instead of his torn old coat, sighed softly, and sank into a
deep, sound, and healing sleep.

He awoke at the sound of somebody entering the room,
opened his eyes and saw Razumikhin, who had opened the
door and now stood on the threshold, hesitating whether to
come in or not. Raskolnikov sat up abruptly and looked at him
as if he were trying to recollect something.

'Oh, you're not asleep. Well, here I am! Nastasya, bring the
parcel!' Razumikhin shouted down the stairs. 'You shall have
an account at once . . .'

'What time is it?' asked Raskolnikov, looking round in
alarm.

'You've had a capital sleep, my dear chap; it's evening, it
must be six o'clock. You have slept for more than six hours . . .'

'Heavens! How could I? . . .'

'What is all this about? It's good for you. What is your
hurry? Have you got an appointment, or something? We have
all time before us. I've been waiting for three hours; I looked
in a couple of times, but you were asleep. I called on Zosimov
twice, but he wasn't in. It doesn't matter, he will be coming . . .
I've been out attending to my own small affairs, too. You
know I finished moving today, with my uncle. I have an
uncle with me now, you know . . . Well now, to the devil

with all that, let's get to business . . . Give the parcel here,
Nastenka. Now we will . . . But how do you feel now, my dear
fellow?'

'I am all right; I am not ill . . . Razumikhin, have you been
here long?'

'I've just told you; I've been waiting three hours.'

'No, but before?'

'What do you mean, before?'

'Since when have you been coming here?'

'But you know I told you not long since; surely you remember?'

Raskolnikov thought. Recent happenings came back to him
dimly, as in a dream. He could not remember without help,
and he looked inquiringly at Razumikhin.

'Hm,' said his friend, 'you've forgotten. I had a sort of idea,
just now, that you were not quite yourself yet . . . But the sleep
has done you good . . . Really, you look much better. That's
fine! Well, let's get on! You'll remember presently. Look at
this, old man.'

He began to undo the parcel, which obviously interested
him greatly.

'This, my dear fellow, is a matter which has been very close
to my heart, believe me. Because we must make a man of you.
We'll begin at the top. Do you see this cap?' he began, drawing
out of the parcel a cap which, while it looked quite decent,
was very ordinary and cheap. 'Won't you try it on?'

'Afterwards—later,' said Raskolnikov, waving it irritably
away.

'Oh no, my dear chap, don't refuse; it will be too late
afterwards, and I shall not sleep all night, because I had to
guess at the size when I bought it. Just right!' he exclaimed
triumphantly, measuring it; 'exactly the size! What to put on
your head, my dear chap, is the very first consideration in
dress; it is a kind of introduction. My friend Tolstyakov has
to take off his lid when he goes into a public lavatory, when
everybody else wears his hat. Everybody thinks he does this
out of servility of spirit, but it is simply because he is ashamed
of the bird's nest he wears on his head; he is a very shame-
faced man! Now, Nastenka, here you have two head-coverings:
this "Palmerston"' (for some unknown reason he applied this
name to Raskolnikov's battered old round hat, which he had
taken from the corner), 'and this jeweller's piece. Put a price
on it, Rodya; what do you think I gave for it? Nastasyuskha?'
he added, turning to her when he saw that he would get no
answer.

'Twenty copecks, I expect,' answered Nastaysa.

'Twenty copecks! You're a fool!' he exclaimed, offended.
'Nowadays even you would fetch more than that. Eighty

copecks, and that only because it's second-hand! It's true, there's a guarantee with it: if you wear this one out, next year you get another free, as true as I'm standing here! Well, now we come to the United States, as we used to call them at school. I warn you, I am proud of the trousers!' and he spread out before Raskolnikov a grey pair, of light-weight wool; 'not a hole, not a mark, and though they have been worn, they are quite serviceable. The waistcoat is the same, a plain one as fashion decrees. As for their having been worn, that really is all the better: it makes them softer, not so stiff . . . You see, Rodya, in order to get on in the world it is enough, in my opinion, to observe the seasons; if you don't ask for asparagus in January, you will save yourself a few roubles; so in relation to the things I've bought. It is summer now, and I've bought summer things, because anyway autumn will demand warmer materials and you will have to throw these away . . . all the more because by that time they will have fallen to pieces of themselves, either from striving after elegance or from inner disorganization. Well, how much do you think for these?— Two roubles and twenty-five copecks! And with the same guarantee, remember: if they wear out you get new ones next year for nothing! At Fedyaev's shop they always deal on those terms: when once you've paid for something, it lasts the rest of your life, because you'll never go there again! Well, now we come to the boots—what do you think of them? Of course, you can see they're not new, but they are good for two or three months, because the workmanship and materials are foreign: the Secretary at the English Embassy sold them last week; he had only worn them for six days, but he badly needed the money. Price, one rouble fifty copecks. Lucky, wasn't I?'

'Maybe they're the wrong size,' remarked Nastasya.

'The wrong size! And what is this?' and he pulled out of his pocket Raskolnikov's grey wrinkled boot, worn into holes and plastered with dried mud. 'I took a sample with me, and they established the right size for me from this monstrous object. So far, everything had gone swimmingly. But about the linen . . . Here to begin with, are three shirts; the material is coarse, but they have the proper fashionable fronts . . . Well, in sum: eighty copecks for the cap, two roubles and twenty-five copecks for the rest of the clothes, total three roubles five copecks; one and a half roubles the boots—because they are really very good ones—total four roubles and fifty-five copecks, and five roubles for all the linen—I got it at the wholesale price—grand total exactly nine roubles fifty-five copecks. Be good enough to accept the change, forty-five copecks in copper; and now, Rodya, you are completely fitted out again, because, in my opinion, your overcoat is not only still serviceable, but even has a certain aristocratic air; that is what it means to order your clothes from Scharmer!⁶ Socks and other things of that sort I leave to you; we have twenty-five roubles left, and you need not worry about Pashenka or the rent; I told you your credit was inexhaustible. Now, my dear fellow, do just change your linen, otherwise some infection might perhaps linger in your shirt . . .'

'Drop it! I don't want to!' Raskolnikov, who had listened with distaste to the strained playfulness of Razumikhin's account of his purchases, waved the suggestion away . . .

'My dear chap, this is impossible! What have I been wearing out shoe-leather for?' insisted Razumikhin, 'Nastasya, don't be modest, help him! There we are!' and in spite of Raskolnikov's resistance, he changed his linen for him. Raskolnikov fell back on his pillow and said nothing for a minute or two.

'They take so long to go away and leave me alone,' he thought. 'Where did the money come from for all this?' he asked at last, with his eyes on the wall.

'The money? Well, I'm hanged! It's your own money, of course. There was a man here from Vakhrushin's a little while ago; your mama sent it; surely you haven't forgotten that as well?'

'Now I remember . . .' said Raskolnikov, after pondering in moody silence for a long time. Razumikhin frowned and looked at him uneasily.

The door opened, and a tall heavy man came in. It seemed to Raskolnikov that there was something familiar about his appearance.

'Zosimov! At last!' cried Razumikhin joyfully.


## CHAPTER IV

Zosimov was tall and stout, with a pale, puffy, clean-shaven face and straight flaxen hair. He wore spectacles, and there was a heavy gold ring on one of his fat, swollen fingers. He must have been about twenty-seven years old. He was dressed in a modish loose light overcoat and light-coloured summer trousers, and his clothes gave a general impression of being loose, fashionable, and spick and span; his linen was irreproachable, and his watch-chain massive. His manner was languid, a mingling of lethargy and studied ease; his pretentiousness, which he strove to conceal, was nevertheless nearly always apparent. His acquaintances found him ponderous, but opined that he knew his business.

6. Scharmer was a famous Petersburg tailor. Dostoevsky himself had his suits made by him.

'I've been to your place twice, my dear fellow . . . You see, he's come round!' exclaimed Razumikhin.

'Yes, yes, I see; well, how are we now, eh?' said Zosimov, looking hard at his patient and sitting down on the sofa at his feet, where he lounged as comfortably as the circumstances allowed.

'He's still under the weather,' continued Razumikhin; 'he almost cried when we changed his linen just now.'

'That's quite understandable, and you could have put it off till later, if he didn't want... The pulse is capital. The head still aching a little, eh?'

'I'm all right; I am quite well!' said Raskolnikov obstinately and irritably, raising himself with flashing eyes; but he fell back again on his pillow at once and turned to the wall. Zosimov watched him.

'Very good . . . everything is as it should be,' he pronounced in his drawling voice. 'Has he eaten anything?'

They told him, and asked what the patient could be given.

'Anything at all . . . Soup, tea . . . He shouldn't have mushrooms or cucumbers, of course, nor beef . . . and . . . well, no need to go on talking now.' He exchanged glances with Razumikhin. 'No more medicine or anything; tomorrow I will see . . . perhaps today it might . . . well, yes . . .'

'Tomorrow evening I shall take him for a walk,' Razumikhin decided. 'We will go to the Yusupov Gardens, and afterwards to the "Crystal Palace".'

'I should not move him tomorrow, or . . . perhaps a little . . . well, we shall see then.'

'It's a great disappointment—I am having a house-warming today, only two steps away; I wish he could be there. If he could just lie on the sofa among us! You will be there? See you don't forget; you promised.'

'Perhaps later, if I can. What arrangements have you made?'

'Nothing much—tea, vodka, herrings, a few patties. Just a few old friends.'

'Who, exactly?'

'Well, they're all from round about here, and, to be accurate, all new acquaintances—except perhaps my old uncle, and even he is new; he only arrived in St. Petersburg yesterday, to settle some small business matters. This is the first time I've seen him for five years.'

'Who is he?'

'Oh, he's vegetated all his life as a district postmaster . . . he has a small pension—he is sixty-five. He's hardly worth mentioning . . . All the same I'm very fond of him. Porfiry Petrovich will be coming; he is the examining magistrate here . . . he's a graduate of the College of Jurisprudence. You must know him.'

'Is he also some connexion of yours?'

'A very distant one. What are you frowning about? Just because you got severely talked to once, aren't you going to come?'

'Much I care for him!'

'All the better. Well, then there are some students, a teacher, one civil servant, one musician, an officer, Zametov . . .'

'Please tell me what you, or he either,' Zosimov nodded at Roskolnikov, 'can possibly have in common with someone like Zametov . . .'

'Oh, these grumblers! You and your principles! . . . you are fixed on your principles as though they were springs; you can't so much as turn round by your own volition. *I* think he is a good man—that's my principle and I don't want to know any more. Zametov is a wonderful man.'

'He has an itching palm.'

'Well, if he has, what of it? What does it matter?' exclaimed Razumikhin, suddenly growing unnaturally irritated; 'was I commending him for looking after himself? I said that in his way he is a good man! And I put it to you straight, look at it all ways—are there so many good people left? I am convinced that nobody would give more than a baked onion for *my* guts, and then only if you were thrown in into the bargain! . . .'

'That's not enough; I'd give two for you myself . . .'

'But I'd only give one for you! Go on, be witty! Zametov is still only a boy and I go very gently with him, because he ought to be won over, not repulsed. If once you repulse a man, you can't set him right, and it is still more so with a boy. With a boy you must go twice as carefully. Oh, you progressive blockheads! You understand nothing! It is not the man you respect, but the office, and so you insult yourselves . . . And if you want to know, perhaps it was a common interest in one particular affair that brought us together.'

'I should like to know what.'

'Well, it's that affair of the house-painter . . . We're going to get him out! There'll be no trouble about it now. The thing is quite, quite clear! We need only put on a bit more pressure.'

'What painter are you talking about?'

'What, haven't I told you about it? I must have. No, wait a bit, I only told you the beginning . . . you know, about the murder of that old woman, the pawnbroker, some official's widow . . . well, now there's a painter involved in it . . .'

'Yes, I had heard about the murder before you told me, and I am interested in it . . . partly, . . . on account of something

... and I saw it in the papers ... But now ...'

'That Lizaveta was killed too!' broke out Nastasya to Raskolnikov. She had remained in the room all the time, near the door, listening.

'Lizaveta?' Raskolnikov's murmur was barely audible.

'Yes, Lizaveta, you know, the dealer. She used to come downstairs. She once mended a shirt for you.'

Raskolnikov turned to the wall, selected one of the white flowers, with little brown lines on them, on the yellowish paper, and began to count how many petals it had, how many serrations on each petal and how many little brown lines. He felt his arms and legs grow numb as if they were no longer there. He did not stir, but looked fixedly at the flower.

'Well, what about the painter?' Zosimov interrupted Nastasya's chatter with marked displeasure. She sighed and said no more.

'They've got him down as a murderer!' went on Razumikhin hotly.

'Have they any evidence?'

'The devil take evidence! However, as far as evidence goes, their evidence isn't evidence at all. That is what we must demonstrate. It's exactly, point for point, the way they took those—what's their names—Koch and Pestryakov ... at the beginning and suspected them. Pah! How stupidly these things are managed; even a quite disinterested onlooker finds it revolting! ... It's possible that Pestryakov will be coming to my place today ... By the way, Rodya, you know about this; it happened before your illness, just the day before you fainted in the office when they were talking about it ...'

Zosimov looked curiously at Raskolnikov, who did not move. Then he remarked:

'Do you know, Razumikhin, I shall have to have a look at you too: what a fussy old woman you are, though!'

'Perhaps I am. All the same, we'll get him out of it!' exclaimed Razumikhin, banging the table with his fist. 'What is the most offensive aspect of all this? Not that what they say is untrue; it is always possible to forgive untruth; untruth is valuable, because it leads to truth. No, what is vexatious is that they set up their falsehood and fall down and worship it! I respect Porfiry, but ... For example, what led them astray in the very first place? The door was fastened, but when they came back with the porter, it was open: therefore Koch and Pestryakov murdered her! That's their logic for you.'

'Don't get so heated; they were simply detained; after all, one can't ... By the way: I must have met this Koch; didn't it turn out that he bought up unredeemed pledges from the old woman, eh?'

'Yes, he's a scoundrel. He buys up notes of hand as well. He'll do anything for a profit. But to the devil with him! I'll tell you what makes me so angry. Can you understand this? I am angry with their routine, their antiquated, banal, hide-bound routine . . . Here, in this one case, an entirely new avenue can be opened up. By psychological data alone it can be shown how one must proceed to find the right trail. "We," they say, "have facts!" But facts aren't everything; at least half the case consists in what you do with the facts!'

'And do you know what to do with the facts?'

'Yes, and it is impossible to keep silent when you feel, when you know by instinct, that you could help matters, if . . . oh! . . . Do you know the details of the case?'

'I am waiting to hear about the painter.'

'Yes, of course! Well, listen to the story: on the third morning after the murder, while they were still fussing about with Koch and Pestryakov (although they could account for every step; the evidence was overwhelming), a most unexpected fact came to light. A certain peasant, Dushkin, proprietor of a tavern opposite that very house, appeared in the office with a jeweller's case with gold earrings in it, and told a long story: "The day before yesterday, in the evening, at approximately eight o'clock" (the day and the hour, notice!) "there came into my place a workman, a painter called Mikolay, who had been in before, and brought me this here little box with these gold earrings with little stones in them, and asked me to lend him two roubles on them, and when I asked him where he got them he said he picked them up in the street. I didn't ask him any more questions"—this is what Dushkin said—"but I gave him a note"—a rouble, that is—"because I thought if it's not me it will be somebody else, and it comes to the same thing, he'll drink it all, and it will be better if I keep the things: safe bind, safe find; and if something happens, or I hear anything, I can hand them in." Well, of course, that's all a pack of rubbish—he lies like a trooper—because I know this Dushkin, and he does some pawnbroking himself, and he's a bit of a fence too, and he never cheated Mikolay out of a thirty-rouble article in order to hand it over. No, he simply lost his nerve. Well, now, dash it, listen. This is Dushkin speaking again: "This here peasant, Mikolay Dementyev, is someone I have known since we was kids; he's from our Government and District, Zaraysk, because I come from Ryazan. Mikolay isn't what you'd call a drunkard, but he likes a drop, and we knew that he was working in that very house, painting, with Mitrey, and he and Mitrey come from the same place. And when he got the note he changed it at once, drank two glasses of vodka, took his change, and went, and I never saw Mitrey with him that time. Next day we heard that Alëna Ivanovna and her sister Lizaveta Ivanovna had been murdered with an axe, and we used to know her, and I got to feeling doubtful about them earrings—because we knew the deceased used to lend people money on their things. So I went in the house to see them and I made inquiries, very careful, bit by bit and quiet-like, and first of all I asked if Mikolay was there. And Mitrey says Mikolay was off on a spree, he didn't come home till daylight, and he was drunk, but he only stayed ten minutes and then went off again, and Mitrey hadn't laid eyes on him since and he was having to finish the job by himself. And the job was on the same staircase as the murder, on the second floor. Well, I listened to all that, but I didn't say nothing to nobody, not then"—this is still Dushkin—"but I found out everything I could about the murder and went back home, but I still felt just as doubtful. And this morning, at eight o'clock"—that was on the third day, you understand—"I see Mikolay coming in, not so to say sober, but not very drunk, he could understand what anyone said to him. He sits down on the bench, and not a word out of him. Besides him there wasn't nobody in the house just then except one stranger, and another man, someone I knew, asleep on a bench, and my two boys. 'Have you seen Mitrey?' says I—'No', says he, 'I haven't.'—'And you haven't been here?'—'Not since the day before yesterday', says he.— 'And where did you sleep last night?'—'On the Sands, near the barges.'—'And where', says I, 'did you get those earrings?'— 'I found them in the street'—but he don't say that in a likely sort of way, and he don't look at us.—'And you've heard, I suppose,' says I, 'that such and such happened that evening, at the very time, on that there staircase?'—'No', says he, 'I haven't'—and he listens with his eyes popping out of his head, and then he turns as white as chalk. Well, I tells him all about it, and then I looks and there he's took his hat and got up to go. Well, I tries to keep him—'Wait a bit, Mikolay,' says I, 'aren't you going to finish your drink?'—and I gives the lad a signal to hold the door shut, and comes out from behind the counter, but he up and out into the street, running he were, and into an alley, and that's the last I sees of him. Well that settled all my doubts; he's the sinner, sure enough . . ." '

'I should think so! . . .' said Zosimov.

'Stop, hear me out. Naturally they were off hot-foot after Mikolay; they detained Dushkin and searched his place, and the same with Mitrey; they turned the barges inside out—and a couple of days later they brought in Mikolay himself; he was detained near the toll-gate, at an inn. He had gone in, taken off his silver cross and asked for a glass of vodka for it. They gave it to him. A few minutes later a woman went into the cow-shed, and saw him through a crack, in the cart-shed next door. He had tied his girdle to a beam and made a noose in it; he was standing on a block of wood and was just about to put his neck in the noose; the woman yelled blue murder, and people ran in: "So that's it!"—"Take me," said he, "to such-and-such a police station; I will confess everything." Well, they took him with due ceremony to such-and-such a station, here, I mean. Then it was this, that, who? how? how old are you?—"twenty-two"—and so on and so forth. Question: "When you were working with Mitrey, didn't you see anybody on the stairs at such-and-such a time?" Answer: "Well, of course, somebody may have gone past, but we had something better to do than watch them."—"And didn't you hear anything, any sort of noise, or something of that sort?"— "We didn't notice anything special."—"And didn't you know, Mikolay, on that same day, that a certain widow had been robbed and murdered, with her sister, on a certain day at a certain time?"—"I hadn't the least idea! I first heard of it from Afanasy Pavlovich, two days later, in a pub."—"Where did you get the earrings?" "I found them in the street."— "Why didn't you turn up at your work next day?"—"Because I went off on a binge."—"Where did you go to?" "Here and there."—"Why did you run away from Dushkin?"—"Because I was very much afraid."—"What were you afraid of?"— "People saying I had done it."—"How could you be afraid of that if you knew you were quite innocent?" . . . Believe me, or believe me not, Zosimov, that question was put in exactly those words; I know it for a fact; my information is reliable! Well, I ask you!'

'Well, all the same, there is some evidence.'

'I'm not talking about the evidence now. I'm talking about the question, about the way they understand reality! Well, never mind! . . . And so they pressed and pressed and squeezed and squeezed, until he confessed: "It wasn't in the street," says he, "but in the flat Mitrey and I were working in, that I found them."—"How did that happen?"—"It was like this; we'd been painting all day, Mitrey and I, right up to eight o'clock, and we were just getting ready to leave, and Mitrey grabbed a brush and daubed my face with paint, full in the mug, and then ran away with me after him. I was running after him yelling blue murder, and just as I got to the bottom of the stairs, near the gate, I ran slap into the porter and some gentlemen—I don't remember how many gentlemen he had with him—and the porter began shouting at me, and the other porter shouted as well, and then the porter's wife came out and began shouting too. Then a gentleman came in through the gate, with a lady, and he cursed us as well, because me and Mitrey were lying right across the gateway; I'd grabbed Mitka's hair and got him down, and I was punching him, and Mitka, who was underneath, got me by the hair as well, and started punching me, but it was only fun, just a friendly rough-and-tumble, no hard feelings. Then Mitka got away and ran off up the street and I ran after him, but I couldn't catch him. So I went back to the flat by myself, to straighten up a bit. I began putting things straight, and waiting for Mitka in case he came back. Then in the entrance, by the door, up against the wall in a corner, I stepped on this box. I looked and saw it lying there wrapped in a bit of paper. I took off the paper and saw there were some little tiny hooks on the box, so I undid the hooks, and there were the earrings . . ." '

'Behind the door, just behind the door? Did you say behind the door?' exclaimed Raskolnikov, raising himself slowly on his arms and staring with troubled, terrified eyes at Razumikhin.

'Yes . . . what then? What is the matter? Why do you ask?' Razumikhin also got up from his place.

'Nothing,' answered Raskolnikov in a barely audible voice, sinking back again and once more turning his face to the wall. There was a short silence.

'He must have dropped off; he's half asleep,' said Razumikhin at length, with a questioning look at Zosimov, who shook his head slightly.

'Well, go on!' he said; 'what happened next?'

'What next? As soon as he saw the earrings he immediately forgot about the flat and Mitka, seized his hat and ran to Dushkin and, as you know, got a rouble out of him, told him the lying story about finding them in the street, and went off on his spree. Concerning the murder he had asserted earlier: "I hadn't the least idea, I only heard about it two days later." "And why haven't you come forward before this?"—"From fear."—"Why did you try to hang yourself?"—"Thinking."— "Thinking what?"—"That they would pin it on me."—Well, that's the whole story. Now, what do you think they have made of all that?'

'What should I think? There *is* a trail there, not much of one, but it's there. Facts. You wouldn't have had them let your painter go free?'

'But they flatly accuse him of the murder now! They haven't the slightest doubt about it . . .'

'Fudge! You're getting excited. What about the earrings? You must agree that if those earrings got into Nikolay's hands from the old woman's trunk just at that very time—you must agree there's got to be some explanation of how they got there. It's no trifle, in such circumstances.'

'How they got there? How they got there?' exclaimed Razumikhin. 'Is it possible that you, a doctor, whose first duty is to study mankind, and who have better opportunities for studying human nature than most people—is it possible that in all this you do not discern the nature of this Nikolay? Is it possible you don't see, at the very first glance, that everything he said at his interrogation is the sacred truth? The things came into his hands just exactly as he says they did. He stepped on the box and picked it up!'

'The sacred truth! But didn't he himself admit that he lied to begin with?'

'Listen to me. Listen carefully: the porter, and Koch, and Pestryakov, and the second porter, and the first porter's wife, and a woman who was with her in the porter's lodge at the time, and Civil Councillor Kryukov, who got out of a cab at the moment and entered through the gate with a lady on his arm—all these eight or ten witnesses testify with one voice that Nikolay brought Dmitri to the ground, with himself on top, and pummelled him, and that Dmitri seized his hair and punched back. They were lying across the way and blocking the entrance; curses rained on them from all sides, but they, "like two small boys" (in the witnesses' own words), lay there one on top of the other, squealing, scuffling, and laughing, both of them yelling with laughter the whole time and with the most comical grimaces, and then chased one another out into the street like children. Do you hear that? Now note carefully: the bodies upstairs were still warm; do you hear, warm?— that's how they were found. If those two, or Nikolay alone, had committed the murder and then broken into the trunk and rifled it, or if they had merely had some share in the robbery, then ask yourself just one question: is a mood such as theirs, shrieks and yells of laughter, childish horseplay in the gateway, compatible with axes and blood, with evil cunning, and wariness, and with robbery? They had just done murder, not more than five or ten minutes before (that emerges from the fact that the bodies were warm), and suddenly abandoning the bodies and leaving the flat wide open, although they knew people had just been there, and leaving their spoils behind somewhere, they began rolling about on the ground like small children, laughing uproariously and attracting attention to themselves—and there are ten witnesses who all agree on it!'

'It's certainly strange; of course, it's impossible, but . . .'

'No, my dear chap, not *but*; if the earrings found in Nikolay's possession on that day and at that time really constitute the most important factual evidence against him—it has been fully explained, however, by his testimony, and consequently is still *disputed evidence*—then we must take into consideration also the facts in his favour, especially as they are *irresistible* facts. But do you think, from the character of our judicial authorities that they will accept, or are capable of accepting, a fact of that kind—based solely on a psychological impossibility, a mental disposition—as irresistible evidence, demolishing all incriminating material evidence of whatever kind? No, they will not accept it, they will not have it on any account, because they have found a box and because a man tried to hang himself, "which he could not have done unless he had known he was guilty!" That is the fundamental question, that is why I get excited! Try to understand!'

'Well, I can see you are excited. Stop a minute; I forgot to ask you: what is there to show that the box and the earrings really came from the old woman's trunk?'

'It has been proved,' answered Razumikhin with apparent reluctance, frowning; 'Koch recognized the thing and indicated the borrower, and he proved conclusively that it really was his.'

'That's bad. Now another thing: did no one see Nikolay when Koch and Pestryakov went upstairs, and can't it be proved somehow?'

'That's just it, nobody did see him,' answered Razumikhin with some annoyance, 'and that is bad; even Koch and Pestryakov didn't notice them as they went past on their way upstairs, although their testimony would not mean very much now. "We saw," they say, "that the flat was open, and that work must be going on in it, but we did not pay any attention to it as we passed and we cannot recollect clearly whether there were workmen in it at the time, or not."'

'Hm. It comes to this, that the only thing in their favour is that they were pummelling each other and laughing. Let us grant that it is powerful evidence, but . . . Let me ask you now: how do you explain the whole episode? How can you account for the finding of the earrings, if he really found them, as he testifies?'

'How do I account for it? There is nothing to account for; it's as clear as daylight. At any rate, the path the investigation must follow is plain and evident, and it is precisely the box that has demonstrated it. The real murderer dropped those earrings. He was upstairs, behind a locked door, when Koch and Pestryakov knocked. Koch acted like a fool and went downstairs; then the murderer slipped out and also started downstairs, because there was no other way out for him. On the way down he hid from Koch, Pestryakov, and the porter in the empty flat, at the exact time when Dmitri and Nikolay had run out of it, and stood behind the door. When the porter and the others had gone past up the stairs, he waited until the sound of steps had died away and went calmly down at the very moment when Dmitri had run out into the street with Nikolay, the little crowd had dispersed, and nobody was left in the gateway. He may even have been seen, without being noticed; plenty of people go past. He dropped the box out of his pocket while he stood behind the door, and did not notice because he had other things to think about. But the box shows quite clearly that it was there that he stood. That's all there is to it!'

'Clever! No, my dear chap, that's clever! It is altogether too ingenious!'

'But why, why?'

'Simply because it is too neatly dove-tailed . . . like a play.'

'Oh!' Razumikhin began, but at that moment the door opened and a new personage came in, a stranger to everybody in the room.

## CHAPTER V

THIS was a gentleman no longer young, starchy and pompous, with a wary and irritable face, who began by stopping in the doorway and looking round with offensively-unconcealed astonishment in his eyes, which seemed to be asking: 'Where on earth have I got to?' Mistrustfully, and with a certain pretence of being shocked and outraged, he scanned Raskolnikov's crowded, low-ceilinged 'ship's cabin'. With the same astonishment he transferred his gaze to Raskolnikov himself, lying undressed, unwashed, and unkempt on his wretched dirty sofa and returning his look with one equally steady. Then, with the same slowness, he began to examine the tousled, unshaven, and dishevelled Razumikhin, who did not move from his place but in his turn looked straight at the visitor with an expression of arrogant inquiry. The tense silence lasted for a minute, but then, as was to be expected, there was a slight alteration in the atmosphere. Realizing, perhaps, from some slight but quite definite indications that an exaggerated rigidity of bearing would accomplish precisely nothing in this 'ship's cabin', the newcomer turned with a softer but still rather stiff courtesy towards Zosimov and asked, articulating every syllable with great distinctness:

'Rodion Romanovich Raskolnikov, a student or former student?'

Zosimov stirred sluggishly and would perhaps have answered if Razumikhin, who had not been asked, had not anticipated him:

'There he is on the sofa! What do you want?'

The familiarity of this shook the starchy gentleman; he was even on the point of speaking to Razumikhin, but he managed to stop himself just in time and hastily turned back to Zosimov.

'That is Raskolnikov!' drawled Zosimov, gesturing towards

the patient, and he yawned, opening his mouth prodigiously wide and keeping it open for a prodigiously long time. Then he slowly inserted his fingers into his waistcoat-pocket, drew out an enormous bulging gold hunter, opened it, looked at it, and returned it equally slowly to its place.

Raskolnikov himself was still lying on his back in silence, with his eyes fixed steadily but vacantly on his visitor. His face, now that he had turned away from the engrossing flower on the wallpaper, was extraordinarily pale and had an expression of intense suffering, as though he had just undergone a painful operation or been subjected to torture. But gradually the newcomer began to awaken in him an ever-intensifying chain of emotions, first attention, then perplexity, then mistrust, and even almost fear. When, however, Zosimov pointed him out as Raskolnikov, he sat up abruptly with a start and said in a defiant but feeble and broken tone:

'Yes! I am Raskolnikov! What do you want?'

The visitor looked at him closely and replied importantly:

'Peter Petrovich Luzhin. I flatter myself that my name is not unknown to you.'

Raskolnikov had been expecting something quite different, and he looked at him dully and thoughtfully without answering, as though this were absolutely the first time he had heard Peter Petrovich's name.

'What? Have you really not yet received a letter with some mention of me in it?' asked Peter Petrovich, a little deflated.

In answer to this, Raskolnikov let himself sink back on his pillow, put his hands behind his head, and turned his eyes to the ceiling. Anxiety showed in Luzhin's face. Zosimov and Razumikhin studied him with even greater curiosity than before, and he seemed at last quite put out of countenance.

'I supposed, indeed I counted on it,' he mumbled, 'that a letter, posted more than ten days, in fact almost a fortnight, ago . . .'

'I say, why should you keep on standing by the door?' interrupted Razumikhin. 'If you have something to say, sit down; you and Nastasya get in each other's way there. Move aside, Nastasyushka, and let him pass! Come this way; here's a chair. Squeeze your way in.'

He pushed his chair away from the table, freeing a narrow space between the table and his knees and waited in a rather awkward posture for the visitor to 'squeeze his way' through the narrow opening. He had chosen his moment so well that it was impossible to refuse, and the visitor hastily pushed past him, stumbling, to the chair, and sat down, looking suspiciously at Razumikhin.

'Don't be upset,' the latter rattled on; 'Rodya has been ill for the past five days, and delirious for three of them, but he is much better now and has even recovered his appetite. This is his doctor here, who has just been having a look at him, and I am a friend of his, another former student, and I am looking after him; so don't be embarrassed, but take no notice of us and go on with your business.'

'I thank you. But shall I not be disturbing the patient with my presence and conversation?' said Peter Petrovich, addressing Zosimov.

'N-no,' drawled Zosimov, with another yawn; 'you may even entertain him.'

'Oh, he's been in his right senses for a long time, in fact since this morning,' continued Razumikhin, whose familiarity seemed to spring from such genuine simple-heartedness that Peter Petrovich began to reconsider his mistrustful attitude, perhaps partly because this impudent ragamuffin had after all introduced himself as a student.

'Your mama . . .' began Luzhin.

'Hm!' commented Razumikhin loudly. Luzhin looked at him inquiringly.

'I didn't mean anything. Go on . . .'

Luzhin shrugged his shoulders.

'. . . Your mama had already begun a letter to you during my sojourn in their neighbourhood. When I arrived here, I purposely allowed some days to elapse before seeking you out, so that I might come to you with full assurance that you had been apprised of everything; but now, to my astonishment . . .'

'I know, I know!' broke in Raskolnikov impatiently, with an expression of irritation. 'So you're the bridegroom, are you? Well, I know about it . . . That's enough!'

Although Peter Petrovich was decidedly offended, he said nothing, but sat visibly striving to understand what all this could mean. There was a minute's silence.

Meanwhile, Raskolnikov, who had turned slightly towards him when he answered, was again gazing at him earnestly, with enhanced curiosity, as though he had not examined him properly before or had been suddenly struck by some new aspect of his appearance; he even raised himself from his pillows to do so. Peter Petrovich's general appearance had indeed something rather special and striking about it, something which justified the appellation of 'bridegroom' flung at him so unceremoniously. To begin with, it was evident, it was even conspicuous, that he had made strenuous use of his few days in the capital in order to get himself fitted out and spruced up in anticipation of his bride's arrival, a harmless and pardonable activity enough. Even his own consciousness of the gratifying change for the better in himself, though perhaps too self-satisfied, might be forgiven in the circumstances, for Peter Petrovich was enrolled among the bridegrooms. All his clothes were newly come from the tailor, and they were all very good, even if they were perhaps a little too new and too obviously designed for a particular purpose. His elegant, spick-and-span round hat testified to the same purpose: he treated it somewhat too respectfully, nursing it carefully in his hands. A coquettish pair of real French lilac-coloured gloves also betrayed the same purpose, if only by the fact that he did not wear them but carried them in his hand for show. In Peter Petrovich's dress light and youthful colours predominated. He was wearing a handsome light-brown summer jacket, light-weight bright-coloured trousers and waistcoat, newly-purchased thin linen, a stock of the finest cambric, with pink stripes; and it must be said that all this suited Peter Petrovich well enough. Even without the help of his youthful clothes, his fresh and handsome face looked younger than his forty-five years. His cheeks were very pleasantly shaded by dark mutton-chop whiskers, which thickened into a handsome bushiness on each side of his shiningly clean-shaven chin. His hair, receding ever so slightly from his forehead, had been combed and curled by a barber, but this circumstance did not make him look comical or foolish, as is so often the case, since curled hair usually makes a man look like a German at his wedding. If there was anything displeasing or unsympathetic in this sedate and quite good-looking countenance it arose from quite other causes. When he had completed his unceremonious scrutiny of Mr. Luzhin, Raskolnikov sank back on his pillow with a malicious smile and resumed his former study of the ceiling.

But Mr. Luzhin was now firmly in control of himself and had apparently decided to ignore all this strange behaviour for the present.

'I regret, with complete and absolute sincerity, that I find you in this state,' he began again, breaking the silence with an effort. 'If I had known of your illness I should have called on you sooner. But, you know, the cares of business! . . . I have besides an extremely important case in the Senate. I do not mention those other cares which you may easily guess at. I expect your people, I mean your mama and sister, at any moment . . .'

Raskolnikov stirred and seemed about to say something; his face showed some perturbation. Peter Petrovich stopped and waited, but as nothing followed he went on:

'At any moment. I have found them quarters for the time being . . .'

'Where?' asked Raskolnikov feebly.

'Not at all far from here, in Bakaleev's house . . .'

'That's on Voznesensky Prospect,' interrrupted Razumikhin; 'there's a cheap hotel occupying two floors of the building; the merchant Yushin runs it; I've been there.'

'Yes, it's a hotel . . .'

'It is a horrible place, dirty and stinking, and its character is suspect; there have been various incidents, and God knows who lives there. What took me there was a disgraceful affair. It is cheap, though.'

'I, of course, could not command such information, since I am myself a newcomer,' retorted Petrovich, nettled. 'I have taken, however, two completely and absolutely clean little rooms, and since it is for an extremely short space of time . . . I have already found our real, that is to say, our future flat,' he went on, turning to Raskolnikov; 'it is being made ready for us. Meanwhile I myself live very inconveniently in rooms, very near here, at Mrs. Lippewechsel's, in the lodgings of my young friend Andrey Semënovich Lebezyatnikov; it was he who told me of the Bakaleev house . . .'

'Lebezyatnikov?' said Raskolnikov slowly, as if remembering something.

'Yes, Andrey Semënovich Lebezyatnikov. He is employed in one of the Ministries. Do you know him?'

'Yes . . . no . . .' answered Raskolnikov.

'Excuse me, I thought from your question that you did. I was at one time his guardian . . . a very nice young man . . . and interested in public affairs . . . I am always glad to meet young people; you learn from them what is new.' Peter Petrovich looked hopefully round at everybody.

'In what respect?' asked Razumikhin.

'In the most serious, so to say, in the most essential respect,' eagerly responded Peter Petrovich, as if glad of the question. 'You see, it is ten years since I was last in St. Petersburg. All these new ideas, reforms, theories, have penetrated even to us in the provinces, but to see the whole picture and see it clearly, one must be in the capital. Well, sir, my meaning was that one sees most and learns most from study of the younger generation. And I confess I was glad . . .'

'Why, exactly?'

'Your question is very far-reaching. I may be mistaken, but it seems to me that I find a clearer point of view, a more, so to say, critical approach, greater practical ability . . .'

'That is true,' put in Zosimov.

'Nonsense! There's no practical ability,' Razumikhin caught him up. 'Practical ability has to be laboriously acquired, it doesn't drop out of the clouds. And for almost two hundred years we've had nothing to do with practical affairs.[7] Plenty of ideas wandering about, no doubt,' he went on to Peter Petrovich, 'and a desire to be good, a rather childish one,

7. Dostoevsky himself believed that Peter the Great's reforms drove a wedge between the Russian people and the educated upper classes.

perhaps; and integrity can be found too, in spite of the enormous number of knaves among us; but there's no practical ability! Practical men, men of business ability, wear white collars, and are prosperous.'

'I do not agree with you,' objected Peter Petrovich, with evident enjoyment. 'Some people go to extremes. There are irregularities, but we must be lenient: the extremes testify to zeal for the cause, and to the anomalous circumstances in which the cause finds itself. If too little has been done, there has not after all been much time. I do not speak of means. In my personal opinion, if you like, something definite has been accomplished; new, beneficial ideas have been propagated, and new and wholesome writings disseminated, in place of the old fantastic and romantic ones; literature has been given a tinge of maturity; many harmful prejudices have been rooted out and held up to ridicule . . . In a word, we have irrevocably severed ourselves from the past[8] and that, in my opinion, is an achievement, sir . . .'

'What a parrot! He's trying to make a good impression,' pronounced Raskolnikov suddenly.

'What?' asked Peter Petrovich, who had not caught this, but he received no answer.

'That is all very just,' Zosimov hastened to interpose.

'Is it not true, sir?' went on Peter Petrovich, with a friendly glance at Zosimov. 'You yourself will agree,' he turned again to Razumikhin, with a hint of triumphant superiority in his manner, and only just saved himself from adding 'young man', 'that there is some advance or, as they say now, progress, at least in the name of science and economic truth . . .'

'Commonplaces!'

'No, sir! If, for example, in earlier times it was said to me: "Love your neighbour" and I acted on it, what was the result?' continued Peter Petrovich, with perhaps excessive haste. 'The result was that I divided my cloak with my neighbour and we were both left half-naked, for according to the Russian proverb: "If you run after two hares, you will catch neither." Science, however, says: love yourself first of all, for everything in the world is based on personal interest. If you love yourself alone, you will conduct your affairs properly, and your cloak will remain whole. Economic truth adds that the more private enterprises are established and the more, so to say, whole cloaks there are in a society, the firmer will be its foundations and the more will be undertaken for the common good. That is to say, that by the very act of devoting my gains solely and

8. Luzhin is paraphrasing and oversimplifying the theories which the progressive radical N. G. Chernyshevsky expressed in various articles and in the novel *What Is to Be Done?* (1863). Chernyshevsky rejected traditional and religious ideas and stressed the influence of environment on man, human rationality and perfectability, and the advisability of seeking one's own advantage. Much of *Crime and Punishment* is meant to be a rebuttal of Chernyshevsky's ideas.

exclusively to myself, I am at the same time benefiting the whole community, and ensuring that my neighbour receives something better than half a torn cloak, and that not by private, isolated bounty, but as a consequence of the general economic advancement. The idea is simple, but, unfortunately, has been too long in finding acceptance, obscured as it is by vaporous ideals and misguided enthusiasms; a certain keenness of intellect, it would seem, is necessary to realize . . .'

'Excuse me, my own intellect is not very keen,' interrupted Razumikhin brusquely, 'and therefore we will stop there, if you please. There was after all some purpose in my remarks, but for three years I have been so sick of this kind of self-congratulatory babbling, this ceaseless inexhaustible flow of platitudes, these monotonous repetitions over and over again of the same old commonplaces, that I swear I blush even to hear them all aired again. You, of course, were anxious to produce a good impression by displaying your knowledge, and that is pardonable; I do not condemn you for it. I, though, only wanted to find out what sort of person you were, because, you see, so many varieties of opportunists have hitched themselves on to the common cause, and so distorted everything they touched in their own interests, that they have befouled the whole cause. Well, enough of that!'

'My dear sir,' Mr. Luzhin was beginning, bridling with an extraordinary assumption of dignity, 'are you trying, and with such lack of ceremony, to imply that I . . .'

'Oh, really, really! . . . How could I? Let us have done with this!' Razumikhin cut him short, and abruptly resumed his former conversation with Zosimov.

Peter Petrovich proved wise enough to accept this explanation. In a minute or two, however, he decided to go.

'I hope that this acquaintance of ours, now that it has been initiated,' he said to Raskolnikov, 'will grow closer, when you are restored to health, in view of the circumstances known to you . . . I particularly wish you a speedy recovery . . .'

Raskolnikov did not even turn his head. Peter Petrovich prepared to rise.

'The murderer was certainly a client,' affirmed Zosimov.

'Quite certainly,' agreed Razumikhin. 'Porfiry does not betray his ideas, but all the same he is interrogating those who pawned things with her . . .'

'Interrogating them?' asked Raskolnikov loudly.

'Yes. What then?'

'Nothing.'

'How does he get hold of them?' asked Zosimov.

'Koch has indicated some of them; the names of others were written on the wrappings of their pledges, and some came of themselves when they heard . . .'

'Well, he must be a cunning and experienced rascal. What audacity! What resolution!'

'That is exactly what he isn't!' interrupted Razumikhin. 'That is where you all go wrong. I say he was clumsy and inexperienced; this was probably his first attempt. Postulate a shrewd and calculating rogue, and the whole affair is most improbable. But suppose him to have been inexperienced, and it emerges that it was nothing but chance that saved him from disaster, and what cannot chance accomplish? Perhaps he did not even foresee the obstacles he would meet with! And how did he manage the affair? He took ten or twenty roubles' worth of things, stuffed his pockets with them, rummaged in the old woman's trunk among old rags—and in the top drawer of the chest of drawers, in a box, there was found fifteen hundred roubles in cash, besides some notes. He didn't even know how to commit robbery, he could only murder! It was the first attempt, I tell you, the first attempt; and he lost his head. And it was not calculation but chance that saved him.'

'You seem to be talking of the recent murder of an old woman,' put in Peter Petrovich, addressing Zosimov. He was already standing with his hat and gloves in his hand, but waiting for a chance to let fall a few more words of wisdom before he left. He evidently went to some trouble to make a favourable impression, and his vanity had conquered his good sense.

'Yes. Have you heard of it?'

'I have heard it talked of.'

'Do you know the details?'

'I cannot say that I do; what interests me is something different, the whole problem, so to say. I do not speak of the increase in crime among the lower classes during the past five years or so, nor of the unbroken series of cases of robbery and arson everywhere; for me the strangest thing is that even in higher social circles crime is increasing in the same way, and, so to say, on parallel lines. In one place we hear of a former student assaulting a postmaster; in another, people of prominent social position have been forging notes; in Moscow, they have caught a whole band of counterfeiters of tickets in the last lottery—and one of the leading spirits was a Reader in Universal History; somewhere else one of our Embassy[9] Secretaries has been murdered for mysterious financial reasons . . . And if now this old pawnbroker woman has been killed by one of her clients, that means he must be a person of some social standing, for peasants do not pawn articles of value. How are we to explain this depravity, so to say, among the civilized elements of our society?'

9. Reported in Moscow newspapers on Sept. 10, 1865.

'Many economic changes . . .' responded Zosimov.

'How are we to explain it?' put in Razumikhin. 'It can be explained precisely by our too deeply ingrained lack of practical ability.'

'How is that, sir?'

'Well, what did that Reader of yours in Moscow answer when he was asked why he had counterfeited tickets?: "Everybody else gets rich by various means, and we wanted to get rich too, as quickly as we could." I don't remember the exact words, but the idea was to do it at other people's expense, as quickly as possible, and without labour. They were used to having everything found for them, to being in leading-strings, to being spoon-fed. When their great hour struck, they revealed what they were . . .'

'But what about morals? And, so to say, principles?'

'What are you making so much fuss about?' broke in Raskolnikov unexpectedly. 'It has worked out in accordance with your own theory.'

'How do you mean, in accordance with my theory?'

'Carry to its logical conclusion what you were preaching just now, and it emerges that you can cut people's throats . . .'

'Oh, come, that's nonsense!' exclaimed Luzhin.

'No, that is not so!' said Zosimov.

Raskolnikov was pale, his upper lip trembled, and he was breathing with difficulty.

'There is reason in all things,' continued Luzhin haughtily; 'an economic idea is not yet an invitation to murder, and if only we assume . . .'

'Is it true,' broke in Raskolnikov again, in a voice trembling with fury, with an undertone of pleasure in being insulting, 'is it true that you told your fiancée, at the very time when you had received her consent, that your greatest reason for rejoicing . . . was that she was poor . . . because it is better to take a wife out of poverty, so that you can dominate over her afterwards . . . and reproach her with the benefits you have heaped on her . . .?'

'My dear sir!' exclaimed Luzhin, in furious irritation. He was blushing and confused. 'My dear sir . . . such a distortion of my meaning! Excuse me, but I am obliged to say openly that the rumours which have reached you, or rather which have been conveyed to you, have not the slightest foundation in fact, and I . . . suspect I know who . . . in a word . . . this shaft . . . in one word, your mama . . . With all her excellent qualities she seemed to me, even before this, to have a somewhat emotional and romantic turn of mind . . . Nevertheless, I was a thousand leagues from supposing that she could put so fantastically perverted a construction on the matter . . . And finally . . . finally . . .'

'Do you know what?' exclaimed Raskolnikov, raising himself on his pillow and fixing him with keen and glittering eyes; 'do you know what?'

'What, sir?' Luzhin paused and waited, with an offended and inquiring expression. The silence lasted for a few seconds.

'This, that if you ever again . . . dare to say so much as a single word . . . about my mother . . . I shall throw you downstairs!'

'What is the matter with you?' cried Razumikhin.

Luzhin turned pale and bit his lip. 'Ah, so that is it, sir! Let me, sir, tell you,' he began deliberately, and exerting all his strength to control himself, but choking with anger nevertheless, 'I realized your hostility from the first, but I remained here on purpose, so as to learn still more. Much may be forgiven a sick man and a relative, but now, sir . . . you . . . never . . .'

'I am not ill!' exclaimed Raskolnikov.

'So much the worse, sir!'

'Take yourself off, and to the devil with you!'

But Luzhin was already leaving without waiting to finish what he was saying, making his way once more between table and chair; Razumikhin stood up this time to let him pass. He went out without a glance at anybody, without so much as nodding to Zosimov, who had for some time been making signs to him to leave his patient alone. As he stooped to go through the door, he lifted his hat with exaggerated care to shoulder level, and the very curve of his back seemed to express resentment at being so shockingly insulted.

'Can people really behave like that?' said Razumikhin, shaking his head in perplexity.

'Go away, go away, all of you!' exclaimed Raskolnikov in a frenzy. 'You torture me; will you leave me alone? I am not afraid of you! I am not afraid of anyone, not of anyone, now! Get out! I want to be alone, alone, alone, alone!'

'Come on!' said Zosimov, signing to Razumikhin.

'Well . . . but ought we to leave him like this?'

'Come on!' repeated Zosimov firmly, and went out. Razumikhin waited a moment in doubt, and then ran to overtake him.

'It might make matters worse, if we crossed him,' said Zosimov on the stairs. 'He must not be irritated . . .'

'What is the matter with him?'

'If only he could be given some sort of push in the right direction, that would be the thing. He had plenty of energy just now . . . You know, he has something on his mind! . . . Something immovable, weighing him down . . . That is decidedly what I am very much afraid of.'

'But there's this fellow, perhaps, this Peter Petrovich. You could tell from what they said that he is marrying Rodya's sister, and that Rodya had a letter about it, just before his illness . . .'

'Yes; the devil prompted him to come just now; he may have upset everything. But did you notice that he was quite indifferent and had nothing to say to anything, except one thing that seemed to rouse him thoroughly: this murder . . .?'

'Yes, yes,' agreed Razumikhin, 'I did notice it. He is both interested and scared. It was that they startled him with in the police office, the day he fell ill; he fainted.'

'You must tell me more about it this evening, and then I shall have something to tell you. He interests me, very much. I shall go back in half an hour to see how he is . . . There won't be any inflammation, though . . .'

'Thank you! Meanwhile, I will wait at Pashenka's and keep an eye on him through Nastasya . . .'

After they had gone, Raskolnikov eyed Nastasya anxiously and impatiently, but she lingered over her departure.

'Will you drink your tea now?' she asked.

'Later! I'm sleepy! Go away!'

He turned with a jerk to the wall; Nastasya went out.

## CHAPTER VI

No sooner had she gone than he got up, fastened the door by its hook, unwrapped the parcel of clothes Razumikhin had brought, and began to dress. Strangely enough, he had now become quite calm; the half-insane ravings of a short time before and the panic fear of the past days had alike vanished. This was the first minute of a strange, sudden tranquillity. His movements were neat and precise, and revealed a resolute purpose.

'Today, today . . .' he muttered to himself. He was aware however, that he was still weak, but an inner tension, so acute that it had resulted in calmness and unshakeable resolution, had endowed him with added strength and self-confidence; he hoped, though, that he would not collapse in the street. When he had finished dressing in the new clothes, he looked at the money lying on the table, hesitated for a moment and put it in his pocket. There were twenty-five roubles. He took also all the small coins, the change from the ten roubles spent by Razumikhin on clothes. Then he quietly undid the hook and went out of the room and down the stairs, glancing through the open kitchen door as he went past; Nastasya was standing with her back to him, stooping to blow out his landlady's samovar. She did not hear anything. And indeed who would have suspected that he would go out? A minute later he was in the street.

It was about eight o'clock and the sun was going down. The heat was still as oppressive as before, but he greedily breathed the dusty, foul-smelling, contaminated air of the town. His head began to feel ever so slightly dizzy; a wild kind of energy flared up in his sunken eyes and pallid wasted face. He did not know, or stop to think, where he was going; he knew only one thing: that he must finish with all *this* today, once and for all, and at once; that otherwise he would not go back home, because *he would not live like this*! But how finish with it? What was he to do? Of this he had no conception, and he refused to think about it. He banished thought. Thought was a torment. He merely knew instinctively that everything must be changed, one way or another; 'somehow, no matter how,' he repeated with desperate, obstinate self-reliance and resolution.

By force of habit, he turned towards the Haymarket, following the usual course of his former walks. Before he reached the Haymarket he came upon a black-haired young man standing in the road before a grocer's shop, grinding out a sentimental ballad on a barrel-organ. He was accompanying a fifteen-year-old girl, who stood before him on the pavement, dressed like a young lady in a crinoline and short mantle, wearing gloves and a straw hat with a flame-coloured feather; all these things were old and worn out. In a coarse, grating, but fairly strong and pleasing voice, she was singing her ballad in the hope of getting a copeck or two from the shop. Raskolnikov stopped near them and listened with two or three bystanders, then took out a five-copeck piece and put it in the girl's hand. She broke off her song abruptly on the very highest and tenderest note and shouted roughly to her companion, 'That will do!' and both trudged away to the next shop.

'Do you like street-singing?' asked Raskolnikov of a passer-by, no longer young, and with the look of an idler, who had been standing by him near the organ-grinder. The man looked oddly at him, in great astonishment. 'I do,' went on Raskolnikov, with an expression as though he were speaking of something much more important than street-singing; 'I like to hear singing to a barrel-organ on a cold, dark, damp autumn evening—it must be damp—when the faces of all the passers-by look greenish and sickly; or, even better, when wet snow is falling, straight down, without any wind, you know, and the gas-lamps shine through it . . .'

'I don't know, sir . . . . Excuse me . . .' muttered the gentleman, frightened alike by the question and by Raskolnikov's strange appearance, and he crossed to the other side of the street.

Raskolnikov went straight on and came to the corner where the dealer and his wife, who had been talking that time to Lizaveta, were usually to be found; they were not there this time. Recognizing the place, he stopped and addressed a lad in a red shirt, who stood yawning at the door of a corn-chandler's shop.

'There is a trader who does business here at the corner, with his wife, a woman from the country, isn't there?'

'All sorts of people do business here,' answered the lad, disdainfully measuring him with his eyes.

'What is he called?'

'What he was christened.'

'Surely you are from Zaraysk, aren't you? Or what Government?'

The lad looked at Raskolnikov again.

'We haven't Governments,[1] your Excellency, in our parts, only Districts; and it was my brother who was smart and went away to work, but I stayed at home, so I don't know, sir. Pardon me, your Excellency, in your generosity.'

'Is that an eating-house, upstairs there?'

'It's a public house, and it has billiards; you can find princesses there . . . Tra-la-la!'

Raskolnikov crossed the square. At the corner a dense crowd was standing; they were all country people. He made his way into the thick of them, looking at people's faces. He felt somehow drawn to talk to everybody. But the peasants took no notice of him; they were all gathered in little clusters, talking noisily. He stopped, thought a moment, and went down the right-hand pavement towards Voznesensky Prospect. Once clear of the square, he came into a lane.

He had often before walked through this short street, which curved round from the square into Sadovaya Street. Recently, whenever he had felt sick of things, he had been drawn to roam about all these parts, 'so as to feel even more nauseated'. Now, however, he was not thinking of anything as he turned into the street. There is in it a large building, all given up to various establishments for eating and drinking; women were constantly coming out of them, dressed as if they were 'just running out to a neighbour's', with bare heads and no outer garments over their dresses. Here and there they gathered in groups on the pavement, mostly near the entrances to the lower floor, where one might go down a couple of steps into various places of entertainment. In one of these at the moment there was a clatter and hubbub that filled the street, a guitar strummed, and somebody was singing; all was merriment. There was a big group of women crowding round the entrance; some were sitting on the steps and some on the pavement, others stood talking together. In the road near by lounged a drunken soldier

1. A "Government" was a large administrative unit in pre-1917 Russia. Peter the Great in 1708 divided the country into such regions. A "District" was a much smaller territorial unit.

with a cigarette, swearing loudly; he seemed to be intending to go in somewhere, but to have forgotten where. One ragamuffin was abusing another, and a man was lying dead-drunk across the pavement. Raskolnikov stopped near the big group of women. Some of them were talking in hoarse voices; they were all in cotton dresses and goatskin shoes, and their heads were bare. Some of them were over forty, but some were only about seventeen: most of them had black eyes.

The singing and all the noise and hubbub down there attracted him . . . From the street he could hear, through the laughter and squealing, somebody dancing with reckless abandonment, beating time with his heels, to the accompaniment of the guitar and the thin remote falsetto of the singing. He listened intently, thoughtfully, sombrely, stooping down to look curiously into the entrance. The thin voice of the singer flowed out to him:

> 'Oh, my fine and darling bobby,
> Do not beat me so unjustly!'—

Raskolnikov strained desperately to hear the words, as though they were of supreme importance.

'Shall I go in?' he thought, 'People are laughing—drunk of course. But wouldn't it be a good idea to get drunk myself?'

'Won't you come in, kind gentleman?' asked one of the women, in a voice that had not yet grown completely husky but was still fairly clear. She was young and—alone of the whole group—not unattractive.

'Hello, here's a pretty girl!' he answered, straightening up to look at her.

She smiled, very pleased at the compliment.

'You're very nice-looking yourself,' said she.

'How thin, though!' commented another in a bass voice. 'Have you just been discharged from the hospital, or something?'

'You lot are all trying to look like generals' daughters, but every one of you's got a snub nose!' broke in a peasant who had just come up, with a sly grinning mask of a face. He was tipsy and his jacket hung unbuttoned. 'High jinks, eh?'

'Now you've come, you can just go away again!'

'I'm going! Toothsome dainties you are!'

He stumbled down the steps.

Raskolnikov moved on.

'Listen, fine gentleman!' one of the wenches called after him. 'What?'

She grew confused.

'Kind gentleman, I shall always be glad to pass an hour with you, but not now. I shouldn't like to have you on my conscience. Give me six copecks to buy a drink, like a kind lover!'

Raskolnikov pulled some coins out of his pockets, three five-copeck pieces.

'Oh, what a kind-hearted gentleman!'

'What is your name?'

'Ask for Duklida.'

'Well really, what sort of behaviour is that?' said one of the group, motioning with her head towards Duklida. 'I simply don't know how she can ask for money like that! I'm sure I should sink through the ground with shame . . .'

Raskolnikov looked at her curiously. She was a pock-marked woman of about thirty, covered with bruises, and her lip was swollen. Her censure was uttered in a quiet and serious manner.

'Where was it,' Raskolnikov thought, as he walked on, 'where was it that I read of how a condemned man, just before he died, said, or thought, that if he had to live on some high crag, on a ledge so small that there was no more than room for his two feet, with all about him the abyss, the ocean, eternal night, eternal solitude, eternal storm, and there he must remain, on a hand's-breadth of ground, all his life, a thousand years, through all eternity—it would be better to live so, than die within the hour? Only to live, to live! No matter how—only to live! . . . How true! Lord, how true! How base men are! . . . And he is worse who decries them on that account!' he added, a minute later.

He came out into another street. 'Ah! The "Crystal Palace"! Razumikhin was talking about it. Only what on earth do I want here? Yes, to read! . . . Zosimov said he had seen something in the newspapers . . .'

'Have you newspapers here?' he asked, entering a very well-ordered and spacious tavern, consisting of several rooms, all rather empty. Two or three customers were drinking tea, and in one of the farther rooms a group of four or five men sat drinking champagne. Raskolnikov thought Zametov was one of them, but from so far away he could not be sure.

'What does it matter?' he thought

'Vodka, sir?' asked the waiter.

'I'll have tea. And bring me some newspapers, old ones, for the last five days or so; it'll be worth a tip to you.'

'Yes, sir. Here is today's, sir. And vodka, sir?'

The tea and the old newspapers appeared. Raskolnikov sat down and began to search through them.[2] 'Izler . . . Izler . . . Azteks . . . Azteks . . . Izler . . . Bartola . . . Massimo . . . Azteks . . . Izler . . . Pah, where the devil . . .? Ah, here are the news items: Woman Falls Downstairs . . . Vodka Causes

---

2. A collection of topical newspaper items follows. In the 1860's Ivan Izler was the "Amusement King" of Petersburg and owned the amusement park Mineral Waters. The boy Massimo and the girl Bartola were midgets exhibited as the last survivors of the "Azteks."

Workman's Death . . . Fire on the Sands[3]. . . Fire in Peter-
burgsky Quarter . . . Another Fire in Peterburgsky Quarter
. . . Another Fire in Peterburgsky Quarter . . . Izler . . . Izler
. . . Izler . . . Izler . . . Massimo . . . Ah, here . . .'

At last he had found what he was looking for, and he began
to read; the lines danced before his eyes, but he read the whole
report and turned eagerly to the succeeding numbers for later
additions. His hands, as he turned over the pages, shook with
feverish impatience. Suddenly somebody sat down next to
him at his table. He looked up. It was Zametov, Zametov
himself, looking exactly the same, with his rings and his watch-
chain, with his dark, curly hair neatly parted and pomaded,
in his fashionable waistcoat, his rather shabby frock-coat and
his not very fresh linen. He seemed cheerful; at any rate his
smile was cheerful and good natured. His swarthy face was a
little flushed with champagne.

'Hello, you here?' he began, in a puzzled tone, and as if
they had been acquainted for ages, 'and it was only yesterday
that Razumikhin was telling me you were still delirious. Very
odd! You know I went to see you . . .'

Raskolnikov had known he would come over to him. He
laid the newspapers aside and turned to Zametov. There was
a smile on his lips, with a hint of irritable impatience in it.

'I know you did,' he answered, 'I heard about it. You looked
for my sock . . . You know, Razumikhin raves about you.
He says you took him to Louisa Ivanovna's—you know, the
one you were doing your best for, that time; you kept winking
at that Lieutenant Squib, and he just wouldn't understand,
do you remember? Yet it hardly seemed possible not to understand—it was clear enough, . . . eh?'

'But what a hot-head he is!'

'Who, the Squib?'

'No, your friend Razumikhin . . .'

'You do pretty well for yourself, Mr. Zametov; you get into
the very nicest places for nothing. Who was that pouring
champagne into you just now?'

'Well, we were . . . just having a drink . . . It did flow pretty
freely.'

'Just a bonus! You turn everything to account!' Raskolnikov
laughed. 'Never mind, my dear boy, never mind!' he added,
slapping Zametov on the back, 'I am not talking like this from
spite, "but in pure affection, playfully", as that workman of
yours said, when he was punching Mitka, in that case of the
old woman.'

'How do you know that?'

'Perhaps I know more than you do.'

3. Around 1865 Petersburg was the scene of numerous fires, which were blamed on revolutionaries and on Poles protesting against the Russian suppression of the Polish uprising
in 1863 and 1864.

'What a queer chap you are, to be sure . . . I suppose you are still very ill. You ought not to be out . . .'

'I seem strange to you?'

'Yes. What are those newspapers you are reading?'

'Newspapers.'

'There is a lot in them about fires.'

'No, I'm not reading about the fires.' He looked mysteriously at Zametov; a mocking smile played about his mouth once more. 'No, not about the fires,' he went on, with a wink. 'Admit, my dear young man, that you are dreadfully anxious to know what I was reading about.'

'I am not anxious at all; I was only asking. Isn't that allowed? Why do you keep on . . .?'

'Listen, you're an educated man, aren't you, a literary man?'

'I reached the sixth class in high school,' answered Zametov with some dignity.

'The sixth! Well, my fine young cock-sparrow! With your hair all combed and curled, and your rings—you're a rich man! Pah, what a pretty little fellow!' Raskolnikov broke into a nervous laugh, straight into Zametov's face. He started back, not so much affronted as struck with astonishment.

'Dear me, how strange you are!' repeated Zametov, very seriously. 'I think you must still be delirious.'

'Delirious? That's a lie, cock-sparrow! . . . So I'm strange, am I? But, you're very curious about me, aren't you, very curious?'

'Yes, very.'

'Well, shall I tell you what I was reading about, what I had been looking for? You see, of course, how many issues I have had brought. Suspicious, isn't it?'

'Well, tell me.'

'All ears, are you?'

'What do you mean, all ears?'

'I'll tell you that later, but now I will declare to you . . . no, better, I'll "confess" . . . No, that's not right either: I will "make a statement", and you shall take it down—that's it! So, I state that I was reading . . . that I was interested in . . . that I was looking for . . . that I was searching . . .' Raskolnikov screwed up his eyes and waited—: 'I was searching—and that is why I came here—for something about the murder of the old woman, the moneylender,' he brought out at last, almost in a whisper, bringing his face very close to Zametov's. Zametov looked steadily back at him, without stirring or moving his face away. Afterwards, what seemed strangest about all this to Zametov was this silence that lasted for a full minute, while they remained looking at one another without moving.

'What does it matter what you were reading?' he exclaimed in a fit of exasperated perplexity. 'And what has it to do with me? What is all this about?'

'It was that same old woman,' Raskolnikov went on in the same whisper, without flinching at Zametov's exclamation, 'that you had begun to talk about, you remember, in the office, when I fainted. Now do you understand?'

'What is all this? What do you mean—"understand"?' said Zametov, almost alarmed.

Raskolnikov's fixed and serious expression was transformed in an instant, and he broke out into the same nervous laughter as before, as if he had not the strength to control himself. And in a flash he remembered, with an extraordinary intensity of feeling, another instant, when he had stood behind a door with an axe, while the bolt rattled, and outside the door people were swearing and trying to force a way in, and he was suddenly filled with a desire to shriek out, to exchange oaths with them, stick out his tongue at them, mock at them, and laugh, laugh, laugh.

'Either you are mad, or . . .' said Zametov, and then stopped as though struck by some thought which had come unexpectedly into his mind.

'Or? Or what? Well, what? Tell me, can't you?'

'Nothing!' answered Zametov angrily. 'We're talking nonsense!'

Both were silent. After his unexpected paroxysmal outburst of laughter, Raskolnikov had become thoughtful and melancholy. He leaned his elbows on the table and propped his head on his hand. He seemed to have completely forgotten Zametov. The silence lasted for some time.

'Why don't you drink your tea? It will be cold,' said Zametov.

'What? Oh, my tea? . . . All right . . .' Raskolnikov took a gulp from his glass, put a piece of bread in his mouth, and then, looking at Zametov, seemed suddenly to remember what he was doing and rouse himself; at the same time, the original derisive smile returned to his face. He went on drinking tea.

'Recently there has been a great increase of swindling,' said Zametov. 'I read not so long ago in the *Moscow Journal* that a whole gang of counterfeiters had been caught. There were quite a lot of them. They had been forging notes.'

'Oh, that was a long time since. I read about it a month ago,' answered Raskolnikov calmly. 'So you think of them as swindlers, do you?' he added with a smile.

'What else could you call them?'

'Them? They were children, greenhorns! They collected fifty people for an undertaking like that! Is it credible? Three would almost have been too many, and even then each one of them would have had to have more faith in the others than he had in himself! Otherwise it would only need one to babble in his cups and the whole thing would go smash! Greenhorns! They hired unreliable people to change the notes at the bank; is that the sort of job to entrust to the first person who comes along? Well, suppose that, raw beginners as they were, they had succeeded, suppose each of them had managed to change a million roubles' worth of counterfeits, what about afterwards? —the rest of their lives? Each one dependent on every other for the whole of his life! Better to hang yourself! But they didn't even know how to change their stuff: here is one changing it in a bank, and when he is handed five thousand his hands tremble. He counts over four thousand, but he takes the rest on trust, without counting, thrusts it into his pocket, and makes off. Well, suspicion is aroused. And everything is ruined because of one fool! No, really it's impossible!'

'For his hands to tremble?' Zametov took him up. 'No, that is possible, sir. I'm quite convinced that it is possible. Sometimes you just can't stand it.'

'What, that?'

'You, no doubt, could? Well, I couldn't! Run into such awful danger for a fee of a hundred roubles! Take a fake note —where?—into a banking office, where they specialize in just such matters—no, I should have to turn tail. Wouldn't you?'

Raskolnikov again suddenly felt the urge to 'stick out his tongue'. An occasional shiver ran down his spine.

'I shouldn't behave like that,' he began long-windedly. 'This is how I should change it: I should count over the first thousand, very carefully, three or four times, looking at every note; then I should start on the second thousand and begin counting it, then when I got to the middle, I should take out some fifty-rouble note and hold it up to the light, turn it over and hold it up to the light again—isn't it a bad one? "I'm afraid of bad money," say I; "a relative of mine once lost twenty-five roubles like that"—and I should tell the whole story. Then when I began to count the third thousand—"No, wait a moment; I think I miscounted the seventh hundred in that last thousand"—; the doubt would grow, I should leave the third thousand and go back to the second—and so on with all five. And when I had finished, I should take a note out of the fifth thousand and another from the second, hold them up to the light again, look doubtful, "please give me others in exchange for these"—and I should have got the cashier into such a stew that he would be aching to get rid of me. Well, finally, it would all be done, I should go and open the door— but no, excuse me, I should go back again to ask some question or get some explanation. That's how I should do it!'

'Pah, what terrible things you say!' said Zametov laughing.

'Only all this is only talk, and in reality you would be sure to trip up. I tell you, it seems to me impossible, not only for you and me, but even for a desperate and experienced man, to answer for himself in such a matter. Here's an example close at hand: an old woman has been murdered in our quarter of the city. Here, then, was a desperate rogue, running the most appalling risks in broad daylight and only saved by a miracle—but all the same, *his* hands trembled; he didn't succeed in carrying out his robbery—he couldn't stand it; it's clear from what we know of the case . . .'

Raskolnikov seemed almost offended.

'Clear, is it? Catch him then, go on!' he cried, taking a malicious pleasure in provoking Zametov.

'He'll be caught, all right.'

'Who'll do it? You? You'll catch him? You'll soon get tired of trying. I'll tell you what you regard as the most important thing: is a man spending freely or not? Here's someone who hadn't any money, and now he's suddenly begun to spend—it must be him! Any child could demolish that argument if he wanted to!'

'But that's just it—that's exactly what they all do,' answered Zametov; 'commit a cunning murder, risk their lives—and then straight into the pub! It is throwing money about that gets them caught. Not everybody is as clever as you, you know. Of course, you wouldn't run off to the pub, would you?'

Raskolnikov frowned and stared at Zametov.

'I suppose you've developed a taste for my methods, and would like to know what I would have done in this case as well?' he threw out, sounding rather displeased.

'Yes, I should,' answered Zametov firmly and gravely. His manner and tone seemed indeed to have grown too serious.

'Very much?'

'Yes, very much.'

'Good. This is how I should have acted,' began Raskolnikov. Once again his face was close to Zametov's, once again he kept his eyes fixed on him, once again he spoke in a whisper, that this time made his hearer shudder. 'This is what I should have done. I should have taken the money and the things and as soon as I left the place, before I went anywhere else, I should have gone to some place that was not overlooked, but had fencing all round, and where there was almost nobody about—perhaps a market-garden or something of that sort. I should have looked into this yard earlier and found a stone weighing a pood or more, somewhere in a corner near the fence, left there, perhaps, from the building of a house; I should have lifted the stone—there would have to be a little hollow under it—and in the hollow I should have put all the things and the money. I should have put them in and rolled the stone over them so that it looked the same as before, I should have pressed it down with my foot, and then I should have gone away. And for a year, for two years, I should not have taken away anything, perhaps for three years—well, now look for your murderer! Vanished into thin air!'

'You're mad!' said Zametov, also for some reason in a whisper, and recoiled suddenly from Raskolnikov. The latter's eyes were glittering, he had grown shockingly pale, and his upper lip trembled and twitched. He leaned as near as possible to Zametov and began moving his lips, but no sound came from them; they remained like this for half a minute. He knew what he was doing, but he could not restrain himself. A terrible word trembled on his lips, as the bolt had trembled *then* on the door: now, now, the bolt will give way; now, now, the word will slip out; oh, only to say it!

'And what if it was I who killed the old woman and Liza-veta?' he said suddenly, and—came to his senses.

Zametov looked at him wildly, and went as white as a sheet. He smiled crookedly.

'Can it really be so?' he said, in a barely audible tone. Raskolnikov looked furiously at him.

'Admit that you believed it! Yes! You did, didn't you?'

'Not at all! Now less than ever!' said Zametov hastily.

'You're caught at last! The cock-sparrow is caught! If you believe it now less than ever, that means that you believed it before!'

'No, certainly not!' exclaimed Zametov, in evident confusion. 'Was that why you startled me, just to lead up to this?'

'So you don't believe it? But what did you begin to talk about that time as soon as I had left the office? And why did Lieutenant Squib interrogate me after I fainted? Here!' he called to the waiter, getting up and taking his cap, 'how much?'

'Thirty copecks altogether, sir,' answered the waiter, hurrying up.

'Here are twenty besides for yourself. Look what a lot of money!'—and he held out to Zametov his shaking hand full of notes. 'Red notes, blue notes, twenty-five roubles. Where does it come from? And where have the new clothes appeared from? Of course, you know I hadn't a copeck. No doubt my landlady has already been questioned . . . Well, that's enough! *Assez causé*! Good-bye, until our next . . . most delightful . . . meeting! . . .'

He went out, shaking all over, with a feeling of wild hysteria mingled with almost unendurable pleasure; and yet his mood was gloomy, and he felt terribly weary. His face was distorted as if he had had some kind of seizure. His fatigue increased rapidly. His energies seemed now to be aroused and summoned up in a moment, at the slightest stimulus, with the first sensation of irritation, and to fail with the same suddenness, as rapidly as his emotion waned.

Zametov, left alone, sat where he was for a long time, in great perplexity. Raskolnikov had unexpectedly overturned all his ideas on a certain point and enabled him to come to a definite conclusion.

'Ilya Petrovich is a blockhead!' he decided finally.

As Raskolnikov opened the door into the street he ran straight into Razumikhin on the steps. Neither saw the other even when a pace separated them, so that they almost rammed their heads together. They stood for some time, measuring each other with their glances. Razumikhin was in a state of utter amazement, but suddenly anger, real anger, flashed menacingly in his eyes.

'So this is where you are!' he shouted at the top of his voice. 'You're supposed to be in bed, and you've run away. And I was ready to look for you under the sofa, and all the attics have been searched! Nastasya very nearly got a beating on your account . . . And this is where he is! Rodka, what does this mean? Tell me the truth! Confess! Do you hear?'

'It means that I was bored to death with all of you, and I want to be alone,' calmly answered Raskolnikov.

'Alone! When you can't walk yet, and your ugly mug is as white as a sheet, and you're panting for breath! Idiot! . . . What were you doing in the "Crystal Palace"? Own up at once!'

'Will you let me pass?' said Raskolnikov, and tried to walk past him. At this, Razumikhin, quite beside himself, seized him fiercely by the shoulders.

'Let you pass? You dare to say that to me? Do you know what I shall do with you this minute? I shall pick you up bodily, tie you into a bundle, carry you home under my arm, and put you under lock and key!'

'Listen, Razumikhin,' began Raskolnikov quietly and apparently quite calmly, 'can't you see that I don't want your kindness? Why will you persist in trying to do good to people who . . . spit on it, . . . people who seriously find your kindness beyond endurance? Tell me, why did you seek me out at the beginning of my illness? For all you know, I might have been glad to die. Surely I've shown you clearly enough today that you annoy me, that I'm . . . sick of you! What you are really trying to do is pester people! I assure you that all you are doing seriously impedes my recovery, because it is a constant irritation to me. You know that Zosimov went away just now so as not to irritate me. Then, for God's sake, you go away as well! What right have you, after all, to restrain me by force? And can't you see that I'm talking now absolutely in my right mind? How, tell me, how can I word my entreaties so that you will at last stop forcing yourself on me and trying to do me good? Perhaps I'm ungrateful, perhaps I am mean and base, only leave me alone, all of you, for God's sake leave me alone! Leave me alone!'

He had begun calmly enough, rejoicing in the thought of all the venom he was preparing to pour out, but by the time he came to the end of his speech he was raving madly and choking with rage, as he had done before, talking to Luzhin.

Razumikhin paused for a moment in thought, and then released his arm.

'Go to the devil then,' he said quietly and almost thoughtfully. 'Stop!' he roared abruptly, when Raskolnikov would have moved away. 'Listen to me. Let me tell you, people of your sort are all, down to the last man, babblers and braggarts! If the slightest thing goes wrong, you make as much fuss as a hen cackling over an egg! Even there you aren't original, but steal from other authors. There isn't a sign of independent existence in you! You're made of candle-grease and you have buttermilk in your veins for blood! I don't trust a single one of you! Your first concern in any circumstances is how not to resemble a human being. Wai-ai-ait!' he cried with redoubled fury, seeing that Raskolnikov was again about to go; 'hear me out! You know, I have some friends coming for a house-warming party today; perhaps they've arrived already. I've left my uncle there—I dropped in just now—to receive my guests. So if you weren't a fool, an utter fool, a confounded fool, a translation from the original—look Rodya, I admit you're an intelligent chap, but you are a fool!—well, if you weren't a fool, you'd be better off going to my place and spending a pleasant evening there than running around aimlessly like this. After all, you have come out, so what's the odds? I'd get in a nice soft arm-chair for you, my landlord has one... A cup of tea, pleasant company... Or no, you shall lie down on the couch—at any rate you will be among us... And Zosimov will be there. You'll come, won't you?'

'No.'

'Rubbish!' exclaimed Razumikhin impatiently. 'You don't know what you'll do; you can't answer for yourself! And you don't understand any of this... I've quarrelled violently with people like this a thousand times and gone running back to them again... You begin to be ashamed of yourself... and go back to the fellow! Now remember, Pochinkov's, third floor...'

'Really, it almost looks as if you would allow anyone to beat you, Mr. Razumikhin, for the satisfaction of doing him good.'

'Who? Me? I should twist his nose if he so much as dreamt of it... Pochinkov's, number 47, in Babushkin's flat...'

'I shall not come, Razumikhin,' Raskolnikov turned and walked away.

'I bet you will!' called Razumikhin after him. 'Otherwise you . . . otherwise I don't want anything to do with you. Hi, stop! Is Zametov here?'

'Yes.'

'Did you see him?'

'Yes.'

'And talk to him?'

'Yes.'

'What about? All right, go to the devil; don't tell me then! Pochinkov's house, 47, Babushkin's, remember!'

Raskolnikov reached Sadovaya Street and turned the corner. Razumikhin looked after him thoughtfully. At last he flung out his hands and turned to go in, but half-way up the steps he paused:

'Devil take it!' he said to himself, almost aloud: 'he talks sensibly enough and as if . . . Really, I'm a fool too! As if lunatics didn't talk sensibly! And I imagine Zosimov was afraid of something like this!' He rapped his forehead with his finger. 'Well, what if . . . oh, how could I let him go alone? Perhaps he'll drown himself . . . Oh, I missed my cue there! It won't do!'

And he ran back in pursuit of Raskolnikov, but the trail was cold already. He spat, and returned at a brisk pace to the 'Crystal Palace' to question Zametov as soon as possible.

Raskolnikov went straight to the Voznesensky Bridge, stopped in the middle of it, leaned both elbows on the parapet, and gazed along the canal. After parting from Razumikhin he had felt so weak that he was hardly able to drag himself so far. He longed to sit down somewhere, or even lie down, in the street. Leaning over the water he looked mechanically at the last pink reflections of the sunset, at the row of buildings growing dark in the thickening dusk, at one distant window, high up in some roof along the left bank, that shone for an instant with flame as the last ray of the dying sun caught it, at the darkening water of the canal. Into the water he peered attentively, until at last red circles began to revolve before his eyes, the houses spun round, the passers-by, the carriages, the embankments, all reeled and swung dizzily. Suddenly he started, saved perhaps from another fainting fit by a strange and ugly sight. He felt someone standing beside him, on his right, and looked up; it was a tall woman wearing a kerchief on her head, with a long, yellow, hollow-cheeked face and red-rimmed, sunken eyes. She was looking straight at him, but apparently without seeing him. With an abrupt movement she rested her right hand on the parapet, raised her right foot and threw it over the railing, followed it with her left, and flung herself into the canal. The filthy water parted and engulfed her for a moment, but then she rose to the surface and drifted gently with the current, face downwards, with her head and legs in the water and her skirt ballooning under her like a pillow.

'She's drowned herself!' cried a dozen voices; people began running up and clustering on both banks and crowding on the bridge round Raskolnikov, who found himself hemmed in and squeezed from behind.

'Oh Lord, that is our Afrosinyushka!' shrieked a woman's tearful voice somewhere near by. 'Oh, good heavens! Save her! Oh, kind friends, pull her out!'

Shouts arose from the crowd: 'A boat, get a boat!'

But there was no need for a boat; a policeman ran down the steps leading to the edge of the canal, threw off his greatcoat and boots, and jumped into the water. His task was not very difficult; the water carried the woman to within two paces of the foot of the stairs, he seized her clothing with his right hand, and with his left clutched a pole held out to him by a colleague; and the drowning woman was quickly pulled out. They laid her on the granite slabs of the landing-place. She speedily recovered consciousness and sat up, sneezing and sniffing and senselessly trying to dry her hands on her wet clothes. She said nothing.

'She's drunk herself to ruination, friends, to ruination,'— this was the same woman's voice, now near Afrosinyushka; 'not long since she tried to hang herself as well; they got her down, though. I had to go to the shop just now, and I left a little girl to look after her—and look what a terrible thing happens! She's a respectable working woman; we live close by, the second house from the corner, just here . . .'

The crowd was dispersing, the police were still busy with the woman, someone shouted a reference to the police-station. . . . Raskolnikov had looked on with a strange feeling of indifference and detachment. Now he felt repelled . . .—'No, it's disgusting . . . water . . . no good,' he muttered to himself. 'Nothing will happen. I needn't expect anything . . . What can the police do? . . . And why isn't Zametov in the office? it's open at ten o'clock . . .' He turned his back to the parapet and looked round him. 'Well, all right then!' he said decidedly, moved away from the bridge and turned towards the police-station. His heart was empty and numb. He did not want to think about anything. Even his dejection had passed, and there was no trace of the energy with which he had left the house 'to make an end of it'. Complete apathy had taken its place.

'Well, after all, this is one way out!' he thought, as he walked slowly and limply along the embankment. 'I shall be finished with it, all the same, because I will it . . . But is it really a way out? Well, it doesn't matter! I shall have my hand's-breadth of ground—ha! What an end, though! Is it really the end?

Shall I tell them or shall I not? Oh . . . the devil! I am tired; oh, to lie down somewhere, or sit . . . soon! The most shameful thing is that I carried it out so stupidly . . . Well, to hell with that, too! Pah, what nonsense runs in my head . . .'

To get to the office he had to go straight on and take the second turning to the left, and then it was only a few steps farther. But as he came to the first turning he stopped and reflected a moment, turned into the lane, and took a round-about route, through two more streets, perhaps aimlessly, perhaps to prolong the journey if only by a minute and gain a little more time. He walked along with his eyes on the ground. Suddenly it was as if someone whispered in his ear. He raised his head and saw that he was standing by *that* house, near the gates. It was the first time he had been there since *that* evening.

An irresistible and inexplicable desire drew him on. He turned in, passed through the gateway, went into the first entrance on the right and began to ascend the familiar stair-case towards the first floor. The steep, narrow stairs were very dark. On every landing he stopped and looked about with curiosity. The window-frame on the first landing had been removed: 'It wasn't like this then,' he thought. On the second floor was the flat where Nikolashka and Mitka had been working. 'Shut up, and the door is newly painted; it must be to let.' Here was the third floor . . . and the fourth . . . 'Here it is!' Perplexity seized him: the door of the flat was open, and there were people in it; he could hear their voices. This was something entirely unexpected. After a short hesitation, he mounted the last steps and went into the flat.

This flat also was being redecorated, and the workmen were inside. This circumstance astonished him; for some reason he had expected to find everything just as he had left it, perhaps even with the corpses in the same places on the floor. But now with its bare walls and empty rooms it seemed somehow strange. He went over to the window and sat down on the sill.

There were only two workmen, both young fellows, but one much younger than the other. They were putting new paper, white, with small lilac-coloured flowers, on the walls, in place of the old, rubbed, faded paper. For some reason Raskolnikov violently disapproved of this, and he looked with hostility at the new paper, as though he could not bear to see everything changed.

The workmen were apparently late and were now hurriedly rolling up the paper ready to go home. They had hardly noticed Raskolnikov's entrance. They were talking about something. Raskolnikov crossed his arms and listened to them.

'She comes in to me, like, in the morning,' the elder of the two was saying, 'ever so early, all dressed up to the nines. "What's all this?" says I, "why do you come parading and strutting up and down in front of me, peacocking about?" So she says: "From now on, Tit Vasilyevich, I want to seem just right to you." So that's how it is, you see! And dressed up! Just like a magazine!'

'What do you mean, uncle, a magazine?' asked the younger. 'Uncle' was evidently his mentor.

'Well, a magazine, little brother, is pictures, like, coloured ones, and the tailor gets them sent to him every Saturday from foreign parts, and they are to show people what to wear, both men and women, see? Drawings, I mean. The men, they're mostly drawn in them short little overcoats, but as for the women, brother, such finery as they have, as you'd give a week's pay just to see them!'

'The things there are in this here St. Petersburg!' enthusiastically exclaimed the younger man; 'there's everything you could possibly think of.'

'Yes indeed, little brother, you can find everything,' stated the other instructively.

Raskolnikov got up and went into the other room, where the trunk, the bed, and the chest of drawers used to stand. The room seemed very small without the furniture. The wallpaper was unchanged; in the corner the place where the icon-stand had been was sharply outlined on it. He looked round and then returned to the window. The older workman was following his movement with a sidelong look.

'What do you want, sir?' he asked abruptly, addressing him. Instead of answering, Raskolnikov stood up again, went out into the passage, and pulled at the bell. The same bell, the same tinny sound! He pulled it again, and then a third time, listening and remembering. The old tormenting frightening sensation began to bring back ever clearer and more vivid memories, he shuddered at every tinkle, and yet he felt more and more pleasure in the sound.

'What do you want? Who are you?' cried the workman, coming out to him. Raskolnikov went in again.

'I want to take the flat,' he said. 'I am looking round.'

'People don't take flats at night; besides, you ought to apply to the porter.'

'I see the floor has been washed; are you going to stain it?' went on Raskolnikov. 'Isn't there any blood?'

'What blood?'

'There was an old woman murdered, and her sister. There was a great pool of blood here.'

'What sort of man are you?' cried the workman uneasily.

'I?'

'Yes, you?'

'You want to know, do you? . . . Well, let's go to the police office, I'll tell you there . . .'

The workman looked at him, puzzled.

'It's time we went, sir; we're late. Come on, Alëshka. We've got to lock up,' said the older workman.

'Let's go, then,' answered Raskolnikov indifferently, and he went out first and walked slowly downstairs. As he came out under the gateway, he called: 'Hi, porter!'

Several people were standing by the gate, watching the passers-by in the street: there were both porters, a country-woman, a man in a long robe, and some others. Raskolnikov went straight towards them.

'What do you want?' answered one of the porters.

'Have you been to the police office?'

'I was there just now. Why do you want to know?'

'Was it open?'

'Yes, it was.'

'Was the assistant there?'

'Some of the time. Why?'

Raskolnikov did not answer, but stood beside him, thinking.

'He came to look at the flat,' said the older workman, coming up to them.

'What flat?'

'The one we're working in. "Why," says he, "has the blood been washed out? There was a murder done here," he says, "and I've come to take the flat." And then he begins ringing the bell, and almost pulls it out. Then he says "Come to the police-station and I'll tell you all about it." Wouldn't take no for an answer!'

The porter, frowning and perplexed, studied Raskolnikov.

'And who are you?' he asked menacingly.

'I am Rodion Romanovich Raskolnikov, a former student, living at Shil's house, here in the lane, not far away, in flat 14. Ask the porter . . . he knows me.' All this was said in a languid and preoccupied tone, while Raskolnikov kept his eyes fixed on the darkening street.

'And what did you go to the flat for?'

'To look at it.'

'What is there to look at there?'

'Why don't you take him to the police?' broke in the man in the long robe, and then was silent again.

Without moving his head, Raskolnikov turned his eyes towards the man, examined him carefully, and then said in the same quiet and languid tone: 'Let us go.'

'You ought to take him!' asserted the man, more boldly. 'Why was he asking about *that*? Has he got something on his mind, eh?'

'Perhaps he's drunk, perhaps he isn't, God knows!' muttered the workman.

'What's it got to do with you?' exclaimed the porter again, beginning to grow really angry. 'Why do you keep on insisting?'

'Are you afraid to go to the police, then?' asked Raskolnikov jeeringly.

'Why should I be? Why do you keep on about it?'

'He's up to something!' exclaimed the peasant-woman.

'Why do you talk to him?' shouted the other porter, a huge peasant with his tunic hanging open and a bunch of keys on his belt. 'Clear out! . . . You're up to some game or other, all right . . . Get out!'

And seizing Raskolnikov by the shoulder, he flung him out so roughly that he almost fell. He recovered himself, however, looked silently back at all of them, and went on his way.

'A queer customer,' said the workman.

'Folks is all queer nowadays,' said the peasant-woman.

'All the same, he ought to have been taken to the police,' added the man in the long robe.

'We don't want to get mixed up in anything,' said the big porter decidedly. 'It's quite sure he's up to something. He was asking for trouble, of course, but if you get yourself mixed up in something, you don't get clear so easily . . . we know!'

'Well, shall I go, I wonder, or not?' thought Raskolnikov, stopping in the middle of the road at a crossing and looking round as if he expected to hear the deciding word from somebody. But no response came from any quarter; everything was blank and dead, like the stones he trod on, dead for him, and for him alone . . . Suddenly at some distance, two hundred paces farther on, at the end of the street, in the gathering darkness, he made out voices, shouts, a crowd of people . . . Some sort of carriage was standing in the middle of them . . . Lights flashed . . . 'What is it?' Raskolnikov turned to the right and approached the crowd. He was ready to grasp at anything, and he smiled coldly as he thought of this, because his mind was firmly made up to go to the police, and he knew with certainty that all would soon be over.

## CHAPTER VII

In the middle of the street stood some gentleman's elegant carriage, harnessed to a pair of spirited grey horses; there were no passengers and the coachman had got down from the box and was standing beside it; someone was holding the horses' heads. A great many people were crowding round, with policemen in the forefront. One of them, with a lighted lantern in his hand, was stooping down to throw the light on something lying on the ground under the wheels. There were constant cries, exclamations, sighs; the coachman seemed half-dazed, and kept repeating every so often:

'What a terrible thing! Oh Lord, how terrible!'

Raskolnikov pressed through the crowd as opportunity offered, and at length saw the object of all the commotion and curiosity. On the ground, plainly unconscious, lay a man who had been crushed beneath the horses' hooves; he was very poorly dressed but his clothes, which were now covered with blood, had once been 'respectable'. Blood was flowing from his face and head, and his head was terribly battered and mutilated. It was evident that his injuries were very serious.

'Oh Lord!' lamented the coachman, 'how can you guard against such things? It isn't as if I was driving very fast, or didn't call out to him, but I was going quite gently and slowly. Everybody saw it: they can all bear me out. He was too drunk to walk straight, that's how it was. I saw him crossing the street, and he was staggering about and nearly falling—I shouted, three times altogether, and pulled in the horses; but he went and fell right under their feet! I don't know if he did it on purpose, or if he was just too unsteady on his legs . . . my horses are young and skittish—they shied, and he screamed— they got more frightened . . . that's how this awful thing happened.'

'That's just how it was!' testified a voice in the crowd.

'He shouted, that's true, he called out to him three times,' said another.

'Exactly three times, everybody heard him!' exclaimed a third.

The coachman, however, was not very distressed or frightened. It was evident that the carriage belonged to some rich and influential personage, who was awaiting its arrival somewhere; the police, of course, were anxious to facilitate this. It remained only to carry the injured man to the police-station and then to the hospital. Nobody knew his name.

Meanwhile Raskolnikov had worked his way through the crowd and was bending nearer. Suddenly, the light of the lantern fell on the unfortunate man's face, and he recognized him.

'I know him, I know him!' he cried, pushing to the very front, 'he is a retired government clerk, called Marmeladov. He lives here, close by, in Kozel's house . . . Get a doctor at once; I will pay, look!' He pulled some money out of his pocket and showed it to the policeman. He was surprisingly agitated.

The police were pleased to have learnt the identity of the injured man. Raskolnikov gave his own name and address as well, and urged them, with as much vehemence as though it were a question of his own father, to carry the unconscious Marmeladov to his own room.

'Here it is, only three doors away,' he said pleadingly, 'in the house of Kozel, the German, a rich man . . . He was probably going home, drunk, now. I know him . . . He is a drunkard . . . He has a family there, a wife and children, and there is a daughter besides. Why take him all the way to the hospital, when there's actually a doctor in the house? I will pay . . . At any rate he'll be looked after by his own people, and at once, but he would die before you got him to the hospital . . .'

He even managed to thrust something inconspicuously into the policeman's hand; the proceeding he suggested was, however, clearly lawful, and, in any case, here assistance was nearer. Helpers were found, and the injured man was lifted and carried away. Kozel's house was some thirty paces away. Raskolnikov walked behind, supporting the head and indicating the way.

'This way, this way! The head must go first up the stairs; turn round . . . that's it. I will pay, I shall be most grateful,' he murmured.

Katerina Ivanovna, as usual, as soon as she had a free moment, had immediately taken to pacing her little room, from the window to the stove and back, with her crossed arms pressed to her breast, talking to herself and coughing. Lately she had taken to talking more and more often to her elder daughter, the ten-year-old Polenka, who, although she understood only a little, yet knew very well that her mother needed her, and therefore always followed her with her great wise eyes and strove her utmost to pretend she understood everything. This time Polenka was undressing her little brother, who had been ailing all day, in order to put him to bed. While he waited for her to change his shirt, which had to be washed during the night, the little boy sat silently in a chair, upright and motionless with a solemn face, and with his little legs stretched out in front of him, squeezed tightly together, heels presented to the room and toes outspread. He was listening to what mama said to his sister, with pouted lips and eyes starting out of his little head, sitting exactly as all good little boys ought to sit when they are being undressed for bed. The still smaller little girl, in absolute rags, stood near the screen waiting her turn. The door to the stairs stood open, to get rid of at least some of the clouds of tobacco-smoke which escaped from the other rooms and constantly drove the poor consumptive into long and torturing fits of coughing. Katerina Ivanovna seemed to have grown even thinner during the past week, and the red stains on her cheeks burned even brighter than before.

'You wouldn't believe, Polenka, you can't even imagine,'

she said as she walked about the room, 'how happily and in what luxury we lived at home with my papa, and now that drunkard has destroyed me, and he will destroy all of you too! Papa was a Civil Colonel, and he almost became Governor; there was only one step higher for him, so that everybody used to come and say to him: "We already look upon you, Ivan Mikhaylovich, as our Governor." When I'—cough—'when I'—cough, cough, cough—'oh, accursed life!' she exclaimed, spitting out phlegm and clutching at her chest, 'when I . . . oh, at the last ball . . . at the Marshal's . . . when Princess Bezzemelnaya saw me . . . she gave me the blessing, later, when I married your papa, Polya . . . she asked at once: "Isn't that the nice girl who did the shawl dance at the end of term?" . . . (That tear must be mended; take your needle and darn it at once, as I taught you, or else tomorrow'—cough—'tomorrow' —cough, cough, cough—'it will tear further!' she cried in a paroxysm of coughing.) 'Prince Shchegolskoy—he was a Gentleman of the Bedchamber—had just arrived from St. Petersburg . . . he danced the mazurka with me, and he wanted to come next day and make an offer; but I thanked him in the most complimentary terms and told him that my heart had long belonged to another. That other was your father, Polya; papa was terribly angry . . . Is the water ready? Well, give me the shirt . . . and where are the socks? . . . Lida,' and she turned to her little daughter, 'you will have to sleep without a shirt tonight, somehow . . . and put your stockings with it . . . They must all be washed together . . . Why doesn't that drunken ragamuffin come? He's worn his shirt till it's like a duster or something, and it's all torn . . . I want to do them all at once, so that I need not tire myself out two nights running. Lord!'— cough, cough, cough, cough. 'Again! What is this?'— she shrieked, seeing the crowd in the entrance and the people crowding into her room with some sort of burden. 'What is this? What are they carrying? Oh God!'

'Where shall we put him?' the policeman was asking, looking round. They had carried Marmeladov, unconscious and covered with blood, into the room.

'On the sofa. Lay him straight on the sofa, with his head this way,' said Raskolnikov.

'He was run over in the street—drunk!' shouted someone from the entrance.

Katerina Ivanovna stood there pale and panting. The children were terrified. Little Lida shrieked, rushed to Polenka and put her arms round her, shaking all over.

When Marmeladov had been laid down, Raskolnikov turned to Katerina Ivanovna.

'For God's sake, be calm; don't be alarmed!' he said quickly. 'He was crossing the road, a carriage ran over him; don't be anxious, he will recover consciousness. I told them to bring him here . . . I have been here, you remember . . . He will come round. I will bear the expense.'

'He's been asking for this!' shrieked Katerina Ivanovna in despair, and rushed to his side.

Raskolnikov quickly saw that this woman was not one of those who instantly swoon away. In an instant a pillow, which nobody had thought of before, appeared under the unfortunate man's head; Katerina Ivanovna began to undress and examine him, busying herself over him without losing her head. She forgot about herself, bit her trembling lips and stifled the cries that tried to escape from her throat.

Raskolnikov meanwhile persuaded somebody to run for the doctor. The doctor, it appeared, lived in the next building but one.

'I have sent for the doctor,' he assured Katerina Ivanovna. 'Do not worry, I will pay him. Isn't there any water? . . . And give me a napkin, or a towel, or something, quickly; we don't know yet what his injuries are . . . He is hurt, but not killed, be assured of that . . . We shall see what the doctor says.'

Katerina Ivanovna hastened to the window; there, in a corner, a large earthenware bowl full of water stood on a broken chair, ready for the nocturnal washing of her husband's and the children's linen. This washing Katerina Ivanovna did with her own hands at least twice a week, and sometimes oftener, for things had got to such a pass that they had practically no change of linen left, but each member of the family had only one garment of each kind. Katerina Ivanovna could not tolerate dirt, and was willing to wear herself out with work that was beyond her strength, at night, while everybody was asleep, so as to be able to dry the wet things by morning and give them back clean, rather than see dirt in the house. She lifted the bowl to carry it to Raskolnikov but almost fell with the weight. He had already found a towel, and he damped it in the water and began to wash the blood from Marmeladov's face. Katerina Ivanovna stood there with her hands clasped to her breast, drawing her breath painfully. She was herself in need of help. Raskolnikov began to understand that he had perhaps done wrong in persuading them to bring the injured man here. The policeman also seemed doubtful.

'Polya!' cried Katerina Ivanovna, 'run to Sonya at once. If she isn't at home, never mind, say that her father has been run over and she is to come at once . . . when she gets in. Quickly, Polya! Here, put a kerchief on your head!'

'Run as fast as ever 'ou can!' shouted the little boy from his chair, and resumed at once his silent upright pose, with his eyes round, his legs stretched in front of him, and his toes spread out.

Meanwhile the room had grown so full that there was not

an inch of floor space left. The police had gone, except one who stayed behind for a time, trying to drive out again the people who had thronged in from the stairs. Practically every one of Mrs. Lippewechsel's lodgers, besides, had flocked out of the inner rooms, crowding at first into the doorway, and then pouring in a mass into the room itself. Katerina Ivanovna flew into a passion.

'You might at least leave people to die in peace!' she cried to the crowd; 'what sort of side-show do you think you've found? With cigarettes!'—cough, cough, cough—'wearing your hats, too! . . . There is one with his hat on! . . . Get out! Show some respect at least for the dying!'

Coughs choked her, but the rebuke had been effective. They even seemed a little afraid of Katerina Ivanovna; the lodgers, one after another, began to press back towards the door, with that strange inward glow of satisfaction which is always found, even among his nearest and dearest, when disaster suddenly strikes our neighbour, and from which not one of us is immune, however sincere our pity and sympathy.

Voices, however, outside the door, were heard referring to the hospital and contending that people ought not to upset the house for nothing.

'People ought not to die!' flashed Katerina Ivanovna, and was in the act of pulling open the door, to let loose a storm on their heads, when she ran into Mrs. Lippewechsel herself in the doorway. The landlady had only that moment heard of the accident and was hastening to restore order. She was an untidy and quarrelsome person.

'*Ach, mein Gott!*' she exclaimed, flinging up her hands. 'Your drunk husband has a horse trampled! He should in the hospital! It iss mine house!'

'Amalia Ludwigovna! I beg of you to consider what you are saying,' began Katerina Ivanovna in a lofty manner (she always adopted this tone in speaking to her landlady, so that the latter should not 'forget her place', and even now she could not deny herself this pleasure). 'Amalia Ludwigovna . . .'

'I haf told you, once for all, you should not dare to say to me Amaly Ludwigovna; I am Amaly-Ivan!'

'You are not Amaly-Ivan, but Amalia Ludwigovna, and since I am not one of your base flatterers, like Mr. Lebezyatnikov, who is laughing outside the door now' (and indeed laughter and a cry of "They're at it again!" could be heard just outside the door), 'I shall always address you as Amalia Ludwigovna, although I really cannot understand why that designation is displeasing to you. You may see for yourself what has happened to Semën Zakharovich: he is dying. Permit him at least to die in peace. I must request you to close that door immediately and allow no one to enter. Otherwise, I assure you, tomorrow your conduct shall be brought to the notice of His Excellency the Governor himself. The Prince knew me in my girlhood, and he remembers Semën Zakharovich, to whom he did many kindnesses, very well. It is well known that Semën Zakharovich had many friends and patrons, whom he himself abandoned in his honourable pride, being conscious of his unhappy failing, but now we are being helped by a noble-hearted young man' (she indicated Raskolnikov) 'of means and influential connexions, whom Semën Zakharovich knew as a child, and be assured, Amalia Ludwigovna . . .'

All this poured out in an ever-increasing torrent of eloquence, until a fit of coughing cut short Katerina Ivanovna's oratory. At the same moment the dying man recovered consciousness and groaned, and she hurried to him. He opened his eyes and they rested, without recognition or understanding, on the figure of Raskolnikov standing close to him. He was drawing deep, laboured breaths at long intervals; blood trickled from the corners of his mouth; drops of sweat stood on his forehead. He did not know Raskolnikov, and his eyes began to wander uneasily. Katerina Ivanovna's look was stern and sad, and tears were flowing from her eyes.

'Oh God, his whole chest is crushed in! Look at the blood, the blood!' she said in despair. 'We must take off all his outer things! Turn yourself a little, Semën Zakharovich, if you can,' she cried to him.

Marmeladov recognized her.

'A priest!' he murmured hoarsely.

Katerina Ivanovna walked away to the window and leaned her forehead against the frame, exclaiming in desperation:

'Oh, accursed life!'

'A priest!' said the dying man again, after a moment of silence.

'They've go-o-one!' shrieked Katerina Ivanovna; he heard the clamour and was silent. His timid anxious glance sought her out; she had returned to his side and stood by his pillow. He seemed a little calmer, but not for long. Soon his eye fell on little Lida (his favourite), who stood in the corner shivering as though with fever and watching him with her wondering eyes childishly intent.

'But . . . but . . .' he indicated her uneasily. He was trying to say something.

'What is it this time?' cried Katerina Ivanovna.

'Bare-footed! bare-footed!' he murmured, with his half-conscious eyes fixed on the little girl's bare legs and feet.

'Be quiet!' exclaimed Katerina Ivanovna irritably. 'You know why she goes barefoot!'

'Thank God, the doctor!' exclaimed Raskolnikov, over-joyed.

The doctor, a neat little old man, a German, came in looking about him with an air of mistrust; he went up to the injured man, felt his pulse, carefully touched his head, and with Katerina Ivanovna's help, unbuttoned his blood-soaked shirt and laid bare his chest. It was all crushed, trampled, and lacerated; several ribs on the right side were broken. On the left, immediately over the heart, was a great yellowish-black mark, left by the cruel blow of a hoof. The doctor frowned. The policeman explained that the unfortunate man had been caught by the wheel and dragged along the roadway for some thirty yards.

'It is surprising that he ever recovered consciousness at all,' whispered the doctor softly to Raskolnikov.

'What is your opinion?' asked he.

'He is dying now.'

'Is there really no hope?'

'None at all! He is on the point of death . . . The head is very badly injured, too . . . Hm. Perhaps I might let some blood . . . but . . . it would do no good. He will certainly be dead in five or ten minutes.'

'But surely you ought at least to try it?'

'Perhaps so . . . However, I warn you that it will be quite useless.'

Now steps were heard approaching again, the crowd in the entrance parted, and the priest, a little old man with grey hair, appeared on the threshold carrying the sacrament. A policeman had gone for him from the scene of the accident. The doctor immediately made way for him, exchanging a significant glance with him as he did so. Raskolnikov begged the doctor to stay, if only for a short time. He shrugged his shoulders and remained.

They all stood aside. The dying man's confession was very short and it is doubtful if he had any clear idea of what was happening; he was capable of uttering only vague broken sounds. Katerina Ivanovna took Lidochka, lifted the little boy from the chair, knelt down in the corner by the stove and made the children kneel in front of her. The little girl only shivered; but the boy, on his little bare knees, raised his hand, crossed himself, and bowed to the ground, knocking his forehead on the floor, a process which seemed to afford him great satisfaction. Katerina Ivanovna was biting her lips to keep back the tears; she also was praying; occasionally she straightened the little boy's shirt, and once, without rising from her knees or ceasing her prayers, she managed to take a shawl from the chest of drawers and throw it round the little girl's shoulders, which were almost bare. Meanwhile the door from the inner rooms began to open again under the pressure of the curious, and in the little lobby the onlookers were crowding thicker and thicker, from every flat on the staircase; but they did not cross the threshold of the room. A single candle lighted the scene.

At this moment Polenka, who had been for her sister, hurriedly pushed through the crowd in the entrance. She came in, out of breath with running, took off her kerchief, looked round for her mother, went to her and said: 'She is coming! I met her in the street.' Her mother made her kneel down next to her. Out of the crowd, noiselessly and timidly, appeared a young girl, and her sudden appearance was strange in that room, in the midst of poverty, rags, death, and despair. Her own clothes were ragged enough, but her tuppenny-ha'penny finery, in the taste and style of her special world of the streets, testified clearly and shamelessly to the purpose for which it had been chosen. Sonya stopped in the lobby, near the door, but without crossing the threshold of the room, utterly forlorn and apparently unconscious of her surroundings; she seemed forgetful alike of her garish fourth-hand silk dress, indecently out of place here with its ridiculous long train and immense crinoline blocking the whole doorway, of her light-coloured boots, of the sunshade she carried with her, although it was useless at night, and of her absurd little round straw hat with its bright flame-coloured feather. From under this hat, worn with a boyish tilt to one side, looked out a thin, pale, frightened little face; the mouth hung open and the eyes stared in terrified fixity. Sonya was small, about eighteen years old, thin but quite pretty, with fair hair and remarkable blue eyes. She kept them fixed on the bed and the priest; she was breathless with the speed of her arrival. At length the whispering among the crowd, or some of the words said, seemed to reach her ears; she cast down her eyes, took a step across the threshold and stood inside the room, but still very near the door.

The confession had been made and the sacrament administered. Katerina Ivanovna again approached her husband's bed. The priest moved away, but turned before he left to say a word of exhortation and solace to Katerina Ivanovna.

'And what shall I do with these?' she interrupted sharply and irritably, indicating the little ones.

'God is merciful. Put your trust in the help of the Most High,' began the priest.

'Ah! Merciful, but not to us!'

'That is sinful, wicked!' he remarked, shaking his head.

'And what is this?' exclaimed Katerina Ivanovna, pointing to her husband.

'It may be that those who were the involuntary cause of your distress will be willing to compensate you, if only for the loss of income . . .'

'You do not understand me!' irritably exclaimed Katerina

Ivanovna, waving her arms. 'Why should there be any compensation? He was drunk and he crawled under the feet of the horses himself! And what income? All I had from him was suffering. He was a drunkard and threw away everything we had in drink! He robbed us and took the money to the public house; he spent their lives and mine in the public house! Thank God he is dying! Our loss will be less!'

'You must forgive in the hour of death. This is sinful, madam; such sentiments are a grievous sin!'

Katerina Ivanovna was busying herself over the injured man, giving him something to drink, wiping the sweat and blood from his face, straightening his pillow, and only occasionally finding time for a word to the priest in the midst of her activities. Now she turned on him, almost beside herself.

'Oh Lord! Those are only words, nothing but words! Forgive! Today, if he had not been run over, he would have come home drunk, with his only shirt dirty and ragged, and gone to bed to sleep like a log, while I splashed about in water till the dawn, washing his old clothes and the children's and drying them out of the window, and as soon as it was light I should have had to sit down and mend them—that is how my night would have been spent . . . So why even talk of forgiveness? I have forgiven him!'

A terrible, deep-seated cough cut short her words. She spat into a handkerchief and thrust it towards the priest, painfully clutching her breast with the other hand. The handkerchief was full of blood . . .

The priest bowed his head and said nothing.

Marmeladov was in the last agony; he did not move his eyes from Katerina Ivanovna's face, bent over him once more. He kept trying to say something to her; moving his tongue with an enormous effort, he even managed to utter some inarticulate words, but Katerina Ivanovna, understanding that he wanted to ask her forgiveness, immediately exclaimed peremptorily:

'Quiet! Don't! . . . I know what you want to say!' The dying man was silent; but then his wandering glance fell on the door, and he saw Sonya.

Until that instant he had not noticed her; she stood in a shadowy corner.

'Who is that? Who is it?' he asked suddenly in a hoarse panting voice, full of agitation, with his alarmed gaze directed to the door, where his daughter was standing. He even tried to raise himself.

'Lie down! Lie down!' exclaimed Katerina Ivanovna.

But with unnatural strength he managed to prop himself on his arm. His wild unmoving gaze remained fixed for some time on his daughter, as though he did not recognize her. Indeed, he had never before seen her in such a costume.

Suddenly he did recognize her, humiliated, crushed, ashamed in her gaudy finery, submissively waiting her turn to take leave of her dying father. Infinite suffering showed in his face.

'Sonya! Daughter! Forgive me!' he cried, and tried to stretch out his hand towards her, but without its support he fell and crashed down headlong from the sofa; they rushed to lift him up, and laid him down again, but he was going. Sonya uttered a feeble cry, ran forward, put her arms round him, and almost swooned in that embrace. He died in her arms.

'He brought his fate on himself!' cried Katerina Ivanovna, when she saw her husband's corpse. 'And what shall I do now? How am I to bury him? And how shall I feed them, tomorrow?'

Raskolnikov went up to her.

'Katerina Ivanovna,' he began, 'last week your late husband told me the story of his life and everything connected with it. You may be sure that he spoke of you with great respect and appreciation. From that evening when I learnt how devoted he was to all of you, and how he loved and honoured you especially, Katerina Ivanovna, from that evening, in spite of his unfortunate weakness, we were friends . . . Permit me now to . . . contribute . . . towards the repayment of a debt to my departed friend. Take this . . . it is twenty roubles, I think— and if it can be of any assistance to you, then . . . I . . . in short, I will come again—I will certainly come again . . . perhaps I may look in tomorrow . . . Good-bye!'

And he hurried out of the room, pushing his way towards the stairs as quickly as he could, through the crowd; among them he suddenly collided with Nikodim Fomich, who had been informed of the accident and had decided to make the necessary arrangements in person. They had not met since the scene in the office, but Nikodim Fomich recognized him at once.

'Oh, is that you?' he asked.

'He is dead,' answered Raskolnikov. 'The doctor has been here, and a priest; everything is in order. Do not distress a very unhappy woman, who is a consumptive besides. Encourage her if you can . . . You are a good man, I know . . .' he added with a smile, looking straight into his eyes.

'But what is this? You are soaked with blood,' remarked Nikodim Fomich, examining by the light of a lantern some fresh stains on Raskolnikov's waistcoat.

'Yes, I am . . . I am all over blood-stains!' said Raskolnikov, with a peculiar look; then he smiled, nodded his head, and turned down the stairs.

He went down quietly, without hurry; he was in a fever again, but unconscious of the fact, and full of a strange new feeling of boundlessly full and powerful life welling up in him, a feeling which might be compared with that of a man con-

demned to death and unexpectedly reprieved. Half-way down
the stairs he was overtaken by the priest returning home;
Raskolnikov silently let him pass, and they exchanged bows
without speaking. Then, when he was descending the last few
stairs he heard hurried steps behind him. Someone was running
after him. It was Polenka, hurrying down behind him and
calling: 'Listen! Listen!'

He turned to her. She ran down the last flight of stairs and
stopped just in front of him, one step higher. A dim light came
from the courtyard. Raskolnikov looked at her nice thin little
face smiling at him and looking at him with childish cheerfulness. She had run after him with a message which evidently
gave her great pleasure.

'Listen, what is your name? . . . And next, where do you
live?' The words came in a rush, in a breathless little voice.

He laid both hands on her shoulders, finding a certain
happiness in looking at her. It seemed to him a very pleasant
thing to do, though he did not know why.

'Who sent you?'

'It was my sister Sonya,' answered the little girl, with a still
more cheerful smile.

'There, I knew it was your sister Sonya.'

'Mama sent me as well. When Sonya was just sending me,
mama came as well and said "Run as quick as you can,
Polenka!"'

'Do you love your sister Sonya?'

'I love her better than anybody!' said Polenka with great
firmness, and her smile grew suddenly serious.

'And will you love me?'

By way of answer, he saw the child's little face brought near
to him and her full little lips naïvely protruded to kiss him.
Suddenly her thin little match-sticks of arms were wound
tightly round his neck, her head rested on his shoulder, and
the little girl began to cry quietly, pressing her face harder
and harder against him.

'It is so sad for poor papa!' she said after a minute, lifting
her tear-stained little face and wiping her eyes with her hands.
'Such dreadful things have been happening lately,' she added
unexpectedly, with that particularly sedate expression that
children strive to adopt when they want to talk like the
'grown-ups'.

'And did papa love you?'

'He loved Lidochka best of all,' she announced very seriously,
without a smile, just like a grown-up, 'because she is little, and
because she's delicate besides, and he always used to bring
her presents; but he taught us to read, and he taught me
grammar and scripture,' she added with pride, 'and mama
didn't say anything, only we knew she liked it, and papa

knew, and mama wants to teach me French, because it is time for me to be educated.'

'And do you know how to pray?'

'Why, of course we do! We have for a long time. I am a big girl, so I pray to myself, but Kolya and Lidochka pray aloud with mama. First they say "Hail, Mary!" and then another prayer: "O God, forgive sister Sonya and bless her" and then "O God, forgive our other papa and bless him," because our old papa is dead, and this one is our other one, and we pray for the old one too.'

'Polechka, my name is Rodion; pray for me too sometimes: "and thy servant Rodion"—just that.'

'I will pray for you all my life,' said the little girl passionately, and then suddenly laughed again, threw herself on him, and hugged him tightly once more.

Raskolnikov told her his name and address, and promised to return the next day without fail. When she left him she was rapturously happy. It was about eleven o'clock when he went out into the street. Five minutes later he was standing on the bridge, on the exact spot where the woman had thrown herself into the water.

'Enough!' he said decidedly and solemnly. 'Away with illusions, away with imaginary terrors, away with spectres! . . . Life is! Was I not living just now? My life did not die with the old woman! May she rest in peace and—enough, old woman, your time has come! Now comes the reign of reason and light and . . . and freedom and power . . . now we shall see! Now we shall measure our strength!' he added arrogantly, as though he were addressing some dark power and summoning it up. 'After all . . . I am very weak at this moment, but . . . I think all my illness has gone. I knew it would, when I came out just now. By the way, Pochinkov's house is only a couple of steps away. I should have to go to Razumikhin's even if it were much farther than that . . . Let him win his bet! . . . Let him laugh, even—it doesn't matter, let him! . . . Strength, strength is what I need; nothing can be done without strength; and strength must be gained by strength—that is something they do not know,' he added proudly and self-confidently, and he left the bridge, though he could hardly put one foot before the other. His pride and self-confidence grew with every minute; in each succeeding minute he was a different man from what he had been in the preceding one. But what had happened that was so special? What had so transformed him? He himself did not know; it had come to him suddenly, as to a man clutching at a straw, that even for him it was 'possible to live, that life was still there, that his life had not died with that old woman'. Perhaps he had been in too much haste to reach this conclusion, but of this he did not think.

'But I asked for "thy servant Rodion" to be remembered in their prayers,' flashed through his mind; 'well, that's just in case!' he added, and laughed at his own childish quibbling. He was in excellent spirits.

He found Razumikhin easily; the new lodger was already known in Pochinkov's, and the porter showed him the way at once. From half-way upstairs he could already distinguish the clatter and lively talk of a large gathering. The door to the staircase stood open; he could hear voices raised in discussion. Razumikhin's room was fairly large, and there were about fifteen people in it. Raskolnikov stopped in the little hall. There, beyond a partition, two servants of the landlord's were busy with two large samovars, various bottles and plates, and dishes of patties and *zakuski* brought from the landlord's kitchen. Raskolnikov sent in for Razumikhin, who came running out, delighted. At the first glance it was evident that he had had much more than usual to drink, and although he practically never got drunk, this time he showed some signs of being affected.

'Listen,' said Raskolnikov hurriedly, 'I only came to say that you've won your bet and that it is true nobody knows what he may do. But I can't come in; I feel too faint to stand. So: hail and farewell! Come and see me tomorrow, though . . .'

'Do you know what? I'll see you home. When you say yourself that you are weak, then . . .'

'What about your guests? Who is that, with curly hair, who just looked this way?'

'That? God knows! Some acquaintance of my uncle's, I suppose, or perhaps he just came without waiting to be invited. I shall leave my uncle with them; he is invaluable; it is a pity you can't make his acquaintance now. But to the devil with all of them! I can't be bothered with them just now; besides, I need some fresh air. My dear chap, you came in the nick of time; another two minutes and I swear I'd have got into a fight! They talk such confounded nonsense . . . You can't imagine what heights of idiotic nonsense a man can finally soar to! But of course you can imagine it—don't we talk rot ourselves? Well, let them talk it if they want to; later on they'll talk sense, no doubt . . . Sit down a minute; I'll get Zosimov.'

Zosimov showed some eagerness as he hurried over to Raskolnikov, and a noticeable and rather odd curiosity. Soon his face cleared.

'You must get some sleep without delay,' he pronounced, having examined his patient as well as he could, 'and take a dose of medicine before you go to bed. Will you take it? I got it ready a short time ago . . . it's a powder.'

'Two if you like,' answered Raskolnikov.

The powder was taken on the spot.

'It is a good idea for you to take him home yourself,' remarked Zosimov to Razumikhin; 'we shall see what happens tomorrow, but things are not at all bad today: there is a decided change since a little time ago. Well, we live and learn . . .'

'Do you know what Zosimov whispered to me just now, as we came out?' blurted Razumikhin, as soon as they were in the street. 'I am telling you this straight out, my dear chap, because he is a fool. Zosimov told me to talk freely to you on the way and make you do the same, and then tell him about it afterwards, because he has an idea . . . that you . . . are mad, or pretty near it. Just imagine that! To begin with, you are three times as clever as he; in the second place, if you aren't a lunatic, why should you care what rubbish he has got into his head?; and in the third place, that lump of flesh specializes in surgery, but now he's cracked on the subject of mental diseases. What set him definitely on your track was the conversation you had today with Zametov.'

'Did Zametov tell you about it?'

'Everything, and he did quite right. I understood all the ins and outs of it then, and so did Zametov . . . Well, in one word, Rodya . . . the point is . . . I'm just a shade drunk just now . . . But that doesn't matter . . . the point is, that that idea . . . you understand? . . . really had got into their heads . . . you understand? That is, none of them dared say it aloud, because it's such ridiculous balderdash, and especially after they'd arrested that painter, it put the extinguisher on all that for good. But why were they such fools? I gave Zametov a bit of a drubbing at the time—this is between ourselves, my dear chap; please don't even hint that you know about it; I have noticed that he is very touchy; it was at Louisa's. But today, today everything has become clear. It was principally Ilya Petrovich. He took advantage of your faint that time in the office, but even he was ashamed of it afterwards; I know for a fact . . .'

Raskolnikov listened avidly. Razumikhin had drunk enough to make him let things out.

'I fainted because it was stuffy and smelt of paint,' said Raskolnikov.

'Why bother to explain? And it wasn't only the paint; your collapse had been coming on for a whole month: Zosimov will bear witness! Only how cut up that boy is now, you simply can't imagine! "I am not worth his little finger!" he says— Yours, that is. He's not a bad chap sometimes, my dear fellow. But the lesson, the lesson you gave him today in the "Crystal Palace"—that put the finishing touch on! You know, you gave him a fright at first, you worked him up into a fever!; you almost made him convinced again of all that monstrous rubbish and then suddenly—you stuck your tongue out at him: "There you are," says you, "you've been caught!" Perfect! He's crushed, he's overwhelmed! You're a master, I swear it; that's just what they need! Oh, why wasn't I there? He was waiting terribly impatiently for you just now. Porfiry would like to know you, too . . .'

'And . . . he as well . . . But why am I supposed to be mad?'

'Well, not exactly mad. It seems, my dear fellow, I've been letting out too much . . . He was struck, you see, by the fact that only this one point interested you . . . Now it is clear why you were interested; knowing all the circumstances . . . and how this irritated you at the time and got mixed up with your illness . . . I'm a little drunk, my dear fellow, only he has some idea of his own, though God knows what it is . . . I tell you he's mad on the subject of mental illness. But you needn't give a damn . . .'

Both were silent for some moments.

'Listen, Razumikhin,' began Raskolnikov, 'I want to tell you something frankly: I've just been at a dead man's house— a clerk who has died . . . I gave all my money to them . . . and besides, I have just been kissed by a creature who, even if I had killed anybody, would still . . . in a word, I saw another creature . . . with a flame-coloured feather . . . but, however, I am wandering. I am very weak, give me your arm . . . the staircase is just here.'

'What is the matter? What is it?' asked Razumikhin anxiously.

'My head feels a little dizzy, but that isn't it; it is that I feel so sad, so sad!—like a woman . . . really! Look, what is that? Look, look!'

'What do you mean?'

'Don't you see? There is a light in my room, do you see? —through the crack . . .'

They were standing at the foot of the last flight, level with the landlady's door, and they could indeed see from below that there was a light in Raskolnikov's room.

'Strange! Perhaps it's Nastasya,' remarked Razumikhin.

'She is never in my room at this hour, and besides she must be in bed long since, but . . . it is all one to me! Good-bye!'

'What do you mean? I am seeing you home. I shall go in with you!'

'I know you will, but I want to shake your hand and say good-bye to you here and now. Well, give me your hand, and good-bye!'

'What is the matter with you, Rodya?'

'Nothing. Come; you will be a witness . . .'

They began to climb the stairs, and the idea came into Razumikhin's mind that Zosimov might be right. 'Oh, dear!

I've upset him with my chatter!' he muttered to himself. Suddenly, as they approached the door, they heard voices in the room.

'What can this be?' cried Razumikhin.

Raskolnikov reached the door first and opened it wide, opened it and stood rooted on the threshold.

His mother and sister were sitting on his sofa, where they had been waiting for him for an hour and a half. Why was it that their arrival was the last thing he expected, and that they were the last thing he had thought of, in spite of the news, repeated that very day, that they were coming, were on the way, would soon arrive? All through that hour and a half they had plied Nastasya with questions in turn, until they had heard everything in the fullest detail. She was standing before them now. They were almost beside themselves with fright when they heard that 'he ran away today', a sick man and certainly, from what they had been told, delirious. 'Oh God, what has become of him?' They had both been crying, and both had suffered untold agonies during that hour and a half of waiting.

A cry of rapturous joy greeted Raskolnikov's appearance. Both flung themselves towards him. But he stood like one dead; a sudden, unbearable thought had struck him like a clap of thunder. He did not lift his arms to embrace them; he could not. His mother and sister clasped him in their arms, kissed him, laughed, cried . . . He took a step forward, faltered, and fell to the ground in a swoon.

Agitation, cries of alarm, groans . . . Razumikhin, who had been standing on the threshold, rushed into the room and seized the invalid in his powerful arms, and Raskolnikov found himself on the sofa in an instant.

'It is nothing, nothing!' cried Razumikhin, 'it is only a faint, a trivial matter! Only just now the doctor said that he was much better, that he was quite well! Water! Look, he's coming to himself now! He's quite come round, see! . . .'

And seizing Dunechka's hand so forcibly that he almost twisted it off, he made her stoop down to see that 'he's quite come round'. Raskolnikov's mother and sister both looked at Razumikhin with tenderness and gratitude as though he were Providence itself; they had learnt from Nastasya what this 'brilliant young man' (as Pulkheria Alexandrovna Raskolnikova herself termed him in intimate conversation with Dunya that evening) had been to their Rodya throughout his illness.

# Part Three

## CHAPTER I

RASKOLNIKOV sat up on the sofa.

He made a feeble gesture to Razumikhin to cut short his flow of warm but incoherent reassurances to his mother and sister, took a hand of each, and sat for a minute or two looking silently from one to the other. This look frightened his mother. It showed not only an emotion so intense as to be painful, but also a sort of insane fixity. Pulkheria Alexandrovna burst into tears. Avdotya Romanovna was pale; her hand trembled in her brother's.

'Go home . . . with him,' he said in a broken voice, indicating Razumikhin, 'until tomorrow; tomorrow, everything . . . When did you arrive?'

'This evening, Rodya,' answered Pulkheria Alexandrovna; 'the train was terribly late.⁴ But, Rodya, nothing could induce me to leave you now. I will spend the night here beside you . . .'

'Don't torment me!' he said, with an irritated gesture.

'I will stay with him!' exclaimed Razumikhin; 'I will not leave him for an instant. As for those people at my place, they can go to the devil for all I care; and if they want to take offence, they can. Anyhow, my uncle is there to look after them.'

'Oh, how can I thank you?' Pulkheria Alexandrovna was beginning, clasping Razumikhin's hand once more, but Raskolnikov interrupted her again.

'I can't stand this, I can't stand it,' he repeated fretfully; 'don't torture me! Enough! Please go away! . . . I can't stand any more!'

'Come, mama; let us at any rate leave the room for a short time,' whispered Dunya, frightened. 'You can see we are too much for him.'

'And am I not even to look at him, after three years?' wept Pulkheria Alexandrovna.

'Wait!' said he, stopping them again. 'You keep on interrupting and my mind gets confused . . . Have you seen Luzhin?'

'No, Rodya, but he knows that we have arrived. We have heard, Rodya, that Peter Petrovich was good enough to call on you today,' said Pulkheria Alexandrovna rather timidly.

---

4. The first railroad in Russia, between Petersburg and Pavlovsk, a suburb, was put in service in 1838. In 1851 Moscow and Petersburg were linked by a railroad line. By 1861 two further railroad lines had been built, from Moscow to Warsaw, and from Moscow to Nizhni Novgorod (today called Gorky).

'Yes . . . he was good enough . . . Dunya, I told Luzhin I should throw him downstairs, and sent him packing . . .'

'Rodya, what are you saying? You really . . . you don't mean to say . . .' began Pulkheria Alexandrovna, startled, but she looked at Dunya and stopped.

Avdotya Romanovna, with her eyes fixed on her brother, waited. Nastasya had already told them as much of the quarrel as she could understand or convey to them, and both had awaited this moment in a torment of doubt and anxiety.

'Dunya,' went on Raskolnikov with an effort, 'I will not have this marriage, and so, tomorrow, the first words you say to Luzhin must be to dismiss him. Then we need never so much as speak of him again.'

'Oh, my God!' exclaimed Pulkheria Alexandrovna.

'Think what you are saying, brother!' began Avdotya Romanovna, flaring up. But she controlled herself at once. 'Perhaps you are not fit just now, you are tired,' she said gently.

'Raving? No . . . You are marrying Luzhin *for my benefit*, and I do not accept the sacrifice. So before tomorrow write him a letter . . . dismissing him . . . Give it to me to read in the morning, and let that be the end of it!'

'That I cannot do!' exclaimed the young woman, offended. 'What right . . .?'

'Dunechka, you are quick-tempered yourself; stop now; tomorrow . . . Can't you see . . .?' exclaimed her mother in fresh alarm, hastening to Dunya. 'Oh, we had better go!'

'He's raving!' exclaimed the tipsy Razumikhin, 'or how would he dare? He'll have got that bee out of his bonnet by tomorrow . . . He really did turn him out today. That's true enough. But then, the other fellow lost his temper too . . . He was holding forth here, showing off his knowledge, but he went away with his tail between his legs . . .'

'So it is true!' exclaimed Pulkheria Alexandrovna.

'Till tomorrow, brother,' said Dunya compassionately; 'let us go, mama . . . Good-bye, Rodya!'

'Listen, sister,' he repeated, with all the strength remaining to him, as she went, 'I am not raving; this marriage is an infamy. I may be infamous, but you should not . . . one is enough . . .; though I am infamous, I would disown such a sister. It is either me or Luzhin! Go now . . .'

'You must be out of your mind! You're behaving like a tyrant!' shouted Razumikhin, but Raskolnikov did not answer, perhaps because he was not strong enough. He lay down and turned towards the wall, completely exhausted. Avdotya Romanova looked questioningly at Razumikhin; her black eyes were flashing and Razumikhin was quelled by her glance. Pulkheria Alexandrovna seemed rooted to the spot.

'I can't possibly leave!' she whispered, almost desperate, to Razumikhin. 'I will stay here somewhere . . . Take Dunya home.'

'And ruin everything!' said Razumikhin, losing his temper, but also speaking in a whisper. 'Come out at least on to the stairs. Give us a light, Nastasya! I solemnly assure you,' he went on, still in a half-whisper, although they were now outside the room, 'that not long since he came very near to striking us, the doctor and me! Do you understand? the doctor himself! And the doctor yielded and left, so as not to annoy him, and I stayed downstairs on guard. But he got dressed and slipped out. And he will slip out again in the night if you upset him, and do himself some injury . . .'

'Oh, what are you saying?'

'Besides, Avdotya Romanovna can't be in an hotel-room without you. Think what sort of place you are staying in! Surely that scoundrel Peter Petrovich would have done better to look for respectable lodgings for you . . . You know I am a little drunk and that is why I . . . became abusive; don't pay any . . .'

'But I shall go to the landlady here,' insisted Pulkheria Alexandrovna, 'and beg her to give Dunya and me a corner for tonight. I cannot leave him like this, I cannot!'

While she spoke she was standing on the landing outside the landlady's door. Nastasya stood on a lower step holding a light for them. Razumikhin was extraordinarily excited. Half an hour before, when he had been taking Raskolnikov home, although he had been, as he was prepared to admit, too talkative, he had felt cheerful and fairly fresh, in spite of the enormous amount he had drunk during the evening. Now his state was one almost of exaltation, and it seemed as though all the vodka he had drunk had mounted to his head again, and with redoubled force. He stood with the two ladies, clasping a hand of each, exhorting them and setting forth his arguments with amazing clarity, and, apparently for greater conviction, squeezing their hands more painfully tight, as if in a vice, with every word, while his eyes devoured Avdotya Romanovna, who seemed not at all disconcerted by this. Once or twice the pain made them try to free their hands from his huge bony ones, but he was so far from realizing what was the matter that he only pulled them more strongly towards him. If they had bidden him throw himself then and there head-first down the stairs to serve them he would have obeyed instantly, without argument or question. Pulkheria Alexandrovna, preoccupied with anxiety for her Rodya, although she felt that this was a very eccentric young man and was squeezing her hand much too painfully, was unwilling, since she regarded him as having been sent by Providence, to attach any importance to all his little eccentricities. But Avdotya Romanovna, although she was equally anxious for her brother, and although she was not of a timorous disposition, felt something very like consternation, and even fear, when she met the wild, flashing, fiery glance of her brother's friend, and only the boundless confidence inspired by Nastasya's account restrained her impulse to run away, dragging her mother with her. She understood also that they might perhaps find it impossible to run away from him now. However, after some ten minutes she found herself much more composed: Razumikhin had the faculty, whatever his mood, of revealing his whole being in one moment, so that everybody knew at once what sort of person he was dealing with.

'You can't go to the landlady; it would be a most terribly stupid thing to do!' he cried, trying to convince Pulkheria Alexandrovna. 'Although you are his mother, if you stay it will drive him to distraction, and then God knows what will happen. Listen, I'll tell you what: Nastasya shall sit with him now, and I will take you both home, because you can't go through the streets alone: here in St. Petersburg, in that respect . . . Well, never mind that! . . . Then I shall hurry straight back here, and I give you my word of honour that within a quarter of an hour I will bring you back a report of how he is, whether he is asleep or not, and so on. Then, listen! I shall go instantly to my rooms—I have some guests there, but they are all drunk, —get Zosimov—that is the doctor who is attending him, he is there too, but he isn't drunk; he never gets drunk!—take him to Rodka and then straight on to you. That means you will have two accounts of him—and one of them from the doctor, you understand, from the doctor himself; that's not at all the same thing as one from me! If the news is bad, I promise faithfully I will bring you back here myself, and if it is good, then you can go to bed. I will spend the night here, but in the passage, so that he won't even hear me, and I will tell Zosimov to sleep in the flat too, so as to be within easy reach. Well, which will be better for him just now, you or the doctor? You know the doctor will be more use, much more use. Well then, go home! You can't go to the landlady; I can, but you can't: she won't allow it, because . . . because she's a fool. She is jealous of Avdotya Romanovna because of me, if you want to know, and of you as well . . . But especially of Avdotya Romanovna . . . She is a completely, an entirely unexpected character! However, I am a fool, too . . . Never mind! Let us go! Do you trust me? Well, do you trust me or not?'

'Come along, mama,' said Avdotya Romanovna. 'I am sure he will keep his promise. He has saved my brother's life already, and if the doctor will really agree to spend the night here, what could be better?'

'See, you . . . you . . . you understand me, because you are an angel!' exclaimed Razumikhin rapturously. 'We are going! Nastasya! Upstairs this instant and sit with him, with a light; I shall be back in a quarter of an hour . . .'

Pulkheria Alexandrovna was not completely convinced, but she raised no further objections. Razumikhin took them both by the arm and drew them down the stairs. However, he worried her a little, too: 'he may be kind and efficient, but is he in a condition to fulfil his promise? Look at the state he's in! . . .'

'Ah, I understand; you think I'm drunk!' said Razumikhin, divining her thoughts and breaking in on them. His enormous strides took him along the pavement at such a pace that the ladies could hardly keep up with him, but he did not notice this. 'Nonsense!—that is . . . I am drunk, fool that I am, but that is not the point: I am not drunk with wine. But, as soon as I saw you, it went to my head . . . But never mind me! Don't pay any attention; I am talking rot; I am beneath you . . . I am infinitely far beneath you! . . . When I have taken you home, I shall pour a couple of buckets of water over my head, from the canal here, and I shall be all right . . . If only you knew how I love you both! Don't laugh, and don't be angry! . . . You may be angry with everybody else, but not with me. I am his friend, and that means I am yours. I want that so much . . . I had a presentiment . . . last year, there was a moment when . . . However, it can't have been a presentiment at all, because now I feel as if you had fallen from the skies. Perhaps I shan't sleep all night . . . Not long since, Zosimov was afraid he might go out of his mind . . . That is why he must not be irritated . . .'

'What are you saying?' exclaimed the mother.

'Did the doctor really say that?' asked Avdotya Romanovna, alarmed.

'Yes, he did, but it is wrong, quite wrong. He gave him some medicine, a powder, I saw it, and then you arrived . . . Ah! . . . It would have been better if you had arrived tomorrow! We did right to come away. And in an hour's time Zosimov will give you a report about everything. *He* is very far from drunk! And I shall no longer be drunk . . . Why did I get so worked up? Because those damned fellows drew me into an argument. I have taken an oath not to agree . . . They talk such rot! I almost came to blows with them. I have left my uncle presiding there . . . Well, would you believe it: they demand complete impersonality, they find the highest enjoyment in it! If one could only not be oneself, if one could be less like oneself than anything! That is what they consider to be the most complete progress. And if it were only their own nonsense they talked, but . . .'

'Listen!' interrupted Pulkheria Alexandrovna diffidently, but this seemed only to increase his fervour.

'What do you think?' cried Razumikhin in a still louder tone. 'Do you think I am annoyed because they talk nonsense? Rubbish! I like people to talk nonsense. It is man's unique privilege, among all other organisms. By pursuing falsehood you will arrive at the truth! The fact that I am in error shows that I am human. You will not attain to one single truth until you have produced at least fourteen false theories, and perhaps a hundred and fourteen, and that is honourable enough in its fashion; but we can't even produce our errors out of our own heads. You can talk the most mistaken rubbish to me, and if it is your own, I will embrace you! It is almost better to tell your own lies than somebody else's truth; in the first case you are a man, in the second you are no better than a parrot! Truth remains; but life can be choked up; there have been instances. Well, what are we all now? We are all, without exception, children in the kindergarten, in respect of science, progress, thought, invention, ideals, desires, liberalism, judgement, experience, and everything, everything, everything, everything! We have been content to rub along on other people's ideas— we have rusted away! That is so, isn't it? What I say is true, isn't it?' exclaimed Razumikhin, shaking and squeezing both ladies' hands. 'Isn't it?'

'Oh, good gracious, I don't know,' said poor Pulkheria Alexandrovna.

'Yes, yes, it's true enough . . . although I don't agree with everything you say,' said Avdotya Romanovna seriously, and exclaimed sharply with pain as he gripped her hand tighter than ever.

'True? You say it's true? Well, after this you . . . you . . .', he cried rapturously, 'you are a fountain of kindness, purity, reason and . . . perfection! Give me your hand, give it me . . . and give me yours too; I must kiss your hands on my knees, here and now!'

And he fell on his knees on the pavement, which fortunately was deserted at this hour.

'Stop, I beg you! What are you doing?' cried Pulkheria Alexandrovna in the greatest alarm.

'Get up, get up!' said Dunya, laughing and alarmed at the same time.

'Not until you have given me your hands! There! I have done; you see I have got up. Let us go on! I am a miserable dolt; I am far beneath you, I am drunk, and I am ashamed . . . I am not worthy to love you, but to worship you is every man's obligation unless he is no more than a brute beast! And I have fulfilled that obligation . . . Here is your hotel, and on this account, at least, Rodion was right to turn Peter Petrovich out!

How dared he send you to such a place? It is disgraceful! Do you know what sort of people are received here? And you his betrothed! You are engaged to him, aren't you? Well, I must tell you after this that your fiancé is a scoundrel! . . .'

'Mr. Razumikhin, you forget yourself . . .' Pulkheria Alexandrovna was beginning.

'Yes, yes, you are right; I have forgotten myself, and I apologize,' said Razumikhin, recollecting himself, 'but . . . but . . . you must not be angry with me for saying what I did! Because I am speaking sincerely, and not for a reason that . . . hm! . . . that would be ignoble; in one word, it is because in you I . . . hm! . . . well, let it be; I need not, I will not say why, I dare not! . . . But all of us saw, when he came in, that that man does not belong to our world. Not because when he came he had had his hair curled at the barber's, not because he was in a hurry to display his intellectual powers, but because he is a spy and a profiteer, because he is quite plainly a Jew and a mountebank. Do you suppose him to be intelligent? No, he is a fool, a fool! Well, is he a match for you? Good God, no! You see, ladies,' and he stood still on the stairs leading up to the hotel, 'although those guests of mine are all drunk, they are honest, and although we do err, because after all I err too, yet by pursuing our errors we arrive at last at the truth because we are on the right path; but Peter Petrovich . . . is not on the right path. Although I was cursing them right and left just now, I respect them all; and though I don't respect him, I like even Zametov, because he's only a puppy! Even that idiot Zosimov, because he's honest and he knows his job . . . Well, that's enough; everything has been said, and forgiven. It has been forgiven, hasn't it? Well, come along. I know this corridor, I've been here; just here, in number three, there was a scandal . . . Well, where are you? What number? Eight? Well, lock your door for the night, and don't let anybody in. I shall be back with news in a quarter of an hour, and then again half an hour later with Zosimov. You'll see! Good-bye! I'm off!'

'Oh dear, Dunechka, what will come of this?' said Pulkheria Alexandrovna, turning to her daughter, full of fear and anxiety.

'Don't worry, mama,' answered Dunya, taking off her hat and cloak. 'It was God Himself who sent that man to us, although he comes straight from some drinking bout. I am sure we can rely on him. And everything he has already done for my brother . . .'

'Oh, Dunechka, God only knows if he will come. And how could I bring myself to leave Rodya? . . . This is not at all, not at all, how I expected to find him! How forbidding he looked, as though he were not glad to see us . . .'

There were tears in her eyes.

'No, mama, that is not true. You didn't observe closely, you were crying all the time. He has been completely upset by this serious illness; that is the reason for it all.'

'Oh, this illness! Something terrible will come of it, something terrible!' said her mother, timidly searching her daughter's eyes, so as to read all her thoughts, and already half-comforted because Dunya was defending Rodya, which must mean that she had forgiven him. And trying to probe her still further, she added: 'I am sure he will change his mind tomorrow.'

'And I am sure he will say the same tomorrow . . . about that,' Avdotya Romanovna cut her short. Here was of course the rub, because this was the point which Pulkheria Alexandrovna now feared to discuss. Dunya went up to her mother and kissed her, and received a silent hug in return. Then her mother sat down to wait anxiously for Razumikhin's arrival, and timidly followed Dunya's movements as she walked about the room with folded arms, deep in thought. This thoughtful pacing from corner to corner was a habit with Avdotya Romanovna, and at such times her mother feared to break in on her reflections.

Razumikhin's sudden, drink-inspired passion for Avdotya Romanovna was of course comical; but seeing her, especially now, as she paced the room with folded arms, pensive and sad, many might perhaps have found other excuses for him besides that of his condition. Avdotya Romanovna was remarkably good-looking, tall, extremely well-made, strong, self-assured, as her every gesture showed, without in the least detracting from the grace and tenderness of her movements. In face she resembled her brother, but it would have been possible to call her a beauty. Her hair was brown, of a slightly lighter shade than her brother's, and her sparkling, almost black eyes were proud and yet at times extraordinarily tender. Her complexion was pale, but not sickly; her face shone with freshness and health. Her mouth was a trifle small, and her dewy scarlet lower lip projected very slightly, like her chin—the only irregularity in that beautiful face, which gave it a rather self-willed look and perhaps a touch of superciliousness. Her expression was rather serious and pensive than merry, but then, how well a smile became that face, and how well her young, free, merry laughter became her! It was understandable that Razumikhin, hot-headed, frank, single-minded, honest, as strong as a hero of legend, and drunk into the bargain, should have lost his head from the first moment, since he had never seen anybody like her. Besides, chance dictated that he should first see Dunya in a radiant moment of love and rejoicing at the reunion with her brother. Later, he saw her lower lip tremble with indignation in response to the arrogant ferocity of Rodya's commands—and he could resist no longer.

He had spoken no more than the truth in his tipsy babbling there on the staircase when he said that Raskolnikov's eccentric landlady, Praskovya Pavlovna, would be jealous not only of Avdotya Romanovna, but perhaps even of Pulkheria Alexandrovna herself. Although Pulkheria Alexandrovna was forty-three, her face retained traces of its former beauty, and besides, like almost all women who preserve into old age their clarity of mind, the freshness of their impressions, and the pure, honest ardour of their hearts, she seemed much younger than her years. Let it be said in parenthesis that the preservation of these things is the only way to keep beauty even in old age. Her hair was beginning to grow grey and thin, little radiating wrinkles had long since appeared round her eyes, her cheeks were hollow and withered with cares and anxieties, but it was still a beautiful face. It was like a portrait of Dunechka twenty years later, without the expressive pout of the lower lip. Pulkheria Alexandrovna was sentimental, but not cloyingly so, diffident and yielding, but only up to a certain point: she would yield much, consent to much, even to things running counter to her convictions, but there always remained a limit of honesty, principle, and firm conviction which nothing could induce her to overstep.

Exactly twenty minutes after Razumikhin left them came two quiet but hurried taps on the door: he had returned.

'I am not coming in; there is not time!' he said hastily, when the door was opened. 'He is sleeping like a baby, soundly and peacefully, and with luck he will sleep for ten hours. Nastasya is with him; I have told her not to leave him until I get back. Now I am going to get hold of Zosimov; he will report to you and then you can get some sleep yourselves. I can see you are completely worn out.'

And he set off along the corridor.

'What an efficient and . . . devoted young man,' exclaimed Pulkheria Alexandrovna, extremely delighted.

'He seems a very nice person,' answered Avdotya Romanovna warmly, as she resumed her pacing about the room.

Nearly an hour later steps were heard in the corridor and there was another knock at the door. Both the women were waiting, this time in complete reliance on Razumikhin's promise; and indeed he had succeeded in bringing Zosimov. Zosimov had immediately agreed to leave the party and go to see Raskolnikov, but he had come to the ladies' room very unwillingly, mistrusting the assurances of the drunken Razumikhin. But his self-esteem was at once appeased, and even flattered; he realized that they had been waiting for him as for an oracle. He sat with them for exactly ten minutes, and managed to convince and reassure Pulkheria Alexandrovna. He spoke with extreme sympathy, but with reserve and forceful seriousness, the picture of a twenty-seven-year-old doctor at an important consultation, not deviating by a single word from the subject or showing the least desire to enter into more private and personal relations with the two ladies. Although he remarked Avdotya Romanovna's brilliant good looks as soon as he went in, he made an immediate effort not to notice her at all during the rest of his visit, and addressed himself exclusively to Pulkheria Alexandrovna. All this gave him immense inward satisfaction. He had found his patient, he said, in a very satisfactory condition. According to his observations, the illness had some psychological causes in addition to the bad material conditions the patient had been living in for the past few months; 'it is, so to say, a product of many complex moral and material influences, anxieties, apprehensions, worries, certain ideas . . . and other things.' Without looking directly at Avdotya Romanovna he perceived that she was listening with special attentiveness, and became more expansive on this subject. To Pulkheria Alexandrovna's timid and uneasy question about 'some suspicions of mental disturbance', he answered, smiling calmly and frankly, that his words had been exaggerated; that, of course, he had observed in his patient a certain fixed idea, some indication of monomania—since he, Zosimov, was particularly interested in this extremely absorbing branch of medicine—but it must be remembered that practically up to that day the patient had been delirious, and . . . and, of course, the arrival of his family would have a salutary, strengthening, and settling effect—'if only new shocks can be avoided,' he added significantly. Then he got up, bowed sedately but affably, and, accompanied by blessings, fervent gratitude, and prayers, went out, after pressing the little hand that Avdotya Romanovna held out to him of her own accord, extremely pleased with his visit and still more so with himself.

'We will have a talk tomorrow; now you simply must go to bed,' insisted Razumikhin, as he left with Zosimov. 'I shall be here with a report tomorrow as early as possible.'

'But what a delightful girl that Avdotya Romanovna is!' remarked Zosimov, almost licking his lips, as they emerged into the street.

'Delightful? Did you say delightful?' roared Razumikhin, flinging himself on Zosimov and seizing him by the throat. 'If you ever dare . . . Do you understand? Do you understand?' he cried, shaking him by the collar and pinning him against the wall. 'Do you hear me?'

'Let me go, you drunken devil!' said Zosimov, struggling free, and then, when Razumikhin had let him go, looked closely at him and began to roar with laughter. Razumikhin stood before him with dangling arms, lost in grave and sombre thoughts.

'Of course, I am an ass,' he said, brooding like a thunder-cloud, 'but then . . . so are you.'

'Well, no, brother; not at all. I don't cherish any impossible dreams.'

They walked along in silence, and it was only as they approached Raskolnikov's flat that Razumikhin, very troubled, spoke again.

'Listen,' he said to Zosimov, 'you're a good chap, but besides all your other bad qualities, you're a womanizer, as I know, and a filthy one. You're a weak and spineless scoundrel, you're capricious, you're self-indulgent, you can't refuse yourself anything, and I call all that filthy, because it leads you straight into the muck. You've grown so soft that I confess I simply can't understand how you can still be a good and even selfless doctor. You sleep on a feather-bed (and you a doctor!) and yet you'll get out of bed to go to a patient. In three years' time you won't do that any more . . . Well, let it go; that isn't the point, but this is: you will spend tonight in the landlady's flat (it took some doing, but I persuaded her) and I in the kitchen; so you'll have the chance of getting more intimately acquainted! Not in the way you think! There's not even a suggestion of that here, brother!'

'I'm not thinking anything!'

'This woman, brother, is all modesty, reticence, shyness, and resolute chastity, and yet at the same time, a few sighs, and she is as melting as wax, yes, as wax. Preserve me from her, for all the devils in hell! A fetching creature! . . . I will repay you, with my life if need be!'

Zosimov laughed more heartily still.

'Well, you are worked up, aren't you? But why me?'

'I assure you it won't be much trouble; you can talk any sort of sloppy nonsense you like, so long as you sit beside her and talk. Besides, you're a doctor; begin curing her of something. I swear you won't regret it. She has a piano, and you know I strum a little; I've got a song there, a genuine Russian one: "I weep scalding tears." She likes real Russian songs—well, so it began with the songs, and you are a virtuoso on the pianoforte, a *maestro*, a Rubinstein . . . I swear you won't regret it!'

'Why, have you given her some sort of promise or something? You've put something in writing perhaps? Did you promise to marry her?'

'No, no, nothing of the sort, absolutely nothing! And she is not like that at all; Chebarov approached her . . .'

'Well then, just drop her!'

'No, that's impossible!'

'Why is it impossible?'

'Well, it just is, and that's all about it! There is a certain element of charm in this business, my dear chap.'

'Well, why did you try to make a conquest of her?'

'I didn't; perhaps I was even conquered myself, fool that I am; but it's absolutely all one to her whether it's you or me, so long as there is someone to sit beside her and sigh. Here, my dear chap . . . I don't know how to express it to you, but here . . . well, you know a lot about mathematics, and you still study it, I know . . . well, begin to go through the integral calculus with her—I swear I'm not joking, I'm perfectly serious—it makes absolutely no difference to her; she will look at you and sigh, for a whole year together. I, among other things, talked to her at great length, two days running, about the Prussian Chamber of Nobles (because what can one talk to her about?)—and she only sighed and glowed! Only don't begin to talk about love—she's so painfully shy—well, and look as if you couldn't tear yourself away—well, that's enough. You'll be terribly comfortable; just like home—read, sit, lie on the sofa, write—. You can even kiss her, if you're careful.'

'But why should I do all this?'

'Oh, I don't seem able to explain it to you anyhow! Look: you two are just like one another! I thought of you before, in fact . . . You will end up that way anyhow, and isn't it all one to you whether it's sooner or later? Here, my dear chap, is the beginning of a feather-bed existence—yes, and more than that! Here you will get drawn in; here is the end of the world, an anchorage, a peaceful haven, the central point of the earth, the three fishes on which the world is based, the essence of pancakes, of rich pies, of the evening samovar, of peaceful sighs and warm jackets and warm stoves to lie on—just as if you were dead and yet still alive—all the advantages of both states at one and the same time! Devil take it, my dear chap, I've been running on, and it's time we went to bed. I sometimes wake up in the night; if I do I will go in and take a look at him. But it doesn't matter, it's unnecessary; everything is all right. Don't bother specially, but if you like, you go in and see him as well. But if you notice anything, delirium, for example, or a temperature or anything, wake me at once. But there won't be anything . . .'

## CHAPTER II

NEXT day, Razumikhin awoke at eight o'clock in a serious and troubled mood. Many new and unforeseen perplexities seemed to have sprung up in him that morning. He had not before so much as dreamed that he would ever experience

such an awakening. He remembered every detail of the previous day, and knew that something out of the ordinary had
happened to him, that he had received an impression of a kind
that he had never known before, and quite unlike all others.
At the same time he clearly realized that the dream that had
set his imagination aflame was in the highest degree unrealizable, so much so that he was ashamed of it, and quickly
transferred his attention to other, more urgent, anxieties and
problems inherited from that 'thrice-accursed yesterday'.

His most horrifying recollection was of how 'ignobly and
disgustingly' he had behaved, not only in being drunk, but in
taking advantage of a young girl's situation to abuse her
fiancé in front of her, out of stupid and hastily conceived
jealousy, when he knew nothing either of their mutual relationship and obligations or, properly speaking, of the man himself.
And what right had he to condemn him so hastily and rashly?
Who had appointed him the judge? Surely such a being as
Avdotya Romanovna was not capable of giving herself to an
unworthy man for money? Therefore there must be some
worth in him. The hotel? But really, how could he know what
sort of place it was? After all, he was having a flat got ready . . .
Pah, how ignobly he had behaved! And what sort of justification was there in the fact that he had been drunk? That
was a stupid excuse, which made him seem still baser. *In vino
veritas*, and here the whole truth had come out, 'that was, all
the foulness of his boorish, jealous heart had come out!' And
was it in any way permissible for him, Razumikhin, to cherish
any such dream? What was he in comparison with this girl—
he, the drunken scoundrel and braggart of yesterday? 'Is such a
ridiculous and cynical comparison possible at all?' He crim-
soned at the thought, and at the same time suddenly recollected how yesterday, on the stairs, he had told them that the
landlady would be jealous of Avdotya Romanovna on his
account. This was quite unbearable. With a wide swing of his
arm he struck the stove with his fist, hurting his hand and
dislodging a brick.

'Of course,' he muttered to himself after a minute, in a
mood of self-abasement, 'of course, I can't gloss over or efface
all this nastiness, now or ever . . . and so I must not even think
of it, but appear before them in silence and . . . fulfil my
obligations . . . also in silence and . . . and not ask forgiveness,
but say nothing, and . . . and now, of course, everything is
ruined!'

All the same, when he dressed he made a more elaborate
toilet than usual. He had no other clothes, and even if he had,
would perhaps not have put them on, would 'purposely' not
have put them on. But in any case he could not go on being a
dirty and slovenly cynic; he had no right to offend other

people's susceptibilities, especially when they needed him and had invited him to come and see them. He brushed his clothes carefully. His linen was always presentable; in this respect he was particularly clean and neat.

This morning he washed with great care—he got soap from Nastasya, and washed his hair, his neck, and, with especial pains, his hands. When, however, it came to the question of whether he should shave his stubble or not (Praskovya Pavlovna still kept the excellent razor that had belonged to her late husband, Mr. Zarnitsyn) it was decided, somewhat emphatically, in the negative: 'Let it stay as it is! What if they should think that I shaved because . . . they certainly will think so! I would not have that for the world!'

And . . . and the chief thing was, he was very coarse and dirty, and had the manners of the pot-house; and . . . and suppose he knew that he, in however small a degree, was a decent fellow . . . well, what was there to be proud of in being a decent fellow? Everybody ought to be decent, and more besides and . . . (he remembered) he had been involved in some things . . . not exactly dishonourable, but all the same! . . . And what designs he had had! . . . Hm . . . 'And to put all this beside Avdotya Romanovna! Oh, the devil! Well, let it be so! I shall be purposely dirty, bawdy, and drunken, and be hanged to it! I shall be worse still! . . .'

Zosimov, who had spent the night in Praskovya Pavlovna's drawing-room, found him in the midst of this monologue.

He was going home, and was in a hurry to take a look at his patient. Razumikhin reported that he was sleeping like a top. Zosimov gave orders that he was not to be disturbed until he awoke of his own accord. He promised to look in himself between ten and eleven.

'If only he is at home,' he added. 'It's the very devil when you have no control over your own patient, and yet you're supposed to treat him. Do you know whether *he* is going there, or *they* are coming here?'

'They here, I think,' answered Razumikhin, who had understood the drift of the question, 'and they will, of course, have family matters to talk of. I shall leave them. You, as the doctor, have naturally more rights than I have.'

'But I'm not their confessor either; I shall just come and then go away; I have plenty of other things to do.'

'One thing worries me,' interrupted Razumikhin, frowning. 'Yesterday, when I was drunk, I let slip various foolish things to him on our way home . . . various . . . among other things, that you were afraid that he . . . might have a tendency to madness.'

'You let that out to the ladies yesterday, as well.'

'I know it was idiotic! I ought to be whipped! But tell me,

had you really a definite idea?'

'Oh, that's nonsense; what definite idea? You yourself described him as a monomaniac when you called me in . . . Well, yesterday we added fuel to the flames, you did, I mean, with those stories . . . about that painter; a good subject of conversation, when perhaps it was that that threw him off balance in the first place! If I had known exactly what happened in the office that time, and that some scoundrel had . . . offended him with that suspicion . . . hm . . . I shouldn't have allowed such talk yesterday. You know these monomaniacs can make an ocean out of a puddle and believe the most fantastic illusions to be real. As far as I remember, half the business became clear to me yesterday from that story of Zametov's. All right! I know a case of a hypochondriac, a man of forty, who could not endure an eight-year-old boy's merry chatter at table, day after day, and killed him! And here you have a man all in rags, an impudent scoundrel of a police officer, an illness just coming on, and a suspicion of that kind! To a hypochondriac who is delirious! In the face of exceptional, lunatic, vanity! And here, perhaps, lies the point of departure of the illness! Well, the devil only knows! . . . By the way, this Zametov is really a nice lad, only . . . hm . . . there was no need for him to repeat all that. He's a terrible babbler.'

'But whom did he tell? You and me.'

'And Porfiry.'

'Well, what if he did tell him?'

'By the way, have you any influence with them, his mother and sister? They ought to be very careful with him today . . .'

'They can be persuaded,' reluctantly answered Razumikhin.

'And why did he behave as he did towards that Luzhin? I shouldn't think she could be averse to a man with money . . . they haven't got a bean, have they?'

'Why all these questions?' exclaimed Razumikhin irritably. 'How should I know whether they have a bean or not? Ask them yourself and perhaps you will get to know . . .'

'Pah, how stupid you are sometimes! You are still feeling the effects of yesterday's drinking. Good-bye; thank your Praskovya Pavlovna from me for her hospitality. She locked herself in and didn't answer the good morning I gave her through the door, but she was up at seven o'clock, for her samovar was carried through the passage from the kitchen . . . I wasn't considered worthy of the honour of seeing her . . .'

At exactly nine o'clock Razumikhin presented himself at Bakaleev's hotel. The ladies had been awaiting him with febrile impatience for a very long time. They had got up at about seven o'clock or even earlier. When he went in he was glowering like a thunder-cloud, and he made his bows awkwardly, and immediately grew furious at himself, of course.

He had reckoned without his hosts; Pulkheria Alexandrovna positively flung herself upon him, seized both his hands, and seemed on the point of kissing them. He looked timidly at Avdotya Romanovna, but even that proud face bore in that moment such an expression of gratitude and friendship, such whole-hearted and to him unexpected esteem (instead of the mocking glances and involuntary ill-concealed scorn he expected) that he might almost have felt easier if he had been met with abuse; as it was, he was almost sheepish. Fortunately, there was a theme of conversation at hand, and he turned quickly to it.

Having learnt that her son 'was not yet awake', but that 'all was well', Pulkheria Alexandrovna declared that this was all for the best, 'because she very, very, very much wanted to talk things over first.' There followed a question about whether he had breakfasted, and an invitation to join them, since they had waited for him before having breakfast. Avdotya Romanovna rang the bell, which was answered by a slovenly ragamuffin. Tea was ordered and, after a long interval, served, but in such a dirty and unseemly fashion that the ladies were ashamed. Razumikhin started an energetic tirade against the place, but, remembering Luzhin, stopped in confusion, and was very glad when Pulkheria Alexandrovna began to ply him with endless questions.

He talked for three-quarters of an hour, continually interrupted and cross-questioned, and managed to communicate as much as he knew of the more important and essential facts of Rodion Romanovich's life during the past year, ending with a circumstantial account of his illness. He left out, however, a good deal which he felt it wiser to omit, including the scene in the police office and its consequences. His story was eagerly listened to, but when he thought he had finished, and satisfied his hearers, he found that as far as they were concerned he had hardly begun.

'Tell me, tell me, what do you think . . . oh, excuse me, I don't even yet know your name,' began Pulkheria Alexandrovna hurriedly.

'Dmitri Prokofich.'

'Well, Dmitri Prokofich, I should very, very much like to know . . . how, in general . . . he now regards subjects . . . that is, I mean . . . how can I express it? Perhaps I had better say, what are his likes and dislikes? Is he always so irritable? What are his desires, his dreams, if I can put it like that? What things influence him now? In one word, I should like . . .'

'Oh, mama, how can anybody answer all that in one breath?' said Dunya.

'Oh, dear, you know I didn't in the least expect to find him like this, not in the least, Dmitri Prokofich.'

'That is very natural,' answered Dmitri Prokofich. 'I have no mother, but my uncle comes here every year, and nearly every time he doesn't even recognize my appearance, and he is a clever man; well, a lot of water has flowed under the bridges in your three years of separation. But what can I tell you? I have known Rodion for a year and a half; he is moody, melancholy, proud, and haughty; recently (and perhaps for much longer than I know) he has been morbidly depressed and over-anxious about his health. He is kind and generous. He doesn't like to display his feelings, and would rather seem heartless than talk about them. Sometimes, however, he is not hypochondriacal at all, but simply inhumanly cold and unfeeling. Really, it is as if he had two separate personalities, each dominating him alternately. Sometimes he is dreadfully taciturn: he has no time for anything—people are always interfering with him—but he spends all his time lying there doing nothing. He never jests, not because he lacks the sharpness of wit for it, but because he has no time for such trifles. He doesn't hear people out. He is never interested in the same things as other people at any given moment. He sets a terribly high value on himself, not, I think, without some justification. Well, what else? . . . I think your arrival will have a most salutary effect on him.'

'God grant it may!' cried Pulkheria Alexandrovna, tormented by Razumikhin's account of her Rodya.

Now at last Razumikhin looked more cheerfully at Avdotya Romanovna. He had glanced at her often as he talked, but fleetingly, turning his eyes away again after a moment. Avdotya Romanovna had listened attentively, now sitting at the table, now getting up and walking about the room in her usual fashion, with folded arms and compressed lips; occasionally she put in a question, without interrupting her thoughtful pacing. She too had a habit of not hearing people out to the end. She wore a dark-coloured dress of thin material with a small diaphanous white scarf knotted round her neck. Razumikhin noticed many indications that the two women were in extremely poor circumstances. Had Avdotya Romanovna been arrayed like a queen, he would probably not have feared her at all; now, perhaps just because she was so poorly dressed and because he was conscious of the narrowness of their circumstances, his heart was filled with apprehension, and he became nervous of the effect of every one of his words and gestures. This served to increase his embarrassment and self-distrust.

'You have told us many curious things about my brother's character and . . . told them in an impartial manner. That was right; I had thought you positively worshipped him,' said Avdotya Romanovna with a smile. 'It seems likely, too, that he ought to have some woman near him,' she added reflectively.

'I did not say that, but perhaps you are right; only . . .'

'What?'

'He really does not love anyone; perhaps he never will,' said Razumikhin.

'You mean he is not capable of loving?'

'You know, Avdotya Romanovna, you are terribly like your brother, in every way!' he blurted out, to his own surprise. Immediately, remembering what he had just been saying about her brother, he was covered with confusion and as red as a lobster. Looking at him, Avdotya Romanovna could not help laughing.

'You may both be mistaken about Rodya,' put in Pulkheria Alexandrovna, rather shocked. 'I am not talking about just now, Dunechka. What Peter Petrovich writes in this letter . . . and what you and I suppose . . . may be untrue, but you can't imagine, Dmitri Prokofich, how capricious and—what shall I say?—cranky, he is. I never could understand his nature, even when he was only fifteen years old. I am convinced that he might suddenly do something with himself now that no other man would think of doing . . . There's no need to look far for an example: do you know how surprised and stunned I was, indeed it almost killed me, when he took it into his head that he was going to marry that . . . what's her name? . . . the daughter of this Mrs. Zarnitsyna, his landlady?'

'Do you know the details of the story?' asked Avdotya Romanovna.

'Would you not think,' continued Pulkheria Alexandrovna warmly, 'that my tears, my entreaties, my illness, my possible death from grief, our poverty, would have stopped him? No, he would have trampled coolly over every obstacle. But surely, surely he loves us?'

'He himself never said anything to me about that affair,' answered Razumikhin cautiously, 'but I have heard something about it from Mrs. Zarnitsyna, who is not a very communicative person either, and what I did hear was perhaps a little strange . . .'

'But what, what did you hear?' asked both women together.

'Well, nothing very particular, really. I only learnt that this marriage, which had been completely settled and was only prevented from taking place by the bride's death, was very much against the wishes of Mrs. Zarnitsyna herself . . . They say the bride, besides, was not even pretty, in fact they say she was very plain . . . and very sickly and . . . and odd . . . but apparently she had some good qualities. She certainly must have had; otherwise it is quite incomprehensible . . . She had no dowry, either, but he would never take a dowry into account . . . It is very difficult to form a judgement of such a case.'

'I am sure she had many virtues,' remarked Avdotya Romanovna shortly.

'God forgive me, but I was glad when she died, although I don't know which of them would have destroyed the other; would he have ruined her, or she him?' concluded Pulkheria Alexandrovna. Then, cautiously, with many hesitations and repeated glances at Dunya, who obviously found them displeasing, she resumed her questions about the scene of the day before between Rodya and Luzhin. This incident plainly worried her more than anything else; she seemed alarmed and agitated by it. Razumikhin told the whole story again in detail, and this time added his own conclusions; he directly accused Raskolnikov of intentionally offending Peter Petrovich, and found his illness but small excuse for him.

'He planned it before his illness,' he added.

'I think so too,' said Pulkheria Alexandrovna, with a dejected air. But she was struck by the discreet and even respectful tone of Razumikhin's references this time to Peter Petrovich, and so was Avdotya Romanovna.

Pulkheria Alexandrovna could not refrain from asking: 'So that is your opinion of Peter Petrovich?'

'I could hold no other of your daughter's future husband,' answered Razumikhin, firmly and warmly, 'and I don't say that only out of ordinary politeness, but because . . . because . . . well, for one reason alone, that Avdotya Romanovna has chosen him of her own free will. And if I was so abusive about him yesterday it was because I was filthily drunk and . . . mad besides; yes, mad, out of my mind; I had completely lost my senses . . . and today I am ashamed of it!' He blushed and said no more. Avdotya Romanovna had also coloured, but she did not break the silence. She had not uttered a word from the moment Luzhin was first spoken of.

Meanwhile Pulkheria Alexandrovna, without her support, was evidently in a state of indecision. At length, stumblingly, with her eyes fixed on her daughter, she explained that one thing was worrying her extremely.

'You see, Dmitri Prokofich,' she began . . . 'Shall I be quite frank with Dmitri Prokofich, Dunechka?'

'Of course, mama,' said Avdotya Romanovna seriously.

'This is how it is,' her mother hurried on, as if a weight had been lifted from her shoulders by this permission to communicate her trouble. 'Very early this morning we received a note from Peter Petrovich, in answer to ours yesterday informing him of our arrival. You see, yesterday he ought to have met us at the station, as he promised. Instead of that, he sent some sort of servant to meet us, give us the address of this hotel, and bring us here. Peter Petrovich had instructed him to tell us that he would come here himself this morning. Instead of that this note arrived from him ... The best thing would be for you to read it: here is the point that most worries me ... you will see at once what that point is and ... tell us your frank opinion, Dmitri Prokofich. You understand Rodya's character best; and are best able to advise us. I must warn you that Dunya made her mind up at once, but I don't yet know what to do and ... I waited for you.'

Razumikhin opened the note, which bore the previous day's date, and read the following:

'Dear Madam, Pulkheria Alexandrovna,

'I have the honour to inform you that, owing to difficulties which arose unexpectedly, I was unable to meet you on the platform, but sent for that purpose a very competent person. I must equally deprive myself of the honour of seeing you this morning, owing to pressing business in the Senate and in order not to impede the family reunion of yourself with your son and Avdotya Romanovna with her brother. I shall have the honour of calling upon you and paying my respects no later than tomorrow at exactly eight o'clock in the evening, and I venture to add my earnest and, I may say, imperative request that Rodion Romanovich shall not be present at our meeting, since he was atrociously and uncivilly offensive to me on the occasion of my visit to him yesterday on his bed of sickness, and besides I personally having to seek an essential and circumstantial explanation of a certain point with you, a matter of which I desire to know your interpretation. I have the honour hereby to give you previous notification that if, despite my request, I do meet Rodion Romanovich, I shall find myself obliged to withdraw immediately, and the consequences must be on your own head. I write this on the supposition that Rodion Romanovich, who appeared so ill at my visit, had completely recovered in the space of two hours, and that he may therefore be able to leave his abode and visit you. I am confirmed in this by the evidence of my own eyes, having seen him in the flat of a certain drunkard, who had been run over and was dying, to whose daughter, a notoriously ill-conducted female, he gave almost twenty-five roubles, on the pretext of funeral expenses, which surprised me greatly, knowing with what pains you had acquired this sum. In conclusion, I present my respectful compliments to Avdotya Romanovna and beg you to accept the assurance of the devoted esteem of

Your humble servant
P. Luzhin.'

'What am I to do now, Dmitri Prokofich?' said Pulkheria Alexandrovna, almost in tears. 'How can I suggest to Rodya that he should not come? Yesterday, he was so insistent that

Peter Petrovich should be dismissed, and now we are told that he himself is not to be received! And when he learns of it, he will come on purpose, and . . . what will happen then?'

'Do whatever Avdotya Romanovna has decided,' answered Razumikhin promptly and calmly.

'Oh dear! She says . . . God only knows what she says, and she will not explain why! She says it will be best, or rather not exactly best, but for some reason she thinks it is absolutely essential, for Rodya to make a point of coming here at eight o'clock, and for them to meet . . . But I didn't want to show him this letter at all, but to arrange some subterfuge with your help, so that he should not come . . . because he is so easily upset . . . And I don't understand at all who this drunkard was who died, or who this daughter is, or how he could give her the last of his money . . . which . . .'

'Which cost you so dear, mama,' added Avdotya Romanovna.

'He was not himself yesterday,' said Razumikhin thoughtfully. 'If you knew what he did in the restaurant, although it was clever enough . . . hm! Something was said about some dead man and some girl or other as we were walking home, but I didn't understand a word of it . . . However, yesterday I myself was . . .'

'Best of all, mama, let us go and see him, and then I am sure we shall see at once what to do. And besides it is quite time—good heavens, it's nearly eleven o'clock!' Dunya exclaimed, glancing at the magnificent gold and enamel watch which hung on a thin Venetian chain round her neck, and which was very much out of harmony with the rest of her attire. 'A present from her fiancé,' thought Razumikhin.

'Oh, it is time we went, quite time, Dunechka!' exclaimed Pulkheria Alexandrovna, with restless anxiety. 'He will think we are angry about yesterday, because we are so long in coming. Oh dear!'

She bustled about as she spoke, putting on her hat and cloak. Dunechka also put on her things. Her gloves were not only shabby, but worn into holes, as Razumikhin noticed, and yet the obvious poverty of their dress gave both ladies that look of special dignity which is always found in those who have the art of wearing poor clothes well. Razumikhin looked reverently at Dunechka and was proud to be her escort. 'That queen,' he thought, 'who mended her own stockings in prison, certainly looked a real queen at that moment, perhaps even more so than in her state appearances and triumphs.'

'Oh dear!' exclaimed Pulkheria Alexandrovna, 'I little thought I should dread a meeting with my own son, with my dear, darling Rodya, as I do now! . . . I dread it, Dmitri Prokofich!' she added, with a faint-hearted expression.

'Don't be afraid, mama,' said Dunya, kissing her. 'Rather

trust him. I do.'

'Oh dear! So do I, but I did not sleep all night!' cried the poor woman.

They went out.

'You know, Dunechka, when I got a little sleep, towards morning, I dreamt of the late Marfa Petrovna... She was all in white ... and she came up to me and took my hand, and shook her head severely, so severely, as though she were blaming me for something ... Does that forebode good or evil? Oh dear me, Dmitri Prokofich, you don't know yet: Marfa Petrovna is dead!'

'No, I didn't know. Who is Marfa Petrovna?'

'It was very sudden! Imagine...'

'Afterwards, mama,' put in Dunya. 'After all, he doesn't even know who Marfa Petrovna was.'

'Oh, don't you? I thought you knew all about it. You must forgive me, Dmitri Prokofich; I have completely lost my wits this last day or two. The fact is that I look on you as our special Providence, and so I am convinced that you know everything. I think of you as one of the family ... Don't be angry with me for saying so. Oh, good heavens! What is the matter with your right hand? Have you hurt it?'

'Yes, I have,' murmured the beatified Razumikhin.

'Sometimes I speak too directly from the heart, and Dunya criticizes me ... But, good God, what a cubby-hole he lives in! I wonder if he is awake yet. And that woman, his landlady, calls it a room! Listen! You say he doesn't like to show his feelings, so perhaps I shall annoy him with my ... weakness ... Won't you teach me to deal with him, Dmitri Prokofich? You know, I am completely at a loss.'

'Don't question him closely about anything if you see that he is frowning and, in particular, don't ask him many questions about his health; he doesn't like it.'

'Oh, Dmitri Prokofich, how hard it is to be a mother! But here are the stairs ... How horrible they are!'

'Mama, you are quite pale; calm yourself, darling,' said Dunya, putting her arm round her mother. 'He ought to be happy to see you, and yet you torment yourself so,' she added, with flashing eyes.

'Wait. I will go ahead and see if he is awake.'

The ladies quietly followed Razumikhin up the stairs, and when they came level with the landlady's door on the fourth floor, they saw that it was ajar and that two lively black eyes were watching them through the narrow opening from the dark interior. When their glances met, however, the door was suddenly slammed with such a noise that Pulkheria Alexandrovna almost cried out with fright.

## CHAPTER III

'HE is better, he is better!' called out Zosimov cheerfully, as they went in. He had arrived some ten minutes earlier, and was sitting in his old place on the end of the sofa. Raskolnikov sat at the opposite end, fully dressed and even carefully washed and combed, as he had not been for a long time. The room seemed to fill up at once, but Nastasya managed nevertheless to crowd in behind the visitors and settled herself to listen.

Raskolnikov really was almost well, especially in comparison with the previous day, but he was still very pale, abstracted, and gloomy. He looked like a man who has been wounded or suffered intense physical pain; his brows were knitted, his lips compressed, his eyes sunken. He spoke rarely and reluctantly, as if under compulsion or to fulfil an obligation, and there was a certain amount of restlessness in his movements.

He needed only a sling or a finger-stall to look exactly like a man with a poisoned finger or a painfully injured arm, or something of that nature.

Even his pale and gloomy countenance, however, lit up for a moment at the entrance of his mother and sister, but this served only to give him an expression of more intensely concentrated torment instead of the diffused anguish that had been there before. The light soon faded, but the torment remained, and Zosimov, watching and studying his patient with all the youthful zeal of the doctor who has only lately begun to practise, was surprised to see that when his family came in he showed not so much gladness as a weary, hidden determination to endure for an hour a new torture, which could not be avoided. He saw afterwards how almost every word of the conversation that followed seemed to touch some sore place in his patient and irritate it; at the same time he was surprised by the way in which yesterday's monomaniac, who had been goaded almost to raving madness by the smallest word, now managed to control himself and conceal his feelings.

'Yes, I myself can tell that I am almost well again,' said Raskolnikov, greeting his mother and sister with a kiss that made Pulkheria Alexandrovna radiant. 'And I don't say that as I said it yesterday,' he added as he turned to Razumikhin and warmly pressed his hand.

'I am really quite astonished at him today,' began Zosimov, who was very pleased to see the newcomers, since in ten minutes he had completely lost the thread of his conversation with his patient. 'In two or three days, if this continues, he will be just as he was, I mean as he was a month ago, or two . . . or perhaps even three. This, you see, has been coming on for a long time . . . hasn't it? Confess now that perhaps you were to blame,' he added with a cautious smile, as though he still feared to irritate his patient.

'Very likely,' answered Raskolnikov coldly.

'I am saying this,' continued Zosimov expansively, 'because your complete recovery now depends chiefly on yourself. Now that it is possible to talk to you, I should like to impress on you that it is essential to remove the original, so to speak, radical causes whose influence caused the inception of your unhealthy condition, and then you will be cured; if not, things will get even worse. I do not know what these fundamental causes were, but they must be known to you. You are intelligent and must certainly have kept yourself under observation. It seems to me that the beginning of your disorder coincided with your leaving the university. You cannot remain without occupation, and therefore hard work and a goal kept firmly before you would, I think, be of great help to you.'

'Yes, yes, you are quite right. I shall re-enter the university as soon as possible, and then everything . . . will run smoothly . . .'

Zosimov, who had begun dispensing this sage advice partly for its effect on the ladies, was naturally rather disconcerted when, at the end of his discourse, he looked at the person he had been addressing and saw a distinctly mocking expression on his face. However, this lasted only for a moment. Pulkheria Alexandrovna immediately began to express her thanks to him, especially for his visit to their hotel the previous night.

'What, did he go to see you during the night?' asked Raskolnikov, somewhat disturbed. 'So you didn't get any sleep after your journey?'

'Oh, Rodya, that all happened before two o'clock. Dunya and I never went to bed before two o'clock at home.'

'I don't know how to thank him either,' went on Raskolnikov, frowning and looking down. 'Setting aside the question of money—you will excuse me for mentioning it—' (turning to Zosimov) 'I do not even know how I have deserved such special attention from you. I simply can't understand it . . . and . . . and it distresses me not to understand; I am quite open with you.'

'Do not worry,' said Zosimov, with a forced laugh. 'Suppose yourself to be my first patient. We doctors who have just begun to practise love our first patients like our own children; some of us indeed almost fall in love with them. And you know I am not very rich in patients.'

'I say nothing about him,' added Raskolnikov, indicating Razumikhin, 'but he has had nothing from me, either, but insults and trouble.'

'What nonsense! You're in a very sentimental mood today, aren't you?' exclaimed Razumikhin.

If he had had more penetration he would have seen that it was very far from being a sentimental mood, but something like the very opposite. But Avdotya Romanovna noticed it. Her eyes followed her brother with anxious attention.

'Of you, mama, I dare not even speak,' he went on, as if it were a lesson he had been studying since morning. 'It is only today that I am able to form some idea of the torments you must have suffered yesterday, waiting for me to return.' So saying, he suddenly held out his hand to his sister, smiling. In that smile there gleamed this time a flash of genuine, unfeigned emotion. Dunya grasped his hand and pressed it warmly, with joy and gratitude. This was the first time he had made any overture to her since the previous day's disagreement. Their mother's face shone with pride and happiness at the sight of the silent but definite reconciliation between the brother and sister.

'Now that's what I absolutely love him for!' murmured Razumikhin, who was always prone to exaggeration, flinging himself round in his chair. 'He is always capable of such gestures! . . .'

'And how well everything becomes him,' thought his mother; 'what noble impulses he has, and how simply and delicately he resolved yesterday's difficulty with his sister, merely by holding out his hand at that moment with such a nice look . . . And what fine eyes he has, and how handsome he is! . . . He is even better-looking than Dunechka . . . But, oh dear, what clothes; how badly he is dressed! Vasya, the errand-boy in Afanasy Ivanovich's shop, is better dressed! . . . Oh, if only, if only I could spring to his side, put my arms round him, and . . . weep—but I am afraid, afraid . . . oh Lord, he is so . . . now, indeed, he speaks kindly, but I am afraid! But what am I afraid of? . . .'

'Oh, Rodya, you would not believe,' she hastened to reply to his last remark, 'how . . . unhappy Dunechka and I were yesterday! Now, when it is all over and done with, and we are all happy again—I can tell you about it. Imagine: we came running here, almost straight from the train, to take you in our arms, and the woman—oh, there she is! Good morning, Nastasya! . . . She broke it to us suddenly, that you were ill with delirium tremens and that in your fever you had just slipped away from the doctor, and out of the house, and that they were looking for you. You would not believe the effect this had on us. I remembered at once the tragic end of Lieutenant Potanchikov, whom we used to know, a friend of your father's—you will not remember him, Rodya—who also had delirium tremens, and who ran out of the house in just the same way, and fell into a well in the courtyard, and they could not recover his body until the next day. And of course we exaggerated things still more. We were on the point of hurrying away to find Peter Petrovich, so that with his help at least . . . because you know we were alone, quite alone,' she wailed pitifully, and then suddenly stopped short, remembering that it was rather dangerous to talk of Peter Petrovich, in spite of the fact that 'everybody was quite happy again'.

'Yes, yes . . . it was all of course . . . very trying . . .' muttered Raskolnikov in answer, but with so absent-minded and inattentive an air that Dunechka looked at him puzzled.

'What the deuce was it I wanted to say besides?' he continued, making an effort to remember. 'Oh, yes: please, mama, and you too, Dunechka, don't think I was unwilling to come to you this morning, but waited for you to come here first.'

'There is no need to say that, Rodya! . . .' cried Pulkheria Alexandrovna in surprise.

'Is he saying these things from a sense of duty, I wonder?' thought Dunechka. 'He is asking forgiveness and making friends again, as though it was part of his job, or as though he had got a lesson by heart.'

'I meant to come as soon as I woke up, but the state of my clothes delayed me; I forgot yesterday to tell her . . . Nastasya . . . to wash out the blood . . . I have only just got dressed.'

'Blood? What blood?' asked Pulkheria Alexandrovna, alarmed.

'It's just . . . don't worry. I got it because while I was wandering about yesterday—I was still a bit light-headed—I came into contact with a man who had been run over . . . a certain clerk . . .'

'Light-headed? But you remember everything,' interrupted Razumikhin.

'Yes, that's true,' answered Raskolnikov, rather uneasily. 'I remember everything, down to the smallest detail, and yet if you were to ask me why I did something, or went somewhere, or said something, I don't think I could give a clear explanation.'

'That is a very well-known phenomenon,' Zosimov joined in. 'Sometimes actions are performed very skilfully, most cleverly, but the aims of the actions, and their origin, are confused, and depend on various morbid influences. It is like a dream.'

'Perhaps it is a good thing that he supposes me to be more or less mad,' thought Raskolnikov.

'But something like that may perhaps take place with people who are quite well,' remarked Dunechka, with a worried look at Zosimov.

'A very true observation,' he answered. 'In that sense, indeed, all of us are very frequently more or less deranged, with the slight difference that the "sick" are a little more deranged than we, and therefore we must inevitably draw the distinction. But a completely harmonious person, it is true, is hardly to be found; in tens, or perhaps hundreds, of thousands you will meet with only one, and then not a very good specimen . . .'

The word 'deranged', carelessly let drop by Zosimov, growing eloquent on his favourite theme, caused foreheads to wrinkle anxiously. Raskolnikov, sitting abstractedly with a strange smile on his pale lips, seemed to pay no attention, but pursued his own train of thought.

'Well, what about this man who was run over? I interrupted you,' exclaimed Razumikhin hastily.

'What?' Raskolnikov roused himself. 'Yes . . . well, I got blood on me when I helped to carry him into the flat . . . By the way, mama, I did something unforgivable yesterday; I must really have been out of my senses. Yesterday I gave away all the money you sent me . . . to his wife . . . for the funeral. She is a widow now, a pathetic creature, consumptive . . . three hungry little orphans . . . in an empty house . . . and there is another daughter . . . Perhaps you would have given her the money yourself, if you had seen . . . But I had no right whatever to do so, I confess, especially as I knew how you had obtained the money. If you want to help people you must have the right, or else *"Crevez, chiens, si vous n'êtes pas contents!"*[5] He laughed. 'Is that right, Dunya?'

'No, it is not,' answered Dunya firmly.

'Bah! You too . . . have your own plans! . . .' he muttered, looking at her almost with hatred and with a mocking smile. 'I ought to have considered that . . . Well, it's praiseworthy; it is better for you . . . you come to a certain limit and if you do not overstep it, you will be unhappy, but if you do overstep it, perhaps you will be even more unhappy . . . However, this is all rubbish!' he added irritably, annoyed at having allowed himself to be diverted. 'I only wanted to say, that I ask your forgiveness, mama,' he finished harshly and abruptly.

'Don't go on, Rodya. I am sure that everything you do is right!' said his mother.

'Don't be too sure,' he answered, with a wry smile. A silence followed. There had been something strained alike in all this talk and the silence, the reconciliation, and the forgiveness, and everybody was conscious of it.

'It is as though they were afraid of me,' thought Raskolnikov, looking frowningly at his mother and sister. The longer Pulkheria Alexandrovna kept silent, indeed, the more timid she became.

The thought occurred to him that it was when they were absent that he really loved them.

'You know, Rodya, Marfa Petrovna is dead!' Pulkheria

5. "Die, dogs, if you are not happy."

Alexandrovna broke the silence.

'Who is Marfa Petrovna?'

'Good gracious! Marfa Petrovna Svidrigaylov! I wrote you a great deal about her.'

'Oh, I remember . . . So she is dead? Really?' said Raskolnikov, looking as if he had just started awake. 'Can she really be dead? What did she die of?'

'Just think, she had a stroke,' Pulkheria Alexandrovna hurried on, pleased at his interest, 'and exactly at the time when I was sending you my letter, in fact on the very same day! Imagine, that horrible man seems to have been the cause of her death as well! They say he beat her dreadfully!'

'Did they really live like that?' he asked, turning to his sister.

'No; quite the contrary, really. He was always very patient and very polite with her. There were many times when he was even too indulgent with her, during those seven years . . . Then suddenly he somehow lost patience.'

'So he's not so horrible after all, if he restrained himself for seven years? Apparently you stand up for him, Dunechka.'

'No, no, he's a horrible man! I can't imagine a worse,' answered Dunya, almost with a shudder. She frowned and relapsed into thought.

'It happened in the morning,' Pulkheria Alexandrovna hurried on. 'Immediately afterwards she ordered the carriage so as to drive into town after dinner, because she always drove into town when such things happened; they say she made a very good meal . . .'

'In spite of her beating?'

'. . . Well, that was always her . . . habit, and as soon as she had dined, she went for her bathe immediately, so as not to be late for the drive . . . You see, she was taking some sort of bathing cure; they have a cold spring there, and she bathed in it regularly every day. As soon as she entered the water she had a stroke!'

'I should think so!' said Zosimov.

'And he had beaten her severely?'

'Really that makes no difference,' replied Dunya.

'Hm! But, mama, why have you such a passion for trivial gossip?' said Raskolnikov, with sudden unexpected irritation.

'Oh, my dear, I really didn't know what to talk about,' burst out Pulkheria Alexandrovna.

'Are you all afraid of me, or something?' he asked with a twisted smile.

'Actually, that is true,' said Dunya, looking directly and severely at her brother. 'As she came upstairs, mama was so terrified that she was crossing herself.'

His face twitched convulsively.

'Oh, why did you say that, Dunya? Please don't be angry,

Rodya . . . How could you, Dunya?' said Pulkheria Alexandrovna in confusion. 'Here I was thinking, all the way in the
train, how we should see each other, and how we should tell
one another all about everything . . . and I was so happy, I
hardly noticed the journey. But what am I saying? I am happy
now, too . . . You shouldn't have said that, Dunya! It makes
me happy just to see you, Rodya . . .'

'Don't go on, mama!' he murmured in confusion, pressing
her hand without looking at her. 'There'll be plenty of time
for us to talk to our hearts' content!'

Then he faltered and turned pale; again that same terrible
feeling of deadly cold swept through him; again he realized
clearly and vividly that he had just uttered a dreadful lie, that
not only would it now never be given to him to talk himself out,
but that now he could never talk *at all*, to anybody. The
impact of this tormenting idea was so strong that for a moment
he completely lost himself, and he stood up and, without a
glance at anybody, made for the door.

'What are you doing?' exclaimed Razumikhin, seizing his
arm.

He sat down again and looked round; they were all looking
at him in wonder and perplexity.

'Why are you all so tiresome?' he exclaimed suddenly. 'Say
something! Don't just sit there! Well, say something! Let us
talk . . . Did we come together just to sit and say nothing? . . .
Say something or other!'

'Thank God! I thought we were going to have a repetition
of yesterday,' said Pulkheria Alexandrovna, crossing herself.

'What is the matter, Rodya?' asked Avdotya Romanovna
mistrustfully.

'Oh, nothing. I just remembered something,' he answered,
and laughed.

'Well, if that's all, it's all right! Otherwise I would have
thought . . .' murmured Zosimov, getting up. 'However, it is
time I went; I will look in again, perhaps . . . if I find you in . . .'

He made his bows and went out.

'What a nice man!' remarked Pulkheria Alexandrovna.

'Yes; nice, excellent, well-educated, intelligent . . .' said
Raskolnikov, talking with great rapidity and with a vivacity
he had not previously shown. 'I can't remember where I met
him, before my illness . . . But I did meet him somewhere,
I think . . . Here is another nice man,' and he nodded towards
Razumikhin. 'Do you like him, Dunya?' he asked with a
sudden inexplicable burst of laughter.

'Yes, very much,' answered Dunya.

'Oh, what a . . . swine you are!' said Razumikhin, blushing
and painfully embarrassed. He stood up. Pulkheria Alexan-

drovna smiled slightly and Raskolnikov roared with laughter.

'Where are you going?'

'I . . . I must go as well.'

'There is absolutely no need for you to go; stay here!' Zosimov has gone, so you must go. Well, don't . . . What time is it? Is it twelve yet? What a charming little watch you have, Dunya! But why are you all silent again? You are leaving me to do all the talking! . . .'

'It was a present from Marfa Petrovna,' answered Dunya.

'It was very expensive, too,' added Pulkheria Alexandrovna.

'Ah! . . . It is almost too big for a lady's watch.'

'I like them like that,' said Dunya.

'So it isn't a gift from her fiancé,' thought Razumikhin, feeling for some unknown reason very pleased.

'And I thought it was a present from Luzhin,' remarked Raskolnikov.

'No, he hasn't given Dunechka anything yet.'

'Ah! . . . Do you remember, mama, that I fell in love and wanted to get married?' he said, looking at his mother, who was struck by the strange manner and tone in which he spoke of it.

'Oh, my dear, yes!' Pulkheria Alexandrovna exchanged glances with Dunechka and Razumikhin.

'Hm! Yes! What can I tell you about her? I don't remember much. She was not very strong,' he went on, with his eyes again fixed on the ground, and absorbed, as it were, in his thoughts; 'she was always ailing; she liked to give to beggars; she was always dreaming of a convent, and once she burst into tears when she began to talk to me about it. Yes, yes . . . I remember . . . I remember very well. She was . . . very plain. I don't really know what attracted me to her; I think it may have been that she was always ill . . . If she had been lame as well, or hump-backed, I might very likely have loved her even more . . .' (He smiled thoughtfully.) 'It was simply . . . a sort of spring fever . . .'

'No, it wasn't only that,' said Dunya vigorously.

He looked at his sister with earnest attention, but seemed not to hear or perhaps not to understand her words. Then, with an air of profound melancholy, he rose, crossed to his mother, kissed her, and returned to his seat.

'You still love her,' said Pulkheria Alexandrovna, moved.

'Her? Still? Oh, yes . . . you are talking of her! No. That might all belong to another world . . . and it is a long time ago. Yes, and everything round me seems as if it were happening somewhere else . . .'

He peered at them.

'Even you . . . it is as if I were looking at you from a thousand miles away . . . But God only knows why we're talking about this. And why keep on asking questions?' he added irritably, and was silent, again deep in thought and biting his nails.

'What a dreadful room you have, Rodya, just like a coffin,' said Pulkheria Alexandrovna, breaking the oppressive silence. 'I'm sure it is responsible for at least half your depression.'

'Room?' said he absently. 'Yes, the room made a big contribution . . . I've thought of that too . . . But if you knew what a strange idea you have just expressed, mama!' he added abruptly, with a mysterious smile.

It wanted but a little more for the company of the family from whom he had been separated for three years, and the intimate tone of the talk combined with the impossibility of finding any subject at all of real conversation, to become absolutely unbearable. There was, however, one urgent matter that simply must be settled, one way or another, that day; he had made up his mind on that point when he woke up. Now he was glad to turn to it as a way of escape from the present difficulties.

'Listen, Dunya,' he began drily and seriously. 'Of course I beg your forgiveness for yesterday, but I think it my duty to remind you that I do not intend to give way on the main point. You must choose between me and Luzhin. I may be no good, but you ought not to do this. It must be one or the other. If you marry Luzhin I shall immediately cease to call you sister.'

'Rodya, Rodya! This really is yesterday all over again,' cried Pulkheria Alexandrovna, distressed. 'And why will you persist in saying you are no good? That I cannot bear. It was just the same yesterday . . .'

'Brother,' said Dunya firmly, and as drily as her brother, 'there is a mistake here on your part. I have been thinking about it since last night and trying to find the mistake. It is all bound up with the fact that you seem to suppose I am sacrificing myself for somebody. That is quite wrong. I am marrying simply for my own sake, because I find things difficult; of course I shall be pleased if I am able to be of some assistance to my family, but that is not the most important factor in my decision . . .'

'She is lying!' he thought, biting his nails in vicious anger. 'She is proud, and unwilling to admit that she wanted to be able to confer benefits on me. Pure arrogance! Oh, ignoble natures! Their love is like hate . . . Oh, how I . . . hate them all!'

'In short, I am marrying Peter Petrovich,' continued Dunechka, 'because it is the lesser of two evils. I am prepared to fulfil honourably all that he expects of me, and so I am not deceiving him . . . Why did you smile just now?'

She coloured and anger flashed from her eyes.

'You will fulfil everything?' he asked, smiling bitterly.

'Within certain limits. The manner and form of Peter Petrovich's proposal showed me at once what he required. Of course he values himself somewhat too highly, but I hope he values me as well . . . Why are you laughing again?'

'And why are you blushing again? You are lying, sister, you are lying deliberately, out of pure feminine obstinacy, just to get your own way in spite of me . . . You cannot have any respect for Luzhin; I have seen him and spoken to him. Therefore you are selling yourself for money, and so, in any case, you are acting basely, and I am glad that you can at any rate blush.'

'That isn't true; I am not lying!' cried Dunechka, losing all her composure. 'I am not going to marry him without the conviction that he will value and esteem me; I am not going to marry him without being sure that I can respect him. Fortunately I can convince myself of that with great certainty, and this very day. And such a marriage is not ignoble, as you call it! And if you were right, if I had really decided on a base action, would it not be pitiless cruelty on your part to talk to me as you have done? Why should you demand from me a heroism which, perhaps, you yourself are not capable of? That is tyranny, despotism! If I destroy anybody it will be myself and nobody else . . . I have not killed anybody! . . . Why are you looking at me like that? Why are you so pale? Rodya, what is the matter? Rodya, dear!'

'Oh dear, he is going to faint, and it is your fault!' cried Pulkheria Alexandrovna.

'No, no . . . rubbish . . . it's nothing! . . . My head felt a little dizzy. It's not a faint . . . You are obsessed with the idea of fainting! Hm! yes . . . what the deuce was I saying? . . . Yes: how do you propose to convince yourself today that you can respect him and that he . . . respects you, wasn't it? . . . as you said you would? I think you said today, or did I mishear you?'

'Mama, show my brother Peter Petrovich's letter,' said Dunechka.

Pulkheria Alexandrovna, with a trembling hand, gave him the letter. He took it curiously. Before opening it, however, he gave Dunya a look of sudden amazement.

'Very odd!' he said slowly, as if suddenly struck by a new idea. 'Why am I making so much fuss? Why all this clamour? You must marry whom you please!'

His words seemed to be meant for himself, but he spoke them aloud, and he continued to look at Dunya for some time, as if he were perplexed.

At last, still with the same expression of wonder, he opened the letter and began to read it slowly and carefully. He read it through twice. Pulkheria Alexandrovna was extremely agitated, and all of them expected something extraordinary.

'I find it very surprising,' he began, after some reflection, as he returned the letter to his mother; his words were not addressed to anyone in particular. 'He is a business man, a lawyer, and his conversation is even . . . pretentious, and yet his letter is really illiterate'.

There was a general stir; this was quite unexpected.

'Well, but they all write like that,' said Razumikhin abruptly.

'Have you read it?'

'Yes.'

'We showed it to him, Rodya, we . . . asked his advice just now,' began Pulkheria Alexandrovna, in some confusion.

'It is only the special legal style,' broke in Razumikhin. 'All legal documents are still written like that.'

'Legal? Yes, it is a legal or a business style . . . It is not perhaps very illiterate, but it is not highly literary; it is commercial!'

'Peter Petrovich does not try to conceal the fact that he has not had an expensive education; he is proud of being a self-made man,' remarked Avdotya Romanovna, rather hurt by her brother's new tone.

'Well, if he is, he has some reason to be; I don't deny it. You, sister, seem to be offended because all I got out of the letter was such a frivolous remark, and you think I talked about trivialities simply out of spite, to crow over you. On the contrary, there came into my mind, in connexion with the style, an idea that is quite vital in the present case. There is one very clear and significant expression there: "on your own head be it," and there is besides the threat of leaving immediately if I come. That threat of leaving is exactly the same as a threat of abandoning you both if you don't obey him, and that after bringing you to St. Petersburg. Well, do you think it is possible to take the same offence at such an expression from Luzhin as if he' (he gestured towards Razumikhin) 'had written it, or Zosimov, or any of us?'

'N-no,' answered Dunechka, more cheerfully. 'I knew quite well that it was too naïvely expressed, and that he is perhaps not a very accomplished writer . . . You were quite right, brother. I did not even expect . . .'

'It is expressed in legal language, and in legal language it must be written like that, but the result was blunter and coarser than he perhaps wished. However, I must disillusion you a little: there is another expression in that letter that is a libel on me, and a very mean one. Yesterday I gave some money to a widow, ill with consumption and crushed by misfortune, not "on the pretext of funeral expenses" but straightforwardly for the funeral; and I did not put it into the hands of the daughter, a girl, as he says, "of notorious character" (and whom

I saw yesterday for the first time in my life), but into those of the widow herself. In all this I see a too hasty desire to vilify me and make mischief between us. Again we have it legally expressed, that is, with too plain a disclosure of the object and with altogether naïve hastiness. He is an intelligent man, but intelligence alone is not nearly enough when it comes to acting wisely. It all gives us a picture of the man, and . . . I do not think that he values you highly. I tell you this solely for your own good, because I sincerely wish you well . . .'

Dunechka did not answer; her decision had already been made; she was only waiting for the evening.

'Then what have you decided, Rodya?' asked Pulkheria Alexandrovna, now even more worried than before by his sudden new *business-like* way of speaking.

'What do you mean: "decided"?'

'Well, Peter Petrovich writes that you must not be there and that he will go away . . . if you come. So . . . will you be there?'

'It is obviously not for me to decide but firstly for you, if you are not offended by Peter Petrovich's demand, and secondly for Dunya, if she also is not offended. I shall do what you think best,' he added drily.

'Dunechka has already decided, and I fully agree with her,' Pulkheria Alexandrovna hastened to say.

'I decided to request you, Rodya, to urge you, not to fail to be with us at this meeting,' said Dunya. 'Will you come?'

'Yes, I will come.'

'And I will ask you to come at eight o'clock as well,' she said, turning to Razumikhin. 'Mama, I am inviting him also.'

'Quite right, Dunechka. Well,' added Pulkheria Alexandrovna, 'let it be as you have decided. It is a relief to me too; I don't like lying and pretending; it will be better if we speak the truth honestly . . . Let Peter Petrovich be angry or not, just as he likes!'

## CHAPTER IV

AT that moment the door opened quickly, and a young woman came in and looked timidly round. They all turned towards her with surprise and curiosity. Raskolnikov did not recognize her at first. It was Sofya Semënovna Marmeladova. He had seen her for the first time on the previous day, but at such a time, in such circumstances, and in such a dress that what remained in his mind was a memory of an entirely different person. Today he saw a simply and even poorly dressed girl, still very young, hardly more than a child, with a modest and becoming manner and a bright but rather frightened face. She was wearing a very simple house-dress and an old and unfashionable hat; but she still carried a sunshade, as she had

done the day before. When she saw a room unexpectedly full
of people, her embarrassment was so great that she quite lost
her head and made a motion to withdraw.

'Oh . . . is that you?' said Raskolnikov in extreme astonishment, and himself became suddenly embarrassed.

It came at once into his mind that his mother and sister
already knew a little, from Luzhin's letter, of a girl of 'notorious' conduct. He had but just now been protesting against
Luzhin's libellous statement and asserting that he had seen
the girl only once, and now suddenly she herself had entered
the room. He remembered also that he had not made any
protest against the expression: 'notoriously ill-conducted'. All
these ideas flashed in a confused way through his brain. But
looking more closely at her he saw that this debased creature
was so humbled that he was filled with pity. When she seemed
about to run away in terror it was as if something turned over
inside him.

'I didn't expect you,' he said hastily, stopping her with a
look, 'Please sit down. I suppose you have come from Katerina
Ivanovna. Excuse me, not here; sit there . . .'

When Sonya came in, Razumikhin, who had been sitting on
a chair close to the door, stood up to let her pass. Raskolnikov
had at first meant to indicate to her the place at the end of the
sofa where Zosimov had sat, but recollecting that it was too
*familiar* a place, since the sofa served as his bed, hurriedly
pointed to Razumikhin's chair instead.

'And you sit here,' he said to Razumikhin, putting him in
Zosimov's place.

Sonya sat down, almost shaking with fright, and looked
timidly at the two ladies. It was plain that she herself did
not know how she could sit down in their presence. This
thought so terrified her that she sprang up again, and in the
greatest embarrassment addressed Raskolnikov.

'I . . . I . . . called for a moment; excuse me for disturbing
you,' she began, stammering. 'I have come from Katerina
Ivanovna; she had nobody to send . . . Katerina Ivanovna
wanted me to beg you most earnestly to come tomorrow morning to the funeral . . . after the mass . . . at the Mitropha-
nyevsky Cemetery, and afterwards at our . . . at her place . . .
for some refreshment . . . Please do her the honour . . . She told
me to ask you to come.'

Sonya stumbled and stopped speaking.

'I will certainly try . . . certainly,' answered Raskolnikov,
who had remained standing, and he too stumbled in his speech
so that he could not finish. 'Do please sit down,' he added
abruptly; 'I must speak to you. Please . . . perhaps you are in a
hurry . . . but be good enough to spare me two minutes . . .'

He moved a chair forward. Sonya sat down again and again

threw a quick, timid, embarrassed look at the ladies and again cast down her eyes.

Raskolnikov's pale face flushed; he shuddered violently and his eyes burned.

'Mama,' he said in a firm and insistent tone, 'this is Sofya Semënovna Marmeladova, the daughter of that unfortunate Mr. Marmeladov, whom I saw run over yesterday, and of whom I have already told you . . .'

Pulkheria Alexandrovna looked at Sonya with narrowed eyes. Although she was disconcerted by Rodya's challenging and insistent glance, she could not deny herself that satisfaction. Dunechka fixed her serious, perplexed gaze on the poor girl's face and watched her steadily. When she heard herself introduced Sonya seemed about to raise her eyes, but became even more embarrassed than before.

'I wanted to ask you,' said Raskolnikov, turning quickly to her, 'how things went with you today. I hope you were not disturbed . . . for example, by the police.'

'No, everything was all right . . . After all, the cause of death was all too clear; we were not worried; but now the lodgers are getting annoyed.'

'Why?'

'Because the body has been there a long time . . . of course the weather is very hot and there is a smell . . . so today, towards vesper time, it will be taken to the cemetery chapel, until tomorrow. At first Katerina Ivanovna did not want that, but now she sees herself that it is necessary . . .'

'Today, then?'

'She asks you to do us the honour of being at the church tomorrow for the funeral, and afterwards at her home for the dinner.'

'Is she arranging a dinner?'

'Yes, just something cold; she particularly wanted me to thank you for having helped us yesterday . . . without you we should have had nothing for the funeral.' Her lips and chin began to quiver, but she mastered her emotion and again sat with downcast eyes.

While they talked Raskolnikov had been watching her closely. She had a thin, a very thin, angular, and pale little face, with rather irregular features and a pointed little nose and chin. She could not have been called even pretty, but her blue eyes were so clear and bright, and, when they lighted up, her whole expression was so simple-hearted and good, that one was involuntarily charmed with her. Her face and her whole person had moreover one characteristic feature: in spite of her eighteen years she seemed almost a little girl still, much younger than her age, little more than a child, indeed, and sometimes there was something almost comically youthful about her movements.

'But surely Katerina Ivanovna could not contrive every-thing, and even plan a meal afterwards, on such a small sum?' asked Raskolnikov, obstinately prolonging the conversation.

'The coffin will be very simple . . . and everything will be simple, so it will not cost much . . . Katerina Ivanovna and I have reckoned it all out, and there will be enough left for us to honour his memory with some refreshment . . . and Katerina Ivanovna wants that very much . . . You can't . . . it is a comfort to her . . . she is like that, as you know . . .'

'I understand, I understand . . . of course . . . Why are you looking round my room? Mama here says it is like a coffin.'

'You gave us all you had yesterday!' she burst out in answer, in a fierce rapid whisper, and then fixed her eyes once more on the floor. Her lips and chin quivered again. She had been struck from the first by the poverty of Raskolnikov's surroundings, and now these words seemed to tear themselves from her of their own volition. A silence followed. Dunechka's eyes brightened, and even Pulkheria Alexandrovna looked kindly at Sonya.

'Rodya,' she said, getting up from her seat, 'we shall, of course, dine together. Come, Dunechka . . . You, Rodya, ought to go for a little walk, and then lie down and rest, and afterwards come to us as soon as you can . . . I am afraid we have tired you out . . .'

'Yes, yes, I will come,' he answered hastily, standing up. 'However, I have something to do . . .'

'But surely you don't intend to stay and dine by yourself?' cried Razumikhin, looking with astonishment at Raskolnikov. 'Why do you say that?'

'Yes, yes, I will come, of course, of course . . . But stay here a minute. You don't need him just now, do you, mama? I am not taking him away from you?'

'Oh no, no! But you will be kind enough to come to dinner, Dmitri Prokofich?'

'Please come,' requested Dunya.

Razumikhin, beaming, bowed his farewells. There followed a moment of sudden strange embarrassment.

'Good-bye, Rodya, or rather *au revoir*; I don't like saying "good-bye". Good-bye, Nastasya . . . oh, I've said it again!'

Pulkheria Alexandrovna meant to bow to Sonya as well, but somehow she did not manage it, and hurried from the room.

But Avdotya Romanovna waited, as it were, her turn, and, as she followed her mother past Sonya, made her a deep and courteous bow. Sonya, confused, bowed hastily with a startled air, and an almost painful feeling was reflected in her face, as if Avdotya Romanovna's politeness and attention were oppressive and even tormenting to her.

'Good-bye, Dunya!' cried Raskolnikov, from the entrance; 'give me your hand!'

'But I did, don't you remember?' answered Dunya, turning to him with awkward tenderness.

'Well, give it me again, then!'

And he squeezed her fingers tightly. Dunechka smiled at him, blushed, quickly withdrew her hand and, also radiantly happy, followed her mother.

'Well, this is splendid!' he said to Sonya, coming back into the room, and looking at her with an expression of serenity. 'Heaven rest the dead, but the living must live! Mustn't they, mustn't they? That is so, isn't it?'

Sonya looked in astonishment at the sudden brightening of his face. He watched her closely and in silence for some moments; in those moments all her father had told him about her passed through his mind . . .

'Oh dear, Dunechka!' said Pulkheria Alexandrovna, as soon as they reached the street, 'I am almost glad to have come away; it is somehow a relief. Well, could I ever have thought yesterday, in the train, that I should be glad for such a reason?'

'I tell you again, mama, that he is still ill. Can you not see it? Perhaps it was worrying on our account that first upset him. We must make allowances, and we can forgive many, many things . . .'

'You didn't make many allowances yourself!' broke in Pulkheria Alexandrovna hotly and jealously. 'You know, Dunya, I looked at the two of you, and you are the absolute image of him, not so much in face as in mind; you are both of a melancholic temper, both moody and hasty, both arrogant, both generous . . . I suppose it is not possible that he is an egoist, eh, Dunechka? . . . But when I think what is going to happen this evening, my heart quite fails me!'

'Don't worry, mama. What must be, will be.'

'But, Dunechka, only think of our situation now! What if Peter Petrovich withdraws?' incautiously said poor Pulkheria Alexandrovna.

'What will he be worth if he does?' answered Dunechka sharply and scornfully.

'We did right to come away now,' Pulkheria Alexandrovna hastily interrupted. 'He had something to do. It will be good for him to go out and get a breath of air . . . it's terribly close in his room . . . but where can one get fresh air here? Even in the streets it is like an unventilated room . . . Stop; move out of the way! You will be crushed; they are carrying something. Why, it is actually a pianoforte! How they push! . . . I am very much afraid of that girl, too . . .'

'What girl, mama?'

'You know, that Sofya Semënovna, who was there just now . . .'

'But why?'

'I have a presentiment, Dunya. Believe me or not, as soon as she came in, I instantly thought there was something there, something very important . . .'

'There is nothing there at all!' exclaimed Dunya, irritated. 'You and your presentiments, mama! He has only known her since yesterday, and when she came in now he didn't recognize her.'

'Well, you'll see! . . . She worries me. You'll see, you'll see! I was quite frightened: she looked at me, she looked at me with such eyes that I could hardly sit still, you remember, when he began to introduce her. It seems very odd to me: look at the way Peter Petrovich writes about her, and yet he introduced her to us, to you as well! So he must be interested in her!'

'It doesn't matter what he writes! People said things, and wrote them, about us as well; have you forgotten that? I am sure she is . . . nice, and that all that is . . . rubbish!'

'God grant it!'

'And Peter Petrovich is a wretched scandal-monger!' snapped Dunechka suddenly.

Pulkheria Alexandrovna winced, and the conversation dropped.

'This is what I want to say to you . . .' said Raskolnikov, taking Razumikhin over to the window.

'Then I will tell Katerina Ivanovna that you will come . . .' said Sonya hastily, preparing to leave.

'One moment, Sofya Semënovna; we have no secrets, you are not in the way . . . I should like another word with you . . . Well, now,' he broke off without finishing his sentence, and turned to Razumikhin. 'I think you know this . . . what's his name? . . . Porfiry Petrovich?'

'Naturally! He's a relative of mine. What is all this?' said Razumikhin, suddenly curious.

'Well, he is now in charge . . . of that case . . . about that murder . . . you were saying so yesterday . . . isn't he?'

'Yes . . . well?' Razumikhin was all agog.

'He was asking for the people who pawned things with her, and there are two pledges of mine there, not worth much, but they are my sister's ring, that she gave me as a keepsake when I came here, and my father's silver watch. They are only worth five or six roubles altogether, but I value them for their associations. Well, what ought I to do now? I don't want to lose them, especially the watch. Just now I was trembling for fear my mother should ask to see the watch, when we were talking about Dunechka's. It is the only thing we have left of my father's. It would make her ill if it were lost. Women! So tell me what to do. I know I shall have to report it to the police.[6] But wouldn't it be better to go to Porfiry himself? What do you think? Something must be done about it as soon as possible. Mama will ask about it before dinner, see if she doesn't!'

'Certainly not to the police, but definitely to Porfiry!' exclaimed Razumikhin, extraordinarily excited. 'Well, how pleased I am! Why are we waiting here? Let us go at once; it's only a step and he is sure to be in.'

'Very well . . . let us go . . .'

'He will be very, very, very pleased to meet you. I have told him a lot about you at different times . . . I was talking about you only yesterday. Come on! . . . So you knew the old woman? Precisely! . . . This has all turned out splen-did-ly! . . . Oh, yes . . . Sofya Ivanovna . . .'

'Sofya Semënovna,' Raskolnikov corrected him. 'Sofya Semënovna, this is my friend Razumikhin, and he's a very good chap . . .'

'If you have to go now . . .' began Sonya, still more embarrassed, and not looking at Razumikhin.

'Yes, we will go!' decided Raskolnikov. 'I will call on you later today. Only tell me, Sofya Semënovna, where do you live?'

He was not exactly confused, but he spoke as if he were in a hurry, and avoided her eyes. Sonya, blushing, gave him her address. They all went out together.

'Aren't you going to fasten the door?' asked Razumikhin, descending the steps behind them.

'I never do . . . Though I've been meaning to buy a lock for two years,' he added carelessly. 'They are fortunate people who have nothing to lock up, aren't they?' he said to Sonya, laughing.

They stopped in the gateway of the house.

'Do you go to the right, Sofya Semënovna? By the way, how did you find me?' he asked, but as if he really wished to say something quite different. He wanted to look into her clear, quiet eyes, but somehow seemed unable to do so.

'Why, you told Polechka the address yesterday!'

'Polya? Oh, yes . . . Polechka! That is . . . the little . . . that is your sister? So I gave her my address?'

'Have you forgotten?'

'No . . . I remember . . .'

'And I heard about you from my poor father that time . . . Only then I did not know your surname, and he didn't know it either . . . But when I got here today, since I got to know your name yesterday . . . I asked: where is there a Mr. Raskolnikov living here? . . . I didn't know that you were a lodger,

6. In the 1860's, Petersburg was divided into twelve police districts and thirty-eight precincts.

like me ... Good-bye ... I will tell Katerina Ivanovna ...'

She was terribly pleased to have got away at last; she hurried along with downcast eyes, to get out of their sight as soon as she could, to cover as quickly as possible those twenty paces before she could turn the corner and be alone at last, and walk rapidly along looking at nobody, noticing nothing, but thinking, remembering, re-creating every word that had been said and every circumstance of her visit. Never, never, had she felt anything like this. A whole new world rose indistinct and unexplored before her eyes. She remembered suddenly that Raskolnikov himself meant to call on her today, perhaps this morning, perhaps almost immediately.

'Only not today, please not today!' she murmured with a sinking heart, as if she were pleading with someone, like a frightened child. 'Oh, good heavens! He is coming to see me ... into that room ... he will see ... oh, heavens!'

Certainly she was in no state to notice at that moment a gentleman, unknown to her, who was assiduously following on her heels. He had accompanied her ever since she came out of the gate. When the three of them stopped to talk for a moment in the street, this passer-by, walking round them, had started as he unexpectedly caught Sonya's words: 'and I asked: where does Mr. Raskolnikov live?' He gave all three a quick but searching glance, especially Raskolnikov, whom Sonya was addressing; then he took note of the house. It was all done in a moment, as he passed by, and then, trying not to attract any attention, he went on, shortening his step as though expecting somebody. He was waiting for Sonya; he had seen that they were saying good-bye and that Sonya was going straight home.

'But where to? I have seen that face somewhere,' he thought. 'I must find out.'

When he came to the corner he crossed to the other side of the street, turned, and saw that Sonya was coming the same way, noticing nothing. When she reached the corner, she also turned into the street. He followed her along the opposite pavement, not taking his eyes off her; after some fifty yards he crossed again to Sonya's side of the street, caught her up, and followed five paces behind her.

He was a man of about fifty, rather tall, stout, with wide sloping shoulders that gave him a round-shouldered look. He was stylishly but comfortably dressed, and had the air of a great gentleman. He carried an elegant cane, with which he tapped the pavement at every step, and his gloves were newly cleaned. His broad face, with its high cheek-bones, was pleasant enough, and his complexion had a fresh colour that did not belong to St. Petersburg. His hair, which was very fair, was still thick, and had only the merest touch of grey in it; his thick, wide, spade-shaped beard was even lighter in colour than his hair. His blue eyes had a cold, watchful, considering look; his lips were very red. He was altogether remarkably well-preserved, and looked much younger than his years.

When Sonya reached the Canal they had the pavement to themselves. Watching her, he had noticed that she was thoughtful and abstracted. Sonya reached the house she lived in and turned in at the gate; he followed her, seeming rather surprised. In the courtyard, she turned to the right, towards the corner where her staircase was. 'Oh!' murmured the stranger, and began to ascend the steps behind her. It was only now that Sonya noticed him. She went up to the third floor, turned along the corridor, and rang at the door of Number 9, which bore the inscription in chalk: *Kapernaumov, Tailor*. 'Oh!' repeated the stranger, full of amazement at this strange coincidence, and rang at Number 8, next door. The doors were about five yards apart.

'You live at Kapernaumov's!' he said, looking at Sonya and laughing. 'He mended a waistcoat for me yesterday. I live here, next door to you, at Madam Gertrude Karlovna Resslich's. How strangely things turn out!'

Sonya looked attentively at him.

'We are neighbours,' he continued with a certain peculiar gaiety. 'I have been in the town only two days. Well, good-bye till we meet again.'

Sonya did not answer; the door opened and she slipped inside. She felt somehow ashamed and shy.

On the way to see Porfiry, Razumikhin was in a peculiarly excited state.

'This is splendid, my dear chap!' he repeated several times, 'and I am glad! I am glad!'

'But why are you glad?' wondered Raskolnikov to himself.

'I didn't know that you too had pawned things with the old woman. And . . . and . . . was this long ago? I mean, is it long since you were there?'

'What a naïve simpleton he is!'

'When? . . . .' Raskolnikov stopped, considering. 'I think I was there two or three days before her death. However, I am not going to redeem the things now,' he said hastily, with special solicitude for the things; 'why, I've only got one rouble in silver again . . . thanks to my cursed delirious state yesterday . . .'

He laid special stress on the last words.

'Oh, yes, yes, yes.' For some reason Razumikhin seemed in a hurry to agree with everything. 'So that is one reason why you were . . . so thunder-struck then . . . and you know, when you were delirious you kept talking about some rings and chains or other! . . . Yes, yes . . . It is clear, everything is clear now.'

'Listen to that! That idea must have taken firm root among

them. Why, this man here would go to the stake for me, and here he is, rejoicing because it is *cleared up* why I mentioned rings in my delirium! That must have confirmed the ideas they were all cherishing! . . .'

'Shall we find him in?' he asked aloud.

'Yes, we shall find him,' said Razumikhin. 'He's a splendid chap, brother, you will see! He's a little awkward. I don't mean that he's not well-bred; when I say he is awkward I mean it in another respect. He is an intelligent fellow, very intelligent, he's nobody's fool, but he is of a rather peculiar turn of mind . . . He is incredulous, sceptical, cynical. He likes to mislead people, or rather to baffle them . . . Well, it's an old and well-tried method . . . He knows his business, knows it very well . . . Last year he investigated and solved a case, another murder, where the scent was practically cold. He is very, very anxious to make your acquaintance!'

'But why should he be?'

'I don't mean in order to . . . You see, recently, since you fell ill, I have been driven to talking about you a great deal . . . Well, he listened . . . and when he heard you were studying law and that circumstances prevented you from finishing the course, he said it was a great pity. And I gathered . . . I mean from all this taken together, not just that one thing; yesterday Zametov . . . You know, Rodya, I talked a lot of nonsense yesterday, when I was drunk, as we walked home . . . and, my dear fellow, I am afraid you may have exaggerated it, you see . . .'

'What do you mean? That I'm supposed to be mad? Well, perhaps it's true.'

He gave a forced smile.

'Yes, yes . . . I mean, hang it, no! . . . Well, everything I said (about other things as well) was rubbish, and just because I was drunk.'

'Why apologize? I am so bored with the whole thing!' exclaimed Raskolnikov, with exaggerated irritation, which was, however, partly feigned.

'I know, I know, I understand. You may be sure I understand. I am ashamed even to speak of it . . .'

'In that case, don't!'

They were silent. Razumikhin's mood was one of wild excitement, and Raskolnikov recognized it with loathing. He was, besides, disturbed by what Razumikhin had just said about Porfiry.

'I shall have to make the most of my illness,'[7] he thought, with a pale face and a thumping heart, 'and as naturally as I

---

7. The original Russian says literally, "I shall have to sing like Lazarus to him." This colloquial expression meant "to beg for help," and it is linked with references to Lazarus elsewhere in the novel.

can. The most natural seeming thing would be not to call attention to it at all. To refrain by an obvious effort! No, an *effort* would be unnatural again . . . Well, we shall see . . . how things turn out . . . presently . . . Is it a good thing or not, that I have come? The moth flying into the candle of itself. My heart is thumping, and that is not a good thing! . . .'

'It's in this grey house,' said Razumikhin.

'The most important thing is, does Porfiry know or doesn't he, that I was in that old witch's flat yesterday . . . and asked about the blood? I must get to know that at the very outset; I must find out from his face, as soon as I go in; o-ther-wise . . . I'll find out, if it's the end of me!'

'Do you know,' he said, turning to Razumikhin with a mischievous smile, 'I have noticed today, my dear fellow, that you have been in a state of extraordinary excitement ever since this morning? Isn't that true?'

'Excitement? I am not in the least excited,' lied Razumikhin.

'No, my dear fellow, I'm right. It's quite noticeable. You were sitting on the edge of your chair, as I've never seen you do before, and twitching as if you had cramp. You kept jumping up for no reason at all. One minute you were angry, the next your ugly mug became as sweet as sugar-candy. You even blushed; you blushed especially red when you were invited to dinner.'

'No such thing! It's a lie! . . . What makes you talk like this?'

'And why are you squirming like a schoolboy? What the devil? You're blushing again!'

'What a beast you are, though!'

'What are you getting embarrassed about? Romeo! Just wait; I'll repeat this today, somewhere! Ha, ha, ha! It will amuse mama . . . and somebody else . . .'

'Listen, listen! Listen to me, this is serious! Really, this . . . what next? The devil!' wound up Razumikhin, full of confusion and cold with fright. 'What are you going to tell them? I, brother . . . Pah! What a cad you are!'

'Just like a June rose! And how well it becomes you, if you only knew. A Romeo six feet tall! And how carefully you have washed today; why, you even cleaned your nails, didn't you? When did that happen before? And as true as I'm alive, you've put pomade on your hair! Bend down!'

'You cad!'

Raskolnikov laughed so heartily that he seemed quite unable to control himself; thus they entered Porfiry Petrovich's flat in a gust of laughter. This was what Raskolnikov wanted; from inside they could be heard laughing as they came in, and still guffawing in the hall.

'Not one word here, or I'll . . . brain you!' whispered Razumikhin furiously, gripping Raskolnikov's shoulder.

## CHAPTER V

RASKOLNIKOV was already going in. He entered looking as if it cost him a great effort to prevent his laughter from bursting out again. Razumikhin, with a thoroughly disconcerted and savage mien, as red as a peony, stumbled shamefacedly after him, lanky and ungainly. His face and his whole appearance were really funny enough at that moment to justify Raskolnikov's laughter. Without waiting to be introduced, Raskolnikov bowed to their host, who was standing in the middle of the room looking inquiringly at them, and shook hands with him, still obviously struggling violently to subdue his hilarity sufficiently to get out a word or two introducing himself. But hardly had he succeeded in regaining a straight face than he glanced again, as if involuntarily, at Razumikhin, and broke down once more: the smothered laughter burst out all the more uncontrollably for the powerful restraint he had put on it before. The extraordinary fury with which Razumikhin met this hearty-seeming laughter lent the whole scene an air of unaffected merriment and, what was more important, naturalness. As if on purpose, Razumikhin added still more to the effect.

'Damn it all!' he roared, waving his arm and bringing down with a crash and a jingle a small round table on which stood a glass of tea.

'Why wreck the furniture, gentlemen? You are damaging Government property,' cried Porfiry Petrovich cheerfully.

This, then, was the scene: Raskolnikov stood there still holding his host's hand, still laughing, but conscious of having gone far enough and waiting for the right moment to stop naturally. Razumikhin, his confusion completed by the fall of the table and the breaking of the tumbler, looked gloomily at the fragments, spat, turned abruptly to the window and stood looking out but seeing nothing, with his back to the room and a terrible scowl on his face. Porfiry Petrovich was laughing, and seemed willing to go on laughing, but it was plain that some explanation must be given to him. On a chair in the corner Zametov had been sitting. He had risen when the visitors entered, and now waited, with his lips stretched into a smile but with perplexity and even incredulity in his eyes as he watched the scene, looking at Raskolnikov in particular with something like bewilderment. His unexpected presence affected Raskolnikov unpleasantly.

'I shall have to take that into consideration, too,' he thought.

'Please excuse me,' he began, with forced embarrassment. 'Raskolnikov . . .'

'Not at all. I am pleased to see you, and your entrance was pleasing too . . . Well, isn't he going to say "Good morning"?'

said Porfiry Petrovich, with a gesture of his hand towards Razumikhin.

'I really haven't the least idea why he's so furious with me. I only said, as we were coming here, that he was like Romeo, and . . . proved it, and that was all, I think.'

'He must have a very serious reason for getting so angry over a word,' laughed Porfiry.

'There speaks the detective! . . . The devil take the lot of you!' snapped Razumikhin, and then, beginning to laugh himself, with a suddenly cheerful face, went up to Porfiry Petrovich.

'Enough of this! We're all fools. To business! My friend here, Rodion Romanovich Raskolnikov, of whom you have heard, in the first place wants to make your acquaintance, and in the second place has a small piece of business to do with you. Hullo! Zametov! How do you come to be here? Do you know each other? Have you been acquainted long?'

'This is something new!' thought Raskolnikov anxiously.

Zametov seemed a little disconcerted, but not extremely so.

'We met yesterday at your place,' he said easily.

'That means Heaven has spared me the trouble; last week, Porfiry, he was pestering me to give him an introduction to you, and now you have managed it between you without me . . . Where do you keep your tobacco?'

Porfiry Petrovich was informally dressed, in a dressing-gown and slippers trodden down at the heel; his linen was spotless. He was a man of about thirty-five, rather short and stout, and somewhat paunchy. He was clean-shaven, and the hair was cropped close on his large round head, which bulged out at the back almost as if it were swollen. His fat, round, rather snub-nosed, dark-skinned face had an unhealthy yellowish pallor, and a cheerful, slightly mocking expression. It would have seemed good-natured were it not for the expression of the eyes, which had a watery, glassy gleam under lids with nearly white eyelashes, which twitched almost as though he were continually winking. The glance of those eyes was strangely out of keeping with his squat figure, almost like a peasant-woman's, and made him seem more to be reckoned with than might have been expected at first sight.

As soon as he heard that his visitor had a 'small piece of business' to do, Porfiry Petrovich invited him to sit on the sofa, installed himself on the other end, and fixed his eyes on him with an air of expecting a speedy exposition of the matter, and that kind of concentrated and almost too serious attention that we find so disconcerting and overwhelming, especially from a new acquaintance, and particularly when the subject we are expounding is, in our own eyes, utterly out of proportion with the extraordinarily weighty consideration it receives. Raskolnikov, however, explained his business shortly and coherently, in clear and exact terms, and felt pleased that he had succeeded fairly well in keeping his eyes on Porfiry. Porfiry Petrovich did not once take his own eyes from his guest. Razumikhin, sitting at the opposite side of the table, followed with restless impatience, constantly turning his eyes from one to the other and back again, which all looked a little silly.

Raskolnikov silently cursed him for a fool.

'You ought to make a statement to the police,' said Porfiry, looking very business-like, 'to the effect that, having learnt of a certain occurrence—of this murder, that is—you desire in your turn to inform the examining magistrate in charge of the investigation that such-and-such things belong to you and that you wish to redeem them . . . or words to that effect . . . but they will write it for you.'

'The fact is that at the present time . . .' began Raskolnikov, trying to seem as embarrassed as possible, 'I am not exactly in funds . . . and even such a trifling sum is not possible for me . . . You see, I should merely like to report now that the things are mine, and that when I have the money . . .'

'That doesn't matter,' answered Porfiry Petrovich, receiving these financial explanations with some coldness; 'if, however, you prefer it, you may write direct to me, to the same effect; that is, having learnt of so-and-so, and offering the information that certain things are yours, you request . . .'

'Can this be done on unstamped paper?' hastily interrupted Raskolnikov, once more interesting himself in the financial side of the matter.

'Oh, yes. Stamped paper is not necessary at all!' Suddenly, with an openly mocking expression, he screwed up his eyes as if he were winking. Perhaps, however, this was only Raskolnikov's imagination, for it lasted only for a moment. At any rate there had been something, and Raskolnikov could have sworn he had been winked at, God alone knew why.

'He knows!' flashed through his brain like lightning.

'Excuse me for troubling you with such trifles,' he went on, a little disconcerted; 'my things aren't worth more than five roubles altogether, but they are especially dear to me for the sake of the people from whom I had them, and I confess I was very much afraid, when I heard . . .'

'Yes, you positively flew up in the air yesterday, when I let out to Zosimov that Porfiry was questioning the people who had pawned things!' agreed Razumikhin with evident purpose.

This was unendurable. Raskolnikov could not restrain himself from turning on him a flashing glance from black eyes burning with rage. But he immediately recollected himself.

'You are laughing at me, my dear fellow, aren't you?' he said, with artfully contrived irritation. 'I confess that I am perhaps too concerned with what you think is rubbish; but I ought not to be considered selfish—or greedy on that account, and in my eyes those two trifling trinkets may be anything but rubbish. I told you just now that that almost worthless silver watch was the only thing left of my father's. You may laugh at me, but my mother has come to see me'—he turned abruptly to Porfiry—'and if she knew'—here he turned quickly back to Razumikhin, trying hard to make his voice tremble—'that that watch was lost, she would be in despair! Women!'

'But really, that's not so! I didn't mean that at all! Quite the contrary,' exclaimed Razumikhin indignantly.

'Have I done well? Did it seem natural? Wasn't it too exaggerated?' Raskolnikov asked himself anxiously. 'Why did I say "women" like that?'

'So your mother has come to see you?' inquired Porfiry Petrovich for some reason.

'Yes.'

'When was this?'

'Yesterday evening.'

Porfiry was silent, as if considering.

'Your things could not possibly be lost in any event,' he went on coldly and quietly. 'Indeed, I had been expecting you here for some time.'

And as though he had said nothing out of the ordinary, he busied himself with procuring an ash-tray for Razumikhin, who was mercilessly scattering cigarette-ash on the carpet. Raskolnikov started, but Porfiry, still concerned over Razumikhin's cigarette, did not appear to see him.

'Wha-at? Expecting him? Do you mean to say you knew he had pawned things *there*?' exclaimed Razumikhin.

Porfiry Petrovich turned back to Raskolnikov.

'Both of your things, the watch and the ring, were in *her* room, wrapped in a piece of paper with your name clearly written on it in pencil, together with the dates on which she had them from you . . .'

'How do you come to be so observant?' began Raskolnikov with an awkward laugh, trying hard to look him straight in the eye; he could not refrain from adding:

'I made that remark just now because there must have been so many people who pawned things . . . that it would be difficult for you to remember them all . . . But you, on the contrary, seem to remember them all so clearly, and . . . and . . .'

'Stupidity! Weakness! Why did I say that?'

'But almost all of them are known now, and in fact you were the only one who had not come to us,' answered Porfiry, with a barely perceptible shade of mockery.

'I have not been very well.'

'I had heard so. I had even heard that something had

seriously upset you. You are rather pale even now.'

'Not at all . . . on the contrary, I am quite well!' broke in Raskolnikov rudely and angrily. His sudden change of tone came from the bad temper seething uncontrollably within him. 'If I speak in anger I shall give myself away,' flashed again through his mind. 'But why do they torment me? . . .'

'Not very well!' interposed Razumikhin; 'what an understatement! Until yesterday he was practically raving . . . Would you credit it, Porfiry, he was barely on his feet again, and as soon as Zosimov and I turned our backs yesterday, he got dressed, slipped away secretly, and went running about the streets till almost midnight? And all this, I tell you, in absolute delirium! Imagine it! A most extraordinary thing!'

'Really, *in absolute delirium*? Please tell me about it,' said Porfiry, shaking his head like a peasant-woman.

'Rubbish! Don't believe him! However, you don't need me to tell you; you don't believe him anyway,' burst out Raskolnikov with excessive rage. But Porfiry Petrovich did not appear to hear these strange words.

'How could you have gone out, unless you were delirious?' asked Razumikhin, suddenly growing heated. 'Why did you go out? What for? . . . And why do it by stealth? Had you any sane idea in your head? Now that all danger is past, I can speak straight out.'

'They got on my nerves yesterday,' said Raskolnikov, turning to Porfiry with an impudently provocative smile, 'and I ran away from them to take rooms where they would not find me; I took a lot of money with me. Mr. Zametov there saw it. What do you say, Mr. Zametov, was I in my right mind or not, yesterday? Settle the argument for us.'

At that moment he would have liked to strangle Zametov; he could not bear the way he sat there in silence and looked at him.

'In my opinion, you talked very sensibly, even cleverly, only you were too irritable,' declared Zametov drily.

'Nikodim Fomich was telling me today,' put in Porfiry Petrovich, 'that he met you very late last night at the home of a clerk who had been run over . . .'

'Well, just take that clerk now!' Razumikhin took him up. 'Weren't you out of your mind there? Giving the widow every penny you had for the funeral! Well, if you wanted to help—you might have given them fifteen or even twenty roubles, so long as you left yourself at any rate three or so, but you simply flung away the whole twenty-five!'

'Perhaps I have found a treasure somewhere, that you know nothing about. Yesterday I felt generous . . . Mr. Zametov knows I found a treasure! . . . Be good enough to excuse us,' he added, turning with trembling lips to Porfiry, 'for taking up half an hour of your time with such wrangling over trifles. It must be very boring for you.'

'Not at all, sir! On the contrary, on the co-ontrary! If only you knew how you interest me! It is interesting both to see and to hear . . . and I admit I am very glad you have at last brought yourself to come and see me . . .'

'What about some tea? My throat is dry!' cried Razumikhin.

'An excellent idea! Perhaps everybody will join us? And wouldn't you like . . . something a little stronger first?'

'Off with you!'

Porfiry Petrovich went out to order tea.

Raskolnikov's thoughts were whirling like a tornado. He felt exasperated.

'What is most significant is that they don't even attempt concealment; there is no standing on ceremony! How did you come to talk about me to Nikodim Fomich, if you knew nothing of me? It comes to this, they don't even want to hide that they are after me like a pack of hounds! They spit in my face quite openly!' He was trembling with fury. 'Well, go straight to the point, don't play with me like a cat with a mouse! That is really uncivilized, Porfiry Petrovich, and perhaps I won't put up with it any longer . . . I will stand up and blurt out the whole truth in your faces; you shall see how I despise you! . . .' He was breathing with difficulty. 'But what if it is all my imagination? What if it is a delusion, what if I am quite mistaken, and it is simply my inexperience that makes me lose my temper and fail to keep up this wretched role I am playing? Perhaps it was all unintentional? All their words are quite ordinary, but there is something in them . . . All of them might be said at any time, but still there is something. Why did he say so directly "in *her* room"? Why did Zametov add that I talked *cleverly*? Why do they take the tone they do? Yes . . . the tone . . . Razumikhin just sat there; why didn't he notice anything? That innocent booby never does notice anything. I'm feverish again! . . . Did Porfiry wink at me, or not? What nonsense; why should he wink? Are they trying to work on my nerves, I wonder, or are they just laughing at me? Either it's all a delusion, or they *know*! . . . Even Zametov is insolent . . . or isn't he? He has thought things over since last night. I thought he would! He is at home here, and yet it is his first visit. Porfiry doesn't think of him as a visitor; he sits with his back to him. They're as thick as two thieves, and undoubtedly *because of me*! I am certain they were talking of me before we arrived! . . . Do they know about that flat? I wish they would get on with things! . . . When I said I had run away to take a flat, he let it pass, he didn't take me up. But it was clever of me to bring in that about the flat; it will be useful later on . . . In delirium? says he . . . Ha, ha, ha. He knows everything about yesterday evening! But he didn't know my mother had come! . . . And that old hag had written down the date with her pencil! . . . Oh no! I shall not give myself away! Really, you have no facts yet, all this is only supposition! No, produce some facts! Even the flat is not evidence, but delirium; I know what to tell them . . . Do they know about the flat? I shan't go away without finding out! Why did I come? But I am getting agitated, and that, perhaps, *is* evidence! Pah, how easily I get upset! But perhaps that's a good thing: I am playing a sick man . . . He is sounding me out. He will get me muddled. Why did I come?'

The thoughts went racing through his head.

It was only a few moments before Porfiry Petrovich returned. He seemed to have grown suddenly cheerful.

'Since your party yesterday, my dear chap, my head . . . In fact I hardly know whether I'm standing on it or my heels,' he began in a quite different tone, smiling at Razumikhin.

'Well, did you find it interesting? I had to leave you at the most interesting point, didn't I? Who won?'

'Nobody, of course. We had arrived at discussing the eternal verities, and we were just floating round in the clouds.'

'Imagine, Rodya, what we were discussing yesterday: is there or is there not such a thing as crime? I told you we were talking damned nonsense.'

'What is there surprising in that? It's an ordinary social question,' answered Raskolnikov absently.

'The question was not put like that,' answered Porfiry.

'Not quite like that, it's true,' agreed Razumikhin at once, beginning to hurry and grow excited, as usual. 'Look, Rodion: listen and tell us your opinion. I want you to. Yesterday I had done my very best with them, and I was waiting for you to turn up; I had told them you were coming . . . It began with the Socialists' view.[8] You know what that is: crime is a protest against the unnatural structure of society—and only that, nothing more, and no other causes are admissible—and that's all! . . .'

'That's not true,' cried Porfiry Petrovich. He was growing visibly more animated, and he kept laughing as he looked at Razumikhin, making him grow still hotter.

'N-nothing else is admitted!' interrupted Razumikhin hotly; 'it is perfectly true! I will show you some of their little books: they explain everything by the "deleterious influence of the environment"—and that's all! Their favourite cliché . . . From that it follows that if society is properly organized, all

---

8. Razumikhin is summarizing the views of French Utopian socialists, especially those of Fourier (1808–93), who proposed "phalansteries" as communal living quarters. Robert Owen (1771–1858) in his *New Views of Society* and Chernyshevsky in *What Is to Be Done?* expressed views on crime similar to those attacked by Razumikhin. The "little books" which he refers to below were pamphlets by Neklyudov.

crimes will instantly disappear, since there will be nothing to protest against, and everybody will immediately become law-abiding. Nature is not taken into account, nature is banished, nature is not supposed to exist! In their philosophy, it is not humanity, following the path of historical, *living*, development to the end, that will finally evolve into the perfect society, but, on the contrary, a social system, devised by some mathematician's brain, will instantly reorganize humanity, make it righteous and innocent in a flash, with greater speed than any living process, and without the aid of living historical development! That is why they are instinctively hostile to history: "there is nothing in it but infamy and stupidity"—and their explanation of everything is simply stupidity alone. That is why they do not like the living process of life: they have no use for the *living soul*. The living soul demands life, the living soul will not submit to mechanism, the living soul must be regarded with suspicion, the living soul is reactionary! But their social system, although it smells of carrion, can be made from india-rubber—and it will be nicely slavish, it will have no will, it will not be alive, it will never rebel! And the result of it all is that their whole effort is directed to nothing but bricklaying and the arrangement of rooms and corridors in a phalanstery. The phalanstery is ready, but nature is not ready for a phalanstery; it wants life; the living process is not yet fulfilled; it is too early for the churchyard. You cannot divert the course of nature by logic alone! Logic can anticipate three possibilities, but there are millions of them! Cut out all the millions and you bring it all down to the question of comfort! A very easy solution of the problem! It is temptingly clear-cut, and there is no need to think! That is the main point—you needn't think. The whole mystery of life can be put on two sheets of printed paper!'

'There's an outburst for you, a regular drum-roll! We must hold him down,' laughed Porfiry. 'Just imagine,' he added, addressing Raskolnikov, 'it was like this yesterday evening, only there were six voices all going in one room, and everybody was fuddled with punch—can you picture it? No, brother, you are mistaken: "environment" means a great deal in crime, I assure you.'

'I know that, but tell me this: a man of forty assaults a ten-year-old girl—was it his environment that made him do it?'

'Well, perhaps it was, strictly speaking,' remarked Porfiry with astonishing authority; 'a crime against a little girl may very well be explained by "environment".'

Razumikhin was all but foaming at the mouth.

'Listen, would you like me to deduce for you this minute,' he shouted, 'that you have white eyelashes simply because the great tower of Ivan the Great is two hundred and fifty feet high, and reason it out clearly, accurately, progressively and even with a shade of liberalism? I will do it! Would you like to bet I can't?'

'Done! Let us listen to his deduction!'

'Damn it all, he's a complete hypocrite!' cried Razumikhin, jumping up and waving his arms. 'It's not worth while talking to you! Of course, he's doing all this on purpose; you don't know him yet, Rodion! Yesterday he took their part as well, just so as to make fools of everybody. And good Lord, the things he said yesterday! And they were delighted with him! ... He's quite capable of keeping this up for a couple of weeks. Last year, for some reason, he assured us he was going into a monastery: he persisted in it for two months! Not long ago he took it into his head to announce that he was getting married, and that everything was ready for the wedding. He even got new clothes, and we were all congratulating him. He hadn't got a fiancée or anything else; it was all a fraud!'

'There you're wrong again! I had got the new clothes before. It was because of the new clothes that I thought of fooling you all.'

'Are you really so fond of mystification?' asked Raskolnikov carelessly.

'Don't you think I am? Just wait, I will take you in too—ha, ha, ha! No, do you see, I will tell you the whole truth. Apropos of all these questions—crimes, environments, little girls—I have just remembered—(but it always interested me) an article of yours: 'Concerning Crime' . . . or some such title, I forget; I don't remember. I had the pleasure of reading it two months ago in *Periodical Discourses*.'

'My article? In *Periodical Discourses*?' asked Raskolnikov, mystified. 'I certainly wrote an article six months ago, when I left the university, in connexion with some book, but I sent it to *Weekly Discourses*, not *Periodical Discourses*.'

'It came out in *Periodical Discourses*.'

'Of course, *Weekly Discourses* has ceased to exist, that is why they did not print it at the time . . .'

'That is true; but when it ceased publication, *Weekly Discourses* was merged with *Periodical Discourses*, and so your article appeared there two months ago. Didn't you know?'

Raskolnikov had indeed known nothing about it.

'Good gracious, but you can ask them to pay you for your article! But what an odd character you are! You live so isolated that you don't know even things like this, that directly concern you. It is a fact, though.'

'Bravo, Rodka! I didn't know either!' exclaimed Razumikhin. 'I shall hurry to the reading-room this very day and ask for the number. Two months ago? What was the date? It doesn't matter, I can find out. Here's a fine trick! Fancy saying nothing about it!'

'But how did you get to know the article was by me? It was signed with an initial.'

'Quite by chance, only a few days ago. Through the editor; I know him . . . I was very interested.'

'I surveyed, I remember, the psychological condition of the criminal throughout the commission of the crime.'

'Yes, and you insist that the act of committing a crime is always accompanied by some morbid condition. Very, very original, but . . . it was not that part of your article that specially interested me, but a certain idea, put forward towards the end, which you unfortunately do not elucidate, but merely refer to in passing . . . In a word, you introduce, if you remember, a hint to the effect that there are persons who are able, or rather, not who are able but who have every right, to commit any wrong or crime, and that laws, so to say, are not made for them.'

Raskolnikov smiled at this forced and deliberate perversion of his idea.

'What? What is this? A right to commit crime? But I suppose not because of "unfavourable environment"?' inquired Razumikhin, with something approaching alarm.

'No, no, not altogether because of it,' answered Porfiry. 'The point is that in his article people are divided into two classes, the "ordinary" and the "extraordinary". The ordinary ones must live in submission and have no right to transgress the laws, because, you see, they are ordinary. And the extraordinary have the right to commit any crime and break every kind of law just because they are extraordinary. I think that is what you say, if I am not mistaken?'

'How can it be? He can't possibly have said that!' muttered the puzzled Razumikhin.

Raskolnikov smiled again. He had at once grasped what they were driving at, and what they wished to push him into saying. He could remember his article; he decided to accept the challenge.

'That is not quite what I say,' he began simply and modestly. 'I admit, however, that you have given an almost correct exposition of it, or even, if you like, a completely faithful one . . .' (He found it almost pleasurable to agree that the account was quite faithful.) 'The only difference is that I do not in the least insist that the extraordinary people are absolutely bound and obliged to commit offences on any and every occasion, as you say I do. I hardly think any such article would have been allowed to be published. I simply intimate that the "extraordinary" man has the right . . . I don't mean a formal, official right, but he has the right in himself, to permit his conscience to overstep . . . certain obstacles, but only in the event that his ideas (which may sometimes be salutary for all mankind) require it for their fulfilment. You are pleased to say that my article is not clear; I am ready to elucidate it for you, as far as possible. Perhaps I am not mistaken in supposing that is what you want. Well, then. In my opinion, if the discoveries of Kepler and Newton, by some combination of circumstances, could not have become known to the world in any other way than by sacrificing the lives of one, or ten, or a hundred or more people, who might have hampered or in some way been obstacles in the path of those discoveries, then Newton would have had the right, or might even have been under an obligation . . . to *remove* those ten or a hundred people, so that his discoveries might be revealed to all mankind. It does not follow from this, of course, that Newton had the right to kill any Tom, Dick, or Harry he fancied, or go out stealing from market-stalls every day. I remember further that in my article I developed the idea that all the . . . well, for example, the law-givers and regulators of human society, beginning with the most ancient, and going on to Lycurgus, Solon, Mahomet, Napoleon and so on, were without exception transgressors,[9] by the very fact that in making a new law they *ipso facto* broke an old one, handed down from their fathers and held sacred by society; and, of course, they did not stop short of shedding blood, provided only that the blood (however innocent and however heroically shed in defence of the ancient law) was shed to their advantage. It is remarkable that the greater part of these benefactors and law-givers of humanity were particularly blood-thirsty. In a word, I deduce that all of them, not only the great ones, but also those who diverge ever so slightly from the beaten track, those, that is, who are just barely capable of saying something new, must, by their nature, inevitably be criminals—in a greater or less degree, naturally. Otherwise they would find it too hard to leave their rut, and they cannot, of course, consent to remain in the rut, again by the very fact of their nature; and in my opinion they ought not to consent. In short, you see that up to this point there is nothing specially new here. It has all been printed, and read, a thousand times before. As for my division of people into ordinary and extraordinary, that I agree was a little arbitrary, but I do not insist on exact figures. Only I do believe in the main principle of my idea. That consists in people being, by the law of nature, divided *in general* into two categories: into a lower (of ordinary people), that is, into material serving only for the reproduction

9. Raskolnikov's views are similar to those expressed by Napoleon III in his book *Life of Julius Caesar*. The newspaper *Golos (Voice)* had recently summarized the English *Saturday Review*'s analysis of Napoleon's ideas about the right of exceptional individuals (such as Lycurgus, Mahomet, and Napoleon I) to transgress laws and even to shed blood. The book appeared in Paris in March 1865; the Russian translation in April!

of its own kind, and into people properly speaking, that is, those who have the gift or talent of saying *something new* in their sphere. There are endless subdivisions, of course, but the distinctive characteristics of the two categories are fairly well marked: the first group, that is the material, are, generally speaking, by nature staid and conservative, they live in obedience and like it. In my opinion they ought to obey because that is their destiny, and there is nothing at all degrading to them in it. The second group are all law-breakers and transgressors, or are inclined that way, in the measure of their capacities. The aims of these people are, of course, relative and very diverse; for the most part they require, in widely different contexts, the destruction of what exists in the name of better things. But if it is necessary for one of them, for the fulfilment of his ideas, to march over corpses, or wade through blood, then in my opinion he may in all conscience authorize himself to wade through blood—in proportion, however, to his idea and the degree of its importance—mark that. It is in that sense only that I speak in my article of their right to commit crime. (You will remember that we really began with the question of legality.) There is, however, not much cause for alarm: the masses hardly ever recognize this right of theirs, and behead or hang them (more or less), and in this way, quite properly, fulfil their conservative function, although in following generations these same masses put their former victims on a pedestal and worship them (more or less). The first category are always the masters of the present, but the second are the lords of the future. The first preserve the world and increase and multiply; the second move the world and guide it to its goal. Both have an absolutely equal right to exist. In short, for me all men have completely equivalent rights, and—*vive la guerre éternelle*—until we have built the New Jerusalem, of course!'[10]

'You do believe in the New Jerusalem, then?'

'Yes, I do,' answered Raskolnikov firmly; he said this with his eyes fixed on one spot on the carpet,· as they had been all through his long tirade.

'A-and you believe in God? Forgive me for being so inquisitive.'

'Yes, I do,' repeated Raskolnikov, raising his eyes to Porfiry.

'A-a-and do you believe in the raising of Lazarus?'

'Y-yes. Why are you asking all this?'

'You believe in it literally?'

'Yes.'

'Ah . . . I was curious to know. Forgive me But, returning to the previous subject—they are not always put to death.

---

10. New Jerusalem, symbolic of the ideal order, after the end of time, is a Heaven on Earth, a new paradise. See the description in Revelation xxi (the Apocalypse). The French phrase means, "Long live perpetual war."

Some, on the contrary . . .'

'Triumph during their lifetime? Oh, yes, some achieve their ends while they still live, and then . . .'

'They begin to mete out capital punishment themselves?'

'If necessary, and, you know, it is most usually so. Your observation is very keen-witted.'

'Thank you. But tell me: how do you distinguish these extraordinary people from the ordinary? Do signs and portents appear when they are born? I mean to say that we could do with rather greater accuracy here, with, so to speak, rather more outward signs: please excuse the natural anxiety of a practical and well-meaning man, but couldn't there be, for example, some special clothing, couldn't they carry some kind of brand or something? . . . Because, you will agree, if there should be some sort of mix-up, and somebody from one category imagined that he belonged to the other and began "to remove all obstacles", as you so happily put it, then really . . .'

'Oh, that very frequently happens! This observation of yours is even more penetrating than the last.'

'Thank you.'

'Not at all. But you must please realize that the mistake is possible only among the first group, that is, the "ordinary" people (as I have called them, perhaps not altogether happily). In spite of their inborn inclination to obey, quite a number of them, by some freak of nature such as is not impossible even among cows, like to fancy that they are progressives, "destroyers", and propagators of the "new word", and all this quite sincerely. At the same time, they really take no heed of *new people*; they even despise them, as reactionary and incapable of elevated thinking. But, in my opinion, they cannot constitute a real danger, and you really have nothing to worry about, because they never go far. They might sometimes be scourged for their zealotry, to remind them of their place; there is no need even for anyone to carry out the punishment: they will do it themselves, because they are very well conducted: some of them do one another this service, and others do it for themselves with their own hands . . . And they impose on themselves various public penances besides—the result is beautifully edifying, and in short, you have nothing to worry about . . . This is a law of nature.'

'Well, at least you have allayed my anxieties on that score a little; but here is another worry: please tell me, are there many of these people who have the right to destroy others, of these "extraordinary" people? I am, of course, prepared to bow down before them, but all the same you will agree that it would be terrible if there were very many of them, eh?'

'Oh, don't let that trouble you either,' went on Raskolnikov in the same tone. 'Generally speaking, there are extremely few people, strangely few, born, who have a new idea, or are even capable of saying anything at all *new*. One thing only is clear, that the ordering of human births, all these categories and subdivisions, must be very carefully and exactly regulated by some law of nature. This law is, of course, unknown at present, but I believe that it exists, and consequently that it may be known. The great mass of men, the common stuff of humanity, exist on the earth only in order that at last, by some endeavour, some process, that remains as yet mysterious, some happy conjunction of race and breeding, there should struggle into life a being, one in a thousand, capable, in however small a degree, of standing on his own feet. Perhaps one in ten thousand (I am speaking approximately, by way of illustration) is born with a slightly greater degree of independence, and one in a hundred thousand with even more. One genius may emerge among millions, and a really great genius, perhaps, as the crowning point of many thousands of millions of men. In short, I have not been able to look into the retort whence all this proceeds. But a definite law there must be, and is; it cannot be a matter of chance.'

'What's the idea? Are you both joking or something?' exclaimed Razumikhin at last. 'You are amusing yourselves at one another's expense, aren't you? Sitting there and poking fun at one another! Are you serious, Rodya?'

Raskolnikov did not answer, but silently lifted towards him his pale and almost sorrowful face. And it seemed to Razumikhin that Porfiry's open, obtrusive, provocative, and *unmannerly* causticity contrasted strangely with that calm and melancholy face.

'Well, my dear fellow, if this is really serious, then . . . Of course you are right when you say that it is not new, but similar to what we have heard and read thousands of times; but what is really *original* in it—and what I am sorry to say, belongs only to you—is that you uphold bloodshed *as a matter of conscience* and even, if you will forgive my saying so, with great fanaticism . . . This, therefore, is the main idea of your article. This *moral* permission to shed blood is . . . seems to me more terrible than official, legal, licence to do so . . .'

'You are quite right. It is more terrible,' Porfiry responded.

'No, you got carried away somehow! That is where the mistake lies. I will read it . . . You were carried away! You cannot think so . . . I will read it.'

'You will not find all this in the article; it is only hinted at there,' said Raskolnikov.

'Yes, yes.' Porfiry was restless. 'I am almost clear now about how you look upon crime, but . . . please forgive me for being so importunate (I am ashamed to be troubling you so much)—

but, you see, although you greatly reassured me just now about mistaken confusion between the two categories . . . I keep worrying about various practical cases! Suppose somebody, some young man, fancies he is a Lycurgus or Mahomet—a future one, of course—and grant that he is to remove all obstacles to that end . . . "I have in front of me," says he, "a long campaign, and money is necessary for it" . . . Well, he begins to acquire supplies for the campaign . . . you know what I mean?'

Zametov in his corner suddenly snorted. Raskolnikov did not even raise his eyes to him.

'I must admit,' he replied quietly, 'that such cases must in fact occur. The rather stupid and conceited, especially the young, are particularly liable to rise to that bait.'

'You do see it. Well, what then?'

'This,' smiled Raskolnikov. 'I am not to blame for it. It does happen, and it always will. He' (he nodded towards Razumikhin) 'said just now that I uphold bloodshed. What then? Society after all is only too well supplied with the weapons of exile, prison, the examining magistrate, hard labour . . . what is there to worry about? Hunt out your thief! . . .'

'Well, and if we find him?'

'It serves him right.'

'Logical enough. And what about his conscience?'

'What concern is it of yours?'

'Well, on the grounds of humanity.'

'Any man who has one must suffer if he is conscious of error. That is his punishment—in addition to hard labour.'

'Well, but the real geniuses,' asked Razumikhin, frowning, 'those to whom you have granted the right to kill, ought surely not to suffer at all, even for the spilling of blood?'

'Why do you say "ought"? There is no question either of permitting or of forbidding it. Let them suffer, if they feel pity for the victims . . . Suffering and pain are always obligatory on those of wide intellect and profound feeling. Truly great men must, I think, experience great sorrow on the earth,' he added, suddenly thoughtful, as though to himself.

He raised his eyes, looked pensively at them all, smiled, and took up his cap. He was too tranquil, compared with his state when he came in, and he felt conscious of it. Everybody stood up.

'Well, grumble at me if you like, be angry if you like; I can't help it,' began Porfiry Petrovich again. 'Let me ask one more little question (I am troubling you a great deal!); I should like to bring in just one little idea, solely so as not to forget . . .'

'Very well; tell me your little idea,' said Raskolnikov, standing waiting before him, pale and serious.

'It is this . . . really, I hardly know how best to express it

. . . it is a very trifling little idea . . . Psychological . . . Well, this is it: when you were composing your article—surely it could not be, he, he, that you did not consider yourself . . . just a tiny bit . . . to be also an "extraordinary" man, one who was saying a *new word*—in your sense, that is . . . Surely that is so?'

'Very likely,' answered Raskolnikov disdainfully. Razumikhin made a movement.

'And if it is so, can you yourself have decided—well, in view of some lack of worldly success, and embarrassed circumstances, or for the betterment in some way of mankind—to step over those obstacles? . . . Well, for instance to kill and steal? . . .'

Again he suddenly seemed to wink at him with his left eye, and laugh noiselessly—exactly as before.

'If I had indeed done so, then of course I should not tell you,' answered Raskolnikov, with haughty, challenging disdain.

'No, really; I was only very interested, just for the comprehension of your article, and only in a purely literary respect . . .'

'Pah, how impudently obvious!' thought Raskolnikov with disgust.

'Allow me to remark,' he answered drily, 'that I do not consider myself a Mahomet or a Napoleon . . . nor anyone whatever of that sort, and consequently, not being them, I am unable to give you a satisfactory explanation of how I should act if I were.'

'Oh, come, who among us in Russia doesn't think himself a Napoleon now?' said Porfiry with sudden dreadful familiarity. This time there was decidedly something special in the intonation of his voice.

'Wasn't it indeed some future Napoleon who last week dispatched our Alëna Ivanovna with an axe?' blurted Zametov from his corner.

Raskolnikov was silent, gazing steadily and resolutely at Porfiry. Razumikhin frowned blackly. Even before this he had begun to notice something. He looked angrily round. There was a minute of bleak silence. Raskolnikov turned to go.

'Are you going already?' asked Porfiry effusively, holding out his hand with excessive amiability. 'I am very, very pleased to have made your acquaintance. As for your application, have no doubts about it. Write just exactly what I told you. Or better still, come and see me there yourself . . . some time soon . . . tomorrow if you like. I am sure to be there round about eleven o'clock. We will arrange everything . . . and have a little talk . . . You, as one of the last who were *there*, could perhaps tell us something . . .' he added, with a most benevolent air.

'Do you wish to interrogate me officially, with all the formalities?' sharply asked Raskolnikov.

'No, why? It is quite unnecessary for the present. You misunderstand me. You see, I don't like to let any opportunity pass, and . . . and I have already talked to all the other borrowers . . . from some of them I took depositions . . . and you, as the last of them . . . Oh, yes, by the way!' he exclaimed, suddenly delighted with something; 'I've just this moment remembered what I was going to say.' He turned to Razumikhin. 'You know how you drummed it into me about that Nikolashka? . . . Yes, I know, I know . . .' turning back to Raskolnikov, 'that the lad is clear, but what could I do? And Mitka had to be worried, too . . . Well, this is the point, the essential thing: when you were going upstairs . . . I think you said you were there between seven and eight?'

'Yes,' answered Raskolnikov, with an unpleasant feeling that he might not have said it at all.

'Well, going past at some time after seven, on the staircase, did you by any chance see, in the open flat on the second floor—you remember?—two workmen, or at any rate one of them? They were painting. Did you notice? It is very, very important for them! . . .'

'Painters? No, I didn't see them,' answered Raskolnikov slowly, as if he were cudgelling his memory. At the same time he was straining every faculty in tortured anxiety to divine as quickly as he might where the pitfall lay, and make sure that he did not miss anything. 'No, I didn't see them, and I didn't in fact notice any flat open . . . but there on the fourth floor' (he had by now triumphantly discovered the trap) 'I remember that a clerk was removing from his flat . . . opposite Alëna Ivanovna's . . . I remember . . . I remember that clearly . . . Soldiers were carrying out some sort of sofa and I was squeezed against the wall . . . But painters—no, I don't remember that there were any painters . . . and I don't think there was a flat open anywhere. No, there wasn't . . .'

'But what are you talking about?' cried Razumikhin suddenly, apparently pulling himself together and realizing something. 'Surely the painters were working on the very day of the murder, and he was there three days before! What makes you ask him about them?'

'Oh, I've got mixed up!' Porfiry struck his forehead. 'Devil take it, this business is driving me out of my senses!' he went on, turning apologetically to Raskolnikov. 'It would have been so important to us, if we could have learnt that they had been seen, in that flat, at some time after seven, that I fancied just now that you could tell us . . . I was quite mixed up!'

'Then you ought to be more careful,' remarked Razumikhin in surly tones.

The last words were spoken in the entrance-hall. Porfiry Petrovich conducted them to the door with extreme politeness. Both were sullen and gloomy when they emerged into the street, and they walked some steps without a word. Raskolnikov drew a long breath . . .

## CHAPTER VI

'. . . I DON'T believe it! I can't believe it!' repeated Razumikhin in bewilderment, trying with all his might to refute Raskolnikov's arguments. They were approaching Bakaleev's, where Pulkheria Alexandrovna and Dunya had long been expecting them. Razumikhin, in the heat of the discussion, kept stopping in the road, embarrassed and excited by the fact that for the first time they were talking plainly of *it*.

'Then don't believe it!' answered Raskolnikov with a cold and careless smile. 'As usual, you noticed nothing, but I weighed every word.'

'You are over-anxious, that is why . . . Hm . . . I admit Porfiry's tone was really rather strange, and that wretch Zametov was particularly odd! . . . You are right, there was something about him—but why? Why?'

'He has been thinking it over since last night.'

'No, on the contrary, on the contrary! If they had had such a brainless idea, they would have done their best to hide it. They would have kept their hands concealed, so as to catch you later . . . But this—it was so reckless and so bare-faced!'

'If they had had facts, real facts, to go on, or any kind of foundation for their suspicions, they would indeed have tried to hide their game, in the hope of a still greater victory (but they would long ago have made a search of my room!). But they have no facts, not one—it is all ambiguous and illusory, a will-o'-the-wisp—that is why they are trying to browbeat me with their impudence. Perhaps he was furious at not having any facts and his annoyance made him break out. Or perhaps he has some design . . . He seems an intelligent man . . . Perhaps he wanted to frighten me by pretending that he knew . . . That, my dear fellow, is your psychology . . . However, it nauseates me to enter into explanations of all this. Drop it!'

'And it is an insult to you, you are outraged! I understand you! But . . . since we have begun to speak plainly (an excellent thing, and I am glad we are doing it at last!)—I will frankly admit now that I have noticed it in them for some time, this idea, but only, of course, the vaguest trace, a creeping suspicion; only why even so much? How can they dare? Where do the hidden roots of it lie? If you knew how furious I am! What, all this just because a poor student, crippled with poverty and hypochondria, on the verge of a cruel illness and perhaps already affected by it (note that!), a prey to anxiety, self-centred, conscious of his own worth, who has spent six months in isolation in his corner, in tattered clothes and boots without soles, stands before some copper or other and suffers his abuse; here he is, confronted with an unexpected debt, an overdue bill in favour of this fellow Chebarov, evil-smelling paint, a temperature of thirty degrees Réaumur,[1] a stifling atmosphere, a crowd of people, talk about the murder of a person he has visited shortly before, and all this on an empty stomach! How on earth could he help fainting? And that, that alone is the basis of all this! What the devil? I know it is very trying for you, but in your place, Rodka, I should have burst out laughing in their faces, or better still, have spat in every one of their ugly mugs, and more than once; and, with due deliberation, as it should always be done, I should have distributed a couple of dozen slaps in the face among them, and left it at that. Cheer up! To hell with them! It's a disgraceful affair!'

'All the same, he summed it up very well,' thought Raskolnikov.

'To hell with them? But there's another examination tomorrow!' he said bitterly. 'Must I really enter into explanations with them? I am annoyed with myself, too, for that degrading scene with Zametov in the tavern yesterday . . .'

'Hang it all! I will go to Porfiry myself. I am related to him, and I'll screw it out of him; he shall lay bare the whole thing to the roots. And Zametov—I'll . . .'

'At last he has guessed right!' thought Raskolnikov.

'Stop!' exclaimed Razumikhin, seizing his friend by the shoulder; 'stop! You are wrong! I have been thinking and you've made a mistake! What sort of trap was it? You say the question about the workmen was a trap? Work it out! If you had done *that*, would you have let it out that you had seen the flat was being painted . . . and seen the workmen? On the contrary, you would have said you saw nothing, even if you had seen them! Who would admit something that told against himself?'

'If I had done *that deed*, I should certainly have said that I had seen the flat and the workmen,' answered Raskolnikov reluctantly and with evident distaste.

'But why testify against oneself?'

'Because only moujiks[2] and very inexperienced greenhorns instantly and flatly deny everything, under questioning. Any man with even a scrap of intelligence or experience will be sure to try to admit, as far as possible, all material facts that

---

1. Thirty degrees Reaumur are equivalent to 99.2 degrees Fahrenheit.    2. Russian peasants.

cannot be avoided; only he will look for other reasons for them, turn them to reveal special and unexpected facets, which will give them a different meaning, and place them in a new light. Porfiry could count on my answering like that, and saying that I had seen them, for the sake of plausibility, and then turning up something to explain . . .'

'But he would have told you at once that the workmen could not have been there two days before and that consequently you must yourself have been there on the day of the murder, between seven and eight o'clock. And you would have been tripped up by a trifle!'

'He counted on that, too; he thought I would not have time to consider, but would hasten to give a plausible answer, forgetting that the workmen could not have been there two days earlier.'

'But how could you forget that?'

'Very easily. It is those trifling details that most easily trip up clever people. The cleverer a man is, the less he expects to be caught out by something simple. In fact to throw the cleverest people off balance you must use the simplest means. Porfiry is not nearly as stupid as you imagine . . .'

'After all this, he's a scoundrel, though!'

Raskolnikov could not help laughing. But at the same time there seemed to him to be something strange in his own liveliness and the readiness with which he had explained the last point, when he had conducted all the previous conversation with sullen distaste and plainly only because it was unavoidable, considering the object he had in view.

'I let myself be carried away,' he thought.

But almost in the same moment he grew uneasy, as if struck by an unexpected and worrying idea. His uneasiness increased. They had reached the entrance of Bakaleev's.

'You go on by yourself,' he said abruptly. 'I shall be back in a minute.'

'Where are you going? We've arrived!'

'I must, I must; I have something to do . . . I will come in half an hour . . . Tell them.'

'Have it your own way. I'll go with you.'

'Why? Do *you* want to torture me as well?' cried Raskolnikov with such bitter exasperation and with such a look of despair that Razumikhin was discouraged. He stood for some time on the steps and morosely watched his friend walk quickly in the direction of his own room. Finally, with clenched teeth and hands, he swore an oath that that very day he would squeeze Porfiry like a lemon, and went upstairs to assuage Pulkheria Alexandrovna's alarm at their long absence.

When Raskolnikov arrived at his own house, his temples were damp with sweat and he was panting. He hurried up the stairs, entered his open door, and fastened it with the hook. Then, frantic with fear, he rushed into the corner, thrust his hand into that hole in the wallpaper where the things had lain, and spent several minutes in searching it minutely, groping in every cranny and in every fold in the paper. When he found nothing, he stood up and drew a deep breath. Going up the steps to the door of Bakaleev's, he had suddenly imagined that one or other of the things, some chain or link or even perhaps a piece of the paper they had been wrapped in, with an inscription in the old woman's hand, might somehow have slipped down and got lost in a crack, to confront him at some later time as unexpected and irresistible evidence.

He stood as if lost in thought and a strange, humble, half-vacant smile played on his lips. At last he picked up his cap and quietly left the room. His ideas were confused. He was still abstracted as he came out to the gate. 'There he is!' called a loud voice; he raised his head.

The porter was standing at the door of his lodge, pointing him out to a little man who looked like a superior workman or small tradesman, but since he was wearing a sort of long robe and a waistcoat, from a distance he resembled a peasant-woman. His head, in a greasy cap, hung down, and his whole figure seemed to stoop. From his flabby wrinkled face he seemed to be over fifty; his sunken little eyes looked hard, morose, and discontented.

'What is it?' asked Raskolnikov, approaching the porter.

The stranger looked sideways at him, frowning, and studied him intently and lingeringly, then he turned slowly round and without a word walked out through the gate into the street.

'But what is it?' cried Raskolnikov.

'That person there was asking if a student lived here—he gave your name and asked who you lived with. You came out just then, I pointed you out, and he went. That's all about it.'

The porter also seemed a little puzzled, but not very, and after standing thinking a moment or two longer he turned round and went back into his lodge.

Raskolnikov dashed out after the stranger, and immediately caught sight of him walking along the other side of the street, at the same even, unhurried pace, with his eyes fixed ruminatively on the ground. He overtook him quickly, and walked for a short time behind him; then he drew level and looked sideways at his face. The man noticed him at once and looked quickly at him, then dropped his eyes again; they walked on thus for about a minute, side by side, without speaking.

'Were you asking the porter for me?' said Raskolnikov at last, in a low voice.

The man made no answer and did not even look at him.
There was silence once more.

'Why do you ... come to ask for me ... and then say nothing?
... What is all this?' Raskolnikov's voice cracked, and his
words seemed unwilling to emerge clearly.

This time the man raised his head and looked at him with
sombre ominous eyes.

'Murderer!' he said suddenly, in a low but clear and distinct
voice.

Raskolnikov went on walking beside him. His knees felt
terribly weak, a chill ran up his spine, his heart seemed to
stop for a moment and then began to thump as though it had
torn loose from its place. They walked on again thus, in
complete silence, for a hundred yards.

The man did not look at him.

'But why do you ... what ... who is a murderer?' muttered
Raskolnikov hardly audibly.

'*You* are,' pronounced the stranger still more distinctly and
impressively, with a smile of triumphant hatred, and again he
looked straight at Raskolnikov's pale face and his staring eyes.
They came to a crossing, and the man turned into the street
on the left and walked on without looking round. Raskolnikov
stood still and watched him for a long time. He saw the man
turn after he had gone some fifty paces and look back at him,
still standing motionless in the same place. It was impossible
to be sure, but it seemed to Raskolnikov that his face again
wore its coldly hostile and triumphant smile.

With languid, feeble steps, with shaking knees and a feeling
of frozen horror, Raskolnikov turned back and mounted to his
room. He took off his cap and laid it on the table, and then
stood there motionless for some ten minutes. Then, drained
of all strength, he lay down on the sofa and painfully stretched
himself out on it, with a feeble groan; his eyes were closed.
He lay there for about half an hour.

He could not think. His mind held ideas, or fragments of
ideas, disconnected and incoherent images—the faces of people
he had known as a child or seen once and never remembered
again, the belfry of the Church of the Ascension, the billiard-
table in some public house, with an officer playing at it, the
smell of cigars in a basement tobacco shop, a tavern, a back
staircase, sloppy with dish-water and strewn with egg-shells,
the Sunday sound of bells borne in from somewhere . . . all
changing and whirling in dizzy spirals. Sometimes an image
pleased him and he tried to cling to it, but it would fade away.
He had a diffused inner feeling of oppression, but it was not
marked; sometimes, indeed, all seemed well . . . A slight shiver
shook him persistently, and this also was an almost pleasurable
sensation.

He heard Razumikhin's hurried steps and his voice, shut his eyes, and feigned sleep. Razumikhin opened the door and stood considering on the threshold for a short space. Then he stepped quietly into the room and cautiously approached the sofa. Nastasya's voice could be heard whispering:

'Don't disturb him. Let him have his sleep out. Then he can have something to eat.'

'Exactly,' answered Razumikhin.

They went out carefully, and closed the door. Another half-hour went by. Raskolnikov opened his eyes and lay on his back with his hands behind his head.

'Who is he? Who is this man who seems to have sprung up from nowhere? Where was he and what did he see? Everything, doubtless. But where was he standing as he looked on? Why has he risen out of the ground only now? And how could he see—could it be possible? Hm . . .,' he went on, turning cold and shuddering, 'what about the jeweller's case that Nikolay found behind the door—was that possible either? Evidence! You overlook one infinitesimal detail—and it builds up to a whole Egyptian pyramid of evidence! A fly was buzzing round, and it saw! Can such things be possible?'

Suddenly he was conscious, with repulsion, of how physically weak he had become.

'I ought to have known it,' he thought, with a bitter smile. 'How, knowing myself, foreknowing myself, dared I take the axe and stain my hands with blood? It was my duty to know beforehand . . . Ah! but really I did indeed know beforehand! . . .' he whispered despairingly.

At times he seemed to stand motionless in contemplation of some particular idea.

'No, those people are not made like this; the *real* ruler, to whom everything is permitted, destroys Toulon, butchers in Paris, *forgets* an army in Egypt, *expends* half a million men in a Moscow campaign, shakes himself free with a pun in Wilno,[3] and when he is dead they put up statues to him; *everything* is permitted to him. No! Such people are plainly not made of flesh, but of bronze!'

A sudden irrelevant thought nearly made him laugh.

'Napoleon, the pyramids, Waterloo—and a vile, withered old woman, a moneylender, with a red box under her bed—what a mishmash even for somebody like Porfiry Petrovich to digest! . . . How could he, indeed? Aesthetic considerations forbid. "Does a Napoleon crawl under an old woman's bed?" he will say. Oh, what rubbish! . . .'

---

3. Napoleon stormed Toulon in 1793 and captured it for the French Revolutionary forces; in 1795 he ruthlessly suppressed a Royalist uprising in Paris; in 1799 he abandoned his army in Egypt in order to return to France, where he took over power by force. Defeated in Russia in 1812, he is supposed to have said about his failure there: "From the sublime to the ridiculous is only a step; let the future generations judge."

At times he felt that he was wandering; he had fallen into a state of feverish exaltation.

'The old hag is nothing!' he thought disconnectedly, with mounting excitement. 'Perhaps the old woman was a mistake, but she is not the point. The old woman was only a symptom of my illness . . . I wanted to overstep all restrictions as quickly as possible . . . I killed not a human being but a principle! Yes, I killed a principle, but as for surmounting the barriers, I did not do that; I remained on this side . . . The only thing I knew how to do was kill! And I could not do that properly either, it seems . . . A principle? Why was that foolish fellow Razumikhin railing at the Socialists just now? They are industrious and business-like people; they work for the "common weal" . . . No, I have only one life given to me, and it will never come again; I do not want to wait for the "common weal". I want to have my own life, or else it is better not to live at all. What then? I only didn't want my mother to go hungry without doing what I could, while we waited for the "common weal". "I," they say, "contribute one brick[4] to the building of the common weal and that gives me full satisfaction." Ha, ha! But what about me? After all, I shall only live once, and after all I also want . . . Oh, aesthetically speaking, I am a louse, nothing more,' he added, suddenly beginning to laugh like a madman. 'Yes, I really am a louse,' he went on, clinging to the idea with malicious pleasure, burrowing into it, playing with it for his own amusement, 'if only because, first, I'm arguing now about being one, secondly, I've been importuning all-gracious Providence for a whole month, calling on it to witness that it was not for my own selfish desires and purposes that I proposed to act (so I said), but for a noble and worthy end . . . ha, ha! Because, thirdly, in the execution of my design I devoted so much attention to securing the utmost justice accurately calculated by weight and measure: from all the lice on earth, I picked out absolutely the most useless, and when I had killed her, I intended to take from her exactly as much as I needed for my first step, and neither more nor less (and all the rest, consequently, would have gone to the monastery for the repose of her soul—ha, ha!) . . . Finally, I am a louse because,' he went on, grinding his teeth, 'because I myself am, perhaps, even worse and viler than the louse I killed, and I *knew beforehand* that I should tell myself so after I had killed her! Can anything compare with such horror? Oh, platitudes! What baseness! . . . Oh, how well I understand the Prophet, on horseback, scimitar in hand: "It is the will of Allah, therefore obey, thou trembling creature!"[5] He is right, he is right, the Prophet, when he establishes a mar-vell-ous battery across

<hr/>

4. "Brick" was frequently used in this sense in a book by Fourier's disciple, Victor Considerant, *Destinée Sociale* (Paris, 1834).

5. From the Koran. Dostoevsky owned a French translation of the Koran.

a street somewhere and mows down the innocent and the guilty, without deigning to justify himself! Obey, trembling creature, and—*do not will*, because—that is not your affair! . . . Oh, nothing, nothing will make me forgive that old witch!'

His hair was damp with sweat, his trembling lips were parched, his immovable gaze was fixed on the ceiling.

'My mother, my sister, how I loved them! What makes me hate them now? Yes, I hate them, hate them physically; I cannot bear them near me . . . A short time ago I went up to my mother and kissed her, I remember . . . To embrace her, and think that if she knew . . . was I to tell her then? It is just the sort of thing I'm capable of . . . Hm! *She* ought to be like me,' he thought, forcing himself to struggle against his growing delirium. 'Oh, how much I hate that old woman now! I think I should kill her again if she came back to life! Poor Lizaveta! Why had she to turn up? . . . It is strange though; I wonder why I hardly ever think of her, as though I had not killed her . . . Lizaveta! Sonya! Poor, meek, gentle creatures, with meek eyes! . . . Why do they not weep? Why do they not groan? . . . They give up everything . . . they look at you meekly and gently . . . Sonya, Sonya, gentle Sonya! . . .'

He had drifted into sleep; it seemed strange that he could not remember how he came to be in the street. It was already late. The twilight had deepened, the full moon was shining brighter and brighter; but the air was particularly stifling. The streets were crowded with people going home from work or out for a walk; there was a smell of lime, and dust, and stagnant water. Raskolnikov was melancholy and anxious; he recollected clearly that he had come out with some definite purpose, that there was something he must hasten to do, but he could not remember what it was. Suddenly he stopped, seeing on the opposite pavement a man standing and waving to him. He crossed the street towards him, but the man turned abruptly and unconcernedly walked away, with lowered head, without looking back or giving any sign that he had summoned him. 'Did he really call me?' wondered Raskolnikov, but began to follow. After some ten paces he suddenly recognized the stoop-shouldered stranger in the long robe, and was terrified. Raskolnikov followed him at a distance; his heart thumped; they turned into a lane—still the man did not turn round. 'Does he know that I am following him?' thought Raskolnikov. The man turned in at the gate of a large house. Raskolnikov hurried to the gate and looked to see if he would not turn round and call him. And in fact, when he reached the other end of the arched gateway and was emerging into the courtyard, he did turn round and again seemed to beckon to him. Raskolnikov at once entered, but when he reached the courtyard the stranger was no longer there. Consequently, he must have turned into the first staircase. Raskolnikov hurried after him. From two flights higher up, indeed, he heard measured, unhastening steps. Strangely enough, the staircase seemed somehow familiar. There was the window on the first floor; the mysterious and melancholy moonlight shone through the panes. Here was the second floor. Oh! This was the same flat where the painters had been working . . . How was it he had not known at once? The steps of the man in front had died away; 'that means he is standing still or has hidden somewhere!' Here was the third floor: should he go any farther? How quiet it was up there, so quiet that it was terrible! . . . But he went on. The sound of his own steps alarmed and frightened him. Heavens, how dark it was! The stranger was probably standing hidden in a corner. Ah, here was a flat with its stair-case door open; he hesitated and went in. It was very dark inside, and empty, as though everything had been removed; very quietly, on tiptoe, he went into the sitting-room: the whole room was bathed in clear moonlight; everything here was as before: chairs, mirror, yellow sofa, and pictures in frames. The huge, round copper-red moon was looking straight through the window. 'The stillness comes from the moon,' thought Raskolnikov; 'she must be asking riddles now.' He stood and waited, waited a long time, while the moonlight grew quieter, and his heart thumped more violently, until it became painful. The stillness continued. Suddenly he heard a momentary dry cracking sound, as if a twig had snapped; then all was silent again. A fly woke up, bumped against the window pane, and set up a whining buzz. At that moment, in the corner between a small cupboard and the window, he saw what looked like a woman's cloak hanging on the wall. 'Why is there a cloak there?' he thought. 'It was not there before . . .' He stole quietly up to it, and realized that someone seemed to be hidden behind it. He moved it carefully aside with his hand, and saw a chair standing there, and the old woman sitting huddled up in it. Her head hung down so that he could not see her face, but it was she. He stood over her. 'She is afraid!' he thought, and stealthily withdrawing the axe from its loop he struck her on the crown of the head, once and again. But it was strange: she did not even stir under the blows; it was as if she were made of wood. He grew afraid, and stooped nearer to look at her, but she bent her head even lower. He crouched down to the floor and looked up into her face from below, looked once and froze where he was: the old woman sat there laughing, overcome with noiseless laughter, striving with all her powers to prevent his hearing it. Suddenly it seemed to him that the bedroom door had opened a crack, and that whispering and laughter were coming from there too. Madness seized him:

he began frenziedly striking the old woman on the head, but with every blow of the axe the sound of whispering and laughter in the bedroom grew stronger and louder, and the old woman shook with mirth. He tried to flee, but the entrance was full of people, all the doors stood open, and the landing and the stairs below were one mass of people, a sea of heads, all looking at him, and all silent, waiting, without a sound . . . His heart laboured, his legs were rooted and would not stir . . . He tried to scream, and . . . awoke.

He drew a deep breath, but the dream seemed strangely to be continuing: his door was wide open and on the threshold stood a complete stranger, looking fixedly at him.

He had hardly opened his eyes before he closed them again. He lay on his back, motionless. 'Is this still the dream, or not?' he thought, and imperceptibly raised his lids a fraction to look; the stranger still stood in the same place, still gazing at him. Suddenly he stepped quietly across the threshold, closed the door behind him, walked to the table, waited there a short time—with his eyes fixed on Raskolnikov the whole time—and gently, noiselessly, sat down on the chair by the sofa; he laid his hat on the floor by his side, propped both hands on his stick and leaned his chin on them. It was plain that he was prepared for a long wait. As far as Raskolnikov could see in quick glimpses through his lashes, the visitor was a man no longer young, stout, with a bushy, light-coloured, almost white, beard . . .

Some ten minutes passed. It was still light, but beginning to grow dusk. Absolute stillness reigned in the room. No sound came from the stairs. Only a large fly buzzed and bumped against the pane. At last, unable to endure any longer, Raskolnikov abruptly raised himself to a sitting position.

'Well, say something! What do you want?'

'Of course I knew very well that you were not asleep, but only pretending,' replied the stranger oddly, with a tranquil smile. 'Allow me to introduce myself: Arkady Ivanovich Svidrigaylov . . .'

# Part Four

## CHAPTER I

'CAN this be the dream continuing?' thought Raskolnikov again. He watched his unexpected visitor warily and mistrustfully.

'Svidrigaylov? Nonsense! That's impossible!' he said at last aloud, in perplexity.

The visitor did not seem at all surprised at this exclamation.

'I have called on you for two reasons; first, because I wanted to become acquainted with you personally, having long known of you through most interesting and favourable reports; and secondly, because I cherish the hope that you will not refuse to help me in a project which directly concerns the interests of your sister, Avdotya Romanovna. It is possible that she is so prejudiced against me that she would not even allow me to come anywhere near her without some recommendation, but with your help, on the other hand, I am confident . . .'

'Your confidence is misplaced,' interrupted Raskolnikov.

'May I ask if it is true that they arrived only yesterday?'

Raskolnikov did not answer.

'I know it was yesterday. I myself, indeed, arrived only the day before yesterday. Well, Rodion Romanovich, I will say this to you: I see no need to justify myself, but be good enough to tell me what was so criminal in my conduct in all that affair, judged sensibly and without prejudice?'

Raskolnikov still watched him without speaking.

'The fact that in my own house I persecuted a defenceless girl and "insulted her with my vile proposals"—is that it? (You see I anticipate you!) But you have only to suppose that I, too, am a man, *et nihil humanum*[6]. . . in one word, that I also am capable of being attracted and falling in love (which after all is not a matter that depends on our will), and everything is explained in the most natural manner. The whole question is: am I a monster or am I myself a victim? And if I am a victim? When I proposed to the object of my affections that she should fly with me to America or to Switzerland, I may have cherished the most honourable sentiments and thought I was furthering

---

6. From a comedy by the Latin poet Terence. The whole saying is: *"Homo sum, et nihil humanum a me alienum puto"* ("I am a human being and consider nothing to do with humanity outside my province").

237

our mutual happiness. Reason, you know, is passion's slave; perhaps, after all, it was to myself I did most harm! . . .'

'That is quite beside the point,' interrupted Raskolnikov with distaste. 'The simple fact is that whether you are right or wrong they find you repugnant, and therefore have no wish to know you. They will have nothing to do with you. Take yourself off! . . .'

Svidrigaylov laughed aloud.

'But you . . . but there is no getting round you!' he said, laughing in the most candid manner. 'I thought I could be artful, but no, you instantly put your finger on the real point!'

'But you are still trying to be artful at this very moment.'

'Well, what then? What then?' repeated Svidrigaylov, still laughing heartily. 'It was what is called *bonne guerre*, and the most innocent of deceptions! . . . All the same, you interrupted me; and, whether or no, I repeat again: there would have been no unpleasantness but for the incident in the garden. Marfa Petrovna . . .'

'They say that you drove Marfa Petrovna into her grave; is that so?' rudely interrupted Raskolnikov.

'Oh, you have heard of that, too? But of course you would have . . . Well, in answer to your question, I hardly know what to say, although my conscience is perfectly clear in that respect. I mean, you mustn't think that I have any misgivings on that score: everything was quite regular and correct; the medical inquiry revealed apoplexy, as a result of bathing immediately after a heavy meal accompanied by almost a bottle of wine, and indeed there was nothing else it could have shown . . . No, sir; but I'll tell you what I have been wondering for some time, especially on my way here in the train; did I not contribute to this . . . unfortunate accident in some degree, by causing some mental disturbance or something of that kind? But I came to the conclusion that it positively could not be so.'

Raskolnikov laughed.

'Why should you want to worry about that?'

'What are you laughing at? Consider: I gave her only a couple of blows with a riding-switch, and it didn't even leave a mark. Please don't think me cynical: I am quite aware that I behaved atrociously, and so on and so forth; but I also know quite well that Marfa Petrovna may even have been pleased at this evidence of passion, so to speak. All that business about your sister had been wrung absolutely dry. Marfa Petrovna had already been obliged to stay at home for two days; she had no fresh excuse for going to town, and they were all bored there with that letter of hers (you heard about her reading the letter?). And suddenly those two blows fell; they might have come from heaven! . . . The first thing she did was to order the carriage! . . . Not to mention the fact that it sometimes happens that women are highly gratified at being outraged, in spite of their apparent indignation. It happens with everybody: mankind in general loves to be affronted, have you noticed? But especially women. You might almost say it's their only amusement.'

At one time Raskolnikov thought of ending the interview by getting up and going away. But a certain amount of curiosity, and even some calculation, kept him back for the time being.

'Do you like fighting?' he asked absently.

'No, not particularly,' calmly answered Svidrigaylov. 'I hardly ever came to blows with Marfa Petrovna. We lived very peaceably together and she was always quite satisfied with me. In all our seven years of marriage I used the whip only twice altogether (not counting a third, quite equivocal occasion): once, two months after our marriage, immediately after we arrived in the country, and again this last time. And did you think I was such a tyrant, a reactionary, a slave-driver? Ha, ha! . . . By the way, do you remember, Rodion Romanovich, how a few years ago, in the days of beneficent publicity, a nobleman—I forget his name—was publicly held up to shame in the press for having thrashed some German woman in a railway-carriage? Do you remember? About that time, in the very same year, I think, there was "the disgraceful affair of the *Century*"[7] (you remember, the *Egyptian Nights*, the public reading. Those black eyes! Oh, where are you, golden days of our youth?). Well, sir, this is my opinion: I don't feel any deep sympathy for the gentleman who administered the thrashing, because after all it . . . well, what is there to sympathize with? But at the same time, I can't help saying that from time to time one comes across such provoking "Germans" that I don't think there is a single progressive who could answer for himself. Nobody looked at the subject from that point of view then, but all the same that is the truly humane point of view, it really is!'

Having said this, Svidrigaylov suddenly laughed again. It was clear to Raskolnikov that this was a man who had firmly made up his mind to something, but would keep his own counsel.

'You must have been several days with nobody to talk to, I suppose?' he asked.

'Almost nobody. Why? Are you surprised to find me so easy-going a person?'

'No, I am surprised because you are almost excessively amiable.'

---

7. The newspaper *Century* in 1861 published an article attacking a lady in the provincial town of Perm, who at a literary party had read Pushkin's work *Egyptian Nights* "shamelessly and with provocative gestures." The progressive press was indignant about the tone and attitude of the *Century* article, as was Dostoevsky's magazine *Time.*

'Because I did not take offence at the rudeness of your questions? Is that it? But . . . why should I be offended? As you asked, so I answered,' he added, with a surprisingly artless expression. 'You know, I take no particular interest in anything,' he went on, musingly. 'Especially now I have nothing to occupy me . . . However, you may believe, if you care to, that I am making up to you with an ulterior motive, especially as I told you myself that I have something to see your sister about. But I will freely acknowledge that I am bored to death, especially these last three days, so that I am very glad to have you to talk to . . . Don't be angry, Rodion Romanovich, but you yourself somehow seem terribly odd to me. Say what you please, but there is something strange about you just now; not, that is, particularly at this moment, but now generally speaking . . . Well, well, I won't go on; don't scowl! Really I am not such a bear as you suppose.'

Raskolnikov looked at him sombrely.

'Perhaps you are not a bear at all,' he said. 'I even think that you are a very well-bred man, or at least know how to behave like one on occasion.'

'I am not particularly interested in anybody's opinion,' answered Svidrigaylov drily and with a touch of haughtiness, 'and therefore why not be a bit of a vulgarian, since that guise is so appropriate to our climate and . . . and especially if one has a natural tendency that way?' he added, with another laugh.

'But I have heard that you have many acquaintances here. You are surely "not without connexions", as it is termed. Why then, in that case, should you have recourse to me, except to further some purpose of your own?'

'It is true that I have friends here,' assented Svidrigaylov, ignoring the main point, 'and I have already met some of them, in the three days that I've been hanging about here. I recognize them as the sort of people I know and I think they recognize me in the same way. That is a matter of course, since I am decently dressed and not reckoned a poor man; the abolition of serfdom has made no difference to me: my income, derived from forests and water-meadows, is not diminished by it. But . . . I won't go to see them. I was bored with them before; this is my third day here and I haven't called on anybody . . . And what a town this is! I wish you could tell me how it has come to be like this. A town of clerks and all kinds of seminarists! It's true I didn't notice much when I was having a good time here before, eight years ago . . . Now I swear I have no confidence in anything but anatomy!'

'In anatomy?'

'As for these political clubs, these Dussauts,[8] these hair-

8. Dussaut's was a famous Petersburg restaurant and hotel.

splitting discussions of yours, or whatever other evidence of progress you may have here—well, they must all get on without me,' he went on, again ignoring the question. 'And I don't want to be a card-sharper, either.'

'Have you ever been one?'

'How could I help it? There was a whole set of us, all highly respectable, eight years ago; we had a very good time; there were rich men among us, and poets, and, you know, we all had the most charming manners. Generally speaking, in our Russian society the very best manners are found among those who are used to being beaten—have you noticed that? Of course, now I've fallen off with being in the country. All the same, in those days I was nearly put in prison for debt by a Greek from Nezhin. Then Marfa Petrovna turned up, bargained with him, and bought me off for thirty thousand silver roubles. (I owed seventy thousand altogether.) We were united in lawful wedlock, and she took me off immediately into the country, like some treasure. She was five years older than me, you know. She loved me dearly. For seven years I never left the country. And note this: all her life she held that document (made out to someone else) over my head, that note for thirty thousand roubles, so that if I had ever had any thought of rebellion, it would have been straight into the trap with me! And she would have done it! Women, you know, see nothing incongruous in all that.'

'And if it hadn't been for that, would you have cut and run?'

'I don't know how to put it. I hardly found that the document hampered me at all. I didn't want to go anywhere, and Marfa Petrovna herself once or twice suggested that I should go abroad, seeing that I was bored. But what would have been the use? I had been abroad before, and I always hated it. I don't know why, but you look at the dawn breaking, the bay of Naples, the sea, and you are sad. The worst of it is, you know, that you really do grieve for something. No, better stay in your own country; here at least one can blame somebody else for everything and find excuses for oneself. Perhaps I might go on an expedition to the North Pole; because *j'ai le vin mauvais*[9] I have no taste for drinking, and there is nothing else left for me to do. I have tried and I know. But I'll tell you what, they say Berg[10] is going to make an ascent in a great balloon on Sunday in the Yusupov Gardens, and that he will take passengers up for a consideration. Is that true?'

'Why, would you go up?'

'I? No . . . I only asked,' murmured Svidrigaylov, as if he were really thinking of something else.

'What does he really want, I wonder?' thought Raskolnikov.

9. "Drinking makes me mean."
10. Berg was an entertainer and adventurer who amused paying crowds by making balloon ascents.

'No, the document was no embarrassment to me,' went on Svidrigaylov thoughtfully. 'I stayed in the country of my own accord. And about a year ago, on my name-day, Marfa Petrovna gave it back to me, and a considerable sum of money besides. She had some capital, you know. "You see how I trust you, Arkady Ivanovich"—those were her very words. Don't you believe that she used those words? But you know, in the country I had become the complete squire; everybody knows me in those parts. And I sent for some books as well. Marfa Petrovna approved at first, but afterwards she was always afraid I should study too much.'

'You appear to miss Marfa Petrovna very much.'

'I do? Perhaps. Yes, it may be so. By the way, do you believe in ghosts?'

'What kind of ghosts?'

'The usual kind, of course!'

'Do you?'

'Well, perhaps not, *pour vous plaire*¹... That is, I don't exactly disbelieve in them . . .'

'Have you ever seen one?'

Svidrigaylov looked at him rather strangely.

'Marfa Petrovna is good enough to visit me sometimes.'

'What do you mean by that?'

'She has already been three times. The first time I saw her was on the very day of the funeral, an hour after we came away from the cemetery. That was the day before I left for here. The second time was on the way here, at Malaya Vishera station, the day before yesterday; the third was two hours ago in the room where I am living. I was alone.'

'And awake?'

'Wide awake. I was awake all three times. She comes, speaks a few words, and leaves by the door, always by the door. You can almost hear her even.'

'I wonder why I thought that something of that kind was certainly happening to you,' said Raskolnikov suddenly, and was immediately filled with astonishment at his own words. He was very excited.

'In-deed? You thought that?' asked Svidrigaylov, surprised. 'Really? Well, didn't I say we had something in common, eh?'

'You never said that!' answered Raskolnikov sharply and with some heat.

'Didn't I?'

'No!'

'I thought I had. Just now, when I came in and saw you lying with your eyes shut, pretending to be asleep, I said to myself at once: "This is the very man!"'

'What do you mean by "the very man"? What are you

---

1. "To please you."

talking about?' cried Raskolnikov.

'Talking about? I really don't know . . .' murmured Svidrigaylov, candidly, seeming puzzled himself.

There was a minute of silence, while they stared at one another.

'What nonsense!' exclaimed Raskolnikov in a tone of annoyance. 'What does she talk about, when she appears to you?'

'She? Oh, the silliest rubbish you can imagine, and (people are very odd!) that makes me really angry. She came in the first time—I was tired, you know, with the funeral, the requiem mass, the prayers, and the meal afterwards, and at last I was alone in the study; I had lit a cigar and sat thinking —she came in at the door, and she said "Arkady Ivanovich, with all the upset today you've forgotten to wind up the clock in the dining-room." Well, all those seven years I had wound up that clock every week, and if I forgot, she always used to remind me. The next day I was on the way here. At daybreak, I got out at a station and got some coffee—I had spent the night dozing fitfully, and I was very tired and could hardly keep my eyes open; I looked up, and suddenly Marfa Petrovna sat down beside me with a pack of cards in her hands. "Wouldn't you like me to tell your fortune for the journey, Arkady Ivanovich?" She was very good at telling fortunes. I shall never forgive myself for not letting her tell it. I took fright and hurried away; it is true that the bell went just then. Today, I was sitting smoking, with an over-loaded stomach after a perfectly wretched dinner brought from a cook-shop—when suddenly Marfa Petrovna came in, all dressed up in a new green silk dress with a long train. "Good afternoon, Arkady Ivanovich! How do you like my dress? Aniska can't make them like this." (Aniska is our dressmaker in the country. She used to be a serf, and she learnt her trade in Moscow—a pretty girl.) She stood in front of me and turned round. I inspected the dress and then I looked very, very carefully at her, and said: "What makes you go to all the trouble of coming to me for such trifles?" "Good gracious, my dear, it's getting impossible to disturb you about anything!" To tease her, I said. "Marfa Petrovna, I want to get married." "That depends on you, Arkady Ivanovich, but it isn't very creditable to rush here and get married again, almost before your wife is buried. If you could even be trusted to choose well! But no, I know it will do neither her nor you any good, and nice people will laugh at you." Then she took herself off, and I seemed to hear her train rustling. What nonsense, isn't it?'

'But perhaps this is all lies, eh?' responded Raskolnikov.

'I don't often lie,' Svidrigaylov answered thoughtfully, as if he had not noticed the rudeness of the question.

'And had you never seen any apparitions before?'

'Y-yes, I had, just once in my life, six years ago. I had a servant, Philka; we had just buried him, and I forgot and called out: "Philka, my pipe!" He came in and went straight to the cabinet where I keep my pipes. I thought: "He is taking his revenge on me," because we had had a fierce quarrel just before his death. "How dare you come into my presence," said I, "with a hole in your elbow? Get out, you rascal!" He turned and went out, and he has never come again. I didn't tell Marfa Petrovna at the time. I wanted to have prayers for his soul, but I was ashamed.'

'You ought to see a doctor.'

'I don't need you to tell me that there is something wrong with me, although I honestly don't know what; it seems to me that I am probably five times as healthy as you. I did not ask you whether you believe that people see ghosts. I asked you whether you believe that ghosts exist.'

'No, nothing would make me believe it!' cried Raskolnikov with some heat.

'What do people usually say?' murmured Svidrigaylov, as though he were talking to himself, with head bent and eyes turned aside. 'They say: "You are sick, and so what you think you see is nothing more than the unreal dream of your feverish mind." But you know, that is not strictly logical. I agree that ghosts appear only to the sick, but that proves only that they cannot appear to anybody else, not that they have no real existence.'

'Of course they don't exist!' insisted Raskolnikov irritably.

'You think not?' went on Svidrigaylov, slowly turning his eyes on him. 'Well, suppose we reason like this (I wish you would help me here): Apparitions are, so to speak, shreds and fragments of other worlds, the first beginnings of them. There is, of course, no reason why a healthy man should see them, because a healthy man is mainly a being of this earth, and therefore for completeness and order he must live only this earthly life. But as soon as he falls ill, as soon as the normal earthly state of the organism is disturbed, the possibility of another world begins to appear, and as the illness increases, so do the contacts with the other world, so that at the moment of a man's death he enters fully into that world. It is a long time since I first developed this argument. If you believe in the life hereafter, you may accept this reasoning too.'

'I do not believe in a life hereafter,' said Raskolnikov.

Svidrigaylov remained thoughtful.

'What if there is nothing there but spiders or something like that?' he said suddenly.

'This is a madman,' thought Raskolnikov.

'Eternity is always presented to us as an idea which it is impossible to grasp, something enormous, enormous! But why should it necessarily be enormous? Imagine, instead, that it will be one little room, something like a bath-house in the country, black with soot, with spiders in every corner, and that that is the whole of eternity. I sometimes imagine it like that, you know.'

'But surely, surely, you can imagine something juster and more comforting than that!' exclaimed Raskolnikov, painfully moved.

'Juster? For all we know, that may be just; and, you know, I would certainly make it like that, deliberately!' answered Svidrigaylov, with a vague smile.

At this monstrous answer a chill seized upon Raskolnikov. Svidrigaylov raised his head, gazed steadily at him, and suddenly laughed aloud.

'No, but think of this,' he cried. 'Half an hour ago we had never seen one another, we look on one another as enemies, and there is still a question to be settled between us; we've dropped the question and just look what nonsense we are talking! Well, wasn't I right when I said we were kindred spirits?'

'Be good enough,' said Raskolnikov irritably, 'to allow me to ask for an immediate explanation of why you have condescended to honour me with a visit ... and ... and ... I am in a hurry; I have no time to spare. I must go out ...'

'Certainly, certainly. Your sister, Avdotya Romanovna, is marrying Mr. Peter Petrovich Luzhin, isn't she?'

'Can't you manage to avoid asking questions about my sister, or mentioning her name? I cannot understand how you dare utter her name in my presence, if you really are Svidrigaylov.'

'But she is exactly what I came to talk about, so how can I help mentioning her?'

'Very well; but say it as quickly as possible!'

'I am convinced that you must already have made up your mind about this Mr. Luzhin (a connexion of mine by marriage), if you have either been in his company for as long as half an hour or heard any faithful account of him. He is not a fitting match for Avdotya Romanovna. In my opinion, Avdotya Romanovna is sacrificing herself, with great nobility and without counting the cost, for ... for her family. It seemed to me, from all I had heard of you, that for your part you would be very pleased if this match could be broken off without harming her interests. Now that I know you personally, I am sure of it.'

'All this is very innocent of you; excuse me, I meant insolent,' said Raskolnikov.

'That is to say that my motives are purely selfish. Don't worry, Rodion Romanovich, if I were considering only my own interests I should not have expressed myself so bluntly. I am not a complete fool. In this connexion, let me tell you a strange psychological fact. A short time ago, justifying my love for Avdotya Romanovna, I spoke of myself as a victim. Well, you must know that now I feel no love for her whatever, none at all, so that even to me it seems very strange, since I really did feel something . . .'

'As a result of idleness and depravity,' interrupted Raskolnikov.

'Well, I am indeed idle and depraved. But your sister has so many excellent qualities that even I could not but be impressed by them to some extent. But it all amounted to nothing, as I see now.'

'And have you seen it for long?'

'I had begun to notice it even earlier, but I finally convinced myself the day before yesterday, almost at the moment of my arrival in St. Petersburg. In Moscow I still imagined that I was coming here to try to win Avdotya Romanovna's hand as Mr. Luzhin's rival.'

'Excuse me for interrupting you. Please cut your story short, if you can, and come straight to the purpose of your visit. I am in a hurry. I have to go out . . .'

'With the greatest pleasure. After I had arrived here and decided to undertake a certain . . . journey, I wished to make the necessary preliminary arrangements. My children have remained with their aunt; they are well provided for and have no need of me. And indeed I am not much of a father! For myself I have taken only what Marfa Petrovna gave me a year ago. It is enough for me. Excuse me, I am coming to the point now. Before this journey which I may perhaps take, I want to settle accounts with Mr. Luzhin. It is not that I dislike him so extremely, but he was the cause of my quarrel with Marfa Petrovna, when I found out that she had contrived this marriage. Now, with your help and perhaps in your presence, I should like to have an interview with Avdotya Romanovna, and tell her firstly that her association with Mr. Luzhin will not only not be of any advantage to her but will probably bring her definite harm. Then, after begging her forgiveness for all the recent unpleasantness, I should ask permission to offer her ten thousand roubles and thus make easier the break with Mr. Luzhin, a break from which I am sure she herself would not be averse if only it appeared possible.'

'But you really are mad!' exclaimed Raskolnikov, more surprised than angry. 'How dare you say such things?'

'I knew you would make a fuss. But to begin with, although I am not rich, I can dispose of ten thousand roubles quite freely; that is to say I have absolutely no need of it, absolutely none. Unless Avdotya Romanovna accepts it, I shall find some more foolish use for it. That is the first point. The second is that my conscience is perfectly clear; there is no ulterior motive behind my offer. You may believe me or not, as you choose, but both Avdotya Romanovna and you will realize it later. The whole point is that I really did cause some trouble and unpleasantness to your sister, whom I greatly respect, and therefore, as I sincerely repent of it, I earnestly desire—not to buy myself off, not to pay for the unpleasantness, but purely and simply to do something for her good, on the basis that I do not really claim the privilege of doing nothing but harm. If my offer contained one-millionth part of calculation, I should not have made it so bluntly, and I should not have offered her only ten thousand roubles when a mere five weeks ago I was offering her much more. Besides, in a very, very short time I may perhaps be marrying another young lady and that fact alone ought to destroy any suspicion that I might have designs on Avdotya Romanovna. Finally, I will say that if she marries Mr. Luzhin, Avdotya Romanovna will be taking the same money, but from another source . . . Don't be angry, Rodion Romanovich. Consider it coolly and calmly.'

Svidrigaylov was himself extremely cool and calm as he said this.

'I beg you to stop,' said Raskolnikov. 'However you look at it, this is unforgivable impudence.'

'Not at all! If that were so, a man could do his fellow men nothing but harm in this world, and would have no right to do a particle of good, because of empty conventions. That is absurd. Surely if, for example, I died and left this money to your sister in my will, she would not then refuse to accept it?'

'Quite possibly she would.'

'No, I won't believe that! However, if the answer is no, there is no more to be said. But ten thousand roubles may be a very good thing on occasion. In any case, I beg you to tell Avdotya Romanovna what I have said.'

'No, I won't tell her.'

'In that case, Rodion Romanovich, I shall be obliged to seek a personal interview, which would mean troubling her.'

'If I do tell her, will you make no effort to see her yourself?'

'I don't know what to say. I should very much like to see her once.'

'There is no hope of that.'

'I'm sorry. However, you don't know me. Perhaps now we may become closer friends.'

'You think we can be friends?'

'Why shouldn't we?' said Svidrigaylov with a smile. He rose and took up his hat. 'I really didn't come here with the intention of troubling you for long, and I wasn't much counting on anything, although this morning I was greatly struck with your face . . .'

'Where did you see me this morning?' asked Raskolnikov uneasily.

'Oh, it was quite accidental . . . I keep fancying there is something very like me in you . . . Don't worry, I am not a bore; I got on well enough with the other card-sharpers, I never bored the great Prince Svirbey, who is a distant relative of mine, I could write about Raphael's Madonnas in Mrs. Prilukova's album, I lived for seven years without a break with Marfa Petrovna, I used to spend the night in Vyazemsky's house²in the Haymarket in the old days, and perhaps I will go up with Berg in his balloon.'

'Well, all right. May I ask if you will be leaving soon?'

'Leaving?'

'Yes, on that journey . . . you spoke of it yourself.'

'The journey? Oh, yes . . . I did speak to you of a journey . . . Well, that's a far-reaching question . . . But if only you knew what you are asking about!' he added abruptly in a loud voice, and laughed shortly. 'Perhaps I may get married instead of making that journey; they are trying to make a match for me.'

'Here?'

'Yes.'

'How have you found time for that?'

'But I do want to see Avdotya Romanovna once. I ask you most earnestly. Well, good-bye . . . Oh, yes! I was forgetting something. Please tell your sister, Rodion Romanovich, that she is remembered in Marfa Petrovna's will for three thousand roubles. That is quite definite. Marfa Petrovna made arrangements a week before her death, and it was done in my presence. In two or three weeks' time Avdotya Romanovna will be able to receive the money.'

'Are you speaking the truth?'

'Yes. Tell her. Well, sir, your servant. I am staying very near here, you know.'

As he left, Svidrigaylov bumped into Razumikhin at the door.

## CHAPTER II

IT was nearly eight o'clock. They were hurrying towards Bakaleev's house, in order to arrive before Luzhin.

'Who was that?' asked Razumikhin, as soon as they reached the street.

'That was Svidrigaylov, the landowner in whose house my sister was insulted when she was governess there. She had to leave, in fact she was turned out by his wife, Marfa Petrovna, because of his amorous advances to her. Later Marfa Petrovna begged Dunya's pardon, and now she has died suddenly. We were talking of her not long ago. I am very much afraid of that

2. A cheap lodging house.

man, I don't know why. He came to St. Petersburg immediately after his wife's funeral. He seems very strange, and he has some plan . . . It is as if he knew something . . . Dunya must be protected from him . . . that's what I wanted to tell you. Are you listening?'

'Protected! What can he do to Avdotya Romanovna? Well, thank you for telling me this, Rodya . . . We will protect her! . . . Where does he live?'

'I don't know.'

'Why didn't you ask him? What a pity! However, I'll find out!'

'Did you see him?' asked Raskolnikov after a short silence.

'Yes, I noticed him; I noticed him particularly.'

'You really did see him? Did you see him clearly?' insisted Raskolnikov.

'Yes, I remember him clearly. I should recognize him among a thousand. I have a good memory for faces.'

They were silent again.

'Hm . . . that's all right . . .' muttered Raskolnikov. 'Otherwise you know . . . I almost thought . . . I still keep thinking . . . that perhaps it was an illusion.'

'What are you talking about? I don't follow.'

'Well,' Raskolnikov went on, with a crooked smile, 'you all say that I am mad; it seemed to me just now that perhaps I really am mad, and have simply seen an apparition.'

'Why do you say that?'

'After all, who knows? Perhaps I really am mad, and everything that has happened all this time has been only my imagination . . .'

'Oh, Rodya, you are upset again! . . . What did he say? Why did he come?'

Raskolnikov did not answer and Razumikhin thought for a minute.

'Well, listen to my story,' he began. 'I looked in on you, but you were asleep. Then we had dinner and then I went to see Porfiry. Zametov was still there. When I tried to begin, nothing came of it. I simply could not find the right words. They seem not to understand, they are incapable of understanding, but they don't let that worry them. I took Porfiry aside, to the window, and began to talk to him, but again it somehow came out wrong: he didn't look at me and I didn't look at him. At last I shook my fist in his face and told him, in a cousinly way, I would beat his brains out. He only looked at me. I spat and came away, and that was all. It was all very stupid. I didn't exchange a word with Zametov. But listen: I was afraid I'd spoilt things for you, but coming downstairs I had an idea—it positively flashed on me: what are we worrying about? If there were any danger to you, or anything like that, well, of course. But really, what is it to you? You have nothing to do with it, so be hanged to them! We shall have the laugh of them afterwards. In your place, I should mystify them a bit more. How ashamed they will be later on! Be hanged to them! Later we can give them a drubbing, but now we will simply laugh at them.'

'Yes, of course,' answered Raskolnikov. 'But what will you say tomorrow?' he thought. It was strange that until this moment it had never entered his head to wonder: 'What will Razumikhin think when he knows?' As he thought this, Raskolnikov looked hard at him. He took very little interest now in Razumikhin's account of his visit to Porfiry; so much water had flowed under the bridges since then! . . .

In the corridor they ran into Luzhin, who had turned up at exactly eight o'clock and was looking for the room, so that all three went in together, but without looking at one another or exchanging greetings. The young men went in first, and Peter Petrovich, to avoid any awkwardness, lingered a little in the passage, taking off his overcoat. Pulkheria Alexandrovna went out to welcome him on the threshold. Dunya was greeting her brother.

Peter Petrovich came in and bowed to the ladies civilly enough, though with redoubled primness. He looked, however, as though he had been somewhat taken aback and had not yet recovered. Pulkheria Alexandrovna, also a little out of countenance, seated everybody at a round table on which a samovar was boiling. Dunya and Luzhin faced each other from opposite sides of the table. Razumikhin and Raskolnikov had Pulkheria Alexandrovna opposite them, Razumikhin nearer Luzhin and Raskolnikov next to his sister.

There was a momentary silence. Peter Petrovich leisurely drew out a scented cambric handkerchief and blew his nose with the air of a virtuous man whose dignity has been wounded and who is firmly resolved to exact an explanation. While he was in the hall, the idea had occurred to him of going away without taking off his coat, thus inflicting a severe and impressive punishment on the ladies and making them realize the whole situation. But he had not been able to make up his mind to this course. Besides, he was a man who did not like the unknown, and there were matters here to be cleared up. If his orders were so openly disobeyed, that meant there was some reason, and consequently it was better to learn what it was first. There would always be time to punish them, and it was in his power to do so.

'I hope your journey was pleasant,' he said formally, addressing Pulkheria Alexandrovna.

'Yes, thank God, Peter Petrovich.'

'I am very pleased to hear it. And Avdotya Romanovna is not too tired, either?'

'I am young and strong, I don't get tired, but it was very trying for mama,' answered Dunya.

'It can't be helped; our national railways are very long. Our so-called "Mother Russia" is vast . . . I, in spite of my own desires, was quite unable to meet you yesterday. I hope, however, that everything passed off without any particular trouble.'

'Alas, no, Peter Petrovich, we felt very downcast,' declared Pulkheria Alexandrovna, with a peculiar intonation, 'and if God Himself had not sent Dmitri Prokofich to us yesterday, we should have been utterly lost. This is he, Dmitri Prokofich Razumikhin,' she added, introducing him to Luzhin.

'I have already had the pleasure . . . yesterday,' muttered Luzhin, with an unfriendly sidelong look at Razumikhin. He frowned and was silent. Peter Petrovich belonged to that order of persons who seem extremely amiable in company and lay special claim to the social graces, but who, as soon as something is not to their liking, lose all their spring and become more like sacks of flour than animated and lively gentlemen. Silence fell again: Raskolnikov remained obstinately dumb, Avdotya Romanovna seemed unwilling to speak for the moment, Razumikhin could find nothing to say. Pulkheria Alexandrovna began to feel anxious again.

'Marfa Petrovna is dead. Have you heard?' she began, resorting to her main topic of conversation.

'Naturally I have heard. I was one of the first to know, and now I have brought you the news that immediately after his wife's funeral Arkady Ivanovich Svidrigaylov left in haste for St. Petersburg. So, at least, I hear from most trustworthy sources.'

'For St. Petersburg? Here?' asked Dunya, exchanging alarmed glances with her mother.

'Just so. And obviously he has some definite purpose, bearing in mind the haste of his journey and the antecedent circumstances in general.'

'Good heavens! Will he not leave Dunechka in peace even here?' exclaimed Pulkheria Alexandrovna.

'I do not think that either you or Avdotya Romanovna has any particular cause for alarm, unless, of course, you yourselves consent to enter into some kind of relations with him. As for me, I am on my guard, and I am now making inquiries to discover where he is staying . . .'

'Oh, Peter Petrovich, you cannot believe how much you have frightened me!' resumed Pulkheria Alexandrovna. 'I have seen him only twice, and I thought him horrible, horrible! I am convinced he was the cause of poor Marfa Petrovna's death.'

'About that it is impossible to reach a definite conclusion. My information is exact. I will not dispute that perhaps he was instrumental in hastening the course of events, so to say, by the moral influence of the affronts he gave her. As for his conduct and his moral character in general, I am in agreement with you. I do not know whether he is rich now, nor exactly what Marfa Petrovna left him; I shall be informed of it in the shortest possible space of time; but here in St. Petersburg, if he has any pecuniary resources at all, he will certainly resume his old courses. He is the most depraved, the most completely abandoned to vice, even of people of his own kind. I have substantial grounds for supposing that Marfa Petrovna, who had the misfortune to fall so deeply in love with him and redeem his debts eight years ago, was of service to him again in another connexion: only her efforts and sacrifices succeeded in suppressing, at the outset, criminal investigations involving a suspicion of brutal and, so to say, fantastic homicide, for which he might very well have been sent on a trip to Siberia. Such, if you wish to know, is the sort of man he is.'

'Good heavens!' cried Pulkheria Alexandrovna. Raskolnikov was listening with great attention.

'Were you speaking the truth when you said you had exact knowledge of this?' inquired Dunya in a severe and impressive tone.

'What I am telling you is only what I myself heard, in confidence, from poor Marfa Petrovna. It must be remarked that from a legal point of view the matter is extremely obscure. There lived, and I believe still lives, here a certain foreigner, a woman called Resslich, who was a small money-lender and had other business interests. A long time ago Mr. Svidrigaylov had very intimate and mysterious relations with this Resslich woman. She had a distant relative, a niece I think, living with her, a deaf-and-dumb girl about fifteen, or perhaps only fourteen, years old. This Resslich hated the girl, reproached her with every morsel she ate, and beat her unmercifully. One day the girl was found hanged in the attic. The verdict was that she had committed suicide. There, after the usual proceedings, the matter ended, but later, information was laid that the child had been . . . cruelly abused by Svidrigaylov. It is true that it was all obscure, as the accusation came from another German, a woman of notorious character whose word could not be credited; finally, no actual written statement was made, thanks to Marfa Petrovna's efforts and her money; it was all limited to rumours. Nevertheless, the rumours were very significant. You, of course, Avdotya Romanovna, heard while you were there the story of the man Philip, who died of brutal ill-treatment, six years ago, before serfdom was abolished.'

'On the contrary, I heard that this Philip hanged himself.'

'Just so, but he was driven, or rather persuaded, to his violent end by the ceaseless systematic persecution and punishments of Mr. Svidrigaylov.'

'I do not know that,' answered Dunya drily. 'I only heard a very strange story about this Philip's being some sort of hypochondriac, a kind of home-grown philosopher, who, the servants said "read himself silly", and about his having hanged himself more because of the mockery than because of the beatings of Mr. Svidrigaylov. While I was there he treated the servants well, and they liked him, even though they did blame him for Philip's death.'

'I see, Avdotya Romanovna, that you are suddenly disposed to find excuses for him,' remarked Luzhin, with an ambiguous smile twisting his lips. 'He is certainly a man of great cunning with the ladies, and very fascinating to them, as the lamentable example of Marfa Petrovna, who died so strangely, serves to show. I only wished to be of service to you and your mama with my advice, in view of the new attempts on his part which are undoubtedly in store for us. As far as I am concerned, I am convinced that the fellow will certainly disappear once more into a debtor's prison. Marfa Petrovna, with her children to consider, was far from intending to settle any land on him, and if she did leave him anything, it must have been the unavoidable minimum, a trifle, a mere nothing, not enough to last a man of his habits a year.'

'Peter Petrovich,' said Dunya, 'please let us stop talking of Mr. Svidrigaylov. It makes me wretched.'

'He has just been to see me,' said Raskolnikov suddenly, breaking his silence for the first time.

There were exclamations on all sides and everybody turned to him. Even Peter Petrovich was roused.

'An hour and a half ago, while I was asleep, he came in, woke me up, and introduced himself,' went on Raskolnikov. 'He was quite at home and cheerful, and is perfectly confident that I shall become a friend of his. Among other things he was most persistent in seeking an interview with you, Dunya, and asked me to act as his intermediary. He has a suggestion to make to you: he told me what it was. Besides this, he reliably informed me that a week before her death Marfa Petrovna had left you three thousand roubles in her will, and you will be able to receive the money in a very short time.'

'Thank God!' cried Pulkheria Alexandrovna, crossing herself. 'You must pray for her soul, Dunya!'

'It really is true,' Luzhin burst out.

'Well, what more?' asked Dunya, urgently.

'Then he said that he was not rich and that all the estate goes to the children, who are now with their aunt. Then he told me he is staying somewhere not far from me—but I don't know where, I didn't ask . . .'

'But what is it, what is it he wants to suggest to Dunya?' asked Pulkheria Alexandrovna fearfully. 'Did he tell you?'

'Yes, he told me.'

'What is it, then?'

'I will tell you afterwards.' Raskolnikov turned to his tea and said no more.

Peter Petrovich took out his watch and looked at it.

'I must go. I have something to do. So I need not be in your way,' he added with an air of some pique, and made to rise from his chair.

'Don't go, Peter Petrovich,' said Dunya. 'You know you intended to spend the evening with us. Besides, you yourself wrote that you wanted to discuss something with mama.'

'Quite so, Avdotya Romanovna,' said Peter Petrovich impressively, sitting down again but keeping his hat in his hands. 'I did indeed desire an explanation both with you and with your respected mama, and on some most important points. But as your brother finds it impossible to discuss some proposal of Mr. Svidrigaylov's in my presence, I am unwilling, and indeed unable, to talk of most extremely important matters in the presence of outsiders. In addition, my most urgent and earnest request has not been fulfilled . . .'

Luzhin's expression was bitter, and he again became majestically silent.

'Your request that my brother should not be present at our meeting was disregarded entirely at my insistence,' said Dunya. 'You wrote that my brother had insulted you; I think that the matter should be cleared up without delay, and that you should be reconciled. If Rodya really did insult you, he *ought to* and *will* ask your pardon.'

Peter Petrovich immediately began to swagger.

'There are some insults, Avdotya Romanovna, which, with the best will in the world, cannot be forgotten. There is a point in everything beyond which it is dangerous to go, for if once you do so, there can be no turning back.'

'That was not, strictly speaking, what I was talking about, Peter Petrovich,' interrupted Dunya with a shade of impatience. 'You must understand plainly that our whole future depends now on whether you clear all this up and make friends as quickly as possible, or not. I tell you candidly at the outset that I cannot see things in any other light, and if you set any value on me at all, this business must be settled once for all today, difficult as it may be. I repeat that if my brother is at fault he will ask your forgiveness.'

'I am surprised that you should put the question in that way, Avdotya Romanovna.' Luzhin was growing more and more irritated. 'Valuing and, so to say, adoring you as I do, I may at the same time find it completely and absolutely possible not to like some member of your family. As an aspirant to the happiness of your hand, at the same time I cannot take upon myself obligations inconsistent . . .'

'Oh, don't be so quick to take offence, Peter Petrovich,' interrupted Dunya with feeling. 'Be the wise and generous person I have always thought and would still like to think you. I have given you a solemn promise, I am engaged to you; trust me in this matter, and believe that I am capable of judging it in an unbiased fashion. The fact that I am undertaking the role of judge is as much a surprise to my brother as to you. When today, after the receipt of your letter, I requested him not to fail to be here at our meeting, I told him nothing of my intentions. Please understand that if you cannot come to terms, I shall be obliged to choose between you: it must be either you or he. That is how the question stands, on your side and on his. I don't want to make any mistake in my choice, in fact I must not. For your sake I must break with my brother; for my brother's sake I must break with you. I can find out now for certain, as I want to, whether he is a brother for me. And about you: am I dear to you, do you prize me, are you the husband for me?'

'Avdotya Romanovna,' said Luzhin, ruffled, 'I find your words too ominous; nay, more, I must call them offensive, in view of the position I have the honour to occupy in relation to you. I will say nothing of the strange and insulting comparison, on the same level, between me and . . . an insolent youth, but your words admit the possibility that the promise you gave might be broken. You say "either you or he" and by that very fact you show how little I mean to you . . . I cannot tolerate this, considering the relations and . . . obligations which exist between us.'

'What?' Dunya fired up. 'I put your interests alongside of everything that has until now been precious in my life, that has until now formed the *whole* of my life, and you are offended because I set *too little* value on you!'

Raskolnikov did not speak, but he smiled sarcastically. Razumikhin was shivering with excitement; but Luzhin would not accept the reproach; on the contrary, with every word he grew more captious and touchy, as though he were beginning to enjoy the dispute.

'Love for the future companion of your life, for your husband, should surpass love for your brother,' he answered sententiously, 'and in any case I cannot be put upon the same footing . . . Although I insisted just now that I did not wish, and indeed was unable, to discuss in your brother's presence all the matters I came here intending to speak of, nevertheless I now propose to seek from your respected mama the explanation, which I must insist on, of a point of the utmost importance, which injuriously affects me. Your son,' he went on, addressing Pulkheria Alexandrovna, 'yesterday, in the presence of Mr. Rassudkin (or . . . I think that is right? Excuse me, I can't remember your surname'—and he bowed graciously to Razumikhin—) 'insulted me by distorting an idea I had expressed to you in private conversation, over coffee, namely, that marriage with a poor girl who has had experience of life's bitterness is in my opinion more advantageous in connubial relations than with one who has known prosperity, for it is more beneficial to the morals. Your son deliberately exaggerated the meaning of my words to the point of absurdity, accusing me of evil intentions and, in my view, basing what he said on your correspondence. I shall count myself happy if you, Pulkheria Alexandrovna, find it possible to persuade me to the opposite effect and thus set my mind at rest to a considerable extent. Please inform me of the exact terms in which you reproduced my words in your letter to Rodion Romanovich.'

'I don't remember,' said Pulkheria Alexandrovna in some confusion. 'I repeated them as I understood them. I don't know how Rodya repeated them again to you . . . Perhaps he did exaggerate something.'

'He could not have exaggerated them without your prompting.'

'Peter Petrovich,' Pulkheria Alexandrovna declared with dignity, 'the proof that Dunya and I did not put a very bad construction on your words is that we are *here*.'

'Well said, mama!' said Dunya approvingly.

'It appears that I am at fault here, too!' said Luzhin resentfully.

'Here you are, always blaming Rodion, Peter Petrovich, and you yourself recently told an untruth about him in your letter,' added Pulkheria Alexandrovna, gaining courage.

'I do not remember writing anything that was not true.'

'You wrote,' said Raskolnikov sharply, not turning to Luzhin, 'that yesterday I gave money not to the widow of the man who was killed, which is what really happened, but to his daughter (whom I had never even seen until yesterday). You wrote it in order to make mischief between me and my family, and for the same purpose you used in addition the vilest terms about the conduct of a girl whom you do not know. All that is gossip of the meanest kind.'

'Excuse me, sir,' answered Luzhin, shaking with anger, 'I enlarged upon your qualities and actions in my letter solely in order to comply with the request of your sister and your mama that I should inform them how I found you and what impression you produced on me. As for the matter alluded to in my letter, find me a single line that is unjust!—show me that you did not waste your money or that in that family, unfortunate though it is, there are no unworthy persons.'

'In my opinion, with all your respectability you are not worth the little finger of the unhappy girl at whom you are casting stones.'

'Does that mean that you could allow yourself to introduce her into the society of your mother and sister?'

'I have already done so, if you want to know. I made her sit down today with mama and Dunya.'

'Rodya!' exclaimed Pulkheria Alexandrovna.

Dunechka blushed; Razumikhin frowned. Luzhin smiled with haughty sarcasm.

'You may see for yourself, if you will, Avdotya Romanovna,' said he, 'whether any agreement is possible between us. I hope that the matter is now cleared up and disposed of once and for all. I will withdraw, in order not to interfere further with the pleasures of a family gathering and the communication of secrets.' He rose and picked up his hat. 'But in going I shall permit myself the liberty of remarking that henceforward I hope to be spared such encounters and, so to say, compromises. I must particularly address this request to you, respected Pulkheria Alexandrovna, especially since my letter was directed to you, and to no one else.'

Pulkheria Alexandrovna felt somewhat affronted.

'It seems that you think you already exercise complete control over us, Peter Petrovich. Dunya told you the reason why your request was not complied with; she meant well. And you wrote to me as if you were giving orders. Are we to regard every wish of yours as a command? I must tell you, on the contrary, that you ought to behave with particular delicacy and forbearance towards us now, because, trusting you, we have abandoned everything to come here, and are consequently practically at your mercy already.'

'That is not quite just, Pulkheria Alexandrovna, especially at the present moment, when Marfa Petrovna's legacy of three thousand roubles has just been announced. It seems to have been very well timed, judging by the new tone in which you have been speaking to me,' he added sarcastically.

'And judging by that remark, we may certainly suppose that you counted on our helplessness,' observed Dunya irritably.

'But now, at least, I can no longer count on it, and I particularly do not wish to hinder the communication of Arkady Ivanovich Svidrigaylov's secret proposals, which he has authorized your dear brother to deliver, and which, I perceive, possess for you a most important, and perhaps a very agreeable, significance.'

'Oh, heavens!' exclaimed Pulkheria Alexandrovna.

Razumikhin could sit still no longer.

'And are you not ashamed now, sister?' asked Raskolnikov.

'Yes, Rodya, I am ashamed,' said Dunya. Pale with anger, she turned to Luzhin. 'Peter Petrovich, go!'

Peter Petrovich appeared not in the least to have expected such an ending. He had had too much confidence in himself, in his power, and in the helplessness of his victims. Even now he could not believe it. He turned pale and his lips quivered.

'Avdotya Romanovna, if I go out of that door now, with such a farewell, depend upon it I shall never return. Think well! I mean what I say!'

'What insolence!' cried Dunya, springing up from her place. 'I do not wish you to return!'

'What? So that's it!' exclaimed Luzhin, quite unable, even at the last moment, to believe in the rupture, and therefore now completely at a loss. 'That's it, is it? Do you know, Avdotya Romanovna, that I should be justified in complaining?'

'What right have you to speak to her like that?' intervened Pulkheria Alexandrovna hotly. 'What could you complain about? What right have you? Would I give my Dunya to such a man as you are? Go away! Leave us altogether! It is our own fault for having entered upon a wrong course, and mine most of all . . .'

'Nevertheless, Pulkheria Alexandrovna,' raved Luzhin in hot anger, 'you bound me by a promise that you are now going back on . . . and finally . . . finally . . . I was involved by it, so to say, in expense . . .'

This last grievance was so much in keeping with Peter Petrovich's character that Raskolnikov, white with rage and with the effort of restraining it, suddenly lost control and—roared with laughter. But Pulkheria Alexandrovna was furiously angry.

'Expense? What expense was that? You are talking of our trunk, I suppose? But surely the guard carried it free of charge for you. And good heavens! You say we bound you! You must think again, Peter Petrovich; it was just the opposite: you bound us hand and foot!'

'That's enough, mama; no more, please!' begged Avdotya Romanovna. 'Peter Petrovich, do me the favour of going!'

'I am going. But one last word!' he said, having by now almost completely lost control of himself. 'Your mama seems to have quite forgotten that I decided to take you, so to say, when the gossip of the town about your reputation had spread all over the district. Scorning public opinion for your sake and vindicating your reputation, I was certainly completely and absolutely entitled to count on being recompensed and even to demand your gratitude . . . And it is only now that my eyes have been opened! I can see that perhaps my action in scorning the general view was completely and absolutely rash . . .'

'Is he asking to have his head broken?' cried Razumikhin, starting up ready to wreak vengeance on him.

'You are a base, malicious person!' said Dunya.

'Not a word! Not a movement!' exclaimed Raskolnikov, holding Razumikhin back; then, advancing until he almost touched Luzhin, he said quietly and distinctly: 'Be good enough to get out! And not another word, or else . . .'

Peter Petrovich, his pale face distorted with rage, looked at him for some seconds and then turned and went out, and rarely indeed has any man carried such vicious hatred in his heart as he now felt for Raskolnikov. He blamed him, and him alone, for everything. It is worthy of note that even as he descended the stairs he still imagined that the game was not utterly lost and that, as far as the ladies were concerned, things might still be set 'completely and absolutely' right.

## CHAPTER III

THE point was that up to the very last minute he had not in the least expected such a break. He had blustered and bullied, never imagining even the possibility that two poor and un-protected women could escape his power. His confidence was greatly strengthened by vanity and that degree of self-reliance which might best be called self-infatuation. Peter Petrovich, who had struggled up from nothing, was full of almost morbid admiration for himself, set a high value on his own brain and capabilities and sometimes, when he was alone, even admired his own face in the mirror. But more than anything in the world he loved and prized his money, got together laboriously and by every means in his power; it raised him to the level of everything that had been superior to him.

When he had bitterly reminded Dunya just now that he had resolved to take her in spite of evil rumours about her, he had spoken with complete sincerity, and even felt the deepest indignation at her 'black ingratitude'. All the same, when he offered his hand to Dunya he was already fully convinced of the baselessness of the stories, which had been publicly refuted by Marfa Petrovna and long since dropped by everybody in the little town, who now warmly defended Dunya. Indeed, he would not have denied that he knew all this at the time. Nevertheless, he still rated very high his decision to raise Dunya to his own level, and considered it heroic. In talking of it to Dunya he had been expressing a cherished secret belief that had more than once aroused his own self-admiration and he could not understand how others could fail to admire his noble action. When he had paid his visit to Raskolnikov, he had entered with the feeling of a benefactor, prepared to reap his reward and taste the sweetness of compliments. And certainly now, as he went downstairs, he considered that he had been grossly insulted and that his virtues had not been recognized.

As for Dunya, he simply could not do without her; giving her up was unthinkable. For several years now he had dreamed voluptuously of marriage, but he went on accumulating money bit by bit, and waited. He dwelt with rapture on the idea of a virtuous maiden, poor (she must be poor), very young, very

pretty, well-born, well-educated and timorous, one who had
known a great many misfortunes, and was completely humble
before him, one who all her life would think of him as her
saviour, reverence him, obey him, admire him and him alone.
How many delightful scenes and episodes, with this seductive
and playful theme, his imagination had created in quiet
intervals of rest from business! And now the dreams of so many
years had almost come true; Avdotya Romanovna's beauty
and education had made an impression on him, her helpless
situation aroused his passion. He had found even more than
he had dreamed of: here was a proud, wilful, virtuous girl,
of a breeding and education superior to his own (he was
conscious of this), and this being would be slavishly grateful
to him all her life for his noble deed, and reverently humble
herself before him, while he exercised absolute and unlimited
dominion over her! . . . It seemed almost providential that
not long before, after prolonged deliberation and forethought,
he had at last resolved to make a decided change in his career
and enter a wider sphere of activity, and at the same time to
climb little by little into higher social circles, as he had long
indulged in pleasant thoughts of doing . . . In one word, he
had determined to try St. Petersburg. He knew that with a
woman's help it was 'completely and absolutely' possible to go
far. The fascination of a charming, virtuous, and well-educated
woman could make his path wonderfully pleasant, attract
friends to him, cast a rainbow-coloured glory over his life . . .
and now all was ruined! This sudden, monstrous break had
come on him like a clap of thunder. It was some hideous joke,
an absurdity! He had been only the tiniest bit overbearing;
he had not even managed to have his say out; he had not
really meant it all, but had got carried away—and it had ended
so seriously! Finally, in his own fashion he really loved Dunya,
in his dreams he was already her lord and master—and then,
suddenly . . . No! Tomorrow, tomorrow at latest, everything
must be restored, the wound must be healed, the breach
repaired and, most important of all; that insolent young puppy,
the cause of the whole thing, must be destroyed. Involuntarily,
with a painful sensation, he remembered Razumikhin . . . but
on that score he soon reassured himself: 'As though such a
person could be put on his level!'·But the one he really was
seriously afraid of was Svidrigaylov . . . In short, he foresaw
a good deal of trouble . . .

'No, I am more to blame than anybody else,' said Dunya,
embracing her mother and kissing her. 'I was blinded by
his money, but I swear, brother, I didn't even imagine he
was such a wretch. If I had seen through him before, nothing
could have tempted me! Don't judge me too harshly, brother.'
'God has delivered us, God has delivered us!' Pulkheria

Alexandrovna murmured, almost unconsciously, as though she had not yet fully realized what had happened.

They were all extremely cheerful, and in five minutes they were even laughing. Sometimes, though, Dunechka, remembering what had happened, grew pale and knitted her brows. Pulkheria Alexandrovna could not understand how she, too, could be glad; only that morning a break with Luzhin had seemed a terrible catastrophe. Razumikhin was in raptures. He did not yet dare to express his delight, but he was feverishly excited, as though a monstrous weight had rolled off his heart. Now he had the right to devote his whole life to them, serve them . . . And who knew what might happen? But he was afraid to pursue his thoughts farther, he feared his own imagination. And Raskolnikov went on sitting in his old place, seeming absent-minded and almost sullen. He, who had been the most insistent on Luzhin's dismissal, now seemed less interested than the others in what had just happened. Dunya could not help thinking that he was still angry with her, and Pulkheria Alexandrovna watched him apprehensively.

'Well, what did Svidrigaylov say to you,' asked Dunya, approaching him.

'Oh yes, yes!' exclaimed Pulkheria Alexandrovna.

'He tried to insist on giving you ten thousand roubles, and besides that, he expressed a desire to see you once, in my presence.'

'See her! Not for anything in the world!' cried Pulkheria Alexandrovna. 'And how dare he offer her money?'

Raskolnikov proceeded to repeat (rather drily) his talk with Svidrigaylov, omitting everything about Marfa Petrovna's ghost, in order to avoid unessential matters, since he felt averse to any but the most necessary conversation.

'What answer did you give him?' asked Dunya.

'At first I told him I would not give you any message. Then he declared that he would use every means in his power to obtain an interview himself. He averred that his passion for you had been a passing fancy, and that now he feels nothing for you . . . He doesn't want you to marry Luzhin . . . But his talk was very confused.'

'How do you explain him to yourself, Rodya? What did he seem like to you?'

'I confess I don't understand him very well. He offers you ten thousand roubles, but he told me he is not rich. He declares he is going away somewhere, and ten minutes later he has forgotten he said anything of the kind. He comes out also with the fact that he wants to get married, and that the match is already being arranged . . . Of course he has some design, and, most likely, a bad one. But again, it is strange to think that he would tackle the matter so stupidly if his intentions were evil . . . Of course, I refused the money on your behalf, once for all.

Altogether he seemed to me very strange . . . even . . . perhaps just a little mad. But I might be mistaken; it may be that he was trying to create a wrong impression. Marfa Petrovna's death seems to have affected him . . .'

'God rest her soul!' exclaimed Pulkheria Alexandrovna. 'I will always pray for her, always! What would have become of us now, Dunya, without that three thousand roubles? It is just as though it had fallen from heaven! Why, Rodya, this morning we had no more than three roubles to our name, and Dunechka and I were wondering how we could pawn her watch somewhere, so that we should not have to ask that man for money until he thought of it for himself.'

Dunya seemed almost thunder-struck by Svidrigaylov's offer. She still stood deep in thought.

'He has some terrible purpose!' she half-whispered to herself, almost shuddering.

Raskolnikov noticed her immoderate alarm.

'I think I am destined to see him again more than once,' he said to her.

'We will watch him! I will track him down!' exclaimed Razumikhin, full of zeal. 'I won't let him out of my sight! Rodya has given me permission. He said to me not long ago: "Look after my sister." Will you give me permission too, Avdotya Romanovna?'

Dunya smiled and gave him her hand, but the worried look did not leave her face. Pulkheria Alexandrovna watched her timidly, but the thought of the three thousand roubles was evidently comforting to her.

A quarter of an hour later they were all engaged in animated conversation. Even Raskolnikov, although he did not talk, had been listening attentively for some time. Razumikhin was holding forth.

'And why, why should you go away?' his excited rhetoric flowed on; 'what will you do in a little town? The main thing is that you are all together here, and you need one another—you need one another very much, if you understand me. If it is only for a little time . . . Accept me as a friend and partner, and I promise you we will devise a marvellous plan. Listen, I will explain it all to you in detail—the whole scheme. It had already occurred to me this morning, before anything had happened . . . This is the point: I have an uncle (I will introduce him to you; he is very nice and most respectable—a dear old man!), and this uncle has a capital of a thousand roubles, but he lives on his pension and does not need it. For two years he has been trying to insist on my borrowing this thousand and paying him six per cent. for it. I can see his idea: he simply wants to help me. But last year I didn't need the money; this year, however, I was only waiting for him to come here and then I meant to borrow it. If you will contribute another thousand out of your three—that will be enough to begin with, and we will make a partnership. And to do what?'

Then Razumikhin began to unfold his plan, explaining at some length that almost all our booksellers and publishers are bad because they have very little knowledge of their wares, while reasonably good books pay, generally speaking, and make a profit, sometimes a considerable one. Razumikhin had been dreaming of a publishing business, having worked for two years for other publishers. He had a fairly good knowledge of three European languages, although he had told Raskolnikov a week before that his German was weak. But this was with the object of persuading his friend to take half the translation and three roubles of the advance payment; he had been lying, and Raskolnikov had known that he lied.

'Why, I ask you, should we let the opportunity slip when we have one of the most important essentials—money of our own?' cried Razumikhin enthusiastically. 'Of course it will need a lot of hard work, but we will work hard, you, Avdotya Romanovna, Rodion, and I . . . Some books yield a famous profit now! The most important foundation for the undertaking is that we shall know just what ought to be translated. We shall translate, and publish, and learn, all at the same time. I can be useful there, because I have had experience. I've been poking my nose into publishing for two years now, and I know all the ins and outs; you don't need to be a saint to make pipkins, believe me! And why, why, let the chance slip? Why, I know— and I've kept the knowledge to myself—two or three books, and the mere idea of translating and publishing them might well be worth a hundred roubles for each one; indeed, for the idea of one of them I wouldn't take five hundred. And yet, do you know, if I told a publisher of them, he might perhaps hum and ha over them, they are such blockheads! As for all the business of printing, paper, selling, leave that to me; I know all the tricks of the trade. We'll begin in a small way, then go on to bigger things, and at least we shall get a living out of it. In any case we shall get our capital back.'

Dunya's eyes shone.

'What you say pleases me very much, Dmitri Prokofich,' she said.

'Of course, I know nothing about it,' put in Pulkheria Alexandrovna. 'Perhaps it is a good idea, but then again, God only knows! It is something new and unknown. We shall, of course, have to stay here, if only for a time . . .'

She looked at Rodya.

'What do you think, brother?' asked Dunya.

'I think it's a very good idea of his,' he answered. 'Needless to say, it is early yet to dream of a publishing house, but we really might issue five or six books with every confidence of success. I know one myself that would certainly go well. As for his knowing how to run the business, there is no doubt of that; he understands it . . . However, you will have plenty of time to make arrangements . . .'

'Hurrah!' shouted Razumikhin. 'Stop a minute, there is a flat here, in this very house, belonging to the same landlord. It is a separate flat, distinct from the hotel and not communicating with it, and it is furnished. There are three small rooms and the rent is moderate. Take it for the time being. I will pawn the watch for you tomorrow and bring you the money and then everything can be settled. The main thing is that you can all three live together, and Rodya can be with you . . . Where are you going, Rodya?'

'What Rodya, are you going already?' asked Pulkheria Alexandrovna in alarm.

'At such a moment!' cried Razumikhin.

Dunya looked at her brother with incredulous surprise. He had his cap in his hands and was getting ready to leave.

'You sound as though you were burying me, or saying good-bye for ever,' he said rather strangely.

He tried to smile, but somehow the smile was not a success.

'But really, who knows? Perhaps we are seeing each other for the last time,' he added unexpectedly.

He had been thinking this to himself, and somehow it said itself aloud.

'What is the matter?' cried his mother.

'Where are you going, Rodya?' asked Dunya in a strange tone.

'I really must go,' he answered confusedly, as though he were hesitating what to say. But his pale face showed a definite resolution.

'I wanted to say . . . as I was coming here . . . I wanted to tell you, mama . . . and you, Dunya, that it would be better if we parted for a short time. I don't feel well, I am not easy . . . I will come to you later, of my own accord, when . . . it is possible. I will remember you, and I love you . . . Leave me! Leave me alone! I had decided this, even before . . . I had firmly decided . . . Whatever happens to me, whether I perish or not, I want to be alone. Forget me altogether. It is better so . . . Don't make inquiries about me. When it is necessary, I will come myself, or . . . send for you. Perhaps it may all come right . . . But now, if you love me, give me up . . . Otherwise I feel I shall begin to hate you . . . Good-bye!'

'Oh God!' cried Pulkheria Alexandrovna.

His mother and sister were both terribly frightened; so indeed was Razumikhin.

'Rodya, Rodya, be reconciled with us, and let us be as we were before!' exclaimed his poor mother.

Slowly he turned towards the door, slowly he walked towards it. Dunya followed him.

'What are you doing to our mother, brother?' she whispered, her eyes blazing with indignation.

He looked sadly at her.

'It's all right. I will come, I shall be coming,' he muttered only half-aloud, as if not fully conscious what he was talking of. He went out of the room.

'Heartless, wicked egoist!' exclaimed Dunya.

'He is ma-a-d, but not heartless! He is out of his mind. Don't you see that? It is heartless of you to call him so!' whispered Razumikhin hotly, close to her ear, while he clasped her hand tightly.

'I will come back,' he exclaimed, turning to Pulkheria Alexandrovna, who seemed dazed and numb, and he hurried from the room.

Raskolnikov was waiting for him at the end of the corridor.

'I knew you would come running after me,' he said. 'Go back to them, be with them . . . be with them tomorrow as well . . . and always. Perhaps . . . I will come . . . if I can. Good-bye!'

And he walked away without offering his hand.

'But where are you going? What do you mean? What is the matter with you? You can't do this sort of thing!' murmured Razumikhin, utterly at a loss.

Raskolnikov stopped again.

'Once for all, never ask me about anything. I cannot answer you . . . Don't come to see me. I may perhaps come here . . . Leave me, but . . . *don't leave them*. Do you understand?'

It was dark in the corridor; they were standing near a lamp. For almost a minute they looked at one another in silence. Razumikhin remembered that minute all the rest of his life. With every moment Raskolnikov's intent and fiery glance pierced more powerfully into his mind and soul. Suddenly Razumikhin shuddered. Something strange had passed between them . . . some idea, something like a hint, something terrible and monstrous, suddenly understood on both sides . . . Razumikhin grew as pale as a corpse.

'Do you understand now?' said Raskolnikov abruptly, with painfully distorted features . . . 'Go back, go to them,' he added, turned away and hastily left the house . . .

I shall not describe that evening in Pulkheria Alexandrovna's room, how Razumikhin returned to them, how he tried to reassure them, how he swore that it was essential to allow the sick man to rest, swore that Rodya would come to them, that he would come every day, that he was very seriously upset, and must not be irritated; how he said that he, Razumikhin, would watch over him, he would get him a good doctor, the very best, he would arrange a consultation . . . In a word, from that evening Razumikhin became a son and a brother to them.

## CHAPTER IV

RASKOLNIKOV went straight to the house on the canal where Sonya lived. It was an old, green-painted house of three stories. He sought out the porter and got from him a vague direction to the tailor Kapernaumov's quarters. In a corner of the courtyard he found the entrance to a narrow, dark staircase, mounted it to the second floor and came out on to a passage that ran round the whole floor on the courtyard side. While he was wandering in the darkness, wondering where to find Kapernaumov's entrance, a door suddenly opened, three paces away from him; automatically he seized it.

'Who is there?' asked a woman's voice, full of alarm.

'Me . . . I was coming to see you,' answered Raskolnikov, walking into the tiny hall. In it a candle in a battered copper candlestick stood on a broken chair.

'You! Good heavens!' exclaimed Sonya weakly, standing as if transfixed.

'Which way is your room? Here?'

And, trying not to look at her, Raskolnikov walked quickly into the room.

A moment later Sonya came in with the candle, put it down, and stood in front of him, completely at a loss, full of indescribable agitation, and visibly frightened by his unexpected visit. Her pale face was suddenly flooded with colour, and tears even stood in her eyes . . . She felt at once sick and ashamed and glad . . . Raskolnikov turned away quickly and sat down at the table. He took in the whole room at a glance.

It was a large room, but very low ceilinged, the only one let by the Kapernaumovs; the locked door to the left led to their other room. Opposite this, in the right-hand wall, was another door, always kept locked, which led into the next flat. Sonya's room was rather like a barn; the irregularity of its angles made it look misshapen. One wall, with three windows which gave on to the canal, was set obliquely, so that one corner, forming a terribly acute angle, seemed to run off into obscurity, and when the light was poor the whole of it could not even be seen properly; the other angle was monstrously obtuse. There was hardly any furniture in this large room. To the right, in the corner, was a bed, with a chair beside it nearer the door. Against the same wall, very close to the door into the other flat, stood a plain deal table covered with a blue cloth, with two cane chairs near it. By the opposite wall, not far from the narrow corner, was a small, plain, wooden chest of drawers, looking lost in the empty spaces. This was all there was in the room. The yellowish, dirty, rubbed wallpaper was darkened in the corners; the room must have been damp and full of charcoal fumes in winter. Its poverty was evident; the bed had not even curtains.

Sonya silently watched the visitor who was so minutely and unceremoniously examining her room, and at last she even began to shake with fright, as though she stood before her judge and the ruler of her destiny.

'I am late . . . Is it eleven o'clock yet?' he asked, still without looking at her.

'Yes,' murmured Sonya. 'Yes, it is!' she repeated hastily, as though this offered her a way of escape. 'My landlord's clock has just struck . . . I heard it . . . It is.'

'I have come here for the last time,' went on Raskolnikov gloomily, although it was, in fact, the first. 'Perhaps I shall never see you again . . .'

'Are you . . . going away?'

'I don't know . . . Tomorrow . . .'

'So you won't be at Katerina Ivanovna's tomorrow?' said Sonya in a trembling voice.

'I don't know. Tomorrow morning everything . . . But that isn't the point; I came to say one word . . .'

He raised his preoccupied glance towards her, and suddenly noticed that he was sitting, while she still stood before him.

'Why are you standing? Do sit down,' he said in a different voice, quiet and kind.

She sat down. He looked at her gently and almost compassionately for some moments.

'How thin you are: just look at your hand! It is quite transparent. Your fingers are like a dead woman's.'

He took her hand. Sonya gave a faint smile.

'I was always like this,' she said.

'When you lived at home too?'

'Yes.'

'Well, of course you were!' He spoke jerkily, and his expression and the sound of his voice had suddenly changed once more. He looked round again.

'This is the place you rent from Kapernaumov?'

'Yes.'

'Are they there, on the other side of the door?'

'Yes . . . They have a room like this one.'

'Just one?'

'Yes.'

'If I lived in your room I should be afraid at night,' he remarked gloomily.

'My landlords are very kind and good,' answered Sonya, still in the same lost, dazed state. 'All the furniture and everything else . . . everything belongs to them. And they are very kind, and the children often come in here . . .'

'Aren't they stammerers or something?'

'Yes, . . . he stammers and is lame besides. His wife is the same . . . She doesn't exactly stammer, but she can't say all her words properly. She is kind, very kind. He is a former house-serf. And there are seven children . . . only the oldest stammers, the others are merely sickly . . . but they don't stammer. How do you know about them?' she added, with some astonishment.

'Your father told me about it, that time. He told me all about you . . . About how you went out at six o'clock and came back after eight, and about how Katerina Ivanovna knelt by your bed.'

Sonya was embarrassed.

'I thought I saw him today,' she whispered hesitatingly.

'Whom?'

'My father. I was in the street, just near here, at the corner, between nine and ten o'clock, and I seemed to see him walking in front of me. It might just have been him. I would have liked to go to Katerina Ivanovna's . . .'

'You were walking the streets?'

'Yes,' whispered Sonya abruptly, again looking down in confusion.

'I suppose Katerina Ivanovna used to beat you, when you lived at your father's?'

'Oh, no. Why do you say that? No!' Sonya looked at him almost with terror.

'You love her, then?'

'Love her? But of course!' Sonya almost wailed, clasping her hands together in distress. 'Oh, you speak of her . . . If only you knew! She is really just like a child . . . I suppose she has really lost her reason . . . from grief. But how clever she used to be . . . how generous . . . how good! You know nothing, nothing at all . . . Oh!'

Sonya said this almost despairingly, wringing her hands in excitement and distress. Her pale cheeks had flushed again, and her eyes looked full of anguish. She was plainly very deeply moved, and longing to speak, to plead, to find expression for something. An almost *insatiable* compassion, if one can use the expression, was depicted in every feature of her face.

'Beat me! What makes you say that? Good heavens, beat me! And even if she had, what of that? What of it? You know nothing, nothing at all . . . She is so unhappy, oh, so unhappy! And she is ill . . . She is seeking justice . . . She is pure. She believes there ought to be justice in everything, and she demands it . . . You might torture her, but she would not act unjustly. She does not see that one can't expect justice from people, and she gets exasperated . . . Like a child, like a child! She loves justice, she loves justice!'

'And what will become of you?'

Sonya looked questioningly at him.

'They are left on your hands, you know. Even before, really, you had to bear the whole burden, and your father came to you for money to drink with. Well, but what will happen now?'

'I don't know,' said Sonya sadly.

'Will they remain where they are?'

'I don't know. They are behind with the rent; and I hear that the landlady said today that she wanted to give them notice, and Katerina Ivanovna says that she won't stay there another minute.'

'What makes her so confident? Is she relying on you?'

'Oh, no, don't speak like that! . . . We are one, we live as one.' Sonya had grown suddenly excited once more, and even angry, exactly like a ruffled canary or some other little bird. 'And besides, what can she do? What else can she do?' she asked, growing more violently excited. 'How she cried today! Her mind wanders, have you noticed? She gets muddled; first she is childishly anxious that everything shall be nice tomorrow, and that we should have a dinner, and everything . . . then she is wringing her hands, coughing up blood, crying, and then suddenly she begins to knock her head against the wall, as if she were utterly desperate. Then she takes comfort again. She pins all her faith on you; she says you will help her, and that she will borrow a little money somewhere and go back to her old home, taking me with her, and open a boarding-school for young ladies, with me to superintend it, and that a wonderful new life is beginning for us. She kisses me, caresses me, comforts me, and she really believes it all, all those fantastic dreams! How can you contradict her? And all day she has been washing, cleaning, mending; with her feeble strength she dragged the tub into the room, and then she couldn't breathe, and had to lie down on the bed. This morning she and I went to the market to buy shoes for Polechka and Lena, because all they had have fallen to pieces; only we hadn't enough money to pay for them, we were a lot short, and she had chosen such nice little boots, because she has very good taste, you don't know. And she began to cry there in the shop, with the shopman there, because she hadn't enough . . . Oh, how sad it was to see her.'

'Well, after that one can understand . . . your living like this,' said Raskolnikov, with a bitter smile.

'And aren't *you* sorry, aren't you sorry for her?' exclaimed Sonya again. 'Yet I know you gave her your last penny, when you had seen nothing. If you had seen everything, good heavens! And how often I have driven her to tears, how often! Even this last week! Yes, I! Not more than a week before he died. I was cruel. And how many times I have behaved so, how many! . . . Oh, how painful it has been all day to remember it now!'

Sonya wrung her hands as she spoke, with the pain of remembering.

'You, cruel?'

'Yes, I, I! I had gone there,' she continued, weeping, 'and my poor father said to me: "Read to me, Sonya," he said, "I have a headache. Read to me . . . here is a book." It was some book he had got from Andrey Semënovich Lebezyatnikov, who lives there; he used always to get such queer books. But I said "I must go," because I didn't want to read, and I had gone there chiefly to show Katerina Ivanovna some collars; Lizaveta, the dealer, had let me have some collars and cuffs cheap, and they were quite new and very pretty, figured ones. Katerina Ivanovna liked them very much; she put them on and looked at herself in the glass and she liked them very, very much: "Please give them to me, Sonya," she said. She said *please*, and she so wanted them. But when could she wear them? It was just that they reminded her of the old, happy days. She looked at herself in the glass and admired herself, and she had had no dresses, none at all, no pretty things, for so many years! And she would never ask anybody for anything; she is proud; she would rather give away her own last possessions, but now here she was asking for them—she liked them so much! But I didn't want to give them away: "What use are they to you, Katerina Ivanovna?" I said. Yes, that is how I spoke to her. I should not have said that to her! She just looked at me, and she was so terribly sad that I had refused her, that it made me sorry to see her . . . And she wasn't sad about the collars, but because I had refused her, I could see that. And now I wish I could change it all, do it all over again, take back all those words . . . Oh, I . . . But why am I saying all this? . . . It makes no difference to you.'

'You knew this Lizaveta, the dealer?'

'Yes . . . Did you know her?' asked Sonya, rather surprised.

'Katerina Ivanovna has consumption, in a very advanced stage; she will soon die,' said Raskolnikov after a silence, ignoring the question.

'Oh, no, no, no!' With an unconscious gesture Sonya seized both his hands in hers, as though imploring him not to let it happen.

'But really it will be better for her to die.'

'No, not better, not better. It will not be better at all!' she repeated in terror, hardly conscious of what she said.

'And the children? Where can they go then, except here?'

'Oh, I don't know! . . .' cried Sonya, almost desperate, clutching her head. It was plain that the idea had occurred to

her many, many times before and that he had only made it
start up again.

'Well, if you become ill and are taken to hospital, while
Katerina Ivanovna is still alive, what will happen then?' he
insisted pitilessly.

'Ah, why do you say that? Why do you say it? It cannot
happen!' Awful terror distorted Sonya's face.

'Cannot happen?' went on Raskolnikov, with a cruel smile.
'Are you insured against it? Then what will become of them?
The whole lot will be turned into the street, she will cough as
she begs, and knock her head against the wall, as she did today,
and the children will cry . . . She will fall down in the street
and be taken to the police and then to the hospital to die, and
the children . . .'

'Oh, no! . . . God will not allow it!' broke at last from
Sonya's over-burdened heart. She had listened with an imploring face, with her eyes on him and her hands clasped in
silent supplication, as though it all depended on him.

Raskolnikov got up and walked about the room. A minute
passed. Sonya stood with hands and head hanging, in terrible
anguish.

'Can't you save, put something away for a rainy day?' he
asked, stopping short in front of her.

'No,' whispered Sonya.

'Of course you can't! Have you tried?' he went on, almost
sneering.

'Yes.'

'And it came to nothing! Of course it did! No need to ask!'

He resumed his pacing about the room. Another minute
went by.

'You don't get money every day?'

Sonya grew more confused than ever, and again colour
flooded her face.

'No,' she whispered, with a painful effort.

'Polechka will probably go the same way,' he said abruptly.

'No! No! That can't be! No!' Sonya almost shrieked in
desperation, as if someone had plunged a knife into her. 'God—
God will not allow such a terrible thing! . . .'

'He lets it happen to others.'

'No, no! God will protect her! God will protect her!' she
repeated, beside herself.

'Perhaps God does not exist,' answered Raskolnikov, with
malicious enjoyment. He looked at her and laughed.

Sonya's face underwent a sudden awful change; a tremor
passed across it. She looked at him with inexpressible reproach; she tried to say something, but she could not utter
a word, and only covered her face with her hands and sobbed
bitterly.

'You say Katerina Ivanovna's mind is deranged; your own mind is deranged,' he said after a short silence.

Some five minutes passed. He went on walking up and down the room in silence, without looking at her. At last he went up to her; his eyes were glittering. He took her by the shoulders with both hands and looked into her weeping face. His piercing eyes were dry and inflamed, his lips twitched violently . . . With a sudden swift movement he stooped, fell to the ground, and kissed her foot. Sonya started back in fear, as though he were mad. Indeed, he looked quite mad.

'Why, why do you do that? To me!' she murmured, turning white, and her heart contracted painfully.

He rose at once.

'I prostrated myself not before you, but before all human suffering,' he said wildly, and walked away to the window. 'Listen,' he added, turning back to her after a minute; 'not long ago I told an offensive fellow that he was not worth your little finger . . . and that I did my sister honour today, seating her beside you.'

'Oh, why did you say that? Was she there?' cried Sonya, frightened. 'An honour to sit with me! But I am . . . a fallen creature . . . Ah, why did you say it?'

'I said it not because of your dishonour and your sin, but because of your great suffering. That you are a great sinner is true,' he added, almost exultantly, 'but your greatest sin is that you have abandoned and destroyed yourself *in vain*. Is that not horrible? Is it not horrible that you live in this filth, which is so loathsome to you, while at the same time you know (you have only to open your eyes) that you are helping nobody by it, and not saving anybody from anything? Tell me,' he said, almost frenziedly, 'how such shame and such baseness can exist in you side by side with other feelings, so different and so holy! Surely it would be better, a thousand times better and wiser, to plunge into the water and end it all!'

'But what will become of them?' asked Sonya faintly, gazing at him with anguish, but also without any apparent surprise at the suggestion. Raskolnikov looked at her strangely.

He had read it all in her look. She must indeed have had that idea herself. Perhaps many times in her despair she had seriously thought of putting an end to everything, seriously enough not to be surprised now when he suggested it. She had not noticed even the harshness of his words. (The meaning of his reproaches and his peculiar view of her shame had of course also escaped her notice, as he saw.) But he fully understood how monstrously she was tormented, and had long been tormented, by the thought of her dishonourable and shameful position. But what, he wondered, what could have prevented her until now from resolving to end it all? And it was only now that he fully realized what those poor little orphans and the pitiful, half-mad Katerina Ivanovna, with her consumption and her way of knocking her head against the wall, meant to Sonya.

Nevertheless, it was clear, again, that Sonya with her character and the upbringing she had in spite of everything received, could not in any event continue as she was. The question remained for him: how could she have stayed in her present situation for so long without going mad, even if it were beyond her strength to throw herself into the water? Of course he understood that Sonya's position in society was fortuitous, was an accident, although unfortunately not exceptional or isolated. But the accidental nature of her position, the certain degree of education she had had, and all her earlier life might, it seemed, have killed her at the very first step on that abhorrent path. What had supported her? Surely it could not be depravity? All her shame had obviously touched her only mechanically; no trace of real corruption had yet crept into her heart; he could see that; it was her real self that stood before him . . .

'Three ways are open to her,' he thought, 'to throw herself into the canal, to end in a madhouse, or . . . or, finally, to abandon herself to debauchery that will numb her mind and turn her heart to stone.' The last idea was repulsive to him, but he was sceptical, he was young, he had an abstract and consequently cruel mind, and therefore he could not but believe that the last course, of yielding to corruption, was the most likely.

'But can that be true?' he cried within his heart. 'Can that creature, who still preserves the purity of her soul, consciously sink at last into the abominable stench of that pit? Is it possible that she already feels the attraction, and that she has only been able to endure until now because vice no longer seems so disgusting to her? No, no, that cannot be!' he exclaimed, as Sonya had earlier. 'No, what has kept her from the canal until now is the thought of sin, and *they*, *those children* . . . And if she has not gone mad before this . . . But who can say she has not? Is her reason really sound? Can sane people talk as she does? Could a healthy mind make her judgements? How can she possibly crouch over her own destruction, above the stinking pit into which she is being drawn, and wave her hands and stop her ears when she is told of the danger? Why does she?— Because she expects a miracle to happen? Probably. And are not all these things signs of madness?'

He clung obstinately to this idea. It was a solution that he preferred to any other. He fixed his eyes intently on her.

'So you pray a great deal to God, Sonya?' he asked her.

Sonya said nothing. He stood and waited for her answer.

'What should I do without God?' she said in a rapid, forceful whisper, glancing at him for a moment out of suddenly flashing eyes, and pressing his hand with hers.

'Well, there it is!' he thought.

'And what does God do for you in return?' he asked, probing deeper.

Sonya was silent for a long time, as though unable to answer. Her flat little chest heaved with agitation.

'Be quiet! Do not ask! You are not worthy! . . ' she exclaimed suddenly, looking at him severely and indignantly.

'That's it, that's it!' he repeated to himself, insistently.

'He does everything,' she said in a rapid whisper, her eyes again downcast.

'That is the solution! That is the explanation!' he decided, watching her with greedy curiosity. He looked with a new, strange, almost painful feeling at that thin, pale, angular little face, at those timid blue eyes that were capable of flashing with such fire, such stern, strong feeling, at that small figure, still shaking with indignation and anger, and it all seemed to him more and more strange, almost impossible. 'She has religious mania!' he repeated firmly to himself.

On the chest of drawers lay a book. He had noticed it every time he passed in his pacing up and down; now he took it up and looked at it. It was a Russian translation of the New Testament. Its leather binding was old and worn.

'Where did you get this?' he called across the room. She was still standing in the same place, a few steps from the table.

'It was brought to me,' she answered unwillingly, without looking at him.

'Who brought it?'

'Lizaveta. I asked her to.'

'Lizaveta! How strange!' he thought. Everything about Sonya seemed stranger and more extraordinary with every minute. He took the book to the candle and began to turn over the pages.

'Where is that about Lazarus?' he asked abruptly.

Sonya looked steadily at the ground without answering. She was standing turned a little away from the table.

'Where is that about the raising of Lazarus? Find it for me, Sonya.'

She glanced at him sidelong.

'You are looking in the wrong place . . . In the fourth gospel . . .' she whispered sternly, without moving towards him.

'Find it and read it to me,' he said. He sat down, with his elbows on the table and his head propped in his hands, and sombrely prepared to listen, with his eyes turned away.

'In two or three weeks' time they will be welcoming her

into the asylum! It looks as though I should be there too, if not worse,' he muttered to himself.

Sonya advanced hesitantly to the table. She had heard his strange request with incredulity, but she took the book.

'Haven't you read it?' she asked, frowning at him across the table. Her voice grew more and more severe.

'A long time ago . . . When I was at school. Read it!'

'And haven't you heard it in church?'

'No, I . . . didn't go. Do you go often?'

'N-no,' whispered Sonya.

Raskolnikov laughed.

'I understand . . . You won't go to your father's funeral tomorrow, then?'

'Yes, I shall. I was there last week . . . I had a requiem sung.'

'Whose?'

'Lizaveta's. She was murdered with an axe.'

His nerves grew tauter and tauter. His head was beginning to swim.

'You were friendly with Lizaveta?'

'Yes . . . She was good . . . She came here . . . not often . . . she couldn't. We used to read together and . . . talk. She will see God.'

The bookish words fell strangely on his ears. And here was again something new: some sort of secret meetings with Lizaveta. And both of them religious maniacs.

'I shall become one myself here! It is catching!' he thought. 'Read!' he exclaimed insistently and irritably.

Sonya still hesitated. Her heart was throbbing. Somehow she dared not read to him. He looked at the 'unhappy madwoman' almost with torment.

'Why? You are not a believer, are you? . . .' she whispered softly, gasping a little.

'Read! I want you to!' he insisted. 'You used to read to Lizaveta!'

Sonya opened the book and found the place. Her hands shook, her voice failed. Twice she tried to begin, but could not utter the first word.

'Now a certain man was sick, named Lazarus, of Bethany' . . . she pronounced at last, with an effort, but after two or three words her voice broke like an over-strained violin string. Her breath caught and her heart laboured.

Raskolnikov half understood why Sonya could not make herself read to him, and the more he understood, the more roughly and irritably he insisted. He knew very well how difficult it was for her to expose and betray all that was *her own*. He understood that those feelings in fact constituted her real long-standing *secret*, cherished perhaps since her girlhood, in the midst of her family, with an unhappy father, a stepmother crazed by grief, and hungry children, in an atmosphere of hideous shrieks and reproaches. At the same time he now knew and knew for certain that although she was troubled and feared something terrible if she were to read now, yet she had a tormenting desire to read, and read for *him* to hear, and read *now*, 'whatever might happen afterwards' . . . He could see all this in her eyes and in her emotional agitation . . . She mastered herself, overcame the spasm in her throat, which had cut off her voice in the first verse, and continued the reading of the eleventh chapter of St. John. She came to the nineteenth verse:

'And many of the Jews came to Martha and Mary, to comfort them concerning their brother.

'Then Martha, as soon as she heard that Jesus was coming, went and met him: but Mary sat still in the house.

'Then said Martha unto Jesus, Lord, if thou hadst been here, my brother had not died.

'But I know, that even now, whatsoever thou wilt ask of God, God will give it thee.'

She stopped again, anticipating with shame that her voice would again begin to quiver and break.

'Jesus saith unto her, Thy brother shall rise again.

'Martha saith unto him, I know that he shall rise again in the resurrection at the last day.

'Jesus said unto her, *I am the resurrection and the life:* he that believeth in me, though he were dead, yet shall he live:

'And whosoever liveth and believeth in me shall never die. Believest thou this?'

'She saith unto him' (and drawing a painful breath, Sonya read clearly but strongly, as though she herself were confessing her faith for all to hear:) 'Yea, Lord, I believe that thou art the Christ, the Son of God, which should come into the world.'

She seemed about to stop, and glanced quickly up at *him*, but then controlled herself and went on reading. Raskolnikov sat listening, motionless, his elbows on the table, his eyes turned away. She read on to the thirty-second verse.

'Then when Mary was come where Jesus was, and saw him, she fell down at his feet, saying unto him, Lord, if thou hadst been here, my brother had not died.

'When Jesus therefore saw her weeping, and the Jews also weeping which came with her, he groaned in the spirit, and was troubled.

'And said, Where have ye laid him? They said unto him, Lord, come and see.

'Jesus wept.

'Then said the Jews, Behold how he loved him!

'And some of them said, Could not this man, which opened

the eyes of the blind, have caused that even this man should not have died?'

Raskolnikov turned and looked at her with emotion: Yes, that was it! Already she was shaking with real, genuine fever. He had expected this. She was approaching the moment of the greatest, the unheard-of miracle, and was filled with immense triumph. Her voice rang like a bell with the power of triumph and joy. Her eyes had grown dark, and the lines of print danced before them, but she knew the passage by heart. In the verse: 'Could not this man, which opened the eyes of the blind . . .' she lowered her voice, and the warmth and passion of it expressed the doubt, reproach, and censure of the blind, unbelieving Jews, who were so soon, in an instant, to fall to the ground as if struck by lightning, sobbing, and believing . . . 'And *he, he* who is also blind and unbelieving, he also will hear in a moment, he also will believe. Yes, yes! Here and now!' she dreamed, and trembled with joyful expectancy.

'Jesus therefore again groaning in himself cometh to the grave. It was a cave, and a stone lay upon it.

'Jesus said, Take ye away the stone. Martha, the sister of him that was dead, saith unto him, Lord, by this time he stinketh: for he hath been dead *four* days.'

Sonya strongly emphasized the word four.[3]

'Jesus saith unto her, Said I not unto thee, that, if thou wouldest believe, thou shouldest see the glory of God?

'Then they took away the stone from the place where the dead was laid. And Jesus lifted up his eyes, and said, Father, I thank thee that thou hast heard me.

'And I knew that thou hearest me always: but because of the people which stand by I said it, that they may believe that thou hast sent me.

'And when he thus had spoken, he cried with a loud voice, Lazarus, come forth.

'*And he that was dead came forth*' (she read, loudly and exultantly, cold and trembling as though her own eyes had seen it) 'bound hand and foot with graveclothes: and his face was bound about with a napkin. Jesus saith unto them, Loose him, and let him go.

'*Then many of the Jews which came to Mary, and had seen the things which Jesus did, believed on him.*'

She read, and indeed could read, no farther, but closed the book and stood up quickly.

'That is all about the raising of Lazarus,' she whispered abruptly and sternly, and stood without moving, turned away from him and not daring to raise her eyes to him, as though she were ashamed. Her feverish trembling continued. The candle-end had long since burned low in the twisted candlestick,

---

3. Four days had passed since the murder of the pawnbroker and Lisaveta.

dimly lighting the poverty-stricken room and the murderer and the harlot who had come together so strangely to read the eternal book. Five minutes or more passed.

'I came to say something to you,' said Raskolnikov loudly and abruptly, with a frown. He got up and went to Sonya, who raised her eyes silently to his. His look was grim and expressed a wild resolution.

'Today I deserted my family,' he said, 'my mother and sister. I shall not go to them now. I have made a complete break.'

'Why?' asked Sonya, stupefied. Her recent meeting with his mother and sister had left a strong, if rather obscure, impression upon her. She heard the news of the rupture almost with terror.

'Now I have only you,' he added. 'Let us go on together . . . I have come to you. We are both alike accursed, let us go together!'

His eyes glittered. 'He is like somebody half-mad!' thought Sonya in her turn.

'Go where?' she asked, frightened, and involuntarily stepped back.

'How should I know? I know only that our paths lie together, and I know it for certain—that is all. We have one goal!'

She looked at him without understanding. She knew only that he was terribly and infinitely unhappy.

'None of them will understand anything, if you talk to them,' he went on, 'but I have understood. I have come to you because I need you.'

'I don't understand . . .' whispered Sonya.

'You will understand afterwards. Haven't you done the same? You too have stepped over the barrier . . . you were able to do it. You laid hands on yourself, you destroyed a life . . . *your own* (that makes no difference!). You might have lived by reason and the spirit, but you will end on the Haymarket . . . But you cannot endure, and if you remain *alone* you will go out of your senses, like me. You are like a madwoman even now; so we must go together, by the same path! Let us go!'

'Why? Why do you say that?' said Sonya, strangely and passionately stirred by his words.

'Why? Because you can't remain like this—that's why! You must judge things seriously and directly at last, and not weep like a child and cry that God won't allow it. What will happen if you really are taken to the hospital tomorrow? She is out of her mind and consumptive, she will soon die, but the children? Won't Polechka be lost? Have you never seen children at the corner of the street, who have been sent out by their mothers to beg? I know where and how such mothers live.

Children cannot remain children there. There a seven-year-old child is depraved and a thief. And yet children are the image of Christ. "Of such is the kingdom of God." He commanded us to love them and cherish them, they are the future of mankind . . .'

'But what must we do? What must we do?' repeated Sonya, crying hysterically and wringing her hands.

'What must we do? Demolish what must be demolished, once and for all, that is all, and take the suffering on ourselves! What? Don't you understand? You will understand afterwards . . . Freedom and power, but above all, power! Power over all trembling creatures, over the whole ant-heap! . . That is the goal! Remember this! These are my parting words to you! This may be the last time I shall talk to you. If I do not come tomorrow, you will hear all about it, and then remember what I say to you now. And at some later time, after many years, you may come to understand what they mean. If I do come tomorrow, I will tell you who killed Lizaveta. Good-bye.'

Sonya started with terror.

'Do you really know who killed her?' she asked, turning cold with horror, and looking at him wildly.

'I know, and I will tell you . . . You, and only you! I have chosen you. I shall not come to ask your forgiveness, I shall simply tell you. I chose you long ago to tell this thing to, when your father talked about you. I thought of it when Lizaveta was alive. Good-bye. Don't give me your hand. Tomorrow!'

He went out. Sonya had looked at him as if he were mad; but she seemed insane herself, and she felt it. Her head was spinning. 'Good heavens! How does he know who killed Lizaveta? What did those words mean? It is terrible!' But all the same, *the idea* did not cross her mind. Never once! Never once! . . . 'Oh, he must be dreadfully unhappy! . . . He had left his mother and sister. Why? What had happened? What were his intentions? What was that he had said to her? He had kissed her foot and said . . . said (yes, he had said it clearly) that he could not live without her . . . Oh, heavens!'

Sonya passed a feverish and delirious night. Sometimes she started up, weeping and wringing her hands, then sank back again into fitful sleep, and dreamed of Polechka, of Katerina Ivanovna, of Lizaveta, of reading the gospel, and of him . . . him with his pale face and burning eyes . . . He would kiss her foot, and weep. Oh, heavens!

Beyond the door on the right, which shut off her room from Gertrude Karlovna Resslich's flat, was another room, which had long been empty. It belonged to Mrs. Resslich's flat, and was to let; cards on the gates of the house and notices stuck to the windows which overlooked the canal advertised this fact. Sonya had long been accustomed to thinking of the room as unoccupied. But all through that interview, behind the door of the empty room, Mr. Svidrigaylov had been concealed, standing and listening. When Raskolnikov went out, he stood there for a moment longer, thinking, then tiptoed into his own room next door, got a chair, and carried it close to the door leading into Sonya's room. The conversation had seemed to him interesting and important, and he had greatly enjoyed it —enjoyed it so much that he had brought the chair so that in future, the next day, for example, he should not be subjected again to the unpleasantness of standing on his feet for a whole hour, but be more comfortably placed and thus enjoy complete satisfaction in every respect.

## CHAPTER V

THE next morning, when, at exactly eleven o'clock, Raskolnikov went into the Criminal Investigation section of the building which housed the police office of the Spasskaya District and asked to be announced to Porfiry Petrovich, he was surprised to be kept waiting so long; it was at least ten minutes before he was summoned. According to his calculations they ought to have pounced on him at once. Meanwhile he stood in the waiting-room, and people who seemed to have no concern with him came and went past him. In the next room, which looked like an office, several clerks sat writing, and it was obvious that not one of them had the least idea who or what Raskolnikov was. He gazed round him with an anxious suspicious air, trying to see if there were not some guard near him, or somebody posted to keep a secret watch on him, so that he should not go away, but there was nothing of the kind. He saw clerks, persons occupied with trivial business, and a few other people, but nobody had anything to do with him; as far as they were concerned, he could go to the farthest ends of the earth. He became more and more firmly convinced that if yesterday's enigmatic stranger, that apparition sprung out of the ground, really had seen everything, really knew everything, he, Raskolnikov, would hardly have been left to stand here and wait in peace. Would they indeed have waited for him until eleven o'clock, when he condescended to come to them? It followed that that man had either not yet reported what he knew or . . . or knew nothing at all, had seen nothing (indeed, how could he have seen?), and consequently that everything that had happened yesterday had been no more than a phantasmagoria created by his sick and excited imagination. Even yesterday, at the time of his intensest alarm and despair, this conjecture had suggested itself to him with growing force. Now, as he turned all these thoughts over in his head, and prepared to renew the conflict, he realized suddenly that he was trembling—and at the idea that he could tremble with fear before the hateful Porfiry Petrovich, anger began to seethe in his heart. More than anything else he dreaded another encounter with that man; he felt infinite, boundless hatred for him, and he even feared that his hatred would make him betray himself. So violent was his indignation that his trembling ceased at once; he was ready to go in with a cold and insolent air, and he promised himself to say as little as possible, but to watch and listen, and this time at least, come what might, to conquer his sick and overstrained nerves. At this moment Porfiry Petrovich sent for him to come in.

Porfiry Petrovich proved to be alone in his office. This was a room neither large nor small, containing a large writing desk standing in front of a sofa upholstered in imitation leather, a bureau, a bookcase in one corner, and several chairs. It was all Government furniture, made of yellow polished wood. In one corner, in the wall, or rather the partition, at the back of the room, there was a closed door; there must be other rooms beyond the partition. When Raskolnikov came in, Porfiry Petrovich at once shut the door behind him, and they remained alone. He had met his visitor with an appearance of great cheerfulness and affability, and it was only a few minutes afterwards that Raskolnikov noticed some signs that he was rather flustered, as though something had happened to put him at a loss or he had been discovered in something very private and secret.

'Ah, my dear chap! Here you are . . . in our territory . . .' began Porfiry, holding out both hands to him. 'Well, do sit down, old man! But perhaps you don't like being called "my dear chap" and . . . "old man" *tout court*, like that? Please don't think I'm being too familiar . . . Sit here, on the sofa.'

Raskolnikov sat down without taking his eyes from him.

'In our territory', the apologies for undue familiarity, the French expression '*tout court*', and so on, were all characteristic. 'He held out both his hands to me, but he didn't actually give me one; he drew them back in time,' he thought, with a flash of suspicion. They were each watching the other, but as soon as their glances met, both turned their eyes away like lightning.

'I have brought you this paper . . . about the watch . . . here! Is that right, or shall I write it out again?'

'What? The paper? Yes, yes . . . Don't worry, it is quite all right,' said Porfiry Petrovich, as though he were in a hurry, and only after he had said it took the paper and looked at it. 'Yes, quite all right. Nothing else is necessary,' he repeated, with the same rapidity, and laid the paper on the desk. A minute later, while he was talking of something else, he took it up again and transferred it to his bureau.

'I think you said yesterday that you wished to question me ... officially ... about my acquaintance with the ... murdered woman,' began Raskolnikov again. 'Why did I put in that *I think?*' flashed through his mind. 'And why am I so worried at having put it in?' came in another flash.

Suddenly he felt that, simply because he was in Porfiry's presence, and had exchanged glances and one or two words with him, his uneasiness had instantly increased to gigantic proportions . . . and that this was terribly dangerous: his nerves were tense, his emotion was increasing. 'This is disastrous! . . . I shall say too much again.'

'Yes, yes, yes! Don't worry! There is plenty of time, plenty of time,' murmured Porfiry Petrovich, who was wandering aimlessly round the table, with occasional dashes, as it were, first to the window, then to the bureau, then back to the table, now avoiding Raskolnikov's suspicious gaze, now suddenly standing still and looking straight at him. This small, plump, round figure, rolling like a ball about the room, and bouncing back off all the walls and corners, produced a very strange impression.

'We have plenty of time, plenty of time! . . . Do you smoke? Have you your own? Here, here's a cigarette,' he went on, handing one to his visitor . . . 'You know, I am receiving you here, but my own flat is just there, on the other side of the partition . . . my official quarters. Just now I am out of it for a time. Some repairs had to be done. Now it's almost ready for me . . . you know, an official flat is a famous thing, isn't it? What do you think?'

'Yes, it is,' answered Raskolnikov, looking at him almost mockingly.

'A famous thing, famous . . .' repeated Porfiry Petrovich, as if he had begun to think of something else. 'Yes, famous!' he almost shouted at last, suddenly turning his eyes on Raskolnikov and coming to a stop two paces away from him. There was something stupid and trivial about this constant repetition that contrasted strongly with the serious, contemplative, and enigmatic look he now bent on his visitor.

All this still further intensified Raskolnikov's bitter malice, and he could no longer resist issuing an ironical and rather indiscreet challenge.

'Do you know,' he said suddenly, looking almost insolently at Porfiry Petrovich, and delighting in his own insolence, 'there must exist, I believe, a lawyer's procedure, a legal method, applying to all sorts of investigations, by which they begin with trivial matters, far removed from the real subject, or even with something serious, so long as it is quite irrelevant, so as to encourage the person being interrogated, or rather to distract his attention and lull his mistrust, and then suddenly and unexpectedly stun him by hitting him on the crown of his head with the most dangerous and fatal question. Am I right? Isn't the principle enshrined in all the rules and precepts to this day?'

'Yes, yes . . . So you think that what I was saying about official quarters . . . eh?' Porfiry Petrovich screwed up his eyes and winked; a look of cheerful slyness passed over his face, his wrinkled forehead became smooth, his eyes narrowed, his features relaxed, and he abandoned himself to prolonged nervous laughter which made his whole body quiver and shake. He was looking straight into Raskolnikov's eyes. The latter, with an effort, began to laugh too, but when Porfiry, seeing him also laughing, went off into guffaws which turned him crimson in the face, Raskolnikov's repulsion overcame his caution: he stopped laughing, scowled, and watched him with a fixed stare of hatred all the time that his long fit of laughter, which seemed indeed deliberately prolonged, lasted. The lack of caution was not all, however, on one side. Porfiry, apparently caught laughing at his visitor to his face, showed very little embarrassment at the aversion this treatment had aroused. To Raskolnikov this seemed very significant, he realized that earlier also Porfiry Petrovich had not been in the least embarrassed, but that perhaps he, Raskolnikov, had fallen into a trap; that there was plainly something here, some sort of motive, he knew nothing of; that perhaps all Porfiry's preparations had already been made, and now, this minute, they would be disclosed, and overwhelm him . . .

He went straight to the point at once, rising and taking up his cap.

'Porfiry Petrovich,' he began resolutely, but in rather violent agitation, 'yesterday you expressed a desire that I should come here for some interrogation' (he stressed the word interrogation). 'I have come, and if you need to ask me any questions, ask them, but if not, allow me to leave. I have no time to spare, I have things to do . . . I have to be at the funeral of the clerk who was run over, about whom you . . . also know,' he added, was immediately angry with himself for the addition, and then grew at once even more agitated. 'I am sick and tired of all this, and have been for a long time . . . It was partly that that made me ill . . . and in one word,' he almost shrieked, feeling that the phrase about being ill was even more out of place, 'in one word, be good enough either to question me or to let me go at once . . . and if you question me, do it in the proper form! Otherwise I shall not allow it; meanwhile, good-bye for the present, since there is nothing for us two to do now.'

'Good Lord! What are you talking about? What is there for me to question you about?' clucked Porfiry Petrovich, with a complete change of tone and aspect, and an instant cessation of laughter. 'Please don't upset yourself,' he fussed now, beginning to wander about once more, and busying himself with making Raskolnikov sit down again. 'There is no hurry, there's no hurry, and all that is pure nonsense! I am, on the contrary, very glad that you have at last come to see me . . . I look upon you as a visitor. And you must forgive me, Rodion Romanovich, old man, for that confounded laughter.—Rodion Romanovich? I think that is your patronymic? . . . I'm all nerves, and you amused me very much by the wittiness of your remark; sometimes, I assure you, I laugh till I shake like a jelly, for half an hour on end . . . I laugh easily. With my constitution I am afraid I might even have a stroke. But sit down, what's the matter? . . . Please, old man, or I shall think you are angry . . .'

Raskolnikov said nothing, but watched and listened, still scowling angrily. He sat down, however, but kept his cap in his hands.

'I will tell you one thing, Rodion Romanovich, old chap, about myself, or rather in explanation of my character,' went on Porfiry Petrovich, still fussing about the room and, as before, apparently trying to avoid meeting his guest's eyes. 'I, you know, am a bachelor, and neither fashionable nor famous, and besides, I have developed as far as I am capable of, grown ripe, and settled down, and . . . and . . . have you ever noticed, Rodion Romanovich, that among us, here in Russia I mean, and especially in our St. Petersburg circles, if two intelligent men, like you and me, who do not know each other very well, but respect one another, so to speak, if two such men come together, for quite half an hour they cannot find anything to talk about—they sit there stiffly and feel awkward? Everybody can find some subject of conversation—the ladies, for instance, or fashionable people, people in high society, can always talk about something, *c'est de rigueur*, but middling people like us, thinking ones, that is, are all awkward and tongue-tied . . . What is the cause of this? Whether it is because we have no interest in public affairs, or because we are very honest and don't want to deceive one another, I don't know. What do you think, eh? Put your cap down though; you look as though you were leaving at once. It makes me uncomfortable to see you . . . And I really am delighted . . .'

Raskolnikov put down his cap, still listening silently and seriously, with a frown, to Porfiry's vague, confused chatter. 'Why, can he really be trying to distract my attention with this stupid talk?'

'I can't very well offer you coffee here, but why not sit and enjoy yourself for five minutes or so with a friend?' Porfiry chattered on without stopping. 'You know, all these official duties . . . Don't mind, old chap, if I keep walking up and down; excuse me, I am very much afraid of offending you, but exercise is simply essential to me. I am always sitting, and I am so glad to move about for a few minutes ... haemorrhoids, you know ... I am always meaning to try gymnastics for it; they say you can see all sorts of quite high officials, even Privy Councillors, skipping with a little rope; what a thing science is, in our day and age! ... Just so ... But about my duties here, interrogations and all those formalities ... you yourself mentioned questioning, old man ... well, you know, Rodion Romanovich, old man, sometimes the questioner is led astray, more than the one he is examining ... You made a very just and penetrating remark on that subject just now, old man.' (Raskolnikov had made no such remark.) 'You get all tangled up! Yes, really; tangled up! And it's all the same thing over and over, over and over, like beating a drum! There is a reform[4] on the way, and we are all to be at any rate called something different. He, he, he! As for our lawyer's procedure, as you so wittily term it—there I am completely in agreement with you. Who is there, tell me, out of all the people accused of crimes, even if they are absolute yokels, who does not know that they will try to lull his mistrust (as you happily express it) with irrelevant questions, and then unexpectedly stun him, he, he, he! by hitting him on the crown of his head, to use your delightful metaphor, as if with an axe, he, he, he! So you really thought that when I talked of my flat I intended ... he, he! You are very ironical. Well, I won't say any more. Oh, yes, by the way—one thing leads to another—you mentioned formalities just now, in connexion with questioning, you know ... But why bother about formalities?—in many cases, you know, they mean nothing. Sometimes just a friendly talk is much more use. The formalities will always be there, if necessary; allow me to assure you of that. But what are they, after all, I ask you? An examining magistrate ought not to be hampered by them at every step. His business is, so to speak, some sort of an art, in its own way ... he, he, he!'

Porfiry Petrovich paused a moment for breath. He had been running on without a break, now throwing off meaningless empty phrases, now slipping in a few enigmatic words, then again wandering off into nonsense. He was almost running about the room, with his fat little legs moving faster and faster, his eyes fixed on the ground, and his right hand thrust behind his back, while his left gesticulated ceaselessly, making various gestures that were always extraordinarily out of keeping with his words. Suddenly Raskolnikov noticed that once or twice, as he scurried about the room, he seemed to pause near the door for a moment, as though he were listening. 'Can he be expecting something?'

4. A reference to reforms of the courts adopted in Russia in 1865.

'But you were really quite right,' Porfiry began again gaily, looking at Raskolnikov with extraordinary artlessness (which made him start and instantly prepare himself for something), 'really right, when you laughed so wittily at our legal forms, he, he, he! Indeed, our profound psychological methods (some of them) are made quite ridiculous, and perhaps even useless, if formalities are allowed to cramp them. Yes . . . I am talking of forms again: well, if I recognize or rather suspect, that this, that, or the other man is guilty, in some case that is in my hands . . . You are reading law, I believe, Rodion Romanovich?'

'I was . . .'

'Then here is an example to guide you, so to speak, in future —but please don't imagine that I am venturing to instruct you: look at the articles on crime you publish! No, only I take the liberty of putting this example before you as a matter of fact—so suppose I consider that this person or that is a criminal, why, I ask, should I worry him before the proper time, even if I have evidence against him? One man, for example, I feel obliged to arrest at once, but another may be quite different, and so why not allow him to go free for a time, he, he? No, I see you do not quite understand, so I will put it more clearly: if I put him in custody too soon, I may by that be giving him, so to speak, moral support. He, he! You are laughing?' (Raskolnikov had no idea of laughing; he sat with compressed lips, with his feverish gaze fixed on Porfiry's eyes.) 'Yet it is true, especially with some types, because people are very different; but of course only practice can guide one. Now you will say: evidence. Well, suppose there is evidence; but evidence, you know, old man, cuts both ways for the most part. I am only an investigator, and fallible like everybody else, I confess; I should like to produce deductions that are, so to speak, mathematically clear; I want to have evidence that is like two and two make four! I want something like direct and incontrovertible proof! But if I put a man in custody at the wrong moment—even though I am sure that it was *he*—I may very likely be destroying my only means of incriminating him further; and why? Because I shall be giving him a definite position, so to speak, I shall give him, as it were, psychological certainty and tranquillity, and once he understands that he is definitely accused, he will retreat from me into his shell. They say that in Sebastopol, immediately after the battle of the Alma,[5] intelligent people were terribly afraid that the enemy would attack at once with all his force and take the town, but when they saw that the enemy preferred a regular siege and was already preparing his trenches, those intelligent people, they say, were thoroughly reassured and highly delighted: if a regular siege was intended,

5. In October 1854, during the Crimean War, Russian armies were defeated on the Alma river and fell back on Sebastopol.

that meant that things would drag on for two months at least! You're laughing again. You still don't believe me? Well, you are right as well. You are right, you are right! These are all special cases, I agree; and the present case is really special! But you ought to bear it in mind, my dear Rodion Romanovich, that the average case, the case for which all the legal forms and rules are devised, which they are calculated to deal with, when they are written down in the textbooks, does not exist at all, because every case, every crime, for example, as soon as it really occurs, at once becomes a quite special case, and sometimes it is absolutely unlike anything that has ever happened before. Very comical things of that kind sometimes occur. Now, if I leave one gentleman quite alone, if I don't arrest him or worry him in any way, but if he knows, or at least suspects, every minute of every hour, that I know everything down to the last detail, and am watching him day and night with ceaseless vigilance, if he is always conscious of the weight of suspicion and fear, he is absolutely certain to lose his head. He will come to me of his own accord, and perhaps commit some blunder, which will provide, so to speak, mathematical proof, like two and two make four—and that is very satisfactory. This may happen even with a boorish peasant, all the more with people of our sort, the contemporary intellectuals, with their one-sided development. Because, my dear chap, a very important point is understanding what side of a man's nature has been developed. And the nerves, the nerves, you seem to have forgotten them. Nowadays, they are all sick, and fine-drawn, and irritable! . . . And everybody is so full of spleen! And I tell you, in its way that provides a mine of information! And why should I worry if a man goes freely about the town? Let him! Let him be at large for a time; I know that he is my prey, and that he can't escape me. Where could he run away to, he, he? Abroad? A Pole will escape abroad, but not my man, especially as I am watching and have taken precautions. Or will he flee into the depths of the country? But the peasants live there, real homespun Russian peasants, and the modern educated man would rather go to prison than live with people as foreign to him as our peasants, he, he! But all this is unimportant, external. What is running away?—it's merely formal; the point isn't that he won't run away because he has nowhere to run to, but that *psychologically* he won't escape, he, he! What an expression! By a law of his nature he wouldn't escape, even if he had somewhere to escape to. Have you ever seen a moth with a candle? Well, he'll be just like that, he'll circle round me as if I were a candle: Freedom will no longer be a boon to him; he will begin to brood, he will get himself into a muddle, entangle his own feet in a net, and worry himself to death! . . . More than that, he himself will provide me with a mathematical proof, of the nature of two and two make four—if only I allow a long enough interval between the acts of the drama . . . And he'll keep on, keep on circling round me, closer and closer, and then, plop! he'll fly straight into my mouth and I'll swallow him, and that will be very satisfactory, he, he, he! Don't you believe me?'

Raskolnikov did not answer, but sat pale and motionless, watching Porfiry's face with the same strained attention. 'The lesson is a good one!' he thought, turning cold. 'It is no longer a case of cat and mouse, as it was yesterday. He is not showing me his strength, and . . . hinting, for nothing: he is much too clever for that . . . He has some other motive, but what? Ah, brother, it's all nonsense your trying to scare me and be so clever! You have no proof, and that man I saw yesterday doesn't exist! You just want to get me confused and worked up beforehand, and then to pounce when I'm in the right condition for you, but you're making a mistake, you'll come a cropper! But why, though, why give me such strong hints? . . . Is he counting on the bad state of my nerves? . . . No, brother, you're mistaken, you'll come to grief, even if you have something up your sleeve. Well, now we shall see what it is.'

And he braced himself as well as he could to meet the unknown and terrible crisis. At moments he longed to throw himself on Porfiry and strangle him then and there. From the time he entered he had been afraid of his own rage. He was conscious of his dry lips flecked with foam, and of his hammering heart. But he was determined not to say a word until the right time came. He knew this to be the right tactics in his position, since he would not only avoid letting anything slip, but also perhaps provoke his enemy by his silence into saying too much. So at least he hoped.

'No, I see you don't believe me. You still think I'm a harmless buffoon,' Porfiry began again, growing more and more cheerful, ceaselessly giggling with pleasure, and once more circling round the room. 'Well, of course, you're right. God created me with such a figure that the only ideas I arouse in other people are comical ones; I'm a clown; but I'll tell you something, and I'll repeat it: you, my dear Rodion Romanovich (excuse an old man), are still a young man, in your first youth, so to speak, and therefore you esteem the human intellect above all things, like all young people. Abstract reasoning and the play of wit tempt you astray. It is exactly like the former Austrian *Hofkriegsrath*,[6] for example (if my

6. Court Council of War. In 1805, the Austrian Army, in which the Allies (Austria, England, Russia) had placed high hopes, and which was commanded by General Mack, surrendered to Napoleon. Tolstoy refers to the events in *War and Peace*, in a part of the novel printed in the February 1866 number of the same magazine which in its July number had printed this part of *Crime and Punishment*.

judgement of military matters is sound, that is); on paper they defeated Napoleon and took him prisoner, calculating and reasoning in the cleverest fashion there in the study, but then, you see, General Mack surrendered with all his army, he, he, he! I can see, I can see, Rodion Romanovich, old man, that you are laughing at me, a civilian, for taking my examples from military history. But what would you have, it's a weakness of mine; I love the art of war, and I like reading all these military histories . . . really, I've missed my vocation. I ought to have had a military career, really. I might not have become a Napoleon, but I should have become a major, he, he, he! Well, my dear friend, now I'll tell you the whole truth, about this *special case*, that is; reality and nature, my dear sir, are very important, and sometimes upset the most penetrating calculations! Ah, listen to an old man, I am speaking seriously, Rodion Romanovich' (and saying this, Porfiry Petrovich, who was barely thirty-five, really seemed to grow old all at once; even his voice changed, and he somehow shrivelled up), 'and besides I'm a very frank person. Am I a frank person, or not? What is your opinion? I think I am completely frank; here I am telling you all these things for nothing, and don't even ask for any reward, he, he! Well, I will proceed: wit, in my opinion, is a wonderful thing; it is, so to speak, the ornament of nature and the solace of life, and what riddles it can set sometimes!—so that a poor devil of an investigator is quite baffled, especially when his own fancy is liable to lead him astray as well, as always happens, since he is only human after all! But the criminal's own nature comes to the rescue of the poor investigator, that's the point! That's what the young person, carried away by his own wit, and "over-stepping all obstacles" (as you so wittily and cleverly expressed it yesterday), doesn't think of. He, let us suppose, will lie, I mean our man, the *special case*, Mr. X, and lie extremely well, in the most marvellously clever fashion; this would seem to be triumph, and he might expect to enjoy the fruits of his wit, and then plop! he will fall in a faint, and that at the most interesting and shocking point! It is illness, we will suppose, and rooms are sometimes stuffy, besides, but all the same! All the same, he has given us an idea! He lied incomparably well, but he couldn't rely on his own nature. That's it, that's where our skill comes in! Another time, tempted by the playfulness of his own wit, he will make a fool of a man who suspects him, he will turn pale *too naturally*, too much as if it were real, and again he's given us an idea! His trickery may be successful at first, but the other will revise his ideas, given time, if he isn't a dunderhead. And it's the same at every step! Why? Because he will begin trying to forestall us, he will thrust himself in where he is not wanted, he will begin to talk incessantly about things he would do better to say nothing about, he will talk in allegories,

he, he! He will come of his own accord and begin asking
why he hasn't been arrested long since, he, he, he!—and this
happens with the sharpest-witted of men, versed in psychology and literature. Nature is a mirror, the very clearest of
mirrors! Look into it and admire! But why are you so pale, Rodion Romanovich? Is it too stuffy for you? Shall I open the
window?'

'Oh, don't trouble, please,' cried Raskolnikov, suddenly beginning to laugh. 'Please don't trouble!'

Porfiry stopped opposite him and after a pause began to
laugh too. Raskolnikov got up from the sofa, abruptly cutting
short his fit of laughter.

'Porfiry Petrovich,' he said loudly and distinctly, although
his trembling legs would hardly support him, 'at last I see
plainly that you definitely suspect me of the murder of that
old woman and her sister Lizaveta. I must tell you that for
my part I had enough of this long ago. If you find that you
have a legal right to prosecute me or arrest me, then do it!
But I will not permit anyone to laugh in my face and torment
me . . .'

His lips began to tremble, his eyes shone with fury, and his
voice rose, although he had been trying to keep it low. 'I will
not permit it,' he shouted, banging his fist violently on the
table. 'Do you hear that, Porfiry Petrovich? I will not permit it!'

'Good heavens! What has brought this on again?' cried
Porfiry Petrovich, apparently thoroughly frightened. 'My dear
fellow! Rodion Romanovich! My dear friend! What is the
matter?'

'I will not permit it!' Raskolnikov shouted again.

'My dear chap, quietly! You will be heard, somebody will
come! And then what could we say to them? Think!' said
Porfiry Petrovich in a frightened whisper, thrusting his face
close to Raskolnikov's.

'I won't permit it, I won't permit it!' repeated Raskolnikov
mechanically, but he had also dropped his voice to a whisper.

Porfiry turned quickly and ran to open the window.

'I'll let some fresh air in! And you must drink a little water,
my dear fellow! You've had an attack!' And he hurried towards
the door to call for water; but there in the corner, luckily,
was a carafe.

'My dear chap, have some water,' he whispered, hurrying
over to him with the carafe. 'It may do you good . . .' Porfiry
Petrovich's alarm and sympathy seemed so natural that Raskolnikov was silent and began to watch him with fierce curiosity.
He did not take the water, however.

'Rodion Romanovich! My dear chap! You'll drive yourself
mad like this, I assure you. Ah! Drink some. Even if it's only
a sip, do drink some water!'

He forced a glass of water into his hand. Raskolnikov began to raise it mechanically to his lips, but then recollected himself and set it on the table with distaste.

'Yes, you've had a little attack! You're going the right way to bring your illness back, my dear fellow,' clucked Porfiry Petrovich with friendly sympathy, although he still looked a little disconcerted. 'Good Lord! How can you be so careless of yourself? Here Dmitri Prokofich came to see me yesterday—I agree, I agree, I've got a nasty sarcastic nature, but just look what people have made of that! . . . Lord! He came yesterday, after you'd gone, we had dinner, and he talked and talked, and I was absolutely flabbergasted; well, thought I . . . good Lord! Did you send him? But sit down, old man, for the love of Christ, sit down!'

'No, I didn't send him. But I knew he had come, and why,' answered Raskolnikov sharply.

'You knew?'

'Yes. What of that?'

'Just this, Rodion Romanovich, old man, that I don't know only about such actions of yours; I am informed about everything! I know that you went to *take that flat*, just before nightfall, when it was getting dark, and began ringing the bell, and asked about the blood and thoroughly puzzled the workmen and the porters. You know, I can understand your state of mind just then . . . but all the same, you'll simply drive yourself mad like that, as true as I'm here! You'll lose your wits! There is indignation seething violently inside you, a generous indignation, at the injuries you have received, first from fate and then from the police, and you go rushing about from place to place, to force everybody, so to say, to speak out and so make an end of it at once, because you are sick of all these stupidities and suspicions. That is so, isn't it? Have I guessed your mood? But in this way you are upsetting not only your own wits, but my Razumikhin's as well; and, really, he is too *good* a person for that, as you know yourself. You are ill, and he is kind and good, and your illness is infectious for him . . . I will tell you, old chap, when you are calmer . . . But sit down, old man, for Christ's sake. Please rest, you are terribly pale; do sit down.'

Raskolnikov sat down; his trembling had ceased, and his whole body felt hot. Stunned with amazement, he listened with strained attention to Porfiry Petrovich, who still seemed alarmed as he pressed his friendly attentions on him. But he did not believe one word he said, although he felt strangely inclined to believe him. He was struck with dismay by Porfiry's unexpected words about the flat: 'What is this?' he thought. 'So he knows about the flat, and he is telling me himself!'

'Yes, we have had an almost exactly similar case in our practice, a case involving morbid psychology,' went on Porfiry in his rapid speech. 'A man falsely accused himself of murder, and how thoroughly he did it! he created a complete but hallucinatory picture, brought forward facts, gave a circumstantial account of it, and got all and sundry muddled and confused, and why? He had been, quite unwittingly, the cause in part, but only in part, of the murder, and when he learnt that he had given the murderer a pretext, he got into a state of depression and stupor, began to imagine things, went completely out of his mind, and persuaded himself that he was the murderer! Finally the Senate High Court tried the case, and the unhappy man was acquitted and put under proper care. One should be grateful to the Senate Court! Alas! Dear, dear, dear! So what then, my dear chap? Why, you may easily drive yourself into a raging fever, if you have these impulses to upset your own nerves, and go about at night ringing bells and asking questions about blood! I've studied all this psychology in my practice. Sometimes, in just the same way, a man feels drawn to jump out of a window or off a church-tower, and the temptation is very strong. So with door-bells . . . Illness, Rodion Romanovich, illness! You have begun to neglect your illness. You ought to consult an experienced doctor, but as it is, what good is that fat fellow of yours? . . . You are liable to become delirious! It is delirium that makes you do all those things! . . .'

For a moment everything seemed to Raskolnikov to be spinning round.

'Can it be possible,' flashed through his mind, 'that he is lying even now? No, impossible, impossible!' He pushed the thought away from him, realizing in time to what degree of rage and fury it might drive him, and feeling that the fury might be violent enough to make him lose his mind.

'I wasn't delirious, I was quite conscious of what I was doing!' he cried, straining all his powers of judgement to fathom Porfiry's game. 'I was conscious, quite conscious! Do you hear?'

'Yes, I hear you, and I understand. Yesterday as well you said you were not delirious, you were particularly emphatic about not being delirious. I know everything you can say! Ah! . . . But listen, Rodion Romanovich, my dear friend, there is at least this circumstance . . . If you really were guilty, or somehow mixed up in this damned business, would you, for heaven's sake, be so emphatic about not having been delirious, but on the contrary, in full possession of your faculties, when you did all that? And so specially insistent on it, with such particular obstinacy—would you?—is it possible, for goodness sake? Quite the contrary, I should say. Indeed, if you really felt you had done something wrong you ought to insist that you certainly were delirious. I am right, aren't I?'

There was something sly about this question. Raskolnikov

recoiled from Porfiry, who was stooping over him, as far as the sofa would allow, and watched him in silent perplexity.

'Then about Mr. Razumikhin, that is about whether he came here yesterday from you or at your instigation, you ought certainly to have said that he came of his own accord, and concealed that you had anything to do with it. But you don't conceal it! You even insist that you persuaded him to come!'

Raskolnikov had never done so. A chill ran down his spine.

'You keep on lying,' he said slowly and faintly, with a sickly smile distorting his lips, 'You want to prove to me again that you know my game, that you know all my answers beforehand,' he went on, aware that he was no longer weighing his words as he should. 'You want to frighten me . . . or else you are simply laughing at me . . .'

As he said this, he continued to look into the face so close to his, and unbridled fury suddenly flashed again in his eyes.

'You are lying all the time!' he cried. 'You yourself know perfectly well that the criminal's best plan is to tell the truth as far as he can . . . to hide, as far as possible, nothing that he can reveal. I don't trust you!'

'What a slippery person you are!' chuckled Porfiry. 'There's no coping with you, old chap. You've got some fixed idea into your head. So you don't trust me? But I tell you that you trust me half-way already, and I'll make you trust me all the way yet, because I sincerely like you and wish you well.'

Raskolnikov's lips trembled.

'Yes, I do, and I will say one final thing to you,' went on Porfiry, lightly touching Raskolnikov's arm in a friendly fashion. 'One last thing: you must watch that illness of yours. Besides, your family is here now; you must think of them. You ought to take care of them and cherish them, but you only frighten them . . .'

'What business is it of yours? How do you know about them? Why are you so interested? You must be watching me, then, and you want to make sure I know it!'

'Good Lord! Why it was you, you yourself, who told me! You don't realize that when you are agitated you tell everything, to others as well as to me. I learnt a lot of interesting details yesterday from Mr. Razumikhin, Dmitri Prokofich. No, you interrupted me, but I tell you that in spite of all your brains, your mistrustfulness makes you unable to take a sensible view of things. For instance, to go back to the same subject, on this question of door-bells: I gave you that precious detail, that fact (for it is a fact to be considered, you know). I gave it you with both hands, I, an examining magistrate! Don't you see anything in that? If I suspected you at all, should I have done that? On the contrary, I should first have lulled your suspicions, and pretended that I had not been informed of the fact; I should have drawn your attention in the opposite direction, and then stunned you, as with a blow on the head with an axe (to use your own expression): "And what," I should have said "were you doing in the murdered woman's flat at ten o'clock, or nearer eleven, at night? Why were you ringing the bell? Why were you asking about the blood? And why did you try to mislead the porter, and get him to go to the police lieutenant at the station?" That's how I should have acted, if I had had even the slightest suspicion of you. I should have taken a statement from you in the proper form, made a search, and perhaps arrested you . . . If I haven't acted like that it follows that I am not harbouring any suspicions! But you have lost the capacity to take a sane view, and I repeat, you see nothing!'

Raskolnikov's whole body quivered, so that Porfiry Petrovich could see it quite plainly.

'You are lying all the time!' he said. 'I don't know what you are aiming at, but you do nothing but lie . . . You weren't talking in that sense a few minutes ago, and I can't be mistaken about that . . . Are you lying?'

'I lying?' rejoined Porfiry, visibly growing a little heated, but still preserving the same cheerfully mocking expression, and apparently not at all worried by what Mr. Raskolnikov might think of him. 'Lying? . . . Well, how was I acting towards you just now (and I an examining magistrate), when I was prompting you, showing you all the ways of defending yourself, supplying all that psychology: "Illness," I said, "delirium, being insulted, melancholia, police officers" and all the rest of it? Eh? he, he, he! There is one thing, however, to be said— all these psychological means of defence, these excuses and evasions, are very insubstantial, and they cut both ways: "Illness, delirium," you say, "fancies, illusions, I don't remember"—that is all very well, but then why is it, old chap, that you see just these illusions in your sick delirium, and not others? There could have been others, couldn't there? He, he, he, he!'

Raskolnikov looked at him proudly and scornfully.

'In one word,' he said loudly and insistently, pushing Porfiry back a little as he stood up, 'in one word, what I want to know is this: Do you admit that I am definitely free from suspicion or *not*? Tell me that, Porfiry Petrovich, tell me definitely and finally, and quickly, at once!'

'Here's a fine fuss! Well, what a fuss you make!' cried Porfiry, with a sly, perfectly cheerful, and unruffled look. 'Why do you want to know, why do you want to know so much, when nobody has even begun to worry you yet? Really you are like a child crying for the fire to play with. And why are you so worried? Why do you thrust yourself upon us? What are your reasons, eh? He, he, he!'

'I tell you again,' shouted Raskolnikov furiously, 'that I cannot any longer endure . . .'

'What? The uncertainty?' interrupted Porfiry.

'Do not taunt me! I will not have it . . . I tell you I won't have it! . . . I can't and I won't! . . . Listen to me!' he shouted, banging the table with his fist again.

'Quietly, quietly! You will be heard! I warn you seriously, look after yourself. I am not joking!' said Porfiry in a whisper, but this time his face had not its former expression of womanish good nature and alarm. On the contrary, now he was *giving orders*, frowning sternly and destroying at one blow, as it were, all mystery and ambiguity. But it was only for a moment. Raskolnikov, perplexed, fell suddenly into a real frenzy; but strangely enough he again obeyed the injunction to speak quietly, although he was in a perfect paroxysm of fury.

'I will not allow myself to be tortured!' As he had before, he suddenly dropped his voice to a whisper, instantly recognizing with anguish and hatred that he felt obliged to submit to the command, and driven to greater fury by the knowledge. 'Arrest me, search me, but be good enough to act in the proper form, and don't play with me! Do not dare . . .'

'Don't worry about the proper form,' interrupted Porfiry, with his former sly smile, apparently even gloating over Raskolnikov. 'I invited you here informally, old man, in a very friendly fashion!'

'I don't want your friendship! I spit upon it! Do you hear? And look: I am taking my cap and going. Well, what will you say now, if you intend to arrest me?'

He seized his cap and went to the door.

'But don't you want to see my little surprise?' chuckled Porfiry, seizing his arm again and stopping him by the door. He seemed to be growing ever more high-spirited and playful, and this made Raskolnikov finally lose control.

'What little surprise? What is this?' he asked, stopping short and looking at Porfiry with terror.

'Just a little surprise. Here it is, just behind the door, he, he, he!' (He pointed his finger at the closed door in the partition, which led into his living quarters.) 'I locked it in, so that it shouldn't run away.'

'What is it? Where? What?' Raskolnikov went to the door and tried to open it, but it was locked.

'It is locked. Here is the key!'

And he showed him the key, which he had taken from his pocket.

'You are still lying!' howled Raskolnikov, no longer restraining himself. 'You lie, you damned clown!' He rushed at Porfiry, who retreated towards the door, but without quailing.

'I understand it all, all of it! You are lying. You are teasing me to make me betray myself . . .'

'But you can't betray yourself any further, Rodion Romanovich, old chap. You're quite beside yourself. Don't shout. I shall
call somebody.'

'You are lying, nothing will happen! Call your people! You
knew I was ill, and you tried to irritate me to madness, so that
I should betray myself, that's what you were after! No, bring
out your facts! I understand it all! You have no facts, you
have only paltry, rubbishy guesses, Zametov's guesses! . . .
You knew my nature, you wanted to drive me mad, and then
stun me with priests and witnesses . . . Are you waiting for
them, eh? What are you waiting for? Where are they? Bring
them out!'

'What witnesses, old man? What an imagination you have!
And to act as you say would not be in accordance with the
forms. You don't understand what the procedure is, my dear
chap . . . The forms are still there, as you will see for yourself!'
muttered Porfiry, with his ear directed to the door.

There seemed really to be some noise at this moment close
to the door, in the other room.

'Ah, they are coming!' cried Raskolnikov. 'You sent for
them! You were waiting for them! You expected . . . Well,
bring them all here, deputies, witnesses, anything you like . . .
bring them! I am ready! I am ready! . . .'

But now a strange thing happened, something so little to be
foreseen in the ordinary course of things, that neither Raskolnikov nor Porfiry Petrovich could have expected such a
*dénouement*.

## CHAPTER VI

AFTERWARDS, remembering that moment, Raskolnikov
recalled it in this way:

The noise outside the door increased suddenly, and the door
opened a little way.

'What is it?' cried Porfiry Petrovich in annoyance. 'I gave
orders not to . . .'

There was no answer for a moment, but there were evidently
several people outside the door, and they seemed to be pushing
somebody away.

'What is it?' repeated Porfiry Petrovich anxiously.

'The prisoner Nikolay has been brought,' said a voice.

'I don't want him! Get out! Wait till you're wanted! . . .
Why is he here? What lack of discipline!' cried Porfiry, rushing
to the door.

'But he . . .' the same voice was beginning again, and was
suddenly cut off.

There were a couple of seconds, not more, of actual struggle;
then somebody seemed to give somebody else a violent push,

and immediately afterwards a very pale man walked straight into Porfiry Petrovich's office.

At first sight, this man's appearance was very strange. He was looking straight before him, but seemed not to see anything. His eyes shone with resolution, but his face was deadly pale, as though he were going to execution. Even his twitching lips were white.

He was still very young, of medium height, thin, with the hair cropped round his head, and spare, parched-looking features. He was dressed like an ordinary working man. The man he had unexpectedly pushed aside burst into the room after him, and managed to seize him by the shoulder; he was a guard. But Nikolay jerked his arm and pulled himself free again. A few curious onlookers crowded in the doorway. Some of them tried to get into the room. All this had happened in the space of little more than a moment.

'Get out! You are too early! Wait until you are sent for! . . . Why did you bring him so soon?' grumbled Porfiry Petrovich, full of annoyance, and seeming very disconcerted. But Nikolay suddenly fell on his knees.

'What do you want?' cried Porfiry in astonishment.

'I am guilty! The sin was mine! I am the murderer!' answered Nikolay abruptly, panting, but in quite a loud voice.

There was a stupefied silence, which lasted for several seconds; even the guard recoiled. He did not approach Nikolay again, but retreated mechanically to the door and stood there without moving.

'What is this?' cried Porfiry Petrovich, emerging from his momentary stupor.

'I . . . am the murderer . . .' repeated Nikolay, after a short pause.

'What . . . you . . . what? . . . Whom did you kill?'

Porfiry Petrovich was clearly at a loss.

Nikolay again said nothing for a moment.

'Alëna Ivanovna and her sister Lizaveta Ivanovna, I . . . killed them . . . with an axe. Everything went black . . .' he added suddenly, and then was silent again. He was still on his knees.

Porfiry Petrovich stood for a short time as if plunged in thought, then abruptly roused himself and waved away the uninvited onlookers. They disappeared at once, and the door was closed. Then he looked at Raskolnikov, standing in the corner with his wild gaze fixed on Nikolay, and seemed about to approach him, but stopped, looked from him to Nikolay and back again, then once more back to Nikolay, and finally turned on Nikolay again as though he could not help himself.

'What do you mean, running ahead with "everything went black"?' he shouted at him almost furiously. 'I haven't asked you anything about that yet . . . Speak out: you killed them?'

'I am the murderer . . . I want to testify . . .' said Nikolay.

'O-oh! What did you kill them with?'

'With an axe. I got it for that.'

'Oh, he's in a hurry! Alone?'

Nikolay did not understand the question.

'Was it you alone who killed them?'

'Yes. Mitka is innocent, he had nothing to do with any of it.'

'Don't be in such a hurry about Mitka! O-oh! . . . How is it then . . . how did you come to run downstairs just then? The porters met both of you, didn't they?'

'I did it as a blind . . . that is why I ran with Mitka,' answered Nikolay quickly, as though he had prepared his reply beforehand.

'Ah, so that's it!' cried Porfiry angrily. 'That's not his own idea; he's picked it up somewhere,' he muttered to himself, and then his eyes fell on Raskolnikov again.

He had evidently been so concerned with Nikolay that he had forgotten about Raskolnikov for the moment. Now he recollected himself, and seemed rather embarrassed . . .

'Rodion Romanovich, my dear fellow! Excuse me,' he said, hurrying over to him, 'I can't . . . would you mind . . . you should not be here . . . and I . . . You see what a surprise! . . . Would you mind? . . .'

And taking him by the arm, he led him towards the door.

'It seems that you didn't expect this,' said Raskolnikov, who had regained much of his courage, although he naturally could not clearly understand any of this.

'Neither did you, old chap. Look how your hand shakes, he, he!'

'You are trembling yourself, Porfiry Petrovich.'

'So I am. I didn't expect this! . . .'

They were already at the door. Porfiry waited impatiently for Raskolnikov to go.

'And aren't you going to show me your little surprise?' asked Raskolnikov suddenly.

'He can talk like that, while his teeth are still chattering, he, he! What an ironical person you are! Well, good-bye for the present.'

'I think we might say simply *good-bye*!'

'That is as God wills, as God wills,' muttered Porfiry, with a wry smile.

As he walked through the outer office, Raskolnikov noticed many eyes fixed on him. In the crowd in the ante-room he picked out the two porters from *that* house, to whom he had suggested going to the police that night. They were standing waiting for something. As soon as he reached the stairs he heard Porfiry Petrovich's voice again behind him. Turning, he saw him panting along after him.

'One word, Rodion Romanovich; as to all the rest of this, it is as God wills, but all the same there are some questions I must put to you, to comply with the formalities . . . So we shall see each other again, you see!'

And Porfiry stopped in front of him with a smile.

'You see!' he added again.

It might have been supposed that he wanted to say something more, but could not bring out the words.

'And you must please forgive me, Porfiry Petrovich, for what I said just now . . . I was angry,' began Raskolnikov, now so much emboldened that he could not resist the desire to show off.

'It doesn't matter, it doesn't matter,' rejoined Porfiry, almost joyfully. 'I myself . . . I have a venomous nature, I am sorry to say! But we shall see each other again—and very many times, if God wills it! . . .'

'And learn to know each other in the end?' rejoined Raskolnikov.

'Yes, in the end we shall get to know each other,' agreed Porfiry, screwing up his eyes and looking at him gravely. 'Are you going to a party now?'

'To a funeral.'

'Oh, yes, to a funeral! Look after your health; keep well . . .'

'I don't know what I can wish you in return,' rejoined Raskolnikov, who had begun to go down the stairs, but turned round to face Porfiry again. 'I would wish you every success, but really, you know, yours is such a funny job!'

'Why funny?' Porfiry Petrovich, who had also turned to go, pricked up his ears.

'Well, just look how you must have teased and tormented that poor Mikolka, psychologically, in your usual way, until he confessed; day and night you must have been trying to prove it to him: "you're the murderer, you're the murderer," and now that he has confessed you'll put him on the rack again: "You're lying," you say, "you aren't the murderer! You can't be! You've picked it up somewhere or other!" Well, after that, what else is it but a funny job?'

'He, he, he! So you noticed that I told Nikolay just now that none of that was his own idea?'

'How could I help it?'

'He, he! You are sharp-witted, very sharp-witted. You notice everything. A really quick mind! You seize on the most comical aspect of things . . . he, he! It is Gogol, isn't it, among our writers, who is said to have that faculty in the highest degree?'

'Yes, Gogol.'

'Yes, Gogol . . . Good-bye till our next most pleasant meeting.'

'Good-bye till then . . .'

Raskolnikov went straight home. He was so confused and bewildered that when he reached home and flung himself down on the sofa, he sat there for a quarter of an hour simply recovering and trying to get his thoughts into some kind of order. He did not even begin to reason about Nikolay; he was dumbfounded; he felt that there was something astonishing and mysterious in Nikolay's confession that he was quite incapable of understanding at this moment. But Nikolay's confession was an actual fact. The consequences of that fact were immediately clear to him: the lie must be exposed, and then they would be on his trail again. But at least he was free until then, and he ought certainly to do something to help himself, for the danger to himself must inevitably return.

But how great was it? The situation was becoming clear. Remembering *roughly*, in general outline, all the recent interview with Porfiry, he could not help shuddering again with fear. He naturally did not yet know everything Porfiry had been aiming at, and therefore could not understand all his moves. But part of his hand had been revealed, and nobody, of course, knew better than he how terrible this 'lead' of Porfiry's had been from his point of view. A little more and he *might* have given the game away completely, even to the factual evidence. Knowing the weaknesses of his character, and having understood him and summed him up correctly at the first glance, Porfiry had taken almost the best possible line with him, though perhaps he had pursued it too vigorously. There was no disputing that Raskolnikov had managed to compromise himself seriously, but, all the same, no *facts* had yet been arrived at; everything was still only inferential. But had he got it right, did he understand it all properly now? What had Porfiry really been driving at today? Had he indeed been preparing some surprise? And what had it been? Was he really waiting for something or not? How would they have parted if Nikolay's arrival had not brought an unexpected climax?

Porfiry had shown almost all his cards; of course, he was taking a risk, but he had shown them and (so it seemed to Raskolnikov) if he had really had anything more, he would have shown it. What had his 'surprise' been? A joke? Had it meant anything, or not? Could it have concealed anything like factual evidence or a definite accusation? The stranger of yesterday? Where had he got to? Where was he today? If, indeed, Porfiry had got hold of something definite, it must be connected with that man . . .

He sat on the sofa with his head hanging down, his face buried in his hands, and his elbows on his knees. A nervous trembling still shook his whole body. At last he rose, picked up his cap, stood thinking for a moment, and turned towards the door.

Somehow he had a presentiment that for today at least he could almost certainly consider himself out of danger. His heart felt suddenly almost light: he was anxious to get to Katerina Ivanovna's. He was too late for the funeral, of course, but he would be in time for the dinner, and there he would see Sonya.

He stopped, thinking, and with a feeble smile on his lips.

'Today, today!' he repeated to himself, 'yes, this very day! I must . . .'

He was on the point of opening the door when it began to open of itself. He started and recoiled. The door was opening slowly and quietly, and suddenly he saw a figure—yesterday's stranger *from under the ground.*

The man stopped on the threshold, looked at Raskolnikov in silence, and then took a step into the room. His appearance was exactly the same as on the day before, the same figure, dressed in the same way, but his face and his look had undergone a considerable change: now he looked melancholy, and after a pause he sighed deeply. It only wanted for him to put the palm of his hand to his cheek and tilt his head to one side and he would have looked exactly like a peasant-woman.

'What do you want?' asked Raskolnikov, terror-struck.

The man said nothing, but suddenly bowed very low, almost to the ground, low enough at least to touch it with one finger of his right hand.

'Who are you?' cried Raskolnikov.

'I am guilty,' said the man quietly.

'Of what?'

'Of evil thoughts.'

They looked at each other.

'I was annoyed. When you came there that time (perhaps you had been drinking) and told the porters to go to the police and asked about the blood, I was annoyed that they left you alone, thinking you were drunk. I was so annoyed that I couldn't sleep. But I remembered your address, and came here yesterday and asked questions . . .'

'Who came?' interrupted Raskolnikov, instantly beginning to remember.

'I did. That is to say I injured you.'

'So you come from that house?'

'Why, I was standing there with them in the gateway, or have you forgotten? I've followed my trade there for years and years. I am a furrier, a working furrier, and I take in work at home . . . but more than anything I was annoyed . . .'

Suddenly Raskolnikov remembered clearly the scene of two days before; he imagined that besides the porters there had been several men standing there, and some women as well. He remembered a voice suggesting that he should be taken straight to the police. He could not remember the face of the man who had spoken, and he did not recognize him even now, but he clearly remembered turning towards him and making some answer . . .

This, then, was what all the previous day's horror resolved itself into. The most terrible thing was the thought that he had almost come to grief, had almost destroyed himself, because of such an *insignificant* circumstance. For it followed that, except for the taking of the flat and the talk about blood, there was nothing that this man could tell. Consequently, Porfiry had nothing either, nothing but *delirium*, no kind of facts, only his *psychology*, which *cut both ways*, nothing definite. Consequently, if no further facts were revealed (and they must not be, they must not, must not!), then . . . what could they do to him? What could they definitely prove against him, even if they arrested him? And Porfiry could only just have learnt about the flat, only now; he could not have known about it before.

'Did you tell Porfiry today . . . that I went there?' he cried, struck by a sudden idea.

'What Porfiry?'

'The magistrate in charge of the investigation.'

'Yes, I told him. The porters didn't go to him, so I went.'

'Today?'

'I was only a minute before you. And I heard it all, the way he was tormenting you.'

'Where? What? When?'

'Why there, behind that partition. I was sitting there all the time.'

'What? So you were the surprise? But how did it all come about? Please tell me!'

'Well,' began the man, 'when I saw the porters wouldn't go when I told them, because they said it was too late, and perhaps they would get into trouble for not going at once, I got annoyed, and I couldn't sleep, and then I began finding things out. I found out all I could yesterday, and today I went there. The first time I went, he wasn't there. I went back an hour afterwards, and I couldn't see him, but the third time they let me in. Well, I began to tell him everything just as it happened, and he began fussing round the room and hitting his chest with his fist, and he said, "What are you rogues doing to me? If I had known about this, I would have sent guards to fetch him!" Then he ran out and called somebody in and began talking to him in the corner, and then he came back to me asking me questions and cursing and swearing. And he blamed me for not going before; and I told him all about everything and I said you didn't dare answer what I said to you yesterday, and that you didn't recognize me. And then he began running round again, beating his breast all the time, and he got angry and ran about, and when they said you were there, he said to me, "Well, go into the next room, and sit there for a bit and don't stir, whatever you may hear," and he brought me a chair himself, and locked me in, and said, "Perhaps I'll ask you to come in." And when they brought Nikolay, he sent me away, after you'd gone. "I shall want you again," says he, "to ask you some more questions" . . .'

'Did he question Nikolay while you were there?'

'When he sent you out, he sent me out straight after, and then began to ask Nikolay questions.'

He stopped, and suddenly bowed again, touching the floor with his finger.

'Forgive me for slandering you, and for my spite.'

'God will forgive you,' answered Raskolnikov. As soon as he had uttered the words, the man bowed to him again, not so deeply this time, but only from the waist, then turned and left the room. 'Everything cuts both ways; now everything cuts both ways,' repeated Raskolnikov to himself again and again. Then, in better spirits than ever before, he too went out.

'Now we shall fight again,' he said with a bitter smile, as he went down the stairs. But the bitterness was directed against himself; he remembered his own 'cowardice' with scorn and shame.

# Part Five

## CHAPTER I

THE morning after his ill-fated interview with Dunechka and Pulkheria Alexandrovna had a sobering effect on Peter Petrovich. To his great displeasure he was compelled little by little to recognize as an accomplished and irrevocable fact what had yesterday appeared to him an almost fantastic occurrence, which still seemed impossible even after it had actually happened. The black snake of wounded self-esteem had preyed on his heart all night. As soon as he got up, Peter Petrovich examined himself in the mirror. He was afraid he might look bilious after the night. But for the time being all was well in that respect, and the inspection of his pale and distinguished face, which had of late grown rather fat, even consoled him momentarily, fully persuading him that he could find another bride, perhaps even a better one, elsewhere. His thoughts returned immediately to reality, and he spat vigorously, a gesture which provoked his young friend and the sharer of his lodgings, Andrey Semënovich Lebezyatnikov, to a silent but sarcastic smile. Peter Petrovich saw the smile, and mentally set it down against his young friend's account. He had set a good many things down there recently. His annoyance redoubled when he suddenly realized that he ought never to have told Andrey Semënovich of the result of yesterday's happenings. That was another mistake he had made yesterday, one made in the heat of the moment, when irritation had made him unduly expansive . . . Throughout the morning, one unpleasantness followed another, as though on purpose to annoy him. Even in the Senate something went wrong with the case that was causing him so much trouble. He was particularly irritated with the landlord of the flat he had taken in anticipation of his imminent marriage and decorated at his own expense: the landlord, a prosperous German tradesman, refused to cancel the newly completed contract and insisted on all the penalties stipulated for in it, although Peter Petrovich was returning the flat to him almost entirely redecorated. Similarly, the furniture shop refused to return a single rouble of the deposit on the furniture which had been bought but not yet delivered to the flat. 'I'm not going to get married simply because I've got the furniture!' said Peter Petrovich to himself, grating his teeth, while the desperate hope flashed through his mind once more: 'Surely everything can't really be irrevocably over and done with. Surely it should be possible to make one more try!' The alluring image of Dunechka wrung his heart once more. He endured a moment of anguish, and, if the mere expression of a wish could have killed Raskolnikov, Peter Petrovich would assuredly have pronounced the wish in that instant.

'Another mistake I made was in not giving them any money,' he thought gloomily, as he returned to Lebezyatnikov's little room; 'why the devil was I such a Jew? It isn't even as if I were being careful of my money. I simply wanted to keep them as badly off as possible and so lead them to see me as their Providence, and now look! . . . Pah! . . . No, my position would have been much better . . . and stronger, if only I had given them some fifteen hundred roubles, for example, for the trousseau, and little gifts, various fancy boxes, dressing-cases, ornaments, materials, and all that sort of rubbish from Knopp's or the English Stores! They would not have cast me off so lightly now! They are the sort of people who would have felt obliged to return both the money and the presents if they refused me, and they would have been sorry to have to do that! Besides, their consciences would have been troubled: "How", they would have said, "can we suddenly drive away a man who has acted with such generosity and delicacy towards us?" . . Hm! I've made a blunder!' And, grinding his teeth again, Peter Petrovich admitted—only to himself, of course—that he had been a fool.

Having come to this conclusion, he reached home feeling twice as vicious and sore as when he had left. The preparations for the funeral dinner in Katerina Ivanovna's room aroused his curiosity. He had heard something about it the day before; he even seemed to remember that he had been invited; but his personal worries had distracted his attention from everything else. He made inquiries of Mrs. Lippewechsel, who was busying herself with the table in the absence of Katerina Ivanovna (who was at the cemetery), and learnt that the dinner would be a very fine one, that almost all the lodgers had been invited, including some who had not known the dead man, that even Andrey Semënovich Lebezyatnikov, in spite of his former quarrel with Katerina Ivanovna, had been included in the invitations, and finally that he himself was not only invited but eagerly expected, since he was almost the most important of all the lodgers. Amalia Ivanovna herself had also been invited with the greatest courtesy, in spite of all past unpleasantness, and was therefore bustling about now, performing housewifely duties and almost enjoying herself. Moreover, she was dressed in her best new black silk, all frills and flounces, and was very proud of herself. All this information gave Peter Petrovich a certain idea, and he went off to his room, or rather to Andrey Semënovich Lebezyatnikov's, rather thoughtfully. The point was that he had also learnt that Raskolnikov was one of those who had been invited.

For some reason, Andrey Semënovich had been at home all the morning. Peter Petrovich's attitude to this gentleman was rather strange, if natural: he had despised and hated him, practically from the day he came to stay with him, and yet he seemed a little afraid of him. His motive for coming here on his arrival in St. Petersburg was not purely niggardly economy. Although this was almost his principal reason, he had another as well. Before he left the provinces, he had heard that Andrey Semënovich, his former ward, was one of the most advanced of the young progressives, and that he even played a prominent part in certain curious and legendary circles. Peter Petrovich was impressed by all this. Those powerful and omniscient groups who despised and denounced everybody, had for a long time inspired him with a peculiar but undefined apprehension. Of course, while he was in the provinces he himself could not acquire even an approximately exact understanding of anything *of that kind*. He had heard, like everybody else, that there existed, especially in St. Petersburg, certain progressives, nihilists, 'denouncers', and so on and so forth, but, like many others, absurdly exaggerated and distorted the idea and meaning of these names. For several years what he had most feared had been *denunciation*, or *exposure*, and this was the principal cause of his constant, exaggerated uneasiness, especially at the thought of transferring his activities to St. Petersburg. In this connexion he was *scared*, as it is called, as little children are sometimes *scared*. Some years ago, in the provinces, while he was still at the beginning of his career, he had met with two cases of cruel 'exposure' of personages of some local importance, to whom he had attached himself, and who had been his patrons. One case had ended particularly scandalously for the personage exposed, and the other had very nearly resulted in the ruin of the person concerned. This was why, when he arrived in St. Petersburg, Peter Petrovich proposed to investigate these movements and if necessary to anticipate possible developments and ingratiate himself with 'our younger generation'. For this purpose he relied on Andrey Semënovich, and he had learned to trot out, after a fashion, current phrases borrowed with a view to interviews with, for example, Raskolnikov . . .

Naturally, he had soon recognized in Andrey Semënovich a singularly commonplace and silly person. But this neither disabused nor encouraged Peter Petrovich. Even if he had been convinced that all progressives were just such simpletons, it would not have allayed his uneasiness. He was not particularly concerned with all the doctrines, ideas, and systems with which Andrey Semënovich bombarded him. He had his own purposes. He simply wanted to find out as quickly as possible what had happened *here*, and how. Had *these people* any power or not? Had he personally any reason to be afraid, or not? If he entered upon any enterprise, would he be denounced, or not? And if he were denounced, what would it be for? What were people denounced for now? Further, could he not ingratiate himself with these people and pull the wool over their eyes, if they really had any power? Ought he to try to do this, or not? Could he not, for example, use them to further his career? In short, there were hundreds of questions to answer.

Andrey Semënovich was a short, thin-blooded, scrofulous creature, a clerk in some Ministry, with hair of an astonishingly pale colour and mutton-chop whiskers of which he was very proud; there was almost always something wrong with his eyes. His heart was soft enough, but his speech was extremely self-assured and sometimes even insolently overbearing; the effect of this, coming from such a manikin, was nearly always comical. Amalia Ivanovna, however, considered him one of her most respectable lodgers; that is to say, he was not a heavy drinker and he paid his rent punctually. In spite of these good qualities, Andrey Semënovich really was rather stupid. He had joined the forces of progress and 'our younger generation' out of conviction. He was one of that countless and multifarious legion of nondescripts, putrescent abortions, and uninformed obstinate fools who instantly and infallibly attach themselves to the most fashionable current idea, with the immediate effect of vulgarizing it and of turning into a ridiculous carica-ture any cause they serve, however sincerely.

Lebezyatnikov, in spite of his great kindness of heart, was also finding it difficult to tolerate his fellow lodger and former guardian, Peter Petrovich. On both sides this state of affairs had come about unexpectedly. Simple though Andrey Semë-novich might be, he had begun to think that Peter Petrovich was fooling him and secretly despised him, and that 'there was something wrong about the fellow'. He had tried to expound Fourier's system and Darwin's theory to him, but Peter Petro-vich, especially recently, had listened very sarcastically, and in the past few days had even begun to jeer. The fact was that he instinctively divined that Lebezyatnikov was not only a foolish and trivial person, but perhaps a fraud as well, and that he had no connexions of any importance even in his own group, but had only heard things at second hand; what was more, he was not very expert even in his own chosen task of *propaganda*, because he got too muddled; and besides, how could he denounce anybody? It may be noted in passing that during those ten days (especially at first) Peter Petrovich had readily accepted some very strange commendations of himself; he had not objected, for example, but had sat silent, when Andrey Semënovich attributed to him a willingness to further the construction in the near future of a new 'commune' somewhere in Meshchanskaya Street, or not to hinder Dunechka if she thought of taking a lover in the first month of their marriage, or not to have his future children christened, and so on—all in the same strain. Peter Petrovich, in his usual manner, did not object when such qualities were attributed to him, and even allowed himself to be praised for them, so pleasant to him was praise of any kind.

Peter Petrovich, who had had occasion during that morning to change several five-per-cent. Government bonds, sat at the table counting packets of bank-notes. Andrey Semënovich, who rarely had any money, wandered about the room and pretended to himself that he regarded all those bundles with indifference, and even with contempt. Nothing could have persuaded Peter Petrovich that Andrey Semënovich could really see so much money with indifference; Andrey Semënovich, in his turn, thought bitterly that Peter Petrovich might be quite capable of holding such an opinion of him, and might, moreover, be glad of this chance to tease and irritate his young friend by displaying the packets of bank-notes and thus making him feel his insignificance and the great difference between them.

He found him, on this occasion, more exasperatingly inattentive than ever, even though he, Andrey Semënovich, had begun to expound his favourite theme, the foundation of a special new 'commune'. The brief comments and replies which escaped from Peter Petrovich in the intervals between the clicks of the balls on the abacus were open and intentionally rude jeers. But Andrey Semënovich 'humanely' ascribed Peter Petrovich's mood to the effect of his having broken with Dunechka, and burned with the desire to talk about this; he had something progressive and proselytizing to say on this subject, which might comfort his esteemed friend and 'undoubtedly' assist his further development.

'What is this funeral dinner they are preparing at that . . . at the widow's?' asked Peter Petrovich suddenly, interrupting Andrey Semënovich at the most interesting point.

'As if you didn't know! I am sure I discussed it with you yesterday, and told you my idea of all these rituals . . . And surely I heard that she had invited you, as well. You were talking to her yourself yesterday . . .'

'I had no idea that that foolish woman, destitute as she is, would throw away on the funeral all the money she got from the other fool . . . Raskolnikov. I was absolutely astonished, as I came past: such preparations, wine . . . Quite a few people are coming. It's quite sickening! . . .' went on Peter Petrovich, enlarging on the subject as though with some purpose. 'What? Did you say that I was invited?' he added suddenly, raising his head. 'When was this? I don't remember it. However, I shall not go. What should I do there? I only spoke a few words to her casually, yesterday, about the possibility of her receiving a grant of a year's salary, as the destitute widow of a civil servant. I suppose that must be why she invited me. He, he!'

'I do not intend to go either,' said Lebezyatnikov.

'I should think not! You beat her black and blue with your own hands. I can understand your feeling ashamed. He, he, he!'

'Who did? Beat whom?' cried Lebezyatnikov, alarmed and blushing.

'You did. You beat Katerina Ivanovna a month ago, didn't you? I heard about it, you know, yesterday . . . So much for your principles! . . . Even the woman's question hasn't worked out very successfully. He, he, he!'

And Peter Petrovich, as though feeling more cheerful, went back to clicking his abacus.

'That is all rubbish, and it is slanderous!' flared up Lebezyatnikov, who always flinched from reminders of this incident. 'It wasn't like that at all! It was different . . . You heard it wrong; all scandal! I was only defending myself. She attacked me first with her finger-nails . . . She plucked out all my whiskers . . . Everybody is allowed to defend himself, I hope. Besides, I don't allow anyone to use violence to me . . . On principle. Because that is almost despotism. What was I to do: just stand there? I only pushed her away.'

'He, he, he!' Luzhin went on laughing maliciously.

'You're only trying to provoke me, because you're in a bad temper yourself . . . And it's all nonsense and has nothing at all, nothing at all, to do with the woman's question.[7] You've got it wrong. I used to think that if it is accepted that woman is man's equal in everything, even physical strength (as some people maintain), there must consequently be equality in such things too. Of course, I decided later that the question ought not to arise, because there ought never to be any fighting; fighting is unthinkable in the future society . . . and of course it is strange to look for equality in fighting. I am not such a fool . . . although fighting does occur . . . I mean it won't occur in the future, but now it still does . . . Bah! The devil! You get

7. In this conversation, here and later, Lebezyatnikov is echoing the progressive ideas about emancipated women and other topics in N. G. Chernyshevsky's novel *What Is to Be Done?* (see note to p. 126 above). He is also carrying to exaggerated lengths the views of another Russian writer, D. I. Pisarev, who stressed practical usefulness as a criterion of value.

people all muddled! It is not because of that unpleasant business that I am staying away from the funeral. My not going is a simple matter of principle, because I don't wish to take part in superstitious ceremonials, that's why! However, it might be possible to go just in order to laugh at it . . . It's a pity there won't be any priests. If there were, I should certainly go.'

'That is, you would accept hospitality and practically spit on it and on your hosts. Is that it?'

'Not at all; merely as a protest. I should go with the intention of being helpful. I might indirectly promote their development and our propaganda. It is the duty of every man to develop others and disseminate propaganda, and perhaps the harsher one's methods the better. I might throw out an idea, a seed . . . From that seed might grow something real. What is there in that to offend them? At first they will be offended, but then they will see that I have been of assistance to them. Look how people blamed Terebyeva (who is in the commune now) because when she left her family and . . . took a lover, she wrote to her mother and father that she did not wish to live in a world of prejudice, and was going to contract a civil marriage, and because it was thought that she was too harsh with her parents, and could have spared them and written more gently. I think that's all nonsense; gentleness is not called for; on the contrary, on the contrary, protest is what is wanted. Look at Varents, who had been married seven years, and abandoned her two children; she made a clean break with her husband, in a letter which said: "I have realized that I cannot be happy with you. I shall never forgive you for deceiving me by concealing that there exists another way of organizing society, in communes. I have recently learnt of this from a great-souled man, and I have given myself to him; together we are founding a commune. I am putting it plainly, because I consider it dishonourable to pretend. Do as you think fit. Do not hope that I shall return to you; it is too late. I wish you happiness." That's how to write letters of that kind!'

'This Terebyeva, isn't she the one you told me has contracted a third "civil marriage"?'

'No, only two, if you look at it in the right way! But if it were four, or fifteen, all that means nothing! And if ever I were sorry that my father and mother were dead, I am sorry now. I have even dreamed of how, if they were still living, I should sting them with my protests! I should have deliberately created a situation . . . Talk about a clean break! I'd have shown them! I'd have surprised them. It's really a pity that I haven't anybody!'

'To surprise? He, he! Well, let that be as you please,'

interrupted Peter Petrovich, 'but now tell me this: I suppose you know the dead man's daughter, that sickly creature. Well, is what they say about her true, eh?'

'What is that? In my opinion, that is, according to my personal conviction, it is the most normal condition for a woman. Why not? I mean to say, *distinguons*. In our present society it is not, of course, entirely normal, because it is forced on her, but in future it will be completely normal, because freely chosen. And even now she had the right to act as she did; she was suffering, and that was her stock, so to speak, her capital, which she had a perfect right to dispose of. Of course, in the future society there will be no need of capital funds; but her role will be given a different significance, under harmonious and rational conditions. As for Sofya Semënovna herself, in present conditions I look upon her action as a spirited concrete protest against the organization of society and I deeply respect her for it; I rejoice to see her!'

'But I was told that it was you who caused her to be driven away from here!'

Lebezyatnikov became positively frenzied.

'That is another slander!' he shouted. 'It was not like that at all, not at all! More falsehood! Katerina Ivanovna got it all wrong, because she did not understand anything! I didn't try to force myself on Sofya Semënovna! I was simply trying to educate her, quite disinterestedly, trying to rouse her to protest . . . All I needed was her protest, and besides, Sofya Semënovna was really unable to stay here any longer!'

'Was she invited to enter the commune?'

'You are still laughing at me, but allow me to tell you it has no effect at all. You don't understand anything! There is no such role in the commune. The communes are founded in order to do away with such roles. In the communes her role will completely change its present character, and what is stupid here will become wise there, what is unnatural here, under present conditions, will become completely natural there. Everything depends on environment and circumstances. The environment is everything, and the man is nothing. I am very good friends with Sofya Semënovna even now, which may serve to prove to you that she never regarded me as her enemy and persecutor. Yes! I am trying now to attract her into the commune, only on a quite different basis, quite different! What do you find so funny? We want to found our own particular commune on a much wider basis than previous ones. We have progressed farther in our convictions. We reject more! If Dobrolyubov rose from his grave I should quarrel with him. As for Belinsky, I should absolutely annihilate him![8] Meanwhile

8. Dobrolyubov and Belinsky were nineteenth-century radical political and literary authors.

I am continuing Sofya Semënovna's education. She has a beautiful nature, beautiful!'

'And so you are taking advantage of her beautiful nature, eh? He, he!'

'No, no! Oh, no! Just the opposite!'

'Well, just the opposite, then. He, he, he! What a thing to say!'

'You must believe me! What reason could I have for deceiving you, I should like to know? On the contrary, I myself find it strange that she is so intensely, even timidly, chaste and modest with me!'

'And you of course are educating her . . . he, he, he!—teaching her that modesty is all nonsense? . . .'

'Not at all! Not at all! Oh, how crudely and stupidly— excuse me—you understand the word education! You don't understand anything at all! Heavens, how . . . unprepared you still are! We are seeking the emancipation of women, but you have only one thing in your head . . . Ignoring altogether the questions of chastity and female modesty as unprofitable in themselves, and even prejudicial, I fully acquiesce in her chastity with me, fully, because that is her right and a matter for her own free will. Of course, if she herself were to say to me: "I want you," I should consider myself very lucky, because I like the girl very much; but as things are now, of course, nobody has ever treated her more politely and courteously than I do, or with more respect for her dignity . . . I wait and hope . . . that is all!'

'It would be better for you to give her some sort of present. I bet you didn't even think of that.'

'I told you you didn't understand anything! Of course, she is in that position, but—this is a different question, quite different! You simply despise her. Seeing a fact which you mistakenly consider deserving of scorn, you refuse to regard a human being in a humane light. You do not know yet what she is like! I am very disappointed about one thing, that she seems lately to have stopped reading, and doesn't borrow any more books from me. She used to. I am sorry, too, that with all the energy and resolution which she showed once, in making her protest, she still has too little self-reliance and, so to speak, independence, too little capacity for rejection, to be able to free herself entirely from certain prejudices and . . . stupidities. In spite of that, she has a wonderful understanding of some questions. For example, she understood the question of kissing hands marvellously well. That is, that it is an insulting mark of inequality for a man to kiss a woman's hand. This was the subject of one of our discussions, and I gave her an account of it immediately afterwards. She listened very attentively to a description of the workers' associations in France, too. Now

I am explaining to her the question of entering rooms in the future society.'

'Oh, and what is that?'

'Recently we have been discussing whether a member of a commune has at all times the right to enter the room of another member, whether man or woman . . . and it was decided that he has . . .'

'And what if he or she is occupied at that moment with the unavoidable demands of nature, he, he?'

Andrey Semënovich was really angry.

'You're always harping on the same string! You keep on and on about those damned "demands of nature"!' he cried, with detestation. 'Pah, I am disgusted with myself for having mentioned those confounded demands, prematurely, when I was expounding the system to you. Damn it all! It's always a stumbling-block to people of your sort, and worse than that—they get parrot-phrases by heart and go round repeating them before they know what it's all about! And as if they were in the right! As if they had something to be proud of! Pah! I have insisted many times that it is not possible to explain this question to beginners before the very end, when they believe in the system and their ideas are properly developed along the right lines. And what, I should like to know, do you find so shameful and despicable even in cess-pits? I should be the first to be ready to clean out any cess-pit you like! There isn't even any self-sacrifice about it! It is simply work, an honourable, socially useful activity, which is worth as much as any other, and may even be worth more than the activities of some Raphael or Pushkin, because it is more useful!'[9]

'And more honourable, more honourable—he, he, he!'

'What does honourable mean? I don't understand such expressions as used to define human activities. "More honourable", "nobler"—that's all rubbish; those are absurdities, antiquated prejudices which I reject! Everything that is *useful* to humanity is honourable. I understand only one word, *useful*! You may snigger if you like, but it is true!'

Peter Petrovich was laughing heartily. He had finished his calculations and put away most of his money. However, for some reason he had left a part of it on the table. This 'cess-pit question' had already, in spite of its triviality, been the occasion of several arguments and quarrels between Peter Petrovich and his young friend. The stupid part of it was that Andrey Semënovich had grown really angry. Luzhin was simply amusing himself, and just now he felt a great desire to tease Lebezyatnikov.

'It's because things went badly for you yesterday that you

9. An allusion to the views of Pisarev expressed in his articles "Realists" and "Pushkin and Belinsky."

are so captious and spiteful,' burst out Lebezyatnikov at last. In spite of all his 'independence' and his 'protests' he was not generally bold enough to oppose Peter Petrovich, and still retained from former years his habit of deference towards him.

'You would do better to tell me,' interrupted Peter Petrovich, in a tone of haughty displeasure, 'whether you can . . . or, rather, whether you are on sufficiently friendly terms with the young person just referred to, to ask her to come here for a few moments. I think they have all got back from the cemetery . . . I can hear people moving about . . . I wish to see her, that young person.'

'What for?' asked Lebezyatnikov, surprised.

'I just want to. I shall be leaving today or tomorrow, and therefore I should like to tell her . . . However, please be here yourself, when I explain. That will be best. Otherwise, you may imagine God knows what.'

'I shan't imagine anything . . . I was only asking. If you have something to say to her, there is nothing easier than to ask her here. I will go at once. And be assured that I will not disturb you.'

Five minutes later Lebezyatnikov returned with Sonechka. She came in feeling extremely surprised, and, as usual, very shy. She was always shy in such circumstances; she had dreaded seeing new faces and making new acquaintances ever since her childhood, and she feared it now more than ever . . . Peter Petrovich greeted her 'nicely and politely', but with a shade of jovial familiarity which, in his opinion, was becoming to a respectable man of solid worth, like himself, in his dealings with a young and, in a special sense, *interesting* creature like Sonya. He hastened to 'reassure' her, and seated her at the table opposite him. Sonya sat down and looked about her—at Lebezyatnikov, at the money lying on the table, and back again at Peter Petrovich—and then her eyes remained glued to his face. Lebezyatnikov turned towards the door. Peter Petrovich got up, signed to Sonya to stay where she was, and stopped Lebezyatnikov on the threshold.

'Is Raskolnikov there? Has he come?' he asked in a whisper.

'Raskolnikov? Yes. Why? Yes, he's there . . . I just saw him come in . . . why?'

'Then I particularly request you to remain here with us, and not to leave me alone with this . . . girl. My business is trifling, but God knows what conclusions will be drawn. I don't want Raskolnikov to tell *them* . . . Do you understand what I am talking about?'

'Yes, I understand!' said Lebezyatnikov, suddenly realizing what he meant. 'Yes, you are right . . . Of course, in my personal opinion you carry your anxiety too far but . . . all the same, you are right. Certainly I will stay. I will remain here

by the window, and not be in your way . . . I think you are
right . . .'

Peter Petrovich went back to the sofa, sat down opposite
Sonya, and looked at her with a very dignified and rather
severe expression, as much as to say, 'Don't get any ideas into
your head, young lady.' This completed Sonya's confusion.

'First of all, Sofya Semënovna, please apologize for me to
your respected mama . . . That is right, I think? Katerina
Ivanovna has taken the place of your own mother?' he began,
still seriously, but quite pleasantly. He evidently had the most
friendly intentions.

'Yes, that is right, my mother's place,' answered Sonya
hurriedly and timidly.

'Well, then, give her my apologies for being obliged, because
of circumstances not depending on me, to be absent from the
dinner, in spite of your mama's kind invitation.'

'Yes; I will tell her; at once,' and Sonya jumped up from her
chair.

'I have not finished yet,' said Peter Petrovich, stopping her
with a smile at her simplicity and ignorance of the way to
behave, 'and you know very little of me, Sofya Semënovna, if
you thought I would disturb you by asking here in person
someone like yourself for such an unimportant reason, concerning nobody but me. I have another object.'

Sonya hastily sat down again. The grey and rainbow-
coloured bank-notes which had been left on the table attracted
her eyes again, but she quickly turned her face away and
raised it towards Peter Petrovich; it suddenly seemed to her
that it was very bad manners, especially for *her*, to look at
somebody else's money. She fixed her eyes on the gold
lorgnettes which Peter Petrovich held in his left hand, and on
the thick, heavy, and very beautiful gold ring with a yellow
stone on the middle finger of that hand, then she turned them
away from that, too, and, not knowing what else to do, ended
by looking straight into Peter Petrovich's eyes again. After a
still more dignified pause, he went on:

'I chanced to exchange a few words in passing with the
unhappy Katerina Ivanovna yesterday. That was enough to
inform me that she was in an . . . unnatural position, if I may
so express it . . .'

'Yes . . . unnatural,' hastily agreed Sonya.

'Or, to put it more simply and understandably, a painful
position.'

'Yes, more simply and underst— . . . yes, painful.'

'Quite so. Therefore, you see, from feelings of humanity
a-a-and so to say, sympathy, I should have liked, for my part,
to be of some service to her, foreseeing her inevitably unhappy
fate. I believe that all that destitute family is now entirely
dependent on you.'

'Allow me to ask,' said Sonya, rising suddenly to her feet, 'whether you spoke to her yesterday of the possibility of a pension. Because she told me that you had undertaken to procure a pension for her . . . Is that true?'

'Far from it. You might even call it ridiculous. I merely made some reference to temporary assistance for the widow of a clerk who has died while in government service—provided she has some influence—but it appears that your late father had not only not served the full term, but had not recently been employed in the civil service at all. In one word, though there might be some hope, it would be of a very flimsy character, because, in fact, there is no right whatever to assistance in this case, quite the contrary . . . And she was already thinking of a pension, he, he, he! A lady who runs away with an idea!'

'Yes, she was thinking of a pension . . . Because she is credulous and good, and her goodness makes her believe everything, and . . . and . . . and . . . her mind works like that . . . Yes . . . excuse her,' said Sonya, and again got up to go.

'Excuse me, you have not yet heard me out.'

'No, not heard you out,' murmured Sonya.

'Sit down, then.'

Sonya, dreadfully confused, sat down for the third time.

'In view of her position, and that of the unfortunate little children, I should like—as I said before—as far as lies in my power, to be of some help, that is, as far as lies in my power, as they say, and no more. Perhaps, for example, it would be possible to get up a subscription for her, or, so to say, a lottery . . . or something of that kind—as is always done in cases of this kind by friends, or even by strangers, but in any case by those desirous of helping people. That is what I intended to speak to you about. It could be done.'

'Yes, very kind . . . God will repay . . .' stammered Sonya, still gazing at Peter Petrovich.

'It can be done, but . . . we will talk of it later . . . that is, we might begin today. We will meet in the evening, talk it over and lay, so to say, the foundation. Come here at about seven o'clock. Andrey Semënovich, I hope, will also make one of us . . . But . . . there is one circumstance which ought to be mentioned beforehand, with due care. It was for this, Sofya Semënovna, that I troubled you to come here. This is what I think: it is impossible to give money into Katerina Ivanovna's own hands, it is dangerous; today's funeral dinner proves it. Not having, so to say, a crust of bread for tomorrow or . . . well, or shoes, or anything, today she buys Jamaica rum, and even, I believe, Madeira, a-a-and coffee. I saw it as I came past. Tomorrow it will all come down on you again, everything to the last crust of bread; it is quite absurd. Therefore the subscription, in my personal view, ought to be organized in such a way that the unhappy widow, so to say, does not know about the money, but only you, for example, know. Am I right?'

'I don't know. It is only just today that she . . . it is only once in a lifetime . . . she very much wanted to remember him, to do him honour, his memory . . . but she is very sensible. However, as you please, sir, and I shall be very, very, very . . . they will all be . . . God will bless you . . . and the orphans . . .'

Sonya burst into tears, unable to finish.

'Quite so. Well, then, bear it in mind; and now be good enough to accept from me personally in the interests of your kinswoman, for immediate needs, what sum I can spare. I am completely and absolutely desirous that my name should not be mentioned in connexion with it. Here you are . . . having, so to say, cares of my own, I am not in a position . . .'

And Peter Petrovich held out to Sonya a carefully unfolded ten-rouble bank-note. Sonya took it, blushed deeply, jumped up, murmured something, and hastily took her leave. Peter Petrovich ceremoniously escorted her to the door. She slipped out of the room at last, agitated and weary, and returned to Katerina Ivanovna in a state of extraordinary confusion.

Throughout this scene Andrey Semënovich had stood there by the window or moved about the room, trying not to interrupt the conversation; when Sonya had gone, he went up to Peter Petrovich and solemnly offered him his hand.

'I heard everything and I *saw* everything,' he said, laying special emphasis on the word *saw*. 'This was noble, I mean humane! You wished to avoid my gratitude, I could see! And although I confess I cannot, on principle, sympathize with private charity, because not only does it not radically destroy the evil, but it even nourishes it, nevertheless I am bound to admit that I saw your action with pleasure—yes, yes, I liked it.'

'Oh, rubbish!' muttered Peter Petrovich, who seemed rather agitated, looking closely at Lebezyatnikov.

'No, it's not rubbish! A man who has been insulted and annoyed as you were by yesterday's happenings, and who is at the same time capable of thinking of other unhappy creatures —such a man, sir . . . although his actions constitute a social mistake—all the same . . . is worthy of respect! I did not expect it of you, Peter Petrovich, especially as according to your way of understanding things—oh! how that still hinders you! How, for example, all the unfortunate events of yesterday upset you,' exclaimed good little Andrey Semënovich, feeling a renewed kindness for Peter Petrovich, 'and why, why do you think you must have this marriage, this *legal* marriage, my very dear, my most generous-minded Peter Petrovich? Why must you have this *legality* in marriage? Well, if you were to beat me for it, I must say that I am glad that it failed, that you are free, that you are not altogether lost for humanity, I am glad . . . You see, I have spoken my mind!'

'Because I don't want, in your civil marriage, to wear horns and bring up other men's children; that's why I want a legal marriage,' answered Luzhin, for the sake of saying something. He seemed thoughtful and preoccupied.

'Children? You said children?' Andrey Semënovich started like a war-horse at the sound of the trumpet. 'Children are a social question, and one of the first importance, I agree; but the problem of the children is solved in another way. Some people even reject children altogether, like every other kind of family life. We will talk about children later, but now let us consider horns![1] I confess I have a weakness for the subject. That nasty Pushkinian guardee's expression is unthinkable in the lexicon of the future. Yes, and what are horns? Oh, what a fallacy! What horns? Why horns? What nonsense! On the contrary, there will be none in civil marriage! Horns are only the natural result of every legal marriage, the correction of it, so to speak, a protest, so that in this sense they are not in the least humiliating . . . And if I am ever—to assume an absurdity —legally married, I shall even be glad of your damned horns; then I shall say to my wife: "My dear, until this moment I only loved you, but now I respect you, because you have shown yourself capable of protesting!"[2] You laugh? That is because you are not strong enough to free yourself from prejudice! Confound it, I understand quite well where the unpleasantness lies when there is deception in legal marriage: but that is only the ignoble consequence of an ignoble state of affairs, in which both the one party and the other are degraded. But when horns are bestowed openly, as in civil marriage, then they don't exist any more, they are unthinkable, they cease even to be called horns. On the contrary, your wife would only be showing how much she respected you, by considering you incapable of opposing her happiness and advanced enough not to take your revenge on her because of her new husband. Confound it, I sometimes imagine that if I were given in marriage—bah, if I got married (irregularly or legally, it's all the same), I might very well provide my wife with a lover, if she took too long about acquiring one for herself: "My dear," I should say to her, "I love you, but even more I wish you to respect me—here you are!" Am I not right in what I say?'

Peter Petrovich sniggered as he listened, but he was not particularly amused. He did not even hear much of all this. He was really thinking of something else, and even Lebezyat-

1. A reference to two libertine epigrams by Pushkin.
2. A parody on a passage in Chernyshevsky's novel *What Is to Be Done?*

nikov perceived this at length. Peter Petrovich seemed excited, and rubbed his hands as he considered something. Afterwards, Andrey Semënovich remembered this and understood it . . .

## CHAPTER II

It would have been difficult to say exactly what were the reasons which had raised the senseless idea of that funeral dinner in Katerina Ivanovna's disordered mind. She had actually squandered on it almost ten roubles out of the twenty Raskolnikov had given her for Marmeladov's funeral. Perhaps Katerina Ivanovna considered it her duty to the dead man to honour his memory 'properly', so that all the lodgers, and especially Amalia Ivanovna, might know that 'he was no worse than they, and probably much better', and that none of them had any right 'to look down his nose' at him. Perhaps the most potent influence on her was that special '*pride of the poor*', which makes many poor people, in observing some of those social rites obligatory in our way of life for all and sundry, exert their utmost efforts and spend the last penny of their savings, simply in order to make as good a showing as their neighbours and not be 'criticized' by them. But most probably Katerina Ivanovna wished, precisely on this occasion, just at this moment when she seemed to be abandoned by everyone on earth, to show all these 'nasty contemptible lodgers' not only that she 'knew how things ought to be done, and how to entertain guests', but also that she had not been brought up for her present lot in life, but in the 'household of an officer and a gentleman, in what might almost be called aristocratic surroundings', and had never been meant for sweeping floors, or washing her children's rags at night. Such fits of pride and vanity sometimes seize the poorest and most downtrodden of people, and may take the form of tormenting and uncontrollable desires. Katerina Ivanovna, moreover, was not downtrodden: circumstances might kill her, but they could not crush her spirit, could not intimidate her or subdue her will. Besides, Sonechka had good grounds for saying that her mind was disturbed. It is true that she could not yet have been definitely and conclusively called deranged, but recently, for the whole of the past year, her poor brain had been too harassed to escape all damage. Doctors say that an advanced stage of consumption also tends to produce some impairment of the mental faculties.

There was neither a great number nor a great variety of wines, nor any Madeira; that had been an exaggeration, but there was wine. There were vodka, rum, and port, all of very poor quality, but all in fair quantity. Besides the traditional *kutya*[3] of boiled rice and raisins, there were two or three varieties of eatables (including pancakes), all from Amalia Ivanovna's kitchen, and two samovars were going at once, so that both tea and punch might be made after dinner. Katerina Ivanovna had bought the provisions herself, with the help of one of the lodgers, a pathetic little Pole, living there for God knows what reason, who had immediately volunteered to run Katerina Ivanovna's errands, and had been dashing about with his tongue hanging out all the morning and all the previous day, apparently trying to make his activity as noticeable as possible. He was constantly consulting Katerina Ivanovna over every trifle, and even went looking for her when she was shopping; he could be heard incessantly calling her 'honoured *Pani*', and at last she grew thoroughly sick of him, although at first she had said she would be quite lost without this 'obliging and generous-hearted' person. It was characteristic of Katerina Ivanovna to paint everybody she came into contact with in glowing colours at first, and to praise them so highly that it sometimes became embarrassing. She would invent circumstances to their credit that had never existed, and herself believed in them most sincerely and whole-heartedly, and then in a moment she would be disillusioned and break with them, repulsing with contempt and harshness the very people she had been almost literally idolizing only a few hours before. She was by nature of a humorous, cheerful, and peaceable disposition, but constant failure and unhappiness had brought her to the point of so *furiously* desiring and demanding that everybody should live in joy and harmony, and *should not dare* to live otherwise, that the slightest discord, the smallest setback, drove her at once almost to madness, and in an instant, from indulging the brightest hopes and fancies, she would fall to cursing fate, smashing and destroying anything that came to hand, and banging her head against the wall. Amalia Ivanovna had also suddenly acquired unusual significance and importance in Katerina Ivanovna's eyes, perhaps only because preparations for this funeral dinner were under way and Amalia Ivanovna had thrown herself whole-heartedly into helping with them; she had undertaken to lay the table, to procure linen and cutlery and so on, and to have the food cooked in her own kitchen. Katerina Ivanovna left everything to her and herself went to the cemetery. Everything had in fact been done very nicely: the table looked quite neat, and although the plates, forks, knives, glasses, cups, and so on, borrowed from different lodgers, did not match, but were of various shapes and sizes, all were set out by the appointed time, and Amalia Ivanovna, in a black dress and with new

3. A dish served at Russian memorial meals for dead persons; it was carried to church for the memorial service.

mourning ribbons in her cap, met the returning funeral party
with a certain pride, conscious of work excellently done. This
pride, though justified, did not please Katerina Ivanovna:
'Really, just as if the table couldn't have been laid without
Amalia Ivanovna!' She disliked the cap with its new ribbons,
too: 'Wasn't this stupid German woman giving herself airs
because she was the landlady, and had consented to help her
poor lodgers out of charity? It looked like it. Charity indeed!
Why, Katerina Ivanovna's papa, who was a colonel, and all
but governor, sometimes had forty guests at table, and persons
like Amalia Ivanovna, or rather Ludwigovna, would not even
have been allowed into the kitchen . . .' However, Katerina
Ivanovna resolved not to give her feelings vent for the moment,
although she decided in her own mind that Amalia Ivanovna
must be taken down a peg or two this very day and reminded
of her proper place, or else she would be fancying God knows
what about herself. Meanwhile, she merely treated her with
coldness. Another unpleasant circumstance helped to increase
Katerina Ivanovna's irritation: at the service, except for the
little Pole, who had just managed to get to the cemetery,
hardly any of the lodgers invited to the funeral had been
present, but now all the poorest and most insignificant of them
had appeared for the dinner, many of them not even quite
sober, the disgusting wretches! But the older and more solid
citizens among them had all stayed away, as if they had
agreed upon it among themselves. Peter Petrovich Luzhin,
who might be called the most respectable of all the people in
the flat, had not appeared, and yet, only the evening before,
Katerina Ivanovna had managed to tell the whole world, that
is to say Amalia Ivanovna, Polechka, Sonya, and the little
Pole, that he was a most noble and generous man, very well-
to-do and with enormous influence, who had been a friend of
her first husband's and received in her father's house, and who
had promised to do his utmost to obtain a considerable pension
for her. We may remark here that if Katerina Ivanovna
boasted of anybody's property and connexions, it was without
any interested motive or personal calculation, but quite disinterestedly, out of the fullness of her heart, so to speak, and
from simple joy in giving praise and ascribing even more than
his real worth to the person she extolled. Like Luzhin, and
probably 'following his example', that 'miserable scoundrel
Lebezyatnikov' also failed to appear. 'Who does he think he is?
He was only invited out of kindness and because he shares a
room with Luzhin and is a friend of his, so it would have been
awkward not to ask him.' A stylish lady and her 'dried-up old
maid' of a daughter were also absent; although they had been
living only a week or two in one of Amalia Ivanovna's rooms,
they had complained several times of the noise and shouting

coming from the Marmeladovs' room, especially when Marmeladov came home drunk, and Katerina Ivanovna had of course been informed of this by Amalia Ivanovna, when she was wrangling with her and threatening to turn out the whole family, shouting at the top of her voice that Katerina Ivanovna was a nuisance to 'respectable lodgers whose shoes she was not fit to untie'. Now Katerina Ivanovna had made a special point of inviting this lady and her daughter 'whose shoes she was supposed not to be fit to untie', all the more determinedly because the lady had always turned haughtily away if they met by chance; Katerina Ivanovna meant to show them that 'people here had nobler thoughts and feelings, and would issue invitations in token that they bore no ill will', and that she herself was not accustomed to living in such circumstances. She had meant to make this, and her late papa's Governorship, clear to them by the conversation at table, and to hint at the same time that there was no reason why they should turn away when they met her, and that it was an extremely stupid thing to do. The fat lieutenant-colonel (really a retired staff-captain) was, alas, absent, but it appeared that he had been 'under the weather' since the morning of the previous day. In a word, the only ones who had appeared were the little Pole, a shabby silent little clerk with a spotty face and a greasy frock-coat, who had an unpleasant smell, and a deaf and almost completely blind old man, who had once worked in some post office and whom someone had been maintaining at Amalia Ivanovna's, nobody knew why, from time immemorial. There was also a drunken retired lieutenant (really a clerk in the commissariat) with a very loud coarse laugh, who, 'just imagine!' had no waistcoat on. One guest sat straight down at the table without even greeting Katerina Ivanovna, and, finally, one person who did not possess a suit would have come in a dressing-gown, but this was so gross an affront to propriety that he was thrust out by the combined efforts of Amalia Ivanovna and the little Pole. The Pole had brought with him two other Poles who had never even lived at Amalia Ivanovna's, and whom nobody had ever seen there before. All this was extremely exasperating to Katerina Ivanovna. 'After all, who were all these preparations made for?' To make more room the children had not even been put at the table, which filled the whole room as it was, but their places had been laid on a trunk in a corner, where the two youngest sat on a bench, and Polechka, as the biggest, was charged with looking after them, feeding them, and wiping their little noses 'like well-brought-up children's'. In short, Katerina Ivanovna was perforce obliged to greet all her guests with redoubled dignity and even haughtiness. Some she eyed very sternly and asked to sit down with great condescension. For some reason she considered Amalia Ivanovna to be responsible for all those who were not present, and suddenly adopted a very off-hand manner with her, as Amalia Ivanovna immediately noticed with extreme resentment. Such a beginning boded no good for the end. At last everybody was seated.

Raskolnikov had arrived at almost the same time as they returned from the cemetery. Katerina Ivanovna was terribly glad to see him, first because he was the only 'educated person' among the guests and 'as everybody knew was preparing to occupy a professorial chair in the university in two years' time', and secondly because he immediately excused himself with great politeness for not having been able to be at the funeral in spite of his own wishes. She almost rushed at him, made him sit down on her left (Amalia Ivanovna was on her right) and in spite of her ceaseless fussing and anxiety that the food should be properly served and that there should be enough for everybody, in spite of the tormenting cough that constantly interrupted her and left her panting for breath, and that seemed to have grown more obstinate during the last two days, she kept up an incessant flow of conversation with Raskolnikov, pouring out in a half-whisper all her accumulated emotions and her justifiable indignation at the failure of the dinner; this indignation alternated with frequent fits of the gayest, most uncontrollable laughter at her guests, and especially at the landlady.

'That cuckoo is to blame for everything. You know who I mean: her, her!' said Katerina Ivanovna, nodding towards the landlady. 'Look at her: her eyes are popping out, she thinks we are talking about her, and she can't catch what we are saying. What an owl! Ha, ha, ha!' Cough, cough, cough. 'And what does she think she is proving with that cap?' Cough, cough, cough. 'Have you noticed that she wants everybody to think she is patronizing me and doing me an honour by being here? I asked her, as a decent respectable woman, to invite nice people, who had known my poor husband, and look at the clowns and sluts she has brought! Look at that one, whose face is not even clean; he's nothing but a lump of dirt on two legs! And those queer little Poles . . . ha, ha, ha!' Cough, cough, cough. 'Nobody has ever seen them here before; I haven't either; well, I ask you, why have they come? All sitting solemnly in a row. Hey, *Pan*,' she suddenly cried out to one of them, 'have you had some pancakes? Have some more! Have some beer! Wouldn't you like some vodka? Look, he's jumped up, he's bowing, look, look! They must be dreadfully hungry, poor things! It doesn't matter, let them eat. They aren't making a noise, at any rate, only . . . only, really, I am afraid for the landlady's silver spoons! . . . Amalia Ivanovna!' she said almost aloud, addressing her, 'if your spoons chance to get stolen, I warn you I won't take the responsibility! . . . Ha, ha, ha!' and she roared with laughter, turning back to Raskolnikov, gesturing towards the landlady again and full of enjoyment of her sally. 'She didn't understand, she didn't understand again! She's sitting there with her mouth open, look: an owl, a real owl, a screech-owl in new cap-ribbons, ha, ha, ha!'

Again her laughter turned into intolerable coughing, which lasted for five minutes. Drops of sweat stood on her forehead, blood appeared on her handkerchief. Silently she showed it to Raskolnikov and then, with hardly a pause, began to whisper to him again with extraordinary animation, and a red flush staining her cheeks: 'Listen, I entrusted her with a most delicate commission, as you might say, that of inviting that lady and her daughter, you understand who I mean? It was necessary to proceed in the most delicate manner, to manage things very skilfully, and she went about it in such a way that that fool of a newcomer, that insolent creature, that provincial nonentity, simply because she is some major's widow and has come here to petition for a pension, and wear out her skirts on the floors of government offices, and at fifty-five years old she rouges and powders (it is well known) . . . and not only does this creature not condescend to put in an appearance, but she doesn't even send an excuse, as common courtesy demands, if she can't come. I can't understand, either, why Peter Petrovich hasn't come. But where is Sonya? Where has she gone? Ah, there she is at last! Why, Sonya, where have you been? It is strange that you can't be punctual even at your father's funeral. Rodion Romanovich, make room for her next to you. There is your place, Sonechka . . . have what you like. Have some galantine, that is the best. The pancakes will be brought in a minute. Have the children been given some? Polechka, have you got everything there?' Cough, cough, cough. 'Good. Be a good girl, Lënya, and don't kick your feet, Kolya; sit still, like a nicely-brought-up little boy. What did you say, Sonechka?'

Sonya hastened to give her Peter Petrovich's apologies at once, trying to speak loud enough for everybody to hear and using the most choicely respectful expressions, purposely composed in the manner of Peter Petrovich and embellished by herself. She added that Peter Petrovich had urgently requested her to inform Katerina Ivanovna that, as soon as he was able, he would come himself to talk to her about *business*, and arrange what could be done for her and undertaken in the future.

Sonya knew that this would soothe and appease Katerina Ivanovna, that she would be flattered, and, most important of all, her pride would be gratified. She sat down next to Raskolnikov, making him a hurried bow and casting at him a quick glance of curiosity. For the rest of the time, however, she avoided either looking at him or speaking to him. She seemed almost absent-minded, although she watched Katerina

Ivanovna's face in order to anticipate her wishes. Neither she nor Katerina Ivanovna was in mourning, for want of suitable clothes; Sonya wore dark brown, and Katerina Ivanovna her only dress, a sober striped cotton print. The news about Peter Petrovich was very well received. Katerina Ivanovna listened with an air of self-importance, and then, in the same consequential manner, inquired after Peter Petrovich's health. Then she promptly whispered to Raskolnikov, almost aloud, that it would indeed be strange for a respectable man of solid worth, like Peter Petrovich, to find himself in such 'extraordinary company', in spite of his devotion to the family and his ancient friendship with her papa.

'That is why I am particularly grateful to you, Rodion Romanovich, for not disdaining my hospitality even in these surroundings,' she added almost aloud; 'but I am convinced that only your special friendship for my poor dear husband persuaded you to keep your word.'

Then once more she surveyed her guests with pride and dignity, and suddenly, with great solicitude, inquired loudly across the table of the deaf old man whether 'he would not care for a little more roast meat, and had he been supplied with port?' The old man did not answer, and for a long time could not be made to understand what he was being asked about, although his neighbours even began to shake him, to amuse themselves. He only gazed about him with his mouth open, which increased the general merriment still more.

'What a dolt! Look at him! Why was he brought? As for Peter Petrovich, I always had full confidence in him,' went on Katerina Ivanovna to Raskolnikov. 'He, of course, is not like' —here she quite overwhelmed Amalia Ivanovna by addressing her loudly and cuttingly, with an expression of great severity—'not like your over-dressed riff-raff who would not even have been admitted as cooks into my papa's kitchen, and my late husband would certainly have done them too much honour if he had received them, even though it was only out of his inexhaustible kindness.'

'Yes, he loved to drink; he loved it, and he certainly drank!' cried the retired commissariat clerk suddenly, as he drained his twelfth glass of vodka.

'My late husband certainly had that weakness, and everybody knows it.' Katerina Ivanovna turned on him in a flash. 'But he was a generous-hearted, good man, who loved and respected his family; his fault was that in the goodness of his heart he trusted all sorts of depraved creatures, and he would drink with God knows who, people who were far beneath him in every way! Just think, Rodion Romanovich, they found a gingerbread cock in his pocket; he was dead drunk, but he had remembered the children.'

'Cock? Did you say a cock?' cried the commissariat clerk. Katerina Ivanovna did not deign to answer him. She sighed thoughtfully.

'Like everybody else, you probably think I was too harsh with him,' she went on to Raskolnikov. 'But I wasn't. He respected me very, very much. He was a good-hearted man! And I was so sorry for him sometimes! He would sit in a corner, watching me, and I would feel sorry for him; I wanted to be nice to him, but then I would think, "If you are nice to him, he will get drunk again." It was only by being severe that I could restrain him a little.'

'Yes, he had his hair pulled more than once,' roared the commissariat clerk again, pouring another glass of vodka down his throat.

'Some fools would be all the better, not only for having their hair pulled, but for a good drubbing. I am not speaking of my poor husband now!' retorted Katerina Ivanovna.

The red patches on her cheeks glowed brighter and brighter, her breast heaved. Another moment, and she would have made a scene. People were sniggering and obviously enjoying themselves. They began to nudge the clerk and whisper to him, evidently hoping to get them both worked up.

'A-llow me to ask what you are referring to,' he began, 'I mean, whose honourable name . . . you were good enough to . . . But that's enough! It's nothing! Widow! I forgive you . . . I pass!' And he returned to his vodka.

Raskolnikov sat and listened with disgust. He ate very little, barely, and only out of politeness and to avoid offending her, touching the food with which Katerina Ivanovna kept piling his plate. His eyes were fixed on Sonya. Sonya grew steadily more anxious and uneasy; she, too, foresaw that the dinner would not end peacefully, and fearfully watched Katerina Ivanovna's growing irritability. She knew that she herself was the principal reason why the two ladies had treated Katerina Ivanovna's invitation with such disdain. She had heard from Amalia Ivanovna that the mother had taken offence at the invitation and had asked 'how she could be expected to let her daughter sit down with *that girl*'. She was afraid that Katerina Ivanovna had somehow learnt of this, and an affront to her, Sonya, meant more to Katerina Ivanovna than offensiveness to herself personally, or to her children, or her papa; it was, in short, a mortal insult and Sonya knew that Katerina Ivanovna would not rest 'until she had shown those two draggle-tails that they . . . &c., &c.' As if on purpose to make matters worse, somebody passed down to her from the other end of the table a plate on which were two hearts pierced by an arrow, moulded from black bread. Katerina Ivanovna flared up at once and remarked across the table in a loud voice that the sender was of course 'a drunken ass'. Amalia Ivanovna, also apprehensive of something unpleasant, and deeply hurt by Katerina Ivanovna's supercilious manner, tried to divert the nasty mood of the company to another object and at the same time to increase her own importance, by beginning suddenly, apropos of nothing, to tell a story about an acquaintance of hers, 'Karl from the chemist's', who took a cab at night, and 'the cabby wished to kill him, and Karl very, very much begged and prayed him not to kill him and cried, and he was feared, and from fear his heart transfixed.' Although Katerina Ivanovna smiled, she immediately observed that Amalia Ivanovna ought not to try to tell stories in Russian. Amalia Ivanovna was even more offended than before and answered that her *'Vater aus Berlin* wass a very, very important man and always his hands in pockets put'. Katerina Ivanovna was too heartily amused to restrain herself any longer, and burst into a fit of laughter that made Amalia Ivanovna begin to lose the last shreds of her patience and self-control.

'Look at the screech-owl!' whispered Katerina Ivanovna, cheerful again, to Raskolnikov. 'She meant to say he kept his hands in his pockets, but it sounded as if he put his hands in other people's pockets.' Cough, cough. 'And have you noticed, Rodion Romanovich, how all these foreigners living in St. Petersburg, without exception, and especially the Germans who come here from all over the place, are stupider than us? You will agree, one simply can't say that "Karl from the chemist's from fear his heart transfixed" or that (snivelling fool!), instead of tying the cabman up, "he prayed and cried and very much begged". The silly creature!—and she thinks it is all very pathetic, and doesn't suspect how stupid she is. I think that drunken clerk is much cleverer than she is; at least you can see that he is a drunkard and has drunk his wits away; but they are all so prim and proper . . . Look at her sitting there with her eyes popping out. She's angry, she's angry! Ha, ha, ha!' Cough, cough, cough.

With her spirits restored, Katerina Ivanovna allowed her attention to stray to all sorts of minor matters, and then began to describe how, with the help of the pension she would obtain, she would open a boarding-school for young ladies in T——, her native town. Raskolnikov had not been informed of this scheme by Katerina Ivanovna before, and she instantly went into all its fascinating details. In some unexplained fashion there suddenly appeared in her hand that same 'Certificate of Merit' of which the late Mr. Marmeladov had told Raskolnikov in the tavern, when he was explaining that his wife, Katerina Ivanovna, when she left school, had danced a shawl-dance 'before the Governor and other important personages'. The certificate was now evidently expected to serve as proof of Katerina Ivanovna's right to conduct a school herself; but, more important, it had been kept in reserve for the purpose of finally discomfiting 'those two dressed-up draggle-tails', in case they came to the dinner, and of showing them quite clearly that Katerina Ivanovna came from a very honourable, one might even say aristocratic, family, was the daughter of a colonel, and was very much better than certain adventuresses, who had recently multiplied so rapidly. The certificate immediately got into the hands of the drunken guests, and Katerina Ivanovna did not try to prevent this since it really stated, *en toutes lettres*, that she was the daughter of a man who had held some civil rank and been decorated, and could consequently almost be thought of as indeed a colonel. Warming to her subject, Katerina Ivanovna proceeded to enlarge on the details of this wonderful and peaceful future in T——, the teachers from the high school, whom she would invite to give lessons in her school, and the respectable old Frenchman, M. Maingot, who had taught her French and was now living out his time in T—— and would no doubt come to her for a very reasonable salary. Finally it came to the turn of Sonya, 'who would go to T—— with Katerina Ivanovna and help her with everything'. Here somebody guffawed at the other end of the table. Katerina Ivanovna, although she instantly tried to pretend that she disdained to notice the laughter, raised her voice and began to talk enthusiastically of Sofya Semënovna's undoubted qualifications to be her assistant, 'her gentleness, patience, self-denial, generosity, and good education'. She tapped Sonya on the cheek and, rising, kissed her warmly twice. Sonya blushed, and Katerina Ivanovna burst into tears, immediately observing that 'she was a silly, nervous creature, and had got too worked up, and it was time she stopped, and since dinner was over it was time to hand round tea'. At this moment, Amalia Ivanovna, now thoroughly disgruntled by the fact that she had not taken the least part in all this conversation, and that nobody was listening to her, risked a last attempt and, with secret misgivings, ventured to express to Katerina Ivanovna two very practical and profound ideas, first, that in the boarding-school to be, they must pay particular attention to the young ladies' clean linen (*die Wäsche*) and that 'they must have absolutely one such good *Dame*, that she should after the linen to care', and secondly, 'that the young ladies must not secretly by night any novels to read'. Katerina Ivanovna, who was really very tired and upset, and who had had enough of this dinner, immediately 'snapped' at Amalia Ivanovna that she was 'talking nonsense', and didn't understand anything; that *die Wäsche* was the linen-maid's concern, not that of the directress of a superior boarding-school; and as for novel reading, that was a most indecorous suggestion, and she begged her to say no more. Amalia Ivanovna flushed and, turning nasty, remarked that she only 'good meant', and 'very much good meant' and that '*Geld* for the room had not paid been'. Katerina Ivanovna at once 'put her in her place', with the retort that she was lying when she said she 'meant good', because she had been badgering her, Katerina Ivanovna, about the rent the day before, while the dead man was still lying there on the table. To this Amalia Ivanovna answered, very logically, that 'those lady she inviting was, but those lady not coming were, because those lady were respectable lady, and to unrespectable ladies could not to come'. Katerina Ivanovna 'scored off her' by observing that, as she was a slut, she was not in a position to judge what genuine respectability was. Amalia Ivanovna was not to be put down, but instantly declared that her '*Vater aus Berlin* a very, very important person wass, and went with both hands in pockets, and always went puff, puff!'; and in order to present a truer picture of her *Vater*, she jumped up from her chair, thrust both her hands into her pockets, inflated her cheeks and began making vague puffing noises to the accompaniment of loud guffaws from the lodgers, who were purposely encouraging her with their approval, in expectation of a fight. Katerina Ivanovna could not brook this, and immediately 'rolled out', for everyone to hear, that perhaps Amalia Ivanovna had never had a *Vater*, but was simply a drunken St. Petersburg Finn, who had probably been a cook somewhere or other, and possibly something worse. Amalia Ivanovna, as red as a lobster, shrieked that perhaps Katerina Ivanovna 'altogether without a *Vater* has been; but she had a *Vater aus Berlin*, and he wore a long frock-coat and ever went puff, puff, puff!' Katerina Ivanovna remarked disdainfully that everybody knew where she came from and that it was stated in pr int on her certificate of merit that her father was a colonel; and that Amalia Ivanovna's father (if she had one at all) was probably a Finnish milkman in St. Petersburg; but most likely she had had no father, because her patronymic was in doubt to this day: was she Ivanovna or Ludwigovna? Here Amalia Ivanovna, driven to frenzy at last, and thumping the table with her fist, began to scream that her *Vater* was called Johann, that he was a *Burgmeister*, and that Katerina Ivanovna's *Vater* had 'quite never a *Burgmeister* been'. Katerina Ivanovna got up from her chair and in a severe and apparently calm voice (although she was very pale and her breathing was laboured) remarked that if Amalia Ivanovna had the effrontery 'to set her rubbishy little *Vater* on a level with her papa once more, she, Katerina Ivanovna, would tear off her cap and trample it under her feet'. On this, Amalia Ivanovna began to run about the room, shouting at the top of her voice that she was the mistress of the house and that Katerina Ivanovna 'must this instant from my flat to depart'; then for some reason she began hastily collecting her silver spoons from the table. Everything was din and uproar. The children began to cry. Sonya hurried to Katerina Ivanovna to restrain her, but when Amalia Ivanovna shouted something about a yellow card, Katerina Ivanovna pushed Sonya away and advanced upon her landlady with the intention of putting her threat about the cap into execution. At this moment the door opened and Peter Petrovich Luzhin appeared on the threshold. He stood there and let his stern and attentive glance travel over the whole company. Katerina Ivanovna hurried eagerly towards him.

## CHAPTER III

'PETER PETROVICH!' she exclaimed, 'you, at least, will protect me! Tell this stupid creature that she must not dare to treat a respectable lady in misfortune in this manner, that there are courts of law! . . . I shall go to the Governor-general himself . . . She shall answer for it . . . Remember my father's hospitality, and protect my orphan children.'

'Excuse me, madam . . . Excuse me, excuse me, madam,' said Peter Petrovich, waving her away. 'As you are aware, I had not the honour of your papa's acquaintance . . . allow me, madam!' (Somebody laughed loudly.) 'In your ceaseless disputes with Amalia Ivanovna I have no intention of taking part . . . I have found it necessary to come here . . . I wish to speak with your stepdaughter, Sofya . . . Ivanovna (I think) . . . at once! Allow me to pass . . .'

Peter Petrovich sidled past Katerina Ivanovna and walked towards the farther corner of the room, where Sonya was.

Katerina Ivanovna remained standing where she was, as if thunderstruck. She could not understand how Peter Petrovich could disown her papa's hospitality. Once she had invented that hospitality, she herself regarded it as gospel. She was impressed, too, by Peter Petrovich's dry, business-like tone, which seemed to convey some contemptuous threat. Everybody had gradually become silent since his entrance. Besides the fact that this 'solid citizen' was sharply out of harmony with all the guests, it was evident that he had come here on business of importance, since probably only an extraordinary reason could bring him into such company, and that, consequently, something was going to happen. Raskolnikov, standing by Sonya, moved aside to let him pass; Peter Petrovich seemed not to notice him. A moment later, Lebezyatnikov also appeared on the threshold; he did not come into the room, but stood there with an expression of peculiar curiosity and even of astonishment; he listened, but for a long time seemed unable to understand.

'Excuse me if I am interrupting you, but the matter is rather important,' remarked Peter Petrovich to the company in general, without addressing himself to any one person. 'I am even glad that there should be people here. Amalia Ivanovna, I humbly request you, as mistress of the flat, to give your attention to my conversation with Sofya Ivanovna.' He turned directly to Sonya, who seemed extraordinarily surprised and even apprehensive, and went on: 'Sofya Ivanovna, immediately after your visit, a banknote of the value of one hundred roubles disappeared from my table in my friend Andrey Semënovich Lebezyatnikov's room. If, in any way whatever, you know where it is now, and will tell us, then I assure you on my word of honour, which I take everybody here to witness, that that shall be the end of the matter. In the contrary event, I shall be obliged to have recourse to more serious measures, and then . . . on your own head be it!'

Complete silence reigned in the room. Even the crying children were quiet. Sonya stood, as pale as death, and looked at Luzhin without speaking. She seemed not to have understood. A few seconds passed.

'Well, what is it to be?' asked Luzhin, looking intently at her.

'I don't know . . . I know nothing about it . . .' said Sonya at last, faintly.

'No? You don't know?' repeated Luzhin, and then paused again for a few moments. 'Think, mademoiselle,' he began again sternly, but still as it were exhorting her. 'Think well. I am prepared to give you more time to reflect. Be good enough to realize that if I were not convinced, I, with my experience, would certainly not run the risk of accusing you so directly, since for so direct and public an accusation, if I were lying, or even mistaken, I should be held, in a certain sense, responsible. I know this. This morning, for my own requirements, I changed some five-per-cent bills of the nominal value of three thousand roubles. I made a note of it in my pocketbook. When I came home, as Andrey Semënovich can bear witness, I began to count the money and when I had counted two thousand three hundred roubles I put that money in my pocketbook, and put the pocketbook in my coat pocket. There remained about five hundred roubles in bank-notes on the table, and among them were three one-hundred-rouble notes. Just then you came (at my request), and all the time you were with me you were very perturbed, and three times in the course of our conversation you hurriedly got up to go, although our conversation was not finished. Andrey Semënovich can testify to all this. You yourself, mademoiselle, will probably not refuse to confirm that I asked you to come, through Andrey Semënovich, for the sole purpose of discussing with you the bereaved and helpless position of your relative Katerina Ivanovna (to whose dinner I was unable to come), and the possibility of helping her by organizing a subscription, or a lottery, or something of the sort. You expressed your gratitude, and even shed tears (I recount everything just as it happened, in the first place to remind you of it, and in the second to show you that my memory retains even the minutest details). Then I took from the table a ten-rouble note and gave it to you, as a contribution from myself for the assistance of your relative. Andrey Semënovich saw all this. Then I accompanied you to the door —still with the same confusion on your part—after which I remained alone with Andrey Semënovich, and, after a conversation with him lasting about ten minutes, Andrey Semënovich went out and I returned to the table where the money was lying, with the intention of counting it and laying it aside, as I had purposed to do before. To my surprise, one of the hundred-rouble notes was missing. Kindly consider, then: I cannot suspect Andrey Semënovich in any way; the very idea is shameful. Neither could I have made a mistake in my accounts, because a minute before your entrance I had finished my reckoning and found the total correct. You will agree that, recollecting your confusion and your haste to be gone, and the fact that you kept your hands on the table for some of the time, and, finally, taking into account your social position and its concomitant habits, I was, so to say, *compelled*, against my will and with horror, to adopt a suspicion which— while of course, it is cruel—is—justifiable! I will add once more that, in spite of my *just* conviction, I know there is nevertheless in my present accusation some risk to myself. But, as you see, I did not let the matter rest, I acted, and I will tell you why; solely, miss, solely on account of your black ingratitude! What? I invite you to visit me, in the interests of your destitute relative, I put into your hands the ten roubles which are all I am in a position to give you, and you immediately, on the spot, repay me for all this by such an action! No, it is not right! You must be taught a lesson! Think well then; nay, I implore you, as your true friend (for you cannot have a better friend than I am at this moment), to reconsider! Otherwise, I shall be inexorable! Well?'

'I did not take anything of yours,' whispered Sonya, terrified. 'You gave me ten roubles; here, take them!' Sonya pulled her handkerchief from her pocket, untied the knot in it, took out the ten-rouble note and proffered it out to Luzhin.

'And so you deny knowledge of the other hundred roubles?' he said insistently and reproachfully, not taking the note.

Sonya looked round. They were all looking at her with terrible, stern, mocking, hateful faces. She glanced at Raskolnikov . . . he was standing by the wall with his arms folded, and looking at her with eyes full of fire.

'Oh God!' burst from Sonya.

'Amalia Ivanovna, the police must be informed, and meanwhile I humbly beg you to send for the porter,' said Luzhin quietly and even gently.

'*Gott der barmherzige*! I haf known that she a thief is!' exclaimed Amalia Ivanovna, throwing up her hands.

'You knew?' Luzhin took her up. 'That means that even before this you had some sort of basis for coming to that conclusion. I beg you, respected Amalia Ivanovna, to remember your words, spoken, moreover, in the presence of witnesses.'

There was a general stir and an outburst of loud conversation on all sides.

'Wha-a-t?' shrieked Katerina Ivanovna, recovering her wits and flinging herself on Luzhin as though a spring had been released. 'What? You accuse her of theft? Sonya? Oh, villains, villains!' She rushed to Sonya and hugged her with her wasted arms.

'Sonya, how dared you take ten roubles from him? How silly of you! Give it to me! Give me the ten roubles at once—here!'

And snatching the note from Sonya, Katerina Ivanovna crumpled it up and flung it with a backward sweep of her arm straight into Luzhin's face. The ball of paper hit him in the eye and fell to the floor. Amalia Ivanovna rushed to pick it up. Peter Petrovich lost his temper.

'Restrain that madwoman!' he cried.

At this moment several more people appeared in the doorway beside Lebezyatnikov, among them the two recently arrived ladies.

'What! Madwoman? I am mad, am I? Fool!' shrieked Katerina Ivanovna. 'You are a fool, you rascally attorney, you vile creature! Sonya, Sonya taking money from him! Sonya a thief! Why, she would be more likely to give it to you, fool!' Katerina Ivanovna laughed hysterically. 'Have you ever seen a fool?' and she turned rapidly from one to another, pointing to Luzhin. 'What? And you as well!' as she caught sight of the landlady. 'You too, you German sausage seller, you assert that "she a thief is", you filthy Prussian hen dressed up in a crinoline! You! You! And she hasn't left the room, and when she came back from seeing you, you villain, she sat down straight away by me; everybody saw her. She sat next to Rodion Romanovich . . . Search her! Since she didn't go out at all, that means the money must be on her! Search then, search, search! Only if you don't find it, then excuse me, my dear man, you shall answer for it! I'll run to the Emperor, the Emperor, to our gracious Tsar himself, I will throw myself at his feet, at once, this very day! I am all alone in the world, they will let me in! Do you think they won't? You are mistaken, I shall get in! I shall get in! I suppose you were counting on her being so meek and gentle, weren't you? Is that what you relied on? But I, brother, am not meek! It will be the worse for you! Search, then! Search, search, go on, search!'

And Katerina Ivanovna frenziedly tugged at Luzhin, trying to pull him towards Sonya.

'I am ready, I will take the responsibility . . . but calm down, madam, calm down! I see only too well that you are not meek! . . . This . . . this . . . what is to be done?' muttered Luzhin. 'The police ought to be present . . . although as it is there are quite enough witnesses . . . I am ready . . . But in any case it is difficult for a man . . . by reason of his sex . . . If with Amalia Ivanovna's assistance . . . although things ought not to be done like this . . . what should we do?'

'Anyone you like! Anybody who wants to may search her!' cried Katerina Ivanovna. 'Sonya, turn out your pockets! See, see! Look, you monster, it's empty, her handkerchief was here, and the pocket is empty! You see! Here's the other pocket, look! You see! You see!'

And Katerina Ivanovna did not so much turn as drag Sonya's pockets inside out, one after the other. But from the second, the right-hand, pocket there flew out a piece of paper which described a parabola in the air and fell at Luzhin's feet. Everybody saw it, and there were many excited exclamations. Peter Petrovich stooped, picked up the paper from the floor with two fingers, raised it where everybody could see, and unfolded it. It was a hundred-rouble bank-note, folded into eight. Peter Petrovich turned round in a circle, holding up the note to show everybody.

'Thief! Out of my flat! Police, police!' howled Amalia Ivanovna. 'They must in Siberia driven be! Get out!'

The air was full of exclamations. Raskolnikov said nothing, but kept his eyes on Sonya except when he occasionally glanced quickly at Luzhin. Sonya still stood in the same place, as though hardly conscious. She did not even seem very surprised. Suddenly her face was flooded with crimson, and she cried out and covered it with her hands.

'No, it wasn't me! I didn't take it! I don't know anything about it!' she cried in a heart-rending wail, and flung herself into the arms of Katerina Ivanovna, who clasped her and held her close as though she would shield her with her body from all the world.

'Sonya, Sonya! I don't believe it! You see, I don't believe it!' cried Katerina Ivanovna, in the face of the plain evidence, rocking her in her arms like a child. She kissed her repeatedly, caught up her hands and kissed them too, lingeringly. 'As if you could have taken it! How stupid these people are! Oh Lord! You are so stupid, stupid!' she cried, turning to them. 'You don't know yet, you don't know her heart, you don't know what she is like! She take it, she! Why, she would strip off her last garment, and sell it, and go barefoot, and give you everything, if you were in need; that's the kind of girl she is! She went on the streets because my children were starving; she sold herself for us!.... Ah, my poor dear husband! Ah, my poor dear dead husband! Do you see this, do you see it? Here is a funeral dinner for you! Oh, heavens! Why are you all standing still? Defend her! Rodion Romanovich, why don't you take her part? Do you believe it, too? Not one of you is worth her little finger, not one of you, not one, not one, not one. Oh God, defend her now!'

The plaints of poor, consumptive, bereaved Katerina Ivanovna seemed to have produced a marked effect on her hearers. There was so much suffering and pathos in the face twisted by pain and wasted by disease, in the parched lips flecked with blood, in the hoarse voice, in the sobs like a crying child's, in the childishly trustful and yet desperate prayer for help, that all of them pitied the unhappy woman. Peter Petrovich at least *pitied* her.

'Madam, madam!' he exclaimed impressively. 'This matter does not involve you! Nobody could accuse you of instigating the theft or of complicity in it, especially as it was you who made the discovery by turning out her pockets; that means that you had no idea of it before. I am completely and absolutely willing to be compassionate if, so to say, destitution was Sofya Semënovna's motive, but why, mademoiselle, did you refuse to confess? Did you fear the disgrace? Was this your first step? You lost your head, perhaps? It is understandable, very understandable . . . But how could you start on such courses? Ladies and gentlemen!'—he turned to the assembled company—'pitying and, so to say, sympathizing, I may be ready to forgive, even now, in spite of the personal insults I have received. And, mademoiselle, let your present disgrace be a lesson to you for the future,' he added to Sonya; 'I shall take no further steps. So be it; I have done. Enough!'

Peter Petrovich cast a sidelong look at Raskolnikov. Their glances met. Raskolnikov's fiery eyes seemed ready to reduce him to ashes. Katerina Ivanovna, meanwhile, appeared no longer to hear what was going on; she was hugging and kissing Sonya like a madwoman. The children had also put their little arms round Sonya, and Polechka, who, although she did not altogether understand what was happening, was drowned in tears and shaking with sobs, had hidden her pretty little face, swollen with crying, against Sonya's shoulder.

'What a foul trick!' said a loud voice suddenly from the doorway.

Peter Petrovich looked round quickly.

'How despicable!' repeated Lebezyatnikov, staring fixedly at him.

Peter Petrovich seemed startled, as everybody observed and remarked upon later. Lebezyatnikov advanced into the room. 'And you dared to call on me as a witness!' he said, going up to Peter Petrovich.

'What does this mean, Andrey Semënovich? What are you talking about?' muttered Luzhin.

'It means that you are a . . . traducer! That is what my words meant!' said Lebezyatnikov hotly, looking at him sternly with his short-sighted little eyes. He was terribly angry. Raskolnikov gazed at him with absorbed attention, as though seizing on and weighing every word. Once more silence reigned in the room. Peter Petrovich seemed at a loss, especially in the first moments.

'If it is me you mean . . .' he stammered. 'What is the matter with you? Are you sane?'

'I am sane enough, and you are . . . a scoundrel! Oh, how vile the whole business is! I listened, I waited to the end, on purpose to understand it all, because, I must confess, I still don't quite see the logic of it . . . I don't understand what your purpose was.'

'But what did I do? Will you stop talking in these idiotic riddles? Or perhaps you have been drinking?'

'You may perhaps drink, base creature, but I don't! I never touch vodka, because it is against my principles! Just think, he himself gave that hundred-rouble note to Sofya Semënovna with his own hands! I saw it, I can bear witness, I will take an oath on it! He did it, he himself!' repeated Lebezyatnikov, looking at each of them in turn.

'Have you gone out of your mind or something, puppy?' squeaked Luzhin. 'She herself, here in front of all of you, she herself asserted a moment ago that she received nothing from me but ten roubles. If that is so, how could I have given it to her?'

'I saw you, I saw you!' asserted Lebezyatnikov in a shout, 'and although it is against my principles, I am prepared to swear any oath you like in court immediately, because I saw how you put it surreptitiously into her pocket! Only I, like a fool, thought you were doing it out of kindness! In the doorway, as you parted from her, when she had turned and you were shaking her hand with one of yours, with the other, the left hand, you slipped the note into her pocket on the sly. I saw you! I saw you!'

Luzhin turned pale.

'What is this nonsense?' he exclaimed haughtily. 'And how could you recognize a banknote, when you were standing by the window? With your short sight, you simply imagined you saw it. You are raving!'

'No, I didn't imagine it. Although I was standing a good

way off, I saw everything, and though it really is difficult to recognize a note from the window—you are right there—it so happens that I know for a certainty that it was indeed a hundred-rouble note, because when you were giving Sofya Semënovna the ten-rouble note—I saw you myself—you took a hundred-rouble note from the table at the same time (I saw this, because I was standing quite near you just then, and because of a certain idea that came to me, I did not forget that you had that note in your hand). You folded it and kept it in your hand all the time. Then I would have forgotten it again, but when you were getting up you transferred it from your right hand to your left and nearly dropped it; then I remembered again because the same idea came back to me, the idea that you wanted to do her a kindness without letting me know. You may imagine that then I began to watch you—and I saw how you managed to thrust it into her pocket. I saw you, I saw you, I am prepared to swear to it!'

Lebezyatnikov was almost breathless. Exclamations, expressing more astonishment than anything else, began to be heard on all sides; some of them, however, were taking on a menacing tone. Everybody crowded round Peter Petrovich. Katerina Ivanovna rushed up to Lebezyatnikov.

'Andrey Semënovich! I misjudged you! Stand up for her! You are the only one on her side! She is an orphan; God sent you to her! Andrey Semënovich, our dear, kind friend!' And Katerina Ivanovna, hardly realizing what she was doing, flung herself on her knees before him.

'Stuff and nonsense!' shouted Luzhin, in a passion of rage. 'You are talking rubbish, sir! "I forgot, I remembered, I remembered, I forgot"—what does it all mean? So I slipped it to her deliberately? What for? What was my purpose? What have I in common with this . . .'

'What for? That is what I cannot understand myself, but that I am speaking gospel truth is a fact! I am so far from being mistaken, you abominable scoundrel, that I remember clearly that that question occurred to me at once, just when I was thanking you and shaking hands with you. Why had you put it stealthily into her pocket? That is, just why did you do it by stealth? Was it only to hide it from me, because you knew I held contrary opinions and repudiated private charity which accomplishes no radical cure? Well, I decided that you really were ashamed to give away such large sums in front of me, and besides, I thought, "perhaps he means to give her a surprise, to astonish her, when she finds a whole hundred roubles in her pocket." (Because some charitable people don't like to make a parade of their good deeds, I know.) Then I thought you wanted to test her, that is, to see if she would come and thank you when she found it. Then, that you wanted to avoid all gratitude, and that . . . how does it go?—that the right hand (isn't it?) should not know . . . something like that, in short. Well, a lot of different ideas came into my head, so that I intended to think them over later, but all the same, I thought it would not be tactful to reveal that I knew your secret. However, yet another point occurred to me: that Sofya Semënovna might lose the money before she noticed it; that is why I decided to come here, call her outside, and inform her that a hundred-rouble note had been put in her pocket. And on the way I called at the Kobylyatnikovs' room to take them *A General Deduction from the Positive Method*, and specially recommend to them Piederit's article (and Wagner's as well)[4]. Then I came here, and what a state of affairs I found here! Now could I, could I, have had all those ideas and deliberations, if I really had not seen you put a hundred roubles in her pocket?'

When Andrey Semënovich had finished his lengthy argument, with the logical conclusion at the end of the speech, he was dreadfully tired, and sweat was pouring off his face. Unfortunately, he was not very skilful at expressing himself in Russian (although he knew no other language), so that he seemed suddenly quite exhausted, even wasted away, after this feat of advocacy. His speech, nevertheless, had produced a remarkable effect. He had spoken with such warmth of conviction that everybody obviously believed him. Peter Petrovich felt that things were going badly for him.

'What concern is it of mine if such silly questions came into your head?' he cried. 'That is not proof. You may have dreamed the whole thing, that's all! And I tell you that you are lying, sir! You are lying and slandering me out of spite against me, out of resentment because I refused to listen to your godless, free-thinking social theories, that's what it is!'

But Peter Petrovich could not manage to twist things to his own advantage. On the contrary, murmurings arose on all sides.

'Oh, so that's your line!' exclaimed Lebezyatnikov. 'Liar! Call the police, and let me be sworn! There is only one thing I can't understand, and that is why he should risk such a vile trick. Wretched, despicable creature!'

'I can explain why he risked it, and if necessary I will swear to it myself,' said Raskolnikov at last, firmly, and stepped forward. He seemed calm and resolute. Simply by looking at him everybody could clearly see that he really did know what all this was about, and that the time had come to unravel the knot.

'Now I can see the complete explanation,' Raskolnikov went

4. Piederit was a German medical author, Wagner a German economist.

on, addressing Lebezyatnikov. 'From the very beginning I suspected some filthy trick; my suspicions were aroused by certain circumstances known only to me, which I will tell you of at once; they are the whole point! Your invaluable evidence has made everything finally clear to me. I beg all of you to listen: This gentleman' (he pointed to Luzhin) 'recently became engaged to a young lady, my sister, Avdotya Romanovna Raskolnikov. But on his arrival in St. Petersburg, at our first meeting, the day before yesterday, he quarrelled with me and I threw him out, as I have two witnesses to prove. He has a very spiteful nature . . . I did not know then that he was lodging here with you, Andrey Semënovich, and that consequently on the very day of our quarrel, that is, the day before yesterday, he saw me, as a friend of the late Mr. Marmeladov's, give some money to his widow, Katerina Ivanovna, for the funeral. He immediately wrote to my mother and informed her that I had given all my money not to Katerina Ivanovna but to Sofya Semënovna, and in addition he referred in the most despicable terms to . . . to Sofya Semënovna's character, that is, he made insinuations about the character of my relations with Sofya Semënovna. All this, you understand, with the idea of making mischief between me and my mother and sister by suggesting that I was squandering the money they had sent to help me, all they had, on unworthy objects. Yesterday, in his presence, and that of my mother and sister, I established the true facts, proving that I had given the money to Katerina Ivanovna for the funeral, and not to Sofya Semënovna, and that I had not even been acquainted with Sofya Semënovna the day before, nor so much as seen her. To that I added that with all his virtues he, Peter Petrovich Luzhin, was not worth the little finger of Sofya Semënovna, whom he had spoken so ill of. When he asked if I would let Sofya Semënovna sit down beside my sister, I answered that I had already done so, that day. He grew angry because my mother and sister refused to quarrel with me without a better reason than his calumnies, and gradually began to say the most unpardonably impertinent things to them. There was a final rupture and he was turned out of the house. All this was yesterday evening. Now I ask for your special attention; think: if he had contrived to show that Sofya Semënovna was a thief, then he would have proved to my mother and sister that he was almost right in his suspicions, that he was justified in being angry with me for setting Sofya Semënovna on a level with my sister, and that in attacking me he had consequently been defending and protecting the honour of my sister and his future wife. In short, by all this he might even have managed to embroil me with my family once more, and of course he hoped to get into favour with them again. I don't speak of the revenge he was taking on me, because he had grounds for supposing that Sofya Semënovna's honour and happiness were dear to me. That is what he counted on doing! That is how I understand the matter. That is all his motive, and there can be no other!'

With these words, or something like them, Raskolnikov ended his speech, which had frequently been interrupted by the exclamations of his audience, all of whom had listened very attentively. In spite of the interruptions he had spoken calmly, curtly, precisely, clearly, firmly. His incisive voice, his air of conviction, and his stern face produced an extraordinary effect.

'That's it! You are right!' corroborated Lebezyatnikov delightedly. 'It must be so, because he did in fact ask me, as soon as Sofya Semënovna came into the room, whether you were here. Had I seen you amongst Katerina Ivanovna's guests? He called me over to the window and asked me secretly. That means he thought it essential that you should be here! You are right! It is all true!'

Luzhin smiled scornfully and said nothing. He had, however, turned very pale. He seemed to be considering how to get out of his fix. He might have been glad to drop the matter and leave, but this was hardly possible at the moment; it would have meant acknowledging the justice of the accusations levelled against him and the fact that he had indeed deliberately slandered Sofya Semënovna. Besides, the guests, who had been drinking fairly heavily, were too excited to allow it. The commissariat clerk, although he did not understand all of it, was shouting loudest of them all, suggesting various measures which Luzhin thought extremely unpleasant. Some people who had not been drinking were also present; they had collected here from every room in the flat. The three Poles were furiously angry and never stopped shouting in Polish, 'The *Pan* is a scoundrel' and muttering threats. Sonya had listened with strained attention, but as though she only partly understood, and looked like a person recovering from a swoon. She had not once taken her eyes from Raskolnikov, feeling that he was her sole protection. Katerina Ivanovna's breathing was harsh and laboured and she seemed in the last stages of exhaustion. More stupid with astonishment than all the rest of them, Amalia Ivanovna stood there with her mouth open and without a thought in her head. She saw only that Peter Petrovich had somehow come to grief. Raskolnikov tried to say something more, but he was not allowed to finish: they were all shouting and crowding round Luzhin with oaths and threats. But Peter Petrovich did not flinch. Seeing that the attempt to incriminate Sonya had completely failed, he now called impudence to his assistance.

'Allow me, ladies and gentlemen, allow me; do not crowd round; let me pass!' he said, pushing his way through them.

'And do me the favour of uttering no threats; I assure you that nothing will come of them. You will accomplish nothing by them, not a jot, but, on the contrary, you, ladies and gentlemen, will answer for trying to force me to conceal a criminal offence. The thief has been unmasked, and I shall prosecute. The law is less blind than you and . . . and it is not drunk and will not believe two acknowledged atheists, agitators, and trouble-makers, when they accuse me for the sake of personal revenge, as they are fools enough to admit themselves . . . Yes! Allow me!'

'I don't want a trace of you left in my room; be good enough to leave immediately! Everything is over between us! And to think of the way I've put myself about, the way I've been explaining things to him . . . for two whole weeks! . . .'

'You know I myself told you, Andrey Semënovich, that I was leaving, and you wished then to get me to stay. Now I will only add that you are a fool, sir! May you be cured of your feeble mind and your short-sightedness! Allow me, ladies and gentlemen!'

He thrust forward, but the commissariat clerk was not going to let him escape so easily; he seized a tumbler from the table, swung it, and launched it at Peter Petrovich, but it flew straight at Amalia Ivanovna. She shrieked and he, thrown off balance by his swing, rolled under the table. Peter Petrovich went back to his room, and within half an hour had quitted the house. Sonya, with her meek nature, had always been conscious that she was more vulnerable than other people, and could be insulted almost with impunity. She had, nevertheless, until this moment thought that she could somehow manage to avoid disaster—by caution, meekness, submissiveness to anybody and everybody. Her disillusionment was too grievous. She was, of course, capable of bearing everything, even this, with patience and almost without murmuring. But at first she found this burden too heavy. In spite of her triumphant vindication, when the first terrified numbness had passed and she was able to realize and understand clearly what was happening, the consciousness of her helplessness in the face of insult and injury oppressed and wrung her heart. She gave way to hysteria and at last, unable to endure any longer, flung herself out of the room, almost immediately after Luzhin left it, and hurried home. Amalia Ivanovna, when the glass struck her, amid roars of merriment, also found it unbearable to have to suffer for what was not her fault. Like a madwoman she rushed shrieking at Katerina Ivanovna, whom she held to blame for everything.

'Away from my flat! This instant! March!' And she began to seize everything of Katerina Ivanovna's that she could lay hands on and hurl them all to the floor. Already almost completely exhausted, nearly fainting, pale, and gasping for breath, Katerina Ivanovna started up from the bed on which she had collapsed, and flung herself on Amalia Ivanovna. But the struggle was too unequal, she was pushed away like a feather.

'What! That godless slander was not enough—this slut must attack me now! What? She drives me out on the day of my poor husband's funeral, after she has eaten at my table, out into the street with my orphaned children! And where can I go?' cried the poor woman, sobbing and panting. 'Oh God!' she exclaimed, with flashing eyes, 'is there no justice? Will you not protect me, widowed and fatherless? But we shall see. There is justice and truth on earth; they do exist, and I will find them! At once; only wait, godless, worthless creature! Polechka, stay with the children until I come back. Wait for me, even if you have to wait in the street! We shall see whether there is justice in the world!'

Throwing over her head the green shawl Marmeladov had spoken of, Katerina Ivanovna made her way through the disorderly and drunken crowd of lodgers who still thronged the room and ran out into the street, wailing and weeping, with a vague intention of going somewhere at once, without delay, and finding justice, whatever the cost. Polechka, terrified, crouched with the children on the trunk in the corner, and waited, shivering, with her arms round the two little ones, for her mother's return. Amalia Ivanovna swept about the room, raging, shrieking, lamenting, and flinging everything she could lay hands on to the floor. The lodgers were all shouting and bawling in a disorderly way, some discussing, as well as they could, what had happened, others quarrelling and cursing one another, others again striking up a song . . .

'Now it is time I went, too!' thought Raskolnikov. 'Well, Sofya Semënovna, let us see what you will have to say now!' And he set off towards Sonya's lodgings.

## CHAPTER IV

RASKOLNIKOV had been energetic and courageous in pleading Sonya's cause against Luzhin, in spite of the burden of fear and suffering in his own soul. But after so harassing a morning he was glad of a chance to escape from the preoccupations that had become unbearable to him, apart altogether from the warm personal feelings involved in his defence of Sonya. Besides, he had already been contemplating, with an alarm that became terror at some moments, his forthcoming interview with Sonya; he felt *obliged* to tell her who had killed Lizaveta, although he foresaw that it would cost him great anguish, which he tried, as it were, to push away from him. When, therefore, he exclaimed, as he left Katerina Ivanovna's:

'Well, what will you have to say now, Sofya Semënovna?' it was probably because he was still wildly, if superficially, elated by his recent victory over Luzhin. But a strange thing happened. When he reached the Kapernaumovs' flat, he experienced a sudden sensation of impotence and fear. He stopped before the door, asking himself, 'Need I really tell her who killed Lizaveta?' The question was a strange one, because at the very same moment he felt not only that he must tell her, but that he could not put it off even for a short time. He did not yet know why he could not, he only *felt* it, and the tormenting consciousness of his helplessness before the inevitable almost crushed him. To escape from his anxious preoccupations, he quickly opened the door and paused on the threshold with his eyes on Sonya. She was sitting with her elbows on her little table and her face hidden in her hands, but when she saw Raskolnikov, she stood up at once and came to meet him, as though she had been expecting him.

'What would have become of me without you?' she said rapidly, as they moved into the room together. Evidently she was in haste to say this one thing to him. Then she waited.

Raskolnikov walked to the table and sat down on the chair from which she had just risen. She stood in front of him, two paces away, exactly as she had the day before.

'Well, Sonya?' he said, suddenly aware that his voice was trembling. 'The whole affair hinged on your "social position and its concomitant habits". Did you understand that just now?'

Sonya looked distressed.

'Please don't talk to me as you did yesterday,' she interrupted. 'Please, don't even begin. There is enough suffering as it is . . .'

She hastened to smile, fearing that he might not like the rebuke.

'I was very foolish to come away. What is happening there now? I wanted to go back at once, but I kept on thinking that you . . . would come here.'

He told her that Amalia Ivanovna was turning them out of their room, and that Katerina Ivanovna had gone off 'to look for justice'.

'Oh God!' exclaimed Sonya. 'Let us go at once . . .'

And she seized her cape.

'It's everlastingly the same thing!' cried Raskolnikov, exasperated. 'You have no thoughts except for them! Stay with me a little.'

'But . . . Katerina Ivanovna?'

'Katerina Ivanovna can wait. Since she has left the house, she will be sure to come here,' he added morosely. 'If you are not here, she will find fault with you . . .'

Sonya sat down, in a torment of indecision. Raskolnikov

remained silent, with his eyes on the ground, considering.

'Assume that Luzhin did not want to do it just now,' he began, without looking at Sonya, 'but if he had wanted to, or if it had somehow been part of his plans, he would have shoved you into gaol, wouldn't he, if it hadn't been for me and Lebezyatnikov?'

'Yes,' she said faintly. 'Yes!' she repeated, distracted and alarmed.

'But you know I might not have happened to be there. And Lebezyatnikov turned up quite by chance, too.'

Sonya was silent.

'Well, and if it had been prison for you, what then? Do you remember what I said to you yesterday?'

Again she did not answer. He waited.

'And I expected you to cry out again, "Oh, don't say it! Stop!"' laughed Raskolnikov, in a rather strained way. 'What, still silent?' he asked after a pause. 'But surely we must talk about something. I should like to know how you would settle a certain "problem", as Lebezyatnikov would say, now.' (He seemed to falter a little.) 'No, I really am serious. Suppose, Sonya, you had known Luzhin's intentions beforehand, and known for a certainty that they meant the ruin of Katerina Ivanovna and the children, and of yourself into the bargain (I put it that way, because you consider yourself of no account). Polechka as well . . . because she is destined to take the same road. Well, then: suppose you were allowed to decide, that either one or the other should go on living, that is, either that Luzhin should live and go on doing evil, or that Katerina Ivanovna should die. How would you decide? Which of them should die? That is my question.'

Sonya looked at him anxiously. She could feel that there was something behind the uncertainty of this speech, which seemed to be approaching some point in a roundabout fashion.

'I had a feeling that you would ask me something like that,' she said, looking at him searchingly.

'Well, perhaps you had. But how would you decide?'

'Why do you ask about what could not happen?' said Sonya distastefully.

'That means that it would be better for Luzhin to go on living and doing mischief! Surely you dare not decide that way?'

'But I can't know God's intentions . . . And why do you ask questions that have no answer? Where is the point of such empty questions? How could it depend on my decision? Who made me a judge of who shall live and who shall not?'

'Oh, if you are going to mix God up in it, we shall get nowhere,' grumbled Raskolnikov sullenly.

'You had better say straight out what you mean,' cried

Sonya in distress. 'You are leading up to something again . . . Did you come here only to torment me?'

She could not restrain herself but burst into bitter weeping. He looked at her in black dejection. Five minutes went by.

'You are right, Sonya,' he said quietly at last. He had changed suddenly; his artificially bold and weakly challenging manner had disappeared. Even his voice had grown suddenly feeble. 'I told you yesterday that I should not come to plead for pardon, and here I seem to have begun by doing just that . . . What I said about Luzhin and about God was for myself . . . I was asking for your forgiveness, Sonya . . .'

He tried to smile, but there was something helpless and incomplete about that pale smile. He bent his head and covered his face with his hands.

Suddenly and unexpectedly a bitter hatred for Sonya seemed to flood his heart. Surprised and almost terrified by this feeling, he lifted his head and gazed at her, meeting her eyes fixed on him with a look of anxiety and anguished care. There was love in that look; his hatred vanished like a shadow. It had not been real; he had taken one feeling for another. All that it meant was that *the moment* had come.

He hid his face in his hands again and bent his head. Suddenly he rose from the chair, his face pale, looked at Sonya, and, without a word, went and sat down mechanically on the bed.

This moment felt to him terribly like that other, when he had stood behind the old woman, after he had freed the axe from its loop, and felt that 'there was not a moment to lose'.

'What is the matter?' asked Sonya, intimidated.

He could not speak. This was not at all, not at all, how he had meant to make his announcement, and he could not understand what was happening to him. She went up to him slowly, sat down on the bed beside him, and waited, without taking her eyes off him. Her heart thumped irregularly. The silence became unendurable; he turned his deathly-pale face towards her; his lips moved impotently, striving to speak. Terror filled Sonya's heart.

'What is the matter?' she repeated, drawing slightly away from him.

'Nothing, Sonya. Don't be afraid . . . It's all rubbish! Really, when you come to think of it, it *is* rubbish,' he muttered, looking like a man wandering in delirium. 'Why did I choose to torture you with this?' he added suddenly, looking at her. 'Really, why? I keep on asking myself that question, Sonya . . .'

He had, indeed, been asking himself the question perhaps a quarter of an hour before, but now he was quite without strength, hardly conscious of what he was doing and trembling from head to foot.

'Oh, how you are torturing yourself!' she said, full of distress.

'It's all nonsense! . . . Listen, Sonya,' (for some reason he smiled suddenly, a pale and impotent smile that lasted for some two seconds) 'do you remember what I wanted to tell you yesterday?'

Sonya waited uneasily.

'I said, when I left, that I might perhaps be saying good-bye for ever, but that if I did come here today, I would tell you . . . who killed Lizaveta.'

She shuddered from head to foot.

'Well, here I am, come to tell you.'

'Then what you said yesterday was really . . .' she whispered with difficulty. 'But how do you know?' she asked quickly, as if she had suddenly recollected herself.

Sonya's breathing was beginning to labour. Her face grew paler and paler.

'I do know.'

She was silent for a minute.

'Do you mean *he* has been found?' she asked timidly.

'No, he's not been found.'

'Then how do you know about *it*?' she asked, again almost inaudibly, and again after almost a minute's silence.

He turned to her and steadily, steadily, looked at her.

'Guess,' he said with the same distorted, feeble smile as before.

A convulsive shudder shook her.

'But you . . . I . . . Why do you frighten me so?' she asked, smiling like a child.

'I must be a great friend of *his* . . . if I know,' went on Raskolnikov, still continuing to keep his eyes fixed on her face, as though it were not in his power to turn them away. 'He did not want to . . . kill Lizaveta. He . . . killed her by accident . . . He meant to kill the old woman . . . when she was alone . . . and he went there . . . But Lizaveta came in . . . He was there . . . and he killed her.'

Another terrible minute went by. They still gazed at one another.

'Can't you guess?' he asked suddenly, with the sensation of a man throwing himself from a tower.

'N-no,' whispered Sonya, almost inaudibly.

'Look well.'

As soon as he had said this an old familiar sensation turned his heart to ice: he looked at her and suddenly in her face he seemed to see Lizaveta. He vividly recalled Lizaveta's expression as he advanced upon her with the axe and she retreated before him to the wall, with one hand stretched out and a childlike fear in her face, exactly like that of small children when they suddenly begin to be frightened, stare anxiously at the object of their fear, shrink back and stretch out their little hands, ready to burst into tears. It was almost the same now with Sonya; just as helpless, just as frightened, she stared at him for some time and then, stretching out her left hand, lightly, almost imperceptibly, rested her fingers on his breast and slowly raised herself from the bed, shrinking farther and farther back, still with her eyes fixed on his face. Her fear suddenly communicated itself to him: the same terror showed in his face and he gazed at her with the same fixity and almost with the same *childish* smile.

'Have you guessed?' he whispered at last.

'Oh God!' burst in a terrible wail from her breast. Powerlessly she fell back on the bed, with her face in the pillow. But after a moment she raised herself quickly, quickly approached him, seized both his hands, and squeezing them as tightly as a vice in her thin fingers, once more fixed her unmoving glance on his face, as though it were riveted there. With this last despairing look she was striving to find and somehow, anyhow, seize upon some last hope. But there was no hope; no doubt remained; it was *true*! Even much later, when she remembered this moment, it seemed strange and wonderful to her that she should have known *at once* that there was no longer any doubt. Surely she could not have said, for example, that she had foreseen something of the kind. And yet now, as soon as he said it, it suddenly seemed to her that she really had foreseen *this* very thing.

'That's enough, Sonya! Stop! Don't torture me!' he begged pitifully.

This was not at all, not at all, how he had thought of making his revelation, but it was the way things had happened.

As if she did not know what she was doing, she jumped up and, wringing her hands, walked into the middle of the room, but quickly came back and sat down again beside him, so close that their shoulders almost touched. Suddenly, as if she had been stabbed, she started, cried out, and flung herself, without knowing why, on her knees in front of him.

'What have you done, what have you done to yourself?' she said despairingly, and, starting up, threw herself on his neck, embraced him and held him tight.

Raskolnikov recoiled and regarded her with a melancholy smile.

'How strange you are, Sonya! You put your arms round me and kiss me, when I tell you *that*. You don't know what you are doing.'

'There is no one, no one, unhappier than you in the whole world!' she exclaimed in a frenzy, not hearing what he said, and suddenly broke into hysterical sobbing.

Long unfamiliar feelings poured like a flood into his heart

and melted it in an instant. He did not withstand them; two tears sprang into his eyes and hung on his lashes.

'Then you will not forsake me, Sonya?' he said, looking at her almost with hope.

'No, no! Never, nowhere!' cried Sonya. 'I will follow you wherever you go. Oh God! . . . Oh, I am wretched! . . . Why, why didn't I know you before? Why did you not come before? Oh God!'

'I have come now.'

'Now! Oh, what can be done now? . . . Together, together!' she repeated, as if beside herself, embracing him again. 'I will follow you to prison!' He felt a sudden shock and the old hostile, almost mocking smile played on his lips.

'Perhaps, Sonya, I don't mean to go to prison yet,' he said.

Sonya looked at him quickly.

After her first passionate and poignant impulse of sympathy for this unhappy being, the terrible idea of murder seized her again. In his changed tone she now suddenly heard the voice of the murderer. She looked at him in bewilderment. She knew nothing yet of the why, the how, the wherefore, of it. Now all these questions sprang at once to her mind. Again she could not believe it. 'He, he a murderer? Can that be possible?'

'What is this? Where am I?' she said in deep perplexity, as if still hardly conscious. 'And how could you, you, the man you are . . . bring yourself to this? . . . It can't be true!'

'But it is. It was to rob her! Stop, Sonya!' he answered wearily and almost with annoyance.

Sonya stood as if stunned, then suddenly cried out, 'You were hungry! You . . . was it to help your mother? Was that it?'

'No, Sonya, no,' he muttered, turning away and hanging his head. 'I was not very hungry . . . I did want to help my mother, but . . . but that wasn't quite it . . . Don't torture me, Sonya!'

Sonya threw up her hands.

'But is this really, really true? Good God, what sort of truth is this? Who can believe it? . . . How could you, how could you give away your last penny, and yet commit murder for gain? Oh! . . .' she exclaimed suddenly. 'That money you gave Katerina Ivanovna . . . that money . . . Good heavens, could that money be . . .?'

'No, Sonya,' he interrupted hastily. 'It was not that money. Calm yourself! My mother sent me the money, through a merchant, when I was ill, and I gave it away the same day . . . Razumikhin saw it . . . he received it for me, indeed . . . That money was mine, my own, really mine.'

Sonya listened in bewilderment, trying with all her might to understand.

'But *that* money . . . I don't even know whether there was any money, though,' he added thoughtfully. 'I took a purse from her neck, a chamois-leather one . . . it was full, tightly crammed . . . but I didn't look inside it; I can't have had time . . . Well, and the things, some sort of studs, and chains—I put them all with the purse, in a courtyard on the Voznesensky Prospect, buried under a stone, the next morning . . . They are still lying there . . .'

Sonya listened with strained attention.

'But then why . . . why did you say it was for money, if you didn't take anything?' she asked quickly, clutching at straws.

'I don't know . . . I had not decided whether I should take the money or not,' he said, again apparently deep in thought, and then suddenly seemed to recollect himself with a brief, hurried smile. 'Oh, what nonsense I've been talking, haven't I?'

The thought occurred to Sonya, 'Is he mad?' But she suppressed it at once. No, it was something else. But she could understand nothing, nothing of all this.

'You know, Sonya,' he said with sudden inspiration, 'I'll tell you what: if I'd killed simply because I was hungry,' he went on, emphasizing every word and looking at her mysteriously but frankly, 'then I should be . . . *happy* now! I want you to understand that!'

'And what would it matter to you,' he cried after a moment, almost in desperation, 'what could it matter to you if I confessed now that I had done wrong? What could you find in such a meaningless triumph over me? Oh, Sonya, was it for that I came to you?'

Sonya seemed about to say something, but remained silent.

'That is why I wanted you to go with me yesterday, because you were all that was left to me!'

'Where did you want me to go?' asked Sonya timidly.

'Not to steal or commit murder. Don't be alarmed, it wasn't for that,' he smiled caustically. 'We are not alike . . . And you know, Sonya, it is only now, only this moment that I realized *where* I was asking you to go yesterday. Yesterday, when I asked you, I didn't know myself where to. I asked you for one reason, I came here for one thing—that you should not leave me. You won't leave me, Sonya?'

She pressed his hand.

'And why, why did I tell her, why did I reveal it to her?' he exclaimed despairingly after a minute, looking at her with infinite pain. 'Now you are waiting for me to explain it, Sonya; you sit and wait, I see, but what shall I say to you? You will not understand a word of it, and will only wear yourself out with suffering . . . because of me! . . . See, you are crying and embracing me again—why do you embrace me? Because I could not carry my burden myself, and have come here to put it on other shoulders: if you suffer it will be easier for me! And can you love such an infamous wretch?'

'But don't you suffer too?' cried Sonya.

Again a wave of the former feeling flooded his heart and for a moment softened him.

'Sonya, I have an evil heart, note that; it explains many things. I came here because I am evil. There are people who would not have come. But I am a coward and . . . an infamous wretch. But . . . let it go! None of this is to the point . . . I must speak now, and I do not know how to begin . . .'

He stopped and considered.

'Oh, we are such different people! . . .' he cried again. 'We don't match. And why, why did I come? I shall never forgive myself that!'

'No, no, it was right to come!' exclaimed Sonya. 'It is better that I should know, much better!'

He looked at her with anguish. 'What if it really is . . .?' he said, as if trying to make up his mind. 'You know, it was like this! This was it: I wanted to make myself a Napoleon, and that is why I killed her . . . Now do you understand?'

'N-no,' whispered Sonya, naïvely and timidly; 'only . . . go on, go on! I shall understand, I shall understand it all inside me!' she implored him.

'You will understand? Good, we shall see!'

He was silent, thinking, for a long time.

'The point is this: on one occasion, I put this question to myself: what if, for example, Napoleon had found himself in my shoes, with no Toulon, no Egypt, no crossing of Mont Blanc, to give his career a start, but, instead of those monumental and glorious things, with simply one ridiculous old woman, who must be killed to get money from her trunk (for that career of his, you understand?)—well, would he have made up his mind to do it if there was no other way? Would he have shrunk from it, because it was so un-monumental and . . . and so sinful? Well, I tell you I tormented myself over that "problem" for a terribly long time, and I was terribly ashamed when at last I realized (quite suddenly) that not only would he not shrink, but the idea would never even enter his head that it was not monumental . . . and he would be quite unable to understand what there was to shrink from. And if there had been no other way open to him, he would have strangled her, without giving her a chance to squeak, and without a moment's hesitation! . . . Well, I also . . . stopped hesitating . . . strangled her . . . following the example of my authority . . . And that is exactly how it was! Does that amuse you? Yes, Sonya, perhaps the most amusing thing about all this, is that that is exactly how it happened . . .'

Sonya was not at all amused.

'You had better tell me straight out . . . without examples,' she said, even more timidly, and hardly audibly.

He turned towards her, looked at her sadly, and took her hands.

'You are right again, Sonya. Of course that's all nonsense, practically nothing but idle words! Look: you know, I suppose, that my mother has almost nothing. It happens that my sister had a good education, and she found herself condemned to scrape up a living as a governess. I was their only hope. I was studying; but I could not keep myself at the university and was obliged to leave it for a time. Even if things could have dragged along like that, it would only have meant that in ten years' time, or twelve, I might (if all went well) hope to become a teacher or a clerk with a salary of a thousand roubles . . .' (He sounded as though he were repeating a lesson.) 'Meanwhile, my mother would have withered away with care and grief, and I would never have been able to make her comfortable, and my sister . . . well, even worse things might have befallen my sister . . . And who would want to spend his whole life passing everything by, turning his back on everything, forgetting his mother, and humbly resigned to the wrongs done to his sister? And for what? In order, having buried them, to acquire new responsibilities—a wife and children, and then to leave them also without a penny or a crust of bread? Well . . . well, and so I decided, having got hold of the old woman's money, to use it for my first years, so that I need not worry my mother, to provide for myself at the university, and to launch myself after the university—and to do all this on a large scale, thoroughly, so as to make a completely new career for myself and set out on a new road of independence . . . Well . . . well, that's all . . . Well, killing the old woman, of course . . . that was wrong . . . Well, that's enough!'

He had dragged himself feebly to the end of his story and now hung his head.

'Oh, you're wrong, you're wrong!' cried Sonya in anguish. 'How could you . . .? No, things are not like that!'

'You see yourself that it's all wrong! . . . But I have told you the honest truth!'

'What kind of truth is that? Oh God!'

'I only killed a louse, Sonya, a useless, vile, pernicious louse.'

'A human being a louse!'

'Of course I know she wasn't a louse,' he answered with a strange look. 'But I am not telling the truth, Sonya,' he added. 'It is a long time since I have told or known the truth . . . This was all wrong; your judgement is sound there. There were quite, quite, quite different reasons! . . . I have not talked to anybody for a long time, Sonya . . . Now my head aches badly . . .'

His eyes shone with the fire of fever. He was almost beginning to wander; an uneasy smile was on his lips. His utter exhaustion was apparent underneath his feverish excitement. Sonya could understand his weariness. Her head also was beginning to feel dizzy. And he spoke so strangely; some of it seemed clear enough, but still . . . 'But how? How? Oh God!' And she wrung her hands in despair.

'No, Sonya, that's all wrong,' he began again, suddenly raising his head as though struck by a new turn of thought that had aroused him again. 'That's not it! Rather . . . suppose (yes, it's much better this way), suppose I am ambitious, envious, malicious, vile, vindictive, well . . . and have perhaps a tendency to madness. (Let's have it all at once! They've talked of madness before, I know.) I told you just now that I couldn't keep myself at the university. But do you know, I might perhaps have done it? My mother would have sent me enough to pay my fees and I could probably have earned money for boots and clothes and food. There was teaching to be got; I was offered half a rouble a lesson. Razumikhin works! But I turned nasty and wouldn't do it. Yes, I turned *nasty*— that's the right word! Then I lurked in a corner like a spider. You've been in my wretched little hole, of course, you've seen it . . . But do you know, Sonya, that low ceilings and cramped rooms crush the mind and the spirit? Oh, how I hated that hole. But all the same I would not leave it. I deliberately stayed in it! For days on end I didn't go out; I wouldn't work, I wouldn't even eat; I just lay there. If Nastasya brought me food, I ate it; if not, I let the day go by without asking, on purpose, out of spite! I had no light at night, and I lay in the dark, because I wouldn't earn the money for candles. I should have been studying, but I had sold my books, and the dust is still lying inches thick on the notebooks and papers on my table. I preferred to lie and think. I spent all the time thinking . . . And all the time I had such dreams, all sorts of strange dreams; no need to tell you what they were! But it was only then that I began to fancy that . . . No, that's not it; I am getting it wrong again! You see, I kept on asking myself, "Why am I so stupid that when other people are stupid and I know for a certainty that they are, I don't even want to be cleverer than they?" Then I realized that if we have to wait for everybody to become clever it will take too long. Then I saw that it will never happen, that people don't change, and nobody can change them, and it's not worth the trouble of trying! Yes, that's it! That's the law of their nature . . . The law of their nature, Sonya! That's it . . . And I know now, Sonya, that the man of strong and powerful mind and spirit is their master! The man who dares much is right in their eyes. The man who tramples on the greatest number of things is their law-giver, and whoever is most audacious is most certainly right. So things have always been, and so they will remain. Anyone who is not blind can see it!'

Although Raskolnikov still watched Sonya as he said this, he had ceased to be concerned whether she understood or not. He was completely in the grip of his fever. He felt a sort of sombre ecstasy. (It really was a very long time since he had talked to anybody.) Sonya understood that this gloomy creed had become his faith and his law.

'I realized then, Sonya,' he went on enthusiastically, 'that power is given only to the man who dares stoop and take it. There is only one thing needed, only one—to dare! I had a thought then, for the first time in my life, that nobody had ever had before me! Nobody! It was suddenly as clear as daylight to me: how strange that not one single person passing through this nonsensical world has the courage, has ever had the courage, to seize it by the tail and fling it to the devil! I . . . I wanted to *have the courage*, and I killed . . . I only wanted to dare, Sonya, that was the only reason!'

'Oh, stop, stop!' cried Sonya, flinging up her hands, 'You have strayed away from God, and God has stricken you, and given you over to the devil! . . .'

'By the way, Sonya, when I used to lie there in the dark thinking of all this, was that the devil confounding me, eh?'

'Be quiet! Don't laugh, it is blasphemous! You don't understand anything at all! Oh God! He will never understand anything!'

'Hush, Sonya, I am not laughing. I know myself that it was the devil dragging me along. Hush, Sonya, hush!' he repeated with gloomy insistence. 'I know all that. I thought it all out and whispered it over to myself, while I lay there in the dark . . . I argued it all out with myself, down to the last detail, and I know it all, all of it! And I got so tired, so tired, of all that rigmarole. I wanted to forget everything and start again, Sonya, without all the chatter. You don't think I was foolish enough to rush headlong into it, do you? No, I went along like a wise man, and that is just what brought me to destruction! You don't think, either, that I didn't know, for example, that if I began questioning and cross-examining myself about whether I had the right to take power, that meant that I hadn't any such right? Or that, if I asked myself, "Is a man a louse?" it meant that *for me* he was not, although he might be one for a man to whom the question never even occurred, and who would march straight ahead without asking any questions at all? . . . If I worried for so long about whether Napoleon would have done it or not, it must be because I felt clearly that I was not Napoleon . . . I endured all the torment of this endless debating, Sonya, and I longed to shake it off;

I longed to kill without casuistry, to kill for my own benefit, and for that alone! I would not lie about it even to myself! I did not commit murder to help my mother—that's rubbish! I did not commit murder in order to use the profit and power I gained to make myself a benefactor to humanity. Rubbish! I simply murdered; I murdered for myself, for myself alone, and whether I became a benefactor to anybody else, or, like a spider, spent the rest of my life catching everybody in my web and sucking the life-blood out of them, should have been a matter of complete indifference to me at that moment! . . . And, most important, it was not money that I needed, Sonya, when I killed; it was not money, so much as something else . . . I know all this now . . . Understand me: perhaps, were I to pursue the same course, I should not commit murder again. I needed to experience something different, something else was pushing me along: what I needed to find out then, and find out as soon as possible, was whether I was a louse like everybody else or a man, whether I was capable of stepping over the barriers or not. Dared I stoop and take power or not? Was I a trembling creature or had I the *right* . . .'

'To kill? Had you the right to kill?' Sonya flung up her hands again.

'O-oh, Sonya!' he cried irritably, and was about to retort, but then remained scornfully silent. 'Don't interrupt me, Sonya! I wanted to prove only one thing to you, that the devil was pulling me along then, and that he made it clear to me after that that I had not the right to travel by that road, because I am just as much a louse as everybody else! He flouted me, and now I have come to you! Take me in! If I were not a louse, would I have come to you? Listen: when I went to the old woman's that time, it was only *to test myself* . . . Understand that!'

'And you committed murder, murder!'

'But really, what kind of murder? Is that how murder is done? Do people go to murder as I went then? I will tell you sometime how I went . . . Did I murder the old woman? I killed myself, not that old creature! There and then I murdered myself at one blow, for ever! . . . But it was the devil who killed the old hag, not I . . . That's enough, Sonya, enough, enough! Leave me alone!' he exclaimed in a sudden convulsion of anguish. 'Leave me alone!'

He propped his elbows on his knees, and clutched his head tightly in his hands.

'How you are suffering!' broke in a tormented wail from Sonya.

'Well, tell me what to do now,' he begged, raising his head and gazing at her with a face monstrously distorted with despair.

'What to do?' she exclaimed, starting up, and her eyes, which had been full of tears, began to flash. 'Get up!' (She seized him by the shoulder, and he stood up, looking at her almost in consternation.) 'Go at once, this instant, stand at the cross-roads, first bow down and kiss the earth you have desecrated, then bow to the whole world, to the four corners of the earth, and say aloud to all the world: "I have done murder." Then God will send you life again. Will you go? Will you go?' she implored him, shaking all over as if in a fit, seizing both his hands and squeezing them tightly in her own, with her burning gaze fixed on him.

He was amazed, thunderstruck, at her sudden exaltation.

'You mean prison, don't you, Sonya? You think I must denounce myself?' he asked gloomily.

'Accept suffering and achieve atonement through it—that is what you must do.'

'No! I shall not go to them, Sonya.'

'But then how can you live? What will you live by?' exclaimed Sonya. 'Is it possible now? How can you speak to your mother? (Oh, what will become of them now?) But what am I saying? After all, you have already abandoned your mother and your sister. Yes, you have abandoned them already. Oh God!' she exclaimed. 'He knows all this himself! You will have ceased to be a human being, and how, how, can you live then? What will become of you?'

'Don't be such a child, Sonya,' he said quietly. 'In what way have I wronged them? Why should I go? What could I say to them? All you have been saying is unreal . . . They destroy millions of people themselves, and count it a virtue. They are rogues and scoundrels, Sonya! . . . I shall not go. What should I say—that I committed a murder and dared not take the money, but hid it under a stone?' he added, with a bitter smile. 'You know they would laugh at me and say, "He was a fool not to take it." A fool and a coward! They wouldn't understand anything, Sonya; they are not fit to understand. Why should I go? I won't go. Don't be a child, Sonya . . .'

'You will destroy yourself, destroy yourself!' she repeated, stretching out her hands to him in desperate supplication.

'Perhaps I am *still* misjudging myself,' he remarked sombrely, as though pondering something. 'Perhaps I am *still* a man and not a louse, and I was in too much of a hurry to condemn myself . . . Perhaps I can still put up a fight!'

There was a supercilious smile on his lips.

'But to bear such torment! And for your whole life long! . . .'

'I shall get used to it . . .' he said, sullenly thoughtful. 'Listen,' he began after a moment, 'Stop crying; it is time to come to the point. I came to tell you the police are after me, trying to catch me . . .'

'Oh!' shrieked Sonya, terrified.

'Well, why do you scream? You wanted me to go to prison; why be frightened now? But this is the point: I will not give myself up. I will fight them again, and they won't be able to do anything. They have no real evidence. Yesterday I was in great danger, and I thought I was lost, but things are better today. All their evidence cuts both ways; I mean I can turn their accusations to my own advantage, do you understand? And I shall do it, because I have learnt my lesson now . . . But they are sure to put me in prison. If it had not been for one accidental circumstance they would certainly have put me there today, and perhaps they may *still* do so before the day is over . . . But that doesn't matter, Sonya: I shall stay there for a little and then they will let me go . . . because they haven't one real proof, and they won't have, I promise you. And it's impossible to convict anybody with what they have. Well, that's enough . . . I only wanted you to know . . . I will try to manage things with my mother and sister so as to reassure them and so that they won't be frightened. My sister, however, seems to be provided for now . . . consequently my mother is, too . . . Well, that's all. But be careful. Will you come and see me in prison, when they arrest me?'

'Oh yes, yes!'

They sat side by side, sad and weary, like shipwrecked sailors on a deserted shore. He looked at Sonya, and thought how much love she had for him, and suddenly it seemed strangely painful and burdensome to be so loved. Yes, that was a strange and terrible feeling! Going to Sonya's, he had felt that she was his only hope, his only way out; he had thought he could lay down a part of his suffering, at least, but now, when her whole heart turned towards him, he was suddenly conscious that his unhappiness was immeasurably greater than before.

'Sonya,' he said, 'better not come and see me when I am in prison.'

Sonya did not answer; she was in tears. Several minutes passed.

'Do you wear a cross?' she asked unexpectedly, as though suddenly remembering something.

He did not understand the question at first.

'No, I suppose you don't. Take this cypress-wood one. I have another, of brass, that was Lizaveta's. Lizaveta and I made an exchange: she gave me her cross and I gave her my ikon. Now I shall begin to wear Lizaveta's, and give this one to you. Take it . . . it is mine! It is my own, you know!' she urged him. 'We are going to suffer together, we will bear the cross together! . . .'

'Give it to me,' said Raskolnikov. He did not want to

distress her. But he drew back at once the hand he had extended for the cross.

'Not now, Sonya. Better give it me afterwards,' he added to reassure her.

'Yes, yes, that will be better, much better,' she took him up enthusiastically. 'When you accept your suffering, you shall put it on. You will come to me, and I will put it on you, we will pray, and then we will go.'

At this moment somebody knocked three times at the door.

'Sofya Semënovna, may I come in?' politely asked a familiar voice.

Sofya rushed to the door in terror. Mr. Lebezyatnikov's blonde head looked into the room.

## CHAPTER V

LEBEZYATNIKOV looked very anxious.

'I have come to you, Sofya Semënovna. Excuse me . . . I thought I should find you here' (he turned abruptly to Raskolnikov); 'that is, I didn't think anything . . . like that . . . but I thought . . . Katerina Ivanovna has gone out of her mind,' he blurted out to Sonya, turning away from Raskolnikov.

Sonya screamed.

'I mean, it looks like it, at any rate. However . . . We don't know what to do, that's the point! She came back . . . I think she'd been turned out of somewhere, and perhaps beaten . . . at least, I think so . . . She had run to Semën Zakharovich's chief, but he wasn't at home; he was dining at some other general's . . . Imagine, she rushed off at once to where they were dining . . . to this other general's, and, imagine, she insisted on having Semën Zakharovich's chief called out, though it seems he was actually at table. You can imagine what happened. She was turned out, of course, and she herself says that she abused him and threw something at him. One may very well imagine it . . . and why she wasn't arrested . . . I don't know. Now she is telling everybody about it, including Amalia Ivanovna, but it is hard to understand her because she is shouting and throwing herself about violently . . . Oh, yes, she is clamouring that since everybody has abandoned her now she will take the children and go out into the streets with a barrel-organ, and the children shall sing and dance, and she will as well, and collect money, and every day they will go under the general's window . . . "Let them see well-born children, whose father was a civil servant, going about the streets as beggars," says she. She is beating all the children and making them cry. She is teaching Lënya to sing "The Little Hut", and the little boy to dance, and Polina Mikhaylovna as well. She is tearing all their clothes and making them little caps, like actors. She herself is going to carry a basin and beat it instead of music. She won't listen to anything . . . Imagine what it's like! It is simply impossible!'

Lebezyatnikov would have gone on even longer, but Sonya, who had been listening almost without drawing a breath, snatched up her cloak and hat and hurried out of the room, putting them on as she ran. Raskolnikov went out after her, and Lebezyatnikov followed him.

'She has certainly gone mad!' he said to Raskolnikov, as they came out into the street, 'only I didn't want to frighten Sofya Semënovna, so I said "it looks like it", but there is no doubt about it. They say that in consumption there are tubercles that attack the brain; unfortunately, I don't know anything about medicine. However, I tried to convince her, but she won't listen to anything.'

'You talked to her about tubercles?'

'Well, not exactly. Besides, she wouldn't have understood. But what I mean is this: if you convince a man logically that he has nothing to cry for, he will stop crying. That's clear. Or don't you think he will stop?'

'That would make living too easy,' answered Raskolnikov.

'No, excuse me, excuse me. Of course, it is rather hard for Katerina Ivanovna to understand; but do you know that in Paris they have been conducting serious experiments on the possibility of curing the mad by the use of nothing but logical persuasion? A professor there, who died recently, a serious scientist, thought they could be cured in this way. His basic idea was that there is no specific organic disorder in lunatics, but that madness is, so to speak, a logical mistake, a mistake of judgement, an incorrect view of things. He would gradually prove the patient wrong, and, just imagine, they say he achieved results. But as he was using douches at the same time, the results of this form of treatment are, of course, subject to doubt . . . At least, it would seem so . . .'

Raskolnikov had not been listening for some time. As they came level with his house he nodded to Lebezyatnikov and turned in at the gate. Lebezyatnikov started, looked round, and hurried on.

Raskolnikov went into his little room and stood in the middle of it. Why had he returned here? He looked around at the discoloured, tattered wallpaper, the dust, his narrow bed . . . From the courtyard came the sound of sharp continuous knocking; somewhere something was being hammered in, a nail, perhaps . . . He went to the window, stood on tiptoes and for a long time gazed into the yard with a look of extraordinary attentiveness. But the yard was empty and whoever was knocking was invisible. In the wing on the left there were open windows here and there; pots of sickly geraniums stood on the window-sills. Linen was hanging outside the windows . . . He knew all this by heart. He turned away and sat down on the sofa.

Never, never before, had he felt so terribly alone!

Yes, once more he felt that he really hated Sonya, especially now when he had made her more unhappy. Why had he gone to plead for her tears? Why did he feel he must spoil her life? How vile!

'I will remain alone!' he said with sudden decision. 'She shall not come to the prison!'

Five minutes later he raised his head with a strange smile. The idea that had suddenly come to him was also strange: 'Perhaps it really would be better to go to Siberia.'

He never knew how long he sat in his room, with vague thoughts crowding into his head. Suddenly the door opened and Avdotya Romanovna came in. She stood still and looked at him from the threshold, as he had done not long before at Sonya, then she came right in and sat down facing him on the chair she had sat in the day before. He looked at her silently, almost vacantly.

'Don't be angry, brother. I have only come for a moment,' said Dunya. She looked thoughtful but not stern. Her eyes were clear and tranquil. He saw that she too had come to him with love.

'Brother, I know *everything*, *everything*, now that Dmitri Prokofich has told me all about it and explained it to me. You are being persecuted and harassed because of a stupid and infamous suspicion . . . Dmitri Prokofich tells me that there is no danger at all, and that you are wrong to distress yourself so. I don't think so, and I *fully understand* that you are filled with indignation, and that this indignation may leave its mark on you for ever. I am afraid it may. I don't judge you, I dare not, for giving us up, and please forgive me for reproaching you before. I can feel myself that if I had had so great a trouble I should have wanted to leave everybody too. I shall not tell mother anything *about this*, but I shall keep talking to her about you, and I shall tell her from you that you will come to us very soon. Don't worry about her, I will make her mind easy, but you must not upset her again; you must come, even if only once. Remember, she is your mother! Now I have only come to say' (Dunya began to get up) 'that if you should happen to need me, or need . . . all my life, or anything . . . you must call me and I will come. Good-bye!'

She turned abruptly and made for the door.

'Dunya!' Raskolnikov stopped her, got up, and went to her. 'Dmitri Prokofich Razumikhin is a very good chap.'

Dunya blushed very slightly.

'Well?' she asked after a moment's pause.

'He is a practical and hard-working man, honest and capable

of true love . . . Good-bye, Dunya.'

Dunya had flushed red; then she became anxious.

'What is this, brother? Are we really parting for ever, that you should make such . . . testamentary dispositions?'

'It doesn't matter . . . Good-bye.'

He turned away from her and walked to the window. She stood there a little longer, looking at him uneasily, and went out full of alarm.

No, he did not feel cold towards her. There had been one moment, at the very last, when he had longed to hold her close in his arms, *say good-bye* to her, and even *tell* her, but he could not make up his mind even to touch her hand.

'Afterwards she would perhaps shudder to remember that I embraced her now, and say that I stole her kiss!'

'And will *she* endure, or not?' he added to himself after some minutes. 'No, she won't; people like *her* are not made for endurance! They can never stand things . . .'

He thought of Sonya.

Cooler air blew in through the window. The light outside was no longer so bright. He snatched up his cap and went out.

Naturally, he could not now take any care of his health, nor did he wish to do so. But all this ceaseless terror and mental turmoil could not be without effect. And if he was not even now lying in a raging fever it was perhaps just because his ceaseless inner trouble kept him for the time being conscious and on his feet, as it were, artificially.

He wandered aimlessly. The sun was going down. A particular sort of dejection had recently begun to show itself in him. There was nothing violent or poignant about it, but it carried with it a premonition of perpetuity, weary, endless years of cold deadening depression, a presage of an eternity on 'a hand's-breadth of ground'. This feeling usually began to distress him even more towards evening.

'With such stupid, purely physical, infirmities, that seem to depend on the sunset or something, how can one help doing stupid things? It was bad enough going to Sonya, but Dunya!' he muttered disgustedly.

Somebody hailed him. He looked round; Lebezyatnikov rushed to him.

'Imagine, I have been to your room. I have been looking for you. Imagine, she had carried out her intention and taken the children away! Sofya Semënovna and I had hard work finding them. She is banging a frying-pan and making the children sing and dance. The children are crying. They stop at crossings and in front of shops. A lot of stupid people are following them about. Come along.'

'And Sonya?' asked Raskolnikov anxiously, as he hurried after Lebezyatnikov.

'She's raving mad. Not Sofya Semënovna, I mean, but Katerina Ivanovna; however, Sofya Semënovna is in a frenzy too. But Katerina Ivanovna is quite beside herself. I tell you, she is definitely mad. They will be taken to the police. You can imagine what effect that will have . . . She is on the Canal now, near the Voznesensky Bridge, quite close to Sofya Semënovna's. It's not far.'

On the Canal bank, not very far from the bridge, and not two houses away from where Sonya lived, there was a knot of people, mostly street urchins. Katerina Ivanovna's hoarse broken voice could be heard from as far away as the bridge. And really it was a strange spectacle, calculated to excite the curiosity of a street crowd. Katerina Ivanovna, in her old dress and the green shawl, wearing a battered straw hat with the brim bent out of shape at one side, really was in a state of absolute frenzy. She was tired and gasping for breath. Her exhausted, consumptive face looked more full of suffering than ever (indeed, in the open air and the sunshine a consumptive always appears worse and uglier than indoors); but she was still in the same excited state and growing more exasperated with every minute. She kept dashing at the children, shouting at them, urging them on, telling them in front of everybody how to dance and what to sing, beginning to explain why all this was necessary, growing desperate over their inability to understand, beating them . .'. Then, breaking off, she would rush back to the crowd; if she saw anybody slightly better-dressed stopping to look, she would immediately begin to explain to him that this, in her words, was what 'children from a respectable, one might even say aristocratic, home' had been reduced to. If she heard laughter or a provocative witticism from among the crowd, she would immediately attack the offenders and begin to wrangle with them. Some of the crowd were laughing, others were shaking their heads, but they all looked anxiously at the madwoman with her terrified children. The frying-pan Lebezyatnikov had spoken of was not there, at least Raskolnikov did not see it; but instead of banging on a frying-pan Katerina Ivanovna beat time by clapping her wasted hands when she made Polechka sing or Lënya and Kolya dance; she even tried to join in the singing herself, but each time her torturing cough made her break off at the second note, and she would lapse into despair again, curse her cough, and even weep. The frightened wailing of Lënya and Kolya made her angrier than anything else. There had really been some attempt at dressing the children up like street-singers. The little boy had on a turban of some red and white material, to make him look like a Turk. There had not been a costume for Lënya, and she was only wearing a red knitted worsted cap (or rather night-cap) of the late Semën Zakharovich's, with a broken piece of white ostrich feather stuck in it which had belonged to Katerina Ivanovna's grandmother and been kept until now in a trunk as a family treasure. Polechka was wearing her usual clothes. She was watching her mother timidly and with great embarrassment, not leaving her side, and trying to hide her own tears; she guessed at her mother's madness and kept looking uneasily about. The street and the crowd terrified her. Sonya was following Katerina Ivanovna about, crying and begging her to go home. But Katerina Ivanovna was not to be persuaded.

'Stop it, Sonya, stop it!' she shouted in rapid, hurried tones, panting and coughing. 'You don't know what you are asking; you might be a child! I have told you that I shan't go back to that drunken German woman's. Let everybody see, let all St. Petersburg see, how a gentleman's children have to beg, though their father served all his life in faithfulness and truth and, one might say, died in the service.' (Katerina Ivanovna had already managed to create this legend for herself and believed in it blindly.) 'Let that worthless little wretch of a general see. And you are being silly, Sonya; how are we to eat now, tell me that? We have been a trouble to you long enough; I won't have any more of it! Oh, Rodion Romanovich, it's you!' she cried, catching sight of Raskolnikov and rushing towards him. 'Please explain to this silly girl that this is the best thing we could do! Even organ-grinders get a living, and everybody can tell at once that we are different. They will see that we are poor orphans of good family who have been reduced to beggary. And that little wretch of a general will lose his job, you'll see! We shall be under his windows every day, and when the Emperor drives past I shall fall on my knees, and put them all in front of me and point to them and say, 'Father, protect them.' He is the father of orphans, he is merciful, he will protect them, you'll see, and that wretched little general . . . Lënya, *tenez-vous droite!*[5] Kolya, you must dance again at once. What are you snivelling for? Snivelling again! But what on earth are you frightened of, little idiot? Oh God, what am I to do with them, Rodion Romanovich? If you knew how stupid they are! What can you do with children like that? . . .'

And, almost crying herself (which did not hinder her incessant, uninterrupted flood of words), she pointed to the whimpering children. Raskolnikov tried to persuade her to go back, and even, thinking to work on her vanity, told her that it was not fitting for her to wander about the streets like an organ-grinder, since she was planning to be the principal of a boarding-school for young ladies . . .

'Boarding-school! Ha, ha, ha! The far-away hills are blue!'

5. "Stand up straight!" The use of French was common among the educated and upper classes in nineteenth-century Russia. Here it is a sign of affectation and pretentiousness.

cried Katerina Ivanovna, her laughter bringing on a fit of coughing. 'No, Rodion Romanovich, the day-dreams are over! Everybody has abandoned us! . . . And that wretched little general . . . You know, Rodion Romanovich, I threw an ink-well at him. It was standing by the visitors' book on the table in the ante-room. I signed my name, threw it at him and ran away. Oh, the vile scoundrels! But I don't care; now I shall feed the children myself, I won't be beholden to anybody! We have burdened her long enough!' (She pointed to Sonya.) 'Polechka, how much have you got? Show me! What, only two copecks? Mean creatures! They won't give us anything, they only run after us with their tongues hanging out! Well, what is that fool laughing at?' (pointing at one of the crowd). 'It's all because Kolka is so stupid; he's a nuisance! What's the matter, Polechka? Speak French; *parlez-moi français.* After all, I have taught you some, you know a few sentences! . . . Otherwise how is anyone to tell you are well-educated children of good family and not like all the other organ-grinders? We're not giving some sort of Punch and Judy show in the street, but singing nice drawing-room songs . . . Oh, yes, what are we going to sing? You keep on interrupting me, and we . . . you see, Rodion Romano-vich, we stopped here to choose what to sing—something Kolya can dance to as well . . . because, as you may imagine, we couldn't prepare any of this beforehand; we must agree on something and rehearse it all thoroughly, and then we shall go to the Nevsky Prospect, where there are far more society people, and they will notice us at once. Lënya knows "The Little Hut" . . . but it's always "The Little Hut"—everybody sings it! We must sing something much more genteel . . . Well, what have you thought of, Polya? You might help your mother! My memory, my memory has gone, or I should have remembered something! At any rate don't let us sing "A Hussar leaning on his sword"![6] Ah, let us sing *"Cinq sous"* in French! I taught it you, you know. And the main thing is that it is in French, so people will see at once that you are a gentleman's children, and that will be much more pathetic . . . We might even sing *"Mal-borough s'en va-t-en guerre"*,[7] because that's a real children's song and it is used in all aristocratic houses as a lullaby:

> *Malborough s'en va-t-en guerre*
> *Ne sait quand reviendra . . .'*

she began singing . . . 'But no, *"Cinq sous"* would be better. Now, Kolya, hands on hips, quickly, and you, Lënya, must go round in the opposite direction, and Polechka and I will sing and clap our hands.

> *Cinq sous, cinq sous*
> *Pour monter notre ménage . . .'*[8]

6. A song to words by K. N. Batyushkov.
7. A popular, traditional French song about the Duke of Marlborough. The two lines mean, "Marlborough is leaving for the wars/He does not know when he will come back."
8. "Five pennies, five pennies/To start our household."

(She went off into a fit of coughing.) 'Put your dress straight, Polechka, the shoulders have slipped down,' she observed between coughs, panting. 'It is specially necessary for you to look nice and tidy now, so that everybody can see you are a gentleman's children. I said at the time that the bodice ought to be cut longer, and made in two pieces. Then you had to put in your advice, Sonya, "Shorter, shorter still", till it has made the child look perfectly dreadful . . . Now you're all crying again! What is wrong, you little sillies? Well, Kolya, begin, quickly! Quickly, quickly—oh, what an impossible child . . .

*Cinq sous, cinq sous—*

Another policeman! Well, what do you want?'

A policeman was in fact pushing his way through the crowd. But at the same time a gentleman in undress uniform and a long cloak, a highly respectable official with an order round his neck (which was very gratifying to Katerina Ivanovna and had some influence on the policeman), came up and silently gave Katerina Ivanovna a green three-rouble note. His face expressed sincere compassion. Katerina Ivanovna accepted the money and bowed politely, even ceremoniously.

'I thank you, my dear sir,' she began, in a rather high-flown manner. 'The reasons which have prompted us . . . take the money, Polechka. You see, noble and generous people, who are ready to give immediate help to a poor gentlewoman fallen on evil days, do exist. You see before you, my dear sir, orphans of good family who, one might even say, have aristocratic connexions . . . And that wretched little general sat there eating grouse . . . and stamping with impatience because I was disturbing him . . . "Your excellency," I said, "protect the poor orphans, because you knew the late Semën Zakharovich very well," I said, "and because his own daughter was basely maligned on the day of his death by the meanest of scoundrels . . ." There's that policeman again! Protect me!' she cried to the official. 'Why is that policeman creeping up to me? We have only just come here to escape one of them on Meshchanskaya Street . . . Well, what do you want, fool?'

'This is not allowed in the streets. Please don't create a disturbance.'

'It's you who are making the disturbance! It is just the same as if I were taking a barrel-organ! What business is it of yours?'

'For a barrel-organ you have to have a licence, and you are doing it on your own, and you are causing a crowd to collect. What is your address?'

'What licence?' wailed Katerina Ivanovna. 'I buried my husband today. Why should I need a licence?'

'Madam, madam, compose yourself,' the official was beginning. 'Come, I will accompany you . . . you ought not to be here in the crowd . . . you are ill . . .'

'My dear sir, my dear sir, you don't know anything!' cried Katerina Ivanovna. 'We will go to the Nevsky Prospect. Sonya, Sonya! Where is she? She's crying, too! What is the matter with you all? Kolya, Lënya, where are you going?' she cried out in sudden fright. 'Silly children! Kolya, Lënya! Where are they going? . . .'

Kolya and Lënya, already terrified out of their wits by the crowd and their mother's crazy tricks, had suddenly, when they saw that the policeman wanted to take them away somewhere, seized each other's little hands and, as if by agreement, run off together. Poor Katerina Ivanovna, weeping and wailing, set off in pursuit. It was an ugly and pitiful sight, as she ran weeping and gasping for breath. Sonya and Polechka hurried after her.

'Bring them back, Sonya, bring them back! Oh, naughty ungrateful children! . . . Polya! Catch them . . . It is for you I . . .'

She stumbled as she ran, and fell.

'She's hurt! She's bleeding! Oh God!' cried Sonya, stooping over her.

Everybody ran up and crowded round. Raskolnikov and Lebezyatnikov were among the first to reach her, and the official also hurried up, with the policeman behind him, muttering, 'Oh dear!' with a despairing wave of his hand, as he foresaw that this would be a troublesome business.

'Be off! Be off!' he said, trying to drive away the people crowding round.

'She is dying!' shouted one.

'She's gone mad!' said another.

'Lord preserve us!' said a woman, crossing herself. 'Have they caught the little boy and the little girl? There they are; they are bringing them. The older one has got them . . . Silly little things!'

But when they looked more carefully at Katerina Ivanovna, they saw that she had not cut herself on a stone, as Sonya thought, but that the blood staining the roadway crimson had gushed out of her throat.

'I know this kind of thing, I've seen it before,' murmured the official to Raskolnikov and Lebezyatnikov. 'That's consumption; the blood flows out like that and chokes them. I saw it happen with one of my relatives not long ago—three-quarters of a pint of blood, all of a sudden . . . But what shall we do? She is dying.'

'This way, this way, to my room!' begged Sonya. 'I live here! . . . In that house there, the second from here . . . Bring her there, quickly, quickly!' She rushed from one to another. 'Send for a doctor . . . Oh God!'

This was decided on, thanks to the efforts of the official, and even the policeman helped to carry Katerina Ivanovna. She was carried almost lifeless into Sonya's room and laid on the bed. The flow of blood had not stopped, but she had begun to come to herself. Besides Sonya, there came into the room Raskolnikov, Lebezyatnikov, the official-looking gentleman, and the policeman, after he had driven away the rest of the crowd, several of whom had accompanied them to the very door. Kolya and Lënya, trembling and crying, were led in by Polechka. Some of the Kapernaumovs had come in as well: the tailor himself, a lame, crooked, odd-looking man with bristly hair and whiskers standing on end, his wife, with an eternally scared look, and several of their children with open mouths and faces set in expressions of perpetual astonishment. Among all these, Svidrigaylov suddenly made his appearance. Raskolnikov gazed at him in surprise, not understanding where he had come from and not remembering to have seen him in the crowd.

There was talk of a doctor and a priest. The official gentleman, although he whispered to Raskolnikov that a doctor could do nothing now, ordered one to be sent for. Kapernaumov went himself.

Meanwhile Katerina Ivanovna had regained her breath and the bleeding had stopped for a time. Her sick eyes looked intently and penetratingly at Sonya, who, pale and trembling, was wiping the drops of sweat from her forehead; at last she asked them to raise her. They sat her up on the bed, supporting her on both sides.

'Where are the children?' she asked faintly. 'Have you brought them, Polya? Oh, you silly children!... Why did you run away?... oh!'

Her parched lips were still flecked with blood. Her eyes moved, looking round the room.

'So this is how you live, Sonya! I have never once been here ... now fate has brought me ...'

She looked at her in distress.

'We have been a drain on you, Sonya ... Polya, Lënya, Kolya, come here ... Well, here they are, Sonya, all of them; take them... from my hands into yours... I have had enough! ... The ball is over!' Cough! '... Put me down, let me at least die in peace ...'

They laid her down again on the pillow.

'What? The priest? ... I don't want him ... you haven't got a rouble to spare for him ... I have no sins ... God ought to pardon me without the priest's help ... He knows how I have suffered! ... And if He doesn't pardon me, so much the worse! ...'

An increasing delirium possessed her. At times she shuddered and moved her eyes, and recognized them all for a moment, but then the delirium seized her again. Her breathing was hoarse and laboured; there was a sort of rattling in her throat.

'I said to him, "Your excellency!" ...' she cried out, gasping after every word. 'That Amalia Ludwigovna ... Oh, Lënya, Kolya! hands on hips, quickly, quickly! *Glissez, glissez, pas-de-Basque!* Stamp! ... Be graceful!

*Du hast Diamanten und Perlen ...* [9]

What comes next? That's what we should sing ...

*Du hast die schönsten Augen.*
*Mädchen, was willst du mehr?*

Well, what next! *Was willst du mehr?*—the things he invents, the blockhead! ... Ah, yes, here's another:

In the mid-day heat, in the Vale of Daghestan ...[1]

Ah, how I loved it ... I used to worship that song, Polechka ... You know, your father ... used to sing it before we were married ... Oh, happy days! ... That's what we must sing! Now, how, how does it ... there, I've forgotten it ... Remind me! How does it go?'

She was extremely agitated and struggling to raise herself. At last, in a terrible, hoarse, broken voice she began to sing, crying out and panting at every word with a look of growing terror:

'In the mid-day heat! ... in the Vale! ... of Daghestan! ... With a bullet in my breast! ...

Your excellency!' she shrieked suddenly, with a heart-rending wail and a gush of tears, 'protect the orphans! You have known the hospitality of the late Semën Zakharovich ... One might even say aristocratic! ...' Cough! She shuddered, coming suddenly to herself, and looked round at them all with a sort of terror, but at once recognized Sonya. 'Sonya, Sonya!' she said gently and tenderly, as though surprised to see her there. 'Sonya, dear, are you here, too?'

They raised her up again.

'Enough! ... The time has come! Good-bye, poor wretch! ... This poor beast has been driven to death! ... I am finished!' she cried, full of despair and hatred, and her head fell heavily back on the pillow.

She had lost consciousness again, but this last phase did not last long. Her bloodless, yellow, wasted face dropped back, her mouth opened, her legs straightened convulsively. She drew a deep, heavy sigh and died.

9. A song set by Franz Schubert to words by Heinrich Heine. The lines quoted mean, "You have diamonds and pearls. You have the most beautiful eyes. Girl, what more do you want?"

1. A famous song by M. A. Balakirev to the words by the poet Michael Lermontov.

Sonya fell upon the body, with her arms about it and her head pressed against the wasted breast, and lay there motionless. Polechka fell at her mother's feet and kissed them, sobbing. Kolya and Lënya did not realize what had happened, but felt that it was something terrible. Each with both hands round the other's shoulders, they stared at one another and then, all at once, both together, opened their mouths and began to scream. They were still in their costumes, one in his turban, the other in the night-cap with the ostrich feather.

How could the 'Certificate of Merit' have made its appearance on the bed, close to Katerina Ivanovna? It lay there by the pillow; Raskolnikov saw it.

He walked to the window. Lebezyatnikov hurried over to him.

'She is dead!' he said.

'Rodion Romanovich, I must say two words to you,' said Svidrigaylov, approaching. Lebezyatnikov instantly gave place to him and delicately effaced himself. Svidrigaylov drew the astonished Raskolnikov still farther into the corner.

'I will take all the arrangements, that is for the funeral and the rest of it, on myself. You know, it takes money, and I told you I had more than enough. I will put these two little fledglings and Polechka into some good institution for orphans, and settle fifteen hundred roubles on each of them for when they come of age, so that Sofya Semënovna may be quite easy about them. And I will pull her out of the mire, because she is a good girl, isn't she? Well, then, will you tell Avdotya Romanovna that this is how I am using her ten thousand?'

'What is the object of all this generosity?' asked Raskolnikov.

'Ah, you're a mistrustful person!' laughed Svidrigaylov. 'You know I told you I had no use for that money. But will you not admit that it can be done simply out of humanity? After all, she wasn't a "louse" ' (he pointed with his finger towards the corner where the dead woman was), 'like some old money-lender. Well, you will agree, "Is Luzhin indeed to go on living and doing mischief, or is she to die?" And if I don't help, probably "Polechka will take the same path to the same end" . . .'

He said all this with an expression of cheerful, insinuating slyness, and without taking his eyes from Raskolnikov. Raskolnikov paled and grew cold as he heard the very expressions he had used to Sonya. He recoiled and looked wildly at Svidrigaylov.

'How . . . do you know?' he whispered, hardly daring to breathe.

'Why, I'm staying at Madam Resslich's, just the other side of the wall here. The Kapernaumovs are here, and Madam

Resslich, an old and most devoted friend of mine, is there. We are neighbours.'

'You?'

'Yes, me,' went on Svidrigaylov, shaking with laughter. 'And I can honestly assure you, my dear Rodion Romanovich, that you interested me strangely. You know I told you we should come together—I foretold it; well, now we have done so. And you shall see how easy-going I am. You shall see that it is possible to live with me . . .'

# Part Six

## CHAPTER I

A STRANGE time began for Raskolnikov; it was as if a mist had fallen round him and enclosed him in unescapable and dreary solitude. Remembering this time afterwards, when it had long gone by, he surmised that his consciousness had become, as it were, blunted, and that this state lasted, with some intermissions, until the final catastrophe. He was firmly convinced that he had been mistaken about many things then; for example, the time and sequence of several happenings. At least, remembering afterwards, and trying to explain his recollections to himself, he learnt a good deal about himself, with the help of other people's testimony. He would confuse one event with another, for example; he would think of one thing as a consequence of something else which had occurred only in his imagination. At times he fell a prey to painful and tormenting anxiety, which sometimes grew to a panic fear. But he remembered also that there were moments, hours, perhaps even days, of complete and overwhelming apathy, which formed, as it were, the reverse side of his previous terror, an apathy like the sick indifference of a dying man. In general, during these last days, he seemed to be trying to avoid a full and clear understanding of his position; there were some facts, urgently demanding immediate consideration, that he found particularly burdensome; and how glad he would have been to get free from certain anxieties, although, had he succeeded in neglecting them, it would have threatened his complete and inevitable ruin.

Svidrigaylov especially worried him; it might almost be said that he could not get past Svidrigaylov. From the time of those ominous and explicit words of Svidrigaylov's in Sonya's room, at the moment of Katerina Ivanovna's death, it was as if the normal flow of his thoughts had received a check. But although this new factor of the situation made him extremely uneasy, he was in no hurry to seek an explanation of it. At times, finding himself in a remote and solitary part of the town, alone at a table in some miserable public house, deep in thought, and hardly knowing how he came there, he would suddenly remember Svidrigaylov; it would become clearly and alarmingly evident to him that he must come to terms with this man as soon as possible, and settle with him finally, as far as he could. Once, walking outside the city, he even fancied that he was waiting for Svidrigaylov and that they had made an appointment to meet there. Another time he woke up before dawn and found himself lying on the ground among some bushes, hardly knowing how he had wandered there. In the few days after Katerina Ivanovna's death he actually did meet Svidrigaylov two or three times, for a very short time, and always in Sonya's room, where he had gone without any clear object. They had exchanged a few short words, never touching on the capital point, as though they had come to an agreement not to mention it for the time being. Katerina Ivanovna's body was still lying there in her coffin. Svidrigaylov was making the funeral arrangements and was very busy. Sonya was also very busy. At their last meeting Svidrigaylov told Raskolnikov that he had brought the question of Katerina Ivanovna's children to a conclusion, and a successful one; that owing to his connexions he had been able to find people with whose help all three orphans could be placed at once in very suitable institutions; and that the money settled on them had also helped considerably, since it was much easier to find places for orphans who had some capital than for those who were destitute. He said something about Sonya as well, promised to call before long on Raskolnikov, and mentioned that 'he would like to ask his advice; he had something that he very much wanted to talk over . . .' This conversation took place in the corridor, near the stairs. Svidrigaylov looked earnestly into Raskolnikov's eyes and suddenly, after a pause, lowered his voice and asked: 'Why, what is it, Rodion Romanovich? You aren't well! Really! You look and listen, but you don't seem to understand. Pull yourself together. Look, let us have a talk; but, unfortunately, I have so much business to attend to, both of my own and of other people's . . . Ah, Rodion Romanovich,' he added suddenly, 'every man needs air, air, air! . . . More than anything!'

He stood aside to allow a priest and a sacristan, who were coming up the stairs, to pass. They were coming to say prayers for the dead. This they did punctually twice a day, by Svidrigaylov's orders. Svidrigaylov went on his way. Raskolnikov stood and thought for a moment, then followed the priest to Sonya's room.

He stood at the door. The service began, quiet, decorous, melancholy. From his childhood, the idea of death and the consciousness of the presence of death had oppressed him and filled him with mystic awe; besides, it was a long time since he had heard the mass for the dead. There was something else here, also, something terrible and disquieting. He looked at the children; they were all kneeling by the coffin, and Polechka was crying. Behind them, weeping softly and almost timidly, Sonya was praying. 'These last few days she hasn't once looked at me or spoken a word to me,' thought Raskolnikov suddenly. The room was bright with sunlight, the incense rose in clouds; the priest read the *Requiem æternam*. Raskolnikov stayed to the end. As he blessed them and took his leave, the priest looked round rather strangely. After the service Raskolnikov went up to Sonya. She grasped both his hands and leaned her head on his shoulder for a moment. The brief gesture bewildered Raskolnikov; it seemed strange. What? Not the slightest repugnance, no trace of loathing for him, not the least tremor of her hands? It showed infinite self-humiliation; so, at least, he understood it. Sonya said nothing. Raskolnikov pressed her hand and went out. He felt terribly over-burdened. If it had been possible for him to go away at that moment and be quite alone, even if it were for the rest of his life, he would have counted himself fortunate. The fact was that although recently he had almost always been by himself, he could not feel that he was alone. He had more than once left the town behind, emerging on to a great highway, and on one occasion into a little wood, but the more solitary his surroundings, the more conscious he felt of the close and disturbing presence of something not so much terrifying as troublesome, so that he would return to the town as quickly as possible and mingle with the crowd, entering an eating-house or a tavern or walking in the Haymarket or the Rag Market. Here he felt easier and more alone. In one tavern, towards evening, there was singing, and he sat listening for a whole hour, and afterwards remembered that he had even enjoyed it. But towards the end he suddenly became uneasy again, as though pangs of conscience had begun to torment him: 'Here I sit listening to songs, but surely that is not what I ought to be doing,' he thought. He realized at once, however, that it was not only this that was disturbing him; there was something that demanded an immediate decision, but he could not put it into words or even formulate it in his thoughts. It was all tangled up. 'No, some kind of struggle would be better than this! Better Porfiry . . . or Svidrigaylov! . . . If there were another challenge of some sort, some attack to meet! . . . Yes, yes!' he thought. He came out of the tavern and set off, almost running. A sudden thought of Dunya and his mother for some reason induced something very like panic in him. It was during the night, before dawn, that he woke up among the bushes on Krestovsky Island, shaking all over with fever; he went home, arriving in the early morning. The fever passed after some hours' sleep, but it was late, two o'clock in the afternoon, when he woke up.

He remembered that this was the day of Katerina Ivanovna's funeral, and was glad that he had not been present. Nastasya brought him something to eat, and he ate and drank with a good appetite, indeed almost greedily. His head felt fresher, and he himself was less restless than for the past three days. He even wondered for a moment at his former fits of panic. The door opened, and Razumikhin came in.

'Ah! He can eat, so he's not ill!' said Razumikhin, and he took a chair and sat down at the table opposite Raskolnikov. He was upset and he did not try to hide it. He spoke with evident vexation but without hurrying or raising his voice much. 'Listen,' he began crisply, 'as far as I am concerned you can all go to the devil, but from what I see now, it is clear to me that I don't understand anything at all. Please don't imagine that I've come to cross-question you. I don't care a rap! I don't want to know! If you began to tell me all your secrets of your own accord, I probably shouldn't even listen to you, but simply spit and go away. I only came to find out for myself, once and for all, whether it is true that you are mad. You see, there is a conviction about you (here and there) that you are either mad or very much inclined that way. I admit I was strongly disposed to support that opinion, judging first by your stupid and odious (and quite inexplicable) actions, and secondly by your recent conduct to your mother and sister. Only a monster and a scoundrel, if he were in his right mind, could behave to them as you have done; it follows that you are mad . . .'

'Is it long since you last saw them?'

'No, it was just now. Haven't you seen them since that time? Tell me, where have you been keeping yourself? I've already been here three times. Your mother has been ill since yesterday, seriously. She wanted to come here. Avdotya Romanovna tried to prevent her, but she wouldn't hear a word: "If he's ill," she said, "if his mind is deranged, who should help him, if not his mother?" All three of us came, because we couldn't leave her to come alone. All the way to your door we kept begging her to compose herself. We came in, and you weren't here; she sat down just here. She sat here for ten minutes, while we stood saying nothing. Then she got up and said: "If he is well enough to go out, that means he has forgotten his mother, and it is unseemly and shameful for her to stand at his door and beg for his kindness as if it were charity." She went back home and went to bed, and now she is in a fever. "I see," she says, "that he has time for *his own girl*." She supposes that *your own girl* is Sofya Semënovna, your fiancée or your lover, I don't know which. I went immediately to Sofya Semënovna's because, brother, I wanted to look into the whole business; I got there and looked in— there was a coffin, and children crying. Sofya Semënovna was trying on their mourning. You weren't there. I saw all this, apologized, went away, and told Avdotya Romanovna. So all that was nonsense, you hadn't got *your own girl*, and so the most likely thing was that you *were* mad. But here you are sitting and devouring roast beef as though you hadn't eaten anything for three days. Well, let's suppose that madmen must eat, too, but although you haven't said so much as a word to me ... I'll swear you're not mad! Whatever else, you're not mad. So to the devil with the lot of you, because there's some mystery here, some secret, and I don't propose to rack my brains over your secrets. I only came to relieve my feelings,' he concluded, getting up, 'by a few curses, and I know what I have to do now!'

'What do you want to do now, then?'

'What business is it of yours what I choose to do?'

'Look, you're thinking of taking to drink!'

'How . . . how did you know that?'

'Well, of course you are!'

Razumikhin said nothing for a minute.

'You've always been a person of sound sense and you've never, never, been mad,' he declared suddenly, with some heat. 'It's true; I am going to take to drink. Good-bye!' And he moved as if to go.

'I was talking to my sister about you, Razumikhin, the day before yesterday, I think.'

'About me? But . . . how could you have seen her the day before yesterday?' Razumikhin stopped suddenly and even turned a little pale. It was possible to guess that his heart was beating slowly and heavily.

'She came here alone, and sat and talked to me.'

'She did!'

'Yes.'

'What did you say . . . about me, I mean?'

'I told her you were a very good, honest, and hard-working person. I didn't tell her you love her, because she knows that herself.'

'She knows it?'

'Of course! Whatever happens to me, wherever I go, you will stay and look after them. I entrust them to you, so to speak, Razumikhin. I say this because I know very well how much you love her, and I am sure your heart is pure. I know, too, that she could love you, and perhaps she already does. Now decide for yourself whether it is better for you to start drinking or not.'

'Rodka . . . you see . . . Well . . . Oh, the devil! And where are you thinking of going? You see, if it's all a secret, let it be! But I . . . I shall discover the secret . . . And I'm convinced it's nothing but a lot of nonsense and awful rot, and that you've made it all up. All the same, you're a splendid chap! A splendid chap . . .'

'But I was just going to say to you when you interrupted me, that you were quite right to decide not to try to unravel these secrets and mysteries. Leave it for a time, and don't worry. You shall know everything at the proper time, that is to say, when you need to. Yesterday somebody said to me that a man needs air, air, air! I must go to him at once and find out what he means by that.'

Razumikhin was excitedly considering an idea.

'He's a political conspirator! That's it! And he is on the point of taking a decisive step—that's it! It can't be anything else, and . . . and Dunya knows . . .' he thought.

'So Avdotya Romanovna comes to see you,' he said, weighing his words, 'and you intend to see a man who says more air is needed, air, and . . . and so that letter, too . . . it's part of the same thing,' he ended, as if he were speaking to himself.

'What letter?'

'She received a letter today that upset her very much. Very much. Very much indeed. I began to talk about you, and she asked me to be quiet. Then . . . then she said that perhaps we should very soon part, then she began to thank me very warmly for something, then she went into her room and locked the door.'

'She had a letter?' inquired Raskolnikov thoughtfully.

'Yes, didn't you know? Hm.'

Both were silent for a short time.

'Good-bye, Rodion. I, brother . . . there was a time . . . however, good-bye. You see, there was a time . . . Well, good-bye! I must go, too. I'm not going to drink. I don't need to now . . . Rubbish!'

He hurried off, but, after he had already closed the door behind him, opened it again and said, looking away:

'By the way! Do you remember that murder, you know, that Porfiry was engaged on; that old woman? Well, the murderer has been found; he has confessed and himself produced all the evidence to prove it. Just think, he is one of those workmen, you remember, those painters that I was standing up for here. Would you believe it, he deliberately staged all that scene of scuffling and laughing on the stairs with his mate, while those people were going up, the porter and the two witnesses? It was all a blind! The cunning and presence of mind of the young puppy! It's hard to credit it, but he gave that explanation himself, and he has confessed everything. And a fine fool I made of myself! Well, in my opinion he's an absolute genius of dissimulation and resourcefulness, a genius at misleading the law, so there's nothing specially surprising about it, I suppose. Such people can exist, no doubt. But I find it much easier to believe in him because he couldn't keep it up, but confessed; that makes him more credible . . . But what a fool I made of myself, what a fool! I was furious in their defence!'

'Tell me where you learnt all this, and why it interests you so much,' asked Raskolnikov, in obvious agitation.

'Well, what next? Why does it interest me? Can you ask? . . . I heard of it from Porfiry and others beside. But it was he who told me most of it.'

'Porfiry?'

'Yes, Porfiry.'

'What . . . what did he say?' asked Raskolnikov fearfully.

'He explained it extremely well. Explained it psychologically, in his usual way.'

'Explained it? He explained it to you himself?'

'Yes, yes. Good-bye! I'll tell you more later, but now I have something to do There . . . there was a time when I thought . . . Well, never mind; later! . . . Why should I drink now? You have made me drunk without it. I am drunk, you know, Rodka! I am drunk without wine. Well, good-bye. I will come again, very soon.'

He went out.

'He's a political conspirator, yes, that's certain, certain!' he concluded definitely as he went down the stairs. 'And he's drawn his sister in; that is very, very likely, in view of Avdotya Romanovna's character. They've been seeing each other . . . Come to think of it, she has given me hints, too. From many of her words . . . and allusions . . . and half-hints, it all emerges quite clearly! And how else can all this muddle be explained? Hm! And I almost thought . . . Oh Lord, what an idea I'd almost got into my head! Yes, that was an eclipse of reasoning, and I ought to beg his pardon. It was that time when he was standing near the lamp in the corridor, that he misled me. Pah! What a nasty, crude, vile idea mine was! A splendid fellow, Nikolka, for confessing . . . And how well this explains other, earlier things, too! His illness, all his odd actions, and even before that, while he was still at the university, the way he was always gloomy and morose . . . But what does that letter mean? Perhaps there is something in that, too. Who was the letter from? I suspect . . . Hm. No, I'm going to ferret it all out.'

As he remembered and considered all that had been said about Dunya his heart seemed to stop. He dashed hastily away.

Raskolnikov, as soon as Razumikhin had gone, got up and, as though forgetting how crowded his little room was, began to bump clumsily round it and . . . sat down again on his sofa. He felt refreshed and renewed; here was struggle again—that meant he had found a way out.

Yes, it meant a way out had been found! Until this, everything had been too oppressive and confining, had crushed him with its overwhelming weight, and a sort of stupefaction had descended on him. From the moment of the scene with Mikolka at Porfiry's he had begun to feel suffocated and hemmed in, without escape. After the scene with Mikolka had come that at Sonya's, the same day; he had not conducted it at all as he might have imagined it beforehand and he had brought it to a very different conclusion . . . his strength, that is to say, had been instantly and radically undermined! At one blow! Indeed, he had agreed with Sonya then, he had agreed in his heart that he could not live alone with such a deed on his mind! And Svidrigaylov? Svidrigaylov was a riddle . . . Svidrigaylov disturbed him, that was true, but not from that point of view. There might be a struggle to come with Svidrigaylov also. Svidrigaylov, perhaps, might also offer a way out; but Porfiry was a different matter.

'So Porfiry had explained things to Razumikhin, had explained them *psychologically*! He had begun dragging in his damned psychology again. Porfiry? But how could Porfiry believe, even for a moment, that Mikolka was guilty, after what had passed between them, after that scene between the two of them before Mikolka arrived, which could not possibly be reasonably interpreted save in *one* way?' (During the past few days Raskolnikov had remembered all that scene with Porfiry in snatches; he could not bear to remember it as a whole.) 'During that interview such words had been pronounced, such gestures had been made, such glances had passed between them, things had been said in such a tone of voice, they had arrived at such a point, that it would take more than Mikolka (whom Porfiry had known through and through from the first word and the first question), more than Mikolka to shake the foundations of his convictions.'

'What wonder? Even Razumikhin had almost begun to suspect! The scene in the corridor, near the lamp, had not been without its effect. He had rushed off to Porfiry . . . But what was Porfiry's idea in duping him like that? What was his purpose in diverting Razumikhin's attention to Mikolka? No, he had certainly had some plan, there was some intention here, but what? It was true that a long time had gone by since that morning—much, much too long, and there had not been a word or a sign from Porfiry. Well, of course, that made matters worse...' Raskolnikov took his cap and went out, still lost in thought. For the first time in all these days, he felt at least sound and sane. 'I must settle with Svidrigaylov,' he thought, 'and as quickly as possible, cost what it may; he, too, seems to be waiting for me to go to him myself.' At this moment such hatred welled up in his weary heart that he might easily have killed either Svidrigaylov or Porfiry. He felt, at least, that he was capable of this, if not now, then later. 'We shall see, we shall see,' he repeated to himself.

But no sooner had he opened his inner door than he ran into Porfiry himself, coming to see him. Raskolnikov froze for a moment, but only for a moment. Strangely enough, he was not very surprised to see Porfiry, and hardly felt afraid of him. He was startled, but then quickly, in a flash, he was ready for him. 'Perhaps this is the denouement! But how could he have approached so quietly, like a cat? I didn't hear a sound. Has he been listening at the door?'

'You weren't expecting a visitor, Rodion Romanovich,' cried Porfiry Petrovich, laughing. 'I've been meaning to drop in for a long time. I was passing, so I thought, "why not look in for five minutes?" Were you going somewhere? I won't keep you. Only just one cigarette, if you will allow me . . .'

'Sit down, Porfiry Petrovich, sit down.' Raskolnikov offered his guest a chair with such apparent pleasure and friendliness that he would have been quite amazed if he could have seen himself. This was the final encounter, the last trial of strength. In just such a way, a man may sometimes endure half an hour of deathly fear from a brigand and when at last the knife is laid to his throat, the fear has vanished. He sat down directly in front of Porfiry and looked at him unflinchingly. Porfiry screwed up his eyes and lit his cigarette.

'Well, speak, speak,' seemed almost ready to burst from Raskolnikov's heart. 'Well? Why, why, why, don't you speak?'

## CHAPTER II

'Oh, these cigarettes!' said Porfiry at last, when he had lighted one and drawn a few breaths; 'they're poison, absolute poison, but I can't give them up! I have a cough, my throat is raw, and I have grown short-winded. I'm cowardly, you know, so not long ago I went to B.—he spends a minimum of half an hour examining each patient; he absolutely laughed when he looked at me: he sounded me and listened. "Tobacco", he said, "is not good for you; your lungs are inflamed." But how am I to give it up? What can I put in its place? I don't drink, that's the trouble. He, he, he! Not drinking a trouble! Everything is relative, you know, Rodion Romanovich, everything is relative!'

'What is this? Is he going to play the same old game again?' thought Raskolnikov disgustedly. The whole of their last interview suddenly came back to him, and the same feeling as before swept over him like a flood.

'I have been here before, the day before yesterday, in the evening; did you know?' went on Porfiry Petrovich, looking round the room. 'I came in, right into the room itself. Just the same as today, I was going past and I thought, "Come, I'll return his call!" I came up and found the room open; I looked round—I waited a while. I went away without even telling the servant I had called. Don't you lock your door?'

Raskolnikov's face had been growing more and more lowering. Porfiry seemed to guess his thoughts.

'I came to have it out with you, my dear Rodion Romanovich, to clear things up. I owe you an explanation; I feel obliged to give it you,' he went on with a smile, and he even patted Raskolnikov's knee. But almost in the same moment his face took on a serious and troubled look; a veil of melancholy seemed to be drawn over it, to Raskolnikov's surprise. He had never seen him look so before, and had not suspected that he could do so. 'It was a strange scene that took place between us at our last meeting, Rodion Romanovich. Perhaps, indeed, it was a strange scene that we played at our first meeting, too, but at that time ... Well, my life now is just one damned thing after another! This is the point: it turns out that perhaps I owe you an apology; I feel that I may. Do you remember how we parted?—your nerves were on edge and your knees were shaking; my nerves were on edge and my knees were shaking. And you know, we treated each other in a way that might be thought neither seemly nor gentlemanly. And we are, after all, gentlemen; that is, we are gentlemen first of all, in any case; that must be understood. You remember, things got to such a point ... that it was quite indecent.'

'Why is he saying this? What does he take me for?' Raskolnikov asked himself bewilderedly, raising his head and gazing hard at Porfiry.

'I have come to the conclusion that it is best for us to be plain with one another,' went on Porfiry Petrovich, turning his head slightly and lowering his eyes, as if he did not wish his glance further to embarrass his former victim, and as if he now scorned to use his earlier tricks and stratagems. 'Yes, sir, such suspicions and such scenes cannot continue for long. Mikolka has solved our problem now, otherwise I don't know to what lengths we might have gone. That damned little tradesman was sitting there behind my partition that time—can you imagine that? You, of course, already know that; and indeed I am aware that he came to see you afterwards; but what you supposed then was not true, I had not sent for anybody, and I had not made any arrangements whatever. You will ask why not. How shall I put it? I was absolutely stunned. I had hardly taken steps even to send for the porters. (No doubt you saw them as you went past.) The idea came to me suddenly, in a flash; I was very strongly convinced of it, you see, Rodion Romanovich. Let me not, I thought—for although I may let one thing slip for a time, yet I seize another firmly by the tail—let me at least not allow my man to get away from me. You are very irritable and touchy, Rodion Romanovich, by nature; too much so, considering all the other fundamental traits of your character and heart, which I fondly hope I have understood to some extent. Well, of course, even then my judgement told me that it doesn't always happen that a man will simply get up and blurt out all the details for you. It does happen, especially when you keep on gnawing away at the last shreds of his patience, but only very rarely. Even I could see that it wasn't likely. No, I thought, I must have some small thing for a foundation. Even if it were only the tiniest detail, and only one, but one that you could take in your hands, a concrete thing, not just a piece of psychology. Because, I thought, if a man is guilty, of course it must be at any rate possible to get something actual and definite out of him and one may sometimes expect the most surprising results. I was relying on your character, Rodion Romanovich, on your character above all! I had great hopes of you then.'

'But you . . . but why do you keep talking like that now?' muttered Raskolnikov at last, not fully understanding what all this was about. 'What is he talking about?' he wondered distractedly. 'Does he really suppose I am innocent?'

'Why do I talk like that? I came to clear the matter up, so to speak. I consider it my bounden duty. I want to lay bare the whole thing down to the foundations, about what happened, the whole story of that, so to speak, darkening of counsel. I made you go through a great deal, Rodion Romanovich. I'm not a monster. I can understand what it must be for a man like you to have brought all this on himself—a man oppressed with cares, but proud, imperious, and, in particular, impatient of wrong! In any case I look on you as a most honourable man and one, indeed, with elements of greatness in you, although I do not agree with all your opinions. I consider it my duty to warn you of this, sincerely and straightforwardly, because above all I have no wish to deceive you. I have felt attached to you since I first knew you. Perhaps you will laugh at such words, coming from me. That is your privilege. I know that you disliked me at sight, because, indeed, there is nothing to like me for. But think what you please, I for my part am anxious to efface your first impression of me by every means in my power, and to show you that I am a man with a heart and a conscience. I speak in all sincerity.'

Porfiry Petrovich waited for a moment in dignified silence. Raskolnikov felt a new wave of terror sweep over him. The idea that Porfiry might consider him innocent suddenly began to frighten him.

'I hardly need tell you in full detail how this all came about,' went on Porfiry Petrovich; 'I think it would be quite unnecessary. And indeed I doubt whether I could. Because how can it be explained circumstantially? First of all there were rumours. What sort of rumours they were, from whom they came, and when . . . and in what connexion your name was brought into the matter . . . I think need not be considered either. As far as I personally am concerned, it all began by chance, by the most casual accident, which might just as easily not have happened at all. What was it? Hm, I don't think I need speak of that either. All this, the rumours and the accident, combined to give me a certain idea. I confess openly, because, if you are confessing anything at all, it had better be everything—that it was I who was the first to light on you. Those jottings of the old woman's on the pledges, and so on and so forth—we may take it didn't amount to anything. You can always count such pieces of evidence in hundreds. I also chanced to learn of the scene in the police office, not just casually mentioned, but discussed in all its details by an excellent witness, who had, without realizing it himself, absorbed the scene with remarkable completeness. You know it was all just one thing added to another, my dear Rodion Romanovich, one thing after another. Well, how could I help turning my mind in a certain direction? Out of a hundred rabbits you'll never make a horse, and a hundred suspicions will never make a proof, as an English proverb says, but that is mere common sense, and we have to try to deal with the passions as well, the passions, because even an examining magistrate is a man. Then, too, I remembered your article in that magazine—you remember, we talked about it at some length on your first visit to me. I scoffed at it then, but that was only to lead you on. I repeat that you are very impatient and far from well, Rodion Romanovich. That you are daring, proud, in earnest, and ... have felt, have felt a great deal, I have long known. I am acquainted with all these feelings, and I read your article with a sense of familiarity. It was conceived in sleepless nights and in a state of ecstasy, with a lifting and thumping of the heart, with repressed enthusiasm. But that proud, repressed enthusiasm of youth is dangerous! I mocked at you then, but now I tell you that I have an amateur's passion for such fiery, young, first literary efforts. Mist, haze, and a chord vibrating through the mist.[2] Your article is absurd and fantastic, but it has flashes of real sincerity, a youthful and incorruptible pride, and the courage of despair; it is gloomy, that article, but that is a good point. I read it at the time and laid it aside and ... as I laid it aside, I thought, "Well, things will not go smoothly for that man." Well, tell me, after such a beginning how could I help being carried away by the sequel? Oh Lord, have I said something? I am not making any allegations now! It is simply what struck me at the time. "What is there here?" I thought. There was nothing, that is, nothing positive, and perhaps absolutely nothing. And to let myself, an examining magistrate, be carried away in that fashion is most unseemly: there I've got Mikolka on my hands, and with facts against him—think what you like of them, but they are facts! And his psychology has been brought into it too; we must devote some attention to him; because this is a matter of life and death. Why am I telling you all this now? So that you may know, and, your mind and heart

2. An inexact quotation from Nikolai Gogol's story "Diary of a Madman."

being what they are, not accuse me of behaving maliciously that time. It was not malicious, I say in all sincerity, he, he! Do you think, I wonder, that I didn't come here at that time to conduct a search? I did, I did, he, he, I was here, when you were lying ill in bed. Not officially, and not in my own person, but I was here. Your room was searched down to the smallest thing, at the first breath of suspicion, but—*umsonst!*[3] I thought, "now this man will come to me, he will come to me of his own accord, and very soon; if he is guilty, he will certainly come. Another might not come, but he will." Do you remember how Mr. Razumikhin began to let things slip out? We had arranged that, to get you agitated; so we deliberately spread rumours, in order that Mr. Razumikhin should blab about them to you, and Mr. Razumikhin is a man who cannot restrain his indignation. Mr. Zametov found your anger and your open daring particularly striking: well, how could anyone blurt out in a tavern, "I killed her!" It was too daring, too audacious, and I thought, "If he is guilty, he's a bonny fighter!" That is what I thought then. I waited for you to come! I waited with the greatest impatience, but you simply crushed Zametov that time, and . . . you know, the point is that all this damned psychology cuts both ways! Well, so I was waiting for you, and I looked out, and my wish was granted—you were coming! My heart absolutely thumped! Ah! Now, what made you come just then? Your laughter, that laughter of yours as you came in, do you remember?—why, I guessed everything then, I saw it all quite plainly, but if I hadn't been waiting for you so specially, I shouldn't have noticed anything in your laughter. That is what it means to be in the right frame of mind! And Mr. Razumikhin—oh! that stone, you remember, that stone, the one the things were hidden under? Why, I can almost see it, in a kitchen-garden somewhere—you did say a kitchen-garden to Zametov, and afterwards, for the second time, in my room? And when we began to examine your article, and you expounded your meaning—every one of your words could be taken in two senses, as if there were another word hidden beneath it! Well, that, Rodion Romanovich, is how I came to run up against a blank wall, and only realized it when I bumped my head on it. "No," I said, "what am I doing? Why," I said, "all of this, down to the smallest detail, can be explained if you wish in an entirely different way, and it would sound even more natural." I had to admit to myself that it would indeed be more natural. It was agony! "No," I thought, "it would be better if I could find just one small fact." And when I heard about those door-bells my heart stood still and a positive shudder ran through me. "Well," I thought, "there's my little fact all right! That's it!" I didn't even stop to consider it, I simply would not. I would have given a thousand roubles at that

3. "In vain!"

moment, of my own money, to have seen you *with my own eyes*, when you walked a hundred yards side by side with that workman, after he had called you murderer to your face, without daring to ask him a single question all the way! . . . Yes, and what about the cold shudder down your spine? And that ringing of door-bells when you were ill and half delirious? So, Rodion Romanovich, how can you wonder, after all that, that I played a few tricks with you? And you, what made you come at just that moment? I'll swear something prompted you, and if Mikolka had not sent us off on a different track . . . do you remember Mikolka just then? Do you remember him well? That was a thunder-clap, if you like! It was a peal of thunder crashing from a cloud, a thunderbolt! Well, and how did I meet it? I didn't believe in the thunderbolt in the least, you could see that yourself! Why should I? Even later, after you had gone, when he began giving me answers that chimed so well with the facts that I was quite surprised, even then I didn't believe a word he said! I was what is called as firm as a rock. "No," thought I, "this is all my eye! What has Mikolka to do with this?"'

'Razumikhin said just now that you believe Nikolay is guilty and that you told him so yourself . . .'

His breath failed and he could not finish. He had listened with indescribable agitation while this man, who had seen right through him, repudiated his own judgement. He dared not, he could not, believe it. Eagerly he had scrutinized the still ambiguous words to find something more precise and definite.

'Oh, Mr. Razumikhin!' cried Porfiry Petrovich, as if he were delighted to have drawn a question from the obstinately silent Raskolnikov. 'He, he, he! Well, Mr. Razumikhin had to be got away somehow: two is company, three is none. Mr. Razumikhin, as an outsider, should not have come running to me all pale . . . Well, never mind him; why bring him into this? As for Mikolka, would you care to know what sort of person he is, as I understand him, I mean? First of all, he is still a lad, not grown up yet, and he is confessing now not because he is scared but because he believes his own inventions, since in his own way he's an artist. Really, don't laugh at my explaining him like that. He is innocent, impressionable, and emotional, and his imagination runs away with him. He can sing and dance and he tells stories so well that, they say, people come from miles round to hear him. He has been to school, too, and he is ready to die of laughing over nothing at all, and every now and then he drinks himself under the table, not really for the sake of getting drunk so much as because somebody plies him with drink—like a child again. And when he stole the jewel-case that time he didn't know it was stealing, because "if I pick it up from the ground, why is that stealing?" And did you know he was a schismatic, and not only that, but one of those simple-minded religious zealots? Some members of his family have belonged to the sects that run away to settle out of the reach of all authority, and it is not long since he himself spent two years under the obedience of some elder in his village. I learnt all this from Mikolka himself and his friends from Zaraysk. And what's more, he was once all for becoming a hermit himself! He was a regular zealot, used to get up in the night to pray, and read himself silly with old books, what they consider the "genuine" ones. St. Petersburg had a very powerful effect on him, especially the female sex—and the vodka, too. He is impressionable, and he forgot the village elder and everything else. I have been told that a painter here got quite attached to him and Mikolka used to go and see him sometimes, and then this affair came along! Well, he felt afraid, he tried to hang himself! He tried to run away! What can be done about the way the common people think of our justice? Some of them find the mere word "trial" terrifying. Whose fault is that? The new courts may make some difference. God grant they may! Well, apparently he has remembered the good elder now that he is in prison; the bible has made its appearance again, too. Do you, Rodion Romanovich, know what some of these people mean by "suffering"? It is not suffering for somebody's sake, but simply "suffering is necessary"—the acceptance of suffering, that means, and if it is at the hands of the authorities, so much the better. In my time there was a most submissive convict in the prison, who for a whole year lay on the stove at night reading his bible, and read and read until he was in such a state, you know, that suddenly, without rhyme or reason, he grabbed a brick and threw it at the governor without the slightest provocation. And how he threw it, too! He deliberately pitched it a yard wide, so that it shouldn't injure him. Well, everybody knows what happens to a prisoner who attacks a prison officer with a weapon; and so "he accepted his suffering". Well, this is the point: I suspect now that Mikolka desires to "accept suffering", or something of the sort. I have good grounds, supported by the facts, for believing this. But he doesn't know that I know it. What, can't you admit that such fantastic creatures are to be found among people of his kind? They often crop up. The elder's influence has begun to work again, especially since Mikolka thought of hanging himself. However, he will come to me of his own accord and tell me everything. You think he will hold out? Just wait, he'll recant yet! I am expecting him at any moment to come to me to take back his statements. I have taken a fancy to Mikolka and I am investigating him thoroughly. And what do you suppose? He, he! On some points he gave me very apt answers, and had evidently got hold of the necessary information and prepared his answers cunningly; but on other points he is simply at sea, and doesn't know the least thing about them; he doesn't know, and he doesn't even suspect that he doesn't know. No, Rodion Romanovich, my dear chap, Mikolka isn't in this at all! This is an obscure and fantastic case, a contemporary case, something that could only happen in our day, when the heart of man has grown troubled, when people quote sayings about blood "refreshing", when the whole of life is dedicated to comfort. There are bookish dreams here, and a heart troubled by theories; there is resolution evident here, for the first step, but resolution of a special kind—a resolve like that of a man falling from a precipice or flinging himself off a tower; this is the work of a man carried along into crime, as it were, by some outside force. He forgot to shut the door behind him, but he murdered, and murdered two people, for a theory. He murdered, but he was not so successful when it came to taking the money, and what he did manage to snatch up he carried away and hid under a stone. The torment he suffered when he crouched behind the door and heard them battering at it and ringing the bell, was not enough for him; no, he must go back to the empty flat, half-delirious, to revive his memory of the bell; he felt compelled to experience once more that cold shiver down the spine . . . Well, grant that he was ill then, all the same there is this: he committed murder, yet he thinks of himself as an honourable man, despises other people and goes about like a martyred angel—no, what has Mikolka to do with all this, my dear Rodion Romanovich? There's no Mikolka in it!'

These last words, after all that had been said before, which had seemed like a recantation, were too unexpected a blow. Raskolnikov shuddered as though he had been stabbed.

'Then . . . who . . . was the murderer?' he could not help asking in a stifled voice. Porfiry Petrovich almost recoiled, as though startled by so unexpected a question.

'Who was the murderer?' he repeated, as though he could not believe his own ears. 'But it was *you*, Rodion Romanovich! You murdered them!' he went on, almost in a whisper, but his voice was full of conviction.

Raskolnikov sprang up from the sofa, stood still for a few seconds, and sat down again without a word. His whole face twitched convulsively.

'Your lip is trembling again, as it always does,' murmured Porfiry Petrovich almost sympathetically. 'I don't think you quite understand me, Rodion Romanovich,' he added after a short pause; 'that is why you are so thunderstruck. I came on purpose to tell you everything, and bring everything out into the open.'

'It was not I who murdered her,' whispered Raskolnikov, like a frightened small child caught red-handed in some misdeed.

'Yes, it was you, Rodion Romanovich, you and nobody else,' whispered Porfiry, with stern conviction.

They were both silent, and the silence lasted for an unbelievably long time, almost ten minutes. Raskolnikov leaned his elbows on the table and ran his fingers through his hair, without speaking. Porfiry Petrovich sat quietly and waited. Suddenly Raskolnikov threw a scornful glance at Porfiry.

'You are up to your old tricks again, Porfiry Petrovich! The same old methods! Really, don't you ever get tired of them?'

'Oh, stop that! What are methods to me now? It would be a different matter if there were witnesses here; but after all, here we are alone, quietly talking to nobody but each other. You can see for yourself that I didn't come here to start you and catch you like a hare. Confess, or don't confess—it's all the same to me now. I am convinced in my own mind, without that.'

'Then why did you come?' asked Raskolnikov irritably. 'I will ask you my earlier question again: if you think I am guilty, why don't you take me to prison?'

'Well, so that is your question! I will answer you in due order: to begin with, it would be of no advantage to me to arrest you straight away.'

'Why not? If you are convinced, you ought . . .'

'Oh, who says I am convinced? For the time being all this is just my dream. Besides, why should I put you there *in peace*? You know yourself, since you are asking me to do it. For example, if I bring that tradesman to give evidence against you, you will say to him, "Were you drunk or weren't you? Who saw me with you? I simply took it for granted you were drunk, and so you were"—and what can I say to you then, especially as your story is much more plausible than his, which is purely a matter of psychology—something that doesn't go well with that mug of his? Besides, you would hit the mark, because the scoundrel is very well known to be a heavy drinker. Moreover, I have admitted to you several times already that psychology is a double-edged weapon, and its second edge is heavier and much sharper, and that except for it I have nothing against you—yet. And although I mean to arrest you all the same, and (contrary to the usual custom) have come myself to explain everything to you beforehand, yet I tell you straight (and this is also contrary to custom) that it won't be any advantage to me. Well, I came here, in the second place . . .'

'Yes, well, in the second place?' (Raskolnikov was still panting).

'Because, as I told you just now, I consider that I owe you an explanation. I don't want you to think of me as a monster, especially since I am genuinely well disposed towards you, believe it or not. Consequently, I have come here, in the third place, with a direct and open invitation to you to come forward with a confession. It will be infinitely better for you, and it will be better for me too—because it will be a weight off my mind. Well, tell me, have I been open with you or not?'

Raskolnikov thought for a minute.

'Listen, Porfiry Petrovich; after all, you said yourself it was only psychology, but now you have gone over to mathematics. Well, what if you are mistaken yourself?'

'No, Rodion Romanovich, I am not mistaken. I have my scrap of proof. I had found it even then; God sent it to me!'

'What proof?'

'I shall not tell you, Rodion Romanovich. But in any case I have no right to delay any longer; I shall arrest you. So use your judgement: it is all the same to me *now*, consequently I am acting solely for your sake. I swear it will be better for you, Rodion Romanovich!'

Raskolnikov's smile was bitter.

'This is not only amusing, it is positively impudent. Why, even if I were guilty (which I don't allow for one moment), why should I come to you with a voluntary confession when you tell me yourself that I shall be *safer* in prison?'

'Oh, Rodion Romanovich, don't put too much trust in what I say; perhaps you won't be absolutely *safe*! After all, it's only a theory, and one of mine besides, and what sort of authority am I for you? Perhaps I am hiding something from you even now. I can't simply come along and reveal everything to you, he, he! Another thing: why should you ask what advantage it will be to you? Surely you know that a reduction of your sentence would follow from it? When would you be coming forward, after all, at what moment? Just think it over! When another has taken the crime on himself and muddled everything up! And I, I give you my solemn word, will so falsify and arrange matters *there* that your appearance shall seem utterly unexpected. We'll do away with all this psychology completely, and I will consign all my suspicions of you to oblivion, so that your crime will seem to have resulted from a clouding of your faculties, as indeed, in all conscience, it did. I am a man of honour, Rodion Romanovich, and I will keep my word.'

Raskolnikov preserved a melancholy silence; he hung his head and remained thoughtful for a long time; finally, he smiled again, but this time his smile was meek and sad.

'Oh, don't!' he said, as if he no longer could conceal anything at all from Porfiry. 'It's not worth while! I don't want your reduction of sentence!'

'Now, that's just what I was afraid of!' exclaimed Porfiry, warmly and almost involuntarily. 'I was afraid of just that, that you would have no use for it.'

Raskolnikov looked at him with a sad and expressive gaze.

'No, don't let yourself loathe life,' went on Porfiry; 'you have a lot before you still. How can you not want a reduction, how can you? You are too impatient!'

'I have a lot of what before me?'

'Of life! How can you prophesy? How much do you know? Seek and ye shall find. Perhaps it is through this that God seeks to bring you to Himself. And the bonds are not eternal . . .'

'The sentence will be reduced . . .' laughed Raskolnikov.

'And you are not afraid of bourgeois scandal, are you? Perhaps, though, you have been afraid of it, but you didn't know it yourself. All the same, you are not a person who should be afraid of such things, or ashamed of volunteering a confession.'

'O-oh, damn all that!' whispered Raskolnikov, with scorn and repulsion, as though reluctant to speak at all. He began to get up, as if he meant to go somewhere, but sank back in evident despair.

'By all means! You have lost faith and you think I am flattering you grossly; but have you lived much yet? Do you understand much? You invented a theory, and you were ashamed because it went wrong and because it turned out to be not even very original! It proved mean and base, it is true, but that does not make you hopelessly mean and base. You are not mean and base at all! At least, you did not deceive yourself for long, but in one leap reached the farthest extremity. Do you know how I regard you? As one of those who would allow themselves to be disembowelled, and stand and face their torturers with a smile—if they had found a faith, or found God. Well, find your faith, and you will live. To begin with, you have needed a change of air for a long time. Perhaps, also, suffering is a good thing. Suffer, then. Perhaps Mikolka is right to desire suffering. I know that you don't believe this—but don't philosophize too subtly; plunge straight into life, without deliberation; don't be uneasy—it will carry you direct to the shore and set you on your feet. What shore? How should I know? I simply believe that there is still much life before you. I know that now you regard my words as a sermon learnt by heart, but perhaps later you will remember them at some time and they will stand you in good stead; that is why I am talking. It's a good thing that you only killed an old woman. If you had invented a different theory you might perhaps have done something a hundred million times as monstrous! Perhaps you ought to thank God; how do you know that He is not sparing you just for that? Keep your heart high and don't be so fearful! Do you flinch from the great fulfilment that confronts you? No, that would be shameful. As you took such a terrible step, now you must take courage. That is justice. Do what justice demands. I know you do not believe me, but it is the sacred truth that life will sustain you. Afterwards you will regain your self-esteem. Now you need only air, air, air!'

Raskolnikov started.

'Who are you?' he cried. 'What sort of prophet are you? From what heights of lofty calm do you utter these all-wise exhortations?'

'Who am I? I am a man who has developed as far as he is capable, that is all. A man, perhaps, of feeling and sympathy, of some knowledge perhaps, but no longer capable of further development. But you—that's another matter: the life God destines you for lies before you (but who knows, perhaps with you, too, it will pass away like a puff of smoke and nothing will come of it). Well, what of it, if you are to pass into a different category of men? With your heart, you will not pine for comfort! What will it matter if nobody sees you perhaps for a very long time? It is not time that matters, but you yourself. Become a sun, and everybody will see you. The first duty of the sun is to be the sun. What are you smiling at again—because I am talking like Schiller? And I am willing to bet that you suppose I am trying now to cajole you by flattery. Well, perhaps that is just what I am doing, he, he, he! Perhaps, Rodion Romanovich, you ought not to believe what I say, perhaps you should never believe me completely—I agree that my ways make it undesirable; but I will add only this—I think you ought to be able to judge how far I am a trickster and how far an honest man!'

'When do you think of arresting me?'

'I can leave you at liberty for a day or two longer. Think it over, my dear chap, and pray. Honestly, it will be to your advantage.'

'What if I run away?' asked Raskolnikov, with a strange smile.

'You won't run away. A peasant would run away, or a modern dissenter—the lackey of another's ideas, because you need only show him the end of your finger and, like Mr. Midshipman Easy, he will believe anything you like for the rest of his life. But you, after all, no longer believe even your own theory, why should you run away? What would you do in hiding? The fugitive's life is hard and hateful, and your first need is for a definite position and existence, and a suitable atmosphere, and what sort of atmosphere would you have? If you ran away, you would come back of yourself. *You can't get on without us.* But if I put you under lock and key—you'll stay there a month, perhaps two, perhaps three, and then, suddenly, you will remember what I say, you will volunteer a confession, perhaps quite unexpectedly even to yourself. An hour beforehand you will not know that you are going to come forward with a confession. You see I am convinced that you will "resolve to accept your suffering"; you don't believe my word now, but you will come to the same conclusion yourself. Because suffering, Rodion Romanovich, is a great thing; don't look at the fact that I am fat myself, that doesn't matter; I still know, and don't laugh at this, that there is an idea in suffering. Mikolka is right. No, you won't run away, Rodion Romanovich.'

Raskolnikov got up and took his cap. Porfiry Petrovich rose as well.

'Are you thinking of going for a walk? It will be a nice evening, if there isn't a storm. However, that might be better if it made it cooler . . .'

He also took up his cap.

'Please don't take it into your head, Porfiry Petrovich,' said Raskolnikov, with grim insistence, 'that I have confessed to-day. You are a strange man, and I have listened to you out of curiosity. But I haven't confessed anything . . . Remember that.'

'Oh, I know that, and I'll remember it. Look, I declare he's trembling. Don't worry, my dear fellow; you shall have it your own way. Go for a little walk; only you mustn't go too far. In case of need, I have one little request to make of you,' he added, lowering his voice; 'it is rather a delicate one, but it is important; if, I mean, if anything happened (not that I think it will and I consider you quite incapable of it), if, by any chance—well, just in case—you should feel a desire during the next forty or fifty hours to put an end to the matter differently, in some fantastic way—by raising your hand against yourself (a ridiculous supposition, you must please forgive me for it), then—leave a short circumstantial note. Just a couple of lines, two little lines—and mention the stone; it would be very generous of you. Well, good-bye . . . Pleasant thoughts and happy new beginnings!'

Porfiry stooped as he went out and seemed to avoid looking at Raskolnikov. Raskolnikov went to the window and waited, burning with impatience, until he judged Porfiry would have left the house and gone some little distance. Then he himself hurriedly left the room.

## CHAPTER III

HE hurried to Svidrigaylov's. What he hoped for from him he did not know himself. But some power over him lay hidden in the man. Once he had recognized this, he could not be easy; besides, the time had come.

One question particularly troubled him as he went: had Svidrigaylov been to see Porfiry? As far as he could judge, he was prepared to swear he had not. He thought it over again and again, remembered every detail of Porfiry's visit, and decided: no, he hadn't, of course he hadn't!

But if he had not been yet, would he go, or not?

He was inclined to think, for the moment, that he would not go. Why? He could not have explained, but even if he could, he would not have troubled his head much with it just now. All this worried him, yet at the same time he could not be bothered with it. It was a strange thing, and perhaps nobody would have believed it, but he felt only feeble, almost absent-minded, concern for the fate that now seemed imminent. Something different and much more important, something extraordinary—which concerned himself, certainly, and no other person, but differently and more vitally—tormented him now. He felt, besides, an infinite moral weariness, although his reason was functioning better this morning than it had done for many days past.

Was it indeed worth while, after all that had happened, to struggle to overcome all these trifling new difficulties? Was it worth while, for example, to try to devise a way of preventing Svidrigaylov from going to see Porfiry, to waste time studying and investigating a Svidrigaylov?

Oh, how tired he was of it all!

Meanwhile he was still hurrying to see Svidrigaylov; could it mean that he expected something *new* from him, some information, some way of escape? A drowning man clutches at a straw! Could destiny, or some instinct, be bringing them together? Perhaps it was only weariness and despair; perhaps he needed not Svidrigaylov but somebody else, and Svidrigaylov had merely happened to turn up. Sonya? But what should take him to Sonya now? Should he plead for her tears again? But the thought of Sonya was terrible to him now. She represented an irrevocable sentence, an unchangeable resolution. He must choose between her way and his own. Especially at this moment he was in no condition to see her. No, would it not be better to try Svidrigaylov, and find out what he meant? And he could not help acknowledging to himself that for a long time he really had felt a kind of need of Svidrigaylov for some reason.

What, though, could they have in common? Even their wrongdoing could not be of the same degree. Moreover, the man was obviously a very unpleasant character, extraordinarily corrupt and depraved, undoubtedly cunning, deceitful, and perhaps malicious. Many tales were current about him. It was true that he was actively concerning himself with Katerina Ivanovna's children, but who could say what that meant or what his motives were? He was a man of endless schemes and designs.

Another thought kept running through Raskolnikov's head now, and he found it terribly disturbing and made efforts to drive it away from him, so painful was it. The train of thought ran thus: Svidrigaylov had persistently put himself in his way, and was still doing so; Svidrigaylov had learnt his secret; Svidrigaylov had had designs upon Dunya. What if he still had? One might say almost with certainty that he had. And what if now, having learnt Raskolnikov's secret and thus got him into his power, he wished to use it as a weapon against Dunya?

This idea had sometimes tortured him even in his dreams, but now, as he walked to Svidrigaylov's, was the first time it had been present to his conscious mind with such clarity. The mere idea filled him with black rage. To begin with, it would change everything, even in his own situation; he would have to reveal his secret at once to Dunechka. Perhaps he would have to give himself up, to save Dunechka from taking some incautious step. That letter! Dunya had received some letter this morning, and who in St. Petersburg could be sending her letters? (Luzhin, perhaps?) True, Razumikhin was on his guard; but Razumikhin did not know anything. Would he perhaps have to disclose everything to Razumikhin, too? The thought was repugnant to Raskolnikov.

In any case, he must see Svidrigaylov as soon as possible, he decided at last. Thank goodness, what he needed to deal with here was not so much details as the gist of the matter; but if, if he was indeed capable, if Svidrigaylov was plotting something against Dunya,—then . . .

All this time, throughout the whole month, Raskolnikov had been so weary that now he could resolve a problem like this in only one way: 'Then I shall kill him,' he thought, with cold despair. A feeling of oppression weighed down his heart; he stopped in the middle of the street and looked round: where was he, and which way had he come? He found himself on the Obukhovsky Prospect, thirty or forty yards from the Haymarket, which he had just crossed. The whole first floor of the building on his left was occupied by a tavern. All the windows were wide open, and the place, judging by the movement of the figures in the windows, was crowded with people. From inside the room came the sound of singing, the thin notes of clarinet and fiddle, the rattle of a Turkish drum. He could hear women's voices squealing. He was about to go back, at a loss to understand why he had turned into Obukhovsky Prospect, when through one of the further windows he suddenly caught sight of Svidrigaylov himself, sitting at a tea-table in the window, with a pipe in his mouth. This produced a strange, almost terrifying impression on him. Svidrigaylov was watching him closely, without speaking, and—another thing which struck Raskolnikov forcibly—seemed about to get up so as to steal away before he was seen. Raskolnikov at once tried to look as though he had not seen him and were looking thoughtfully at something else, but continued to watch him out of the corner of his eye. His heart was hammering with alarm. He was right; Svidrigaylov was plainly very anxious not to be seen. He had taken the pipe out of his mouth and was trying to get out of sight, but apparently, having risen and moved away his chair, he suddenly realized that Raskolnikov had seen him and was watching him. Something passed between them that resembled the moment of their first meeting, at Raskolnikov's, when he had been dreaming. A mischievous smile appeared on Svidrigaylov's face, growing steadily broader. They both knew that each was watching the other. At last Svidrigaylov broke into loud laughter.

'Well, well! Come in, if you like. I am here!' he called through the window.

Raskolnikov went up into the restaurant.

He found him in a very small room, with one window, adjoining the larger room where shopkeepers, clerks, and people of that sort were drinking tea at a score of small tables, to the screeching of choruses by a wretched group of singers. The click of billiard balls could be heard from somewhere. On the table in front of Svidrigaylov stood an open bottle of champagne and a half-full glass. There was a boy in the room also, who held a little barrel-organ in his hands, and a healthy red-cheeked girl of eighteen, with her striped skirt tucked up and a beribboned Tyrolean hat on her head. Paying no attention to the choruses in the next room, she was singing a popular song in a rather hoarse contralto, to the accompaniment of the organ . . .

'Well, that's enough!' Svidrigaylov interrupted her as Raskolnikov entered.

The girl immediately broke off and stood waiting respectfully. The same expression of serious respect had been on her face as she sang her servants'-hall rhymes.

'A glass, Philip!' shouted Svidrigaylov.

'I won't have any wine,' said Raskolnikov.

'As you please. This wasn't for you. Drink, Katya! You won't be wanted any more today; be off with you!' He poured her a full glass of the wine and put down a yellow note. Katya tossed off the wine as women do, swallowing twenty times without pausing for breath. Then she picked up the note, kissed Svidrigaylov's hand, which he solemnly gave her for the purpose, and went out of the room, taking the boy with his organ in her wake. They had been brought in from the street. Svidrigaylov had not been a week in St. Petersburg, and already everything round him was established on a patriarchal footing. The waiter, Philip, was already an 'old friend' and cringed obsequiously. The door to the other room could be locked; Svidrigaylov seemed quite at home in the little room and spent, perhaps, whole days in it. The tavern was dirty and greasy, and not even fifth-rate.

'I was going to your place to look for you,' began Raskolnikov, 'but why did I suddenly turn into the Obukhovsky Prospect just now from the Haymarket? I never come this way. I always turn right from the Haymarket. And this is not the way to your place. But I turned along here, and here you are! Strange!'

'Why don't you say straight out it's a miracle?'

'Because it may be only coincidence.'

'Oh, all you people are the same!' laughed Svidrigaylov. 'Even if you believe a miracle has occurred, you won't admit it. After all, you say yourself that it only "may be" a coincidence. And you can't imagine, Rodion Romanovich, how afraid everybody here is of having his own opinions. I am not talking about you. You have your own opinion, and you have shown you were not afraid to hold it. That is what made me curious about you.'

'Nothing else?'

'Surely that is enough.'

Svidrigaylov was obviously exalted, but only very slightly; he had drunk only half a glass of wine.

'I think you came to see me before you discovered that I was capable of possessing what you call my own opinion,' remarked Raskolnikov.

'Oh, that was different. Everyone has his own affairs. Talking of miracles, I must tell you that you seem to have been asleep this last two or three days. I told you the name of this tavern myself, and there is nothing miraculous in your having come straight here; I explained how to get here and told you where it was and the times when you could find me here. Don't you remember?'

'I had forgotten,' answered Raskolnikov, astonished.

'I can well believe it. I told you twice. The address registered itself in your memory automatically; you turned down here automatically and unconsciously came the right way to this address. Even while I was speaking to you then, I didn't think you were taking it in. You are very transparent, Rodion Romanovich. And another thing: I am sure lots of people in St. Petersburg talk to themselves as they walk about. It's a town of half-crazy people. If we had any science in this country, the doctors, lawyers, and philosophers could conduct very valuable researches in St. Petersburg, each in his own special sphere. There are few places which exercise such strange, harsh, and sombre influences on the human spirit as St. Petersburg. What can be accomplished by climate alone! Besides, this is the administrative centre of all Russia and that character must be reflected in everything. That, however, is not the point now, but this is: I have several times observed you from a distance. You come out of the house with your head held high. After twenty paces it is beginning to droop and your hands are folded behind your back. Your eyes are open, but obviously you see nothing of what is in front of you or all round. At last your lips begin to move and you talk to yourself, sometimes unclasping your hands and flourishing them in the air, and then finally you stand still for quite a time in the middle of the road. This is very bad. Perhaps somebody else notices you, besides me, and it won't do you any good. It's really all one to me, and I don't want to cure you, but you, of course, understand me.'

'Do you know that I am being followed?' asked Raskolnikov, looking searchingly at him.

'No, I don't know anything about it,' answered Svidrigaylov, with apparent surprise.

'Well, let us leave me alone,' frowningly muttered Raskolnikov.

'Very well, we will leave you alone.'

'Tell me, rather, if you come here to drink, and twice told me to come to you here, why, when I looked through the window from the street just now, you tried to hide yourself and to get away. I saw you very clearly.'

'He, he! Why, when I was standing on your threshold, did you lie on your sofa with your eyes closed and pretend you were asleep, when you weren't asleep at all? I saw you very clearly.'

'I might have had...my reasons...you know that yourself.'

'I might have my reasons, too, although you don't know them.'

Raskolnikov leaned his right elbow on the table, rested his chin on the fingers of his right hand, and fixed his unwavering gaze on Svidrigaylov. For about a minute he studied his face, which he had always wondered at. It was a rather strange face, almost like a mask: red and white, with a very light-coloured beard and still quite abundant fair hair. The eyes seemed somehow too blue, and their gaze too massive and unmoving. There was something terribly unpleasant in the handsome face, so extraordinarily young for its years. Svidrigaylov's light summer clothes were foppishly elegant, and his linen particularly so. There was a large ring, set with a valuable stone, on his finger.

'Must I really still trouble about you as well?' said Raskolnikov, coming with feverish impatience direct to the point. 'Although you could perhaps be a most dangerous person if you chose to do me harm, I won't let myself be racked any more. I will show you that I don't value myself as highly as you seem to think. I have come to tell you straight out that if you still retain your former intentions with regard to my sister, and if to further them you think of making use of what you have recently found out, I will kill you before you can get me put in prison. You may take my word for this: you know that I am capable of keeping it. Secondly, if you wish to tell me anything —because all this time it has seemed to me that there was something you wanted to say to me—tell me quickly, because time is precious and very soon it may be too late.'

'Where are you going in such a hurry?' asked Svidrigaylov, examining him curiously.

'Everybody has his own affairs,' said Raskolnikov grimly and impatiently.

'You, yourself, were demanding just now that we should be frank,' remarked Svidrigaylov, with a smile, 'but at the very first question you refuse to answer. You think all the time that I have some design, and so you regard me with suspicion. Well, that is quite understandable in your situation. But I shall not undertake the labour of convincing you of the contrary, however much I may wish to be friends with you. The game really isn't worth the candle. And I wasn't intending to say anything so very special to you.'

'Then what did you want with me? You did seek me out persistently, didn't you?'

'Simply as a curious subject for observation. I was pleased with the fantastic nature of your position, that's what it was. Besides, you are the brother of a person in whom I was greatly interested, and, finally, I had heard a dreadful amount about you from that same person, from which I concluded that you had great influence with her; that's enough, isn't it? He, he, he! However, I admit that your question is quite complicated and that it is difficult for me to answer. Well, for example, here you have come to me now, not only with a definite object, but for something new. That's true, isn't it? Isn't it?' insisted Svidrigaylov, with a mischievous smile. 'Well, then, imagine that I, while I was still on my way here, was counting on you too to tell me something *new*, and on managing to borrow something from you! You see what we rich men are!'

'Borrow what?'

'How can I tell you? How should I know what? You see this wretched tavern I spend all my time in, and I enjoy it, or rather, I don't exactly enjoy it, but one must have somewhere to sit. Well, take that poor Katya—did you see her? . . . Well, if I, for example, were a gourmet or an epicurean clubman— but as it is, look at what I can eat!' (He pointed to the corner, where a tin tray on a little table held the remains of an unappetizing beef-steak and potatoes.) 'By the way, have you had dinner? I've had a bite, and I don't want anything more. I don't drink wine, for example, at all. I never touch any kind but champagne, and of that one glass lasts me all the evening, and even then I get a headache. I ordered this now to help me pull myself together, because I am getting ready to go somewhere, and you find me in a peculiar mood. That was why I tried to hide just now, like a schoolboy, because I thought you might hinder me; but I think' (he took out his watch) 'I can

spend an hour with you; it's half-past four now. Believe me, if
only I were something—a landowner, say, or a father, an officer in the Lancers, a photographer, a journalist . . . but I'm
nothing. I have no speciality. Sometimes it is almost boring.
Honestly, I thought you would tell me something new.'

'But who are you, then, and why have you come here?'

'Who am I? You know: a gentleman, who served two years
in the cavalry, then knocked about here in St. Petersburg, then
married Marfa Petrovna and lived in the country. There's my
biography for you!'

'You are a gambler, I think?'

'A gambler? No. A card-sharper is not a gambler.'

'And you were a card-sharper?'

'Yes, I have been that, too.'

'And were you ever caught and thrashed?'

'It did happen. What then?'

'Well, that means you might challenge someone to a duel . . .
and altogether it could be lively.'

'I won't argue with you, and besides, I am no master of
philosophy. I confess I came here as soon as I could more on
account of women.'

'As soon as Marfa Petrovna was buried?'

'Yes,' smiled Svidrigaylov with winning frankness. 'What of
that? You seem to find something wrong in my talking like
that about women.'

'You mean, do I approve or disapprove of debauchery?'

'Debauchery? So that's what you think! However, I will
take things in order and answer you first about women in
general; I am inclined to be talkative, you know. Tell me, why
should I put any restraint on myself? Why should I give up
women, if I have any inclination for them? It's something to
do, at any rate.'

'So all you hope for here is a spell of debauchery?'

'Well, why not? Debauchery if you will! You seem to like
the word! But I like a straight question, at any rate. In "debauchery" there is at least something constant, based on nature,
indeed, and not subject to fantasy, something that exists in the
blood as an eternal flame, always ready to set one on fire, and
not to be readily extinguished, for a long time to come, perhaps
for many years. You will agree that in its way it is an occupation.'

'Why be glad of that? It is a disease, and a dangerous one.'

'Oh, so that's what you think? I agree that it is a disease,
like everything else that goes to extremes—and it is an essential
part of it, that it goes to extremes—but, to begin with, it is one
thing with one person and something different with another, and,
in the second place, one must of course observe measure in all
things, and make calculations, however mean; but then, what can

one do after all? If it were not for it, one might have to shoot one-self without more ado. I agree that a respectable man is morally obliged to put up with boredom, but you know, all the same ...'

'And could you shoot yourself?'

'Well, there it is!' Svidrigaylov parried, with an expression of aversion. 'Do me a favour, and don't speak of that,' he added hastily, and without any of the swaggering tone of his earlier words. Even his face looked different. 'I confess to an unpardon-able weakness, but I can't help it: I am afraid of death and don't like to hear it spoken of. Do you know that I am a bit of a mystic?'

'Ah, Marfa Petrovna's ghost! Why, does it still appear?'

'Don't mention that; I haven't seen it in St. Petersburg yet. The devil take it!' he cried, with an irritated look. 'No, we had better ... but ... Hm! Unfortunately, time is getting short, and I can't stay with you long. I'm sorry. I could have told you some-thing.'

'What takes you away—a woman?'

'Yes, a woman. A quite unforeseen chance ... no, that's not what I want to talk about.'

'Well, and the squalor, has the squalor of this no effect on you any longer? Have you already lost the strength to stop?'

'And do you claim to have strength as well? He, he, he! You surprise me, Rodion Romanovich, even though I knew before that it would be like this. You to talk about debauchery and aesthetics! You a Schiller! You an idealist! It was bound to be like this, of course, and it would have been surprising if it had been otherwise, but all the same it does seem strange when it actually happens ... Oh, dear, I'm sorry that time is short, because you yourself are a very curious study! By the way, do you like Schiller? I'm terribly fond of him.'

'What a lot of boasting you do, though!' said Raskolnikov, with some distaste.

'No, honestly I don't!' answered Svidrigaylov, guffawing. 'But I won't argue, perhaps I do boast; but, after all, why not, if it's harmless? I lived in the country with Marfa Petrovna for seven years, and so now that I have got hold of an intelligent man like you—intelligent and in the highest degree interesting —I simply delight in letting myself run on. Besides, I have drunk this half-glass of wine, and it has gone to my head the least bit. And, most important of all, there is something that I am very worked up about, but I ... won't speak about that. Where are you going?' he asked suddenly, in alarm.

Raskolnikov was on the point of rising. He felt stifled and uncomfortable and it seemed to him that it had been a mistake to come here. He was convinced that Svidrigaylov was the most shallow and worthless scoundrel on the face of the earth.

'Oh, sit still! Stay a little longer!' begged Svidrigaylov.

'Order yourself some tea, at least. Do stay a little, and I won't talk any more nonsense, about myself, I mean. I will tell you a story. Would you like me to tell you how a woman tried, as you would put it, to "save" me? It will answer your first question, even, since that person was—your sister. May I tell you? It will help to kill time.'

'Very well, but I hope you . . .'

'Oh, don't worry! Besides, Avdotya Romanovna can inspire only the deepest respect even in a thoroughly bad character like me.'

## CHAPTER IV

'You know, perhaps (and indeed I told you so myself),' began Svidrigaylov, 'that I was in the debtor's prison here, with an enormous debt and not the slightest prospect of getting the means to pay it. There is no need to go into the details of how Marfa Petrovna bought me out. Do you know to what lengths of foolishness love can drive a woman? She was an honest creature, and not at all stupid (although completely uneducated). But just imagine, this same honest, jealous woman, after many scenes of frenzied reproach, actually stooped to a sort of bargain with me, which she kept all through our marriage. The point was that she was considerably older than me, and besides she was always chewing a clove or something. I was sufficiently brutal, and honest enough in my own way, to tell her straight out that I could not be absolutely faithful to her. This admission drove her wild, and yet I think my brutal frankness pleased her in a way: "If he tells me this in advance," she said, "it means he doesn't want to deceive me," and that is of the first importance to a jealous woman. After a lot of weeping we made a verbal contract, like this: first, I was never to leave Marfa Petrovna, but always remain her husband; second, I was never to be absent from her without her permission; third, I was never to set up a permanent mistress; fourth, in return for this, Marfa Petrovna was to allow me to cast an eye occasionally at the house servants, but never without her secret knowledge; fifth, God preserve me from falling in love with a woman of our own class; sixth, if I fell a victim, which God forbid, to a great and serious passion, I was bound to disclose it to Marfa Petrovna. On this last point, however, Marfa Petrovna's mind was fairly easy all along; she was an intelligent woman and consequently could only regard me as a rake and a profligate, who was not capable of loving seriously. But an intelligent woman and a jealous woman are two different things, and that was where the disaster came from. To form an impartial judgement of some people, however, one must first discard some preconceived opinions and one's habitual attitude to the ordinary persons and objects surrounding us. I feel able to rely on your good sense, more than on anybody else's, indeed. You may perhaps have already heard a great many ridiculous and laughable things about Marfa Petrovna. She had certainly some absurdly funny ways, but, I tell you straight, I am sincerely sorry for all the innumerable griefs I caused her. Well, that's enough, I think, for a becoming *oraison funèbre* on the tenderest of wives from the fondest of husbands. On the occasion of our quarrels, I mostly kept silent and didn't lose my temper, and this gentlemanly behaviour was almost always effective; it influenced and even pleased her; there were times when she was even proud of me. But all the same she could not bear your sister. How did it come about that she risked taking such a beauty into her house as a governess? I explain it by the fact that Marfa Petrovna was an ardent and impressionable woman and that she simply fell in love herself—literally fell in love—with your sister. Well, Avdotya Romanovna! I knew very well, at the first glance, that it would be a bad business, and—what do you think?— made up my mind not even to look her way. But Avdotya Romanovna herself took the first step—do you believe that, or not? Will you believe, too, that at first Marfa Petrovna went so far as to be angry with me for my constant silence about your sister, and for listening with such indifference to her own continual rapturous praises of Avdotya Romanovna? I can't understand what she wanted! Well, of course, Marfa Petrovna told Avdotya Romanovna all about me in the greatest detail. She had an unfortunate trick of telling all our family secrets to absolutely everybody, and incessantly complaining to everybody about me; so she was hardly likely to omit her wonderful new friend. I suppose that they never talked of anything else but me, certainly there is no doubt that Avdotya Romanovna learnt all those sombre and mysterious stories that are told about me . . . I am willing to bet that you have heard something of the sort, too.'

'Yes, I have. Luzhin accused you of being the cause of a child's death. Is that true?'

'Do me the favour of leaving all that vulgar gossip alone,' replied Svidrigaylov impatiently and with distaste. 'If you are determined to hear about all that nonsense, I will tell you myself one day, but now . . .'

'There was talk of a servant of yours in the country, too, and how you were supposed to be the cause of what happened to him.'

'Please, that's enough!' interrupted Svidrigaylov again, with manifest impatience.

'I suppose that wasn't the servant who came and filled your pipe after he was . . . dead . . . that you told me about yourself?' asked Raskolnikov, with steadily increasing irritation.

Svidrigaylov looked hard at Raskolnikov, and a hint of jeering spite seemed to gleam for an instant in his eyes like a flash of lightning, but he restrained himself and answered with great urbanity:

'Yes, that was the one. I can see that you find all that extraordinarily interesting, and I shall consider it a duty to satisfy your curiosity in every particular at the first favourable opportunity. Hang it, I can see that to some people I really might appear a romantic figure. You may judge then, after that, how grateful I was bound to feel to Marfa Petrovna for having told your sister so many mysterious and interesting things about me. I can't judge what impression they made on her, but in any case, it was all to my advantage. In spite of Avdotya Romanovna's real aversion for me, and my persistently gloomy and forbidding aspect, she grew sorry for me at last, sorry for a lost soul. And when a girl's heart begins to feel *pity* for a man, then of course she is in the greatest danger. She begins to want to "save" him, and make him see reason, and raise him up, and put before him nobler aims, and awaken him to a new life and new activities—well, everybody knows what can be dreamt of in such circumstances. I realized at once that the bird had flown into the net of its own accord, and I began to make preparations in my turn. You seem to be frowning, Rodion Romanovich. There is no need; the affair, as you know, came to nothing. (Devil take it, what a lot of wine I'm drinking!) You know, from the very beginning I always thought it was a pity that your sister had not chanced to be born in the second or third century of our era, as the daughter of a ruling prince somewhere, or some governor or pro-consul in Asia Minor. She would doubtless have been one of those who suffered martyrdom, and she would, of course, have smiled when they burnt her breast with red-hot pincers. She would have deliberately brought it on herself. And in the fourth or fifth century she would have gone into the Egyptian desert and lived for thirty years on roots, ecstasies, and visions. She is the kind of person who hungers and thirsts to be tortured for somebody, and if she does not achieve her martyrdom she is quite capable of jumping out of a window. I have heard something of a certain Mr. Razumikhin. They say he is a sensible young man; I suppose he is a seminarist.[4] Well, let him take care of your sister. In short, I think I understood her, and I consider that it does me credit. But at that time, at the beginning, that is, of an acquaintance, you know yourself that one is always somehow more frivolous and stupid than usual; one makes mistakes and sees things in

4. A seminarist could be the son of a Russian orthodox priest enrolled in a seminary school, as well as a person studying for the priesthood. Razumikhin's name (derived from *razum*, meaning reason, good sense) sounds like the names typically given by bishops to graduates of seminaries upon their completing the school, a time when they often were assigned new names.

the wrong way. Hang it, why was she so pretty? It was not my fault. In one word, with me it began with an uncontrollable fit of sensual passion. Avdotya Romanovna is terribly chaste, to a positively unheard-of degree. (Notice this; I tell you it about your sister as a fact. She is perhaps even morbidly chaste, in spite of the depth of her intelligence, and it will do her harm.) There happened to be a certain girl in the house, Parasha, black-eyed Parasha, who had just been brought from another estate as a maid-servant, and I had never seen her before. She was very pretty, but incredibly stupid: burst into tears, raised a yell that could be heard all over the place, and caused a scandal. Once, after dinner, Avdotya Romanovna deliberately sought me out when I was alone in the garden and with flashing eyes *demanded* that I should leave poor Parasha alone. It was almost our first private conversation. I, naturally, considered it an honour to fulfil her wish, and tried to pretend that I was embarrassed and discomfited, and, in short, played my part not too badly. Then began negotiations, secret conversations, moral lectures, sermons, entreaties, supplications, even tears—would you believe it, even tears! That shows how far the passion for conversion will go in some girls! Of course, I put the blame for everything on my destiny, made out that I was avid and greedy for light, and finally brought into play the greatest and most reliable means of subjugating a woman's heart, which never disappoints anybody and always produces a decisive effect on every single woman, without exception. I mean, of course, flattery. There is nothing in the world harder than straightforwardness, and nothing easier than flattery. In straightforward dealing, if there is one-hundredth part of a false note, the result is immediate dissonance and, in consequence, trouble. But in flattery every single note can be false and the effect will be agreeable, and it will be listened to with some pleasure; the pleasure may indeed be somewhat crude, but it is still pleasure, for all that. And, however gross the flattery may be, at least half of it will certainly seem to be true. This holds for every stage of development and every social level. Even a vestal virgin can be seduced by flattery, not to mention ordinary people. I can't help laughing when I remember how I once seduced a lady who was devoted to her husband, to her children, and to virtue. What fun it was, and how little trouble! And the lady really was virtuous, in her own way at least. My whole strategy consisted in being crushed and prostrate before her chastity the whole time. I flattered her unconscionably, and no sooner did I obtain so much as a glance or a pressure of the hand than I reproached myself for having taken it by force, declaring that she had resisted me, and resisted me so strongly that I should certainly never have won any favours if I had not been so depraved; that she, in her innocence, did not anticipate my cunning and yielded without intention or knowledge, unaware of what she did, and so on and so forth. In short, I attained my ends, and the lady remained convinced that she was innocent and chaste, that she was neglecting none of her duties or obligations, and that she had fallen quite by accident. And how angry she was with me when at long last I told her that in my honest opinion she had been seeking satisfaction just as much as I had. Poor Marfa Petrovna was also terribly susceptible to flattery and if I had only wanted I could have possessed myself of all her property while she was still alive. (But I am drinking an awful lot of wine and talking too much.) I hope you won't be angry if I say now that the same effect began to appear even with Avdotya Romanovna. But I was stupid and impatient and spoiled everything. More than once, even before this (and especially on one occasion) Avdotya Romanovna found the expression of my eyes terribly displeasing, if you will believe me. To put it shortly, there was a flame in them that flared up more strongly and less guardedly all the time, and it frightened her and at last she came to hate it. There is no need to go into details, but we parted. Then I again acted stupidly. I allowed myself to turn all her moral propaganda to the crudest mockery; Parasha appeared on the scene again, and she was not the only one—in short, we had a perfect pandemonium. Ah, Rodion Romanovich, if you had only once in your life seen how your sister's eyes can flash fire! It doesn't matter if I have drunk a whole glassful of wine and am tipsy now, I am telling the truth; I assure you, I dreamed of that look; in the end I couldn't bear even to hear the rustle of her dress. Really, I thought that I should have a fit or something; I had never imagined that I could get into such a frenzy. In one word, a reconciliation was essential to me; but it was quite impossible. And can you imagine what I did then? To what depths of stupidity a man can be reduced by frenzy! Never undertake anything in a frenzy, Rodion Romanovich. I calculated that Avdotya Romanovna was a beggar, after all (oh, excuse me, I didn't mean to say that . . . but does it make any difference what word you use, if it means the same?), that, in short, she had to earn her own living, and that she had to help to keep both her mother and you (oh, hang it, you are scowling again . . . ), so I decided to offer her all my money (I could have realized up to about thirty thousand at the time) on condition that she would run away with me here, to St. Petersburg. Naturally, I would have sworn to give her eternal love, blissful happiness, and so on and so forth. Believe me, I was so enamoured that if she had said: "Cut Marfa Petrovna's throat or poison her and marry me"—I would have done it on the spot! But the whole thing ended in the disaster that you already know about, and you can judge for yourself to what a pitch of fury I was driven when I heard that Marfa Petrovna had got hold of that rascally clerk, Luzhin, and all but succeeded in contriving a match between them—which in reality would have amounted to exactly the same thing as I had suggested. Wouldn't it? Wouldn't it? It would, wouldn't it? I notice that you have begun to listen very attentively ... an interesting young man ...'

Svidrigaylov impatiently thumped the table with his fist. He had become red in the face. Raskolnikov saw clearly that the glass or glass and a half of champagne he had drunk, without noticing, in constant small sips, had affected him for the worse, and he resolved to profit by the opportunity. He was very suspicious of Svidrigaylov.

'Well, after all that, I am quite convinced that you came here with my sister in mind,' he said bluntly and openly to Svidrigaylov, so as to irritate him still more.

'Oh, drop it!' Svidrigaylov seemed to pull himself up sharply. 'Why, I told you . . . and besides your sister can't stand me.'

'I am convinced of that, too, but that isn't the point.'

'You are convinced of it?' (Svidrigaylov screwed up his eyes with a mocking smile.) 'You are right, she doesn't like me; but never try to answer for what is between a husband and his wife, or a lover and his mistress. There is always one little corner which remains hidden from all the world, and is known only to the two of them. Will you vouch for Avdotya Romanovna's having looked on me with aversion?'

'From some words and hints you dropped while you were telling your story, I notice that you still have your own views, and your own urgent designs on Dunya—vicious ones, of course.'

'What? Did I let words and hints of that kind escape me?' Svidrigaylov was naïvely startled, but paid not the slightest attention to the epithet applied to his designs.

'You are still doing so. Well, for example, what are you so afraid of? Why were you so startled?'

'I am afraid, am I? Afraid of you? You ought rather to be afraid of me, *cher ami*. All the same, what rot! ... However, I'm drunk, I can see; I very nearly let things out again. Damn the wine! Hi, there! Water!'

He seized the bottle and without more ado threw it out of the window. Philip brought some water.

'That's all nonsense,' said Svidrigaylov, wetting a towel and applying it to his head. 'I can confound you with one word, and reduce all your suspicions to nothing. Do you know I'm getting married?'

'So you have already told me.'

'Did I? I'd forgotten. But I couldn't have spoken positively then, because I hadn't even seen my future wife; I was only thinking of it. Well, now I am engaged, and the thing is done, and, if only I hadn't something urgent to do, I should certainly take you to see them at once—because I want to ask your advice. Oh, hang it! I've only ten minutes left. Look at my watch. But all the same, I will tell you about it, because it's something very interesting, in its way, my marriage. Where are you off to? You're not going again?'

'No, I won't go now.'

'You won't go away at all? We shall see! I will take you there, truly, only not now; now it will soon be time for me to leave. You turn to the right, and I to the left. Do you know this Resslich? This same Resslich, in whose house I am living now, eh? Do you hear? No, what do you think? she is the same one they talk about, you know, about one of her girls in the water, in the winter . . . well, are you listening? Do you hear me? Well, she was the one who cooked it all up for me; you're bored, she said, you must find something to amuse you. I'm a moody, gloomy person, you know. Do you think I've a cheerful disposition? No, it's moody: I don't do any harm, but I sit in a corner, and sometimes I haven't a word to say for three days on end. This Resslich is a tricky piece of work, I can tell you, and this is what she has in mind: I shall get tired of my wife and leave her, and my wife will fall into her hands, and be put into circulation by her, among our own class, that is, and higher ones. There is, she says, an invalid father, a retired official, who sits in his arm-chair and has not been able to move his legs for three years. There is, she says, a mother as well—a very sensible lady, mama. The son is serving somewhere in the provinces, and doesn't help them. The married daughter never goes to see them, and they have two little nephews on their hands (as though their own weren't enough), and they took their younger daughter away from school before she finished her education. She will be just sixteen in a month's time, that is, she will be marriageable in a month. She is the one meant for me. We went there; it was very funny. I introduced myself:—a landowner, a widower, bearing a well-known name, with such-and-such connexions, and with money—what does it matter that I am fifty and she is not yet sixteen? Who will consider that? Well, but it's tempting, eh? It's tempting, you know! Ha, ha! If you could have seen me talking to papa and mama! It would have been worth paying to get in, simply to see me then. She came in, dropped a curtsy—still in short skirts, imagine! An unopened bud. She coloured up, blushing like the dawn (she had been told, of course). I don't know what you think about women's faces, but to my mind these sixteen years, these still childish eyes, this modesty and tearful shyness—to my mind, they are better than beauty. But in addition to all this, she was a little picture! Fair hair in tight little ringlets like a lamb's coat, pouting rosy little lips, tiny feet—charming! . . .

Well, we had made each other's acquaintance, and I explained that for domestic reasons I was in a hurry, and so the next day, the day before yesterday, that is, we were betrothed. Since then, whenever I go, I take her on my knee at once, and don't let her go . . . Well, she blushes like the dawn, and I kiss her every minute; mama, of course, impresses on her that "this" (so she says) "is your husband, and things must be so"—and, in one word, it suits me down to the ground. This present condition, of being betrothed, is perhaps really better than marriage. There is in it what is called *la nature et la vérité*. Ha, ha! I have had one or two talks with her—she is far from stupid; sometimes she will steal a look at me that positively burns through me. And you know, she has a little face like a Raphael Madonna's. Has it ever struck you that the Sistine Madonna really has a fantastic face, a face of melancholy and almost simple-minded piety? Well, hers is something like that. The day after we received her parents' blessing I took with me fifteen hundred roubles' worth of things: a *parure* of diamonds and another of pearls, a silver dressing-case—as big as this—with all sorts of fittings, so that even that little Madonna face of hers flushed with pleasure. Yesterday I took her on my knee—very unceremoniously, no doubt—she blushed crimson and tears started to her eyes, but she did not want to betray how deeply stirred she was. Everybody was out of the room for a moment, and we were left quite alone, and suddenly she threw herself on my neck (it was the first time she had done so of her own accord), put both her little arms round me, kissed me, and swore to be a good, true, and obedient wife to me and make me happy, to spend her whole life, every minute of her life, for me, and to sacrifice everything else, and in return all she wished was to *have my respect*; beyond that, she said, "I want nothing, nothing, nothing—no more gifts." You will agree that to hear such an avowal, alone, from a little sixteen-year-old angel in a muslin dress, with a mass of little curls, blushing with maidenly shame and with tears of enthusiasm in her eyes—you will agree that it is rather a temptation. It is, is'nt it? It is worth something, eh? Isn't it? Well . . . well, listen . . . well, let us go and see my fiancée . . . only not just now!'

'In short, this monstrous difference in years and knowledge of life whets your sensual appetite! But surely you will not really marry like that!'

'Why not? Certainly I shall. Every man considers himself, and that man has the gayest life who is most successful in deceiving himself. Ha, ha! But why are you standing up so stoutly for virtue? Spare me, I am only a sinful man! He, he, he!

'And yet you have settled Katerina Ivanovna's children. However . . . however, you had your own reasons for that . . . I understand it all now.'

'I like all children. I like them very much,' laughed Svidrigaylov. 'Apropos of that, I could tell you a very curious story,
that is not finished yet. On the first day I arrived here I visited
various resorts, absolutely plunging into filth after those seven
years. You have probably noticed that I have not been in a
hurry to rejoin my old set, the friends and acquaintances of
former times. Indeed, I intend to get on without them as long
as I can. You know, in the country with Marfa Petrovna the
memory of those places was an endless torment to me, those
mysterious places in which a man who knows how can find
many things. But hang it! The common folk get drunk; educated young people with nothing to do consume themselves
with unrealizable dreams and fancies, and stultify themselves
with theories; Jews have flocked here and are hoarding up
money; all the rest lead lives of debauchery. I found the
town fairly reeking with its familiar odours from the first
moment. I chanced one evening on a so-called dance—it
was in a horrible den (but I like my sewers filthy), and, of
course, there was a *cancan* of an unheard-of kind, such as there
never was in my day. Yes, sir, there has been progress there.
Suddenly, I looked and saw a little girl of about thirteen, very
nicely dressed, dancing with an expert, and with another
*vis-à-vis*. Her mother was sitting in a chair by the wall. Well,
you can imagine what that *cancan* was like! The little girl was
confused and blushing, and at last, feeling herself insulted, she
began to cry. The expert seized her and began to spin her
round and posture in front of her, and everybody laughed and
—at these moments I love our public, even our *cancan* public—
they laughed and shouted, "That's right, serves them right!
Children shouldn't be brought here!" Well, I didn't care, and
it wasn't any business of mine, whether they were logical or
not in soothing their consciences in that way. I had at once
made up my mind on my own position, and I went and sat
down by the mother, and began talking to her about my being
also newly arrived, and what ignorant boors these were, who
could not distinguish genuine worth or give it proper respect;
I gave her to understand that I had plenty of money, and
offered to take them home in my carriage. I took them home
and got acquainted with them; they were staying in poky little
lodgings and had only just come to St. Petersburg. The mother
declared that she and her daughter could only take my acquaintance as an honour. I learned that they possessed neither
stick nor stone of their own, and had come here on business
connected with a petition to some Minister. I offered them my
services and money; I learned that they had gone to the dance
by mistake, thinking that it really was a dancing class; I offered
to assist the young lady's education with lessons in French and
dancing. They were delighted to accept, taking it for an honour,

and our acquaintanceship has continued till now . . . If you like, we will go and see them—only not just now.'

'That's enough. No more of your wicked, base stories, you vile, disgusting, salacious creature!'

'A Schiller, a Russian Schiller, an absolute Schiller! *Où va-t-elle la vertu se nicher?* You know, I shall go on telling you things like this, on purpose to hear your outcries. Delightfully amusing!'

'Of course! Don't I seem ludicrous even to myself just now?' muttered Raskolnikov bitterly.

Svidrigaylov laughed uproariously; then at last he summoned Philip, settled his bill, and got up to go.

'Well, I'm quite drunk, *assez causé!*' he said. 'A great pleasure!'

'Of course, you would find it a pleasure!' exclaimed Raskolnikov, as he also rose. 'Naturally an accomplished rake like you, with some monstrous scheme of the same sort in his mind, enjoys talking of such adventures, especially in circumstances like these and to a man like me . . . It excites him.'

'Well, if it's like that,' answered Svidrigaylov, with some astonishment, 'if it's like that, you're a pretty fair cynic yourself. At any rate, you have all the makings of a very considerable one. There are many things you know how to recognize, many . . . and, indeed, you are capable of doing many things, too. Well, but that's enough. I am sincerely sorry to have had so little conversation with you, but I shall not lose touch with you . . . Only wait a little . . .'

Svidrigaylov left the tavern, and Raskolnikov followed him. Svidrigaylov was not very drunk; the wine had gone to his head for a moment, but the effect was passing with every minute. He was preoccupied with something, something very important, and his brows were knitted. He was plainly disturbed and excited by the expectation of something. In the past few minutes his tone to Raskolnikov seemed to have changed, becoming ruder and more mocking. Raskolnikov had perceived this and was also disturbed. He had become very suspicious of Svidrigaylov and resolved to follow him.

They came out on to the street.

'Your way lies to the right and mine to the left, or perhaps the other way round, only—*adieu mon plaisir*. Good-bye for the present.'

He turned right, towards the Haymarket.

## CHAPTER V

RASKOLNIKOV followed him.

'What does this mean?' exclaimed Svidrigaylov, turning round. 'Surely I said . . .'

'It means that I will not part from you now.'

'Wha-a-t?'

They both stopped, and stood for a minute, measuring each other with their eyes.

'From all your half-drunken talk,' said Raskolnikov abruptly and harshly, 'I have come to the positive conclusion that you not only have not given up your vile designs on my sister, but are pursuing them more actively than ever. I know that my sister received a letter this morning. You have been in a fever of impatience all this time . . . Suppose you have managed to dig up a wife on the way; that doesn't mean anything. I want to satisfy myself personally . . .'

Raskolnikov could hardly have defined exactly what he wanted at that moment, or just what it was of which he wished to satisfy himself personally.

'So that's it! Do you want me to call the police?'

'Call them!'

Again they stood face to face for a minute. At last, Svidrigaylov's expression suddenly changed. Satisfied that Raskolnikov was not to be frightened by threats, he assumed a cheerful and friendly air.

'What a man! I didn't mention your affair, on purpose, although of course I am itching with curiosity. A fantastic business. I nearly put off speaking of it till another time, but really, you would provoke a dead man . . . Well, let us go, only let me tell you first that I am only going home for a moment now, to get some money; after that I shall lock up my room, take a cab, and go out to the Islands for the evening. Well, what good will it do you to follow me?'

'I shall go to your lodgings, all the same, but to see Sofya Semënovna, not you, to apologize for not going to the funeral.'

'As you please, but Sofya Semënovna is not at home. She has taken the children to a lady, an elderly lady of high rank, whom I used to know a very long time ago, and who is the patroness of some orphanages. This lady was enchanted when I took her the money for all three of Katerina Ivanovna's nestlings, and gave her more money for the orphanages as well. I finally told her all Sofya Semënovna's story, without any concealment or disguise. It produced an indescribable effect. That is why Sofya Semënovna has been summoned to appear this very day at the hotel where my titled lady, who has come up for a time from the country, is staying.'

'It doesn't matter. I will call all the same.'

'As you like, only I am not going with you; but what does it matter to me? Here we are at home. Tell me, aren't you—I am sure you are—suspicious of me just because I have been so delicate and not worried you with questions up to now . . . you understand? It seemed extraordinary to you, I'll bet! Well, that shows what you get for being delicate!'

'And listening at doors!'

'Oh, that's what you're after?' laughed Svidrigaylov. 'Yes, I should have been surprised if you had let that pass, after all. Ha, ha! I did understand a little, if not much, of what you had been up to, that time ... there ... and were telling Sofya Semënovna about, but, all the same, what is it all about? Perhaps I am quite out of date, and can't understand anything any more. Explain it to me, my dear fellow, for God's sake! Instruct me in the latest ideas.'

'You couldn't hear anything. It's all lies!'

'But I'm not talking about that, not about that at all (although I did hear something); no, I was talking about the way you keep on sighing all the time. The Schiller in you is always getting into a muddle. Now it seems one mustn't listen at doors. If that is so, go and explain to the authorities how "this extraordinary thing," you must say, "happened to me in such-and-such a way: a slight mistake revealed itself in my theory". If you are so sure that one can't listen at doors, but any old woman you like can be knocked on the head, then you'd better be off at once to America somewhere. Run away, young man! Perhaps there is still time. I am speaking in all sincerity. You haven't any money, is that it? I'll give you enough for your journey.'

'I am not thinking of that at all,' interrupted Raskolnikov disgustedly.

'I understand (but don't trouble yourself: you needn't say anything unless you want); I understand what questions are occupying your mind—moral ones, aren't they? Questions appropriate to a man and a citizen? But let them be; why should they concern you now? He, he! Because you are still a man and a citizen? But if so, you shouldn't have got yourself into this; don't thrust yourself into other people's affairs. Well, shoot yourself; or don't you want to?'

'You seem to be deliberately trying to annoy me, so that I shall leave you ...'

'What an odd creature you are! But here we are; do come in. You see, that is Sofya Semënovna's door; look, there is nobody in. Don't you believe me? Ask the Kapernaumovs; she leaves her key with them. Here is Madame de Kapernaumov herself, eh? What? (She is a trifle deaf.) Has she gone out? Where to? Well, did you hear that? She isn't here, and she won't be back, perhaps, until very late tonight. Well, now let us go to my rooms. I believe you wanted to call there, too, didn't you? Well, here we are. Madam Resslich is not at home. She is a woman who is always on the go, but she is a very good woman, I assure you ... and perhaps she might have been of use to you, if you had been a little more sensible. Well, now please observe: I take this five-per-cent bond from the bureau (look

what a lot of them I still have!), but this one is destined for the
*bureau de change* today. Well, did you see? I have no more time
to lose. The bureau is locked, the door is locked, and we are
on the staircase again. Well, let us take a cab, shall we? I really
am going to the Islands. Wouldn't you like a drive? Look, I'll
take this carriage to Elagin Island, shall I? Do you refuse?
Can't you stand it any longer? It doesn't matter, come for a
drive! I think it may be going to rain; but never mind, we'll
have the top down . . .'

Svidrigaylov was already sitting in the carriage. Raskolnikov had decided that his suspicions were not justified, at
least for the moment. Without a word in reply, he turned and
walked back towards the Haymarket. If he had looked round
even once as he walked, he might have seen that Svidrigaylov,
after no more than a hundred yards, had paid off the cab and
was once again on the pavement. But it was too late now to see
anything; he had turned the corner. Intense loathing drove
him away from Svidrigaylov's neighbourhood. 'How could I,
even for one instant, hope for anything from that hardened
scoundrel, that debauched, licentious brute?' he could not
help exclaiming. In fact, however, the judgement Raskolnikov
had pronounced was too hasty and ill-considered. There was
something about Svidrigaylov that was at least out of the
ordinary, if not mysterious. As far as his sister was concerned,
Raskolnikov remained convinced that Svidrigaylov would not
leave her in peace. But the constant turning of everything over
and over in his mind was becoming intolerably burdensome
to him.

In his usual way, once he was alone, he fell into deep thought
before he had gone twenty yards. Coming up on to the bridge,
he stopped by the parapet and gazed down at the water. Close
beside him as he stood there was Avdotya Romanovna.

He had met her at the entrance to the bridge but had walked
past without seeing her. Dunechka had never before encountered him in this state in the street, and she was struck with
dismay. She stopped, uncertain whether to call out to him.
Suddenly she saw Svidrigaylov approaching hurriedly from
the direction of the Haymarket.

His movements seemed secretive and cautious. He did not
come on to the bridge, but stood to one side on the pavement,
taking every care to prevent Raskolnikov's seeing him. He
had noticed Dunya some time before, and he began to make
signs to her. They seemed to be meant to ask her not to call or
disturb her brother, but to come to him.

This Dunya did. She went quietly past her brother and up
to Svidrigaylov.

'Let us go quickly,' he whispered. 'I do not wish Rodion
Romanovich to know of our meeting. I must tell you that I

have been sitting with him, not far from here, in a tavern where he had sought me out, and it was only with difficulty that I got away from him. He has learnt somehow of my letter to you and suspects something. Surely it wasn't you who told him? But if not, who was it?'

'Now we have turned the corner,' interrupted Dunya, 'and my brother will not see us. Let me make it clear that I shall go no farther with you. Tell me what you have to say here; it can all be said in the street.'

'In the first place, it is quite impossible to say it in the street; in the second place, you ought to hear Sofya Semënovna as well; in the third place, I have some papers to show you . . . Well, and finally, if you will not agree to come to my room, I refuse to enter into further explanations, and I shall leave you immediately. Further, I beg you to remember that I am completely possessed of your beloved brother's very extraordinary secret.' Dunya paused irresolutely, turning her searching gaze on Svidrigaylov.

'What are you afraid of?' he observed quietly. 'The town is not the country. And even in the country you did me more harm than I did you, and here . . .'

'Has Sofya Semënovna been told?'

'No, I haven't said a word to her, and I am not even sure that she is at home now. She probably is, however. She buried her stepmother today; it is not the sort of day on which she is likely to go out visiting. I don't want to say anything about this to anybody until the time comes, and I am even a little sorry that I have told you. In this matter the slightest indiscretion amounts to a complete betrayal. Here is where I live, in this house here that we are coming to. Look, there is our porter; he knows me very well; see, he is bowing to us. He sees that I have a lady with me, and has certainly taken note of your face; that will please you if you are very afraid and suspicious of me. Excuse me if I am putting it too crudely. I am in lodgings here. Sofya Semënovna, who is also in lodgings, has the adjoining room. The whole floor is let out in rooms. But why are you frightened, like a child? Am I so very terrible?'

Svidrigaylov twisted his features into a condescending smile, but he was no longer in a mood for smiling. His heart was thumping and his breath caught in his throat. He deliberately raised his voice, to conceal his mounting excitement. Dunya, however, was so irritated by his saying that she was childishly frightened of him and thought him terrible, that she failed to notice this peculiar excitement.

'Although I know that you are a man . . . without honour, I am not in the least afraid of you. Lead the way,' she said with apparent calm, although her face was very pale.

Svidrigaylov stopped at Sonya's door.

'With your permission I will inquire whether she is at home. No. That is unfortunate. But I know she may come very soon. If she has gone out, it can only have been to see a certain lady about those orphan children. Their mother is dead. I have interested myself in the case and made arrangements for them. If Sofya Semënovna doesn't return in ten minutes, I will send her to see you this very day, if you wish. Well, here is where I live. These are my two rooms. My landlady, Mrs. Resslich, is through that door. Now please look here, and I will show you my most important proofs: this door leads from my bedroom into two empty rooms, which are to let. Here they are . . . you must please look at them rather carefully . . .'

Svidrigaylov rented two fairly large furnished rooms. Dunechka looked round mistrustfully, but she could see nothing out of the ordinary in the furnishings or arrangement of the rooms, although there was something to see, that Svidrigaylov's apartment, for example, was between two others that were almost unoccupied. His door did not open straight off the corridor, but was reached through two rooms belonging to his landlady, which were almost empty. From his bedroom Svidrigaylov, opening a locked door, had shown Dunechka another apartment, this one to let and also empty. Dunechka stopped on the threshold, not understanding why she was requested to look, but Svidrigaylov hastened to explain.

'Look here, in this large second room. Notice that door; it is locked. Near the door stands a chair, and there is only that chair in the two rooms. I brought it from my own room, so that I could listen more comfortably. Here, immediately behind the door, is Sofya Semënovna's table; she was sitting there talking to Rodion Romanovich. And I listened here, sitting on the chair, on two successive evenings, each time for about two hours—and of course I was able to learn something, don't you think?'

'You listened?'

'Yes, I listened. Now let us go into my rooms; there is nowhere to sit here.'

He led Avdotya Romanovna back into the first of his rooms, which he used as a sitting-room, and asked her to sit down. He himself sat down at the other end of the table, at least two yards from her, but his eyes seemed to glitter with the same flame that had once so frightened Dunechka. She shuddered and again looked mistrustfully round. The gesture was involuntary; she plainly did not wish to reveal her mistrust, but the isolated situation of Svidrigaylov's rooms had at last impressed her. She would have liked to ask whether his landlady, at least, was at home. but, out of pride, she did not put the question. She was, besides, suffering an incomparably greater anguish than fear for herself. Her distress was unendurable.

'Here is your letter,' she began, laying it on the table. 'Can what you write possibly be true? You hint at a crime committed by my brother. The hint is too plain for you to dare to retract it now. I must tell you that I had heard this stupid story before and that I do not believe a word of it. The suspicion is ridiculous and vile. I know the story, and how and why it was invented. You cannot have any kind of proof. You promised to prove it: speak then! But I tell you beforehand that I do not believe you! I don't believe you! . . .'

Dunechka had spoken rapidly and hurriedly, and colour flooded her face for a moment.

'If you didn't believe me, how could you have taken the risk of coming to see me alone? Why did you come? Simply from curiosity?'

'Don't torment me, speak, speak!'

'One thing is certain, that you are a brave young woman. I swear I thought you would ask Mr. Razumikhin to accompany you here. But he was not with you, or anywhere about; I looked. That was courageous; it means that you wished to protect Rodion Romanovich. But everything about you is godlike . . . As for your brother, what shall I say? You yourself saw him just now. What did he look like?'

'Is that all you have to go on?'

'No. I have his own words. He came here to see Sofya Semënovna on two evenings in succession. I have shown you where they sat. He made a full confession to her. He is a murderer. He killed an old woman, a moneylender, with whom he had pawned things; he killed her sister as well, a dealer called Lizaveta, who arrived unexpectedly during her sister's murder. He killed them both with an axe he had taken with him. He killed them in order to steal, and he did steal; he took money and some things . . . He himself told all this, word for word, to Sofya Semënovna, who is the only one who knows his secret, but who had no part in the murder either in word or deed. On the contrary, she was just as frightened as you are now. Don't be uneasy, she will not betray him.'

'This cannot be true!' murmured Dunechka, with pale stiff lips; she felt suffocated. 'It cannot be. There was not the slightest reason, no cause . . . It is a lie! A lie!'

'He robbed her, that was the only reason. He took money and things. It is true that, by his own confession, he made no use of either the things or the money, but hid them somewhere under a stone, where they still are. But that was because he did not dare use them.'

'But is it likely that he could rob and plunder? Or that he could even dream of it?' cried Dunya, starting up from her chair. 'You know him, you have seen him. Could he be a thief?'

She was almost imploring Svidrigaylov; she had forgotten all her fear.

'There are thousands, millions, of possible combinations and arrangements, Avdotya Romanovna. A thief steals, but then he knows himself to be a scoundrel; but I have heard of a man of good family who robbed the mail, and who knows, perhaps he thought he was doing something respectable! Of course I should not have believed this, any more than you do, if I had heard it at second hand. But I believed my own ears. He explained his reasons, too, to Sofya Semënovna, but at first she could not believe her own ears, although at last she had to believe her own eyes. After all, he himself told her.'

'But what . . . reasons?'

'It is a long story, Avdotya Romanovna. Here you have . . . how can I put it? . . . a kind of theory, the same sort of thing which makes me, for example, consider that a single piece of wrongdoing is allowable, if the chief aim is good. One single evil and a hundred good deeds! Besides, it galls a young man of merit and exorbitant ambition to know that if only he had, for example, some three thousand roubles, it would make all the difference to his whole career, the whole future course of his life, but that the three thousand is lacking. Add to this the irritations of hunger, cramped quarters, rags, and a clear consciousness of the full beauty of his social position, and that of his mother and sister. And above all vanity, vanity and pride, though God only knows there might be good qualities too . . . I don't blame him, please don't think I do; it's no business of mine. Then there was this particular little theory of his—a theory of sorts—according to which people are divided, do you see, into the common mass and the special people, those, that is to say, for whom, because of their elevated position, laws are not written, but who, on the contrary, frame laws for the others, the common mass, the rabble. Well, as a theory it may pass, it's *une théorie comme une autre*. Napoleon had a terrible fascination for him, or rather, what particularly attracted him was the fact that so many men of genius had not heeded the isolated misdeed but marched straight over it, without reflection. He seems to have persuaded himself that he too was a man of genius, that is to say, he was convinced of it for a period. He suffered, and still suffers, greatly from the thought that, although he was capable of conceiving the theory, it was not in his nature to overstep the bounds of the law, without pausing to reflect, and that it follows that he is not a man of genius. Well, that, for a young man with a due share of self-esteem, is humiliating, especially in our day . . .'

'And the pangs of conscience? So you would deny him any moral feeling? Is he really like that?'

'Ah, Avdotya Romanovna, everything is mixed up now, though that is not to say that it was ever particularly straightforward. The minds of the Russian people in general are broad, Avdotya Romanovna, like their country, and extraordinarily inclined to the fantastic and the chaotic; but it is disastrous to have a broad mind without special genius. Do you remember how often we two discussed this theme, and in this strain, sitting on the terrace in the garden, in the evening after supper? You were always reproaching me with that breadth of mind. Who knows, perhaps at the very time we were talking he was lying here and making his plans. In our educated Russian society, Avdotya Romanovna, there are no sacred traditions: at most someone may possibly frame some for himself out of books . . . or deduce something from old chronicles. But such people are the more learned sort, and, you know, all more or less simpletons, so that a man of the world would think their procedures quite unbecoming to himself. However, you know my general opinions; I make it a rule to condemn absolutely nobody, since I never do anything myself and don't intend to. But we have spoken of this more than once before. I was even fortunate enough to gain your interest in my opinions . . . You are very pale, Avdotya Romanovna.'

'I know that theory of his. I have read his article, in a magazine, about people to whom everything is permitted . . . Razumikhin brought it to me . . .'

'Mr. Razumikhin? An article by your brother? In a magazine? Is there one? I didn't know. It must be interesting. But where are you going, Avdotya Romanovna?'

'I want to see Sofya Semënovna,' said Dunya faintly. 'Which way does one go? She may have come in, and I must see her at once. Let her . . .'

Avdotya Romanovna could not finish what she was saying; her breath literally failed her.

'Sofya Semënovna will not return before night, I suppose. She should have been here very quickly, and if she was not, it means she will be very late . . .'

'Ah, so you have been lying to me! I see . . you lied . . . you were lying all the time! . . . I don't believe you! I don't believe you!' cried Dunechka frenziedly, quite losing her head.

Almost fainting, she sank on to a chair hastily placed for her by Svidrigaylov.

'Avdotya Romanovna, what is the matter? Don't faint! Here is some water. Take a sip . . .'

He sprinkled her with water. Dunechka shuddered and came to herself.

'The effect was too violent!' muttered Svidrigaylov to himself, frowning. 'Avdotya Romanovna, calm yourself! I tell you, he has friends. We will save him, rescue him. Would you like me to take him abroad? I have money; I can get a ticket in three days. As for his having killed, he may yet accomplish much good in expiation. Calm yourself. He may yet be a great man. Now how are you? How do you feel?'

'An evil man! He is still sneering. Let me go . . .'

'Where? Where do you want to go?'

'To him. Where is he? Do you know? Why is this door locked? We came in by it, and now it is locked. When did you contrive to lock it?'

'After all, we couldn't shout the subject of our conversation all over the place. I am not sneering at all, only I was tired of talking in that strain. Where are you going in such a state? Do you want to betray him? You will drive him to madness and he will give himself away. I tell you they are already on his trail, they have hit the scent. You will only give him away. Wait a little; I saw him and talked to him just now; he can still be saved. Wait. Sit down and we will consider it together. That was why I asked you to come here, so that we could talk about it in private and consider it wisely. Please sit down!'

'How can you save him? Can he possibly be saved?'

Dunya sat down, and Svidrigaylov sat beside her.

'It all depends on you, on you and on you alone,' he began, with flashing eyes, almost in a whisper, stumbling, and hardly articulating some words from excitement.

Dunya recoiled from him in fear. He also was trembling violently.

'You . . . one word from you and he is saved! I . . . I will save him. I have money, friends. I will get him away at once, and I will get a passport, two passports. One for him, the other for me. I have friends; practical people . . . Would you like me to get another passport for you . . . for your mother? . . . What need have you of Razumikhin? I love you so . . . I love you infinitely. Let me kiss the hem of your dress, let me! Let me! It is more than I can bear to hear it rustle. Say to me, "Do this!" and I will do it. I will do anything. I will do the impossible. Whatever you believe in, I will believe in too. I will do anything, anything. Don't look at me like that, don't! I tell you, you are killing me . . .'

He was almost raving. It was as if something in his mind had suddenly given way. Dunya sprang up and flung herself towards the door.

'Open the door, open the door!' she called through the door to anybody who might be outside, and shook it. 'Please open it! Is there nobody there?'

Svidrigaylov controlled himself and got up. A smile of malicious mockery forced itself on to his still trembling lips.

'There is nobody at home there,' he said slowly and deliberately; 'my landlady has gone out and you are wasting your breath shouting like that. You are only getting needlessly worked up.'

'Where is the key? Open the door at once, at once, wretch!'

'I have lost the key and I shall not be able to find it.'

'Oh? Then you are using force!' cried Dunya, as pale as death, and rushed to the corner of the room, where she barricaded herself with a little table that happened to stand near. She did not scream; but she fixed her eyes on her tormentor and followed his every movement. Svidrigaylov remained standing in his place, facing her from the opposite side of the room. He had succeeded in regaining control of himself, at least outwardly. But his face was still pale and the mocking smile had not left it.

'You spoke just now of "force", Avdotya Romanovna. If I do intend force, you can judge for yourself whether I have taken suitable measures. Sofya Semënovna is not at home and it is a long way to the Kapernaumovs, through five locked rooms. Finally, I am at least twice as strong as you and, besides, I have nothing to fear because you will not be able to complain afterwards. You will not want to betray your brother, will you? Besides, nobody will believe you: for what purpose should a young girl have visited a single man in his rooms? So, even if you sacrifice your brother, you won't prove anything; "force" is very difficult to prove, Avdotya Romanovna.'

'Scoundrel!' whispered Dunya indignantly.

'As you please, but note that I was speaking only of a supposition. In my personal belief you are quite right: violence is an abomination. I was simply showing you that your conscience would have nothing to reproach you with if you were ... if you wished to save your brother voluntarily, in the way I have suggested. I mean you would simply be yielding to circumstances, or even to force, if we can't manage without that word. Think of this: your brother's fate, and your mother's as well, are in your hands. I will be your slave ... all my life ... I will wait here ...'

Svidrigaylov sat down on the sofa, some yards away from Dunya. She had no longer the slightest doubt of his unshakeable determination. Besides, she knew him ...

Suddenly she took a revolver out of her pocket, cocked it, and rested the hand that held it on the little table. Svidrigaylov sprang up.

'Aha! So that's it!' he exclaimed in astonishment, but still smiling maliciously. 'Well, that entirely changes matters! You yourself are making things very much easier for me, Avdotya Romanovna. Where did you get that revolver, though? Not from Mr. Razumikhin? Why! That revolver is mine! An old friend! And I looked all over for it! ... The lessons in shooting, which I had the honour to give you in the country, were not entirely wasted, then.'

'The revolver did not belong to you, but to Marfa Petrovna, whom you killed, wretch! There was nothing of yours in her house. I took it when I began to suspect what you were capable of. Dare to move one step forward, and I swear I will kill you!'

Dunya was in a frenzy. She kept the revolver cocked.

'Well, and what about your brother? I ask out of curiosity,' said Svidrigaylov, still standing in the same place.

'Denounce him, if you will! Don't stir! Not a step! I will shoot! You poisoned your wife, I know you did. You are a murderer yourself! . . .'

'Are you quite certain that I poisoned Marfa Petrovna?'

'Yes! You hinted as much to me; you spoke to me about poison . . . I know you went for some . . . you had it ready . . . It was you! It was certainly you . . . wretch!'

'Even if that were true, it would have been because of you . . . you would have been the cause of it.'

'You are lying! I always hated you, always . . .'

'Ah, Avdotya Romanovna! You seem to have forgotten how you softened towards me in the heat of propaganda and grew tender . . . I could see it in your eyes; do you remember the evening, and the moonlight, and a nightingale singing?'

'Lies!' (Dunya's eyes flashed with furious rage.) 'Lies and vile slander!'

'Lies? Well, perhaps so. I lied. Woman should not be reminded of such things.' (He smiled.) 'I know you will shoot me, you pretty little wild creature. Well, shoot then!'

Dunya raised the revolver and looked at him with her great black eyes flashing fire in her white face. Her lower lip was pale and quivering, but her resolve was firm and she estimated the distance between them and waited for the first move on his part. He had never seen her look so beautiful. The flame that shone in her eyes as she raised the revolver seemed to set him on fire, and his heart contracted with pain. He took a step forward and a shot rang out. The bullet grazed his scalp and lodged in the wall behind him. He stood still and laughed softly:

'The wasp has stung me! She aims straight at the head . . . What's this? Blood!' He took out his handkerchief to wipe away the blood which flowed in a thin trickle down his right temple. The bullet seemed barely to have grazed the skin. Dunya lowered the revolver and stared at Svidrigaylov not so much in terror as in a sort of wild perplexity. It was as though she did not understand what she had done or what was happening.

'Well, you missed! Fire again, I will wait,' said Svidrigaylov softly, still laughing, if rather sourly. 'If you behave like this, I shall have time to seize you before you have got the revolver cocked!'

Dunechka shuddered, hastily cocked the gun, and again levelled it.

'Leave me alone!' she said desperately. 'I swear I will shoot again . . . I . . . will kill you! . . .'

'Well . . . at three paces it is impossible not to kill. But if you don't kill me . . . then . . .' His eyes gleamed, and he took two more paces forward.

Dunechka pulled the trigger, and the gun misfired.

'You didn't load properly. It doesn't matter! You have another cap there. Put it right. I'll wait.'

He stood in front of her, two steps away, waiting and gazing at her with wild determination in his sombre eyes, inflamed with passion. Dunya realized that he would rather die than let her go. And . . . she would certainly kill him now, at two paces! . . .

Suddenly she flung down the revolver.

'She has given up!' said Svidrigaylov in amazement, and drew a deep breath. Some burden seemed to have lifted suddenly from his heart, and it was perhaps not only the fear of death, which, indeed, it is doubtful if he had felt in that moment. The relief he felt was from another emotion, gloomier and more melancholy, which he could not have defined in all its force.

He went up to Dunya and gently laid his arm round her waist. She did not resist, but her whole body shook like a leaf and she looked at him with imploring eyes. He tried to say something but, although his lips moved, he could not speak.

'Let me go!' implored Dunya. Svidrigaylov started, struck by the sudden difference in her tone.

'So you do not love me?' he asked softly.

Dunya shook her head.

'And . . . you cannot? . . . Not ever?' he whispered in despair.

'Never!' whispered Dunya.

In Svidrigaylov's soul there was an instant of terrible, silent struggle. He gazed at Dunya with an indescribable expression. Suddenly he took away his arm, turned round, and walked quickly away to the window, where he stood for a moment in silence. 'Here is the key!' (He had taken it from the left-hand pocket of his overcoat and laid it behind him on the table, without looking or turning round.) 'Take it; leave quickly! . . .'

He still gazed fixedly out of the window.

Dunya approached the table to take the key.

'Quickly! Quickly!' repeated Svidrigaylov, still without moving or turning round. But the sound of his voice had something terrible in it.

Dunya understood, seized the key, hurried to the door, unlocked it hastily, and rushed from the room. A minute later she was running like a mad woman along the canal towards Voznesensky Bridge.

Svidrigaylov stayed some three minutes longer by the window; at last he turned round, looked about him, and slowly passed his hand over his forehead. There was a strange smile on his face, the weak, pitiful, mournful smile of despair. The blood, which was already almost dry, smeared his palm; he looked at it bitterly, then wetted a towel and washed his temple. The revolver Dunya had flung away from her caught his eye as it lay near the door. He picked it up and looked at it. It was a small old-fashioned weapon which fired three shots; there were still two charges and one percussion cap in it. It could be fired once more. He stood and thought for a moment, then thrust it into his pocket, took his hat, and went out.

## CHAPTER VI

ALL that evening until ten o'clock he spent in wandering between various taverns and brothels. He picked up Katya again somewhere, and she sang another of her servants'-hall songs, about a certain 'villain and tyrant' who 'kissed Katya'.

Svidrigaylov bought drinks for Katya, the organ-grinder, some singers and servants, and two little clerks. He had drawn these clerks into the company because they both had crooked noses, one twisted to the right and the other to the left. Svidrigaylov was much struck with this circumstance. Finally, they persuaded him to go to a pleasure-garden, where he paid for all of them to go in. This garden contained one frail three-year-old fir tree and three bushes. A 'Vauxhall',[5] really a bar which served tea as well, had been built in it, and besides there were a few green tables and chairs. The public was entertained by a chorus of very poor singers and some drunken German from Munich as a red-nosed, but extremely melancholy, clown. The clerks got into an argument with some other clerks and almost came to blows. They asked Svidrigaylov to settle the dispute. He listened to them for about a quarter of an hour, but they shouted so loud that there was not the slightest hope of discovering what it was all about. What seemed to be the most firmly established was that one of them had stolen something and even managed to sell it then and there to a Jew who happened along, but then he had refused to share the proceeds with his companion. It turned out that the object he had sold was a teaspoon belonging to the 'Vauxhall'. The loss was discovered and the affair began to take on a troublesome aspect. Svidrigaylov paid for the spoon, got up

5. Vauxhall was a famous London entertainment garden, dating from the seventeenth century; its name came to be applied to outdoor restaurants and gardens throughout Europe.

and left the garden. It was about ten o'clock. During all this time he had drunk nothing at all, and in the 'Vauxhall' had ordered for himself only tea, and that merely for the sake of appearances. The evening had been sultry and overcast. Towards ten o'clock heavy clouds began to pile up overhead, there was a clap of thunder, and rain swept down in a deluge. It fell not in drops but in streams that beat upon the ground like a waterfall. The lightning flashed incessantly, and the flashes lasted while one might count five. Wet through to the skin, Svidrigaylov went home, locked his door, opened his bureau, took out all his money, and tore up some papers. Then, thrusting the money into his pocket, he was about to change his clothes, but when he looked out of the window and heard the thunder and the rain he shrugged his shoulders, took his hat and went out, leaving the door unlocked. He went straight to Sonya. She was at home.

She was not alone; Kapernaumov's four little children were with her. Sofya Semënovna was giving them tea. She greeted Svidrigaylov silently and politely, looked in surprise at his wet clothes, but said nothing. The children fled in unaccountable terror.

Svidrigaylov sat down at the table and asked Sonya to sit beside him. She timidly prepared to listen to him.

'Sofya Semënovna,' he said, 'I may, perhaps, be going to America, and as this is probably the last time we shall see each other, I have come to complete some arrangements. Well, did you see the lady today? I know what she told you, you need not repeat it.' (Sonya, blushing, had made some slight movement.) 'People like that always follow the same old lines. As far as your little brother and sisters are concerned, they are definitely provided for and I have paid over the money destined for each of them into trustworthy hands and taken receipts for it. You had better keep the receipts, in case they are needed. Here you are. Well, now that is done. Here are three five-percent bonds, worth three thousand roubles altogether. Take these for yourself, for yourself personally, and let this be between ourselves. Nobody is to know of it, whatever you may hear. You will need them, because, Sofya Semënovna, to live as you have been doing is wrong and now you will have no further need to do so.'

'You have been so very good to me, and those orphaned children, and their poor mother,' said Sonya hurriedly, 'that if I have given you so little thanks up to now, . . . I don't want you to think . . .'

'Stop. Say no more.'

'But this money, Arkady Ivanovich, I am very grateful to you, but I really don't need it now. I have only myself to keep.

Please don't think I am ungrateful, but if you want to do good with this money, then . . .'

'It is for you, for you, Sofya Semënovna, and, please, without any discussion, because I really have no time. And you will need it. Rodion Romanovich has two ways open to him: a bullet through the brain, or Siberia.' (Sonya looked at him wildly and began to tremble.) 'Don't be disturbed; I know everything, and from his own lips, but I am not a talker. I shall not tell anybody. You did right to tell him that he should go and confess everything of his own accord. It would be much better for him. Well, if it is to be Siberia—he will go, and I suppose you will follow him. That is so, isn't it? Isn't it? Well, if so, that means you will need the money. You will need it for him, do you understand? If I give it to you it is all the same as if I gave it to him. Besides, you promised to pay Amalia Ivanovna, as well; I heard you. Why is it, Sofya Semënovna, that you take all these debts and obligations on yourself so recklessly? It was Katerina Ivanovna who was in debt to the German woman, not you, so you should let the German go hang. That's not the way to live in this world. Well, if ever anybody asks you—tomorrow, say, or the day after—about me or anything to do with me (and you will be asked), don't mention my having been to see you now, and don't show anybody the money or tell them anything about my having given it to you. Well, now good-bye.' He stood up. 'My kind regards to Rodion Romanovich. By the way: until the time comes keep the money with Mr. Razumikhin. Do you know him? Oh, of course you do. He is all right. Take it to him tomorrow or . . . when the time comes. Until then hide it carefully.'

Sonya had also jumped up and was gazing fearfully at him. She was longing to say something, to ask questions, but at first she did not dare, and indeed did not know how to begin.

'How can you . . . how can you go now, in such rain?'

'What, mean to go to America and be afraid of the rain! He, he! Good-bye, Sofya Semënovna, my dear. May you live long to be a blessing to others. By the way . . . tell Mr. Razumikhin that I sent him my greetings. Say it in those words: Arkady, you must say, Ivanovich Svidrigaylov sends you his greetings. Don't fail.'

He went, leaving Sonya bewildered and frightened, and filled with vague and distressing forebodings.

It appeared later that at some time after eleven o'clock that same evening he made another extremely odd and unexpected visit. It was still raining. He was wet through when, at twenty minutes to twelve, he entered the crowded little flat of his fiancée's parents, at the corner of the Maly Prospect and the

Third Line, on Vasilyevsky Island. He had some difficulty in gaining admittance, and at first his presence caused consternation; but, when he wished, Arkady Ivanovich had extremely charming manners and he immediately succeeded in dispelling the first (and very intelligent) suspicion of his bride's prudent and sensible parents, that he had got so drunk somewhere or other that he did not know what he was doing. The sensible and soft-hearted mother wheeled out her invalid husband in his arm-chair to Arkady Ivanovich and then, in her usual way, proceeded to discuss subjects remote from all that concerned her. (She was a woman who never attacked questions directly, but, if it were absolutely necessary for her to get accurate information about something, such as what day Arkady Ivanovich would be pleased to appoint for the wedding, she always first brought into play various little smiles and rubbings of her hands, and then began to ask curious and even eager questions about Paris and the life of the court there, in due course bringing the subject round by slow degrees to the Third Line on Vasilyevsky Island.) At any other time, of course, all this was received with respect, but on this occasion Arkady Ivanovich proved somehow peculiarly impatient, and brusquely expressed a wish to see his fiancée, although he had been informed at the very beginning that she had already gone to bed. Naturally, she made her appearance. Arkady Ivanovich at once told her that he was obliged to leave St. Petersburg for a time on very important business, and had therefore brought her various notes to the value of fifteen thousand roubles in silver, which he asked her to accept from him as a gift, since he had long meant to make her this trifling present before their marriage. The particular logical connexion of the gift with his imminent departure, and with the absolute necessity of arriving in pouring rain at midnight, was not, of course, made at all clear by these explanations, but things went off very well, nevertheless. Even the inevitable ohs and ahs, questions and wondering exclamations were unusually restrained and subdued; on the other hand, there were ardent expressions of gratitude, reinforced by tears from the very sensible mother. Arkady Ivanovich rose, laughing, kissed his fiancée, tapped her cheek, reaffirmed his intention of returning soon, and, seeing in her eyes, as well as childish curiosity, a silent, serious question, thought for a moment and kissed her again. At the same time he experienced a moment of real vexation that his present would immediately be locked away in the care of the most sensible of mothers. He went out, leaving them all in a state of extraordinary excitement. But the tender mama, in a rapid undertone, at once began to resolve some of their more pressing doubts, declaring that Arkady Ivanovich was a great man, a man of affairs, with great connexions, a rich man—

God only knew what he might have in his mind; he might take it into his head to go away, or to give away money, and consequently there was no reason to be surprised. Of course, it was strange that he was wet through, but Englishmen, for example, were even more eccentric than that, and besides, none of these worldly and fashionable people cared what might be said of them, and they did not stand on ceremony. Perhaps he even came like that on purpose, to show that he was not afraid of anybody. But the most important thing was not to say a word about this to anybody, because nobody knew what might be the consequences, and the money must be put under lock and key at once, and, of course, the best thing about all this was that Fedosya was still in the kitchen, and, above all, above all, nothing must be confided to that sly vixen Resslich, and so on, and so on. They sat and whispered until almost two o'clock. The young lady, however, had gone to bed much earlier, full of wonder and rather melancholy.

Meanwhile, just at midnight, Svidrigaylov crossed the Tuchkov Bridge towards Petersburgsky Island. The rain had ceased, but a blustering wind had risen. He was beginning to shiver. For a minute he gazed with peculiar interest, and even with a questioning look, at the black water of the Little Neva, but he soon found it very cold standing near the water, and he turned and walked along the Bolshoy Prospect. He walked steadily down the endless avenue for almost half an hour, stumbling sometimes in the darkness on the wooden pavement, but always intently scanning the right-hand side of the avenue in search of something. Somewhere there, nearly at the end of the Prospect, he had recently noticed as he went past a fairly large hotel, built of wood; its name, as far as he could remember, was something like 'The Adrianople.' He was not mistaken; in that remote spot the hotel was so conspicuous that it was impossible to miss it, even in the dark. It was a long wooden building, black with age, and in spite of the lateness of the hour there were still lights and signs of life about it. He went in and asked the ragged waiter who met him in the corridor for a room. The waiter looked him over, pulled himself together, and led him to a cramped and stuffy room, somewhere at the farthest end of the corridor, in a corner under the stairs. But there was no other; all the rest were occupied. The ragged waiter looked inquiringly at Svidrigaylov.

'Is there any tea?' asked Svidrigaylov.

'There might be, sir.'

'Is there anything else?'

'Veal, vodka, hors d'œuvre.'

'Bring me tea and some veal.'

'Don't you want anything else?' asked the waiter, apparently somewhat puzzled.

'No, nothing.'

The ragged waiter retreated, quite disillusioned.

'A marvellous place this is!' thought Svidrigaylov. 'Why didn't I know that? I, too, probably look as if I were coming back from some *café-chantant*, and had had some adventures on the way. I wonder, though, who stays here.'

He lit a candle and looked more closely at the room. It was a tiny hutch of a place, hardly big enough to hold him, with one window; a filthy bed, a stained deal table, and a chair occupied almost all the floor-space. The walls looked as though they had been roughly knocked together from boards, and the wall-paper was dirty and faded, and so dusty and torn that, although its original colour (yellow) could still be guessed at, it was quite impossible to make out its pattern. At one place, where the stairs went up, the wall and ceiling sloped obliquely like those of an attic. Svidrigaylov put down his candle, sat on the bed, and fell into thought. But after some time his attention was distracted by a strange incessant whispering, which sometimes rose almost to a shriek, coming from the adjoining hutch. This sound had never ceased since he went in. He listened; somebody was almost tearfully scolding and upbraiding somebody else, but he could hear only one voice. Svidrigaylov got up and shaded the candle with his hand; light at once shone through a crack in the wall. He went up and looked through it. In the room, which was slightly larger than his own, were two guests. One, in his shirt-sleeves, a man with extraordinarily curly hair and an inflamed red face, stood in the pose of a public speaker, with his legs wide apart to preserve his balance, and pathetically, beating his breast, reproached the other for his beggary and lack of social standing, and reminded him that he had plucked him out of the gutter and could drive him back there when he would, and that only the finger of God sees everything. The object of the tirade sat on the chair with the expression of a man with an irresistible desire to sneeze which he cannot gratify. He glanced occasionally at the orator with a dull and sheepish eye, but he plainly had no idea what the trouble was and it was even doubtful whether he heard anything that was said. On the table, where the candle had nearly burned down, stood an almost empty decanter of vodka, glasses, bread, cucumbers, tumblers, and a long-emptied tea service. Svidrigaylov studied this picture carefully, and then indifferently moved away from the crack and sat down again on the bed.

The seedy waiter, returning with the tea and veal, could not refrain from asking again whether he did not want something more; receiving a negative answer once more, he finally took himself off. Svidrigaylov pounced on the tea, to warm himself, and drank a glassful, but his appetite was quite gone and he could not eat anything. He was evidently beginning to be feverish. He took off his overcoat and jacket, rolled himself in a blanket and lay down on the bed. He felt annoyed: 'I ought to have been well for this occasion,' he thought, and laughed shortly. The room felt stuffy, the candle burnt dimly, the wind howled outside, a mouse scratched somewhere in a corner, and the whole room smelt of mice and some kind of leather. He lay in a half-dream, with the ideas chasing each other through his mind. He would have liked to find some object on which his thoughts could fix themselves. 'There must be a garden of some sort outside the window', he thought; 'I can hear the trees rustling. How I dislike the sound of trees at night in storm and darkness! A nasty sensation!' And he remembered how repulsive he had found it just now, when he was passing the Petrovsky Park. This reminded him of the Tuchkov Bridge and the Little Neva and he seemed to feel cold again, as he had then, standing above the water. 'I have never liked water, even in landscapes,' he thought again, and once more laughed shortly at a certain strange idea: 'You would think I ought to be quite indifferent to all these questions of aesthetics and comfort now, and here I have grown as particular as a wild animal fastidiously choosing a place . . . in similar circumstances. I ought just to have turned into Petrovsky Park. I suppose I thought it was too dark, or too cold. He, he! Are pleasant sensations so nearly essential to me? . . . By the way, why not put out the candle?' (He blew it out.) 'My neighbours have gone to bed,' he thought, no longer seeing the light through the crack. 'Now, Marfa Petrovna, now you would do very well to pay me a visit; it is dark, the place is apt, and the choice of time would be original. But of course, it is just now that you will not come . . .'

For some reason he suddenly remembered how, an hour before he carried his design against Dunechka into effect, he recommended Raskolnikov to entrust her to Razumikhin's care. 'The fact is that I said that mostly to torment myself, as Raskolnikov guessed. What a rascal that Raskolnikov is, though! He has brought a lot on himself. He may become a great rogue in time, when the nonsense has left him, but now he wants to live *too much!* In that particular people like him are wretches. Well, the devil take him; let him do as he likes, it's nothing to me.'

He could not sleep. Little by little the image of Dunechka as he had last seen her began to glimmer before him, and a sudden tremor shook him. 'No, now I must throw this off,' he thought, rousing himself; 'I must think of something else. It is strange and laughable: I never greatly hated anybody, I never even felt particularly revengeful, and that is a bad sign, a bad sign! I didn't like quarrelling either, and never got heated

—another bad sign! And how much I promised her! Oh, the devil! But she might indeed have re-moulded me somehow . . .'
He fell silent, and clenched his teeth; again Dunya's image rose before him, exactly as she had been when, after firing once, she became terribly frightened and lowered the revolver, gazing at him, half-stunned, so that he might have seized her twice over and she would not have raised a hand to defend herself, if he had not reminded her himself. He remembered how at that moment his heart had contracted with pity for her . . . 'Oh, to the devil with it! These thoughts again! I must throw them all off, throw them off! . . .'

He was slipping into forgetfulness; his feverish trembling had ceased; suddenly he seemed to feel something running over his arm and leg under the blanket. He jumped: 'Damn it, I'm hanged if it isn't a mouse!' he thought. 'It's the veal I left on the table . . .' He felt extremely reluctant to unroll himself from the blanket and get up in the shivering cold, but again something unpleasant touched his leg; he tore off the blanket and lit the candle. Shaking with feverish chill he stooped down to look at the bed—there was nothing there; he shook out the blanket and a mouse darted out on the sheet. He tried to catch it, but the mouse, without jumping down from the bed, ran to and fro in zigzags, slipped from between his fingers, ran over his hand, and disappeared under the pillow; he flung the pillow aside, but instantly felt something jump under his shirt and run over his body and down his back. He shuddered with nerves and woke up. The room was dark, he was lying on the bed, still wrapped in the blanket, and the wind howled outside the window. 'How horrible!' he thought with disgust.

He got up and sat on the edge of the bed with his back to the window. 'I should do better not to sleep at all,' he decided. But it blew cold and damp from the window; without getting up, he pulled the blanket towards him and wrapped himself in it. He did not light the candle. He did not think of anything, and did not wish to think; but dreams and fragmentary ideas without beginning or end, or any coherence, rose before him one after another. He fell into a kind of half doze. The cold or the darkness, the dampness or the wind whistling outside the window and shaking the trees, one of these perhaps aroused in him a stubborn fanciful mood and longing—at any rate, his mind began to dwell persistently on flowers. He imagined a charming landscape; a bright, warm, almost hot day, a holiday—Whit Sunday.[6] A rich luxurious country cottage in the English style, overgrown with sweet-scented flowering plants and with flower-borders all round it; a porch twined with climbing plants and surrounded by beds of roses; a light, cool staircase, richly carpeted and banked with rare flowers

6. Whit Sunday, the feast of the Pentecost, in the Russian Trinity Feast, celebrated in Russia on the fiftieth day after Easter, usually at the end of May or beginning of June.

in Chinese vases. He particularly noticed great bunches of delicate white narcissi in jars in the windows, with their heavy aromatic fragrance, hanging their heads on their long thick stalks of clear green. He was reluctant to leave them, but he went on up the stairs and into a large, high-ceilinged drawing-room, and again, everywhere, in the windows, round the doors standing wide open to the balcony, on the balcony itself, everywhere there were flowers. The floor was strewn with fragrant freshly cut hay, the windows were open, a cool, fresh, gentle breeze blew into the room, birds were chirping under the windows, and in the middle of the room, on tables shrouded in white satin, stood a coffin. It was lined with heavy white silk, bordered with thick white frilling, and surrounded on all sides by wreaths of flowers. Among the flowers lay a young girl in a white tulle dress, and the hands closely folded over her breast were like marble. But her loosened hair, her bright fair hair, was wet; there was a garland of roses on her head. Her stern, set profile looked as though it too were carved in marble, but the smile on her pale lips was full of infinite, unchildlike grief and immense bitterness. Svidrigaylov knew her. There were no lighted candles, no holy icons, beside the coffin, and no prayers were heard; she was a suicide, drowned. She was no more than fourteen, but that heart had been broken, and had destroyed itself, savagely wounded by the outrage that had amazed and horrified her young childish conscience, overwhelmed her soul, pure as an angel's, with unmerited shame, and torn from her a last cry of despair, unregarded, but defiantly shrieked into the dark night, into the blackness, the cold, the torrents of spring, while the wind howled . . .

Svidrigaylov roused himself, got up from the bed, and reached the window in one stride. The wind whipped furiously into his crowded little room and clung coldly, like hoar-frost, round his face and his breast, covered only by his shirt. Under the window there must indeed be a garden of sorts, a pleasure-garden, it seemed; probably there was music and singing there in the daytime, and tea was carried out to be drunk at little tables. Now rain spattered in at the window from the trees and bushes, and it was as dark as a cellar, so that it was barely possible to distinguish objects as faintly darker patches in the blackness. Svidrigaylov, stooping down and leaning with his elbows on the sill, stared into the obscurity for a full five minutes. Through the gloom of the night sounded a cannon shot, then another.

'Ah, the signal![7]The water is rising,' he thought; 'towards morning, in the lower parts of the town, it will swirl through the streets and flood the basements and cellars, the sewer-rats will come up to the surface, and amid the rain and the wind

7. There were five different categories of signals by cannon shots, corresponding to various levels of flooding.

people will begin, dripping wet and cursing, to drag their rubbish to the upper floors ... What time is it now?' No sooner had the thought crossed his mind, than a clock somewhere near, ticking away in a great hurry, struck three. 'Aha, in an hour it will be light! Why wait for that? I will go at once, I will go straight across to Petrovsky Island and pick out somewhere a tall bush, dripping with rain, so that the slightest touch will bring a million rivulets splashing down all over my head ...' He fastened the window, lit the candle, pulled on his waistcoat and overcoat, put his hat on his head and went out with his candle into the corridor to look for the tattered waiter (sleeping in some corner among candle-ends and all sorts of trash), pay for his room, and leave the hotel. 'This is the very best time, I could not choose a better!'

It took a long time to walk the whole length of the narrow corridor; he found nobody, and was just about to shout when in a shadowy corner, between an old cupboard and a door, something caught his eye, something that seemed to be alive. He stooped down with the candle and saw a child—a little girl, no more than five years old, shivering and crying, her clothes dripping like a wet dish-cloth. She did not seem afraid of Svidrigaylov but looked at him with dull wonder in her big black eyes. Now and then she caught her breath sobbingly, as children do when they have stopped crying after a long time and are beginning to be comforted, but still from time to time break into sobs again. The child's little face looked pale and exhausted, and she was stiff with cold. 'How did she come here? She must have hidden herself and stayed here all night.' He began to question her. The little girl became lively all at once and began to babble in her childish way. There was something about 'mummy', 'mummy will be cwoss', about a cup that was 'bwoke'. The little girl chattered without ceasing, and it was possible to make out from what she said that she was the neglected child of some drunken cook, probably in that hotel, and that her mother bullied and thrashed her; that she had broken 'mummy's' cup the evening before and been so frightened that she had run away, and after cowering outside in the rain for a long time had crept in here and hidden behind the cupboard. She had crouched all night in the corner, crying and shivering from the damp, the darkness, and the fear that she would be severely thrashed. He carried her into his room, set her on the bed, and began to undress her. The torn shoes on her bare feet were as wet as though they had lain in a puddle all night. When he had undressed her, he laid her on the bed and swathed her from head to foot in the blanket. She fell asleep at once. When he had finished, he relapsed again into moody thoughts.

'Well! Here I am, getting myself involved!' he thought suddenly, with heavy anger. 'How absurd!' Irritated, he took up his candle, to go and find the waiter at all costs, and leave as quickly as possible. 'Oh, the little girl!' he thought with an oath, as he was opening the door, but he turned back once more to see whether she was asleep, and how she was sleeping. Carefully he lifted the blanket. The little girl was sound and peacefully asleep. She had grown warm under the blanket, and there was colour in her pale cheeks. But it was strange, the colour seemed brighter and stronger than the usual rosiness of childhood. 'It is the flush of fever,' thought Svidrigaylov, but it looked almost more like the flush of wine—as though she had been given a whole glassful to drink. Her scarlet lips seemed to burn and glow, but what was this? Suddenly it seemed to him that the long black lashes stirred and fluttered, as though they were about to lift, and from under them looked, with an un-childlike wink, a sly, sharp eye, as though the child were not asleep, but only pretending. Yes, it was true; her lips parted in a smile; the corners of the mouth quivered, as if she were still restraining herself. But now she had ceased to control herself at all, and it was a laugh, a downright laugh; an impudent invitation gleamed from that unchildlike face; it was corruption, it was the face of a courtesan, the brazen face of a mercenary French harlot. Now, without further concealment, both eyes were open, enveloping him with their shameless, burning glance, inviting him, laughing . . . There was something monstrous and infinitely offensive in that laugh, in those eyes, in all that nastiness in the face of a child. 'What! A five-year-old!' whispered Svidrigaylov in real horror. 'This . . . what is this?' But now she turned to him, all her little face glowing, and stretched out her arms . . . 'Accursed creature!' cried Svidrigaylov in horror, raising his arm to strike her . . . But at that moment he awoke.

He was still on the bed, rolled as before in the blanket; the candle had not been lighted, and daylight was already whitening the windows.

'Nightmares all night long!' He raised himself, feeling jaded and angry; his bones ached. There was a thick mist outside, and nothing could be seen through it. It was nearly five o'clock; he had overslept! He got up and put on his still damp jacket and overcoat. He felt in his pocket for the revolver, took it out and correctly replaced the percussion cap; then he sat down, took out a notebook and wrote a few lines in large letters on the front page, where they must be seen, read them over and sat pondering with his elbows on the table. The revolver and the notebook lay by his elbow. Newly awakened flies clustered on the untouched veal, which also stood on the table. He watched them for some time and at last began trying to catch one of them with his free right hand. He tried for a long time, until he was tired with his efforts, but quite unsuccessfully. Finally, catching himself in this interesting occupation, he roused himself with a start, got up, and resolutely walked out of the room. A minute later he was in the street.

A thick milky mist covered the city. Svidrigaylov walked along slippery, greasy, wooden pavements towards the Little Neva. His mind still held the illusory vision of its waters rising in flood during the night, and pictured Petrovsky Island, the wet paths, the soaking grass, the dripping trees and bushes and at last that one bush . . . In an effort to think of something else, he looked disapprovingly at the houses. The avenue was empty of cabs and passers-by. The little bright-yellow wooden houses, with their closed shutters, looked dirty and dejected. The cold and damp were penetrating his whole body and making him shiver. Occasionally he came across signs outside little shops and market-gardens, and he conscientiously read each one. The wooden pavement had come to an end, and he was passing a large stone building. A dirty, shivering cur, with its tail between its legs, crossed his path. A man in a greatcoat lay, dead-drunk, face down on the pavement; he passed him and went on. A tall watch-tower caught his eye on the left. 'Bah!' he thought. 'This is a good enough place; why go to Petrovsky? At least there will be an official witness . . .' He almost smiled at this new idea and turned into Syezhinskaya Street. Here stood the large building with the watch-tower. Near the big closed gates a little man, wrapped in a soldier's grey greatcoat and wearing a copper helmet that made him look like Achilles, was leaning his shoulder against the wall. He looked with sleepy indifference at Svidrigaylov as he approached. His face had the eternal expression of resentful affliction which is so sharply etched on every Jewish face, without exception. For a short time the two, Svidrigaylov and Achilles, stood contemplating one another in silence. At length Achilles decided that it was out of order for a man who was not drunk to be standing two yards away and staring at him without a word.

'Vell, vot do you vant here already?' he asked, without moving or changing his position.

'Nothing, brother. Good morning to you!' answered Svidrigaylov.

'So go somevere else.'

'I am going to foreign parts, brother.'

'Foreign parts?'

'To America.'

'America?'

Svidrigaylov took out the revolver and cocked it. Achilles raised his eyebrows.

'Vot now, this is not the place for jokes!'

'Why shouldn't it be the place?'

'Because it isn't.'

'Well, brother, it doesn't matter. It's a good place . . . If you are asked, say I said I was off to America.'

He lifted the revolver to his right temple.

'But you can't do that here! This is not the proper place!' Achilles, whose eyes had been growing rounder and rounder, started forward.

Svidrigaylov pulled the trigger . . .

## CHAPTER VII

THAT same day, but towards seven o'clock in the evening, Raskolnikov was making his way towards his mother's and sister's flat in Bakaleev's house, where Razumikhin had installed them. The entrance to the staircase was on the street. As Raskolnikov approached, he seemed to hang back as though he were in two minds whether to go in or not. But he had made up his mind; nothing would have made him turn back. 'Besides, it makes no difference. They don't know anything yet,' he thought, 'and they have got used to finding me unaccountable . . .' His clothes were dreadful, dirty, threadbare, torn and wrinkled after a whole night in the rain. His face was almost distorted with exhaustion, the result of physical fatigue, foul weather, and an inward strife prolonged for almost twenty-four hours. All night he had been alone, God knows where. But at least he had made up his mind.

He knocked at the door; his mother opened it. Dunechka was not there. The maid also happened to be out for the moment. At first Pulkheria Alexandrovna was dumb with joyful amazement; then she seized his hand and drew him into the room.

'Well, here you are!' she began, stammering with joy. 'Don't be angry, Rodya, because my welcome was so foolish and tearful; I am laughing really, not crying. Do you think I am crying? No, I am happy, but it is a foolish way I have; the tears come. It has been like this since your father's death; I cry for everything. Sit down, my darling, you must be tired; I can see you are. Oh dear, you have got yourself into a sadly dirty state.'

'I was out in the rain yesterday, mama . . .' Raskolnikov was beginning.

'Oh no, no!' burst out Pulkheria Ivanovna, interrupting him. 'You thought I was beginning to ask you questions straight away, like a foolish old woman, as I used to; don't be alarmed. Really I understand, I understand everything; now I have learnt how things are done here and really it is more sensible, I can see that for myself. I have come to the conclusion, once for all, that I mustn't expect to understand the considerations that decide your actions, or demand an account of them from you. You may have God knows what plans and business in your mind, or all sorts of ideas may have sprung up in you; am I to be always jogging your elbow to ask you what you are thinking about? You see I . . . Oh Lord, why am I dashing about like a scalded cat? . . . Look, Rodya, I have been reading your article in the magazine for the third time; Dmitry Prokofich brought it for me. Well, I sighed when I saw it. "See how foolish you are," I thought to myself; "this is what he is busy with, this is the answer to the riddle! Clever people are always like that. He has new ideas, perhaps, in his head just now; he is thinking about them, and I worry and disturb him." I am reading it, my dear, and of course there is a lot that I don't understand; but that must be so: how could I?'

'Show me, mama.'

Raskolnikov took the paper and glanced for a moment at his article. Inconsistent as the feeling might be with his mood and circumstances, he experienced the strange and painfully sweet sensations of the author who sees himself in print for the first time; but then, he was only twenty-three. It lasted only for a moment. After reading a few lines, he frowned and a terrible anguish squeezed his heart. All his inward strife of the past months returned to him in an instant. Annoyed and disgusted, he flung his article down on the table.

'But, Rodya, however foolish I may be, all the same I can tell that in a very short time you will be one of the first, if not the very first, among our men of learning. And people dared to think you were mad! Ha, ha, ha! You don't know, but they really did think that. Wretched crawling worms, how can they understand what true intellect is? And you know, Dunechka, Dunechka too almost believed they were right—as if they could be! Your poor father twice sent something to a magazine —first a poem (I have the manuscript still, I will show it to you some time), and then a whole novel (I copied it out for him, at my own request), and how we both prayed that they would be accepted—but they weren't! A few days ago, Rodya, I was terribly grieved to think of your clothes, the way you live, and what you have to eat. But now I see that I was just being foolish again, because you could get anything you wanted tomorrow, with your brains and talents. It is just that for the moment you have more important things to occupy you and don't want . . .'

'Isn't Dunya at home, mama?'

'No, Rodya. I very often don't see her; she leaves me by myself. I am grateful to Dmitry Prokofich; he comes to sit with me, and talks about you all the time. He is very fond of you and he respects you, my dear. I am not saying that your sister is not very considerate. I really am not complaining. She has her own character, and I have mine; she has acquired some secrets of her own, too; well, I have no secrets from either of you. Of course, I am firmly convinced that Dunya is too wise, and besides, she loves both me and you . . . but I really don't know what it is all leading to. Here you have made me so happy now, Rodya, by coming, and she has gone out somewhere; when she comes, I shall say, "Your brother has been while you weren't here, and where have you been spending your time?" You mustn't spoil me too much, Rodya: if you can, come, if not, it can't be helped; I shall wait. Whatever happens, I shall know you love me, and I can be content with that. I shall read your writings, I shall hear about you from everybody, and from time to time you will come to see me—what could be better? You have come now, haven't you, to comfort your mother? I can see . . .'

Here Pulkheria Alexandrovna suddenly burst into tears.

'There I go again! Don't look at your foolish mother! Oh Lord, why do I go on sitting here?' she cried, jumping up. 'There is some coffee, and I don't even offer you some! You see what an old woman's selfishness means. I'll get it at once!'

'Mama, don't bother. I am going at once. That is not what I came for. Please listen to me.'

Pulkheria Alexandrovna timidly came to him.

'Mama, whatever happens, whatever you hear about me, whatever anybody says about me, will you love me just as you do now?' he asked with a full heart, seeming not to think of his words or weigh them.

'Rodya, Rodya, what is wrong? How can you ask such a thing? Who will say anything to me about you? And I shouldn't believe anybody, no matter who it was; I should simply send them packing.'

'I came to assure you that I have always loved you, and now I am glad that we are alone, glad even that Dunya is not here,' he went on in the same impulsive way. 'I came to tell you plainly that, although you will be unhappy, you must be sure that your son loves you more now than himself, and that all you have been thinking about my being cruel and not loving you is false. I shall never cease to love you . . . Well, that's enough; I thought that I must do this, begin with this . . .'

Pulkheria Alexandrovna silently embraced him, pressing him close to her and weeping softly.

'I don't know what is the matter with you, Rodya,' she said at last. 'I have been thinking all this time that you were simply bored with us, but now I see from all this that there is some great misfortune in store for you, and that is why you are sad. I foresaw it long ago, Rodya. Forgive me for talking about it. I think about it all the time, and I can't sleep at night. Last night your sister was talking in her sleep all night, and all about you. I made some of it out, but I couldn't understand it. I've been going about all day as if I were under sentence of death, waiting for something and full of foreboding, and now it has come! Rodya, Rodya, where are you going? Are you going away somewhere?'

'Yes.'

'I thought so! But you know I can go with you, if you need me. And Dunya; she loves you, she loves you dearly, and perhaps Sofya Semënovna could come with us, if you want her; you see, I am even willing to accept her as a daughter. Dmitri Prokofich will help us to make our plans to go together . . . but . . . where . . . are you going?'

'Good-bye, mama.'

'What? This very day?' she cried out, as though losing him for ever.

'I can't . . . It is time. I must .. .'

'But can't I go with you?'

'No, but kneel down and pray to God for me. Your prayers perhaps will reach him.'

'Let me make the sign of the cross over you, and bless you! Yes, that is right, that is right. Oh God, what are we doing?'

Yes, he was glad, very glad that nobody else was there, and that he was alone with his mother. It was as though, after all those dreadful months, his heart was all at once softened. He fell down before her and kissed her feet, and they wept, with their arms about one another. And she was not surprised; this time she did not question him. Indeed, she had understood for a long time that something terrible was happening to her son, and now a dreadful moment had come for him.

'Rodya, my dear, my first-born,' she said, sobbing 'now you are just like the little boy you used to be; you would come to me just like this, and put your arms round me and kiss me. When your father was still alive and we were poor, it was a comfort to have you with us, and when I buried your father, how often we used to weep over his grave with our arms round each other, like this. And if I have wept for a long time now, it is because my mother's heart had a presentiment of disaster. As soon as I saw you the first time, in the evening, you remember, when we had only just arrived here, I guessed everything simply from the way you looked at me, and my heart failed me; then today, when I opened the door, and looked at you, "Well," I thought, "the fatal moment has come". Rodya, Rodya, surely you are not going away immediately?'

'No.'

'You will come here again?'

'Yes . . . I will come.'

'Rodya, don't be angry, I can't even venture to ask questions. I know that I mustn't dare, but all the same, just tell me in two little words: are you going a long way?'

'A very long way.'

'What is there there? Some work, a career for you?'

'What God sends . . . only pray for me . . .'

Raskolnikov went to the door, but she caught at him and looked into his eyes with an expression of despair. Her face was disfigured with fear.

'That's enough, mama,' said Raskolnikov, bitterly regretting that he had ever thought of coming.

'It's not for ever? Surely it's not good-bye for ever? You will really come, come tomorrow?'

'Yes, yes, I will come. Good-bye.'

At last he tore himself away.

The evening was fresh, warm, and bright; the weather had begun to clear early in the morning. Raskolnikov went home; he was in a hurry. He wanted to finish all he had to do before sunset. Meanwhile he didn't wish to encounter anybody. As he went up to his flat he noticed that Nastasya left her samovar and attentively followed his progress with her eyes. 'Can there be somebody in my room?' he thought. The idea that it might be Porfiry filled him with repulsion. But when he reached his room and opened the door he saw Dunechka. She was sitting all alone, lost in thought, and seemed to have been waiting for a long time. He stopped on the threshold and she got up, startled, from the sofa and stood before him, her eyes fixed on his face with a look of terror and unfathomable sorrow. From that look he realized at once that she knew everything.

'Shall I come in or go away again?' he asked mistrustfully.

'I have been with Sofya Semënovna all day; we were both waiting for you. We thought you would be sure to go there.'

Raskolnikov went in and wearily sat down.

'I feel rather weak, Dunya, and I am very tired. And yet I should have liked to be in full control of myself, at any rate just now.'

Warily he raised his eyes to her.

'Where were you all night?'

'I don't remember very well; you see, sister, I wanted to reach a definite decision and I found myself walking near the Neva many times; I do remember that. I should have liked to end things there, but . . . I decided against it . . .' he whispered, again looking mistrustfully at Dunya.

'Thank God! We were so afraid of that very thing, Sonya Semënovna and I. So you still believe in life; thank God, thank God!'

Raskolnikov smiled bitterly.

'I did not believe in it, but just now, as I stood with my mother's arms round me, we both wept; I do not believe, but

I have asked her to pray for me. God knows how that comes about, Dunechka; even I don't understand any of it.'

'You have been to see mother? Have you told her?' cried Dunya, horrified. 'Could you really bring yourself to tell her?'

'No, I didn't tell her . . . in so many words; but she understood a great deal. She has heard you talking in your sleep. I am sure she half-knows already. Perhaps I did wrong to go and see her. I don't even remember myself why I went. I am a despicable creature, Dunya.'

'Despicable, when you are prepared to go to meet your suffering? You are going to meet it, aren't you?'

'Yes. Now. And it was to escape the shame that I wanted to drown myself, Dunya, but the thought came to me, when I was already standing on the bank, that if I had hitherto considered myself strong, then the shame should not frighten me now,' he said, hastening on. 'Is that pride, Dunya?'

'Yes, Rodya, it is pride.'

The almost extinct fire flared up again in his lustreless eyes; it was as though he were pleased that he could still be proud.

'And you don't think, sister, that I was simply afraid of the water?' he asked, with an ugly smile, looking into her face.

'Oh, stop, Rodya!' exclaimed Dunya bitterly.

There was a silence that lasted for some two minutes. He sat with his eyes on the floor; Dunechka was standing at the other end of the table and watching him in anguish. Suddenly he got up.

'It is late, I must go. I am going to give myself up immediately.'

Big tears rolled down her cheeks.

'You are crying, sister, but can you give me your hand?'

'Did you doubt it?'

She clasped him fiercely.

'Surely, by advancing to meet your punishment, you are half atoning for your crime?' she cried, pressing him close and kissing him.

'Crime? What crime?' he cried, in a sudden access of rage. 'Killing a foul, noxious louse, that old moneylender, no good to anybody, who sucked the life-blood of the poor, so vile that killing her ought to bring absolution for forty sins—was that a crime? That is not what I am thinking of, and I do not think of atoning for it. And why are you all pressing in on me from all sides with your "crime, crime!"? It is only now that I clearly realize the full absurdity of my faint-heartedness, now when I have made up my mind to face this unnecessary shame! It was simply my own baseness and incompetence that made me reach my decision, and perhaps the thought of benefit to myself, as that . . . Porfiry . . . suggested! . . .'

'Brother, brother, why are you saying this? You really did spill blood!' cried Dunya, in despair.

'Which everybody sheds,' he put in almost frantically, 'which flows and has always flowed on this earth in torrents, which is poured out like champagne, and for which men are crowned in the Capitol[8] and afterwards called benefactors of mankind. Look a little more closely and consider it carefully. I myself wanted to benefit men, and I would have done hundreds, thousands, of good deeds, to make up for that one piece of stupidity—not even stupidity, but simple clumsiness, since the whole idea was not nearly as stupid as it seems now, when it has failed . . . (failure makes anything seem stupid!). By that stupidity I meant only to put myself in an independent position, to take the first step, to acquire means, and then everything would have been expiated by immeasurably greater good . . . But I, I failed even to accomplish the first step, because I am a miserable wretch! That's what it all amounts to! All the same, I shan't look at it with your eyes: if I had succeeded, I should have been crowned, but now I shall fall into the trap!'

'No, that's wrong, that's quite wrong! Brother, why do you say these things?'

'Ah, it's the form that's wrong, the form is not aesthetically satisfactory! Well, I definitely don't understand why smashing people with bombs in a regular siege is formally more respectable! Regard for aesthetic considerations is the first sign of inability to act! . . . Never, never have I recognized this more clearly than now, and I understand less than ever why what I did is a crime! Never have I been stronger, never have I held my convictions more firmly, than now! . . .'

His white, exhausted face was flushed with colour. But, as he uttered the last exclamation, his eyes unexpectedly met Dunya's, and he read so much anguished feeling for him in her look that he involuntarily stopped short. He felt that, whatever else, he had made two poor women unhappy, that he was, in any case, responsible for that.

'Dunya, my dear! If I am guilty, forgive me (although, if I am guilty, I cannot be forgiven). Good-bye! Don't let us quarrel. It is time, it is quite time I went. Don't follow me, I beg you. I have to go somewhere else . . . But go at once and stay near mother. I beg you to do that! This is my last and most urgent request to you. Don't leave her, all the time; I left her in a state of agitation that I am afraid she will not be able to bear: she will die or go out of her mind. Be with her! Razumikhin will be with you; I have told him . . . Don't cry for me: I shall try to be honourable and manly all my life, although I am a murderer. Perhaps one day you will hear me spoken of. I shall not disgrace you, you will see; I may yet prove . . . But now, good-bye for the moment,' he finished hastily, again noticing a

8. The French emperor Napoleon III wrote in his book *The History of Julius Caesar,* a translation of which was published in Petersburg in 1865, and which made a great impression on Dostoevsky, that Julius Caesar was awarded the title of Supreme Priest and Tribune after he had cruelly killed many pirates.

strange expression come into Dunya's eyes at the promises in his last words. 'Why are you crying so? Don't cry, don't cry; we are not parting for ever! . . . Oh, yes! Stop a minute! I had forgotten . . .'

He went to the table, picked up a thick dusty book, opened it, and took out from between two pages a small water-colour portrait on ivory. It was a picture of his landlady's daughter, his former fiancée, who had died of fever. This was the strange girl who had wanted to enter a nunnery. He gazed for a minute at the expressive, delicate little face, kissed the portrait, and gave it to Dunechka.

'I talked to her a good deal *about that*, and to her alone,' he said thoughtfully. 'I confided to her heart a great deal of what afterwards turned out so monstrously. Don't distress yourself,' he went on, turning to Dunya; 'she did not agree with me, any more than you do, and I am glad she is not here now. The main thing is that now everything is going to be different. My whole life will be snapped in two,' he cried out suddenly, returning again to his own torments, 'everything, everything, and am I prepared for that? Do I want it? They say it is a necessary part of my ordeal. But what purpose is served by all these senseless trials? Shall I be better able to recognize that purpose then, when I am crushed with suffering and idiocy, and senilely impotent after twenty years of prison, than I am now? What shall I have to live for then? Why do I now acquiesce in such a life? Oh, I knew I was a miserable wretch when I stood at dawn today on the bank of the Neva!'

Together they went out at last. It was hard for Dunya, but she loved him. She walked away, but when she had gone fifty yards she turned round again and looked at him. He was still in sight. When he reached the corner he too turned round; their eyes met for the last time; when he saw that she was watching him he impatiently, even irritably, waved her on, and himself turned sharp round the corner.

'I am cruel, I know,' he thought, beginning to be ashamed of his irritated gesture. 'But why should they love me so much, when I am not worthy of it? Oh, if only I were alone and nobody loved me, and if I had never loved anyone! *All this would never have happened*! I wonder if my spirit will really grow so humble in the next fifteen or twenty years that I shall whine and whimper before people, branding myself a criminal with every word I utter. Yes, exactly, exactly! That is just why they are deporting me now, that is what they want . . . Look at all these scurrying about the streets, and every one of them is a scoundrel and a criminal by his very nature, and worse still, an idiot! But try to save me from exile and they would all go mad with righteous indignation! Oh, how I hate them all!'

He began to consider earnestly 'by what process it might

come about that he would finally humble himself before all of them instinctively, out of conviction. And yet why not? Of course, it must be so. Would not twenty years of unrelieved oppression crush him in the end? Water wears away a stone. And why,. why live after this? Why am I going there now, when I know that it will all happen according to the book, and not otherwise?'

He had already asked himself that question a hundred times since the previous evening, but all the same he went.

## CHAPTER VIII

IT was already dusk when he entered Sonya's room. She had been waiting for him all day in terrible agitation. She and Dunya had waited together for much of the time. Dunya, remembering how Svidrigaylov had said the evening before that Sonya 'knew about it', had gone to her in the morning. We shall not repeat all the details of the women's talk and their tears, or of what close friends they became. Dunya carried away at least one comfort from their interview, that her brother would not be alone; he had gone to Sonya first with his confession; when he felt the need of another human being, he had gone to her; and she would follow wherever fate sent him. Dunya did not even need to ask questions, she knew it was so. She regarded Sonya almost with awe and at first embarrassed her by treating her with such reverence. Sonya was almost ready to burst into tears; she thought of herself, on the contrary, as unfit even to look at Dunya. The lovely image of Dunya, when she bowed to her with such gracious politeness at their first meeting at Raskolnikov's, had remained with her ever since as one of the most beautiful and unattainable visions of her life.

Dunya at last grew impatient and left Sonya, in order to wait for her brother in his own room; she had thought all the time that he would go there first. Sonya immediately began torturing herself with the fear that he might really commit suicide. Dunya felt the same fear. But they had each been trying ceaselessly all day to persuade the other by every sort of argument that it could not happen, and they had felt less anxious while they were together. Now that they had parted, however, neither could think of anything else. Sonya remembered how Svidrigaylov had told her the day before that two courses were open to Raskolnikov—Siberia or . . . She knew, besides, his vanity, his arrogance, his self-esteem, his want of faith. Could it be that only a faint heart and the fear of death had kept him alive, she wondered desperately. The sun was setting. She stood by the window, looking out sadly and fixedly, but nothing could be seen from it but one blank unwhitewashed wall of the next house. At last, when she was completely convinced that the unhappy Raskolnikov was dead, he came into the room.

A joyful cry escaped her. But when she looked attentively at his face she grew pale.

'Yes,' he said, smiling. 'I have come for your crosses, Sonya. It was you who sent me to the cross-roads; why, now that it has come to the point, do you shrink back?'

Sonya looked at him in amazement. His tone seemed to her strange, and a cold shudder ran through her, but after a minute she realized that the tone and the words were both artificial. While he spoke to her his eyes were turned away, as if he wanted to avoid looking directly at her.

'You see, Sonya, I have decided that perhaps it will be better this way. There is one circumstance . . . Well, it would take too long to tell, and there is no need. Do you know what annoys me, though? It makes me angry that all those stupid, bestial faces will soon be crowding round me, gaping and goggling at me, asking stupid questions I shall be forced to answer, pointing their fingers at me . . . Pah! You know, I am not going to Porfiry; I am sick of him. I would rather go to my friend the Squib. How I shall surprise him, what a sensation I shall produce! But I ought to be cooler; I have been getting too full of bile lately. Would you believe that I all but shook my fist at my sister just now, simply because she turned round to look at me for the last time? What a filthy state of mind to be in! Ah, that is what I have come to! Well, where are the crosses?'

He seemed not to be himself. He was unable to stay in any one place for more than a moment or concentrate his attention on any one object; his thoughts cut across one another; he talked incoherently; his hands trembled slightly.

Silently Sonya took the two crosses, of cypress-wood and copper, from the drawer, made the sign of the cross over herself and over him, and hung the little cypress-wood cross on his breast.

'This, then, is a symbol that I am taking up my cross. He, he! As if my earlier sufferings had been mere trifles! The wooden one, that's the peasant one; the copper one, Lizaveta's, you take for yourself. Show me; was she wearing it . . . then? I know of two things like these, a silver cross and a little ikon; I threw them back on the old woman's breast. They would be truly appropriate now; I ought to put them on . . . But I am talking nonsense and forgetting the real point; I am scatter-brained, somehow! . . . You see, Sonya, I came specially to warn you, so that you should know . . . Well, that's all . . . I really only came for that. (Hm. I thought all the same that I should have more to say.) Well, you wanted me to go, and here I shall be in prison and your wish will be fulfilled; so why are you crying?

You, too? Stop, that's enough! How difficult you are making it for me!'

But feeling had been awakened in him; his heart contracted as he looked at her. 'She, why should she be concerned?' he thought to himself. 'What am I to her? Why should she weep, why should she try to look after me, as if she were my mother or Dunya? She's determined to be a nursemaid to me!'

'Make the sign of the cross, and pray, once at least,' Sonya begged in a timid shaking voice.

'Oh, if you wish: just as you like. And with all my heart, Sonya, with all my heart . . .'

But he wanted to say something different.

He made the sign of the cross several times. Sonya seized her shawl and put it over her head. It was a green woollen shawl, probably the one Marmeladov had spoken of, the 'family shawl'. Raskolnikov thought of that for a moment, but he did not ask about it. He had begun to feel very conscious that his mind was wandering wildly and that he was painfully agitated. This alarmed him. It suddenly struck him, too, that Sonya meant to go with him.

'What are you doing? Where are you going! Stay here, stay here! I shall go alone,' he cried in petty annoyance, and went to the door, almost seething with malice. 'What need is there for a regular procession?' he grumbled as he went out.

Sonya was left standing in the middle of the room. He had not even said good-bye to her; he had already forgotten her; a mutinous and poignant doubt had welled up in his breast.

'But am I doing right, is all this the right thing?' he wondered again, as he went down the stairs. 'Is it really impossible to stop now and revise all my intentions again . . . and not go?'

All the same, he went. Suddenly he felt conclusively that he need ask himself no more questions. As he went out into the street, he remembered that he had not said good-bye to Sonya, he had left her standing there in the room, in her green shawl, not daring to stir because of his outburst. He hesitated for a moment. In that moment an idea flashed on him with great clarity, as though it had been lying in wait to strike him at last.

'Why and for what purpose did I go to her now? I told her I had some business with her, but what business was it? I had absolutely no business at all! To announce that I *was going*? What of that? There's something to call necessary! Do I love her? No, surely I don't? Why, I drove her away just now like a dog. Well, did I, in fact, need to get the crosses from her? Oh, how low I have fallen! No—I wanted her tears, I wanted to see her terror, and watch her heart being torn and tormented! I wanted something, anything, to cling to, some excuse for delay, some human being to look at! I, who had such confidence in myself, such visions of what I would do!

I am a beggarly, worthless scoundrel, I am a miserable wretch!'

He was walking along the canal bank, and had not much farther to go. But when he came to the bridge he stopped, turned across it, and walked towards the Haymarket.

He looked eagerly right and left, gazing intently at everything he saw, but unable to concentrate his attention on any: everything slipped away from him. 'In a week, or a month, I suppose I may be taken somewhere in a prison van over this bridge, and look down at this canal—shall I remember this?' came into his mind. 'This sign here, shall I read these same letters then? Look, *Association* is written here; well, I must remember that *a*, the letter *a*, and look at it again in a month's time, at that same *a*; how shall I look at it then? What shall I be feeling or thinking then? . . . Oh God, how petty all this must be, all these present . . . preoccupations of mine! Of course, it must all be very curious . . . in its way . . . (ha, ha, ha! the things I think of!). I am becoming childish, posing to myself; why am I disgracing myself? Pah, how people jostle! Look at that fat man—he must be a German—who elbowed me; does he know who it was he was pushing? There is a peasant-woman with a baby, begging; odd that she should consider me more fortunate than herself. I must give her something just for the joke of it! Ha, there's a five-copeck piece still left in my pocket; where did it come from? Here you are . . . take it, little mother!'

'God bless you!' whined the beggar.

He entered the Haymarket. He found it distasteful, very distasteful, to rub elbows with the crowd, but he went just where the crowd seemed thickest. He would have given the whole world to be alone; but he himself felt that he would not have remained alone for a single minute. There was a drunken man making a disgusting spectacle of himself; he kept trying to dance, but he could not keep his balance. The people were pressing round him. Raskolnikov pushed through them and stood watching the drunken man for several minutes; then he laughed shortly and abruptly. A moment later he had quite forgotten the man and did not even see him, although he was looking at him. He walked away at last, not even conscious of where he was, but when he came to the centre of the square a sudden sensation came over him, a feeling that mastered him all at once, seized him body and soul.

He had suddenly remembered Sonya's words: 'Go to the cross-roads; bow down before the people, and kiss the ground, because you are guilty before them, and say aloud to all the world, "I am a murderer!"' A shudder shook his whole body at the remembrance. He was so crushed by the weight of all the unescapable misery and anxiety of all this time, and especially of these last hours, that he almost flung himself on the possibility of this new, complete, integral sensation. It had come down on him like a clap of thunder; a single spark was kindled in his spirit and suddenly, like a fire, enveloped his whole being. Everything in him softened on the instant and the tears gushed out. He fell to the ground where he stood . . .

He knelt in the middle of the square, bowed to the ground, and kissed its filth with pleasure and joy. He raised himself and then bowed down a second time.

'Look, here's a chap who's had a drop too much,' remarked a youth near him.

Laughter answered him.

'It's because he's going to Jerusalem, lads, and he's saying good-bye to his family and his country. He's bowing down to the whole world and kissing the famous city of St. Petersburg and the soil it stands on,' added a workman who was slightly drunk.

'He's still quite a young lad!' put in a third.

'Respectable, too!' said someone else soberly.

'Nowadays you can't tell who is respectable and who isn't.'

All these exclamations and observations acted as a check on Raskolnikov and stilled the words 'I am a murderer', which had perhaps been on the tip of his tongue. He endured the remarks calmly, however, and without looking round walked straight down the street leading in the direction of the police office. As he went he caught a glimpse of something that did not, however, surprise him; his feelings had forewarned him that it was bound to happen. While he was bowing down to the ground for the second time, in the Haymarket, he saw Sonya standing fifty yards away from him on his left. She was trying to hide from him behind one of the wooden booths standing in the square, and it was plain that she had accompanied him all along his distressful way. In that moment Raskolnikov knew in his heart, once and for all, that Sonya would be with him for always, and would follow him to the ends of the earth, wherever destiny might send him. His heart contracted . . . but—now he had come to the fatal place . . .

He entered the courtyard briskly enough. He must go up to the third floor. 'I'll go up, anyhow,' he thought. He had a general feeling that it was still a long way to the fatal moment, that he had a great deal of time left and could still reconsider many things.

The spiral staircase was as dirty and littered as ever, the doors of the tenements still stood open, the same kitchens emitted the same reeking fumes. Raskolnikov had not been back since that first time. His legs felt numb and ready to give way but they still carried him. He stopped for a moment to regain his breath and pull himself together, so that he might go in *like a man*. 'But why? What for?' he thought, when he suddenly became conscious of his action. 'If I must drink this cup does it make any difference? The viler the better.' The figure of Ilya Petrovich, the Squib, flashed in that instant before his inward eye. Must he really go to him? Could he not go to some other? To Nikodim Fomich, perhaps? Turn back at once and go straight to the superintendent's flat? At least things would go off in a less official atmosphere . . . 'No, no! To the Squib, the Squib. If I must drink, let it be all at once . . .'

Feeling cold and barely conscious, he opened the office door. This time there were very few people there, only a house-porter and a peasant. The doorman did not even trouble to look out from behind his partition. Raskolnikov went through into the next room. 'Perhaps even yet I need not say anything,' flashed through his mind. In this room one of the clerks, in a frock-coat, not a uniform, was arranging himself at a desk to write something. Another clerk was settling down in a corner. Zametov was not there. Neither, of course, was Nikodim Fomich.

'Is nobody in?' asked Raskolnikov, turning to the personage at the desk.

'Who is it you want to see?'

'Aha! Fee, fi, fo, fum, I smell the blood . . . how does it go? . . . I've forgotten! Your humble servant, sir!' suddenly exclaimed a familiar voice.

Raskolnikov started. The Squib stood before him; he had emerged from the third room. 'It is fate,' thought Raskolnikov. 'Why is he here?'

'Have you come to see us? On what business?' cried Ilya Petrovich. (He was apparently in an excellent temper, and even a trifle exalted with drink.) 'You are too early, if you come on business. I am only here by chance . . . However, anything I can do . . . I confess, Mr. . . . Mr. . . . Excuse me . . .'

'Raskolnikov.'

'Of course, Raskolnikov! You surely couldn't suppose I had forgotten! Please don't think me that sort of person . . . Rodion Ro . . . Ro . . . Rodionovich, isn't it?'

'Rodion Romanovich.'

'Yes, yes, yes! Rodion Romanovich, Rodion Romanovich! I had it on the tip of my tongue. I have even asked about you many times. I confess that I have been sincerely sorry ever since that you and I . . . I was told afterwards that you were a young author and a scholar besides, and, so to speak, the first steps . . . Oh Lord! How many young scholars and men of letters have not been distinguished by some unconventionality to begin with? My wife and I—we both have the highest respect for literature, and my wife is passionately fond of it . . . Literature and art! Let a man be a gentleman and he can acquire everything else by his talents, knowledge, intelligence, and genius. The hat—well, what does a hat signify, after all? Hats are as common as blackberries; I can go and buy one at Zimmermann's, but what is under the hat, what is covered by the hat, that I can't buy . . . I confess I even thought of calling on you to put myself right with you, but I thought perhaps you . . . However, I haven't even asked you: do you really want something? They tell me your family has come here.'

'Yes, my mother and sister.'

'I have already had the honour and pleasure of meeting your sister . . . a person of great charm and culture. I confess I was sorry we got so heated with one another that time. A queer thing! And if, on account of your fainting-fit, I eyed you in a certain way—well, that was brilliantly explained later! Fanaticism and bigotry! I can understand your indignation. Perhaps you are changing your address because of your family's arrival?'

'N-no, I only . . . I came to ask . . . I thought I should find Zametov here.'

'Oh, yes! Of course you have become friends; I heard of it. Well, Zametov isn't here—you've missed him. Yes, we have lost Alexander Grigoryevich! We've been deprived of his presence since yesterday; he's been transferred . . . and when he left he quarrelled with everybody . . . most discourteously . . . He is a giddy-pated fellow, nothing more: he might even be thought promising; but you can have all our brilliant youngsters! It appears he wants to take some examination or other, but really it's all for the sake of talking about it here and showing off, that's all the examination amounts to. It's not at all like, for example, you or that Mr. Razumikhin, your friend. You have chosen a learned career and you are not to be turned aside by failures! To you all the beauty of life, one might say, *nihil est;*[9] you are an ascetic, a monk, a hermit! . . . For you a book, a pen behind your ear, learned researches—that's what makes your spirit soar! I myself am a little . . . Have you read Livingstone's Journals?'[1]

'No.'

'I have. But there are such a lot of nihilists now, all over the place; and indeed it is easy to understand why; what times these are, I ask you! You and I, however . . . of course, you aren't a nihilist, are you? Tell me frankly, frankly!'

'N-no.'

'No. You know, you can be open with me, you needn't hesitate, any more than if you were talking to yourself. Duty is one thing, but . . . you thought I was going to say *friendship*

9. "Nothing is," "nothing exists." An allusion to the negativism of the nihilists.
1. The travel accounts of the English explorer of Africa, David Livingstone, were published in London in 1865. Dostoevsky could also have heard about Livingstone from his friend, the critic N. N. Strakhov, who was finishing his translation of Livingstone's travel book about his journey in Zambezi at the time that Dostoevsky was writing the concluding parts of *Crime and Punishment.*

is quite another. No, you were wrong! Not friendship, but the sentiments of a citizen and a human being, the feeling of humanity and of love for the Supreme Being. I may be an official and obliged to do my duty, but I am always bound to feel the man and the citizen inside, and to be answerable for him . . . You were speaking of Zametov. Zametov will get involved in some French sort of scandal over a glass of champagne or Russian wine in a disreputable establishment—that's your Zametov for you! And I, perhaps, am consumed, so to speak, by devotion to duty and the loftiest feelings, and besides I have importance, rank, status! I am married and have a family. I am doing my duty as a man and a citizen, and who is he, I should like to know? I ask you, as a gentleman by education. Then there are an extraordinary number of midwives cropping up all over the place.'

Raskolnikov raised his eyebrows questioningly. Ilya Petrovich had evidently been dining, and his words seemed to come rattling and scattering out for the most part as empty noises. But part of them he did understand; his look was inquiring, since he did not know where all this was leading.

'I am talking of those short-haired females,' went on the garrulous Ilya Petrovich. 'It is my own idea to call them midwives and I think the name is very satisfactory.[2] He, he! They push themselves into the Academy and study anatomy; well, tell me, if I fall ill am I going to call in a girl to cure me? He, he!'

Ilya Petrovich laughed, delighted with his own wit.

'It is, let us suppose, that his thirst for education is insatiable; but he is educated and that's enough. Why abuse it then? Why insult decent people as that scoundrel Zametov does? Why did he insult me, I ask you? Then again, look what a lot of these suicides there are; you can't imagine. All these people who get through their last few shillings and then kill themselves . . . Why, only this morning we had the case reported to us of a gentleman newly arrived in St. Petersburg. Nil Pavlovich! Nil Pavlovich, what was his name, that gentleman we have just heard shot himself on Peterburgsky Island?'

'Svidrigaylov,' answered a hoarse voice indifferently from the other room.

Raskolnikov started.

'Svidrigaylov! Svidrigaylov has shot himself!' he cried.

'What? Do you know Svidrigaylov?'

'Yes . . . I know him . . . He has not been here long . . .'

'Yes. He arrived recently. He had lost his wife, he was a

---

2. Short hair was a mark of the emancipated women of the period. The only occupations open to women at the time were teaching or midwifery. Women tried to enter the Russian universities in the 1860's. Only the Medical Academy admitted them. There followed a mass exodus of Russian women to Swiss universities.

man of dissolute conduct, and suddenly he shot himself, in a way too shocking to be imagined . . . He left a few words in a notebook to say that he died in his right mind and to ask that nobody should be blamed for his death. This one, they say, had money. How well did you know him?'

'I . . . had met him . . . My sister used to be their governess . . .'

'Ah, ah, ah! . . . So then you can tell us something about him. Did you suspect anything?'

'I saw him yesterday . . . He . . . was drinking . . . I didn't know anything.'

Raskolnikov felt as though a crushing weight had descended on him.

'You look pale again. The atmosphere here is so close . . .'

'Yes, it is time I went,' murmured Raskolnikov. 'Excuse me for troubling you . . .'

'Not at all. Whenever you like! It has been a pleasure, and I am glad to say so . . .'

Ilya Petrovich even held out his hand.

'I only wanted . . . I came to see Zametov . . .'

'I understand, I understand. It has been a pleasure.'

'I . . . am very glad . . . Good-bye . . .' smiled Raskolnikov.

He went out; he swayed. His head was reeling and he seemed to have no feeling in his legs. He began to go downstairs, leaning his right hand against the wall. He thought that a porter with a book in his hand pushed past him on his way upstairs to the office, that a dog began to bark furiously somewhere lower down, and that a woman shouted and threw a rolling-pin at it. He reached the foot of the staircase and went out into the courtyard. There, not far from the entrance, stood Sonya, deadly pale; she looked at him wildly, desperately. He stopped before her. Her face expressed pain, weariness, and despair. She threw up her hands. He forced himself to smile, a lost, hideous smile. He stood there for a moment, smiled again, and turned back to the office.

Ilya Petrovich had sat down and was rummaging among some papers. Before him stood the peasant who had jostled against Raskolnikov as he passed him on the stairs.

'A-a-ah! You again! Have you left something? . . . But what is the matter?'

Raskolnikov, white to the lips, walked slowly forward with a fixed stare until he reached the table, leaned his hand upon it, and tried vainly to speak; there emerged only incoherent sounds.

'You are ill. A chair! Here, sit down, sit on that chair. Water!'

Raskolnikov let himself fall on the chair without taking his eyes from Ilya Petrovich's face, which was full of unpleasant surprise. They looked at one another and waited. Somebody brought water.

'It was I . . .' began Raskolnikov.

'Drink some water.'

Raskolnikov waved aside the water and spoke quietly and brokenly, but distinctly.

'*It was I who killed the old woman and her sister, Lizaveta, with an axe, and robbed them.*'

Ilya Petrovich opened his mouth. People ran in from all sides.

Raskolnikov repeated his statement. . .

# Epilogue

## CHAPTER I

SIBERIA. On the bank of a wide remote river stands a town, one of the administrative centres of Russia; in the town is a fortress, in the fortress is a prison. In the prison Rodion Raskolnikov, second-class convict,[3] had been confined for nine months. It was almost eighteen since the day of the murder.

The legal proceedings had passed off without any great difficulty. The criminal had firmly, exactly, and clearly reaffirmed his statement, neither confusing the circumstances nor extenuating them in his own interest, neither misrepresenting the facts nor forgetting the smallest particular. He described the murder in minute detail, explained the mystery of the *pledge* (the piece of wood with its strip of metal) which was found in the dead woman's hand, told how he had taken the keys from the body, and gave a description of the keys, the trunk, and its contents; he even enumerated some of the objects which were lying in it. He cleared up the mystery of Lizaveta's murder, and related how Koch arrived and knocked at the door, and how the student came after him, and repeated everything that had passed between them. He told how he afterwards ran downstairs and heard the shouts of Mikolka and Mitka, how he hid in the empty flat and how he then went home. Finally, he directed them to the stone near the gates of the courtyard in Voznesensky Prospect, and the purse and the other things were found under it. In a word, everything was made perfectly clear. The examining magistrates and the judges found it very surprising, among other things, that he had hidden the purse and the other property under the stone without making any use of them, and were most astonished of all that not only did he not remember all the details of the objects he had himself stolen, but he was even uncertain of their number. In particular, the circumstance that he had never once opened the purse and did not know exactly how much it contained seemed incredible. (There were, in fact, three hundred and seventy roubles and

---

3. A decree of 1845 divided the forced labor to which convicts in Russia could be sentenced into three classes: (1) work in mines; (2) work in fortresses; (3) work in industrial plants, particularly in distilleries and saltworks. Dostoevsky himself was classified in the second category of forced labor.

sixty copecks in it; from long lying under the stone some of the biggest notes, at the top, had almost perished.) They spent a long time trying to discover why the accused should be lying in this one particular, when he so freely and accurately acknowledged his guilt in every other respect. In the end some of them (especially some who were psychologists) even admitted the possibility that he really did not know what was in the purse because he had hidden it under the stone without looking inside it, but from this they concluded that the crime itself could have been committed only in a state of temporary mental derangement, so to speak, as the result of homicidal mania expressed in murder and robbery for their own sakes, without motive or calculation. This conclusion coincided happily with the latest fashionable theory of temporary insanity, which our contemporaries so often try to apply to various criminals. Besides, Raskolnïkov's long-standing hypochondria was testified to by many witnesses, including Dr. Zosimov, his former fellow students, his landlady, and the servant. All this powerfully assisted the conclusion that Raskolnikov was not quite like the ordinary murderer and robber, but that something different was involved here. To the extreme annoyance of those who upheld this opinion, the criminal hardly tried to defend himself; to the crucial questions, what had made him commit murder, and what had prompted him to rob, he replied plainly, with the bluntest accuracy, that the motive of the whole thing lay in his wretched position, his poverty and helplessness, his desire to furnish for the first steps of his career the security of the three thousand roubles, at least, that he counted on finding in his victim's possession. His resolve to murder was the consequence of his unstable and cowardly nature, which was moreover exasperated by privation and failure. When he was asked what had induced him to volunteer a confession, he answered that it was sincere remorse. All this was said almost callously . . .

The sentence, however, was more merciful than might have been expected in view of the nature of the crime, perhaps just because the criminal not only did not try to exculpate himself, but even betrayed a desire to magnify his guilt. All the strange and peculiar circumstances were taken into account. The prisoner's illness and poverty up to the time of the crime did not admit of the slightest doubt. The fact that he made no use of the things he stole was accounted for as the effect partly of newly awakened remorse, partly of the criminal's incomplete command of his mental powers at the time. The circumstance of Lizaveta's unpremeditated murder served to strengthen this last assumption: a man commits two murders and yet forgets that the door is open! Finally, his coming forward with a confession, at the very time when the whole matter had been inextricably entangled by the false self-accusation of a melancholic and fanatic (Nikolay), and when not only was there no clear evidence against the real criminal but there was even practically no suspicion of him (Porfiry Petrovich had fully kept his word)—all this contributed to the mitigation of the defendant's sentence.

Other circumstances, besides, strongly favouring the prisoner, were quite unexpectedly brought to light. Razumikhin unearthed somewhere and put forward testimony that Raskolnikov, while he was at the university, had helped a poor consumptive fellow student with his last resources and almost entirely supported him for six months. When the student died, Raskolnikov looked after the old and ailing father who survived him (and whom the son had maintained by his own efforts almost since his fourteenth year), eventually found a place for him in the hospital, and, when he too died, buried him. All this information had a favourable influence on Raskolnikov's fate. His former landlady, the mother of his dead fiancée, the widow Zarnitsyna, gave evidence that while they were living in another house, near Five Corners, Raskolnikov had, during a fire, rescued two little children from a burning room, and had himself been injured in doing so. This evidence was carefully investigated and sufficiently well authenticated by many witnesses. In short, the prisoner was condemned to penal servitude in the second class for a term of no more than eight years, in consideration of his voluntary confession and various extenuating circumstances.

At the very beginning of the legal proceedings Raskolnikov's mother fell ill. Dunya and Razumikhin had found means to remove her from St. Petersburg for the whole time of the trial. Razumikhin had picked out a town on a railway line, not far from St. Petersburg, so that he could closely follow the course of the trial and at the same time see Avdotya Romanovna as often as possible. Pulkheria Alexandrovna's illness was of a rather strange nervous kind, accompanied by at least partial, if not complete, mental derangement. Dunya, returning from her last interview with her brother, found her mother ill, feverish, and delirious. That evening she and Razumikhin agreed on the answers they would give to her mother's questions about her brother, and even worked out together a complete story of Raskolnikov's having gone away to a distant place on the Russian frontier on a private mission which would bring him in the end both money and fame. But they were surprised to find that neither then nor later did Pulkheria Alexandrovna ask them anything about this. On the contrary, she herself produced a complete account of her son's sudden departure; she told them with tears how he had come to say good-bye to her and gave them to understand by hints that she alone knew many very important and mysterious facts, and that Rodya had many powerful enemies and therefore must hide himself. As for his future career, it seemed it was certain to be brilliant when some hostile circumstances were overcome; she assured Razumikhin that her son would in time be a great political figure, as was proved by his article and his literary brilliance. She was incessantly reading the article, sometimes even aloud; she all but slept with it. Nevertheless, she hardly even asked exactly where Rodya was, in spite of the fact that they avoided talking to her about it, which might have been enough in itself to arouse her mistrust. They began at last to be frightened by Pulkheria Alexandrovna's strange silence on some points. She did not complain, for instance, that there were no letters from him, although earlier, in her little provincial town, she had lived only in the hope and expectation of soon receiving a letter from her beloved Rodya. This circumstance was so inexplicable that it greatly worried Dunya; the idea came to her that perhaps her mother had a foreboding of something terrible in her son's fate, and was afraid to ask lest she should learn of something even more terrible. At all events, Dunya saw clearly that her mother's reason was impaired.

Once or twice, however, it happened that she led the conversation in such a way that it was impossible to answer her without mentioning exactly where Rodion now was; but when the answers were perforce unsatisfactory and suspicious, she fell at once into a sad, gloomy, and silent mood which lasted for a considerable time. Dunya realized at last that it was too difficult to lie and invent, and came to the definite conclusion that it was better to preserve complete silence on certain points; but it became more and more clearly evident that the poor mother suspected something terrible. Dunya recalled among others those words of her brother's, about how their mother had overheard her talking in her sleep on the night before that last fatal day, after her scene with Svidrigaylov; had she learnt anything then? Often, sometimes after several days or even weeks of dismal brooding silence and speechless tears, the sick woman roused herself almost hysterically and began to talk, hardly pausing for breath, of her son, of her hopes, of the future . . . Her fancies were sometimes very strange. They humoured her, assenting to everything she said (and perhaps she saw clearly that they were only humouring her), but still she talked . . .

Five months after the criminal had volunteered his confession, his sentence followed. Razumikhin saw him in prison whenever it was possible; so did Sonya. Finally came the separation; Dunya swore to her brother that their parting was not for ever; Razumikhin did the same. Firmly lodged in Razumikhin's young and ardent brain was a plan to lay, during the next two or three years, at any rate the foundations of his future livelihood as well as he could, to accumulate at least a little money, and to emigrate to Siberia, where the soil was rich in every sense, but there were too few inhabitants, too little labour, and too little capital; then he would settle in the town where Rodya was and . . . they would all begin a new life together. They all wept when they said good-bye. During the past few days Raskolnikov had been very thoughtful; he asked about his mother a great deal, and was constantly uneasy about her. His tormented anxiety about her worried Dunya. When he learned the details of his mother's illness he became very depressed. For some reason he was extremely silent with Sonya during all this time. She had long since made all her preparations, with the help of the money Svidrigaylov had left with her, to follow the party of convicts in which he was included. She and Raskolnikov had never made the slightest allusion to this, but both knew that it would be so. At their very last parting, he smiled strangely at his sister's and Razumikhin's passionate assurances of a happy future when he came out of prison, and predicted that his mother's illness would soon end disastrously. At last he and Sonya set off.

Two months later Dunechka and Razumikhin were married. It was a quiet and sorrowful wedding. Porfiry Petrovich and Zosimov were among those who were invited to it. For some time Razumikhin had looked like a man whose mind is firmly made up. Dunya believed blindly that he would carry out all his plans; she could not, indeed, do otherwise, for he revealed an iron determination. He began attending university lectures again, among other things, so as to complete his studies. They were always framing plans for the future; both resolutely counted on emigrating to Siberia in five years' time. Until then, they relied on Sonya . . .

Pulkheria Alexandrovna joyfully blessed her daughter's marriage to Razumikhin, but after it she became still more melancholy and troubled. In order to give her a moment of pleasure, Razumikhin told her about the student and his infirm old father, and about how Rodya had suffered from burns in saving the lives of two little children a year ago. These stories brought Pulkheria Alexandrovna's already disordered mind to a pitch of feverish exaltation. She was always talking about them and even beginning conversations in the street (although Dunya always accompanied her). In public vehicles or in shops, wherever she could find a hearer, she led the conversation round to her son, his article, his helping of the student, his being injured in a fire, and so on. Dunechka did not know how to stop her. Besides the danger of this morbidly exalted state of mind, there always threatened the disastrous possibility that somebody might remember Raskolnikov's name from the trial and speak of it. Pulkheria Alexandrovna had learned the address of the mother of the two little children saved from the fire, and was determined to go and see her. Her agitation increased at length beyond all measure. Sometimes she would suddenly begin to cry, and she often fell ill, her mind wandering feverishly. One morning she roundly declared that by her reckoning Rodya ought soon to be with them, and that she remembered his telling her, when he said good-bye, that they must expect him in nine months. She began to put the flat in order and prepare for their reunion, arranging the room she intended for him (her own), cleaning the furniture, washing curtains and hanging up new ones, and so on. Dunya was worried but she said nothing, and even helped her to arrange the room for her brother's arrival. After an anxious day, filled with incessant fancies, happy dreams, and tears, she became ill in the night and by the morning was delirious. She developed a burning fever and two weeks later she died. In her wanderings words escaped her from which it could be concluded that she suspected far more of her son's terrible fate than they had supposed.

It was a long time before Raskolnikov learnt of his mother's death, although a correspondence with St. Petersburg had been established at the very beginning of his exile in Siberia. It was carried on through Sonya, who wrote punctually every month to Razumikhin and punctually every month received a reply from St. Petersburg. At first Sonya's letters seemed to Dunya and Razumikhin somewhat dry and unsatisfactory, but in the end they both found that they could not have been better written, since from these letters there finally emerged a most complete and accurate picture of their unhappy brother's lot. Sonya's letters were full of the most prosaic actuality, the simplest and clearest description of every circumstance of Raskolnikov's life as a convict. They contained neither statements of her own hopes, nor speculations about the future, nor descriptions of her feelings. Instead of attempts to explain his psychological condition and his inner life generally, there were only facts, his own words, that is, and detailed reports of his health, of what he expressed a wish for at their interviews, the questions he asked her or the commissions he entrusted to her. All this she communicated with extraordinary minuteness. In the end, the picture of their unhappy brother stood out in relief, exactly and clearly drawn in his own words; there could be nothing misleading about it, because it consisted wholly of factual reports.

Dunya and her husband could derive little consolation from these reports, however, especially in the beginning. Sonya invariably informed them that he was sullen and uncommunicative, and almost completely uninterested in the news she always carried to him from her letters. He sometimes asked about his mother, and when at last, seeing that he had already divined the truth, she told him of Pulkheria Alexandrovna's death, she saw to her amazement that even this did not touch him very deeply, so far, at least, as she could judge from his outward appearance. She told them, among other things, that although he seemed so wrapped up in himself and so wilfully remote from everybody else, his attitude to his new life was very direct and simple; he had a clear understanding of his position, did not expect any immediate improvement in it, cherished none of the frivolous hopes so natural in his situation, and showed almost no surprise at anything in his new surroundings, so little resembling all he had known before. She told them that his health was satisfactory. His work he performed without either reluctance or eagerness. He was almost indifferent to what he ate, but the food was so bad, except on Sundays and holidays, that in the end he was glad to take a little money from her in order to procure his own tea every day; about everything else he asked her not to trouble herself, asserting that all this concern for him only irritated him. Sonya told them besides that all the accommodation in the prison was shared in common, that although she had not seen the inside of their barracks she inferred that they were crowded, hideous, and insanitary, that he slept on a piece of felt stretched over bare boards and that he had no desire to arrange things differently for himself, but that he lived so poorly and roughly not out of any preconceived plan or purpose but simply from inattention and outward indifference to his lot. Sonya's letters did not disguise that not only was he not interested in her visits but, especially at first, he was irritated by her presence and monosyllabic or even rude to her; but in the end he became used to their interviews and found they had grown necessary to him, so that he sadly missed them when for a few days she was ill and unable to visit him. On holidays she saw him at the prison gates or in the guardroom, to which he would be summoned for a few minutes, but on week-days she visited him at work, making her way to the workshops, the brick-works, or the warehouses on the banks of the Irtysh. Sonya informed them that she herself had been fortunate enough to acquire some acquaintances and patrons in the town, and that she did sewing and, since there was no dressmaker in the town, had become indispensable in many houses; but she did not mention that through her Raskolnikov had also come under the protection of the authorities, or that his labours were lightened, and so on. At last the news came (Dunya had noticed signs of alarm and anxiety in the most recent letters) that he was shunning everybody, that the other convicts had begun to dislike him, that for days together he did not speak, and that he was becoming very pale. Suddenly, in her last letter, Sonya wrote that he was seriously ill in the prison ward of the military hospital . . .

## CHAPTER II

HE had been ill for a long time, but it was not the horrors of a convict's life, nor the heavy work, nor the food, nor his shaven head and ragged clothing that had broken him: what did all that hardship and suffering matter to him? He was even glad of the hard work; physical exhaustion at least brought him a few hours of peaceful sleep. And what did he care for the food—that thin cabbage soup with cockroaches in it? In his former life, when he was a student, he had often not had even that. His clothes were warm and appropriate to his way of life. The fetters he did not even feel. Was he to be ashamed of his shaven head and parti-coloured coat? But before whom? Before Sonya? Sonya feared him, and was he to feel ashamed before her?

What was it then? He did, in fact, feel ashamed even before Sonya, whom he tortured because of this by his rough and contemptuous manner. But he was not ashamed of his shaven head or his fetters; his pride was deeply wounded, and it was the wound to his pride that made him fall ill. How happy he would have been if he could have put the blame on himself! Then he could have borne anything, even shame and infamy. But although he judged himself severely, his lively conscience could find no particularly terrible guilt in his past, except a simple *blunder*, that might have happened to anybody. He was ashamed precisely because he, Raskolnikov, had perished so blindly and hopelessly, with such dumb stupidity, by some decree of blind fate, and must humble himself and submit to the 'absurdity' of that decree, if he wished to find any degree of peace.

An objectless and undirected anxiety in the present, and endless sacrifice, by which nothing would be gained, in the future, was all the world held for him. And what did it signify that in eight years he would be only thirty-two and still able to begin a new life? What would he have to live for? What could be his aim? What should he strive for? To live in order to exist? But he had been ready a thousand times before to sacrifice his existence for an idea, a hope, even for a fancy. Mere existence had always meant little to him; he had always desired more. Perhaps it was just because of the strength of his desires that he had considered himself a man to whom more was permitted than to others.

If only fate had granted him remorse, scalding remorse, harrowing the heart and driving sleep away, such remorse as tortured men into dreaming of the rope or deep still water! Oh, he would have welcomed it gladly! Tears and suffering—they, after all, are also life. But he did not feel remorse for his crime.

He might at least have raged at his own stupidity, as before he had raged at the monstrous and infinitely stupid actions that had brought him to prison. But now when he was in prison, and *free*, he had reconsidered and reweighed all his former actions, and found it completely impossible to think them as stupid and monstrous as they had seemed to him before, at that fatal time.

'How,' he thought, 'how was my idea more stupid than any of the other ideas and theories that have sprung up and multiplied like weeds all over the world, ever since the world existed? One need only look at the matter with a broad and completely independent mind, free from all the common influences, for my ideas not to seem so very . . . strange. Oh, you tuppenny-ha'penny prophets of denial, why do you stop half-way?'

'What makes what I have done seem to them so monstrous?' he asked himself. 'The fact that it was a . . . crime? What does the word mean? My conscience is easy. Of course, an illegal action has been committed; of course, the letter of the law has been broken and blood has been spilt; well, take my head to satisfy the letter of the law . . . and let that be all! Of course, if that were the case, many benefactors of mankind who did not inherit power but seized it for themselves, should have been punished at their very first steps. But the first steps of those men were successfully carried out, and therefore *they were right*, while mine failed, which means I had no right to permit myself that step.'

This was the sole sense in which he acknowledged his crime, that he had not succeeded and that he had confessed.

Another thought added to his suffering: why had he not killed himself? Why, when he stood on the bank of the river, had he chosen rather to confess? Was there really such strength in the will to live, and was it so difficult to overcome it? Had not Svidrigaylov, who feared death, overcome it?

He tortured himself with these questions, unable to realize that perhaps even while he stood by the river he already felt in his heart that there was something profoundly false in himself and his beliefs. He did not understand that that feeling might have been the herald of a coming crisis in his life, of his coming resurrection, of a future new outlook on life.

He preferred to see in all this only the dull bondage of instinct, which he could not shake off, and which he was still not strong enough to break (because of his weakness and worthlessness). He looked at his fellow convicts and marvelled: how all of them, also, loved life and cherished it! It seemed to him, indeed, that it was more loved and prized, more highly valued, in prison than in freedom. What terrible sufferings and hardships some of them had borne, the tramps, for example! How could one ray of sunlight mean so much to them, or the virgin forest, or a cool spring in some remote and hidden solitude seen once years before, that the tramp dreams of and longs for like a lovers' meeting, with the green grass all round it and a bird singing in the bushes? When he looked round him he saw even stranger things.

There was much in his prison surroundings, of course, that he did not and would not see. He lived, as it were, with his eyes cast down; he could not bear to look at the loathsome spectacle. But in course of time he began to find many things surprising and, almost against his will, to notice what he had not previously suspected. The most surprising thing of all, in general, was that terrible unbridgeable chasm which lay between him and all the others. It was as if he and they belonged to different races. They regarded him, and he them, with mistrust and hostility. He knew and understood the general reasons of his separateness, but he would never have admitted that these causes would be in fact so deep-rooted and strong. The prison contained some Polish exiles, who were political prisoners. These simply looked on all the rest as ignorant serfs and despised them; but Raskolnikov could not take that view; it was clear to him that in many ways, though ignorant, they were wiser than the Poles. There were Russians, also, who looked down on them—a former officer and two seminarists; Raskolnikov clearly saw their mistake.

He himself was disliked and avoided by everybody. In time they even began to hate him. Why, he did not know. Men who were far more culpable than he despised him and laughed at his crime.

'You are a gentleman!' they said. 'You shouldn't have gone to work with an axe; it's not at all the thing for a gentleman.'

In the second week of Lent it was his turn, with the rest of his barrack, to prepare for the sacrament. He went to church and prayed with the others. Out of this, he himself did not know why, a quarrel arose one day; they all turned on him in fury:

'You're an atheist! You don't believe in God!' they shouted. 'We must kill you.'

He had never spoken to them about God or religious beliefs, but they wanted to kill him as an atheist; he did not reply to them, but was silent. One of the convicts rushed at him in a perfect frenzy. Raskolnikov awaited him calmly and silently; not a muscle of his face quivered. The guard managed to get between him and his attacker in time, or blood would have been shed.

There was a question which he could not answer: why was Sonya so well liked by everybody? She did not try to ingratiate herself with them; they rarely met her, except occasionally at work, when she came to see him for a minute. Nevertheless, they all knew her, knew besides that she had followed *him*, and knew how and where she lived. She did not give them money or perform any particular services for them. Once only, at Christmas, she brought a gift of pies and loaves for the whole prison. But little by little closer connexions developed between Sonya and them: she wrote letters for them to their families and posted them. When their relatives came to the town, the convicts told them to leave goods and even money for them in Sonya's care. Their wives and sweethearts knew her and visited her. And when she appeared where they were working, to visit Raskolnikov, or when she met a party of prisoners on their way to work, they would all take off their caps and bow to her. 'Little mother, Sofya Semënovna, you are our kind, affectionate mother,' these coarse, branded criminals would say to the slight little creature. She would smile and bow to them; they were all pleased when she smiled at them. They liked even the way she walked, turning round to watch her, and praising her; they praised her even for being so small; they could not find enough to say in her praise. They even went to her when they were ill.

Raskolnikov was in hospital all through the latter part of Lent and Easter. When he began to recover he remembered the dreams that had visited him while he lay in his fever and delirium. He had dreamt in his illness that the whole world was condemned to fall victim to a terrible, unknown pestilence which was moving on Europe out of the depths of Asia. All were destined to perish, except a chosen few, a very few. There had appeared a new strain of trichinae, microscopic creatures parasitic in men's bodies.[4] But these creatures were endowed with intelligence and will. People who were infected immediately became like men possessed and out of their minds. But never, never, had any men thought themselves so wise and so unshakable in the truth as those who were attacked. Never had they considered their judgements, their scientific deductions, or their moral convictions and creeds more infallible. Whole communities, whole cities and nations, were infected and went mad. All were full of anxiety, and none could understand any other; each thought he was the sole repository of truth and was tormented when he looked at the others, beat his breast, wrung his hands, and wept. They did not know how or whom to judge and could not agree what was evil and what good. They did not know whom to condemn or whom to acquit. Men killed one another in senseless rage. They banded together against one another in great armies, but when the armies were already on the march they began to fight among themselves, the ranks disintegrated, the soldiers fell on their neighbours, they thrust and cut, they killed and ate one another. In the towns, the tocsin sounded all day long, and called out all the people, but who had summoned them and why nobody knew, and everybody

---

4. In 1865–66, articles about previously unknown microscopic creatures, called "trichinae," appeared in the Russian press, and a booklet was published about diseases supposedly caused by them.

was filled with alarm. The most ordinary callings were abandoned, because every man put forward his own ideas, his own improvements, and there was no agreement; the labourers forsook the land. In places men congregated in groups, agreed together on some action, swore not to disband—and immediately began to do something quite different from what they themselves had proposed, accused one another, fought and killed each other. Conflagrations were started, famine set in. All things and all men were perishing. The plague grew and spread wider and wider. In the whole world only a few could save themselves, a chosen handful of the pure, who were destined to found a new race of men and a new life, and to renew and cleanse the earth; but nobody had ever seen them anywhere, nobody had heard their voices or their words.

It distressed Raskolnikov that this ridiculous fantasy lingered so painfully and sadly in his memory, and that he could not shake off for so long the impressions of his delirious dreaming. The second week after Easter was passing in a succession of warm, clear, spring days; in the prison ward the windows were opened (they were barred and guarded by a sentry). Sonya had been able to visit him in the ward only twice during the whole course of his illness; each time she had to beg for permission and it was hard to get. But she often went into the yard, under the hospital windows, especially in the evening, sometimes only to stand and look for a moment at the windows of the ward from a distance. One evening Raskolnikov, who had almost completely recovered, had fallen asleep; when he woke up, he went by chance to the window and caught sight of Sonya in the distance, standing by the gates of the hospital; she seemed to be waiting for something. It was as if something pierced his heart at that moment; he shuddered, and moved hastily away from the window. The next day Sonya did not come, nor the next after that; he realized that he was waiting anxiously for her. At length he was discharged. When he reached the prison he learnt from the other convicts that Sofya Semënovna had been taken ill and was in bed and not able to go out.

He was very disturbed and sent to inquire after her; he soon heard that her illness was not dangerous. When she in her turn heard that he was anxious and worried about her, Sonya sent him a note, written in pencil, informing him that she was much better, that she had simply had a slight cold, and that she would soon, very soon, come to see him at his work. As he read the note, his heart beat heavily and painfully.

The day was again bright and warm. Early in the morning, at about six o'clock, he went off to his work on the river-bank, where gypsum was calcined in a kiln set up in a shed, and afterwards crushed. Three convicts altogether had been sent there.

One of them, with the guard, had gone to the fortress for a tool, the other began splitting wood and putting it in the kiln. Raskolnikov went out of the shed on to the bank, sat down on a pile of logs and looked at the wide, solitary river. From the high bank a broad landscape was revealed. From the other bank, far away, was faintly borne the sound of singing. There, in the immensity of the steppe, flooded with sunlight, the black tents of the nomads were barely visible dots. Freedom was there, there other people lived, so utterly unlike those on this side of the river that it seemed as though with them time had stood still, and the age of Abraham and his flocks was still the present.⁵ Raskolnikov sat on and his unwavering gaze remained fixed on the farther bank; his mind had wandered into day-dreams; he thought of nothing, but an anguished longing disturbed and tormented him.

Suddenly Sonya appeared at his side. She had come up almost soundlessly and sat down beside him. It was early; the chill of the morning still lingered. She wore her shabby old pelisse and the green shawl. Her face still bore traces of her illness; it was thinner and paler and hollow-cheeked. She gave him a joyful welcoming smile, but she held out her hand as timidly as ever.

She always stretched out her hand to him timidly, sometimes even half withdrawing it, as if she feared he would repulse her. He always grasped it reluctantly, always greeted her with a kind of irritation, sometimes remained obstinately silent all through her visit. There had been occasions when she had quailed before him and gone away deeply hurt. But this time their hands remained joined; he gave her a rapid glance, but said nothing and turned his eyes to the ground. They were alone; there was nobody to see them. The guard had turned away.

How it happened he himself did not know, but suddenly he seemed to be seized and cast at her feet. He clasped her knees and wept. For a moment she was terribly frightened, and her face grew white. She sprang up and looked down at him, trembling. But at once, in that instant, she understood. Infinite happiness shone in her eyes; she had understood, and she no longer doubted that he loved her, loved her for ever, and that now at last the moment had come . . .

They tried to speak, but they could not. Tears stood in their eyes. They were both pale and thin, but in their white sick faces there glowed the dawn of a new future, a perfect resurrection into a new life. Love had raised them from the dead, and the heart of each held endless springs of life for the heart of the other.

5. An allusion to John 8:33.

They knew they must wait and be patient. They had seven more years before them, and what unbearable sufferings and infinite happiness those years would hold! But he was restored to life and he knew it and felt to the full all his renewed being, and she—she lived only in his life!

The same evening, after the barrack was locked, Raskolnikov lay on his plank-bed and thought. Today it had even seemed to him that the other convicts, formerly so hostile, were already looking at him differently. He had even spoken to them and been answered pleasantly. He remembered this now, but after all, that was how it must be: ought not everything to be changed now?

He was thinking of her. He remembered how ceaselessly he had tormented her and harrowed her heart; he remembered her pale thin little face; but those memories now hardly troubled him: he knew with what infinite love he would now expiate all her sufferings.

And what were all, *all* the torments of the past? Everything, even his crime, even his sentence and his exile, seemed to him now, in the first rush of emotion, to be something external and strange, as if it had not happened to him at all. But this evening he could not think long or coherently of anything or concentrate his attention on any idea, and indeed he was not consciously reasoning at all; he could only feel. Life had taken the place of logic and something quite different must be worked out in his mind.

There was a New Testament under his pillow. Mechanically he took it out. It was hers, the very one from which she had read to him the raising of Lazarus. At the beginning of his prison life he had been afraid that she would pester him with religion, talk about the gospels and press books on him. But to his great astonishment she did not once speak of it, and never even offered him a New Testament. He himself had asked her for it not long before his illness and she had brought it to him without a word. He had not yet opened it.

He did not open it even now, but an idea flashed through his mind: 'Could not her beliefs become my beliefs now? Her feelings, her aspirations, at least . . .'

She also had been full of agitation all day, and at night she even became feverish again. But she was so happy, and her happiness was so unexpected, that it almost frightened her. Seven years, *only* seven years! At the dawn of their happiness, both had been ready, for some few moments, to think of those seven years as if they were no more than seven days. He did not even know that the new life would not be his for nothing, that it must be dearly bought, and paid for with great and heroic struggles yet to come . . .

But that is the beginning of a new story, the story of the gradual renewal of a man, of his gradual regeneration, of his slow progress from one world to another, of how he learned to know a hitherto undreamed-of reality. All that might be the subject of a new tale, but our present one is ended.

# THE NAMES OF THE
# PRINCIPAL CHARACTERS

Russian middle names are not given names, but patronymics—derivatives of the first name of the person's father. Hence all siblings will have the same patronymic. The masculine and feminine forms differ slightly. Alternate forms of the names are enclosed in parentheses.

**Raskólnikov, Rodión Románovich** (**Ródya, Ródenka, Ródka**)
————, **Pulkhéria Alexándrovna**, his mother
————, **Avdótya Románovna** (**Dúnya, Dúnechka**), his sister
**Razumíkhin, Dmítri Prokófich**, his friend
**Alëna** (**Alyóna**) **Ivánovna**, moneylender
**Lizavéta Ivánovna**, her sister
**Marmeládov, Semën** (**Semyón**) **Zakhárovich**, ex-government clerk
————, **Katerína Ivánovna**, his wife
————, **Sófya Semënovna** (**Semyónovna**) (**Sonya, Sónechka**)
————, three other children: **Polína Mikháylovna** (**Pólya, Pólenka, Pólechka**); **Lëna** (**Lyóna**) (**Lída, Lídochka**); **Kólya** (**Kólka**)
**Svidrigáylov, Arkády Ivánovich**, landlord, Dunya's former employer
————, **Márfa Petróvna**, his wife
**Lúzhin, Peter Petróvich**, Dunya's fiancé
**Lebezyátnikov, Andréy Semënovich** (**Semyónovich**), his friend
**Lippewéchsel, Amália Ivánovna**, Marmeladovs' landlady. (She calls herself **Ivanovna**, but Mrs. Marmeladova calls her **Amalia Lúdwigovna**, which annoys her, since the patronymic calls attention to her German origin.)
**Zosímov**, a doctor
**Zamëtov** (**Zamyotov**), **Alexánder Grigórevich**, chief police clerk
**Porfíry Petróvich**, examiner

## Significant Roots of Characters' Names

**Raskolnikov:** *raskol* = schism, split. *Raskolniki* are the members of religious sects, some of which date back to the great seventeenth-century Russian Orthodox schism.
**Razumikhin:** *razum* = reason, good sense.
**Lebezyatnikov:** *lebezit* = to fawn on someone, cringe, ingratiate oneself (it might also possibly recall the word *lebed*, "swan").
**Marmeladov:** *marmelad* = jam, jelly.
**Sonya:** for *Sofya* (Greek "wisdom").
**Lippewechsel:** a blatantly German name, which, like her German accent and broken Russian, might have struck Dostoevsky's public as slightly comic.

The Russian word for "crime," in the title of the novel and elsewhere, is *prestuplenie*, from *pre* (across, trans-) and *stuplenie* (a stepping), so that etymologically it is similar to the English "transgression." The root meanings of "stepping across" some barrier, as both essential and analogous to the criminal, are played on in the text in a manner which is lost sight of in the translation, since our word "crime" does not have the same derivation.

# Backgrounds and Sources

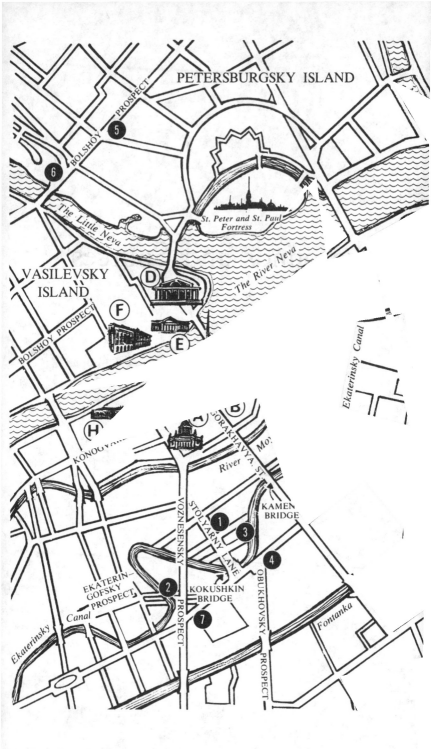

PETERSBURGSKY ISLAND

BOLSHOY PROSPECT

5

6

The Little Neva

St. Peter and St. Paul Fortress

The River Neva

VASILEVSKY ISLAND

BOLSHOY PROSPECT

D

F

E

Ekaterinsky Canal

H

KONOGVA

A

B

GORAKHAVYA ST.

River Mo

VOZNESENSKY PROSPECT

STOLYARNY LANE

KAMEN BRIDGE

1

3

4

EKATERIN-GOFSKY PROSPECT

2

KOKUSHKIN BRIDGE

OBUKHOVSKY PROSPECT

Ekaterinsky Canal

7

Fontanka

*Map* · 469

# *The St. Petersburg of* Crime and Punishment

**Places important in *Crime and Punishment***

1  Raskolnikov's room (No. 9, Srednaya Meshchanskaya Street).
2  The pawnbroker's room.
3  Sonya's room.
4  Haymarket Square (where Raskolnikov bows and kisses the earth).
5  Place of Svidrigaylov's suicide.
6  Tuchkov Bridge.
7  Yusupov Gardens.

**Important Petersburg Locations**

A  St. Isaac's Cathedral.
B  The Admiralty Building.
C  The Winter Palace and the Ermitage (Tsar's Palaces).
D  The Bourse (Stock Exchange).
E  Academy of Sciences.
F  Leningrad University.
G  Falconnet's statue to Peter the Great.
H  The Senate.

**General Note**

Petersburg was built early in the eighteenth century by Peter the Great, close to the Gulf of Finald, in a marshy region around the river Neva, which flows westward to the sea. A system of canals and small rivers drained the location of Petersburg; the city continued (and continues to this day) to have the character of a city criss-crossed by rivers and canals, with many bridges.

The area around the Haymarket, where Sonya and Raskolnikov lived, was a slummy section. Most of the locations which Dostoevsky had in mind have been identified; artists have painted the houses and even the doorways important in the novel. For the identification of houses referred to in *Crime and Punishment*, the editor is indebted to an unpublished radio script prepared, for Leningrad Radio, by Dostoevsky's grandson, Andrey Fyodorovich Dostoevsky, who was a specialist in the study of the Petersburg backgrounds of Dostoevsky's writings, and to *Literaturnye pamyatnye mesta Leningrada* (Leningrad, 1959), a book edited by A. M. Dokusov, which discusses Leningrad places important in literature.

On the map, it is possible to trace exactly Raskolnikov's various walks (his three trips from his room to the pawnbroker's, as well as his usual route to the university, with a view of the city from the bridge), Sonya's route from Raskolnikov's room to her own, and Svidrigaylov's last journey before his suicide.

The observant reader will note that "Kameny Bridge" (p. 1 in our text of the novel) ought to read "Kokushkin Bridge." (Dostoevksy's text used only the initial, "K—— Bridge." Somewhere along the line, an editor substituted "Kameny"—erroneously, as the map makes clear, since Dostoevsky's text shows that Raskolnikov must have turned towards Kokushkin Bridge on his way to Alena Ivanovna.)

## From Dostoevsky's Notebooks†

Here ends the *story* and begins the *diary*[1]

The chief question which finally he formulates to himself clearly and puts positively: Why did my life come to an end. Rebellion. God doesn't exist etc.

I must do that. Freedom of will does not exist. Fatalism    [II, 1, 78]

The general main thing. NB:

In all these six chapters he must write, talk, and represent himself to the reader partly as if he were not in his right mind.    [II, 6, 81]

Chapter II. NB. Every minute there must leap out in the midst of the story absolutely unnecessary and unexpected details.

June 16. Two days later, at night, I started to write and sat there for four hours. This will be a document.

They will never find these pages. The board under the window can be lifted out and nobody knows that. It has lifted out for a long time and I have known about it for a long time. In case of need, one can lift it up and again put down like that so that even if someone else touched it, he would not lift it up. He won't even think of it. There, under the board, I hid everything. I took out two bricks.    [II, 45, 100–101]

All that as swiftly as possible. The event and then begins the

† Dostoevsky's notebooks to *Crime and Punishment* occupy three longhand notebooks covering in the original approximately 135, 152, and 150 pages respectively, or, in the Russian printed version of all three, a total of 182 book pages. The text was published in the original order, without any sorting out, in 1931 by I. I. Glivenko, under the title *Iz arkhiva F. M. Dostoevskogo, Prestuplenie i nakazanie* (Moscow and Leningrad, 1931) and in 1970 in a "organized form" with various versions of the novel and the notes and outlines printed separately, in logical and chronological sequence, in F. M. Dostoevsky, *Prestuplenie i nakazanie*, ed. L. D. Opulskaya and G. F. Kogan, Literaturnye pamiatniki (Moscow: Nauka, 1970). The 1931 edition has been translated into English by Edward Wasiolek, *The Notebooks for Crime and Punishment* (Chicago: The University of Chicago Press, 1967). Internal evidence indicates that Dostoevsky kept the notebooks in 1865 and 1866. They are working notebooks—not meant for publication. In them Dostoevsky wrote down various ideas, drafts, and random notes. They contain memoranda to himself; tentative ideas for future plotting and character development; drafts of scenes, some of which were later used with various changes, and others which were abandoned and never used in the printed version; doodles; drawings; thoughts on the narrative method to be used. The notebooks thus represent the "creative laboratory" or the workshop of Dostoevsky while composing *Crime and Punishment*. The selections in this volume are followed by numbers which refer first to the notebook (in the order of writing, II, I, III), then to the page of the notebook, then to the page in Glivenko's Russian edition.

1. During one stage of writing, Dostoevsky wanted to have *Crime and Punishment* told in the first person, as a journal or as a confession made by Raskolnikov. Later entries in the notebook show his consideration of alternative ways of narrating the novel; others are drafts of the novel told as a "Confession."

corruption of his own psychology. Because only now he regained consciousness.

1 All that after being with Zametov in the restaurant and the article in the *Voice* and the story of Nastasya and all the information . . . He got the purse. NB

2 Got the purse. That purse I put so I'd never take it and now I have taken it myself.

NB The main thing. After his illness some kind of brutality and full self-justification and when all that tottered, the letter from his mother. [II, 95, 144]

Note to the "Confession"

NB. Yes, go and tell them. They will say it is stupid. He killed, without a reason, he took 280 rubles and things worth twenty rubles. If he had taken 15,000 or if I had killed and robbed Kraevsky, then they would not laugh (then they would see the aim and they would believe that I had big plans). But now I'd have to endure laughter and contempt. They will say—the little fool, he killed without a purpose. He imagined he would take care of himself with two hundred and would make everybody happy. They will not believe my plan when I explain it. Oh shame, shame. The most disgusting shame is sure to come on me. Oh mean creature. I call them low and foul and yet I myself care about their opinion. I am ready for nothing, nothing. Life has not given me anything. [II, 149, 162–3]

Meanwhile the action at his mother's. What is the matter with him. Razumikhin. The mother is afraid. Isn't he in difficulties. Burdened? All of them together go to see him. They find *her* there. She is insulted. He quarrels. Razumikhin quarrels with him. *She* a letter to him. Mother is glad the true cause of his bad state of mind has been discovered and that it is not greed, not a bad feeling, not fear that they have come to be a burden on his neck. He goes to see *her*. They insult her on the street. He meets Razumikhin at her place. Quarrel. He tells her what he is and that he is worse than she. A scene. She is terrified. He goes home full of presumption. Marmeladova on the street with children. He to Razumikhin who is also there: There, there. Fever, to the hospital. The children to a home. Mother's question: not with her? At the mother's. Razumikhin announced as bridegroom. His doubts. Perspective of the future. Speaks with Razumikhin. The latter hurried to the rescue. *She* looks for him. He is sick, at her place. (Razumikhin comes often) He ran away from her (and from their compassion) all over town. Storm. Christ. Veuve Capet. Why do they moan? Crevez chiens si vous n'êtes pas contents. Fire? (Razumikhin is there too) All of them are there. (Mother's

## 472 · *Backgrounds and Sources*

exultation) Singed, he goes home.[2] Two words to Razumikhin. The latter first terrified, then captivated. To Haymarket to bow down, to hers, to say goodby. Tell mother. Lieutenant Porokh (Powder). Revelation.

Mix up all questions in this novel. The subject is such, the story should be told impersonally and not in his person. If confession, then it must be to the last extreme, everything must be made clear. So that every moment of the story is clear. (Full frankness fully serious, to the point of naïveté, only one thing is essential.)

NB Take into consideration: with a confession, at other points it will not be modest and it will be difficult to imagine for what purpose it was written.

But from the author's point of view. Too much naïveté and frankness necessary. One must imagine an author an omniscient and infallible being, holding out one of the members of the new generation for everybody to see. [I, 107, 59–60]

Another plan
Narration from the author's point of view, as if by an invisible but omniscient being, but not leaving him even for a minute, even with the words "all that happened unexpectedly." [I, 109, 61]

Farewell to mother. Have you not suffered?
Mother with Marmeladova.
I am doing harm to everybody.
I acted stupidly, when, for instance, I told her. If I had taken advantage of love and that is all.
But would that be honorable. Can one endure that? I harm everybody. A bullet in the head. He comes to say goodby.
*She* stops him.
End it differently.
Repent and begin another life. Out of despair there comes a new perspective.
Fire.
That is one thing, by heroism you will expiate it. You will redeem it. To reeducate oneself.
Beginning of the novel.
The tone.
AT FIRST:
We went to the old woman to look around and half light-

2. Apparently Dostoevsky contemplated including a major scene in which Raskolnikov would rescue someone from a burning building. This scene, as well as the apparition of Christ, referred to in several notes, are not included in the final version, which, however, does make passing references to Raskolnikov's heroic conduct at a fire. The fire as well as the vision of Christ may be presumed to have been intended as steps in Raskolnikov's regeneration.

heartedly and himself he almost does not believe he will do it. So—in any case.

THEN continuation and side issues. Even in the manner of humor. As if he himself does not expect that THAT can happen.

FURTHER. The murder is done almost unexpectedly. (I myself did not expect it.) The story about the panic, fear, and sickness. This ends with Marmeladov's death.

FINALLY. Suddenly: a gloomy sadness and endless pride and struggle lest life die altogether, and that life should be.

NB. From this crime itself begins his moral development, the possibility of such questions as earlier were impossible.

In the last chapter, in jail, he says that without the crime he would not have discovered in himself such questions, wishes, feeling, needs, striving, development.

NB. Second Part. Confession. The story of the murder. I myself did not expect it and all that time in the story there follows as though surprise at himself, as though surprise on the side. And then full judgment of himself (two weeks later calm)

Third Part. Full of pride. The mother's and sister's arrival. They chased out the bridegroom. Caprices. Against Razumikhin. Scenes with the sister. Conversation at the lamp. Suspicion of Marmeladova: I *cannot* love you. Finally suddenly terror and despair. Wonderings. Meeting with Marmeladova. He explains everything. Bullet through the head. She stops him. She runs away from him. She took Sasja. A vision. Christ. Why do they not rebel and grumble? He goes to say goodby. She stops him [I, 122–123, 69–70]

The chief idea. Eureka!

The novel begins with him with Marmeladova in the highest state of humiliation and despair. . . . . Quarrel with Marmeladova. She says—Repent. She shows him perspective of new life and love (not a word about love).

Finally he turns himself in, conquered. [I, 124, 71]

To the characterization of Sonya.

After Marmeladova's death, when he calls her saintly, she says with fright: Oh what are you saying. I am a great sinner. When he thinks she is talking about the yellow ticket and says so, Sonya (weary of his confused words on that theme) says to him: I am not speaking about that, but I have been ungrateful. I sinned often against love. She tells the story (she tells it masterfully) how the humiliated and downtrodden Marmeladova once wanted an embroidered collar which belonged to Sonya and asked her for it, and she did not give it to her, the collar got lost, and now, if only she had the collar and she asked for it—I'd give it, I'd give everything.

Sonya tells many anecdotes about her father. Sometimes gaily and at other times sufferingly-martyr-like. [I, 134, 74]

The Russian nation always suffered like Christ, says Sonya. The characters of arithmetic kill, and direct faith saves. All became confused. Nothing to believe in, ..othing on which to make a stand. But direct faith is also a prejudice. Believe in the beauty of the Russian element (Sonya.)

NB From that time on there begin scenes in various places, a few intrigues. She with Sonya (letters by Sonya to him), mother against Sonya, Razumikhin's with the daughter, the Investigator, a young man, and his walks. He begins to work in order to live, brings to Marmeladova. [I, 36/111, 76]

He in front of Sonya on his knees. I love you. She says to him: "Give yourself up to the court." Must be you do not love me, he says. She is silent. His walks. Fire. (He is decorated) Mother, sister at his bedside. Reconciliation with all. His joy, a joyful evening. In the morning, towards service, bows to the people. Farewell. I shall come, Sonya says.

* * *

NB Turn yourself in, Sonya says. [I, 37/111, 77]

The Idea of the Novel

1 Orthodox View. What Orthodoxy is.

2 There is no happiness in comfort. Happiness is purchased by suffering.

3. Man is not born for happiness. Man earns his happiness, and always by suffering. There is no injustice there, for knowledge and consciousness of life (i.e. directly felt by body and soul, i.e. by all life process) is acquired by experience pro and contra, which one must get through on one's own. (by suffering, such is the law of our planet, but that direct knowledge, felt by life process is such a great joy that one can pay for it by years of suffering.)

In *his* image in the novel is expressed the idea of extraordinary pride, arrogance, and contempt for all society. His idea is to take that society into his power. Despotism is a trait of his. It goes to meet him.

NB In writing it, do not forget that he is 23 years old.

He wants to rule—and does not know the means.

Take power as quickly as possible and get rich. And the idea of murder came into his head.

NB Express all that in Razumikhin's evening party.

NB To the novel: Find and put into the novel a Russian merchant (Babushkin), an industrialist, so that then he can give Razumikhin a job at 3000. [III, 3–4, 167–168]

Svidrigaylov. If I were a socialist naturally I should go on living because I'd have something to do. There are no people with stronger convictions than socialists. And in life, conviction is the main thing. Go and take his convictions away. He feels that he loses the stuff of life. For him conviction is the main thing. Wherein lies conviction? The main idea of socialism is mechanism. There man is made man by mechanics. Rules for everything. Man himself is removed. They took away the living soul. It is understood that it is possible to be calm—it is real reaction, and those people say they are progressives! Lord, if that is progress, then what is reaction. . . . . Socialism is the despair ever to put man in order. They build despotism and say it is freedom. And lest he swaggered too much, they love terribly the view that man himself is only mechanics. [III, 62, 173]

The chapter Christ (like Oblomov's dream)[3] ends with a fire. After the fire he came to say goodby to her. No, I am not yet ready, I am full of pride and falseness. I am only just beginning all the process of transformation—in jail. [III, 67–68, 177–178]

Capital and Main Thing.
Never even a word was spoken about love between them. But Sonya, beside having fallen in love with him the evening of her father's death, right away was impressed because in order to calm her, he told her that he had killed, therefore he respected her so much that he did not fear to open himself to her completely. He, not speaking to her about love, saw that she is necessary to him like air, like everything and he loved her without limit. [III, 108–109, 192]

The Conclusion of the Novel
Raskolnikov goes to shoot himself.
Svidrigaylov: I'd go to America gladly right now, but nobody wants to.
Svidrigaylov to R. on the Haymarket: Shoot yourself, maybe I'll shoot myself too. Did you notice that lately more strange things have happened. Two women drowned, someone threw himself out of the window and finished it all. The times are becoming playful. Isn't it like spiders. . . .
Svidrigaylov is despair, the most cynical.
Sonya is hope, the most unrealizable.
Raskolnikov himself must say that. He attached himself pas-

3. In Goncharov's novel *Oblomov*.

sionately to both of them.

Svidrigaylov: Shoot yourself, it is not in your character to remain alive, there are two roads for you: either confess or shoot yourself. . . .

And if we sat in the House of Deputies, busy, and worked away with all our force, to overthrow the cabinet, worked on finance—then what?

That would be lower than the present state. Nastier— [III, 150, 216–217]

# From Dostoevsky's Letters†

## To A. A. *Kraevsky (Petersburg, June 8, 1865)*

\* \* \* I ask you for three thousand rubles, now, as an advance for a novel which I formally obligate myself to send to the office of *Ot. Zapisky*[1] no later than early this October. \* \* \* NB. My novel is called "The Drunkards" and it will be connected with the current problem of drunkenness. Not only is the problem examined, but all its ramifications are represented, most of all depictions of families, the bringing up of children under these circumstances, and so on. It will be no less than twenty signatures[2] but maybe even more. 150 rubles for each signature.[3]

## Draft, to M. N. *Katkov (first half of September, 1865)*

May I hope to place a story in your magazine R. V. [*Russian Messenger*]? I have been writing it here in Wiesbaden, for two months already, and I am now finishing it. It will be five to six signatures long. There remains two week's work or maybe more to be done. In any case, I can say that probably in a month and no later, it ought to reach the office of R. V.

---

† Four of the letters that follow have been drawn from *Pis'ma* ("Letters") ed. Dolinin (Moscow, 1928): I, 408 (Kraevsky); I, 430, 432 (Vrangel); IV, 280–81 (Katkov, 1866); I, 437–38 (Korvin-Krukovskaya). The draft of the letter to Katkov appears on pp. 160–62 of Glivenko's edition of Dostoevsky's notebooks, *Iz arkhiva Dostoevskogo* (Moscow, 1931); we do not know for certain whether Dostoevsky sent it to Katkov. The letters have been translated by George Gibian.

1. *Fatherland Notes.* Kraevsky was editor of this magazine.

2. A signature is one printer's sheet, which, when folded and cut, occupies sixteen pages in a book.

3. It is clear from this letter and that to Katkov below (September, 1865) that Dostoevsky had two ideas for two different novels or stories, about drunkards and about a murderer. That of the murderer originally was intended to be only a story or short tale. The two plots merged in the process of Dostoevsky's working on them, and he incorporated the idea of the drunkards (in the form of the Marmeladov subplot) in *Crime and Punishment*. Kraevsky did not accept Dostoevsky's offer of a novel as against a cash advance Dostoevsky then concluded a contract with Stellovsky described in his letter to Korvin-Krukovskaya.

The idea of the story cannot run counter to your magazine's; on the contrary. It is a psychological account of a crime. A young man expelled from the university, a bourgeois by origin and living in extreme poverty, lighthearted, unstable in his ideas, has surrendered to several strange, "unfinished" ideas which are in the air. He decided to get out of his bad position at one stroke. He decided to kill an old woman, a Titular Councillor's wife, who lent money on interest. The old woman is stupid, deaf, sick, greedy, takes usurious interest rates, is mean, and oppresses the life of another person—she torments her younger sister who is working for her. "She is good for nothing, what is she living for? Is she useful to anybody?" Those questions drive the young man out of his mind. He decides to kill her, rob her, in order to make happy his mother, who lives in a provincial district, to rescue a sister, who lives at a landlord's estate as a companion, from the lecherous molestations of the head of that landlord's family, molestations which threaten to ruin her—to finish his studies, go abroad, and then be honest the rest of his life, firm and unyielding in the fulfillment of his human duty to mankind. Which of course will redeem the crime, if one can call crime that act towards the old, deaf, stupid, mean, and sick woman who does not know herself what she is living for and who a month later might have died anyway. Although such crimes are terribly difficult to perform— i.e., almost always they leave behind crude, visible clues, and so forth, and they leave terribly much to chance, which almost always betrays . . . . . he, in an entirely accidental manner, succeeds in performing his plan both quickly and successfully.

He spends almost a month after that until the final catastrophe; almost no suspicions existed or could exist against him. There, too, the psychological process of the crime develops. Insoluble problems arise for the murderer; unsuspected and unexpected feelings torment his heart. The truth of God and the law of the earth take their toll, and he ends by being forced to denounce himself, forced, even if he should perish in jail, to rejoin people. The feeling of isolation and separation from mankind which he felt as soon as he committed the crime wore him down. The law of truth and human nature took its toll, . . . . the criminal himself decides to accept torments in order to redeem his act. But it is difficult for me to clarify fully my idea. Beside this, my story makes allusion to the idea that the punishment meted out by the law to the criminal deters the criminal far less than the lawgivers think, because he himself requires it morally.

I saw this in even the most undeveloped people, in the coarsest cases. I wanted to express this in an educated man of the new generation, in order to make the idea more clearly and palpably visible. Some events of the most recent time convinced me that my subject is not at all eccentric, particularly the murderer being an educated and even good man. Last year in Moscow they told me about a student expelled from the university after the Moscow student affair when he decided to rob a postcoach and kill the postman. There is much evidence in our newspapers about the unusual instability of ideas which impel people to terrible acts. (The seminarist who killed a girl after an agreement with her in a barn and whom they took an hour later at lunch.) In a word, I am convinced that my subject is partly justified by our contemporary days.

Naturally in this presentation of the idea of my story, I have left out the whole plot. I guarantee the interest of it, I do not take it on myself to judge the artistic quality of it. I have written many, too many very, very bad things, in a hurry, to beat a deadline, etc. This time I have written without hurrying and passionately; I shall try, if only for my own sake, to finish it as well as possible.

### To A. E. Vrangel (Petersburg, February 18, 1866)

\* \* \* I am sitting over my work like a prisoner. It is the novel for the *Russian Messenger*. It is a long novel in six parts.[4] Towards the end of November a lot was written and finished. I burned it all. Now I can confess it. I did not like it myself. A new form, a new plan carried me away and I started afresh. I work day and night and still I work too little. I calculate that every month I must send in to the *Russian Messenger* up to six signatures. That is terrible. But I'd send them in, if I had freedom of mind. The novel is a poetic thing, it demands calm of mind and of imagination. My creditors are tormenting me, they threaten to send me to jail \* \* \*

Two weeks ago the first part of my novel came out in the first, January issue of the *Russian Messenger*. It is called: *Crime and Punishment*. I have already heard many enthusiastic comments. It contains bold and new things.

### To M. N. Katkov (Petersburg, April 25, 1866)

\* \* \*

All nihilists are socialists. Socialism (particularly in its Russian form) demands especially the severing of all connections. They

4. In the *Russian Messenger*, the novel was divided into three parts; in the separate edition, into six. The six-part structure of the novel coincides with the six-part arrangement of the separate book edition (two volumes, 1867, published by Bazunov). The change from the division into three parts to six came in the interval between the first and second issue of the *Russian Messenger*, no earlier than the end of February.

are completely certain that on the *tabula rasa* they will immediately build a paradise. Fourier was convinced that all it will take is to build one phalanstery and the whole world will immediately be covered by phalansteries; those are his own words.[5] And our Chernyshevsky said that he only needed to talk to the people for a quarter hour and immediately he would convince them to convert to socialism. Moreover, in our poor little defenseless Russian boys and girls, there is one more, eternally persisting, fundamental point upon which socialism will base itself for a long time to come: enthusiasm for the good, and the purity of their hearts. Frauds and foul people there are many among them. But all those high school students, schoolboys of whom I have seen so many, converted to nihilism so purely, so selflessly in the name of honor, truth, and true welfare. They are defenseless against these absurdities and accept them as if they were perfection itself. Sound science of course will eradicate it all. But when will it come? How many victims is socialism going to swallow until then? Last of all: sound science, even when it takes root, will not wipe out the weeds so quickly, because sound science is still only science, and not the direct form of civic and social reality. The poor little people are convinced that nihilism gives them that full manifestation of their civic and social reality and freedom.

### To A. V. *Korvin-Krukovskaya* (*June 17, 1866*)[6]

\* \* \* Imagine what has happened to me (something amusing and very typical). Last year I was in such a bad financial situation that I was forced to sell the right to publish all I had previously written, all at once, to a speculator, Stellovsky, a rather bad man, a publisher who understands nothing. But in our contract was a clause in which I promise him to complete for his edition a novel at least twelve signatures long. If I don't send it in by Nov. 1, 1866 (the last deadline) then he, Stellovsky, has the right to publish free of charge in the course of ten years in any way he wants, all that I shall have written without any payment to him. . . . I signed. November 1 is four months away. I thought I could buy myself out from Stellovsky, by paying a forfeit, but he does not want to. I begged him for a three months' extension—he does not want to and tells me openly that he is convinced I do not have the time to write a novel twelve signatures long, particularly since I have only written half of the one for the *Russian Messenger*, so it is more advantageous for him not to agree to an extension and a forfeit, because then everything I shall later write will belong to him. I want to do an unusual and eccentric thing: write thirty

5. Phalansteries were communal dormitories and social units proposed by the French Utopian socialist Charles Fourier (1772–1837).

6. The maiden name of the famous woman mathematician better known as Sonia Kovalevskaya.

signatures in four months,[6] on two separate novels. I shall write one in the morning, the other in the evening, and finish in time.[7] I am convinced that not one of our other writers, past or present, dead or alive, wrote under such conditions as those under which I write all the time. Turgenev would die at the mere thought. If they only knew how depressing it is to ruin an idea which was born in you, about which you became enthusiastic, about which you know that it is good—and to be forced to ruin it, knowingly!

## A Passage from an Early Draft†

For some reason at that moment I suddenly remembered extraordinarily vividly how abominably I had behaved in the office, how I had fawned on that filthy Ilya Petrovich and had played up to him; how vilely I had acted all that morning and prayed that I would succeed in hiding the things, acted meanly until the very moment . . . But no, that wasn't it, that wasn't the main thing, that wasn't what pained me the most, not those recollections . . .

I could not myself clearly describe what a sudden, altogether new feeling of dejection suddenly overwhelmed me there at the bench. Maybe precisely because I wasn't able to give myself a full explanation of it I felt it even more painfully. I only felt that some kind of a new and long anxiety had begun, an altogether unforeseen and unthought of one which all my strength would now have to go to dealing with. And the main thing was that I myself didn't want to believe in that dejection and anxiety.

That is not dejection, but sickness, I decided in the end. That was not IT. It is the whole past month that is making itself felt. It's a fever, maybe even hunger, and not dejection. I'll get better,

6. Equivalent to 480 pages of a book.
7. Dostoevsky succeeded in completing his works and escaped Stellovsky's clutches. In his emergency he decided to hire a stenographer and to dictate his novels to her. On October 4, 1866, Anna Grigorevna Snitkina applied to him for a position as stenographer. She helped him with the last part of *Crime and Punishment* and with the novel *The Gambler* for Stellovsky. She became his second wife and was of great help to him personally and professionally. (See Bibliography for her *Reminiscences*.) For further remarks on Dostoevsky's method of working and his practice of dictating his novel, see Chulkov's comments.
† Manuscripts of the novel for the most

part have disappeared. Dostoevsky himself said that he burned the first version, when he was carried away by enthusiasm for his "new plan," and the final manuscript from which the novel was set in type has been lost, with the exception of two small fragments. However, a few chapters have been preserved in manuscript form, and they were published for the first time in the Literary Monuments edition of the novel in Moscow in 1971. Some of them vary considerably from the printed text. The passage translated here is from an early version which was narrated in the first person by Raskolnikov. It corresponds to pages 92–94, Part Two, Chapter II, in the text of the novel, above.

and things will be different. Hm. Yes. Maybe *yesterday* also upset me too much. I couldn't stand it. My nerves. It had to be like that. Even a reasonable person is sometimes afraid to go into a dark room. Nerves, too. Besides, how vilely I had been forced to act yesterday and today—to lie, humiliate myself, fawn, to hide the things, how I had to debase myself! . . . Well, that added to it, the nerves from not being used to it. Nerves and delirium.

Why, why am I here? Why do I feel an alien? Why am I on "another planet"? Where did those words pop into my head from, there at the bench? Why did I feel so disgusted now at the bench? Am I not myself the sole judge of myself? Of course, delirium . . . I couldn't bear the fact. Well, I couldn't stand it, but I will stand it. I knew beforehand that this delirium must be, must come in its time. I foretold it a month ahead of time. So what? I must endure it. I must get better. To give my blood, if only it had been possible to avoid spilling that blood, and I know that I'm saying this sincerely. What do I have to be afraid of? I'm a brick that fell on the old woman's head; I'm a plank that fell down on her. I knew all that beforehand; and if I left the bench and drew a blank, it is the despondency, it is the hunger, illness, fever, nerves. I'll look after myself, and the sickness and the nerves will pass. I'll start to live and will look at the thing clearly. What am I worth? I want to live and I will live. I take the task on myself deliberately, not like a fool . . . Wait: where am I going now? I am going to see a man. A month ago I decided that the very next day I would go to see that man, that I would begin with that. So I will go there. If only for the sake of exactness I will go there.

It was thus, if one can even approximately put it into words, that my melancholy was beginning to speak within me. I went to see a certain student, Razumikhin, my former friend, also expelled like myself, who now lived on the Vasilyevsky Island. When I walked off the Nikolaevsky Bridge, some kind of peculiar impatience seized me: faster, faster, I wanted to see Razumikhin, as if that would decide everything. I didn't even feel tired. Besides, it seemed I had reached that limit of tiredness after which you cease to feel it, and something different takes over.

Razumikhin was at home, in his little room on the fourth floor above the Little Neva, and opened the door himself. He was studying, writing. He was a kind and cheerful fellow, thin, badly shaven, with black hair and large black eyes. He was not stupid but very simple, sometimes he became very wild, and was known to be a very strong man. Once, at night when he was with a group of friends, he knocked down with one blow a policeman seven feet tall. Razumikhin was also remarkable because he could stand almost everything, he could sleep even on the roof, and endure extraordinary hunger.

Once he did not heat his room all winter and said that one sleeps better that way. We were not great friends, only comrades. We had not seen each other for five months. But having decided to see him, I didn't even stop to realize that it meant I should see him face to face ... In a word, I can't express the revulsion I suddenly felt at finding myself in his place. All my gall arose in me.

You? he shouted, looking me up and down in amazement. Are things as bad as that? You are better dressed than we are, he added, looking at my rags. Sit down, you must be tired. When I collapsed on the oil-cloth covered sofa, which was in worse condition even than mine, he realized that I was ill.

But you're seriously ill. He tried to feel my pulse. I snatched my hand away.

No, don't, I said, I came ... this is why: I don't have any pupils ... I should like ... however, I don't need any pupils.

Do you know, you are delirious, he said after a silence.

No. Goodbye. I got up from the couch.

But wait, wait! You are so freakish.

No, don't, I said, snatching away my hand.

What the deuce did you come for then? Have you gone clean off your head? You know—this is almost an insult. I won't let you go like this.

Well listen: I came to see you because except for you I don't know anybody who could help me ... begin ... because you are simpler and kinder than anybody. But now I see that I don't want any pupils. So no—I don't need your pity or your help either. I don't need anything. Leave me in peace. Alone. Goodbye. Goodbye.

Stop a minute, you chimney sweep. You are quite mad.[1]

1. From here on, the text is the same as on page 94, above.

# Essays in Criticism

# N. STRAKHOV

## [The Nihilists and Raskolnikov's New Idea]†

Nihilist men and women have been represented in our novels
and stories for a long time. . . . What did Dostoevsky do? He
took on a very much deeper and more difficult task than that of ridi-
culing the ugliness of empty and anemic natures. His Raskolnikov
may suffer from youthful depression and egoism, but he represents
a man gifted with a strong mind and warm heart. He is not a
phrase-monger devoid of blood and nerves; he is a real man. This
young man also constructs a theory, but a theory which because
of the force of his greater vitality and larger power of mind runs
more deeply and more definitely counter to life. * * *

For the first time, an unhappy nihilist, a nihilist suffering in
a deeply human way, is depicted before us. * * * The author
took nihilism in its extreme form, at the point beyond which there
is no further place to go. * * * The task of the novel is to show
how life and theory fight each other in man's heart, to show that
struggle in the form in which it reaches its highest degree, and to
show that victory was won by life. * * *

It is odd to argue that Raskolnikov is not insane. In the novel
itself there are characters close to Raskolnikov who watch his
torments and do not understand the sources of the strange behavior to which his inner torments lead him and who begin to
suspect that he may be losing his mind. But then the mystery
is solved. Something immeasurably less probable is revealed: he
is not an insane man, but a criminal.

The novel is written in an impersonal manner, with the author
not speaking in abstract terms about the minds and characters of
his heroes, but making them act, think, and feel directly. Particularly the principal character, Raskolnikov, is hardly at all described
by the author speaking in his own person, but rather he is everywhere *shown* to be a man endowed with a clear mind, firm character, and noble heart. He is such in all his actions except for the
crime. Thus he is regarded by the other characters, above whom
he towers in every way possible. This is how the investigator
Porfiry speaks about Raskolnikov to his face: "I can understand
how some despondent man could endure all this, but a proud,
masterful, and impatient man, particularly an impatient man! In

† Strakhov was a friend of Dostoevsky
(as well as a friend and collaborator
of Tolstoy). The following extracts are
taken from Strakhov's review of *Crime*
*and Punishment* in two issues of
*Otechestvennye zapiski*, 171 (1867),
329, 334–36, and 339–40. Translated
by George Gibian.

any event I consider you a most noble man who even has the makings of greatness of mind." Even the horrible thing done by Raskolnikov indicates to people who know him closely the power of his mind, albeit a perverted mind which has lost its way. * * * The author clearly wants to represent a strong soul, a man full of life, not one who is demented and weak. The secret of the author's intention is particularly clearly revealed in the words which he put in Svidrigaylov's mouth when he explains her brother's conduct to Raskolnikov's sister: "Russian people are broad people." The author wants to depict the broad Russian nature, that is, a living nature, little inclined to walk the beaten, worn path of Russian life, capable of living and feeling in various ways. The author took such a nature, alive and at the same time undefined, and surrounded it with a milieu which had become confused, in which particularly the sacred traditions had long since ceased to exist. * * * Svidrigaylov himself, who utters such a general accusation against our educated society . . . represents something after the fashion of the old generation of the same nature and of the same society, who are the counterparts of Raskolnikov, the member of the new generation. Despite the fantasticality of Svidrigaylov, one can nevertheless see in him the familiar traits of that educated and well-to-do class which recently departed from us. Debauchery, cruelty to serfs reaching the point of homicide, secret crimes, the lack of anything sacred in their souls—it is towards those things that the broad Russian natures hurled themselves in order to spend their energies on something. Raskolnikov is also a man who very much wants to live, who quickly needs a way out, who needs something to do. Such people cannot remain inactive. The thirst for life, no matter what kind of life, as long as it comes now, as quickly as possible, leads them to absurdities, to the breaking of their souls, and even to complete destruction.

\* \* \*

The very essence of the crime of Raskolnikov is that it is a murder for a principle. It was not the three thousand rubles that attracted Raskolnikov. Strange as it may be to say so, it is true that if he could have obtained that sum by stealing, cheating at cards, or by some other petty fraud, he hardly would have decided to do it. He was attracted by the killing of a principle, by permitting himself that which is most forbidden. A theorist, he did not know that in killing a principle, he was at the same time making an attempt at the very life of his own soul. But having killed, he understood, by the terrible sufferings, what kind of crime he had committed.

Such were the tasks which the author set before himself, huge tasks of incomparable seriousness. The general theme of Dostoevsky's novel is the extremely deep perversion of the moral sense and the subsequent return of the soul to truly human feelings and concepts.

# LEO TOLSTOY

## [How Minute Changes of Consciousness Caused Raskolnikov to Commit Murder]†

\* \* \*

The mainspring which activates all human life lies not in human beings' moving their arms, legs, and backs, but in their consciousness. In order for a human being to do something with his legs or arms, it is first necessary for a certain change to take place in his consciousness. This change, which defines all subsequent actions of that person, is always minute, almost imperceptible.

The painter Bryullov[1] once made a correction on a student's sketch. The pupil, looking at the transformed sketch, said: "You hardly at all touched my study, yet it has become entirely different." Bryullov answered: "Hardly-at-all is where art begins."

That saying is strikingly true, not only in relation to art, but also in relation to all life. One can say that true life begins where hardly-at-all begins, at the point where changes occur which seem to us infinitely small, barely perceptible. True life does not take place where large external changes occur, where people move, collide, fight, kill one another. It takes place where hardly-at-all differentiating changes are made.

Raskolnikov's real life did not take place when he was killing the old woman or her sister. When he was killing the first old woman and still more her sister, he was not living his real life; rather, he was acting like a machine, he was doing something that he was not capable of doing: he was firing a charge which had been loaded inside him a long time before. One old woman had been killed, the other stood there in front of him, the axe was in his hand.

Raskolnikov's real life took place not when he was facing the old woman's sister, but before he had killed either old woman, when he had not yet stood in a strange apartment in order to murder, when he

† An excerpt from the essay "Why Do Men Stupefy Themselves?" Tolstoy's essay was written in 1890, when he was sixty-one, as an introduction to a book on drunkenness by P. S. Alexeev. These pages have been translated for this volume by George Gibian from the text in *Polnoe Sobranie Sochineniy* (Moscow-Leningrad, 1933) 27: 279–81. The essay is vintage Tolstoy and illustrates his approach to literature as a repository of illustrations and lessons on moral and psychological life. It deserves to be far more widely known than it is in Western countries.
1. K.P. Bryullov (1799–1852) was a famous Russian painter.

had not yet held an axe in his hand, and did not have a loop in the overcoat on which he hung the axe—it took place before he had even thought of the old woman, when he was lying at home on his sofa, not thinking at all about the old woman or even about whether one could, on the basis of an individual's decision, wipe another human being, a superfluous and harmful being, off the face of the earth. His real life took place when he was thinking about whether or not he ought to live in Petersburg, whether or not he should accept money from his mother, about questions which had nothing to do with the old woman. The decision whether or not he would kill the old woman was made then, in that animal sphere of life completely independent of reality. Those decisions were not made when he stood in front of the other woman with an axe in his hand, but rather when he was not yet acting but only thinking, when only his consciousness was active, when barely perceptible changes were taking place in that consciousness. It is then that the greatest possible lucidity of thought is particularly important for the correct solution of the question which arises, and it is then that one glass of beer, one smoked cigarette can impair the solution to the problem, hinder its solution, deafen the voice of the conscience, and cause the question to be decided in favor of one's lower animal nature, as it was with Raskolnikov.

The changes are just barely perceptible, but their consequences are colossal, terrible. The instant when a human being makes a decision and begins to act can change many material things. Houses, fortunes, peoples' bodies can perish, but nothing that is brought about is more important than that which is deposited in the human being's consciousness. Consciousness limits what can take place. From barely perceptible changes which take place in the area of consciousness, the most unimaginably important, limitless consequences can follow.

\* \* \*

# SERGEI V. BELOV†

## The History of the Writing of the Novel

\* \* \*

Three notebooks with drafts and notes for *Crime and Punishment* have been preserved, that is, three manuscript versions of the novel: the first, short version ("the novella"); the second, lengthier version; and the third, final version. These correspond to the three stages of [Dostoevsky's]

† These pages have been translated for this volume by George Gibian from S. V. Belov, *Roman F. M. Dostoevskogo "Prestuplenie*    *i Nakazanie": Kommentariy (F. M. Dostoevsky's Novel* Crime and Punishment: *A Commentary* (Moscow, 1984) 22–29.

work: the Wiesbaden stage (the letter to Katkov); the Petersburg stage (from October to December 1865), when Dostoevsky launched his "new plan"; and, finally, the last stage (1866).

All three manuscript versions of the novel have been published three times. The last two publications, by G. F. Kogan and L. D. Opulskaya, are on a high scholarly level. These publications of the drafts of *Crime and Punishment* gives us the opportunity to take a clear look into Dostoevsky's creative laboratory and at his searching, stubborn grappling with words and with narrative forms.

The Wiesbaden novella, as well as the second, lengthier version, were still cast in the form of a confession by the criminal: "I am on trial, and I shall tell it all. I shall write down everything. I am writing for myself, but let others read it, too, all my judges, too, if they want to. This is a confession. I shall keep nothing back." But in the course of the work, when the material of the novel "The Drunkards" merges with the "confession," and the conception becomes complicated, the earlier form of a confession told by the murderer who had cut himself off from the world and had completely moved inside his "fixed idea" becomes too narrow for the new psychological and social contents. Dostoevsky settles on a "new form"—authorial narration. In November 1865 he burns the first version, the novella.

In the third, final version, a very important entry appears: "Narration by myself, not by *him*. If it were a confession, it should be too much so, to the last extreme, everything would have to be made clear. So that every moment of the story is clear. NB To be taken into consideration: if told as a confession, at some points it will be immodest, and difficult to imagine for what purpose it has been written. But if told by the *author*, much naïveté and openness are needed. One must assume an author who is an omniscient, infallible being, exhibiting one of the members of the new generation for everybody to see."

The drafts in the notebooks to *Crime and Punishment* make it possible for us to trace how long Dostoevsky looked for an answer to the main question of the novel: why did Raskolnikov commit the murders? The answer did not come easily to the author. In the original conception of the novella (letter to Katkov), it was "simple arithmetic": to kill one worthless, harmful, and rich being, in order to use the money to make many beautiful but poor people happy: "My poor mother, my poor sister. I meant it for you. If it is a sin, I decided to take it on me, but only so that you would be happy"; "to die proudly, having paid with a mountain of helpful good deeds for the trivial and ridiculous crime of my youth."

In the second, extensive version, Raskolnikov still presents himself as a humanist thirsting to defend the humiliated and injured ones: "I am not a person who would permit a scoundrel to destroy a defenseless, weak creature. I join in, I want to join in." But the paradoxical idea of a murder out of love for others, a murder of a human being out of love for mankind, gradually becomes covered over with Raskolnikov's will to power. Till now, Raskolnikov does not seek power out of vanity. He wants to acquire power in order to devote himself entirely to service to human beings; he wants to use power only for the good of people: "I take power, I acquire the strength, whether force or money, to do harm. I bring happiness." His prayer after he comes home from the Marmeladovs: meekly: "Lord! If the murder of this blind, stupid old woman, who is of no use to anybody, is a sin, when I had wanted to dedicate myself—to consecrate myself, then condemn me. I judged myself severely, it was not vanity."

But Dostoevsky penetrates still more deeply into the soul of the criminal and, behind the idea of the good heart which lost its way, discovers murder for the sake of love of humanity, for the sake of good deeds. He discovers what was for him the most horrible and monstrous idea—the "Napoleonic Idea," the idea of power for the sake of power, the idea dividing mankind into two unequal parts: the majority—the trembling creatures—and the minority—the masters, called from birth to the mission of ruling over the majority, standing outside the law and having the right, like Napoleon, to transgress against the law and to break the divine order of the world, for the sake of the ends which they require. In the third, final version the "Napoleonic Idea" reaches its full maturity. "Is it possible to love them? Is it possible to suffer for them? Hatred for mankind"; "Lack of love for mankind and suddenly the idea about the old woman"; "The idea of extreme pride, haughtiness, and contempt for this society is expressed in the novel in *his character*. His idea: to take this society in his power. Despotism—that is his character trait." "He wants to rule—and does not know by what means. To grasp power as fast as possible and to become rich. The idea of murder came to him full blown. NB Whatever I might be, what I might then do, whether I should be a benefactor of humanity or whether I would suck out its vital juices like a spider,—that does not matter to me. I know that I want to rule, and that is enough." "Listen: there are two sorts of people. The higher natures can step across obstacles."

Thus, in the creative process, in Dostoevsky's bringing the conception of *Crime and Punishment* to its maturity, in the character of Raskolnikov, two contradictory ideas clashed: the idea of love for people and the idea of contempt for them. The notebooks with drafts for the novel show the torments Dostoevsky went through as he looked for a way out: either to drop one of the two ideas, or to keep both. In the second, extended version there is the entry: "*The main anatomy of the novel*. After the sickness and so forth. Put the line of the action definitely on a real footing and get rid of all indefiniteness; that is, in one way or another make clear the whole murder and make his character and relationships clear." But the disappearance of one of the two ideas would have significantly simplified and impoverished the concept of the novel, and Dostoevsky decides to combine both ideas, to show a man in whom, as

Razumikhin says about Raskolnikov in the final text of the novel, "two antithetical characters take each other's place in turn."

Dostoevsky also agonized as he struggled to find a conclusion to the novel. One of his notes reads: *"The ending of the novel. Raskolnikov goes to shoot himself."* But that was the ending only for the "Napoleonic idea." The writer also sketches in an ending for the "idea of love," when Christ himself saves the repentant sinner: "A vision of Christ. He asks the people for forgiveness."

But what will be the end of a man uniting in himself both antithetical principles? Dostoevsky understood very well that such a man will accept neither the authorial judgment, nor the juridical one, nor that of his own conscience. Raskolnikov acknowledges only one court over himself, the "Supreme Court," the court of Sonya Marmeladova, that same Sonya in whose name he had raised the axe, that same humiliated and injured Sonya, one of those women who had always suffered, ever since the earth has existed.

After he has killed the old women, Raskolnikov not only does not experience repentance, but believes in his theory more than ever. Even when he goes to the police station in order to turn himself in, he does not think that there is anything for him to repent of. Despite his conviction that he was right, he goes and denounces himself, and accepts punishment for his crime, which, in his opinion, he had not committed. Something higher than the considerations of reason wins over his will. This struggle between the conscience protesting against the bloodshed and reason justifying the bloodshed is what constitutes the spiritual drama of Raskolnikov. And when the conscience (the moral instinct which Raskolnikov cannot understand) finally conquers, and Raskolnikov is already languishing in prison, his reason still does not surrender, but refuses to acknowledge that it had been mistaken.

Even his confession in his opinion proved not that his theory was false, but that he himself was not one of those great people who can break moral laws: "I spent so many days tormenting myself: would Napoleon have gone [to confess], or not? I felt clearly that I was not Napoleon . . ." This is what rips Raskolnikov to pieces: he turned out to be an ordinary human being subject to the moral law.

He wanted to have "freedom and power, but mainly power! Over all trembling creatures, over the entire anthill!" He was to have received that power after he had freed himself from the moral law. But the moral law showed itself to be stronger than he, and he lost. . . . Only in prison, literally on the last page of the novel, a revolution took place in Raskolnikov's soul: he was born into a new life. The moral sense won. Such was Raskolnikov's tragedy. Conscience and nature turned out to be stronger than theory, in spite of its logical invulnerability.

What did the error of Raskolnikov's theory consist in? Raskolnikov wanted to base it on logic, to rationalize something which in its very essence does not permit such a logical grounding, such a rationalization.

He wanted to find a fully rational morality and by way of a logical path arrived at its full rejection. Raskolnikov sought proofs of the moral law through the path of logic and did not understand that the moral law does not require proofs, for it receives its supreme sanction not from the outside, but from within itself. Why does the personality of each human being represent something sacred? No logical reason can be adduced, but such is the law of human conscience, a moral law. It is not without a purpose that Dostoevsky wrote in his preparatory materials for the novel, "There is only one law, the moral law."

No matter what the origin of this law may be, it exists in the soul of man, as a reality, and it does not allow itself to be broken. Raskolnikov tried to breach it, and he was defeated. Everyone is bound to be defeated in this way if he possesses the moral sense, and breaches the moral law, the law of human conscience.

Naturally, he who lacks the moral sense is able to shed blood with absolute calm, without feeling any pangs of conscience. Svidrigaylov commits his crimes without feeling any tragedy in his soul. Those who possess no conscience do not need to ask themselves whether they have the right to kill another human being; they do not need any moral justification for their actions. But Raskolnikov is a human being with a conscience, and conscience avenges itself on him for his flouting of the moral law.

The moral law proclaims that every human personality is a supreme sacred entity. Countless numbers of unnoticeable transitional stages exist between the highly moral person and the criminal: at which of these points does a human personality cease to be sacred?

In the image of Raskolnikov, Dostoevsky refutes the rejection of the sacredness of the human personality. He proves through the entire contents of the novel that any human personality is sacred and untouchable and that all people are equal in this regard.

All, even the most ideal criteria of goodness, truth, and reason, fade before the greatness and significance of the reality of the human being, before his spirituality.

The idea of the supreme value and sacredness of the human personality found a powerful expression and defense in *Crime and Punishment*. The thought of the untouchability and sacredness of any human personality plays the main role in understanding the ideological meaning of the novel. If one were to summarize this ideological meaning briefly, one could do it through the biblical prohibition, Do not kill. One cannot kill a human being. The famous revolutionary Rosa Luxemburg wrote about Dostoevsky, for a good reason: "Exactly in the same way in which Hamlet's mother's crime ripped apart all links between human beings for Hamlet, so for Dostoevsky 'the times were out of joint' when he faced the possibility that a human being could be allowed to kill another human being. He does not find peace; he feels the responsibility for this horror rests on him and on each of us."

That is why in the third, final version of the novel, there appears the following entry: *"The Idea of the Novel. I. Orthodox (Pravoslavnoe) Views, what does Orthodoxy consist of.* There is no happiness in comfort, happiness is brought by suffering. Such is the law of our planet. This immediate knowledge, which is experienced through the process of living, is such a great joy that we can pay for it with years of suffering. Human beings are not born to happiness. Human beings earn happiness, and always through suffering. There is no injustice in this, for knowledge and awareness of life (which are felt immediately, by the body and spirit, i.e., through the whole process of life) are acquired by experience *pro* and *contra*, which one must pull through on one's own."[1]

The idea of Orthodoxy was to be expressed in Raskolnikov's having a "vision of Christ," after which he was to repent. "But," as Y. Karyakin writes, "instead of the ready-made scheme, a different solution won out: 'Sonya and love for her broke him down.' (Cf. in the novel: "Love resurrected them.")

In the drafts we read:

NB The last line of the novel.
The ways in which god finds man are inscrutable.

But Dostoevsky concluded the novel with different words, which are an example of the victory of the artist over his prejudices and, at the same time, express the doubts which tormented Dostoevsky. . . . The contradictions in him are so scorching that all traditional faith burns away in their fire. Of course, if conscience comes from god, then atheism is amoral. But what if the revolt against god originates in conscience, in the name of man? What if conscience does not accept any theodicy, that is, no exculpation of god for the evil which exists in the world? Does this mean that the highest morality and atheism are compatible? That is the chief question which draws and frightens Dostoevsky. Many times he answered: they are incompatible, but then there is the incontrovertible fact that Dostoevsky really had doubts until the day he died whether God existed, but he never doubted conscience. He did not translate the words "conscience," "love," and "life," as the word "religion," but rather he translated the word "religion" as the words "conscience," "love," and "life." The artistic world that he created turns around the human being, not around God. The human being is the only sun, and in this world, he must be the sun!

---

1. The last two paragraphs of Belov's article are indebted to, and quoted from, the influential, religiously oriented Soviet study of Dostoevsky's *Crime and Punishment*, Yuri Karyakin's *Samoobman Raskolnikova* (Raskolnikov's Self-Deception) (Moscow, 1976).

# GEORGY CHULKOV

## [Dostoevsky's Technique of Writing]†

What place does *Crime and Punishment* occupy among the works of Dostoevsky? On one hand, this novel completes the cycle of social motifs going from *The Poor Folk* through *The Insulted and Injured* and *The Notes from the House of the Dead*. The theme of the Marmeladovs is the same familiar theme of people ruined by poverty, of their impotent effort at passive protest. But on the other hand, the theme of Raskolnikov and Svidrigaylov moves into the foreground, partly prepared for by *Notes from the Underground*. This is the beginning of a new narrative cycle, where the theme of "revaluation of values" is the basis of the artist's intention. Raskolnikov will naturally be followed by other moral rebels not content with the passive protest of the "insulted and injured." In the drafts of the notebooks, both narrative themes are reflected.

It is curious that the theme of Marmeladov is written almost without variants, and the drafts relating to it are very close to the canonical text. Here, as a sample, is a part of the monologue of the "Drunkard" as it is written in the rough draft in the notebook:

> Clerk. Nobody can endure contempt for himself. Oh, dear sir, you think I am saying this out of pride, or spite, or the desire to justify myself. Oh, dear sir! I know, I know, there are great hearts who perish under thousand tons of oppression, without saying anything, keeping silent, and doing their work. They are not the ones who have reached high rank and built themselves houses. I am not talking about them. . . . I am speaking about God's angels. And such a God's angel is my daughter, who gave me today thirty kopeks—an angel even if she has a yellow ticket, and—such is my wife, yes my wife, too. But dear sir, even if I talk about God's angels, I am not an angel. We are miserable, we are fallen, we are the ones who have perished. So let us have perished! But, dear sir, who will feel sorry for us? It is necessary that people feel sorry for one! And who will feel sorry for us, for us, us poor ones, perished ones, turned into cattle! And my wife, my lawful wife! Sir, you may see me looking like a pig, but she is a lady. Yes, my dear sir, a lady. A lady. I am a scoundrel, but she is a lady. If she only felt sorry for me. I know that even when she tears into me like a hurricane, she does it out of pity. Yes, it is so. But God, if

† From Georgy Chulkov, *Kak rabotal Dostoevsky* (Moscow, 1939), pp. 132–34, 141–46, 313–15, 326. Translated by George Gibian. Chulkov was a Symbolist poet, a literary critic, and a scholar.

she knew how to pity me without tearing into me like a hurricane. My dear sir! Then, maybe I'd wake up. No. Hm. No, I should not wake up. I'd drink up everything, everything. I'd even sell her last stockings and drink them. Anyway, I have already drunk them, and her mohair kerchief I have taken, and she caught cold in the winter. My dear sir. Have you seen a sow? A fed up, mean sow? Well, that's what I am. (Again he took a drink out of his bottle.) And my daughter did feel sorry for me. Why did she give me thirty kopeks? She knew very well I would spend it on drink. And still she gave it to me. Why? Because she felt sorry for me. That is how God's angels feel sorry: whether you are a sinner or not, still they feel sorry for you and weep for you and pamper you and love you. People say that pity is harmful. No, it is good. For even if the thirty kopeks went for wine, which is harmful and bad, still her deed entered my heart and suffering. I suffer and I weep—I live by that.

\* \* \*

If we read the monologue of Marmeladov corresponding to these extracts,[1] it is not difficult to notice how the final version differs in comparison with the first sketches. The changes are chiefly stylistic, being directed towards verbal economy. Repetitive expressions are deleted, as are epithets and exclamations. \* \* \*

Such is the subject of the "poor clerks" and the "unhappy prostitute." The second topic is not a sentimental one, but "an underground topic," the subject of Raskolnikov.

From Dostoevsky's letter to Vrangel we know that in the end of November 1865 he was not satisfied with what he had written about Raskolnikov and that he burned his manuscript.[2] In his notebook, however, a significant fragment of that very same burned version, or one close to it, is preserved. Why did Dostoevsky burn that original text? Evidently because the first person narrative was insufficiently suited to give the reader an impression of all the complexity of psychology and plot. Much in the original version, however, was considered by Dostoevsky to have been successful, and before he gave up the subjective narration, he transferred very skillfully the first person narration into an objective narration in the author's person.

\* \* \*

Dostoevsky's notebooks to *Crime and Punishment* differ significantly from notebooks devoted to other novels in one respect. The drafts to *Crime and Punishment* are less rich in variants and less diverse than the drafts to *The Idiot, The Raw Youth,* and

---

1. See the final text of the novel, pages 12–20, above [*Editor*].

2. See Dostoevsky's letter, p. 478, above [*Editor*].

The Possessed. Essentially, there were only two main plans in Dostoevsky's intentions in the period of Crime and Punishment, which later fused into one—the plan of "The Drunkards" and the plan of Raskolnikov. The personage of the hero himself was not subjected to significant changes, such as those in the drafts to The Idiot, where the character of the Idiot was originally radically different from the character of Prince Myshkin in the canonical text.

The composition of Crime and Punishment also differs from the composition of other novels through the unity and goal-orientation of the action. The novel about Raskolnikov does not have that complexity of material which is so characteristic of The Possessed, for example, or The Raw Youth. The interest of the story does not lose thereby, since all the properties of a "criminal novel" are present in Crime and Punishment—lively interest in the outcome of events—but Dostoevsky concentrated all his artistic dialectic on one basic theme. Sonya Marmeladova is necessary to him only as an antithesis to the murderer-for-an-idea. The social background (the poverty of the Marmeladovs and of Raskolnikov's own family) is essential for the clarification of material conditions of the crime, whereas the character itself of the crime becomes intelligible only in the conditions of a bourgeois society torn apart by contradictions, which Dostoevsky knew how to depict with the highest artistry. True, the novel has one other theme—that of Svidrigaylov and Dunya. Some commentators even consider Svidrigaylov and not Raskolnikov to be the chief hero of the novel. But this view can hardly be argued convincingly, if only because Svidrigaylov does not appear until the fifth part of the novel and plays an important role only in the last, sixth part. That is of course a formal observation, but even substantively, Svidrigaylov is needed in the composition of the novel as the crooked mirror to Raskolnikov himself, and Svidrigaylov's ideas caricature his ideas. In keeping with Dostoevsky's intention, Raskolnikov, despite his crime, accepts prison as "a new life," whereas Svidrigaylov, although he refrains from the last crime (in the duel with Dunya), nevertheless puts a bullet through his head. One must suffer from decadent perversity to see in Dostoevsky's novel compassion for Svidrigaylov rather than a terrible verdict passed on him.

The sharpness of the negative arguments which Dostoevsky puts into his heroes' mouths more than once gave grounds for doubt that a positive principle in his books existed. However, in the very days when Dostoevsky was writing Notes from the Underground, the work which marked the beginning to all the confessions and doubts of Dostoevsky's great skeptics—among whom Svidrigaylov is not the last—Dostoevsky's first wife was dying in Moscow. That event is noted by Dostoevsky in his small notebook. It gives us the clue to an understanding of his world view. In that note, quite unacceptable to a skeptical way of thinking, one hears the voice of Sonya Marmeladova, who guides Raskolnikov and asks him to return to people, through repentance and prison. All of Raskolnikov's tragedy lies in the fact that his extreme individualism leads him to a murder for an idea, and murder convinces him that through crime, man loses all the threads which tie him to humanity. The idea of "humanity" of course is refracted in a peculiar manner in Dostoevsky's thought, but in analyzing his books, if we are not to be formalists, we must find the central idea which guided him in writing his works. This idea consists in this: no moral prohibitions will help man to enter into a real communication with other people, with humanity, with the whole world, nor will they save him from individualism, in the last analysis a suicidal individualism, if he does not find in life some kind of *point d'appui*, some kind of ultimate incarnation of living reality, expressing in itself all the perfection of possible harmony. Dostoevsky saw that reality in the myth of Christ. For him, Christ was not an abstract mythology, it was a real truth, and he used it as a criterion of good and evil. The moral problem about the right of man to commit a crime for the sake of other, higher goals has been presented more than once. Balzac put it forth in artistic form in the novel *Père Goriot*, where the hero Rastignac finds himself in a situation rather close to Raskolnikov's. That has already been noted by others [L. Grossman]. However, in that novel which Dostoevsky knew well (in one of the scenes of *Crime and Punishment* he reproduces quite closely the contents of the dialogue between Rastignac and a fellow student) there is not to be found that mythology which to Dostoevsky appeared the decisive one. That is why Rastignac in one version of the novel is ready to "transgress" the moral barrier without a catastrophe ensuing, and in another version he remains in doubts and vacillations, since Balzac's hero does not have that criterion of truth which makes Raskolnikov's moral theme so tragic.

In summing up the results of Dostoevsky's work in the years 1865–66, we must admit that the novel written by him in that period was the first fully successful attempt at that new narrative form which was discovered only by him, and discovered for the first time despite the fact that he had not a few predecessors and teachers. He himself often named his literary favorites who influenced him. Among them the leading ones were Balzac, Dickens, George Sand, Hoffmann, and Victor Hugo. Their influence is without any doubt. But his own artistic achievement was immeasurably richer than what he found in the great Europeans. * * * [Like Pushkin Dostoevsky] remained original and free. * * *

Wherein lies the uniqueness of Dostoevsky's novel? It consists in a whole number of original artistic devices. * * * He dramatized the narrative form of the novel. If in other writers we find such a theatricalization from time to time as an exception in their narrative experiments, in Dostoevsky on the contrary this artistic device remains basic. His novels are in their essence tragedies, and therefore all their elements of narration are scenic and theatrical.

Raskolnikov's dialogues with Porfiry, Svidrigaylov, Sonya, and other characters are dramatic to the highest degree. Each reply, though it may seem unexpected, seems to conform to the scene and arouses keen interest. All of Dostoevsky's dialogues are ideological and psychological duels, and the reader, as if he were a spectator, follows with tense excitement the rapier thrusts of the duelists. Dostoevsky's novels are always catastrophic. Expectation of catastrophe also calls forth a purely theatrical pathos. All these devices would be a very bad means of affecting the reader if all of them were not conditioned by inner inevitability. The secret of those devices lies in the author's high art with which he preserves the organic unity of his intention. Therefore there is no room in his novels for mechanical effects.

* * *

The landscape, settings, the outside appearance of heroes in Dostoevsky's novels are like theatrical stage directions. That is why descriptive elements are either absent in his novels or very laconic. Sometimes, of course, the descriptions, without losing the nature of a stage direction, develop into rather long protocol-like accounts. This device makes it possible for Dostoevsky to give the reader an impression of confidence in the accuracy of the facts. This device, which at first sight seems "naturalistic" because of its bareness, achieves the author's aim of convincing the reader of the authenticity of the account. Such a hyperbolic "naturalism" is theatrical and decorative in its essence and naturally has nothing in common with vulgar naturalism.

* * *

Most writers make several provisional, rough drafts between the first plan (of which there is most often only one, but sometimes two or three) and the final version. Writers work chiefly on these intermediate versions, improving the language, style, enriching the text with new images and situations, and in general perfecting their work. In Dostoevsky, on the contrary, the entire center of equilibrium has been transferred to the original search. Other writers (Tolstoy, Turgenev, Pisemsky, Goncharov) complicate the chosen theme by new ideas and images, landscapes, details of everyday life, dialogues, lyrical digressions, but the theme does not depart from the original plan. Dostoevsky uses a different artistic method. He was always in the grip of strong artistic turmoil. Before he settled on some theme, he had had to lead an inner struggle with parallel themes. That struggle was often very complicated. * * *

When he reached the stage where the original artistic aim, the ideological center of his work, and the dominant chord of artistic motifs became clear to himself, he then wrote his "night programs," examples of which we know from his notebooks to *The Brothers Karamazov*. He then dictated to the stenographer in the daytime, and next day he corrected the text prepared by Anna Grigorievna and returned it to her for a final transcription. Sometimes he copied it over himself. Such was his method of work.

Sometimes, too, he sacrificed a substantial part of his work if he came to the conclusion that the chosen device did not achieve his aims. Such was the history of the text of *Crime and Punishment*, when he decided to write several printer's sheets over. * * *

Not every writer can use a stenographer, even if he does have a detailed program of his narrative text in hand. Dostoevsky could use such a technique, because his novels are built chiefly on dialogue. According to eyewitness accounts, Dostoevsky was a marvellous reader and an inspired interpreter, and his dictation was something like theatrical improvisations. This corresponded fully to his poetics, to the form of his novel-tragedies, in which everything was scenic. He improvised the final text, being guided by the plans he had prepared as if by a scenario. * * *

One scholar has called Dostoevsky's novels "ideological novels." Such a definition of their genre requires clarification and could mislead the reader, for the word "ideology" has a suggestion of rationalism which contradicts the real contents of the definition. . . . Dostoevsky's novels are filled with the sharpest contradictions and the most daring irrational symbols. Almost all writers placed some central idea or complex of ideas at the center of their large works, but no one besides Dostoevsky used ideas as artistic material. This is the exceptional peculiarity of Dostoevsky's work. His artistic or rather poetic "I" was always the center of a tremendous number of ideas not abstracted from reality and linked to it inseparably. These idea-feelings, these idea-forces, actually *operate*, under specific social conditions. They arise, enter into battles, develop, diminish, find their rival-ideas, and win or die defeated. The acting personages of his novels do not merely represent certain characters or express social types; they are bearers of living ideas. Ideas in Dostoevsky's novels are, so to speak, living creatures.

# K. MOCHULSKY

## [The Five Acts of *Crime and Punishment*]†

"Crime and Punishment" is a tragedy in five acts with a prologue and an epilogue.

The *prologue* (the first part) depicts the preparation and perpetration of the crime. The hero is enveloped in mystery. The impoverished student is afraid of his landlady; we find him in a state of illness that "resembles hypochondria." He goes to a money-lender to pawn his silver watch, and talks about a certain "venture." "I want to undertake a *venture* of those proportions, and yet at the same time I am frightened by nonsense such as this! . . . Am I really capable of *it?*" The word "murder" is not spoken. "My God!" Raskolnikov cries out as he is leaving the money-lender's apartment, "how disgusting *this* all is! . . . Is it really possible that *such an appalling thing* could have entered my mind! . . . Above all it's filthy, obscene, vile, vile!" This "distorted dream," which for a whole month has filled his being as he sat deliberating in his corner, now provokes within him spasms of revulsion. And so on the very first pages of the novel we find the hero in a state of intense conflict. He does not believe that he is in fact capable of carrying out the "venture." This idea of his is purely theoretical. "I've learned to spout nonsense as I lie whole days and nights in my corner and think . . . So, I'm amusing myself for the sake of fantasy—toys." The dreamer abhors his own practical inability; the romantic is aesthetically repulsed by the "vileness" of murder. This division within the hero's consciousness is the beginning of his self-knowledge. Two motifs are struck in the tavern scene with Marmeladov—the endlessness of human sorrow and the inefficacy of sacrifice (Sonya). His mother's letter presses the hero to face some decision. His own sister is preparing to sacrifice herself, by having sold her life to the contemptible businessman Luzhin. She is stepping forth onto Sonya's

† From Konstantin Mochulsky, *Dostoevsky: His Life and Work*, translated by Michael A. Minihan (Princeton University Press, 1967), pp. 300–313. Mochulsky was an émigré Russian scholar. His book, originally published in Paris in 1947, is the best one-volume general study of Dostoevsky available in any language.

road. "Sonechka, Sonechka Marmeladova, eternal Sonechka, so long as the world stands!" Raskolnikov exclaims. And this sacrifice is being made for him. Can he accept it? And if he refuses to accept it, what then awaits him? Poverty, hunger, destruction?

"Or should one renounce life completely," he says, "and docilely accept one's fate as it is, once and for all, and stifle everything in oneself, after having renounced any *right to act, to live, and to love?*" The dilemma is posed in its most acute form. Christian morality preaches humility and sacrifice, but Raskolnikov has lost his faith. He is an atheistic humanist; for him the old norms of truth and justice have become lies. He is convinced that humility and sacrifice ultimately lead only to ruin. And what does one do—accept this destruction? Is it possible that man has no *right to life?* It is immoral to transgress the old moral law, but is bringing oneself to ruin and destruction moral? "All this present anguish was engendered in him a very long time before. It matured and became concentrated, taking the form of *a terrible, violent, and fantastic question.*"

His mother's letter is the turning point in the hero's fate. Up until now he had been lying on his sofa resolving abstract questions; now life itself demands that he take immediate action. The dreamer is taken by surprise. For a month he has been amusing himself with his "fantastic idea"; "now it appeared suddenly not as a dream at all, but under a new, frightening and as yet completely foreign aspect, and he suddenly *became aware* of this himself . . . His head began to pound and everything grew dark before his eyes." A new level of consciousness has been reached: the idea is beginning to take on substance. Nonetheless the hero cannot reformulate his entire being in one stroke. Reason embraces the new "idea," but "nature" continues to live within the framework of the old moral order. Little by little the abstract dream seizes possession of his consciousness. "Nature" struggles with it in desperation, is horrified by it, strives not to believe in it, pretends that it does not know it. In order to weaken its resistance, the author introduces the motif of sickness. The hero's pathological condition is repeatedly underlined: after the murder he lies for four days in a state of nervous delirium and this illness perdures through the end of the novel. Thus by his very example Raskolnikov proves the reasonableness of his theory. Did he not maintain in an article entitled "About Crime" that "the act of committing a crime is always accompanied by sickness"? Only illness can ultimately succeed in demolishing the disillusioned romantic's "nature," in overcoming the aesthete's revulsion when faced with the "vileness" of murder. In the end "nature" declares open warfare upon the "distorted dream." All of Raskolnikov's compassion, all his anguish and horror when confronted with world-evil, finds expression in his nightmare about the horse. Mikolka beats the nag about the eyes with a shaft, and then finishes it with a crowbar. The hero sees himself as a child. "He begins to cry. His heart rises within him; tears come streaming down . . . Letting out a scream he forces his way through the crowd over to Roan. He clasps his arms around its dead, blood-soaked head and kisses it, kisses it on the eyes, on the lips." This cruel deed fills him with mystical horror. He sees murder for the first time not as an algebraic symbol, but as blood that has been poured forth, and he is appalled. He too will kill a creature, just as Mikolka did . . . blood will flow—sticky, warm blood. Raskolnikov renounces his plan . . . "Lord! Why, even if I have the choice, I will not do such a thing. Lord, show me the way that I am to follow—I renounce this accursed dream of mine." This nightmare that brought him back to childhood, resurrects his childhood faith, and the atheist turns and appeals to God. He grew up in a religious family. "Remember, my precious," his mother writes him, "how when you were a child, when your father was still alive, you used to mouth your prayers at my knees, and how we all were happy then." "Nature" rejects the poison that is in its system—the thought of crime. Raskolnikov exalts in his deliverance: "Freedom! Freedom! He was now free from that spell, from that sorcery, the fascination, from the temptation." But this victory on the side of good does not perdure for long. The idea has already penetrated into his subconscious, and after this final outburst of rebellion it becomes his driving force, his *destiny*. The hero no longer exercises control over his life; he is drawn forward. Mysterious occurrences steadily lead the murderer to his victim. By pure chance he comes upon the Hay Market, and there by chance he learns that tomorrow at seven o'clock the old woman will be alone. "His initial feeling of surprise turned to horror. He did not decide anything rationally, and he absolutely could not reason, but with all his being he suddenly felt that he no longer had either freedom to reason or to will."

On the day of the murder he acts mechanically: "As though someone were leading him by the hand and dragging him along irresistibly, blindly, with unnatural force, without objections. Just as though he had fallen like a piece of cloth into the wheel of a machine and it was beginning to draw him into the apparatus." By willing a murder man betrays himself to the powers of dark necessity. He is stripped of his freedom and acts with the automatism of a person walking in his sleep. Everything takes place unexpectedly and by chance: he takes the axe not from the kitchen as he had planned, but from the porter's lodge; he accidentally kills Lizaveta; forgets to lock the door; he has no idea of how to commit the robbery. "It was as though he were in a delirium . . . He forgot himself. He was not asleep, but in a state of oblivion." The prologue ends with the murder. As yet neither the hero nor the readers know the real reason for the crime.

The *first act of the tragedy* (the second part) portrays the crime's immediate effects upon the criminal's soul. It deals a terrible spiritual blow to Raskolnikov. He comes down with an attack of nerves and fever. He is close to madness and wants to do away with himself. "What, can it really have begun already? Can *my decimation be this close* already?" He tries to pray and laughs at himself. Laughter gives way to despair. He is summoned to the police bureau because of a debt that he has not paid his landlady. He concludes that his crime has been discovered and he prepares to throw himself on his knees and confess everything. In the office his nerves fail to hold out and he falls into a faint. This is the fatal moment in his destiny: the murderer attracts the attention of the clerk Zametov and this latter tells the prosecuting magistrate Porfiry Petrovich about the strange student. The counteraction against Raskolnikov is set in motion as a result of this fainting spell; this serves to fasten the first thread of the net in which the magistrate eventually envelops him. The criminal is betrayed by "nature." In the storm of feelings and sensations that have engulfed the murderer, one begins to predominate. "A dismal sensation of acutely painful, infinite *solitude and alienation* became consciously apparent in his soul." He awaited the punishment with which the pangs of conscience would afflict him; there was none. There was, however, something else: a mystical awareness of his estrangement from the human family. The murderer has stepped beyond something more than the moral law: *the very basis of the spiritual world itself*. After he has buried the stolen articles under a stone, he suddenly asks himself a question: "If in fact this whole thing was done with a purpose and not just frivolously, if you really had a definite and set *design*, then why didn't you look and see how much money there was?" The humanist-dreamer has suffered defeat. He displayed his utter helplessness in the course of the action; he grew frightened, committed blunders, lost his head. If in fact he had killed the old woman in order to rob her, then why is he not interested in the stolen goods? Or the deed was perpetrated "frivolously," and the humanistic motivation served only as a pretext. The *crisis* within his conscience is underlined by his illness and loss of memory which lasts over a period of three days. When the hero finally comes to himself, the old man, the sensitive "friend of humanity," in him has already died. Raskolnikov is aware of his infinite solitude and is not overwhelmed by it. He "cut himself off from all and everything as though with a pair of scissors." He finds people unbearable. " 'Let me be, let me be, all of you,' Raskolnikov cried out in a rage, 'And will you leave me alone, once and for all, you tormentors? I'm not afraid of you! Get away from me! I want to be alone, alone, alone, alone.' " Thus a new consciousness is born—the consciousness of a strong personality, fiendishly proud and solitary. His fear, his faint-heartedness, the sickness have passed. The hero senses a terrible energy that has been aroused within him; he feels that they are suspicious of him, that they are following him, and with ravishing glee he throws himself into the battle. Upon meeting Zametov in a tavern, he casts an insolent challenge at him: ". . . And what if it was I who killed the old woman and Lizaveta?" He experiences "a wild, hysterical sensation in which, nonetheless, there was an element of unbearable delight." He goes to the old woman's house, enters her apartment, tries the little bell, asks about the blood. As he is leaving, he informs the porter of his name and address. This new, forceful spirit which has begun to burn within him, overcomes his body, the opposition of "nature" is broken. The bold fighter remembers his fears and spectres with contempt. "So there *is* life!" he exclaims. "My life didn't end along with the old woman's! May she rest in the Kingdom of Heaven. And then that's enough, my good lady; it's time you went to your repose! Now the kingdom of reason and light has come! and . . . of will and strength . . . And we'll see now! We'll try our strength now!" he adds arrogantly as though adverting to some dark force and defying it. The tragic hero throws down a challenge to fate. The new *strong individual* is endowed with "animal-like cunning," unheard-of boldness, a will to live and diabolical pride.

The *second act* (part three) relates the process of the strong individual's struggle. The author intensifies our new impression of the hero by means of various indirect characterizations. Razumikhin remarks about his comrade: "I know Rodion: morose, sombre, *haughty and proud* . . . Sometimes . . . cold and *insensible* to the point of being inhuman. Really, it's just as if there were *two* opposing characters in him which alternately replace one another . . . *He sets a terribly high value upon himself,* and not completely without reason . . . *He does not love anyone* and never will." Pukheriya Aleksandrovna describes the fantastic plan her son had had to marry his landlady's consumptive daughter. "Do you think," she adds, "my tears, my supplications, my illness, my death perhaps from grief, our poverty would have stopped him then? *He would have stepped most calmly over all the obstacles.*" Thus Raskolnikov's "second character" is revealed to us as being diametrically opposed to the first. We see that he has deceived himself in saying that he was going to sin for the sake of his mother's happiness; why, he "would have stepped most calmly over" her very death in order to satisfy a simple caprice.

The hero recognizes the fact that Porfiry suspects him, and proceeds to challenge him. He cannot bear inactivity and uncertainty. He is impatient to "try his strength." During the course of his first meeting with the prosecuting magistrate, he expounds his theory of "exceptional people." "The exceptional man has the right . . . that is, not a legally established right, but he himself has the right to permit his conscience to step over . . . certain obstacles." Razumikhin perceives the terrible essence of this theory: "What's original in these ideas," he says, "is that ultimately you are allowing a man to shed blood in accord with the design of his conscience . . . Why, this license to shed blood according to your conscience . . . it's, it's, in my opinion, more terrible than an official authorization to shed blood, a legal one." What is terrible is that Raskolnikov's theory does not merely negate Christian morality, it goes further; it sets another—an anti-Christian code of morality in its stead. The "strong individual" is not without conscience: he has *his own conscience which authorizes the shedding of blood.* The proud demon is sad in his lonely grandeur. "It seems to me," Raskolnikov says, "truly great people experience an immense sadness while on earth." The whole tragedy of man-Godhood is expressed in these few words.

And suddenly the hero founders; after this first encounter Raskolnikov faces an utter humiliation. An artisan comes to him, and in a "quiet, but clear and distinct voice" says: "murderer." Who is this man and what did he see? Does it mean that there is evidence against him? Does it mean that he was not even capable of committing murder? "And how could I, knowing myself, *having misgivings about myself,* have dared take up an axe and soil myself with blood . . ." No, he is not a strong individual. "I was in a hurry to step beyond . . . I didn't do away with a human being; I did away with a principle! It was the principle that I did away with, and I didn't get to step beyond. I remained on the other side." . . . . The very fact that he has misgivings about himself and does not believe in his strength, attests to his shameful weakness. No, he is not a Napoleon, but an "aesthetic louse," "even more foul and disgusting than the louse that he has killed." "Oh, the vulgar banality! Oh, the baseness! Oh, now I understand the 'prophet' with his scimitar, on his steed: Allah commands and you, obey—'trembling creature'!" This crisis culminates in a terrible dream. Raskolnikov takes up an axe and strikes the old woman across her skull; but she inclines her head forward and "breaks out in a quiet, hardly audible laugh." The victim laughs at her murderer: she is alive. He strikes again and again; she laughs more heartily. *It is impossible to kill her: she is immortal.* And yet it was not so long ago that Raskolnikov mockingly bid her final farewell: "That's enough, my good lady; it's time you went to your repose!" Now all the people around him are like corpses, while the dead woman continues to live. He has cut himself off from the living "as though with a pair of scissors," but it is impossible for him to be separated from her: they are joined together forever . . . by blood.

The *third act* of the tragedy (part four) carries Raskolnikov's struggle to its ultimate climax. The hero has apparently triumphed, but his victory is only veiled defeat. He awakes from his terrible dream; there standing before him is Svidrigaylov, the man who has abused his sister. Raskolnikov is tragically divided: there are "two opposing characters" within him. The "strong individual" convulsively struggles against the humanist, torturously frees himself from "principles" and "ideals." Svidrigaylov is exactly the same as Raskolnikov, but he has already succeeded in completely "curing himself" of all moral prejudices. He is the embodiment of one possible resolution of the hero's fate. There exists a metaphysical similitude between them. "We have a certain point in common," says Svidrigaylov, "We are *berries from the same tree*." They both follow along the same path, but Svidrigaylov is more free and bold than Raskolnikov and he pursues it to its very end. The student "has stepped beyond," "has authorized the shedding of blood in accord with his own conscience," but for all that he continues to uphold "humanism," "justice," "what is noble and beautiful."

Svidrigaylov tells Raskolnikov that eternity strikes him as a country bath-house: "covered with soot and with spiders crawling along all the corners." The latter asks in disgust: "And really, really, you see nothing more comforting, more just than that?" Svidrigaylov answers with derision: is it for him, a murderer, to talk about justice! Can he preach morality! What hypocrisy! Why won't he hand over ten thousand to Dunya from the man who has abused her? Why, "the end justifies the means"! Raskolnikov has abolished the old morality, and yet he still clings to beauty, honor, and all the rest of humanistic rubbish. Svidrigaylov is more consistent: good and evil are merely relative concepts; all things are permissible—all things are one and the same. What is left is universal boredom and vulgar banality. And he is bored. He has amused himself in whatever ways he could: he was a card-sharper, spent some time in prison, sold himself to his late wife for 30 thousand. Perhaps he will take a flight in a balloon or set off on an expedition to the North Pole. He has visions, the shreds of other worlds, but what crude banalities! Svidrigaylov's boredom is not psychological, but rather metaphysical. The ultimates merge together; good and evil are indistinguishable— a deformed infinity, indifference, absurdity. Svidrigaylov is not a simple villain: generously he lets Dunya go, he contributes money, helps the Marmeladovs. He tests his freedom in evil and finds that it has no end. For a time he is engaged by his passion for Dunya. He shoots himself out of boredom. The superman can find nothing to do in the midst of people. His strength finds no outlet for itself, and so it becomes self-destructive.

Svidrigaylov is a voluptuary. There are terrible crimes upon his conscience: his wife's murder, the suicide of his servant Filipp and of the fourteen-year-old girl whom he abused. He loves the most filthy debauchery, but his conscience is at peace and he has a "fresh complexion." He is placed next to Raskolnikov to serve as his dark and somber double. He is born of the hero's nightmare; he emerges out of his dream. The hero asks Razumikhin: "You actually saw him,—saw him clearly? Hm . . . in that case—But then you know, it struck me . . . it all seemed to me that perhaps this was just a fantasy . . ." In exactly the same way after his nightmare Ivan Karamazov asks Alyosha if he has seen his visitor. Svidrigaylov is Raskolnikov's "devil."

This meeting with his double marks a new stage in the hero's consciousness. Being convinced of his defeat ("Not a Napoleon, but a louse") he begins to lose his sense of reality. He lives in a state of delirium, is no longer capable of distinguishing dream from reality (Svidrigaylov's appearance). Precipitously the action moves on to its dénouement.

In opposition to this scene with Svidrigaylov stands the scene with Sonya; the evil angel is counterbalanced by the good angel, the "bath-house with its spiders" by the resurrection of Lazarus. Svidrigaylov showed Raskolnikov that the demonic way leads only to the boredom of non-being. Sonya points out another way and discloses the image of Him who said: "I am the way." The murderer can be saved only by a *miracle*, and Sonya passionately prays for a miracle. Just as in the case of the conversation with Svidrigaylov, the dialogue with Sonya proceeds to soar to metaphysical heights. Sonya answers the hero's arguments about the absurdity of sacrifice, the futility of compassion, and the inevitability of ruin and destruction, *by her faith in a miracle*. "God, God will not permit anything so awful." " 'But it is possible that this God doesn't even exist,' Raskolnikov answered with a certain malicious pleasure." Suddenly he asks Sonya to read to him from the Gospels "about Lazarus." She believes that "even he, he—though he is blinded and does not believe, now he too will hear, he too will believe, yes, yes, immediately, now." The reading is over. Raskolnikov has received an answer to his mute question: "What is it she's waiting for—a miracle? Yes, it must be. *But really isn't this a sign of insanity?*" The miracle did not take place. The murderer's faith was not restored, and he only concluded that Sonya was mad: she actually believes in the resurrection of a corpse that has been dead for four days!

He calls Sonya "a great sinner"; she is as guilty of damning her soul as he. "You have ruined a life . . . your own (it's the very same thing)."

These terrible five words in parentheses—"(*it's the very same thing*)"—are filled with malice and a fiendish lie. To lay down one's life for one's friends is *the very same thing* as destroying the life of one's neighbor! In horror Sonya asks: "And what—and what should one do?" "What should one do?" answers the demon, "*Wreck and demolish* what one has to, once and for all, that's what; and then take the suffering upon yourself. What? You don't understand? You'll understand later. *Freedom and power*, but mainly, power! Over every trembling creature and over the whole ant-hill!" The reading of the Gospel occasions an outburst of diabolic pride. Ruin and destruction are set in opposition to the Resurrection ("wreck and demolish what one has to"); love of power stands and defies humility; the figure of the man-god opposes the image of the god-man.

The criminal's pride leads him to challenge Porfiry Petrovich to a second encounter. He demands that "an interrogration take place in accord with legal form." The magistrate analyzes in detail his conduct after the murder, enumerates his blunders and shows that "psychologically he will not run away." The hero's hatred mounts with each minute. At last he can endure it no longer. " 'You're lying about everything,' Raskolnikov began to shout, 'You're lying, you damned punchinello . . . You're lying and mocking me so that I will give myself away!" And suddenly we are confronted with an unexpected peripeteia. Porfiry had intended to expose the murderer on the basis of the artisan's testimony, but instead Nikolay the painter comes and confesses that it was he who killed the old woman. Raskolnikov laughs at the evidence that the magistrate had wanted to produce, at his "psychology about the double cutting-edge." "Now we will still go on struggling with one another!" he exclaims proudly.

The *fourth act* (part five) marks a slowing-up in the action before the culmination of the catastrophe. Its major section is devoted to the scene in which the characters gather for Marmeladov's funeral dinner. In the course of this second meeting with Sonya, the strong individual arrives at the final stage of his self-knowledge. With scorn he rejects as "rubbish" the idea that the crime was committed out of humanistic motivations. "Nonsense! I simply committed murder! *I committed murder for myself, for myself alone*," Raskolnikov declares. He performed an experiment; he was resolving the enigma of his own personality. "I had to *find out*, and find out quickly whether I was merely a louse just like everybody else, or whether I was a *man*. Will I be able to step beyond, or won't I? Am I a trembling creature, or do I possess the right?" He nurtures the greatest possible contempt for the human "herd." This "trembling creature" must be made to submit to the iron rod. The strong individual rises in revolt against the order of the world . . . "Suddenly it struck me as clear as the sun how strange it is that up till now not a single man has ever dared or does dare, just casting aside all this absurd rubbish, to take everything quite simply by the tail and send it flying to hell. I . . . I wanted to have this daring and I committed murder." Raskolnikov continues the revolt begun by the man from the underground ("and isn't it up to us to send all this common sense flying . . . to hell") and prepares the way for the despotism of the Grand Inquisitor. A morality of force leads to a philosophy of violence. The superman is revealed as the Prince of this world—the Anti-Christ. Raskolnikov summarizes disdainfully: "I wanted to turn myself into a Napoleon, and for that purpose I even committed murder." He concedes his mistake: the man who doubts his right to seize power does not have any such right, and consequently he too is a "louse" just like everyone else. "Was it really the old woman that I killed? I killed myself." Sonya says: "God has struck you down; He has handed you over to the devil." The murderer actually accepts this explanation: "Why, I myself am aware of the fact that the devil has been pulling me along . . . And it was the devil that murdered the old woman; I didn't do it." Oh, now it makes no difference to him who is guilty of his defeat—the devil or God. Since it is clear that he is only a "louse," why not admit that someone was amusing himself at his expense? Sonya tells him to kiss the ground, to give himself up, "to accept suffering and through it to redeem himself." He does not believe in suffering or in redemption. Sonya's love conjures up "bitter hatred" in him. He will give himself up because he is "a coward and a wretch," but he will never submit himself to humiliation and repent. Once again pride flares up within him: "Perhaps I still am a man and not a louse, and I have been too quick to condemn myself. I will still continue to struggle."

He does not reject his theory of strength and power. "Sonya understood that this somber catechism had become his faith and law."

The *fifth act* (the sixth part) presents the catastrophe. The author depicts the parallel ruin of the two "strong individuals"—Raskolnikov and Svidrigaylov. The murderer has a premonition of his end: he is in a state of semi-delirium, wanders about the streets without purpose, sits down in a tavern, then falls asleep somewhere in the bushes . . . "The lack of air in all this congestion began to suffocate him." Porfiry Petrovich's arrival resolves this tension. The magistrate analyzes the whole "psychological process of the crime" and gives him an historic definition. "Here we find a fantastic, gloomy business, *a contemporary affair, an incident of our own times*, sir, when the human heart has grown troubled, when the phrase is quoted that 'blood refreshes' . . . Here we have bookish dreams, sir, here *a heart that has been exasperated by theories.*" As though struggling for air, Raskolnikov asks: "So . . . who then . . . committed the murder?" "Porfiry Petrovich started back in his chair just as though this were completely unexpected and he was astonished at the question. 'What—who committed the murder?' he pronounced as though not believing his ears. 'But *you* committed the murder, Rodion Romanovich! It was you who committed the murder, sir.'"

After the "strong personality" has been defeated, it is then exposed. Svidrigaylov follows in Porfiry Petrovich's place. The latter has pointed out Raskolnikov's theoretical mistake ("a bookish dream"); the former discloses his moral hypocrisy. "No, I'm talking about the fact," he says, "that you keep on moaning and moaning now. *Every moment one sees the Schiller*[1] *in you* . . . And if you really feel that one has no right to stand by a door and eavesdrop, but that it is alright to crack open old women with whatever happens to fall into one's hands, for one's own pleasure, then you'd better hurry and set out for some place or other in America! I understand what questions you have on your mind—moral ones, right? The questions that face the citizen and the human being? Well, you just set them aside. Of what interest are they to you now? Ha! Ha! Because you're still a citizen and a human being? And if so, then you shouldn't have butted into this affair. One shouldn't undertake anything that is not for one's own advantage."

Svidrigaylov, Raskolnikov's double, laughs at him, just as Ivan Karamazov's double, the devil, amuses himself at his expense. They both embody a strong individual's doubt in himself. Now the hero is faced with only two possibilities: either to shoot himself or give himself up. He does not have enough strength of will to commit suicide, and so he surrenders himself to the authorities. This is not a sign of penitence but of pusillanimity: for him punishment is an "unnecessary shame" and "senseless suffering." He reflects contemptuously: "And how can this have come about that in the end I . . . will be humbled, will be humbled through my conviction?"

Raskolnikov goes to Sonya in a state of irritation and gloom, and asks for a cross: "This symbolizes the fact that I am taking the cross upon myself, ha! ha!" His laugh is blasphemous and shows his hatred for Sonya who is sending him to this disgraceful end . . . Remembering her words: "Bow down to the people," he falls upon his knees in the street, but he cannot confess: "I have murdered." He goes into the police station, and comes out again. He sees Sonya standing in the courtyard, and once again goes into the building and

1. Friedrich Schiller (1759–1805), German poet and dramatist, came to stand for enthusiastic, romantic idealism in the eyes of many nineteenth-century Russians.

at last declares: "It was I who killed the old widow and her sister Lizaveta with an axe and then robbed them."

Raskolnikov's tragedy ends with an *epilogue*. The criminal has now spent a year and a half in penal servitude. Sonya has followed him to Siberia, but nonetheless he "tortures her by his contemptuous and rude manner." Has he changed? No, he is the same—solitary, morose, proud. "He examined himself thoroughly and severely and his obdurate conscience could find no particularly terrible fault in his past, except perhaps a simple blunder which might have happened to anyone . . . *He did not repent of his crime.*"

" 'Well, why is it that my act seems so distorted to them?' he used to say to himself, 'Because it was evil? What does the word "evil" mean? *My conscience is at peace.*' " In the words "My conscience is at peace," the final truth about Raskolnikov is suddenly revealed. He is in fact a superman. He has not been defeated; it is he who has conquered. He wanted to try out his strength and he found that there were no limits to it. He wanted "to step beyond" and he stepped beyond. He wanted to show that the moral law has no relevance for him, that he stands beyond the confines of good and evil, and now his conscience is at peace. He has not been ruined because "his rupture with mankind has proved a source of torment" for him—oh no, he loves his proud solitude—or because "his nerves did not hold out"—"nature surrendered its place"—all that is nonsense. His strength would have been sufficient. It is not without reason that Porfiry Petrovich considered him a "bold fighter," and Svidrigaylov said to him: "You yourself are a thorough-going cynic. You have, at any rate, enormous stuff in you, You can conceive of a great deal, a great deal, *but then you can accomplish a great deal as well.*" Nor has he been ruined because of the fact that Porfiry has caught him in his "psychology of the double cutting edge." He is not cowed even by Porfiry. It is only while serving his sentence that he comes to understand the reason for his downfall. "He was ashamed precisely because he, Raskolnikov, had come to his ruin so blindly, desperately, onerously and stupidly, *through some decree of blind fate.*" This last feature crowns his majestic image. None of his adversaries is worthy of the strong individual; he has but one single enemy—fate. *Raskolnikov has been brought to destruction like a tragic hero in battle with blind Destiny.* But how could the author present this bold truth about the new man to the readers of Katkov's well-meaning journal in the 1860's? He had to cover it by throwing an innocent veil over it. He did this, however, hurriedly, carelessly, "just before the final curtain." While the hero is in the labor camp, just after recovering from his illness, he casts himself at Sonya's feet . . . and he begins to love: "Their sick and pale faces already shone with the dawn of a renewed future, *of a total resurrec-tion into a new life*. They had been resurrected by love." "But," the author adds discreetly, "this begins a new story . . ." The novel ends with a vague anticipation of the hero's "renewal." It is prom-ised, but it is not shown. We know Raskolnikov too well to believe this "pious lie."

"Crime and Punishment" resuscitates the art of ancient tragedy in the form of a contemporary novel. Raskolnikov's story is a new embodiment of the myth of Prometheus' revolt and the tragic hero's destruction in the course of his struggle with Fate. But Dostoevsky, the great Christian writer, adds an infinitely more profound dimen-sion to the metaphysical significance of the myth. It is to the Rus-sian people themselves that the author consigns the rôle of passing final judgment upon the "strong individual." On one occason they "all fell upon him at once in a fury. 'You're an atheist! You don't believe in God!' they shouted at him. 'You must be killed!' "

This judgment as it is expressed by the people, conveys the *reli-gious idea* of the novel. Raskolnikov's "heart has grown troubled"; he has stopped believing in God. For Dostoevsky atheism reverts invariably to the deification of man. If there is no God, then I my-self am God. The "strong individual" sought to free himself from God—and he has succeeded. His freedom proved to be infinite. But in this infinity ruin awaited him. Freedom from God shows itself as sheer demonism; renunciation of Christ as *slavery to Fate*. After having traced the course of atheistic freedom, the author leads us to the religious basis of his world-outlook: *there is no freedom other than freedom in Christ; he who does not believe in Christ stands subject to the power of Destiny.*

# JOSÉ ORTEGA Y GASSET

## [Why Dostoevsky Lives in the Twentieth Century]†

While other great names are setting, carried down into oblivion by the mysterious revolution of the times, that of Dostoevski has established itself firmly in the zenith. Perhaps the present fervent

† "Dostoevski and Proust," in José Or-etga y Gasset, *The Dehumanization of Art and Other Essays on Art, Culture and Literature* (rev. ed., copyright © 1968 by Princeton University Press; Prin-ceton Paperback, 1968), pp. 74–80. Re-printed by permission of Princeton Uni-versity Press.

admiration of his work is a trifle exaggerated, and I would rather reserve my judgment for a serener hour. At any rate, he has escaped from the general shipwreck of nineteenth century novels. But the reasons usually given to explain his triumph and his ability to survive seem to me erroneous. The interest his novels arouse is attributed to their material: the mysteriously dramatic action, the utterly pathological character of the personages, the exotic quality of those Slavic souls so different in their turbulent intricacy from our clear and neat dispositions. All this may contribute to the pleasure we draw from Dostoevski; only it is not sufficient reason. Moreover, there is a certain questionable quality to these features that makes them as well suited to repelling as to attracting us. We remember that those novels used to leave us with a mingled feeling of pleasure and uneasy confusion.

The material never saves a work of art, the gold it is made of does not hallow a statue. A work of art lives on its form, not on its material; the essential grace it emanates springs from its structure, from its organism. The structure forms the properly artistic part of the work, and on it aesthetic and literary criticism should concentrate. If too much stress is laid on the subject of a painting or a poem, sensitive nerves smell the Philistine. No doubt, as there is no life without chemical processes, thus there is no work of art without a subject. Just as life cannot be reduced to chemistry but begins to be life only when it has imposed upon the chemical laws other original processes of a new and more complex order, so the work of art is what it is thanks to the form it imposes upon the material or subject.

I have often wondered why even experts find it difficult to recognize that form, which to the uninitiated may seem abstract and inefficient, is the true substance of art. The author's or the critic's point of view cannot be the same as that of the unqualified reader who is concerned exclusively with the ultimate and total effect the work has on him and does not care to analyze the genesis of his pleasure.

As it is, much has been said about what is going on in Dostoevski's novels and very little about their form. The extraordinary quality of the events and emotions this formidable writer describes has fascinated the critics and prevented them from penetrating into what, at first sight, seems accidental and extrinsic but in reality forms the essence of the work: the structure of the novel as such. Hence a curious optical delusion. The turbulent, wayward character of his personages is ascribed to Dostoevski himself, and the novelist is looked upon as one more figure in his own novels—which indeed seem begotten in an hour of demoniacal ecstasy by some nameless elemental power, akin to the thunder and brother of the winds.

But all this is mere fancy. An alert mind may indulge in such colorful pictures but will soon dismiss them for the sake of clear ideas. It may be that the man Dostoevski was a poor epileptic or, if one so desires, a prophet. But the novelist Dostoevski was an *homme de lettres*, a conscientious craftsman of a sublime craft, and nothing else. Many a time have I tried in vain to convince Pío Baroja[1] that Dostoevski was, above all, a past master of novelistic technique and one of the greatest innovators of the form of the novel.

There is no better example of what I have called the sluggish character of the genre. Dostoevsky's books are almost all extremely long. But the story that is told is usually quite short. Sometimes it takes two volumes to describe what happens in three days, indeed, in a few hours. And yet, is there anything more intense? It is an error to believe that intensity is achieved through an accumulation of occurrences. Just the opposite; the fewer the better, providing they are detailed, i.e., "realized." Here, as in many other instances, the *multum non multa* applies. Density is obtained not by piling adventure upon adventure but by drawing out each incident through a copious presentation of its minutest components.

The concentration of the plot in time and space, so characteristic of Dostoevski's technique, brings to mind, in an unexpected sense, the venerable unities of classical tragedy. This aesthetic rule, which calls for moderation and restraint, now appears as an efficient means of bringing about the inner density, the high pressure, as it were, within the body of the novel.

Dostoevski never tires of filling pages and pages with the unending conversations of his personages. Thanks to this abundant flow of words the imaginary persons acquire a palpable bodily existence such as no definition could contrive.

It is extremely interesting to watch Dostoevski in his cunning ways with the reader. To a perfunctory observation, he seems to define each of his personages. When he introduces a figure he nearly always begins by briefly giving a biography of that person and thus makes us believe that we know well enough with what kind of man we are dealing. But no sooner do his people begin to act—i.e., to talk and to do things—than we feel thrown off the track. They refuse to behave according to those alleged definitions. The first conceptual image we were given of them is followed by another in which we see their immediate life, independent of the author's definition; and the two do not tally. At this point, the reader, afraid to lose sight of the personages at the crossroads of these contradic-

1. Pío Baroja y Nessi was a Spanish novelist contemporary with Ortega [*Editor*].

tory data, sets forth in their pursuit by trying to reconcile the discrepant facts to make a unified picture. That is, he gets busy to find a definition himself. Now this is what we are doing in our living intercourse with people. Chance leads them into the ambit of our life, and nobody bothers officially to define them to us. What we have before us is their intricate reality, not their plain concept. We are never quite let into their secret, they stubbornly refuse to adjust themselves to our ideas about them. And this is what makes them independent of us and brings it home that they are an effective reality transcending our imagination. But is not then Dostoevsky's "realism"—let us call it that not to complicate things—not so much a matter of the persons and events he presents as of the way the reader sees himself compelled to deal with these persons and events? Dostoevski is a "realist" not because he uses the material of life but because he uses the form of life.

In this ruse of laying false scent Dostoevski indulges to the degree of cruelty. Not only does he refuse clearly to define his figures beforehand, but as their behavior varies from stage to stage they display one facet after another and thus seem to be shaped and assembled step by step before our eyes. Instead of stylizing the characters Dostoevski is pleased to have their ambiguity appear as unmitigatedly as in real life. And the reader, proceeding by trial and error, apprehensive all the time of making a mistake, must work out as best he can the actual character of those fickle creatures.

Owing to this device, among others, Dostoevski's books, whatever their other qualities, have the rare virtue of never appearing sham and conventional. The reader never stumbles upon theatrical props; he feels from the outset immersed in a sound and effective quasi-reality. For a novel, in contrast to other literary works, must, while it is read, not be conceived as a novel; the reader must not be conscious of curtain and stage-lights. Reading Balzac, for example, we are on every page thrown out of the dream-world of the novel because we have bumped into the novelistic scaffolding. However, the most important structural peculiarity of Dostoevski's novels is harder to explain; I will return to it later.[2]

But let me here add that this habit of confusing instead of defining, this condensation of time and space, in brief, this sluggishness or *tèmpo lènto* are not peculiar to Dostoevski alone. All novels that are still readable employ more or less the same methods. As a West European example we may mention all the great books of Stendhal. *Le rouge et le noir*, a biographical novel which relates a few years of a man's life, is composed in the form of three or four pictures, each

2. Unfortunately, Ortega did not do so [*Editor*].

proceeding within its bounds like an entire novel of the Russian master.

In the last great example of prose narrative—Proust's colossal work[3]—this inner structure becomes even more manifest and is, in a way, carried to an extreme. So slowly does the action move that it seems more like a sequence of ecstatic stillnesses without progress or tension. Reading this "remembrance of things past" we feel convinced that the permissible measure of slowness is overstepped. Plot there is almost none; and not a whit of dramatic interest. Thus the novel is reduced to pure motionless description, and the diffuse, atmospheric character, which is in fact essential to the genre, appears here with exaggerated purity. We feel the lack of a firm and rigid support, of something like the ribs in an umbrella. Deprived of its bones, the body of the novel is converted into a cloudy, shapeless mass. That is why I have said before that action and plot may play a minor part in a modern novel, but that they cannot be entirely dispensed with. They fulfill the same function—a mechanical function, it is true—as the string of a necklace, the ribs of an umbrella, the poles of a tent.

# ERNEST J. SIMMONS

## The Art of *Crime and Punishment*†

In Dostoevsky's fiction previous to *Crime and Punishment* the unified contemplative experience of his art had been expressed largely through the medium of the central figure of the story. His treatment was restrictive and intensive rather than expansive. He was never to have the large epic sweep of a Tolstoy, nor did he even pretend to the limited but inclusive "slice of life" that Turgenev portrayed. With *Crime and Punishment*, however, one detects a broadening of the base of experience that he desired to reflect in fiction. The accumulated happenings of the last twenty years of his life seemed suddenly to have thrust upon him the central problem of human thought—the relation of man to the

3. *Remembrance of Things Past* (1913 to 1927) [*Editor*].
† From *Dostoevsky: The Making of a Novelist* by Ernest J. Simmons. Copyright 1940 by Oxford University Press, Inc. Pp. 158–171. Reprinted by permission.

world. Henceforth in his imaginative writings, as well as in his journalistic articles, he wrestles with various phases of the problem. In *Crime and Punishment* the hero of course holds the centre of the stage in most of this ethical and moral speculation. In this respect, however, Dostoevsky by no means neglects the secondary characters, one or two of which actually challenge comparison in artistic finish and interest with Rashkolnikov himself.

Perhaps the most striking and memorable is Sonya Marmeladova. She is first mentioned in the novel by her father in his remarkable confession to Raskolnikov in the tavern. This favourite indirect method of introducing a character is employed most effectively here. The father's description of how his daughter was forced to become a prostitute makes an immediate impression which creates eager suspense until the actual appearance of Sonya on the scene. The horror of her position is only intensified by its profoundly despairing effect on her human derelict of a father. In his description of this tragic incident in Sonya's life there is an unusually clear anticipation of her whole nature. She is an outstanding representative of Dostoevsky's Meek characters and one of the most noteworthy of all his female creations.

In one of the notebooks, Dostoevsky jotted down a few brief characterizing phrases which are elaborated in the complete portrait of the novel: "Sonya is always meek and has no humour at all; she is always grave and quiet." The father describes her as "a gentle creature with a soft little voice, fair hair and such a pale, thin little face." (Part I, Chapter II) She is utterly unequal to the struggle with life. It terrifies her. To all the miseries of poverty and squalor are added continual family quarrels and the extra insults reserved for a step-daughter. Yet in this Marmeladov household of drunkenness, starvation, beatings, wailing children, and screaming scenes Sonya moves like a furtive, unbidden shadow. All her actions, her very voice, suggest meekness and submissiveness. Even on those extremely rare occasions when she becomes agitated or angry—as much as she can be angry—Dostoevsky is careful to describe the emotion as indicative of the softness and humbleness characteristic of her nature: "Sonya was agitated again and even angry, as though a canary or some other little bird were to be angry." (Part IV, Chapter IV) Joined to her fear of life is a conviction that she is a burden to everyone and ought to be helping her poverty-stricken family. Attempts at honest labour fail. Then, in a moment of despair, circumstances literally oblige her to take the other way out. The necessity to live by charity can never degrade a woman as prostitution does, and for a woman of Sonya's meek and devout nature it is the lowest form of existence.

Dostoevsky's feminine characters of the Meek type are all of lowly origin, as though he were convinced that their special attributes would seem natural and plausible only among women close to the soil or crushed by poverty. Complete passivity exists in them to an equal degree, and they accept humbly and uncomplainingly everything that fate sends their way. The humility and submissiveness of Sonya, however, contain a more poignant and extreme quality because of her dishonourable calling, for she is the only prostitute among the Meek characters. This is why she experiences such horror when Raskolnikov declares that she is as honourable as his mother and sister.

There is an interesting bit of dialogue in the notes between Sonya and Raskolnikov which is only partially reflected in the novel. Sonya says to him: "In comfort and wealth you would not be able to see anything of the distress of people. God sends much unhappiness to him whom He loves very much and in whom He has much hope, so that he may learn and see more for himself, because the misery of people is more obvious in their unhappiness than in their happiness. Perhaps there is no God, he says to her. She wanted to reply, but suddenly she burst into tears. Why, what should I be without God?"

Here Dostoevsky places in Sonya's mouth his own doctrine of earning one's happiness by suffering, the lesson that Raskolnikov is forced to learn at the end of the novel. At first the hero calls her a "religious maniac." In truth, a large element of mysticism, subtly attuned to her meekness, is deeply rooted in her fatalistic nature. Later characters in this group reflect it to an even greater degree. Sonya is convinced that the acts of her life depend upon some mysterious, all-powerful force, and in this dependence is expressed her complete incapacity. This supernatural power, of course, is God. When Raskolnikov asks her what God does for her, she whispers, "He does everything." (Part IV, Chapter IV) She unquestioningly accepts everything He sends, whether it be good or bad. If, in His infinite wisdom, He visits her with suffering, she willingly submits for she cannot pretend to judge the ways of God. This deep faith is Sonya's only hope in life, for it always enables her to entertain the expectation of something better. As Raskolnikov divines, she believes not only in God, but in all His miracles.

The relationship between Sonya and Raskolnikov is of the utmost importance, for upon it turns the ultimate fate of both. His intellectual pride forces him to hate everything she represents. In his amazing categories of humanity, Sonya would occupy the lowest place among those despised "ordinary people" who are born to be submissive. On the other hand, Sonya also appeals to all the finer instincts of his nature. The submissive aspects of his own dual personality lead him to see in this prostitute an embodiment of Christian love and the very image of chastity.

Their love for each other, however, is strangely evasive in all its external manifestations, but it is quite representative of similar relations between such characters in later novels. In his art Dostoevsky, like Tolstoy, realized that love is expansive only in hidden ways, and that its loftiest expression should be treated as a secret thing. The undercurrent of passion may run high in the lives of his characters, but the verbal expression of it is carefully subdued in his pages. Ordinarily, the experience of love for Dostoevsky's Doubles is a torturing, hopeless struggle between pride and submissiveness, which expresses itself through the conflicting emotions of love and hate. This was made clear in the discussion of Natasha Ikhmeneva in *The Insulted and Injured*. There is a suggestion of this contradiction in Raskolnikov, but his destiny is worked out on a much broader psychological basis. For artistic reasons Dostoevsky deliberately mutes every outward show of love between Sonya and Raskolnikov. In the hero's case a confession of love would have amounted to an act of submission foreign to the dominant pride of his nature. His authoritarian theory of greatness has no place for love; he can neither give nor receive it. In the notes Dostoevsky reminds himself of this characteristic for future development in the very first meeting of Sonya and Raskolnikov: "He descends with her at the Marmeladovs'; behaves rudely so as not to give her an excuse to fall in love with him." He is soon in love with Sonya himself, but it is an affection that never shows itself by any outward demonstration; it develops imperceptibly, like a thing of the spirit, and manifests itself only in the irresistible affinity between these strange, shy beings. Throughout the notes Dostoevsky continually warns himself not to allow any expression of love on their part, which he obviously considered to be an artistic and psychological fault in this particular situation. A note such as the following is repeated in various forms: "N.B. There is not a word of love between them. This is a *sine qua non*."

With Sonya, certainly, any active expression of love would have been contrary to the characteristic emotional features of her type. All the passive and submissive traits of the Meek characters are most clearly evinced in their relations with the opposite sex. One hesitates to call this relationship love, since the sex element is virtually negligible. The Meek woman in love is utterly devoid of passion. In love, as in nearly everything else, she is destined to play the role of the sufferer. She considers herself infinitely below the person loved, and if there is any response to her affection, her happiness is not that of satisfied desire but of gratitude. Curiously enough, if her love is not returned, it appears to make no palpable difference in her life.

As a prostitute, however, Sonya's selflessness in love surpasses that of the other Meek characters, such as Darya Shatova in *The Possessed* and Sofiya Andreevna in *A Raw Youth*. Despite Raskolnikov's crime, she feels herself immeasurably beneath him in every respect, and her love is one of utter self-abnegation. She is willing to give all and she demands absolutely nothing in return. Even in that last scene in Siberia, when their intimate future together is symbolized by Raskolnikov's acceptance of their mutual lot of salvation by suffering, Sonya's role is still that of passive submission.

From the point of view of the novelist's art, the material for the characterization of Sonya would seem to have nothing more viable in it than the stuff of a picture of "still life." It is a tribute to Dostoevsky's genius that he was able to breathe the breath of real life into this exceptional figure. If she reminds one at times of an allegorical personification of some abstract virtue in a medieval morality play, she transcends her allegorical significance by the sheer force of the novelist's art. Perhaps it would be better to say that Sonya is a kind of living universal symbol of crushed and suffering humanity that bears within itself the undying seed of joyous resurrection.

The other members of the family have nothing in common with Sonya, emotionally or spiritually, unless it be her father. Marmeladov has something of Sonya's deep religious feeling, of her conviction that God will receive the lowliest sinner if only he be contrite and humble of heart. Marmeladov is a unique creation. He takes his place, although a lesser one, among that memorable company of exaggerated, off-centre heroes of world literature to which belong Don Quixote, Parson Adams, Uncle Toby, and Micawber. This may appear to be an ill-assorted group, but like all these famous figures, Marmeladov strikes us as comical, even ridiculous, and at the same time the ridiculous in him is never far removed from an abiding pathos that makes us pity while we smile. It is very likely that Micawber and his long-suffering brood were in Dostoevsky's mind when he conceived Marmeladov and his family. The seriousness and psychological depth in the portrayal of this chronic drunkard, however, make him much less a caricature than Dickens's amiable creation. The abundant detail with which Marmeladov and his family are drawn may be accounted for by the fact that Dostoevsky had originally intended to write a full-length story about them.

Nothing could be more effective as a piece of characterization than Marmeladov's own revelation of his nature to Raskolnikov in the tavern. Beneath the verbiage, pomposity, and unintentional humour of this inimitable confession is revealed the soul of a man who has experienced every feeling of degradation in an unequal, hopeless struggle to preserve his human dignity. Nowhere else in his fiction is Dostoevsky's intense sympathy for the poor and downtrodden more feelingly expressed than in his treatment of Marmeladov and his family. The frequent quarrels, the dying of Marmeladov, and the funeral feast provide an unexampled picture of human misery. And the last chapter of Part III, in which the deranged mother takes her children out on the streets to beg, is almost too excruciating in its realistic details. One experiences the sensation of being shut up in a madhouse; the scene is the stuff of nightmares.

The mysterious Svidrigaylov, no less than Valkovsky in *The Insulted and Injured*, gives one the eerie feeling of coming to grips with a human phantom. The identification suggests itself naturally enough, for Svidrigaylov belongs to the same type of Self-Willed characters. So obvious is their similarity that it scarcely requires any pointing out. The shamelessly frank confession of Svidrigaylov to Raskolnikov in the tavern is almost an exact duplication of Valkovsky's confession to Ivan Petrovich in the tavern. The setting, thoughts, criminal adventures, frank admission of immorality, and even some of the turns of expression are repeated in the scene in *Crime and Punishment*. Svidrigaylov is especially addicted to Valkovsky's dominating passion—women. Debauching young girls, which runs so strangely through Dostoevsky's fiction, is a particular feature of Svidrigaylov's immoral nature.

It is clear from Dostoevsky's notes on this characterization that he kept constantly in mind the criminal type of Orlov and Petrov, which he had described in *The House of the Dead*. The notes continually emphasize the fierce, unreasoning, peculiarly instinctive criminal nature that lies behind the cynical and, at times, genial exterior of Svidrigaylov. To take only one example: under the heading "N.B. Primary Point," he writes: "Svidrigaylov is conscious of mysterious horrors within himself which he will tell no one but lets slip out as facts. He has convulsive, animal-like urges to rend and to kill; coldly passionate. A wild beast. A tiger."

Despite their close resemblance, there is one important difference between Valkovsky and Svidrigaylov. Although Valkovsky is a land-owning noble, Dostoevsky never explains how he manages to retain his high social status while he appears to spend most of his time with the riffraff of the city. This difficulty is avoided in the case of Svidrigaylov. He is a noble, but a bankrupt one who has already breathed prison air. After each adventure he falls lower and lower in the social scale, and in the end he is quite alienated from his class. The descent is a logical one, and his criminal actions psychologically correspond with the loss of his original social status. This is not true of Valkovsky, whose inconclusive actions at the end of *The Insulted and Injured* seem to reflect an uncertainty in Dostovesky's own mind concerning the psychological development of the character. There is no uncertainty about the ultimate fate of Svidrigaylov. For the entirely Self-Willed type, whose rational or instinctive actions represent a criminal force directed against society, there can be only one solution—death. Svidrigaylov fulfils his development by committing suicide.

If Dostoevsky has scorn for any of the characters in the novel, it is for Luzhin, the would-be suitor of Raskolnikov's sister. One gathers from the notes that Dostoevsky originally intended Luzhin to be more complex and his actions more extensive than they actually are in the novel. The notes suggest that he becomes involved in a series of intrigues which would have contributed greatly towards his fuller development along typical Dostoevskian lines. At first Dostoevsky has him "falling terribly in love with Sonya." He pursues her without success and then makes indecent proposals. Her flat rejection provokes his violent antipathy. It is difficult to understand why Dostoevsky dropped this whole intrigue in the finished novel. Its inclusion would have made more plausible Luzhin's vile attempt to prove Sonya a thief, and, besides, the excluded action is all of a piece with his disgusting personality.

On the whole, the pettiness, nastiness, and money-grubbing aspects of Luzhin are strikingly portrayed. Razumikhin sees through his hypocritical humanitarianism, and his own self-communings reveal the baseness of his "noble" love for Raskolnikov's sister. In voluptuous dreams he had already possessed Dunya. She was young, pretty, of good birth and education. But she was very poor and would humble herself, worship him as her saviour. He was convinced that he would have boundless power over her and that she would be slavishly grateful to him all her life for his heroic condescension in marrying her. Besides, he would make use of her in his climb to greater business success.

The traits of Luzhin's nature were precisely those which Dostoevsky despised in real life—the cautious, reasoned, calculating, middle-of-the-road bourgeois attitude, bourgeois hypocritical respectability, and a petty sense of self-importance. Luzhin has nothing of the largeness, generosity, intense passion, or impulsiveness which Dostoevsky admired in real men and women as well as in his imaginary creations.

These admirable qualities that Luzhin lacked are to be found in the genial Razumikhin. Once again Dostoevsky's notes indicate aspects of Razumikhin's character, and to a lesser degree of Dunya's, which do not appear in the novel itself. For in the notes Dostoevsky describes him as a "very powerful nature," and he drafts a series of incidents which bring out this characteristic. The incidents have to do with the relations between Razumikhin and Sonya. At first Razumikhin becomes her protector, but apparently Dunya resents these attentions and through her instigation he insults Sonya. No reason is given for Dunya's enmity, unless it be the implied one of jealousy. Eventually the generous soul of Razumikhin is again won over by Sonya, and he has a terrible scene with Dunya on this score. These incidents in the notes do not appear in the finished novel, and Razumikhin's relations to Sonya are only briefly referred to. Clearly this dramatic opposition would have brought out the fine, generous nature of Razumikhin and would have clarified his rather vague relations to Dunya. The notes indicate that Dostoevsky had intended to throw in relief pointed contradictions in Dunya's nature which his heroines often possess. Her affection for Razumikhin, it appears, was to assume the more decided emotional expression of the split personality in love, and largely through the agency of Sonya. Although the final version of her character is not entirely clear, she emerges as a lovable, wise, but strong-willed woman. One can only guess why Dostoevsky omitted these significant incidents and additional points of character development. Either the novel had already grown too long and he could not fit in these further details, or else he felt that these incidents, involving Dunya and Razumikhin, were essentially episodic and that the architectonic features of the work demanded that he centre his attention on the main figure of Raskolnikov.

The remaining minor characters of *Crime and Punishment* do not require any special attention here. However small their roles may be, it is surprising how well Dostoevsky individualizes them with a few strokes. Raskolnikov's mother is ineffably human. Her cares, joys, and sorrows over her erring son, whose strange behaviour she cannot possibly understand, reflect a natural maternal exaggeration. The long letter she writes to Raskolnikov to tell of the proposed marriage of Dunya shows all the love and self-sacrifice for a son and daughter who have left her far behind in everything but affection.

The police inspector, Porfiri, is endowed with Dostoevsky's own powerful dialectical method. He bears little resemblance to the scientific sleuth of the modern detective story, but he is no less real for that. What he may lack in scientific technique he compensates by possessing a deep sense of human values which is never devoid of a sympathetic understanding of his victim. Not only was Dostoevsky intensely interested in criminal psychology, but he sought special knowledge in crime detection and legal procedure. This expert information is revealed in the police inspector's handling of Raskolnikov's case. Evidence of Dostoevsky's careful checking of details is to be found in the notebooks. For example, against the direction: "They place him [Raskolnikov] under surveillance," he reminds himself that the legality of this action must be checked by the note: "Is it possible to do this?" In Porfiri's subtle psychologizing one perceives Dostoevsky's mind at work. In fact, through the police inspector he seems to be projecting his own opinions on Raskolnikov's crime and his moral need for punishment.

On the whole, the faults of *Crime and Punishment* as a work of art are not very serious. Critics have censured the melodramatic element, but the unusual fact, in this novel of crime, is that the melodrama is rarely overdone. The murder of the old pawnbroker and Lizaveta is one of the best pieces of expository narrative in literature. This scene cannot be called melodrama. It is so intensely imagined that the author appears to be describing a vividly realized experience of his own. The cold logic of events is never sacrificed to extra-melodramatic effects. If anything, Dostoevsky consistently underwrites this unforgettable account of crime. He is not always so successful in other scenes, however, where the action crackles with horrific effects. For example, there is more melodramatic exaggeration than artistic measure in the scene in the locked room where Dunya shoots from close range at the imperturbable Svidrigaylov and manages to miss him.

Coincidence is an ever-present trap for weary novelists, and in this respect Dostoevsky nodded rather frequently in *Crime and Punishment*. It is perhaps the principal artistic blemish in the work. Coincidence, of course, may be justifiable in a novel, for it is a legitimate part of the pattern of reality. In real life, however, coincidental happenings do not violate the laws of probability, and in fiction our credibility is forfeited if coincidence is overworked. Dostoevsky certainly carries the matter too far in *Crime and Punishment*. Svidrigaylov is allowed to pass Sonya precisely at the moment when she asks Raskolnikov an important question. Svidrigaylov overhears the reply which significantly affects the action. Lebezyatnikov bumps into Raskolnikov on the crowded city streets just when he is looking for him. Indeed, such opportune meetings in the busy city occur frequently and create the impression that Dostoevsky took the easiest way out when it was necessary to get his characters together. Following this line of least resistance, he often ignored the time-sequence. In one of the notebooks he boldly declares: "What is time? Time does not

exist; time is a cipher; time is the relation of being to unbeing."
On occasions the action is so telescoped that time indeed does
not seem to exist. And this compressed action and time-sequence
literally force him to group his characters in a most improbable
manner: Luzhin lives in the same house as the Marmeladovs, and
Svidrigaylov hires quarters in Sonya's house. The restricted stage,
which recalls the misdirected application of the unities in some
bad imitations of classical drama, results in forced situations and
unbelievable coincidences.

Apart from these faults, however, there is little else to quarrel
with in *Crime and Punishment* as a work of art. Dostoevsky's
powerful dialectic admirably satisfies the realistic demands of the
reader, for the author rarely fails to present, with equal persuasive-
ness, both sides of the intellectual, moral, and spiritual contradictions which evolve out of his hero. Although Dostoevsky may seem
at times to sympathize with Raskolnikov's unique theory of murder,
this fact does not interfere with his convincing presentation of
the negative side. In the struggle between good and evil that
goes on in the mind of Raskolnikov, Dostoevsky does not hesitate
in the end to take a positive stand on the side of the good. This
does not mean that he projected, in a didactic manner, his personal
moral or ethical discrimination into a work of art. He clearly
recognizes that the moral and artistic spheres are quite distinct
from each other, for he never confuses his own morality, which
is primarily concerned with the way men behave in the real world,
with the morality of art which is not, or should not be, conditioned by the personal factors of ordinary life.

As a story, however, the common interest of *Crime and Punishment* does not rest in any dialectics, morality, or in the author's
central idea, although these features definitely contribute to make
the novel what it is. As Dostoevsky himself described it, the novel
is the "psychological account of a certain crime," and it is the
compelling, high seriousness of this drama of crime as it is cast
against a throbbing background of real life that attracts the average
reader. The intensity of the step-by-step revelation of Raskolnikov's
plan, the thrilling description of the murder, and then the equally
intense psychological analysis of the disintegration of all the rational forces that had driven him on to kill—this is the essential
and vital story that never loses its grip on the reader's imagination
and emotions. Over all radiates a spiritual glow, so characteristic
of Dostoevsky's great novels, that illumines at once the darkest
recesses of the minds of the proud and humble, of the criminal
and morally debased and inspires them to seek a deeper meaning
in life through suffering to ultimate salvation.

# GEORGE GIBIAN

## Traditional Symbolism in *Crime and Punishment*†

It may seem paradoxical to claim that critics have not sufficiently concerned themselves with Dostoevsky's attack against rationalism in *Crime and Punishment*; yet this aspect of the novel has frequently failed to receive adequate attention, not because it has been overlooked, but because often it has been immediately noticed, perfunctorily mentioned, and then put out of mind as something obvious. Few writers have examined the consequence of the anti-rationalistic tenor of the novel: the extent to which it is paralleled by the structural devices incorporated in the work.

Dostoevsky held that dialectics, self-seeking, and exclusive reliance on reason ("reason and will" in Raskolnikov's theories and again in his dream of the plague) lead to death-in-life. In *Crime and Punishment* he set himself the task of exposing the evils of rationalism by presenting a laboratory case of an individual who followed its precepts and pushed them to their logical conclusion. By working out what would happen to that man, Dostoevsky intended to show how destructive the idea was for individuals, nations, and mankind; for to him the fates of the individual and the nation were inseparably interlocked. In *The Possessed* we find a passage which applies perfectly to Raskolnikov if we substitute his name for the "nation" of which Dostoevsky is speaking here. The statement could serve as a basic text for *Crime and Punishment*: "Not a single nation has been founded on principles of science and reason. There never has been an example of it, except for a brief moment of folly. . . . Nations are built up by another force which sways and dominates them, the origin of which is unknown and inexplicable. . . . It is the spirit of life, as the Scriptures call it, 'the river of living water,' the drying up of which is threatened by the Apocalypse."[1]

The underlying antithesis of *Crime and Punishment*, the conflict between the side of reason, selfishness, and pride, and that of acceptance of suffering, closeness to life-sustaining Earth, and love,

† Reprinted by permission of the Modern Language Association of America from *PMLA*, LXX (1955), 979–96.
1. All references to *The Possessed* (*The Devils*) and *Crime and Punishment* are to the trans. by David Magarshack, Penguin Books. Quotations have been checked with the text in *Polnoe sobranie sochineniy* (St. Petersburg, 1885), Vol. III. and, where necessary, I have taken the liberty of making changes in Magarshack's translation.

sounds insipid and platitudinous when stated in such general fashion as we have done here. Dostoevsky, however, does not present it in the form of abstract statement alone. He conveys it with superb dialectical skill, and when we do find direct statements in the novel, they are intentionally made so inadequate as to make us realize all the more clearly their disappointing irrelevancy and to lead us to seek a richer representation in other modes of discourse. Such a deliberately unsatisfactory formulation is, for example, Raskolnikov's utterance after his temporary decision not to go through with the murder, his twice repeated "No, I just couldn't do it! I just couldn't do it!" Equally inadequate is Sonya's attempt at explaining why she could not take the life of another human being, even under the worst circumstances. All she can say in answer to Raskolnikov's cruel, harassing questions is to stammer, "To kill?" It is significant that Sonya, the wisest person in the book, is the most inarticulate of the major characters of the novel.

Symbolism is the method of expression with which we are primarily concerned here, but it is far from being the only indirect, non-intellectual manner of expression on which Dostoevsky depends. Oblique presentation is another means which he uses; one example is the introduction of the subject of need for suffering. The idea is first presented in a debased and grotesque form by Marmeladov. His confession of how he had mistreated his family, of his drinking, and of the theft of money—to Raskolnikov, a stranger whom he has met in the tavern—is almost a burlesque foreshadowing of Raskolnikov's later penance, the kissing of the earth and his confession at the police station. Marmeladov is drunk, irresponsible, and still submerged in his selfish course of action; he welcomes suffering but continues to spurn his responsibilities; he is making a fool of himself in the tavern. His discourse throughout calls for an ambiguous response. Raskolnikov's reaction may be pity, agreement, laughter, or disgust; the reader's is a mixture and succession of all those emotions.

Thus the important ideas summed up in Marmeladov's "it's not joy I thirst for, but sorrow and tears" are introduced in a derogatory context and in an ambivalent manner, on the lowest, least impressive level. Yet the concept is now present with us, the readers, as it is with Raskolnikov—even though it first appears in the guise of something questionable, disreputable, and laughable—and we are forced to ponder it and to measure against it Sonya's, Raskolnikov's, Porfiry's and others' approaches to the same subject of "taking one's suffering."

A simple, unequivocal statement, a respectable entrance of the theme on the stage of the book, would amount to a reduction of life to "a matter of arithmetic" and would release the reader from the salutary, in fact indispensable task of smelting down the ore for himself. Compare Dostoevsky's technique to the remarks in Hegel's *Phenomenology of Mind*: "The truth is not like stamped coin that is issued ready from the mint and so can be taken up and used" and "Dogmatism . . . is nothing else but the view that truth consists of a proposition which is a fixed and final result or again which is directly known."[2] Among the many writers who shared with Dostoevsky a sense for the desirability of oblique, seemingly inappropriate, even grotesque statement are Plato and Kierkegaard. Plato's *Symposium*, for instance, is a third-hand report, composed of conflicting speeches, parables, myths, and Socrates' dialectical probing, as well as his version of the teaching of a remote source, Diotima. The dialogue takes place in an atmosphere of drinking and jesting; truth emerges from the whole complex structure instead of from one outright affirmation or abstract statement. Kirkegaard, too, opposed flat assertion and believed in the ironic or humorous manner of communicating truths which vanish in an attempt at direct formulation.

In *Crime and Punishment* the reader, as well as Raskolnikov, must struggle to draw his own conclusions from a work which mirrors the refractory and contradictory materials of life itself, with their admixture of the absurd, repulsive, and grotesque. The oblique presentation of ideas was Dostoevsky's favorite technique also in his other novels, in which no pat answer is true. In *The Notes from the Underground* he turned a monologue into a multiple drama by dividing the personality of the speaker into several warring component parts, and by drawing the reader into the struggle as a participant with whom the Underground Man argues, whose supposed responses are clearly indicated, and who is as actively present as the audience in one of Browning's dramatic monologues. In *The Idiot* some of the most significant ideas are stated by Ippolit with scorn and with the purpose of rejecting them, and by Lebedev in drunkenness and with the intention of parody and ridicule; yet like Balaam the speakers bless what they intend to curse. In *The Brothers Karamazov* the indirect, dramatic, and oblique presentation is developed to the highest degree. An almost Talmudic method of anecdotal exposition is used by Dostoevsky, in conjunction with inner dialogues of Ivan and his Devil, imaginary dialogues between the Grand Inquisitor and his silent auditor, Christ, and exterior dramatic dialogues between most of the various possible combinations of two speakers taken from the repertory of the four Karamazov brothers, principally Ivan and Mitya, Alyosha and Mitya, Alyosha and Ivan, and Ivan and Smerdyakov.

2. Trans. J. B. Baillie in *Hegel: Selections*, ed. J. Lowenberg (New York, 1929), pp. 33, 35.

Traditional symbolism, that is, symbolism which draws on images established by the Christian tradition and on those common in Russian non-Christian, possibly pre-Christian and pagan, folk thought and expression, is an important element in the structure of *Crime and Punishment*. The outstanding strands of symbolic imagery in the novel are those of water, vegetation, sun and air, the resurrection of Lazarus and Christ, and the earth.[3]

Water is to Dostoevsky a symbol of rebirth and regeneration. It is regarded as such by the positive characters, for whom it is an accompaniment and an indication of the life-giving forces in the world. By the same token, the significance of water may be the opposite to negative characters. Water holds the terror of death for the corrupt Svidrigaylov, who confirms his depravity by thinking: "Never in my life could I stand water, not even on a landscape painting." Water, instead of being an instrument of life, becomes for him a hateful, avenging menace during the last hours of his life. In him the drying out of "the river of living water" mentioned in the remark quoted above from *The Possessed* has taken place, and the events of the last hours of his life are introduced by water in another, frightening form: "Towards ten o'clock the sky became overcast with fearful clouds. There was a clap of thunder, and it began to pour with rain. The rain did not come down in drops, but lashed the earth with whole torrents of water. . . . Soaked to the skin, Svidrigaylov came home . . . listening to the thunder and rain, he changed his mind, took his hat, and went out without locking up his room." His errands, such as the visits to his child-fiancée and to Sonya, take place in the rain. "To plan to go to America [his riddling phrase for suicide] and to be afraid of the rain!" he says with grim irony to Sonya. He dislikes the Neva and feels cold when he merely thinks of the river. Returning from his fiancée, "Svidrigaylov, at precisely twelve o'clock, was crossing Tuchkov Bridge in the direction of the Petersburg suburb. The rain had ceased, but the wind was still howling. He was beginning to shiver, and for a moment he looked at the black waters of the Little Neva with a sort of special curiosity, and even wonderingly. But he soon felt very cold on the bridge." Rain blows in from the garden into the window of his room in the shabby hotel in which he passes his last night; Svidrigaylov thinks of the rain and flood, both of which he associates with images of evil, discord, and death:

3. Outstanding among the several writers who have discussed certain aspects of Dostoevsky's symbolism are Vyacheslav Ivanov, *Freedom and the Tragic Life* (New York, 1952); L. A. Zander, *Dostoevsky* (London, 1948); K. Mochulsky, *Dostoevsky* (Paris, 1947); N. O. Lossky, *Dostoevsky i ego khristianskoe miroponimanie* (New York, 1953); Romano Guardini, *Religiöse Gestalten in Dostojewskis Werk* (Munich, 1951). Their interests are for the most part theological or limited to only one or two groups of images; they are not concerned with how symbolism contributes to the structure of one particular novel.

"The water is rising," he thought. "By morning it will rush into the streets in the low-lying parts of the town, the basements and cellars will be under water, and drowned rats from the cellars will be floating on the surface. . . . Why not leave this place now, go straight to Petrovsky Park, choose a large bush drenched with rain, so that just touching it with my shoulder millions of drops will shower down on my head, and—"

Indeed it will be in the cold and in the rain that he will put a bullet in his head. Instead of being a positive force, water is for him the appropriate setting for the taking of his own life.

When Raskolnikov is under the sway of rationalism and corrupting ways of thinking, this also is indicated by Dostoevsky by attributing to him negative reactions to water similar to those of Svidrigaylov. In Raskolnikov, however, the battle is not definitely lost. A conflict still rages between his former self—which did have contact with other people and understood the beauty of the river, the cathedral (representing the traditional, religious, and emotional forces), and water—and the new, rationalistic self, which is responsible for the murder and for his inner desiccation. When, after the murder, he is trying to hide the stolen property, it occurs to him that he might "get rid of it all" by throwing everything "into the Canal, and there won't be any traces left [in the original the phrase reads *i kontsy v vodu, i delo s kontsom*, literally 'all remnants go in the water and everything is finished,' a saying which continues the water symbolism] and all will be over." But of course "it was not so easy to get rid of it." The possibility of throwing it in the Neva presents itself to him; he asks, "Why the Neva? Why the water?" The river still seems to him an improper or an impossible place for obliterating the consequences of his crime.

His state of mind is made quite clear soon afterwards, again by a representation of his reactions to water: "He . . . turned with his face to the Neva, in the direction of the Palace. There was not a wisp of cloud in the sky, and the water was almost blue, as happens only rarely on the Neva. The cupola of the cathedral, which nowhere appears to better advantage than when seen from there—from the bridge, about twenty yards from the little chapel —glittered in the sunshine, and in the clear air every ornament on it could be plainly distinguished. . . . This magnificent view always struck a strange chill into his heart; this gorgeous sight filled him with blank despair. He had always wondered at this gloomy and enigmatic impression of his." There is still left in Raskolnikov an instinctive reaction to water (and to beauty) as an instrument of life, although this receptivity, which had been full-blown and characteristic of him in his childhood, is now in his student days overlaid by the utilitarian and rationalistic theories. (In contrast to

Svidrigaylov, who feels clearly and unequivocally depressed by the contemplation of beauty.) But Raskolnikov also realizes that his trends of thought have banished him, like Cain, from the brotherhood of men and clouded his right and ability to enjoy beauty and the beneficent influences of life symbolized by water; hence his perplexity and conflict.

A small but significant incident connects with the Neva scene and carries on its theme of not-belonging. A woman who mistook Raskolnikov for a beggar gives him a twenty-kopek piece; mankind, through a stranger actuated by spontaneous pity (to Raskolnikov a rationally unjustifiable emotion), still includes Raskolnikov within its community. But Raskolnikov has placed himself outside of society consciously through his concept of the superman and of man-made reason and will-controlled morality which discounts all tradition and feeling, and unconsciously through his crime. Therefore he cannot accept an act based upon sympathy: "He opened his hand, stared at the coin, and raising his arm, he flung it with a violent movement into the water; then he retraced his steps and went home. He felt as though he has cut himself off with a pair of scissors from everyone and everything at that moment." He underlines his isolation and break with the past by choosing to throw the coin, here the token of kindness and human sharing, "into the water."

At one point Raskolnikov comes close to degrading himself so far as to have the same reactions as Svidrigaylov. For he too at least considered death by water: "I went to the Neva many times. . . . I wanted to end it all there, but—I couldn't make up my mind," he tells Dunya, and even as late as immediately before his confession and surrender, he still asked himself, "Why, why live?" But the forces of life were strong in him and prevented him from doing the same as Svidrigaylov.

When Raskolnikov is in a positive spiritual state opposed to his crime and favorable to his living in union with other men, this also is revealed by his different reaction to the Neva. The dream of the mare, for example, makes him feel that he will be unable to carry out his plan: "The thought of it actually made me feel sick and filled me with horror. No, I couldn't do it! I just couldn't do it!" Under the influence of his sudden change of mind, he "crossed the bridge [and] gazed calmly and quietly at the Neva, and at the bright, red sunset. In spite of his weakness, he did not feel tired. . . . He was free! He was now free from all those obsessions, magic spells, delusions, witchcraft!" For a short interval his feeling of liberation and the ascendancy of a life-sustaining attitude lead him to derive happiness and calm from the river rather than "chill" and "blank despair," as he did when he was the self-assertive, rationalistic Raskolnikov.

A cogent expression of the dominant significance of water to Raskolnikov is available in his dream of the oasis: "He kept daydreaming, and his day-dreams were all so strange: mostly he imagined himself to be somewhere in Africa, in Egypt, in some sort of oasis. The caravan is resting, the camels are lying down peacefully; palms are growing in a circle all around; they are all having their meal, but he is drinking water all the time, straight from a little stream that flowed babbling close by. And it is so cool, and the wonderful, blue, cold water is running over stones of many colors and over such clean sand, which here and there glittered like gold."

The stream here represents Raskolnikov's desire to be saved from his criminal plan. He is attracted by the possibility of a restful, serene life (expressed here, as frequently elsewhere in the novel, by the cluster of images of water, vegetation, and restfulness) which would be very different from the horrible existence (represented in the first dream by the beating of the mare) into which, Raskolnikov subconsciously realizes, his life will develop if he perseveres in his determination to kill the pawnbroker.

The dream is the last attempt by his subconscious to hold out to him a way of life opposite to that to which his reason and will have committed him. It is a desperate and unheeded call which he scornfully rejects as a sign of a passing disease. Symbolism of water is the language used to express the conflict; Raskolnikov's reaction to water is a gauge of his inner state.

Related to the many references to the river and rain, and often closely associated with them, are two other groups of symbolic imagery: that of vegetation (shrubbery, leaves, bushes, flowers, and greenness in general) and that of the sun (and the related images of light and air).

In contrast to the dusty, hot, stifling, and crowded city, a fitting setting for Raskolnikov's oppressive and murderous thoughts, we find, for example, "the greenness and the freshness" of the Petersburg islands. Before the murder, Raskolnikov walked over to them and "the greenness and the freshness at first pleased his tired eyes, used to the dust of the city, to the lime, and the huge, enclosing, confining houses. Here there were no bad smells, no oppressive heat, no taverns. . . . The flowers particularly attracted his attention." He made his way "into some bushes, lay down on the grass and fell asleep at once," and had the dream of the mare and Nikolka. The natural surroundings reawakened in him the feelings of his youth, through which he came close to avoiding his crime and to finding regeneration without having to pass through the cycle of crime and punishment. It is significant that it was in that particular setting that the dream foreshadowing the murder came to him, with the mare standing for the pawnbroker and all the victimized women of the novel, and with Raskolnikov—this time not a tormentor and criminal, but a child-bystander—sympathizing with the victim and wishing to save her.

By the same token, vegetation exercised the opposite effect on Svidrigaylov: it repelled him. In the inn on the night of his suicide, when he heard the leaves in the garden under his window, he thought, "How I hate the noise of trees at night in a storm and in darkness." Whereas Raskolnikov received a healthy warning during his short sleep "under a bush," Svidrigaylov uses the sordid setting of an amusement park which "had one spindly three-year-old Christmas tree and three small bushes" merely for vain distraction on the eve of his suicide, and contemplates killing himself under "a large bush drenched with rain." In him all positive elements had been rubbed out or transformed into evil. The forces symbolic of new life, vegetation as well as rain, either became hateful to him or were perverted by him to serve his destructive purposes, just as he had abused all the relationships of his life: in marriage giving hate instead of love, in presents to his fiancée aiming at causing embarrassment and shock instead of pleasure, and in his relations with his servant domineering and bullying instead of guiding.

Svidrigaylov's perversion of instruments of life is manifested in his dream of the fourteen-year-old girl whom he had driven to suicide—significantly, to suicide by drowning. He first dreams of a profusion of flowers:

> Whether it was the cold, or the darkness, or the dampness, or the wind howling under the window and shaking the trees, but he felt an overpowering and persistent inclination and craving for the fantastic, and yet all he could think of were flowers. He saw flowers everywhere. He fancied a delightful flowering landscape. A bright, warm, almost hot day, a holiday—Trinity day. A magnificent, sumptuous country cottage in the English style, overgrown with masses of fragrant flowers, with flower-beds all round it . . . climbing plants and . . . beds of roses . . . exotic flowers . . . bunches of tender, white and heavily scented narcissi, drooping on their thick, long, bright-green stalks. He felt reluctant to leave them, but he ascended the staircase and entered a large, high-ceilinged room, and again there were flowers everywhere—at the windows, by the open doors leading to the large balcony, and on the balcony itself. The floors were strewn with freshly mown fragrant hay.

The flowers suggest the last outburst of his craving for life which is doomed to end in failure; the luxuriant vegetation already contains something sickly and artificially exuberant and unnatural, and turns out to be a setting for the opposite of life—death; and the death is one which Svidrigaylov himself had brought about through a violation of the girl. A deceptively attractive picture is only a preparation for the shock of the object within it: "The windows were open, a fresh, cool, light breeze came into the room, the birds were chirping under the windows, and in the middle of the room, on tables covered with white satin shrouds, stood a coffin. . . . It was garlanded with flowers. A young girl, smothered in flowers, lay in it. . . . A wreath of roses encircled her head."

In his other writings Dostoevsky frequently used symbolism of vegetation to express the forces of life and regeneration. In *The Diary of a Writer* he wrote: "Mankind will be regenerated in the garden and through the garden it will be restored, that is the formula," and went on to attack the strivings of the bourgeoisie after progress through industry and social means as salvation through the "Crystal Palace," hostile and diametrically opposed to salvation through "the garden."[4] In his later works Dostoevsky frequently concentrated the meaning of vegetation and "the garden" into "a leaf." In *The Possessed*, for instance, Kirilov tells Stavrogin, "I saw a yellow leaf recently, a little green, wilted at the edges. Blown by the wind. When I was a boy of ten I used to shut my eyes deliberately in the winter and imagine a green leaf, bright green with veins on it, and the sun shining," and then in answer to Stavrogin's contemptuous objection, "What's that? An allegory?" proceeds both to deny an allegorical significance and to confirm, by implication, the symbolical one: "Not an allegory, just a leaf, one leaf. A leaf's good. All's good." Of the many similar associations of plants with life in *The Brothers Karamazov*, one example will have to suffice here as a parallel to Dostoevsky's earlier practice in *Crime and Punishment*, Ivan's "I have a longing for life, and I go on living in spite of logic. . . . I love the sticky little leaves as they open in the spring."[5]

The symbolism of water and vegetation has pagan and Russian folkloristic origins, but it is not devoid of Christian antecedents and connotations. Baptism is rebirth through water: Jeremiah 1.13 reads "They have forsaken . . . the fountain of living waters, and hewed them out cisterns, broken cisterns that can hold no water"; and the *locus classicus* for water of life as well as the tree of life is chapter twenty-two of the Book of Revelation: "And he showed me a pure river of water of life, clear as crystal, proceeding out of the throne of God and of the Lamb. In the midst of the street

4. Trans. Boris Brasol (New York, 1949), I, 417. Gerhard Gesemann, "Das Goldene Zeitalter: ein Kapitel über Dostojewski," *Die Dioskuren* (München, 1923), II, 275–303, and Leonid Grossman, *Tvorchestvo Dostoevskogo* (Moscow, 1928), pp. 112–113 discuss the role played in Dostoevsky's writings by nature in the form of a "garden" or "landscape."

5. Trans. Constance Garnett (New York, 1943), p. 273.

of it, and on either side of the river [in New Jerusalem] there was the tree of life which bare twelve manner of fruits, and yielded her fruit every month: and the leaves of the tree were for the healing of the nations. And there shall be no more curse."

Similarly to water and vegetation, sunshine, light in general, and air are positive values, whereas darkness and lack of air are dangerous and deadening. The beauty of the cathedral flooded by sunlight ought to be felt and admired: "The cupola of the cathedral . . . glittered in the sunshine, and in the clear air every ornament on it could be plainly distinguished." During the service of the dead at the Marmeladovs', an occasion which helps to stir Raskolnikov's conscience and brings him closer to the beneficent influence of Sonya, "The room was full of sunshine; the incense rose in clouds; the priest read, 'Give unto her, O Lord, eternal peace.' " Sunshine is again associated with beauty, calm, and religion. The sun is a symbol of those forces of life which combat deadly theory.[6] Raskolnikov had also been disturbed by the sunlight which lit up the room of the pawnbroker during his trial visit, and thought to himself on that occasion, fearfully remembering the murder he was planning: "So the sun will be shining then, too, I suppose." The light of the sun and the crime seem incompatible to him. Before the murder, he looks up from the bridge at the "bright, red sunset" and is able to face the sun as well as the river with calm, but after the murder, "in the street it was again unbearably hot—not a drop of rain all during those days. . . . The sun flashed brightly in his eyes, so that it hurt him to look and his head was spinning round in good earnest—the usual sensation of a man in a fever who comes out into the street on a bright, sunny day." The sun is pleasant for a man in good spiritual health, but unbearable for a feverish creature of the dark, such as Raskolnikov had become. His room is like an animal's lair, hidden from the sun and any source of light or air: "On his return from the Hay Market, he flung himself on the sofa and sat for a whole hour without moving. Meanwhile it got dark; he had no candle, and indeed it had never entered his head to light one." Sonya's room, in contrast, is large and has several windows: "Sonya's room was rather like a shed, it was in the shape of an irregular quadrangle. . . . The wall with the three windows looking out on to the canal cut across the room obliquely." Svidrigaylov, on the other hand, is submerged in unrelieved darkness. He is a nocturnal animal who seems in appropriate surroundings during his wandering in the dark on the night of his suicide.

6. Mochulsky, *Dostoevsky*, p. 242, makes this point. An elaborate discussion of the symbolism of the sun in the Western Middle Ages is available in H. Flanders Dunbar, *Symbolism in Medieval Thought and Its Consum-* *mation in the Divine Comedy* (New Haven, 1929). Her study serves as an interesting comparison with Dostoevsky's Orthodox use of the sun as one component of Sophia, see below.

The light of the sun, as well as the beauty of nature and the sea, displeases him: "The sunrise, the bay of Naples, the sea—all that makes you feel so damnably depressed! The horrible thing is that it really makes you yearn for something."

Absence of air reinforces the lack of light suggestive of inner heaviness. Raskolnikov, whom Svidrigaylov tells that people need air, feels physically and mentally suffocated when he is summoned to the police-station: "There's so little fresh air here. Stifling. Makes my head reel more and more every minute, and my brain too." Later he tells his friend Razumikhin: "Things have become too airless, too stifling." Airiness, on the contrary, is an indication of an advantageous relation between outward circumstances and Raskolnikov's inner state. The warning dream of the mare comes to Raskolnikov in a setting not only of greenness but also of abundance of fresh air: "The green vegetation and the fresh air at first pleased his tired eyes, used to the dust of the city, to the lime and mortar and the huge houses that enclosed and confined him on all sides. The air was fresh and sweet here: no evil smells."

When we turn to specifically Christian symbolism in *Crime and Punishment*, we find the outstanding images to be those of New Jerusalem, Christ's passion, and Lazarus. New Jerusalem is an important concept throughout Dostoevsky's work.[7] It constitutes one of the main themes of *The Possessed*, where the revolutionaries seek a false New Jerusalem, an inhuman, oppressive pseudo-millennium. A similar tension between what Dostoevsky considered the proper ultimate goal of man, the true New Jerusalem, and the mistaken aims of utilitarians, socialists, and rationalists in general exists in *The Notes from the Underground*, *The Brothers Karamazov*, and elsewhere. It is often reinforced by references to the context of New Jerusalem in the Book of Revelation, which is particularly frequently mentioned in *The Possessed* and *The Idiot*.[8] In *Crime and Punishment* Porfiry asks Raskolnikov, "Do you believe in New Jerusalem?" The significance of Raskolnikov's positive answer lies in the fact that the New Jerusalem which he means is the Utopian perversion of it, to be built upon foundations of crime and individual self-assertion and transgression (*prestuplenie*). It is the "Golden Age," as Raskolnikov called it in the draft version in Dostoevsky's notebook: "Oh why are not all people happy? The picture of the Age of Gold—it is already present in minds and hearts. Why should it not come about? . . . But what right have I, a mean murderer, to wish happiness to people and to dream of

7. Gesemann discusses the concept of New Jerusalem in Dostoevsky, with special attention to *The Possessed*, *A Raw Youth*, and *The Dream of a Ridiculous Man*.
8. The Book of Revelation was one of Dostoevsky's favorite books; he often referred to it in conversation, and was enthusiastic over Maykov's translation of it. Grossman, *Tvorchestvo*, p. 163.

the Age of Gold?"[9]

The confession of Raskolnikov is described in terms reminiscent of Christ's passion on the road to Golgotha: he goes on "his sorrowful way." When Raskolnikov reads in his mother's letter of Dunya's having walked up and down in her room and prayed before the Kazan Virgin, he associates her planned self-sacrifice in marrying Luzhin with the Biblical prototype of self-assumed suffering for the sake of others: "Ascent to Golgotha is certainly pretty difficult," he says to himself. When Raskolnikov accepts the cypress-wood cross from Sonya, he shows his recognition of the significance of his taking it—the implied resolve to seek a new life though accepting suffering and punishment—by saying to Sonya, "This is the symbol of my taking up the cross."

One of the central Christian myths alluded to in the novel is the story of Lazarus. It is the Biblical passage dealing with Lazarus that Raskolnikov asks Sonya to read to him. The raising of Lazarus from the dead is to Dostoevsky the best *exemplum* of a human being resurrected to a new life, the road to Golgotha the best expression of the dark road of sorrow, and Christ himself the grand type of voluntary suffering. "I am the Resurrection and the Life" is the refrain in this book of a man who lost his life and found it again.

The traditional emphasis of the Eastern Church is on Resurrection—of the Western, on the Passion.[1] In *Crime and Punishment* both sides are represented: the Eastern in its promise of Raskolnikov's rebirth, the Western in the stress on his suffering. Perhaps at least part of the universality of the appeal of the novel and of its success in the West may be due to the fact that it combines the two religious tendencies.

External evidence of Dostoevsky's bent to think of the action in terms of its Christian archetypes exists in Dostoevsky's notebook. On the same page we find the following somewhat enigmatic entries:

When she is persuading him, i.e. before the farewell.
Well kiss the gospel, kiss it, read it.

Lazarus, arise.

And then when Svidrigaylov gives her money.
I myself was dead Lazarus, and Christ raised me from the dead.

NB Sonya follows him to Golgotha, forty paces behind.[2]

9. I. I. Glivenko, *Iz arkhiva F. M. Dostoevskogo: Prestuplenie i nakazanie* (Moscow-Leningrad, 1931), p. 89.
1. See, e.g., N. S. Trubetzkoy, "Introduction to the History of Old Russian Literature," *Harvard Slavic Studies* (Cambridge, Mass., 1954), II, 95–96.
2. Glivenko, *Iz arkhiva*, p. 204. There are further references to Christ on pp. 73, 76, and 177.

It is clear that here Dostoevsky made a point of pulling out of context and putting alongside each other, in the form of a brief list, the drafts of three tentative fragmentary passages which have only one thing in common: the fact that they are Biblical allusions. The link between them is that all three explicitly draw a parallel between the action of the novel and the gospel accounts of Lazarus' resurrection and Christ's road to Golgotha. Moreover, the draft version of *Crime and Punishment* contained a chapter entitled *Christ*; Raskolnikov was to have seen a vision of Christ himself. This was replaced in the final text by the reading of the gospel by Sonya.

The notebook proves that Dostoevsky thought of the pervasive Biblical references as a connected series which was to be noticed; the individual parallels, scattered as they are in the final version of the novel, are to be thought of together, as a steady accompaniment to the story of Raskolnikov, an underpinning of allusions to Christ's and Lazarus' deaths and rebirths.

The Christian symbolism is underlined by the pagan and universal symbolism of the earth. Sonya persuades Raskolnikov not only to confess and wear the cross, but also to kiss the earth at the crossroads—a distinctly Russian and pre-Christian acknowledgment of the earth as the common mother of all men.[3] The earth is the source of fertility and the sanction for all family and community ties. It is fitting to confess to the earth: "Go at once, this very minute, and stand at the crossroads, bow down, first kiss the earth which you have defiled, and then bow down to the whole world, to all four sides—and then say to all men aloud, I am a murderer! Then God will send you life again." In bowing to the earth and kissing it, Raskolnikov is performing a symbolic and non-rational act; the rationalist is marking the beginning of his change into a complete, organic, living human being, rejoining all other men in the community. By his crime and ideas, he had separated himself from his friends, family, and nation, in one word, he had cut himself off from Mother Earth. By the gesture of kissing the earth, he is reestablishing all his ties.

Alyosha and Zosima in *The Brothers Karamazov* and Marya Lebyatkina in *The Possessed* show similar reverence for the earth, which stands for matter organized into a single cosmos, possessed of lifegiving power, and raised to the high level of a personal being almost directly connected with God.[4]

3. The importance of Mother Earth in Russian thought has been frequently discussed. See esp. R. V. Pletnyov, "Zemlja," in A. L. Bem, ed., *O Dostoevskom: sbornik statey* (Prague, 1929), I, 153–162; Zander, *Dostoevsky*, pp. 36–65; and Georgy Fedotov, *Stikhi dukhovnye* (Paris, 1935), passim. My article "Dostoevsky's Use of Russian Folklore," in the *Journal of American Folklore*, 1956, Slavic issue, deals with the relationship between folk literature and Dostoevsky's works in general, including the theme of Mother Earth.

4. Zander, p. 52.

When Raskolnikov kisses the earth at the crossroads, the meeting place of men, a bystander sarcastically suggests that he may be saying goodby to his "children and his country" and leaving on a pilgrimage to Jerusalem. There is deep irony in the mocking words. Raskolnikov is indeed saying goodby—to Petersburg, for he will be sent to Siberia. At the same time he is taking farewell of his false ideal of the New Jerusalem. In another sense, he *is* now about to embark on a search for a new ideal, another New Jerusalem— and in this sense he will be a pilgrim, seeking personal regeneration which is to replace his earlier social-rationalistic ideal. Thus at the turning point of the novel, there is a fusing of the Christian symbolism of taking up the cross and New Jerusalem with the primeval symbolism of Gaea, Mother Earth.

Now that we have examined selected examples of symbolism in the novel, let us take a look at the epilogue as a test of insights we may have gained into the structure and unity of the novel, for the epilogue is the culmination and juncture of the various strands of images which we have encountered earlier.

The epilogue has been called unprepared for, weak, and disjointed. These strictures are natural if we pay attention exclusively to "rational" aspects of the book and look for connections between the epilogue and the body of the novel only in the realms of outward plot and explicit statement. It is true that the regeneration of Raskolnikov is not presented as fully or as dramatically as the events leading to its inception; yet its beginning and its future course are indicated sufficiently by other means. The frequent undervaluation of the epilogue may be symptomatic of the lack of attention to Dostoevsky's communication through the symbolic pattern of the novel.

If we approach the epilogue with the various preparatory strands of images clearly in our minds, what do we find? Raskolnikov is in a Siberian city on the banks of "a broad, deserted river," a reprise of water imagery. He has relapsed into isolation from his fellow men; he is sunk into apathy and gloom: "He looked at his fellow-prisoners, and was surprised at them: how they all loved life! How highly they prized it! It was in prison, it seemed to him, that people loved and prized life more than outside it. What terrible agonies and tortures some of them had endured—the tramps, for instance. Did a ray of sunshine or the primeval forest mean so much to them? Or some cold spring in some far-away, lonely spot which the tramp had marked three years before and which he longed to see again as he might long to see his mistress, dreamed of it constantly, and the green grass around it, and the bird singing in the bush?" Here, then, we see the state of the soul of the unregenerate Raskolnikov, the Lazarus before the rebirth, expressed by Dostoevsky through the symbolic imagery to which the novel has made us accustomed—water and vegetation. The love for life (which Raskolnikov does not yet comprehend) is represented by a spring with green grass and bushes around it.

When the regeneration of Raskolnikov begins, it is expressed in a manner still more closely linked to previously introduced imagery. His dream of the plague condemns Raskolnikov's own rationalism. It shows people obsessed by reason and will losing contact with the soil: "They gave up tilling the ground." The plague-infected men become frenzied and kill each other. In contrast to Raskolnikov's earlier bow to the earth, the men in his dream have abandoned the earth. The dream is an expression of a new way of looking at reason and will—a way diametrically opposed to Raskolnikov's previous exaltation of those two faculties and rejection of all else. This dream of the plague, coming immediately before the start of the hero's regeneration, may also be another reminiscence of the Book of Revelation with its last seven plagues coming just before the millennium and the establishment of the New Jerusalem.

The epilogue then goes on to emphasize that it is the second week after Easter—the feast of Christ's passion, death, and resurrection; and that it is warm, bright spring—the season of the revival of dead nature, again a coupling of Christian and non-Christian symbolism of rebirth such as we have encountered earlier in the novel.

The crucial final scene which follows takes place on "a bright and warm day," and "on the bank of the river." The river which Raskolnikov sees now is no longer a possible means for committing suicide nor a sight inducing melancholy; it is the river of life. Calm countryside opens up before Raskolnikov across the river, where he sees nomads' tents on a steppe flooded with sunlight. They seem to be men of the age of Abraham and his flocks, truly free and living people, not living dead as Raskolnikov had been. Now he can identify himself with these nomads, although he has only one thing in common with them, the most important thing of all— humanity. A short time before, he had been cut off from his fellow-prisoners and all mankind, even those who ought to have been very close to him, his friends and family. About his life in Siberia we had been told: "What generally surprised him most was the terrible, unbridgeable gulf that lay between him and all those other people. It seemed to him that they belonged to quite different nations. . . . He knew and understood the general reasons of this separation, but he would never before have admitted that those reasons were so deep-rooted or strong." His feeling at present, when without direct contact or community of interests he can sense his kinship with the nomads of Siberia, is in contradiction also to the earlier state of his feelings indicated in the episode of his throwing away the alms given him by the woman in Petersburg. The change in him now, towards the end of the novel, is marked by the fact that he feels no longer isolated from men representing, through the allusion to Abraham, humanity of the past as well as of the present.

Then appears Sonya, and with her arrival comes the moment when Raskolnikov is suffused with love for his guide and savior. Sonya plays in the novel a part comparable to that performed by Beatrice and Lucia taken jointly in the *Divine Comedy*. Her name is a clue, as so often happens with Dostoevsky's emphatically significant names. Sonya stands for Sophia, which in Russian thought occupies a position far more important than merely that of its literal meaning, wisdom. To Vladimir Solovyov, S. N. Bulgakov, Alexander Blok, and many others, the concept of Sophia supplemented that of the divine trinity. It has been variously defined as "cosmic love" or love for "the divine ground of the created world"; through contemplation of Sophia one can merge all that is visible, admire its beauty, and penetrate to its essence.[5] Vivid response to all that lives is a joining with the creator in creating and preserving the world; Sophia is a blissful meeting of god and nature, the creator and creature. In Orthodox thought Sophia has come close to being regarded as something similar to the fourth divine person.[6] Love for Sophia is a generalized ecstatic love for all creation, so that the images of flowers, greenness, landscape, the river, air, the sun, and water throughout *Crime and Punishment* can be regarded as being subsumed in the concept of Sophia and figuratively in the person of Sonya, the embodiment of the concept. Sonya sees that all exists in God; she knows, and helps Raskolnikov to recognize, what it means to anticipate the millennium by living in rapt love for all creation here, in this world.

It was Sonya who had brought Raskolnikov the message of Lazarus and his resurrection; she had given him the cypress cross and urged him to kiss the earth at the crossroads. On the evening of the day when, by the bank of the river and in the presence of Sonya, Raskolnikov's regeneration had begun, the New Testament lies under his pillow as a reminder of the Christian prototype of resurrection which had been stressed earlier in the novel. Against the background of all the important symbols of the book, Easter, spring, Abraham's flocks, the earth of Siberia, the river, the dream, and Sonya, the drama within Raskolnikov's mind assumes its expressive outward form.

There follow several explicit statements of what happened. We

5. Zander, p. 62.                        6. Zander, pp. 48–49 and 62.

read that "the dawn of a full resurrection to a new life" was already shining "in their faces, that love brought them back to life, that the heart of one held inexhaustible sources of life for the heart of the other," and that "the gradual rebirth" of Raskolnikov would follow. But the power of the general, overt statements depends on the indirect, oblique, dramatic, and symbolic statements which preceded them and prepared the ground for our acceptance of them. If we sense the full significance of the statement that now "Raskolnikov could solve nothing consciously. He only felt. Life had taken the place of dialectics," for example, it is because we have seen dialectics and apathy dramatized in Luzhin, Lebezyatnikov, Raskolnikov, and Svidrigaylov, and resurrection in Sonya and various symbols throughout the novel of which the epilogue is a climax and a recapitulation.

In a passage which Janko Lavrin calls "one of the best clues to Dostoevsky the psychologist," Jung described "the working of the intellect" as "thinking which is a mere equation, and from which nothing comes out but what we have put in," and went on to say: "But beyond that there is a thinking in primordial images—in symbols which are older than historical man; which have been ingrained in him from earliest times, and, eternally living, outlasting all generations, still make up the groundwork of the human psyche. It is possible to live the fullest life only when in harmony with these symbols; wisdom is a return to them. . . . Science and these symbols are incommensurables."[7] In *Crime and Punishment* Dostoevsky wishes to demonstrate that "a simple sum of arithmetic," something very similar to Jung's "mere equation" and "working of the intellect," may be not only sterile, but even actively destructive.

The similarity between Jung and Dostoevsky is interesting, but it is not as relevant as the parallels to be found in the works of G. H. Schubert, whose treatise on dreams, *Die Symbolik des Traumes* (1816 and many other editions), influential on the Continent throughout the nineteenth century, is important for an understanding of Dostoevsky's use of dreams and symbolism in general. Schubert's ideas probably reached Dostoevsky indirectly, through their reflections in the writings of E. T. A. Hoffmann and others.[8] Like Dostoevsky, Schubert believed that the rationalism dominant since the eighteenth century forbade to man's waking state much that was essential to life and which therefore took refuge in man's mental life during sleep. In a foreshadowing of

7. "The Stages of Life," in *Modern Man in Search of a Soul* (New York, 1934), pp. 129–130, quoted in Janko Lavrin, *Dostoevsky: a Study* (New York, 1947), pp. 53–54.

8. A related direct influence which stressed the unconscious was that of C. G. Carus' *Psyche*, discussed in my article "C. G. Carus' *Psyche* and Dostoevsky," in the *American Slavic and East European Review*, October 1955.

Freud's theory of repression and disguised reappearance, he wrote: "When waking man turns to lies, then at least uncorrupted dreams must speak the truth. . . . Materialism wanted to laugh out of existence the whole subject [of dream symbolism] as a dream of the night; but in the dream and in the night there was a terribly effective force which did not allow itself to be rejected and denied."[9] Schubert referred to the laws governing the processes of dreams as "a higher algebra which is quicker and easier than ours and knows how to reveal the poet hidden in us" and believed that "in the dream the soul seems to speak quite a different language. . . . Ideas follow a different law of association than usual. The connections between ideas take a much quicker, shorter, and more spirited course or flight than those of the waking state, in which we think more in words. In that language [of dream symbolism] we express more in a few moments through a few hieroglyphic, strangely connected images which present themselves to us in quick sequence or alongside each other or together, than we could explain in several hours by using words."

All artists of course use the symbolic language of the imagination, but there is particular appropriateness in its presence in *Crime and Punishment*. The manner and form of expression is suited to the content. In attacking rationalism, Dostoevsky did not rely solely on the weapons of his opponent, but used the whole gamut of his artistic resources, among which oblique and symbolic devices played an important part. His deft use of symbolism gives his novel added power and effectiveness.

# PHILIP RAHV

## Dostoevsky in *Crime and Punishment*†

> *When thought is closed in caves*
> *Then love shall show its roots in deepest hell*
> —WILLIAM BLAKE

Is this the type of narrative nowadays called a psycho-thriller? Yes, in a sense it is, being above all, in its author's own words, the psychological account of a crime. The crime is murder. But in itself this is in no way exceptional, for the very same crime

9. Page xvi in 1862 ed. The passage is quoted from Schubert's *Geschichte der Seele*.
† From *Partisan Review*, Vol. XXVII,

No. 3 (Summer, 1960), pp. 393–425. Reprinted by permission of the author and *Partisan Review*.

occurs in nearly all of Dostoevsky's novels. Proust once suggested grouping them together under a single comprehensive title: *The Story of a Crime*.

Where this novel differs, however, from the works following it is in the totality of its concentration on that obsessive theme. Virtually everything in the story turns on Raskolnikov's murder of the old pawnbroker and her sister Lizaveta, and it is this concentration which makes the novel so fine an example of artistic economy and structural cohesion. Free of distractions of theme and idea, and with no confusing excess or over-ingenuity in the manipulation of the plot, such as vitiates the design of *A Raw Youth* and reduces the impact of *The Idiot, Crime and Punishment* is the one novel of Dostoevsky's in which his powerful appeal to our intellectual interests is most directly and naturally linked to the action.

The superiority of this work in point of structure has been repeatedly remarked upon, but what has not been sufficiently noted is its extraordinary narrative pace. Consider the movement of Part I, for instance. In this comparatively short section (coming to eighty-four pages in Constance Garnett's translation), we get to know the protagonist fairly well, to know the conditions of crushing poverty and isolation under which he lives and the complex origins of his "loathsome scheme"; we see him going through a rehearsal-visit to the victim's flat; we listen to Marmeladov's sermon in the pothouse, to the recital of his domestic woes, including the circumstances that forced his daughter Sonya to become a prostitute; we witness the drunken old man's homecoming and the hysterical violence with which he is received by his wife; then we read with Raskolnikov the long letter from his mother, learning a good deal about his family situation; we dream with him the frightful dream, looking at once to the past and to the future, of the beating to death of the little mare; finally, after several more scenes of the strictest dramatic relevance, we are brought to a close-up of the double murder, probably the most astonishing description of its kind in fiction, and watch the murderer returning to his lodgings where, after putting back the axe under the porter's bench, he climbs the stairs to sink on his bed in blank forgetfulness.

Thus in this first section of seven chapters a huge quantity of experience is qualitatively organized, with the requisite information concerning the hero's background driven into place through a consummate use of the novelistic device of foreshortening, and with the swift narrative tempo serving precisely as the prime means of controlling and rendering credible the wild queerness of what has been recounted. For this wild queerness cannot be made to yield to explanation or extrinsic analysis. To gain our consent—to enlist, that is, our poetic faith—the author must either dramatize or perish, and for full success he must proceed with the dramatic representation at a pace producing an effect of virtual instantaneousness. To have secured this effect is a triumph of Dostoevsky's creative method—a triumph because the instantaneous is a quality of Being rather than of mind and not open to question. As the vain efforts of so many philosophers have demonstrated, Being is irreducible to the categories of explanation or interpretation.

The artistic economy, force and tempo of Part I is sustained throughout the novel. (The epilogue, in which hope and belief play havoc with the imaginative logic of the work, is something else again.) There is no wasted detail in it, none that can be shown to be functionally inoperative in advancing the action and our insight into its human agents. And it is important to observe that the attaining of this fullness and intensity of representation is conditional upon Dostoevsky's capacity to subdue the time element of the story to his creative purpose. Readers not deliberately attentive to the time-lapse of the action are surprised to learn that its entire span is only two weeks and that of Part I only three days. Actually, there is no real lapse of time in the story because we are virtually unaware of it apart from the tension of the rendered experience. Instead of time lapsing there is the concrete flow of duration contracting and expanding with the rhythm of the dramatic movement.

Least of all is it a chronological frame that time provides in this novel. As the Russian critic K. Mochulsky has so aptly remarked, its time is purely psychological, a function of human consciousness, in other words the very incarnation of Bergson's *durée réelle*.[1] And it is only in Bergsonian terms that one can do it justice. Truly, Dostoevsky succeeds here in converting time into a kind of progress of Raskolnikov's mental state, which is not actually a state but a process of incessant change eating into the future and expanding with the duration it accumulates, like a snowball growing larger as it rolls upon itself, to use Bergson's original image.

This effect is partly accomplished by the exclusion from Raskolnikov's consciousness of everything not directly pertaining to his immediate situation. From beginning to end he is in a state of crisis from which there is no diversion or escape either in memory or fantasy. The import of what he thinks, feels, and remembers is strictly functional to the present. Thus he thinks of his mother, who is involved in the action, with distinct alternations of feelings, while his dead father hardly exists for him. He belongs to the past, and so far as Raskolnikov is concerned the past is empty of affect. The one time he evokes his father's figure is in the anguished

1. *Dostoevskii: zhizn i tvorchestvo* (Paris, 1947), pp. 243 ff.

dream of the beating to death of the little mare, and his appearance in that dream is singularly passive, manifestly carrying with it no charge of emotion. This dream, enacting a tragic catharsis, is introduced with calculated ambiguity. Is the dreamer actually remembering an episode of his childhood or is he imagining the memory? In any case, though the dream is of the past its meaning is all in the present. The pitiful little mare, whipped across the eyes and butchered by Mikolka and a crowd of rowdy peasants, stands for all such victims of life's insensate cruelty, in particular such victims as Sonya and Lizaveta whose appeal to Raskolnikov is that of "poor gentle things . . . whose eyes are soft and gentle." Also, the mare stands above all for Raskolnikov himself, and in embracing her bleeding head in a frenzy of compassion it is himself he is embracing, bewailing, consoling. He is present in the dream not only as the little boy witnessing an act of intolerable brutality but as at once its perpetrator and victim too. The dream's imagery is entirely prospective in that it points ahead, anticipating the murder Raskolnikov is plotting even while exposing it as an act of self-murder. Its latent thought-content is a warning that in killing the pawnbroker he would be killing himself too, and it is indeed in this light that he understands his deed afterwards when, in confessing to Sonya, he cries out: "Did I murder the old woman? I murdered myself, not her! I crushed myself once and for all, forever." The cathartic effect of the dream is such that upon awakening he recovers the sense of his human reality, feeling "as though an abscess that had been forming in his heart had suddenly broken . . . he was free from that spell, that sorcery, that obsession." But the catharsis is momentary, and he no sooner hears that the pawnbroker will be alone in her flat the next evening than he is again gripped by his obsession.

Another instance of the functional character of Raskolnikov's memory is the way he recalls the invalid girl to whom he had once been engaged. "I really don't know," he says, "what drew me to her then . . . she was always ill. If she had been lame or hunchback, I believe I would have liked her even better." This is a meaningful admission, and it is curious that the numerous commentators on the novel should have unanimously ignored it. It is as if they all wanted to spare Sonya. For what prompts this memory if not his involvement with Sonya, who is in her own way ill too? In the eyes of the world and likewise of Raskolnikov in some of his moods she is a morally deformed creature, an outcast, and "a religious maniac" to boot. Physically too, the description of the invalid girl has much in common with that of Sonya.

Yet, for all his living in the present, Raskolnikov wills and acts with his whole past back of him; and it is for a very good reason that we are not permitted to gain a privileged understanding of his past in the sense of entering a series of his mental states anterior to the action. By denying us such intimacy the author effectively prevents us from rationalizing the mystery of the crime and its motive—the mystery which is never really solved but toward the solution of which everything in the novel converges. Now the study of Dostoevsky's manuscripts has shown that he was himself disturbed no end by the indefiniteness and uncertainty of Raskolnikov's motive, and he wrote a note reminding himself that he must once and for all clear up the uncertainty and isolate the "real" motive in order "to destroy," as he put it, "the indefiniteness and explain the murder this way or that way" (*tak ili etak*). Fortunately he was able to forget this injunction as the novel progressed. For his basic idea of his hero's motivation is such as to identify it with the totality of his consciousness, and to have changed that conception to a more conventional one would have led to the withering of that fine insight; and what that insight comes to, in the last analysis, is that human consciousness is inexhaustible and incalculable. It cannot be condensed into something so limited and specific as a motive. The consciousness is ever obliging in generating a sufficiency of reasons, but it is necessary to distinguish between reasons and motives. Not that motives have no existence; they exist, to be sure, but only on the empirical plane, materializing in the actual practice of living, primarily in the commitment of action. Existentially speaking, the acting man can be efficient and self-assured only insofar as his consciousness is non-reflective. Raskolnikov, however, is above all a man of reflection, and his crime is frequently described in the book as a "theoretical" one, "theoretical" not only in the sense of its being inspired by a theory but also in the sense that theory, that is to say abstraction, is of its very essence: no wonder he carries out the murder in the manner of a sleep-walker or of a man falling down a precipice. The textual evidence shows that what his crime mainly lacks is empirical content, and that is what some critics had in mind, I think, in defining it as a pure experiment in self-cognition. Thus it can be said of this murderer that he produces a corpse but no real motive. His consciousness, time and again recoiling upon itself in a sickening manner, consumes motives as fast as it produces them.

*Crime and Punishment* may be characterized as a psycho-thriller with prodigious complications. It is misleading, however, to speak of it as a detective story, as is so often done. It is nothing of the sort, since from the outset we know not only the murderer's identity but are also made to enter into some of his innermost secrets. True, the story is almost entirely given over to detection—not of the criminal, though, but of his motive. Inevitably it turns out that there is not one but a whole cluster of motives, a veritable *embarras de richesses* and if the criminal himself is in his own fashion constrained to take part in the work of detection it is because he is soon lost in the maze of his own motivation. Never quite certain as to what it was exactly that induced him to commit murder, he must continually spy on himself in a desperate effort to penetrate his own psychology and attain the self-knowledge he needs if he is to assume responsibility for his absurd and hideous act. And this idea of him as the criminal in search of his own motive is precisely what is so new and original in the figure of Raskolnikov.

His knowing and not knowing is in a sense the worst of his ordeal. He is aware of several motives that keep eluding him as his thought shifts among them, and there are times when they all seem equally unreal to him. To sustain himself in the terrible isolation of his guilt he must be in complete possession of a single incontrovertible motive representing his deepest self, his own rock-bottom truth. But he no sooner lays hold of this truth than he catches himself in a state of mind that belies it, as, for example, in the scene when right after burying the loot—a purse and some trinkets of jewelry—he suddenly stops in the street to confound himself with a simple and terrifying question: "If it had all really been done deliberately and not idiotically, if I really had a certain and definite object, how is it that I did not even glance into the purse and didn't know what I had there. Then why have I undergone these agonies and have deliberately undertaken this base, dirty and degrading business?" This is but one of several passages in which the abstraction—so to speak—of the crime, its lack of empirical substance, is brought home to us. There is an intrinsic incongruity between this criminal and his crime which is exhibited by the author with masterful indirection, and nowhere to better effect than when Raskolnikov makes his confession to Sonya. In the course of it, though straining as hard as he can to discover and at long last seize the motive that impelled him, he still cannot stop wavering and giving various and contradictory explanations of his act. He begins by stating that he murdered "for plunder," but when Sonya cries: "You were hungry! It was to help your mother? Yes?" he at once retracts that explanation, muttering: "No, Sonya, no . . . . I was not so hungry . . . . I certainly did want to help my mother, but that's not the real thing either . . . ." A little later he adds that if he had simply killed the old pawnbroker because of hunger he would be *happy* now, exclaiming that he really wanted to become a Napoleon and that is why he killed her. Yet still later we hear him say that the argument from Napoleon is "all nonsense" as he reverts to the explanation from poverty and simple need. Soon enough, however, he strikes again the Napoleonic note, accounting for the murder now as a matter of wanting to have the daring: "I only wanted to have the daring . . . that was the whole cause of it"; he claims that he killed "not to gain wealth and power" but for himself alone so as to find out quickly whether "he was a louse like everybody else or a man," whether he was a "trembling creature" or one who has "the right" to step over barriers. Still another cause, more immediately psychological in bearing, is introduced when he speaks of his airless cupboard of a room, that room where he turned sulky and sat "like a spider," where he would not work but simply lay for hours thinking. It is chiefly this perpetual thinking, this desperate resort to sheer reflection, which is the source of the mystifications that torment him. Though it is his consciousness which did him in it is to his empirical self that he absurdly looks for the justification it cannot supply; so that in the end, for all the keenness with which he explicates his act to Sonya, we are still left with a crime of indeterminate origin and meaning.

The indeterminacy is the point. Dostoevsky is the first novelist to have fully accepted and dramatized the principle of uncertainty or indeterminacy in the presentation of character. In terms of novelistic technique this principle manifests itself as a kind of hyperbolic suspense—suspense no longer generated merely by the traditional means and devices of fiction, though these are skillfully brought into play, but as it were by the very structure of human reality. To take this hyperbolic suspense as a literary invention pure and simple is to fail in comprehending it; it originates rather in Dostoevsky's acute awareness (self-awareness at bottom) of the problematical nature of the modern personality and of its tortuous efforts to stem the disintegration threatening it. Thus Raskolnikov, like Stavrogin and other protagonists of Dostoevsky's, is represented throughout under the aspect of modernity (the examining magistrate Porfiry Petrovich sees him very specifically as "a modern case") understood as spiritual and mental self-division and self-contradiction. It is in this light that the search for the true cause of the crime becomes ultimately intelligible, the search that gives the novel at once its form and meaning, taking us where no psycho-thriller before or after *Crime and Punishment* has even taken us, into a realm where only the sharpest psychological perception will see us through and into still another realm where our response to ideas is impetuously solicited: ideas bearing on crime and its relation to psychic illness on the one hand and to power and genius on the other; ideas about two kinds of human beings, ordinary and extraordinary, with the former serving as mere material for the latter who arrogate to themselves the right "to overstep the line" and remove moral obstacles at will; ideas concerning the supernal value of suffering and the promise of deliverance in Christ.

The principal characters (Raskolnikov, Svidrigaylov and others) are the carriers of these ideas, and if we are not to sever the unity of thought and action, theory and practice, prevailing in the Dostoevskean world, it is necessary to take their ideas for what they are, without reducing them, with the purely psychological critics, to a species of "interesting" rationalization, or, with the formalistic critics, to mere "fictive matter" drawn fortuitously from the intellectual sphere. That we must first of all regard the ideas as dramatic motivation goes without saying; but that should not deter us from also accepting them as given on the level of thought. "I killed not an old woman but a principle," declares Raskolnikov. What is that principle and why does he want to kill it? The answer to such questions has been much simplified or, worse still, credulously taken for granted.

From the Christian standpoint Raskolnikov is easily enough perceived to be a kind of Lazarus whom Sonya strives to raise from the dead. Yet if he comes forth from the tomb it is only after experiencing the ecstasy and terror of having touched for one moment the secret springs of freedom and power. "What, then, is to be done?" asks Sonya. This is indeed the fateful question which reverberates throughout the whole of Russian literature and to which all the leaders of Russian thought, from Chaadayev to Lenin, sought to provide an answer. Raskolnikov, too, accepts the challenge. "Break what must be broken," he replies, "once and for all, and take the suffering on oneself. . . . Freedom and power! Over all trembling creation and all the antheap! . . . That is the goal, remember that!" No wonder that though apparently renouncing that goal in yielding to Sonya's entreaties that he save himself through penance and submission, he nevertheless remains essentially unrepentant to the end. At the very least it can be said that he remains so deeply divided in his mind as to give himself up more because of confusion and despair than because of any real change of heart. About his regeneration we are told only in the epilogue, when at long last the pale sickly faces of the murderer and the saintly prostitute become "bright with the dawn of a new future." But this happy Siberian aftermath is the beginning of something altogether new and different. As the author observes in the last paragraph of the text, it "might be the subject of a new story but our present story is ended."[2] We, as critical readers, can-

2. It might indeed have been the subject of a new story. However, Dostoevsky, as a number of critics have noted, appears to have been incapable of carrying out his declared intention to depict the renewal of life on Christian foundations. On this score the late Leo Shestov made one of the most sardonic notations: *"Crime and Punishment* ends with the promise to picture the Christian rebirth of the hero. His words sound as if he were binding himself with a sacred vow. And, in point of fact, as a professed teacher

not overmuch concern ourselves with such intimations of ultimate reconcilement and salvation. Our proper concern is with the present story, with the story as written.

Dostoevsky wrote the first of his four great novels in monthly installments for the *Russky Vestnik*, where it ran serially between January and December, 1866. He was following his usual course of producing a long work under the immediate pressure of editors and printers. In this instance, however, he appears to have encountered very few difficulties in meeting the magazine's schedule. And the ease with which he accomplished the actual composition may have been partly due at least to the fact that the narrative mode he had adopted after considerable experimenting and much vacillation, the mode, that is, of telling the story from the standpoint of the "omniscient author," justified itself in practice, allowing him to make the most of his material without strain or hindrance.

The strain had indeed told on him in the late months of 1865, when while living in Wiesbaden he had written an incomplete draft of the novel in the form both of a diary and of a murderer's confession. Those versions turned out to be so unsatisfactory, chiefly because of the cramping effects of the method of narration in the first person, that he was forced to scrap them. The economy of interest he had been trying to enforce by means of that method proved to be too much of a good thing, and he now took exactly the opposite tack, expanding the interest where formerly he had compressed it. Into the new expansive scheme he introduced the figures of Svidrigaylov and Porfiry Petrovich, who have nothing in common besides the fact that both represent possible attitudes toward Raskolnikov, viewpoints or perspectives enabling us to see at once more clearly and more variously the significance of his case. Dostoevsky also introduced into his revised scheme the basic ele-

of humanity, was not Dostoevsky in duty bound to let us in on the secret of the new reality and fresh possibilities that opened up to Raskolnikov? Yet our preceptor never managed to fulfill that sacred vow. The same promise is encountered again in his foreword to *The Brothers Karamazov*, where we are told that in order to portray his real hero, Alyosha, he would need to write still another volume, as if the existing book with its thousand pages lacked sufficient space to accommodate the 'new life.' In the three novels he produced after *Crime and Punishment* there is no mention of the sacred vow. Prince Myshkin cannot be taken into account here. If he is the one representing the 'renewal' awaiting mankind . . . then there is no point whatever in looking toward the future. . . . No, compared to Dostoevsky's other heroes Prince Myshkin is a misfit. This novelist understood only restless, fractious, struggling people whose search is never ended. No sooner did he undertake to show us a man who has found himself and achieved tranquility than he fell into fatal banalities. One thinks, for instance, of the elder Zosima's dreams of 'the coming wonderful union of men.' What is this 'wonderful union' if not another of those idyllic pictures of the future which even the socialists —so maliciously ridiculed in his cellar by the narrator of *Notes from the Underground*—have by now learned to do without?" *Dostoevskii i Nitsshe: filosofiya tragedii* (St. Petersburg, 1903).

ments of a tale, entitled *The Drunkards*, which he had just sketched out in outline and in which he was proposing to enter into "all the ramifications" of the then rather topical subject of alcoholism rampant among the city poor, with the emphasis falling on "the picture of a family and the bringing up of children under such circumstances." It is in this somewhat fortuitous manner, or so it would seem on the face of it, that the Marmeladov sequence, so reminiscent of the author's earlier vein in its pathos of indigence and harrowing exposition of the Petersburg misery, as the Russians are wont to call it, came to be included in the account of Raskolnikov's crime.

But the fortuitousness is more apparent than real. There is an inner logic, both of content and structure, in his combination of subject matter from which the novel gains enormously—and this can be said even while conceding that the rather stagey woes of the Marmeladovs are inducive of some moments of weariness. A somewhat Dickensian family with deviations toward Russian intensity, they are of course the very embodiment of the Petersburg misery. But Raskolnikov is also a child of that misery, patently belonging to the world of the insulted and injured, though in him the humility and submissiveness of that world's human mixture are turned inside out. He is the first of its inhabitants to attempt its redemption by making a bid, in however futile and hideous a fashion, for freedom and power.

Intrinsically his figure is a composite of the typical protagonists of Dostoevsky's earlier and later fiction. Morbidly estranged as he is from life and ceaselessly brooding in his cupboard of a room, he at once brings to mind certain traits of *the* underground man as well as of the daydreaming recluse portrayed in such stories of the 1840's as *The Landlady* and *White Nights*—the recluse who, suffering from nearly pathological depression and nameless guilt-feelings, keeps to himself and lives a life of wishful fantasy. At the same time Raskolnikov represents a startling departure from the recluse type in that, having overcome the latter's masochistic need for self-abasement, his aggression is no longer turned inward but outward. He is quite as much a fantast as the daydreaming recluse, but his fantasy has left behind it all *Schwärmerei* and noble aspiration *a la* Schiller: it has taken on the color of blood. A complete egoist on one side of his nature at least and a surprisingly candid one at that, he is filled with the wrath of outraged pride and a furious impatience to break out from his trapped existence even at the risk of self-destruction. Moreover, to see him from this angle of vision, as the Dostoevskeian hero in process of evolution, is to note another new element in him, namely, that he is an intellectual *pur sang*, recklessly yielding himself to the passion of thought and caught at last in the toils of an idea, mastered by it to the point of monomania. Thus the novel of which he is the protagonist has a double aspect. In virtue of its carryover of the theme of the Petersburg misery, it brings to a close the series of so-called social narratives which, from *Poor Folk* to *The Insulted and Injured*, is dominated by a consistent motif that has been aptly defined as that of "the impotent protest of powerless people." In its second aspect, however, the novel throws off the limitations of the earlier theme, attaining the higher goals of its author's greater or ultimate period.

Raskolnikov's involvement with the Marmeladov clan enabled Dostoevsky to solve what must have been his main compositional problem: How to portray with entire cogency a hero who is a solitary and monomaniac acting throughout in a mood of "morbid irritability" verging on madness without succumbing to him, that is to say, without letting him take the lead to the degree of making the world over in his image? This is but another way of formulating one of the principal difficulties which forced Dostoevsky to abandon the first versions of the book. For to have permitted Raskolnikov, as first-person narrator, to absorb the story unto himself would surely have resulted in its impoverishment, producing an impression of life closing in, a claustrophobic effect diminishing the hero's stature in our eyes and turning him into an altogether special case.[3] And this is where the Marmeladovs come in exactly, that for all the grimness of their situation and its grotesque features they still somehow exist within the bounds of the normal, whereas Raskolnikov is decidedly outside it; hence their presence adds considerably to the story's quota of circumstantial realism, helping to overcome the hazard implicit in Raskolnikov's malaise. For we must keep in mind that his story, which on one side is an account of a crime open to explanation on the seemingly objective grounds of material need and a sinister "nihilistic" theory, is converted on the subjective side into an analysis of an extreme pathological condition or soul-sickness, if you will.

The episodes dealing with Svidrigaylov, the would-be seducer of Raskolnikov's sister Dunya, have an engrossing interest of their own, but they also serve the same functional purpose of reducing the protagonist's remoteness from the common human measure. In order to heighten the dramatic tension and explore to the end the complex meanings of Raskolnikov's plight, it was positively necessary to involve him in intimate human associations, notwith-

3. The special or clinical case is precisely what no master of the narrative medium will let himself in for. Dostoevsky did let himself in for it once, in the early *nouvelle, The Double*, which, for all its startling effects, cannot be rated otherwise than as a failure. He never repeated that youthful error. In lesser talents, however, this error becomes habitual, for in coping with the extremes of morbidity or irrationality they are frequently lured into betraying the shared sense of human reality.

standing the feeling of absolute aloneness, or "agonizing, everlasting solitude," into which he is plunged by his murderous act. It is a feeling brought on by the guilt he refuses to acknowledge and strains every nerve to repress; and what better way was there of dramatizing the struggle within him between guilt and scornful pride than by showing him entering almost in spite of himself into relations with people who for reasons both good and bad are intent on penetrating his isolation? Sonya, his "chosen bride" and Christian mentor, is of course the chief agent of this turn of the plot, but so in his own paradoxical fashion is Svidrigailov. The latter, however, is so fascinating a character in his own right, exercising an appeal nearly matching that of the hero, that at times he threatens to run away with the story; certainly the scene of his suicide and of the dream-haunted night that precedes it are perfectly realized incidents and among the marvels of the book. It must have called for the nicest management on the author's part to hold him to his subordinate position. But that was only part of the task Dostoevsky set himself in undertaking to unify the three thematic elements at his disposal: the major theme of Raskolnikov's crime and its consequences and the strongly contrasted minor themes of the lowly and good Marmeladovs on the one hand and of the wealthy immoralist Svidrigaylov on the other. And it is the achieved integration with its fine contrapuntal effects which makes for verisimilitude of a higher order, for novelistic truth and density, and for structural cohesion.

But though the Svidrigaylov sequence is successfully integrated into the main action, there is no denying that he is invested with an originality and expressive power that invite comment. It will not do to see him, in the fashion of most critics of Dostoevsky, as being merely Raskolnikov's double, representing the pole of self-will in his character. The formal abstractness of this traditional approach to Svidrigaylov cannot do him justice; and so far as the element of self-will is concerned, Raskolnikov, like all "the children of darkness" in Dostoevsky, has more than enough of it in himself and is in no need of Svidrigaylov's services. No, the latter has an independent existence in the novel though his position in it is structurally subordinate; his function is not simply that of ministering to its hero. There is no innate relationship between the two, no affinity of the mystical order such as is posited in so many Dostoevsky studies. Actually Svidrigaylov enters the novel by way of the external plot or intrigue (his pursuit of Dunya), yet once he is in it he provides the story not only with an additional perspective on Raskolnikov but also with the psychosexual vitality which it otherwise lacks, for both Raskolnikov and Sonya are singularly sexless. Svidrigaylov exemplifies a distinct character-type in

Dostoevsky, the type of the nihilist in the realm of sensuality. He is a more elaborate and refined version of the rather coarse-grained libertine Valkovsky in *The Insulted and Injured* and he anticipates the figures of Stavrogin and the elder Karamazov in the later novels (like Stavrogin he is guilty of outraging a little girl). In this character-type, sensuality becomes a flight from the vertiginous consciousness of freedom and from a kind of ennui which has gone beyond the psychological and has acquired a metaphysical status. Thus Svidrigaylov believes in ghosts who "are as it were shreds and fragments of other worlds" and who appear only to people whose psyche is prepared to receive them. He rejects all dogma, including that of the atheists, as he is given to relativizing all possible ideas, whether of belief or unbelief. Whereas Raskolnikov does not believe in a future life, Svidrigaylov speculates that perhaps the future life does exist but that there are only "spiders there or something of that sort." "We always imagine eternity as something beyond our conception, something vast, vast! But why must it be vast? Instead of all that, what if it is one little room, like a bathhouse in the country, black and grimy and spiders in every corner, and that's all eternity is?" As for vice, he chides Raskolnikov for his moral prejudices, contending that in sexual vice "there is at least something permanent, founded indeed upon nature and not dependent on fantasy, something present in the blood like an ever-burning ember, forever setting one on fire and maybe not to be quickly extinguished even with years. You agree that it's an occupation of a sort." Admitting that it is a disease, like everything that exceeds moderation, he defends his indulgence in it by claiming that to give it up would mean that he would be forced to shoot himself. Clearly, his métier is not the simple-minded villainy of melodrama but a species of objective cruelty (as in his doing away with his wife and driving his footman to suicide) which is in a sense a form of meditation upon life beyond good and evil translated into practice. Therefore he is at the same time capable of acts of sympathy and kindness, as when he helps the Marmeladov orphans and lets Dunya go after cornering her. Good and evil are never ends to him but simply the available, even if sometimes redundant, means of convincing himself that it is possible to continue living. Hence the actions he performs strike one as transpiring somewhere outside himself, for they are at bottom experiments conducted by a self which is itself an experimental projection.

It has been observed often enough that every literary artist genuinely an innovator creates his own audience. This is certainly true of Dostoevsky, in whose sphere we have now learned to move without undue strain but who shocked his contemporaries by his open and bold reliance on melodrama and by the seeming fantasticality of his characters. The Russian reader had learned by that time to identify the unhurried, equable, lifelike realism of writers like Turgenev, Goncharov and Tolstoy with the higher norms of the novel; and what those writers scrupulously avoided above all was the sensational and excessive. Dostoevsky was hard put to it to persuade the reader that he too, despite his startling deviations from the newly-established norms, was a realist. Hence while writing *Crime and Punishment* he fretted over the thought that his story would gain no credence from the public; and since he had long been trying to defend himself against the charge of insufficient regard for the real, he was pleased to note, shortly after the appearance of the first installment of the novel, that a crime curiously similar to the one he was describing had been committed by a Moscow student and reported in the newspapers. He at once seized upon this item as confirming his own "special view" of the relation between art and actuality. "What the majority call fantastic and exceptional," he wrote to the critic Strakhov, "sometimes signifies to me the very essence of reality. . . . In every issue of the newspapers you come upon accounts of the most real facts and amazing coincidences. For our writers, who are unconcerned with them, they are fantastic. But being facts they are reality none the less."

But this appeal to actual life—formless, disorderly and inconsequent life with its "most real facts and amazing coincidences"—is unworthy of the genius of Dostoevsky. In spite of his opposition to such radical-minded simplifiers of the relation of art and life as Chernyshevsky, Dobrolyubov and Pisarev, critics exceedingly influential in their time, he was himself far from immune to the idea then prevailing in his intellectual milieu that the work of art was useless and perhaps even immoral in its inutility unless directly validated by life or "reality," understood in the simplest empirical sense of these terms. Dostoevsky was after all a Russian writer of his generation, a generation ideologically inspired to exalt life over art and seeking to justify the latter by citing the gifts of illumination and hopes of betterment it ostensibly brings to life. Where Dostoevsky twisted that common assumption to suit his creative practice was by claiming to discern the essence of reality not in its typical everyday manifestations but in the exceptional and fantastic. He was unable to go beyond that formula toward the assertion of a symbolic rather than literal correspondence between life and the fictive worlds of his own devising. Hence the speciousness of his argument from life in his literary apologetics, as in his pointing to life's "amazing coincidences" in the letter to Strakhov quoted above. The fact is that no coincidence copied from life can make in the least plausible the kind of coincidences, even the minor ones, you find in *Crime and Punishment*, such as the prosperous and respectable bourgeois Luzhin turning up in the same slum-lodging with the starving Marmeladov family or Svidrigaylov, a rich man, finding no better place to stay in Petersburg than in the very same house where Sonya lives, a house in which his flat adjoins the room where she practices her trade and conducts those incredible conversations with Raskolnikov upon which he eavesdrops with the greatest relish. It is plain that Svidrigaylov is situated where he is in order to make it possible for him to learn Raskolnikov's secret at the same time as he confides it to Sonya; an important turn of the plot depends on it. This is a calculated coincidence different in kind from those, however improbable, that life offers. It belongs to the stock-in-trade of melodrama, and Dostoevsky learned the use of it in his assiduous reading of Hoffmann, Dickens, Balzac, Sue, and a host of lesser authors of crime-thrillers and adventure stories.

It is in literature rather than in unprocessed life that you find some of the sources of this novel, including its major plot-element of a murder committed by someone who stands in no personal relation to the victim. Also, the Napoleon motif, on which so many changes are rung by Dostoevsky, is clearly transposed by him to a Petersburg setting from mid-nineteenth-century French fiction, Balzac and Stendhal in particular, both of whom glorified Napoleon (the former covertly and the latter overtly) and justified their ambitious plebeian heroes by appealing to his illustrious example. Thus Raskolnikov may be seen as a Russian version of Julien Sorel and Eugène de Rastignac—the young man on the make who comes to the capital from the provinces intent on a career and a conquest. It is especially Balzac's *Le Père Goriot* that suggests an influence in the design of Raskolnikov's story. In his essay on Dostoevsky[4] Georg Lukács mentions the anecdote of the Chinese mandarin in Balzac's novel as containing the hint that the Russian writer might have developed. The relevant passage is worth citing in full. It occurs in a dialogue between Rastignac and his friend the medical student Bianchon:

> "What makes you look so serious?" asked the medical student, taking his arm [Rastignac's] to walk up and down in front of the palace with him.
> "I am bothered by troublesome thoughts."
> "Of what kind are they? You know that thoughts can be cured."
> "How?"
> "By yielding to them."
> "You are laughing at me, without knowing what I mean. Have

4. *Der russische Realismus in der Weltliteratur* (Berlin, 1949), p. 178.

you read Rousseau?"

"Do you remember the place where he asks the reader what he would do, if he could become rich by killing an old mandarin in China, by the sole act of his will, without stirring from Paris?"

"Yes."

"Well?"

"Pooh! I have already come to my thirty-third mandarin."

"Don't joke. Come, suppose you knew it were possible, and that a nod from you would do it, should you consent?"

"Is he a very old mandarin? But young or old, sick or well, my goodness—the deuce. No, I shouldn't."

And Bianchon concludes his argument in favor of sparing the Chinaman by warning Rastignac against a rash solution of the problem posed at "the entrance of life," against the attempt to cut that Gordian knot with his sword. "If you mean to act thus," he says, "you must be an Alexander or else you will be sent to the gallows." Unlike Rastignac, however, Dostoevsky's hero confides in no one and sets out to cut the Gordian knot without in the least resembling an Alexander or a Napoleon, though hoping that his crime might possibly prove him to belong to their superior breed.

It seems to me, too, that Dostoevsky drew on *Le Père Goriot* for far more than the germinal anecdote of the Chinese mandarin. Svidrigaylov's posture vis-à-vis Raskolnikov is in certain respects strongly reminiscent of Vautrin's relation to Rastignac in Balzac's novel. We know that Svidrigaylov is missing from the early drafts of *Crime and Punishment*, and it is not improbable that when it came to composing the final version Dostoevsky decided to introduce a character playing Vautrin to his own Rastignac. Consider that both Vautrin and Svidrigaylov are older men who assume the role of mentors in the ways of the world, that both have insinuating manners and appear cheerful and obliging when it suits them, that both are sexual deviants (the Frenchman is a homosexual and the Russian has very special tastes in underage girls), and that both are predatory types who make no secret of their immorality. Moreover, some of the ideas that Vautrin communicates to Rastignac turn up in Raskolnikov's thought virtually without modification, as if he had absorbed the lesson addressed to his French prototype. Vautrin declares, for instance, that there are but two courses open to a man, blind obedience or open revolt, and that he can make his way in the world either "by the splendor of genius or the adroitness of corruption. He must burst like a cannonball into the ranks of his fellow-men, or he must move among them like the pestilence. Honesty is of no use. Men yield to the power of genius; they hate and calumniate it . . . but they yield to it if it persists, and kneel to it when they find that they cannot suppress it." There is a remarkable parallel between this formulation and Raskolnikov's view, passionately expounded to Sonya, that "whoever is strong in mind and spirit will have power over men. Anyone who is greatly daring is right in their eyes. . . . I divined that power is only vouchsafed to the man who dares to stoop and pick it up. There is only one thing, one thing needful: one has only to dare." Clearly, Vautrin's genius who bursts like a cannon-ball among his fellow-men bears an uncommon resemblance to Raskolnikov's criminal of genius who dares assert the right inherent in his superiority and whose criminality is soon forgiven or forgotten as he becomes a lawgiver and leader among men. However, in constructing Raskolnikov's theory of the relation between power and genius, Dostoevsky borrowed from more than one source; Balzac is but one of them.

It is possible to speak if not of a school then surely of a Petersburgian genre in Russian literature, of which Dostoevsky is in fact the leading practitioner. Pushkin's *The Bronze Horseman* is doubtless the outstanding poem of that genre, as Gogol's "The Overcoat" is the outstanding story and *Crime and Punishment* the outstanding novel. One must be aware of its author's profound response to Petersburg and of the masterly way in which he appropriated it to imaginative purposes in order to perceive that as the scene of Raskolnikov's crime the city is one of the essential constituents of the story, more foreground than background, a unique urban setting charged with multiple meanings, of which one of the more urgent emerges from Dostoevsky's preoccupation with the Petersburg misery and his depiction of it in a manner demonstrating his solidarity with its victims. As a novelist of the modern metropolis he was of course in the line of Balzac and Dickens, by whom he was greatly influenced, though there is a marked difference in his representation of the city and theirs. Balzac's Paris, as Arnold Hauser has remarked, is still a romantic wilderness, "a theatrical setting painted in chiaroscuro contrasts, a fairyland in which dazzling riches and picturesque poverty live side by side,"[5] whereas Dostoevsky describes the metropolis in somber colors, taking us into its reeking taverns and coffin-like rooms, bringing to the fore its petty-bourgeois and proletarian types, its small shopkeepers and clerks, students, prostitutes, beggars and derelicts. True as this is, there is also something else in Dostoevsky's vision of Petersburg, a sense not so much of romance as of poetic strangeness, a poetic emotion attached to objects in themselves desolate, a kind of exaltation in the very lostness, loneliness and drabness which the big city imposes on its inhabitants, as is so poignantly brought out in the

5. *The Social History of Art* (New York: Alfred A. Knopf, Inc., 1952), Vol. 2, p. 854.

scene when in an evening hour Raskolnikov stops on a street corner to listen to a sentimental song ground out on a barrel-organ and sung by a girl in a cracked and coarsened voice:

> "Do you like street music?" said Raskolnikov, addressing a middle-aged man standing idly by him. The man looked at him, startled and wondering.
> "I love to hear singing to a street organ," said Raskolnikov, and his manner seemed strangely out of keeping with the subject. "I like it on cold, dark, damp evenings—they must be damp —when all the passers-by have pale green, sickly faces, or better still when the wet snow is falling straight down, where there's no wind—you know what I mean? and the street lamps shining through it. . . ."
> "I don't know. . . . Excuse me. . . ." muttered the stranger, frightened by the question and Raskolnikov's strange manner. . . .

Catching Raskolnikov talking to himself on the street, Svidrigailov says to him: "This is a town of crazy people. . . . There are few places where there are so many gloomy, queer influences on the soul of man as in Petersburg." There is indeed something peculiarly Petersburgian about Raskolnikov, and not merely in the sense that he belongs to its "proletariat of undergraduates." The crime he commits—in the idea of it, namely, which is so strange an amalgam of the abstract and artificial with the sheerly fantastic —corresponds intrinsically to the character of this city, frequently described in exactly such terms.[6] It is in the heat and stench of its slums, as he wanders endlessly through the streets, that Raskolnikov spawns his idea, which he himself likens to "a spell, a sorcery, an obsession." And afterwards, having carried his idea to its terrible conclusion, though not at all in the bravura manner of a Napoleon but rather like a man deprived of reason and will

6. The ambiguity of Petersburg in its odd blending of the real and the unreal is what Dostoevsky tried mainly to capture. *A Raw Youth* there is an especially suggestive passage in which young Arkady speaks of a Petersburg morning as being at the same time infinitely prosaic and infinitely fantastic: "On such a wild Petersburg morning, foul, damp and foggy, the wild dream of some Hermann out of Pushkin's 'Queen of Spades' (a colossal figure, an extraordinary and regular Petersburg type . . . the type of the Petersburg period) might, I believe, strike one as a piece of solid reality. A hundred times over, in such a fog, I have been haunted by a strange and persistent fancy: 'What if this fog should part and float away? Would not all this rotten and slimy town go with it, rise up with the fog, and vanish like smoke, and the old Finnish marsh be left as before and in the midst of it, perhaps, to complete the picture, a bronze horseman on a painting, over-driven steed?'"

The bronze horseman is Falconet's statue of Peter the Great, but implicitly the reference is of course to Pushkin's famous poem of that title. Hermann is the protagonist of Pushkin's story "The Queen of Spades," in whom some scholars have discerned an early model of Raskolnikov. For like Dostoevsky's hero, Hermann is under the spell of Napoleon and he too, daring all on one throw, kills an old woman in an attempt to wrest from her the secret that will make his fortune. What the two characters share, basically, is the Petersburgian power-urge combined with the peculiar Petersburgian dreaminess.

power by mental illness, on the very next day he resumes his wanderings about the city in a state more often than not bordering on delirium.

St. Petersburg was far more the capital of the Russian empire than of the Russian land. It was erected on the Finnish marshland with cruel haste and at the cost of many lives by the edict of Peter the Great, who undertook, with the savage rationality typical of belated and alien converts to progress, to transform his backward domain all at once into an efficient state militarized along modern lines. The self-will and precipitate style of this operation brought into being a city without roots in the past or in the vast rural hinterland, the center of alienation and of everything novel and foreign violating the national traditions and the patriarchal mode of life. It was in Petersburg that in a fashion peculiar to it the imperial bureaucracy exerted itself to westernize the country from above while the turbulent and seditious "proletariat of undergraduates," impelled by other motives and a nobler vision, strove to effect the same end from below. Thus the material brutality of the caste pressing down upon society from the top met its counterpart in the tragic spiritual brutality of the dissident intelligentsia forcing the issue lower down.

No wonder the Slavophils hated Petersburg. Khomyakov, a leading ideologue of their faction, spoke of it as a city of dead beauty, where "all is stone, not only the houses but the trees and inhabitants as well." The Marquis de Custine, visiting the capital in 1839, could not believe that it would endure. "I have seen no place that is more penetrated with the instability of human beings," he wrote. Penetrated with the instability of human beings—a marvelously apt phrase which we can apply to the Dostoevskean world as a whole with but a slight shift of context. You will find this singular instability in Raskolnikov, to be sure, but you will also find in him more than a trace of that savage rationality characterizing the champions of the Petersburg period in Russian history and subsequently the revolutionary elite. He emerges from that "literate world of reckless youth," as Bakunin called it, in which the latter professed to see the hope of the revolution, and he is the epitome of those traits of which Alexander Herzen gave an account of incomparable precision in his *Memoirs.* "We are greatly given," he noted, "to theoretical pedantry and argumentativeness. This German propensity is in us associated with a special national element—which we might call the Araktcheyev[7] element—a ruthlessness, a passionate rigidity, and an eagerness to dispatch their victims.

7. Alexis Araktcheyev (1769–1834), a high official and trusted adviser of Alexander I in the closing years of his reign, put into effect such inordinately cruel administrative practices as to give rise to the dread term *Araktcheyev-china.*

To satisfy his grenadier ideal, Araktcheyev flogged living peasants to death; we flog to death ideas, arts, humanity, past leaders, anything you like. In dauntless array we advance step by step to the limit and overshoot it, never sinning against logic but only against *truth*; unaware, we go on further and further, forgetting that real sense and real understanding of life are shown precisely in stepping short before the extreme. . . ."

In truth Raskolnikov is one of those young men whose coming was foreshadowed with fear by Joseph de Maistre, the author of *Soirées de St. Pétersburg*, when he observed, in discussing the peasant uprisings of the eighteenth century, headed by such leaders as Emelian Pugachev, an obscure and illiterate Cossack, that if another such revolt ever took place in Russia it would be headed by a Pugachev "armed with a university degree." But the hour of the university Pugachevs had not quite struck when Raskolnikov set out entirely on his own, cut off from any social effort or collective historical action, to remove "certain obstacles." Proclaiming the necessity of breaking once and for all what must be broken, in other words, of killing not simply an old woman but the principle of authority bolstered by the moral law, he yet proceeds to commit not an act of political terror but another crime altogether that inevitably stamps him as no more than a common criminal, a criminal from egoism. He is a dissenter and rebel (*raskol*, the word from which his name derives, means *schism* or *dissent*), in essence the type of revolutionary terrorist of that period, whose act of terror is somehow displaced unto a private object. The terrorist is a political criminal, and if he is to be vindicated at all it is by an appeal to historical necessity; no such appeal is open to Raskolnikov.

Of course he has at his disposal a theory justifying his crime, and I have already indicated one source of it in Balzac. Another and more important source, to my mind, is Hegel's concept of the historic hero (the agent of the World-Spirit) and his victims. The enormous influence of the Hegelian philosophy in Russia during the late 1830's and the 1840's is well known; the period of this influence coincides with Dostoevsky's youth and it would have been impossible for him to escape it. But that he was in fact concerned with it is shown, moreover, by his letter (of February 22, 1854) from Siberia to his brother Mikhail asking that he send him, among other books, Hegel's *Philosophy of History*.[8] It is strange that this source, far from esoteric, should have been overlooked. I imagine that scholars and critics have been so carried away by the apparent analogy between Raskolnikov (in his theory of

8. "Send me the Koran, and Kant's *Critique of Pure Reason*, and if you have the chance of sending me anything not officially, then be sure to send Hegel, particularly Hegel's *Philosophy of History*. Upon that depends my whole future."

himself, that is) and Nietzsche's Superman as to have missed a more substantial likeness, though one which is more in the nature of a caricature than an exact replica. It is only in the vulgarized popular version of the Superman that Raskolnikov's theory reminds us of him; so far as Nietzsche's actual idea of the Superman goes, as a product of a mutation of the human species, there is no resemblance. It is in Hegel rather that we discover a direct and obvious source of Raskolnikov's notion of inferior and superior men, the superior ones having the right to commit breaches of morality while inferiors are obliged to mind their business, which is to stay put in the common rut. Now what Dostoevsky has done in devising Raskolnikov's justification is to convert into a theory of human nature what is in Hegel not a psychological theory at all but a theory of men as subjects and objects of history. Hegel's world-historical individual—such as Alexander or Caesar or Napoleon, the very names invoked by Dostoevsky's protagonist—performs the grandiose tasks set for him by the *Weltgeist* irrespective of moral considerations; he can do no other, for, as Hegel puts it, "the history of the world moves on a higher level than that of morality." These heroes may "treat other great and even sacred interests inconsiderately—a conduct which subjects them to moral reprehension. But so mighty a figure may trample down many an innocent flower, crush to pieces many things in its path." Thus as the subject of history he rides roughshod over its mere objects or victims. Dostoevsky gives us a parody-version of Hegel's theory of two types of men by abstracting it from its historical logic. This enables him to entangle Raskolnikov in what is in truth a comedy of mistaken identity: an obvious victim of the historical process—a small man in search of personal security and happiness—laughably taking himself for its hero. In this sense he is no better than a clown, and he does indeed laugh at himself from time to time. "One sudden idea made him laugh. Napoleon, the pyramids, Waterloo, and a wretched skinny old woman, a pawnbroker with a red trunk under her bed. . . . It's too inartistic. A Napoleon creep under the old woman's bed! Ugh, how loathsome!"

However, though Raskolnikov refuses the historical action of the political rebel, and, instead of throwing a bomb at a general or even the Czar himself, crushes the skull of an old woman with an axe, there is still something in his deed, for all its weird abjectness and ugliness, which in some sense comes through to us as a protest against the Petersburg misery and the ethics justifying it. One cannot but agree with Alberto Moravia's statement in his essay "The Marx-Dostoevsky Duel" that though "Raskolnikov had not read Marx and regards himself as a superman beyond good and evil, he was already, in embryo, a people's commissar."[9] Moravia is one of the very few Western commentators on the novel who has not overlooked its aborted political meaning, which emerges again and again, as when Raskolnikov dissociates himself from his friend Razumikhin's abuse of the socialists. He understands very well that rebellion can take another form, the collective form advocated by the socialists. After all, what the socialists want, he remarks to himself, is the happiness of all. As it happens, however, he is not the one "to put his little brick into the happiness of all," for what he wants is to live properly here and now. Into his manuscript Dostoevsky inserted the following passage (later deleted) into a speech of Raskolnikov's: "What care I what will come to pass in the future? Is it possible to live at present? I cannot pass by with indifference all these horrors, this suffering and misery. I want power." Power for what purpose? Presumably to do good, to alleviate the suffering and misery. He is in a state of fatal self-contradiction, however, in that he attempts to further a common end of an altruistic character with egoistical and purely private means. In order to test his strength he needs more than anything else the support of a social faith. This is plainly seen by the examining magistrate, Porfiry Petrovich, who is the one figure in the story who can be said manifestly to speak for the author, and it is he who says to Raskolnikov: "You made up a theory and then were ashamed that it broke down and turned out to be not at all original! It turned out something base, that's true, but you are not hopelessly base! . . . How do I regard you? I regard you as one of those men who would stand and smile at their torturer while he cuts their entrails out, if only they have found faith or God." It is significant that the phrase is "faith or God," not faith in God, as if to say that there are other faiths besides the traditional one.

That Raskolnikov stands in an inauthentic relation to his crime is thus confirmed by the author's spokesman in the novel. The crime does not truly belong to him, and that is the reason he affects us as being almost ludicrously inadequate to his deed, as when he faints in the police station the day right after the murder, even though there is as yet no suspicion attached to him, and calls attention to himself in other ways too. In spite of all his protestations to the contrary, he is prostrate with guilt and the yearning for punishment. It is not that he lacks the strength to kill and bear the responsibility for it to the end, but that he killed for himself alone, deranged by unconscious urges and over-conscious theories, rather than for the common cause to which his "nihilistic" generation was dedicated; and that is also the secret of Sonya's hold

9. *Encounter*, November 1956.

on him. There is no social substance in his anarchic individualism, as there is none in Sonya's idea of Christian salvation.

Sonya, "the eternal victim so long as the world lasts," is a small thin girl of eighteen, every feature of whose face reflects "a sort of insatiable compassion." Raskolnikov turns to her in his need because, as he tells her: "We are both accursed, so let us go together." She is the very embodiment of meekness and humility (far more so than Myshkin or Alyosha), and only Dostoevsky, with his uncanny powers of representation, could have brought her to life without blundering into mawkish sentimentality. But though he so brilliantly persuades us of her reality as a novelistic creation, this in itself in no sense constitutes a "proof" of her idea of Christian salvation. She proves quite as much the Nietzschean negation of it. It appears to me that it is precisely in his characterization of Sonya, rather than of Raskolnikov, that Dostoevsky's insight coincides with that of Nietzsche; the fact that the Russian arrives at that insight by way of assent, and the German by way of dissent, is scarcely to the point here. Thus Nietzsche speaks in his *Antichrist* of "that queer and sick world into which the Gospels introduce us—as in a Russian novel, a world into which the scum of society, nervous disorders, and 'childlike' idiocy seem to be having a rendezvous." Sonya is truly an inhabitant of that world, and she has the stirring charm of the mixture it exhibits—"a mixture of the sublime, the sickly and the childlike." Nowhere in literature do we find so striking a confirmation of Nietzsche's idea of the evangelical type as in the figure of Sonya. What is that type? It is one in whom "the incapacity for resistance becomes morality," who experiences "any resistance, even any compulsion to resist, as unendurable *displeasure* . . . and finds blessedness (pleasure) only in no longer offering any resistance to anybody, neither to evil nor to him who is evil—love as the only, as the *last* possible way of life." Significantly, Sonya's faith is not one that has been attained through struggle. When Raskolnikov challenges her faith, she answers with simple pathos: "What should I be without God?" This is the kind of faith which, as Nietzsche said, "has been there from the beginning; it is as it were an infantilism that has receded into the spiritual."[10] Plainly, Sonya's faith is of a sort that offers no solution to Raskolnikov, whose spiritual existence is incommensurable with hers. No wonder that the epilogue to the novel, in which he finally seems to be preparing himself to accept her outlook, has struck many readers as implausible and out of key with the work as a whole.

A few weeks after Dostoevsky's death in January 1881, a ter-

---

10. *The Portable Nietzsche,* edited by Walter Kaufman (New York: The Viking Press, Inc., 1954), pp. 602 ff.

rorist of the People s Will party by the name of Andrey Zhelyabov took part in the successful attempt on the life of Alexander II. He was caught and brought to trial, and this is what he had to say to the court: "I was baptized in the Orthodox Church but I reject Christianity, although I acknowledge the essential teaching of Jesus Christ. This essential teaching occupied an honored place among my moral incentives. I believe in the truth and righteousness of that teaching and I solemnly declare that faith without works is dead and that every true Christian ought to fight for the truth and for the rights of the oppressed and the weak, and even, if need be, to suffer for them. Such is my creed." Evidently the blood he shed did not weigh on Zhelyabov's conscience, for he went to his death on the gallows calm and impenitent. Raskolnikov, cheated of Zhelyabov's fate, goes to a Siberian prison in the same state of perplexity and outrage with which he undertook to carry out his "loathsome scheme." But, then, it was a hideous old harpy he killed, not the Czar of all the Russias.

Whatever the manifest theme of the novel, its latent theme is not that of crime as such or the criminal's innate need of punishment but the right to violent rebellion. It was the violence that Dostoevsky condemned, even as he was secretly drawn to it, fearing that if let loose it would tear down the authority both of heaven and earth, and Raskolnikov goes down to defeat to prove his creator right.

In its aspect as a polemic against the radical generation of the 1860's—whose obscurantist rationalism and notion of enlightened self-interest as the motive-force of human conduct Dostoevsky began satirizing in Notes from the Underground—the novel depends on the sleight-of-hand of substituting a meaningless crime for a meaningful one. But if that were all, Crime and Punishment would not be the masterpiece it undoubtedly is. The very substitution of one type of crime for another set problems for Dostoevsky which he solved brilliantly by plunging his hero into a condition of pathology which ostensibly has nothing to do with the "heroic" theory by means of which he justifies himself. In his article "On Crime" Raskolnikov wrote that the perpetration of a crime is always accompanied by illness, and that is an exact description of his own case, though he believes himself to be another kind of criminal altogether, one acting from rational calculation and in the interests of a higher idea; the irony of his self-deception is among the finest effects of the book. And it is astonishing how well Dostoevsky was able to preserve the unity of his protagonist's character, to present him as all of a piece in spite of the fact that we are dealing not with one but with several Raskolnikovs. There is Raskolnikov the altruist and there is Raskolnikov the egoist, "a despot by nature"; there is the crypto-revolutionary Raskolnikov and there is the self-styled genius who demands power as his right and as the guaranty of his freedom; then of course there is the neurotic who acts out his illness through a murder intellectually rationalized but inexplicable except in terms of an unconscious drive. After all, he conceives an "insurmountable repulsion" to Alyona Ivanovna, the old moneylender, weeks before he elaborates his murderous plan. Dostoevsky confronted the hazard of these contradictions with unequalled mastery. His capacity to combine them creatively in a single brain and a single psyche, while staving off the danger of incoherence at one end and of specious reconciliation at the other, is the measure of the victory scored in this novel by the imaginative artist in him over the ruthless polemicist.

# JOSEPH FRANK

## The World of Raskolnikov†

Most Western criticism of Dostoevsky, when it is not searching his work for religious sustenance, approaches him from a psychological or biographical point of view. The overwhelming and immediate impression made by Dostoevsky's works on first reading is that of a passionate exploration of abnormal states of divided consciousness; and it has been only natural to assume that so masterly a portrayal of internal psychological conflict could only come from direct experience. Hence Dostoevsky's biography has been endlessly explored, analysed, and speculated about in the hope of uncovering some traumatic key to his creations.

Russian criticism since the Bolshevik Revolution has, of course, taken a different tack. It has tried to interpret him either in socio-psychological terms (he is a member of the "dispossessed and root-less petty-bourgeois intelligentsia," whose characters reflect all the abnormalities of this class), or it has engaged in genuine historical investigation and turned up numerous interesting relations between Dostoevsky's novels and the cultural history of his time. (In fairness, I should also mention the excellent stylistic researches of such critics as Leonid Grossman,[1] Yuri Tynyanov, and V. V. Vinogra-

---

† From *Encounter*, June 1966, pp. 30–35. Reprinted by permission of the author and *Encounter*. 1. See the passages from Grossman's essay, pp. 618–24 [*Editor*].

dov, which form the basis for our contemporary understanding of Dostoevsky's art.) Since Dostoevsky, however, is still the most brilliant and devastating opponent of the men who provide the foundations for present Soviet culture—not Marx and Engels, but the Russian radical tradition of Belinsky and Chernyshevsky—Soviet historical study of Dostoevsky is inevitably handicapped in scope and myopic in interpretation.

Without accepting the theoretical premises of the Soviet approach to Dostoevsky, I believe, nonetheless, that the Russians are right in stressing the social and cultural dimensions of his work. For the exclusive Western emphasis on psychology and personal biography as a means of access to Dostoevsky's mind and art is unquestionably very limiting and very falsifying. I should probably argue the same in the case of any writer; but since my subject at the moment is not critical method, I shall only say that, of all the great modern writers, this type of biographical criticism seems to me *least* illuminating as regards Dostoevsky.

If Dostoevsky has one claim to fame, it is certainly as a great *ideological* novelist—perhaps not the greatest, for that would involve comparisons with Sterne and Cervantes, but at least the greatest in the 19th century. And if his status as such is so generally accepted, it must be because his creative imagination was stimulated primarily by the problems of his society and his time rather than by his personal problems and private dilemmas. Or, to put the point the other way round, he was always able to project these private dilemmas in terms that linked up with the sharp conflict of attitudes and values occurring in the Russia of his time.

This is the reason why psychology in Dostoevsky's novels, vivid and unforgettable though it may be, is invariably only an instrument or tool used for a thematic purpose that is ultimately moral-ethical and ideological in import—ideological in the sense that all moral values are connected in Dostoevsky's sensibility with the future destiny of Russian life and culture. More particularly, he saw all moral and ethical issues in the light of the inner psychological problems posed for the Russian intelligentsia by the necessity of assimilating (and living by) alien Western European ideas. Dostoevsky's extensive journalism of the early 1860s (most of which has not yet been translated) or, more accessibly, his travel-articles about Europe, *Winter Notes on Summer Impressions* (1863), contain a whole history of Russian culture conceived in terms of this inner struggle. We cannot take even the first step towards understanding his major aim as a novelist, if we do not realise that he wished to portray the *new* types and modalities of this perennial Russian inner struggle springing up all around him in the turbulent and evolving Russia of the 1860s and 1870s.

It is from this point of view that we must take very seriously Dostoevsky's claim to "realism" for his novels—a claim which, in my opinion, is entirely justified. But let us be clear about the nature of this "realism" and the nature of Dostoevsky's imagination. He knew very well that he was not a "realist" in the sense of getting the normal, middle range of private and social experience on the page. This was why he spoke of his bent for "fantastic realism"; but what he meant by this term was something very clear and very specific. He meant that the process of his creation would invariably start from some doctrine that he found prevalent among the Russian radical intelligentsia. It was there in black-and-white in the magazines or novels everybody was reading, and in this sense was perfectly "real"—particularly since Dostoevsky believed in the reality of ideas. But then he would take this doctrine and imagine its most extreme consequences *if* it were really to be put into practice and carried through in all its implications; and this was where his psychological gifts came in to aid him in dramatising the "fantasy" of this idea relentlessly translated into life.

Dostoevsky was perfectly well aware that the extremism he depicted in such a character as Raskolnikov was not at all the way in which the vast majority of the radical intelligentsia would hold the doctrines in question, or the way in which it would affect their lives. But then, the people who accepted the theories of Leibniz in the 18th century bore little resemblance in real life to Dr. Pangloss and his pupil Candide. Nonetheless, we cannot deny that *Candide*[1] dramatises a "real" fact of 18th-century culture. (It is suggestive that among the unfinished projects that Dostoevsky left at the time of his death was that of writing a Russian *Candide*.) Exactly the same relation obtains between the theories of Dostoevsky's protagonists, the acts to which their theories drive them, and the Russian culture of their time. Indeed, I think the best way to define Dostoevsky's particular uniqueness as a novelist is to call him a writer whose imagination naturally inclined to the *conte philosophique*, but who, happening to be born in the century of the realistic novel, possessed enough psychological genius to give his characters verisimilitude and to fuse one *genre* with the other. This, by the way, is one reason for the often-noted resemblance between *Notes from Underground* and *Le neveu de Rameau*,[2] aside from the fact that

1. Voltaire's philosophical tale of 1759.

18th-century mechanical materialism was as important in the Russia of the 1860s as it had been in the France of Diderot.

I should now like to apply this general view of Dostoevsky to some of the problems involved in the interpretation of his first great novel, *Crime and Punishment*. If Dostoevsky invariably began with some doctrine of the Russian radical intelligentsia, what was his starting-point in this case? An answer to this question will, I believe, not only provide an entry into the book, but also explain why *Crime and Punishment* emerged when it did in Dostoevsky's development. Ordinarily, this novel is linked with his prison-term in Siberia, first because of his use of this setting in the Epilogue, and secondly because this period was supposed to have focused his attention on the problem of crime and the psychology of the criminal. None of this needs to be denied; but if this were the whole story, it is impossible not to wonder why Dostoevsky did not write *Crime and Punishment* when he came out of imprisonment and wrote so many other things instead. The truth is that the novel as we know it could not have been conceived before 1865 because the situation of Russian culture that Dostoevsky could imagine as Raskolnikov had not existed before that time.

If we look at Russian culture in the early and mid-1860s—and this means, for our purposes, the doctrines of the radical intelligentsia—we can easily spot the "reality" that is incarnated in Raskolnikov. In the first place, all the radical intelligentsia were convinced that the theories of English Utilitarianism solved all the problems of ethics and personal conduct. This has caused a great deal of confusion because only in Russia do we find this peculiar blend of French Utopian Socialism, with its belief in the possibility of a future world of love and moral perfection, held conjointly with a view of human nature stemming from the egoistic individualism of Bentham and Mill. Even more, the Russian radicals believed in the doctrine of what they called "rational egoism" with their usual passionate extremism and fanaticism. To find anything similar to their belief in abstract reason as an infallible guide to the complexities of the moral life, we should have to go back to William Godwin. And I bring in Godwin's name here both because he had a direct influence in Russian through N. G. Chernyshevsky, the intellectual mentor of the radicals in the early 1860s, and also because the Russian cultural situation at this time closely parallels that of England in the period of the French Revolution.

2. Diderot's tale in dialogue, *Rameau's Nephew*, written 1762–79 and published in 1823.

Like Godwin, the Russians also strove to develop an ethics which —in the graphic words of Hazlitt's *The Spirit of the Age*—tried "to pass the Arctic Circle and Frozen Regions, where the understanding is no longer warmed by the affections. . . ." And no better commentary has ever been written on *Crime and Punishment* than the passage in *The Prelude* where Wordsworth explains how abstract reason dupes itself in its dialectic with the irrational:

> This was the time, when, all things tending fast
> To depravation, speculative schemes—
> That promised to abstract the hopes of Man
> Out of his feelings, to be fixed thenceforth
> For ever in a purer element—
> Found ready welcome. Tempting region that
> For Zeal to enter and refresh herself,
> Where passions had the privilege to work,
> And never hear the sound of their own names.

The last two lines of this passage define the theme of *Crime and Punishment* with far more exactitude than the mountain of critical literature on Dostoevsky. Indeed, if we are to understand the position of Dostoevsky and his intellectual allies (Apollon Grigoriev and Nikolai Strakhov) as they confronted the Russian radicals of the 1860s, we can do no better than to take as a guide the reaction of the first generation of English Romantics to the French Revolution. Moreover, if Godwin stimulated the radicals, then the works of Carlyle, who was an especial favourite of Apollon Grigoriev, furnished sustenance for the anti-radical camp.

Thus it is by no means accidental that we find Raskolnikov's crime planned on the basis of a Utilitarian calculus; this was the very essence of the matter for Dostoevsky. And we see too that, exactly like Godwin, Raskolnikov believes that his reason can overcome the most fundamental and deeply rooted human feelings. Godwin argued, it will be recalled, that reason would (or should) persuade him to leave his mother or sister burning in a fire and rescue Fénelon instead because, as he writes in *Political Justice*, "the illustrious Bishop of Cambrai was of more worth" to humanity. Whatever a Freudian might think of this argument, Godwin believed that it followed with impeccable logic from a Utilitarian calculus taking as its ultimate standard the universal good of humanity. Raskolnikov's conviction that he would be able to commit a perfect crime is based, we should notice, on exactly the same type of reasoning.

Ordinary criminals, Raskolnikov had theorised, rob and steal out of need or viciousness; and they break down at the moment of the crime, leaving all sorts of clues scattered about, because they inwardly accept the justice and validity of the law they are breaking. The irrational forces of their conscience interfere with the rational lucidity of their action. But, he was convinced, nothing of the kind would happen to him because he knew that his so-called crime was not a crime. Reason had persuaded him that the amount of harm his crime would do was far out-weighed by the amount of good it would allow him to accomplish. Hence his irrational conscience would not trouble and distort his reason, and he would not lose control of his nerves and make blunders.

This is one way in which the very conception of Raskolnikov springs from the ideology of the Russian radicals in the mid-1860s, and shapes the basic psychological conflict in the book between reason and the irrational. But another essential ideological component is derived from the evolution of Russian left-wing ideas between 1860 and 1865. In this period, for various reasons, we find a shift from the ideals of Utopian Socialism, with its semi-religious glorification of the people, to that of an embittered élitism, which stressed the right of a superior individual to act independently for the welfare of humanity.

The most important event in Russian culture between 1863 and 1865 was a public quarrel between two groups of radicals—the old Utopian Socialists, and the new Nihilists. Dostoevsky's magazine *Epoch* printed a number of articles analysing and commenting on this momentous dispute, and immediately recognised with great perspicacity, that it marked a fateful moment in the evolution of radical ideas. "The sons have taken up arms against the fathers, one generation replaces another," ironically wrote Strakhov, then the chief critic of *Epoch*; "a thick journal, once progressive, has turned out to be backward, and in its place stands another thick journal, which has succeeded in going farther along the path of progress." Even more relevant is that Dostoevsky himself wrote an article about this internecine warfare between the radicals called "Schism (*Raskol*) Among the Nihilists"; and this is what the whole episode is still called in histories of Russian culture. All this was just a few months before Dostoevsky, after the collapse of *Epoch*, sketched out in a letter his idea for a story about a murder committed by a young student acting under the influence of certain "strange, incomplete ideas"; and we can, I think, relate this schism among the Nihilists to *Crime and Punishment* in two ways.

One is in the difference that Dostoevsky draws between the comic and harmless Utopian Socialist in the novel, Lebezyatnikov, and Raskolnikov himself, who is no longer a Utopian Socialist but a true Nihilist. The Utopian Socialist is in favour of peaceful propaganda, conversion to the cause by reason and persuasion (which is why he lends books to Sonia), and he believes that the salvation of humanity hinges on communal living arrangements. These matters had still been important just two years before, in the period of *Notes from Underground*; but things in Russia moved very fast, and it was now out-of-date. Raskolnikov looks on all this as ineffectual nonsense; he feels that time is running out, that it is necessary to act now and not be content with Utopian dreams of the future, and that the superior individual has the right and the obligation to strike a decisive blow by himself.

A second reflection of this new situation may be found in Raskolnikov's famous article "*On Crime.*" For every idea in this text, it would be possible to supply a parallel quotation from *The Russian Word*, the "thick journal" that had become the Nihilist organ. The main spokesman for the Nihilists was Dimitri Pisarev, best known for his attacks on art as being useless—which is, of course, merely another application of the Utilitarian calculus. And if we go back and read Pisarev and his group, we find these undeniably genuine left-wing radicals exhibiting the utmost contempt for the people on whose behalf they presumably wish to change the world. We also find them using the arguments of Social Darwinism to establish the justice of the ineradicable distinction between the weak and the strong, and the *right* of the strong to trample on the weak and unworthy.

Indeed, one of the most pugnacious contributors to *The Russian Word*, Bartholomew Zaitsev, who later in exile became a follower of Bakunin, even defended Negro slavery on the ground that Negroes were biologically inferior and would otherwise be wiped out entirely in their struggle for life against the White race. This opinion was repudiated by the majority of the radicals, although Pisarev defended Zaitsev's premises if not his conclusions. Even though a minority opinion, however, this was exactly the sort of *consistent* application of Utilitarianism-cum-Nihilism that Dostoevsky believed revealed the true moral consequences of the new radical ideology. This context explains the "Nietzschean" aspects of Raskolnikov, which have been so often commented upon. Thomas Masaryk noted some of these "Nietzschean" elements in Pisarev and Russian Nihilism as far back as 1913, in his indispensable book *The Spirit of Russia*; but nobody has paid the slightest attention to them since, or brought them into any relation with Dostoevsky.

All this, I hope, has now placed us in a better position to understand what Dostoevsky was trying to do in *Crime and Punishment*. His aim, in my view, was to portray the inescapable contradictions in this radical ideology of Russian Nihilism. To do so, he adopted his usual procedure (in his mature work) of imagining its "strange, incomplete ideas" put into practice by an idealistic young man whose character traits embody its various conflicting aspects. Now Dostoevsky knew very well that the emotional impulses inspiring the average Russian radical were generous and self-sacrificing. They were moved by love, sympathy, altruism, the desire to aid, heal and comfort suffering—whatever they might believe about the hard-headedness of their "rational egoism." The underlying foundation of their moral nature was Christian and Russian·(for Dostoevsky the two were the same), and in total disharmony with the superimposed Western ideas they had assimilated, and on whose basis they believed they were acting. Hence over and over again in Dostoevsky's major works we find him dramatising the inner conflict of a member of the Russian intelligentsia torn between his innate feelings and his conscious ideas, between the irrational (which, by the way, is never Freudian in Dostoevsky but always moral as in Shakespeare) and the amorality of reason in one form or another.

In *Crime and Punishment*, Dostoevsky set himself the task of portraying this conflict in the form of a self-awakening, the gradual discovery by Raskolnikov *himself* of the unholy mixture of incompatibles in his ideology. This is why Raskolnikov seems to have one motive for his crime at the beginning of the book and another towards the end, when he makes his famous confession to Sonia. Many critics have pointed to this seeming duality of motive as a weakness in the novel, an artistic failure on Dostoevsky's part to project his character unifiedly. On the other hand, Philip Rahv quite recently has maintained that this is precisely what makes the book great—that in failing to provide a clear and single motive Dostoevsky reveals "the problematical nature of the modern personality," or the startling fact "that human consciousness is inexhaustible and incalculable."

Both these views, however, are equally and egregiously wrong.[3] The whole point of the book lies precisely in the process by which Raskolnikov moves from one explanation of the crime to another, and in so doing discovers the truth about the nature of the deed he committed. Even without the historical background I have sketched

3. Philip Rahv's useful essay, "Dostoevsky in *Crime and Punishment*," has been widely reprinted and widely read since its original appearance in *Partisan Review* in 1960. It therefore seems advisable to correct an important error of fact that Mr. Rahv's essay has no doubt had the effect of propagating. [See p. 533, above—*Editor*.]

Mr. Rahv believes that he has discovered a long-overlooked "source" for Raskolnikov's theory of "the great man" in Hegel's *Philosophy of History*. As evidence of Dostoevsky's acquaintance with this text, he cites a letter of Dostoevsky's (22 February 1854) in which, among a list of other books requested, Dostoevsky says "be sure to send Hegel, particularly Hegel's *Philosophy of History*. . . ." A comparison with the original, however, reveals that Dostoevsky asked for Hegel's *History of Philosophy* and not the *Philosophy of History*.

in, this should be abundantly clear to anyone who has some respect for Dostoevsky's capacity as a craftsman, and who studies the curious and original construction of the first part of the novel.

Why, for example, does Dostoevsky begin his narrative just a day before the actual commission of the crime, and convey Raskolnikov's *conscious* motivation in a series of flashbacks? One reason, of course, is to obtain the brilliant effect of dramatic irony at the close of Part I. For the entire process of reasoning that leads to Raskolnikov's theory of the altruistic Utilitarian crime is only explained in detail in the tavern-scene, where Raskolnikov hears his very own theory discussed by another student and a young officer; and this scene is the last important one just before the crime is committed. (It may be well, incidentally, to recall that when the officer doubts the possibility of anyone committing such a crime, the student retorts that, if this were so, "there would never have been a single great man." The "great man" component of Raskolnikov's theory is thus there from the very first, and is not unexpectedly tacked on later.) Temporally, the tavern-scene and the murder itself are at the very opposite ends of a single time-sequence; but they are telescoped together deftly by Dostoevsky's narrative technique—and for a very important purpose. And if we grasp the thematic significance of Dostoevsky's dramatic irony here, I think it will give us a model to illuminate the whole vexed question of Raskolnikov's motivation.

The purpose of Dostoevsky's juxtaposition and telescoping of the time-sequence is obviously to undermine Raskolnikov's *conscious* motivation for the reader. The hypnotic hysteria in which he kills the old pawnbroker could not reveal more clearly, in an objective, dramatic fashion, that Raskolnikov's crime is not being committed according to his altruistic, Utilitarian theory. Whatever Raskolnikov may have believed about himself, he is now acting in the grip of other forces and not on the basis of the theory, which is still fresh in our minds because we have met it only a page or two before. Dostoevsky's technique is thus intended to force the reader, if he is at all attentive, to pose to himself the question of what Raskolnikov's *true* motive can possibly be.

Now I believe that the entire construction of the first part of the book is intended to give an answer to this question in the same objective, dramatic fashion. Part I consists of two alternating sequences of episodes. In one sequence, composed largely of flashbacks, we learn about Raskolnikov's past, his desperate family situation, and all the circumstances pushing him towards the crime. All these scenes build up the altruistic side of his character, and reinforce our sense of his essential goodness, humanity, and sympathy for suffering. It is this aspect of his nature which forever distinguishes him from a real criminal, and that makes him think of expiating his crime—if one can really call it a crime—by future services to humanity. But then we also see him in *action* in this part, in the series of episodes with Marmeladov and his family, and with the young girl on the boulevard. And in these scenes we notice a very significant dialectic occurring, which undermines the foundations of his altruistic, Utilitarian theory in exactly the same way as the later dramatic irony; this latter is, indeed, only the final crescendo of this whole masterly sequence.

In each of these episodes, Raskolnikov at first responds purely instinctively to the spectacle of human misery and suffering, and he spontaneously rushes to help and to succour. But at a certain point, a total transformation of his personality occurs from one moment to the next. Suddenly he withdraws, becomes indifferent and contemptuous, and instead of pitying mankind he begins to hate it for being weak and contemptible. In each case, this change of feeling is indicated to be the result of the application of a Utilitarian calculus. For example, he is starving and yet leaves all his money at the Marmeladovs; but as he walks out he begins to laugh at himself scornfully for this gesture. Why? Because, he thinks, "after all they have Sonia and I need it myself." This leads him into reflections on how despicable human beings are because they can become accustomed to anything—like living off the income of a prostitute daughter.

The same situation occurs at greater length with the girl on the boulevard, who has clearly once already been violated and who is in danger of falling into the hands of another seducer. Raskolnikov at first springs to her aid, but then again turns away with a cold revulsion of feeling. "Let them eat themselves," he says to himself (after all, a good Darwinian sentiment). And then he ponders the Malthusian proposition that a "percentage" has to go that way anyhow for the protection of society, so that pity and sympathy are totally misplaced. The "percentage" theory has recently been traced in Russian scholarship to an article of Zaitsev's in *The Russian Word*, who used it for the philanthropic purpose of arguing that, since vice and crime were inevitable natural phenomena, it was wrong to punish their perpetrators. Dostoevsky's use of the same idea for Raskolnikov, however, is perhaps more logical in taking the greatest good of the greatest number as a standard.

Each step, then, in the *backward* process of revealing Raskolnikov's conscious, altruistic motive for the contemplated crime is accompanied by another episode moving *forward* in time that undercuts it, and that reveals the *true* effect of his ideas on his feelings. In each case the reader can see clearly that when Raskolnikov acts under the influence of his Utilitarian ideas, he unleashes in himself a cold and pitiless egomaniac who hates humanity although he continues to believe that he loves it. This repeated dramatic illustration of how Raskolnikov's ideas twist and distort his feelings may perhaps explain why even those critics who taxed Dostoevsky with inconsistency of motive have never gone so far as to claim that his supposed artistic lapse seriously damaged the novel. Clearly, these critics could feel the inner unity of Raskolnikov, even though, on the basis of their misreading of the book, it was impossible for them to explain what this unity was or how it was obtained.

I have perhaps said enough now to explain why it is really no surprise when Raskolnikov confesses to Sonia that he had committed the crime for himself alone, and solely to see whether he was strong enough to have the right to kill. This is merely his own self-recognition of what Dostoevsky has been making the reader feel ever since the first pages of the book. Let me conclude, however, with a few more observations on Dostoevsky's extremely skilful handling of the relation between structure and theme in *Crime and Punishment*.

In Part II, Dostoevsky begins to close the gap that exists between the reader's awareness of Raskolnikov and Raskolnikov's awareness of himself. For in Part II, as he begins to recover from his illness, Raskolnikov starts to ponder all the anomalies of the crime and to realise that he no longer knows *why* it was committed. At this point he is confronted with his old article *"On Crime,"* which reveals to what extent egomania had always been an inseparable part of the Utilitarian love of humanity. Dostoevsky withholds the full development of this motif, though he had carefully foreshadowed it earlier, until it becomes relevant both to answer Raskolnikov's own questions about his crime and to crystallise and define the reader's earlier impressions. The experience of the crime, however, has now shown Raskolnikov that the feelings which inspired his altruistic love of humanity cannot co-exist in the same sensibility with those necessary to be a Napoleon, a Solon, or a Lycurgus. For the true great man, possessed by his sense of mission, cannot have any thoughts to spare for the suffering humanity on whom he tramples for their own future happiness.

Once Raskolnikov's original theory breaks apart in this way, he is then confronted with the choice between non-Utilitarian Christian love and self-sacrifice in Sonia or total amorality leading to self-destruction in Svidrigailov. The construction of the latter half of the book thus clearly reflects its purpose, which was to persuade Dostoevsky's readers among the radical intelligentsia that they had to choose between a doctrine of love and a doctrine of power. Both were embodied, as I have tried to show, in the strange mixture of impulses and ideas that went by the name of Russian Nihilism.

And that Dostoevsky's attacks did have some effect may be indicated by the change that occurred in Russian radical ideology in the 1870s, when "rational egoism" was abandoned for a secularised Christian ethics of love.

As a footnote, let me add that I have always been intrigued by the information that the high-strung young Pisarev broke down and wept when he read *Crime and Punishment*. Was there any shock of recognition involved in this response? If so, it did not prevent him from immediately writing an article, which has since become a classic in Russian criticism, proving that Raskolnikov's crime was really caused by hunger and malnutrition.

# NICHOLAS BERDYAEV

## [Dostoevsky, the Nature of Man, and Evil]†

\* \* \*

*Crime and Punishment* is different from the books mentioned above [*The Idiot, Raw Youth, The Possessed*]. In it human destiny is not worked out collectively in the restless surroundings of personal relations; Raskolnikov discovers the bounds of human nature by communing with and making his experiments upon himself. He is a child of darkness, but there is nothing enigmatical about him as about Stavrogin or Ivan. He represents a less advanced stage upon the road of human wilfulness, he has not yet reached their degree of complexity. It is not Raskolnikov who is a puzzle, it is his crime, in which the man exceeds his own limitations. But perverse inclination has not yet radically modified human nature in him. Raskolnikov, like the hero of *Letters from the Underworld*, puts forward problems and riddles: Versilov, Ivan Karamazov, Stavrogin are themselves these problems and riddles.

Dostoievsky was more than anything else an anthropologist, an experimentalist in human nature, who formulated a new science of man and applied to it a method of investigation hitherto unknown. His artistic science or, if it be preferred, his scientific art studied that nature in its endless convolutions and limitless extent, uncovering its lowest and most hidden layers. He subjected man to a spiritual experiment, putting him into unusual situations and then taking away all external stays one after another till his whole

† From *Dostoievsky* by Nicholas Berdyaev. Originally published by Sheed and Ward, 1934. Pp. 44–50 and 95–101.

social framework had gone. Dostoievsky pursued his study according to the methods of dionysian art, and when he made his way into the deep places of human nature he took his whirlwinds with him. His work is an anthropology-in-motion in which things are seen in such an atmosphere of flame and ecstasy that they have meaning only for those who are themselves involved in the tempest. He leads us into the pitch darkness of man's innermost recesses—and there a glimmer of light must be found. Dostoievsky wants to kindle that spark. So he takes man and emancipates him completely, from law, from the cosmic order, and follows up his destiny in this state of freedom until he reveals whither it has inevitably led him. That was what interested Dostoievsky: what happens to man when, having liberty, he must needs turn aside to arbitrary self-will. Only then can the depth of human nature be seen; all the while existence is normal and firmly established it remains hidden, so Dostoievsky's interest begins from the moment that man sets himself up against the objective established order of the universe, cuts himself off from nature and his organic roots, and manifests his arbitrary will. When he has repudiated nature and the organized life he casts himself into the hell of the city and there treads his miserable path in expiation of his sin.

It is very instructive to compare the respective conceptions of man of Dante, Shakespeare, and Dostoievsky. For Dante (as for St. Thomas Aquinas) man is an organic part of the objective order of the world, the divine cosmos. He is one of the grades in the universal hierarchy: Heaven is above him, Hell below; God and Satan are realities belonging to the universal order, imposed on man from without, and the seven circles of Hell with their terrifying torment serve only to confirm the existence of this objective divine order. God and Satan, Heaven and Hell are not revealed within the human spirit and by human experience: they are given to man from outside and they have a reality equal to that of objects in the material world. This conception of the world, of which Dante was so great an interpreter, is strictly in line with that of the men of antiquity, and man's faith in the heaven with its hierarchical choirs above and the gehenna below was not shaken until the Renaissance. From that time on there is an absolutely new notion of the world. When the humanist era was established, with its self-affirmation and shutting-up of man within the walls of nature, Heaven and Hell were closed—but an infinity of worlds was opened. There was no longer a single cosmos with an ordered hierarchy; the infinite empty sky of the astronomers was not like Dante's sky, the mediaeval heaven, and that terror which Pascal experienced before "endless space" may be understood: man was lost in those vast solitudes which were no longer subject to any cosmic order. So he turned inward to himself, entering the psychic realm, and took refuge more and more in the earth, frightened of being separated from her in face of that new and strange infinitude.

This is the humanistic period of modern times, in the course of which man's creative forces have been played out. He is no longer bound by any objective world-order, given from above: he feels free. This is the Renaissance, and Shakespeare was one of its greatest geniuses. His work set forth for the first time the psychic human world, endlessly complex and varied, full of emotion and passion, strength and energy, boiling over with the play of man's powers. The heaven and hell of Dante have no place in Shakespeare's work, which, especially with respect to the place man holds in it, was determined by the humanistic conception of the world, a conception directed towards its psychic and not its spiritual aspect, away from man's ultimate spiritual self. Man renounced the centre of his soul and remained at the periphery. Shakespeare, a superb psychologist, was *the* psychologist of humanist art.

Dostoievsky appeared at another epoch and further stage in the history of mankind. For him, too, man does not belong to the objective world-order of which Dante's man was a part. During the course of the modern period man had tried to confine himself to the surface of the earth and to enclose himself within a purely human universe. God and Satan, Heaven and Hell were definitively relegated to the regions of the unknowable as having no communication with this world, until at length they were deprived of all reality. Man himself became a flat creature in two dimensions—he had lost that of depth; his soul was left to him but his spirit had gone. But the time came when the creative and joyous energy that marked the Renaissance dried up, and man began to feel that the earth was not so solid under his feet as he had thought: sudden rumblings were heard and the volcanic nature of the underworld was manifested. In man himself an abyss opened and therein God and Heaven, the Devil and Hell were revealed anew. At first one could only grope about in these depths, for the daylight of the world of the soul and of her material earth was fading and the abrupt kindling of a new light had not yet taken place.

The modern age served its apprenticeship to human freedom and man's powers were given full opportunity, but at the end of that period this experiment in liberty was carried over to another plane and another dimension, and it is there that man's destiny is now working itself out. Human freedom abandoned the psychic world in whose daylight it had existed since the Renaissance and plunged into the depths of the spiritual world. It is like a descent into Hell. But there man will find again not only Satan and his kingdom, but also God and Heaven; and they will no longer be revealed in accordance with an objective order imposed from without but by way of a face-to-face meeting with the ultimate depths of the human spirit, as an inwardly revealed reality. All Dostoievsky's work is an illustration of this. Therein man has a very different place from that given to him by Dante or Shakespeare: he neither forms part of an unchangeable objective order nor exists on the surface of the earth or of his own soul. Spiritual life is restored to him, and he has found it in himself: that is to say that, according to Dostoievsky, the spiritual life is imminent in man and not transcendent. But it must be clearly understood that this does not imply that he denied all transcendental reality.

The first manifestations of newly-freed man are exaggerated individualism, self-isolation, and rebellion against the exterior harmony of the world; he develops an unhealthy self-love which moves him to explore the lower regions of his being.

\* \* \*

Evil is essentially contradictory, and optimistically to conceive it as indispensable to the evolution of good and to try to remove its antinomy in the name of reason is to see only one aspect of it. The good that can be derived from evil is attained only by the way of suffering and repudiation of evil. Dostoievsky believed firmly in the redemptive and regenerative power of suffering: life is the expiation of sin by suffering. Freedom has opened the path of evil to man, it is a proof of freedom, and man must pay the price. The price is suffering, and by it the freedom that has been spoiled and turned into its contrary is reborn and given back to man. Therefore is Christ the Saviour freedom itself. In all Dostoievsky's novels man goes through this spiritual process, through freedom and evil to redemption. The *staretz* Zosima and Alyosha have known evil, and come through it to a higher state. Alyosha is by no means free from the troubles that arise from being a Karamazov: his brother Ivan and Grushenka both remark on it and he feels it himself; but in the mind of Dostoievsky he is the man who has emerged victorious from the test of freedom. That is how a human destiny should work out.

To speak of wrongdoing raises the question of what is allowable. Everything? It is a question that always troubled Dostoievsky, and he was always putting it in one form or another: it is behind *Crime and Punishment* and, to a considerable extent, *The Possessed* and *The Brothers Karamazov*. Free man is faced with this dilemma: Are there moral norms and limits in my nature or may I venture to do anything? When freedom has degenerated into self-will it recognizes nothing as sacred or forbidden, for if there be no god but man then everything is allowable and man can try himself out at will. At the same time he lets himself get obsessed by some fixed idea, and under its tyranny freedom soon begins to disappear—a process that Dostoievsky has set out with all his power. It was the case with Raskolnikov. He does not give the impression of a free man at all but of a maniac possessed by vicious delusions; there is no sign of that moral independence that goes with self-purification and self-liberation. Raskolnikov's fixed idea is to experiment with the uttermost limits of his own nature and that of mankind in general. He regarded himself as belonging to the pick of the world, one of those remarkable people whose mission is to confer benefits on humanity at large. He believed nothing to be impossible, and was anxious to prove it in himself. Dostoievsky simplified Raskolnikov's theorem by reducing it to the terms of an elementary question: Has a very unusual man, who is called to the service of his fellows, the right to kill a specimen of the lowest sort of human creature, who is only a source of evil to others, a repulsive and aged usuress, with the sole object of contributing to the future good of mankind? In *Crime and Punishment* he set out most forcefully that such a thing is forbidden us and that the man who does it is spiritually lost.

All things are *not* allowable because, as immanent experience proves, human nature is created in the image of God and every man has an absolute value in himself and as such. The spiritual nature of man forbids the arbitrary killing of the least and most harmful of men: it means the loss of one's essential humanity and the dissolution of personality; it is a crime that no "idea" or "higher end" can justify. Our neighbour is more precious than an abstract notion, any human life and person is worth more here and now than some future bettering of society. That is the Christian conception, and it is Dostoievsky's. Even if he believes himself a Napoleon, or a god, the man who infringes the limits of that human nature which is made in the divine likeness falls crashing down: he discovers that he is not a superman but a weak, abject, unreliable creature—as did Raskolnikov. His experiment with his freedom and his strength had a disastrous result: instead of killing a stupid and dangerous old woman he had killed himself, and after his crime, which was an unalloyed experience, he lost his freedom and was crushed by his own powerlessness; even his pride was gone. He had learned, in fact, that it is easy to kill a man but that spiritual and not physical energy is expended in the doing of it. Nothing "great" or "marvelous," no world-wide echo, followed the murder, only a nothingness that overwhelmed the murderer. The divine law asserted itself, and Raskolnikov fell beneath its power. Christ came for the fulfilling of that law and not for its destruction: the freedom of the New Testament does not overturn the law of the Old but shows it in relation to a yet higher world; and it was the immutable biblical law whose force Raskolnikov felt.

Men of real genius, authentic benefactors of mankind, do not look on themselves as supermen for whom all things are lawful; on the contrary, they do great things for the world by sacrificing themselves to that which they put above man. Raskolnikov was a divided, riven being, from whom freedom was already alienated by his inner unhealthiness, whereas the truly great are integral and jealous for their own unity. Dostoievsky showed the folly of claiming to be a superman, a lying idea that is the death of man: this claim and all its cognate aspirations sooner or later collapse into a state of pitiable weakness and futility which is no longer human, and against it the true nature of religious and moral consciousness stands out with everlasting majesty. The sin and the powerlessness of man in his pretension to almightiness are revealed in sorrow and anguish; the tortured conscience of Raskolnikov is a witness not only to his transgression but also to his weakness.

The case of Raskolnikov illustrates the crisis of Humanism, what its morality leads to, the suicide of man by self-affirmation; it is played out, as the emergence of a visionary superman with a "higher" morality proves. There is no humanitarianism left in Raskolnikov, who is cruel and without pity for his neighbour: concrete, living, suffering men must be sacrificed to the idea of a superman. But Dostoievsky taught the religion of love for one's neighbour, and he denounced the falsity of this disinterestedness in favour of some far-away end out of sight and reach of mankind: there *is* a "far-away" principle, it is God—and he tells us to love our neighbour. The idea of God is the only supra-human idea that does not destroy man by reducing him to being a mere means. God reveals himself by his Son, and that Son is perfect God and perfect man, the God-man in whose perfection the divine and human are made one. Any other sort of superman debases man into an instrument, and thus the man-god kills true manhood, as can be seen in the example of Nietzsche. The Marxian ideal of an inhuman collectivism is equally deadly for mankind.

Dostoievsky studied the results of man's obsession by his own deification under several forms, individual and collective. One consequence is that there is an end to compassion, there is no more mercy. Compassion is a ray of the truth by which Christianity enlightened the world, and a renouncement of this truth completely changes one's attitude towards one's fellows. In the name of his Magnificence the Superman, in the name of the future happiness of some far-away humanity, in the name of the world-revolution, in the name of unlimited freedom for one or unlimited equality for all, for any or all of these reasons it is henceforth lawful to torture and to kill a man or any number of men, to transform all being into a means in the service of some exalted object or grand ideal. Everything is allowable when it is a question of the unbounded freedom of the superman (extreme individualism), or of the unbounded equality of all (extreme collectivism). Self-will arrogates to itself the right to decide the value of a human life and to dispose of it. The control of life and the judgment of mankind do not belong to God; man, as the depository of the "idea of the superman," takes them upon himself and his judgments are pitiless, impious and inhuman at the same time. Raskolnikov is one of the individuals possessed by this fallacious notion in whom Dostoievsky examined the progress of self-will: Raskolnikov answered the question whether or no he had the right to kill a human being in furtherance of his "idea" solely by reference to his own arbitrary will. But the answering of such a question does not belong to man but to God, who is the unique "higher idea." And he who does not bow before that higher will destroys his neighbour and destroys himself. That is the meaning of *Crime and Punishment*.

# VYACHESLAV IVANOV

## The Revolt Against Mother Earth†

\* \* \*

The apostate from humanity as One being made of soul and spirit—he who renounces humanity, and consequently Mother Earth—such a one "splits off"[1] and thus himself becomes split: the intellectual and criminal Raskolnikov, who is saved by the self-sacrifice of a meek feminine soul; or, on the other hand, the martyr to the faith in humanity as a spiritual integer, the holy "Idiot" Myshkin, who loves the Earth more than his primitive memory of the other-worldly home, and has come to rescue the feminine soul from bondage and desecration—for Dostoevsky these two are the poles of a *single* conception. The Luciferian self-

† From *Freedom and the Tragic Life* by Vyacheslav Ivanov (1952, Noonday Press, pp. 72–85), by permission of Farrar Straus & Company, Inc. and the Harvill Press, Ltd., London.

1. In Russian, Raskolnikov comes from the word "Raskol", that means "split", "schism", "heresy"; Raskolnik", "apostate", "heretic".

assertion of the personality that strives meanly to preserve itself, and greedily to increase its wealth, is opposed to the generous self-surrender of the soul that, following the precept of the New Testament, does not fear to lose itself.

The opposition in shown between alienation from Earth[2] and oneness with it; between defection from men and union with them; between efforts to rise from poverty and weakness to power and fame, and the renunciation and impoverishment ($\kappa\acute{\epsilon}\nu\omega\sigma\iota\varsigma$) of an over-abundant spiritual force born in the light of grace; between the slow climb towards the light, and the sudden plunge into darkness—like that of a shooting star.

All these contrasts illustrate also the respective motives of the myths of those two antithetical works, *The Idiot* and *Crime and Punishment*. Before studying the former, let us contemplate the underlying mythical conceptions of the latter.

2

The action of *Crime and Punishment* takes place in St. Petersburg. Dostoevsky could discover no more suitable location and background for the tragedy of the illusive presumption and rebellion of One against All, of the individual against Heaven and Earth. Nowhere else, in his opinion, did the *genius loci* produce so dreadful a fever of the soul, such fantastic, and at the same time abstract, visions and ventures of delirium.

Is not St. Petersburg itself—that magnificent city conjured, in the teeth of the elements, from the northern swamps—is it not, as we read in the novel *A Raw Youth*, a purely imaginary and contrived conception? Is not its relation to the essence of Russia like that of a mirage to reality, of a deceitful mask to the true countenance? Is not the "St. Petersburg period" in Russian history the epoch of the great cleavage between actuality and appearance; of a form of consciousness—presumptuous and illusory, because its roots in the nation are snapped—which withers up man's sense of his organic union with Mother Earth, and thus of the living reality of God and of the world?

This was approximately the verdict also of the Slavophils—to this extent, at least, they agreed with Dostoevsky. But they were content with delivering this verdict, and enquired no further: for they had no understanding of the antithesis in the Russian soul, whereas Dostoevsky had a full and penetrating comprehension of this antithesis, in its dialectical inevitability. Moreover, Dostoevsky shared Pushkin's love for the equivocal creation of that mighty magician, Peter the Great, with all its enigmatic and dangerous

---

2. "Man, if he'll be man in-fact, Let him make eternal pact With his pious Mother Earth, With the soil that give him birth." These words from Schiller's "Eleusinian Festival", the Credo of Dimitri Karamazov, are also Dostoevsky's Credo.

ambiguities.

It is inevitable that beneath the horse of the Bronze Rider in Senate Square there should writhe a serpent. (The Revolution is a logical corollary of Peter's work; and the anarchist Raskolnikov obviously belongs to the Revolution's serpent-brood.) Yet, without the Empire, would the Russian spirit have been able to develop into a universal spiritual power? Such was Pushkin's train of thought at the time when he wrote *The Bronze Rider;* and Dostoevsky swore by this master's words.

Literary-historical research has already pointed out the extent to which *Crime and Punishment* is derived from Pushkin's St. Petersburg tale *The Queen of Spades.* Dostoevsky himself emphasizes the deep significance of this tale: according to Dostoevsky, the character of its hero personifies the mood of the entire St. Petersburg period. There is, indeed, an unmistakable similarity between the two works; but it is not merely the result of a simple imitation or reshaping of a literary model. The correspondence between them is a product of the identity of their basic mythical conceptions: the two tales are, as it were, variations on the same myth.

Pushkin's young officer, Hermann, a man of no family or fortune (in other words a plebeian and upstart, to his elegant and wealthy friends), and the hungry genius, the student Raskolnikov, are essentially akin; even though the former is a thoroughly selfish and loveless character, whereas the latter has a tender love for his mother and sister, who shyly and surreptitiously suffer deprivations in order to help him, and has a greater sense of grievance on their behalf than on his own.

Common to both are: social envy and personal ambition; an introverted and impenetrable nature, which seeks to shape day-to-day experiences into abstract patterns; the iron control of a passionate temperament by a will concentrated upon a single purpose; an almost pathological combination of unbridled fancifulness and cold calculation; moral scepticism; and, lastly, an unconscious magical urge to subjugate reality to their own demands—that which people who come in contact with either of these characters feel as something uncanny and daemonic in their natures.

Hermann, despite his modest, sober, strictly regulated mode of life, is generally regarded by his comrades as one who has "at least three crimes" upon his conscience; his comrades are repeatedly struck by his suddenly emergent resemblance to Napoleon. Raskolnikov's thoughts turn to Napoleon, as if drawn by a magnet: he admires Napoleon's daring, and his talent for crime.

The destinies of the two young men are also similar: both of them encounter—and this is where the mythical element enters

—a terrifying old woman, whom they seek to rob of the treasure she is guarding; both incur the guilt of killing the Parca, and must suffer her posthumous revenge. For the mummy-like old Countess of the story, who takes with her to the grave the magic method of becoming rich, entrusted to her by Saint-Germain, is certainly the same deathless being who appears in the novel as an odious female money-lender.

What is the fatal Power that lurks behind these masks? Is not this female avenger, arising from the darkness, one of those earth-powers that can bring both woe and weal; that know the secrets of the Fates and keep subterranean riches under lock and key? Is she not an emissary of Mother Earth, rising in wrathful resistance against the over-audacious and presumptuous demands of visionary pride and rapacious high-handedness; against the wild attempt to annul by violence the decisions of eternal Themis?

If one seeks an explanation for her in the realm of myth, she can clearly be none other than a chthonian being. And the fact that she is, indeed, none other, is sufficiently expounded in Dosto-evsky's variation on the theme; for clearly all his works are con-cerned with man's revolt against Mother Earth, the latter's resent-ment and her appeasement by the expiation demanded by her and made unto her.

3

The mythical element in the fundamental idea presented by *Crime and Punishment* is most plainly revealed in the mere plan of the work's central theme; which, without Dostoevsky's being aware of it—he is simply following popular tradition—might almost have served as the plot (*hypothesis*) for a play by Aeschylus, and can therefore be much better expressed in the technical language of ancient tragedy than by the concepts of modern ethics: the turbu-lent revolt of human arrogance and insolence (*hybris*) against the primitively-sacred decrees of Mother Earth; the preordained in-sanity of the evil-doer; the wrath of the Earth over the blood that has been shed; the ritual purification of the murderer—who is hunted by the Erinyes of spiritual anxiety, but is not yet re-pentant in the Christian sense—by the kissing of the Earth in the presence of the people assembled to try him; and the discovery, through suffering, of the right path ($\pi\acute{a}\theta\epsilon\iota$ $\mu\acute{a}\theta\sigma$).

This kiss of submission, indeed, is the symbolic climax of the entire action, which is, as it were, overshadowed by the invisible, gigantic figure of Gaia. It symbolizes the conflict and reconciliation between her and the proud son of Earth. The latter, aspiring to superhuman power, supposes that the more he alienates himself from the organic, the universal and the primitively real—whose vigour he has hitherto drawn from the all-nourishing mother-soil—

the more he will exalt himself; and is thus driven to appease his hunger with the poisonous weeds of the wilderness that he creates within himself. ("The wilderness spreads woe unto him who carries the wilderness within him"—these are the very words of Nietzsche!) The hero of *Crime and Punishment* is guilty in the sight of Earth, and receives absolution through his expiation made unto Earth. When he has done this, then she, the patient and silent, who in her universal acceptance has taken his guilt upon herself, at the end reveals herself to the convalescent, in the manifestation of her boundless pastoral steppes, where still "the air of the Patriarchs" blows, and consoles and strengthens him.

How differently would the ambitious wiseacre have fared, had he acquired soon enough the wisdom of simple Brutus of the Roman saga; who, when told by the oracle that the *summum imperium* would go to him amongst those present who first should kiss his mother, at once fell down and touched the Earth with pious lips. "*Terram osculo contigit scilicet quod ea communis mater omnium mortalium esset.*"—Livy, I, 56.

### 4

*Crime and Punishment* was Dostoevsky's first great revelation to the world, and the main pillar of his subsequent philosophy of life. It was a revelation of the mystic guilt incurred by the personality that shuts itself up in solitude, and for this reason drops out of the comprehensive unity of mankind, and thus also out of the sphere of influence of moral law. A formula had been found for negative self-determination by the individual: the name for it was—isolation. Raskolnikov's incarceration within himself, which was a result of the supreme decision of his free will (a will cut off from the universal whole), finds its final expression in the crime he commits. The sequence is not from crime to self-incarceration, but the converse: for from the latter arises the attempt to ensure the strength and autarky of the solitary personality —an attempt which, on the plane of external events, expresses itself as a crime.

It seemed to Dostoevsky that no symbolic action was expressive enough to convey a sense of the strange and almost incomprehensible—because so anomalous—spiritual condition of one who. like Cain, rejects God and man, shunning and fleeing all that lives. When Raskolnikov, after accepting the kindly gift that had been offered to him in error, later flung the small silver coin into the Neva, he knew that by this action he was severing the last bond between himself and mankind. Within the framework of the story we do not meet the rebel repentant of the murder he has committed, but merely one who refuses to endure the isolation which, under the mad illusion that it was a gauge of spiritual grandeur, he has voluntarily brought upon himself.

Worth noting is the dual character, deliberately emphasized by the author, of Raskolnikov's actions. On the one hand, all the circumstances, even the most trivial, array themselves in such a fashion that each separately and all collectively impel, adjure and force him to commit the deed that is apparently so contrary to his nature: a deed that results from some strange prompting from without, and is thereupon immediately regarded by Raskolnikov as an inexorable destiny. All his hesitation, all attempts to resist, are annulled by chance incidents, and conduce inevitably to the fatal step; as if his whole life were a torrent that with all its force surges irresistibly towards the huge precipice close ahead. On the other hand, Raskolnikov's whole environment appears to be in some sort a product of his imagination; and he who by chance puts the thought of murdering the old woman into his mind only gives utterance to something hidden and dormant within him. Raskolnikov himself creates this world of his. He is a magician of self-incarceration, and conjures up at will his miraculously created world of madness. He is also, however, the prisoner of his own phantom. He is saved by Sonia, who asks only one thing of her beloved: that he should acknowledge the reality of man and mankind outside of himself, and should solemnly declare his acceptance of this new and, to him, strange faith by an act of confession before all the people.[3]

Here we have an expression of the most important lesson that Dostoevsky learnt from inner experience during his exile. When, after his years in Siberia, he relates that he came to know the Russian people by sharing its ignominy and humiliation, and achieved union with it in suffering, and that in the same time he made himself acquainted with the Gospel, this confession has for us a double significance. There is no question here of a mere rapprochement between the "uprooted intellectual" of yesterday and the typical—indeed, according to Dostoevsky (*The House of the Dead*) the strongest and most significant—representatives of the Russian people's psyche, of the "people" in the empirical

---

3. *Cf.* the author's *Kluefte, ueber die Krisis des Humanismus* (Skythen-Verlag, Berlin), p. 36. "It is worth noting that the creator of *Crime and Punishment* agrees with Aeschylus (*cf.* the *Oresteia*) concerning the problem of purification after the shedding of blood: for the penitent's act of taking upon his shoulders the Cross held out to him by God Himself, of going into the market-place, kissing the earth and making full confession before all the people—is not all this essentially the same as Oedipus' abandoning his newly-attained throne, making a humble pilgrimage to Phoebus, and thus ratifying his inward purification by the verdict of the sacred national Areopagus?

"This mystic universalization of the conscience, this elevation of the universal human principle as a new power and a new value, such as do not reside in any single individual, to a level higher than any ever attainable by the individual's 'beautiful humanity'; and this view of the criminal as an apostate who is in need of reunion with the Whole: these things, it is plain, are not humanism."

sense of the word: for this no Gospel would have been necessary. No, we are in the presence of something greater: for Dostoevsky the people itself is the all-unifying, universal human principle, which, in all its sinfulness and humiliation, embraces God and stands opposed to the isolated personality that is in conflict with God.

In all Dostoevsky's later dicta on the subject of the people it is equally evident that he is speaking of the people's supra-empirical essence, into which strike all the roots of the personality that has vanquished its solitude and become aware of its Ego as a limb of the universal body. And this Christian people, *spiritually* incorporated in the Church and regarded by Dostoevsky as *one* soul, seems to him in a sense to merge into the concept of Earth as a mystical being; so that the apostate and rebel is, in Dostoevsky's view, a sinner not only against the Church, but also *contra naturam*.

5

The announcement of salvation through atonement—of the manner in which the personality discovers itself anew in God, by overcoming its illusory autarky of isolation—finds its climax in the Apotheosis and the cult of the Passion. In suffering man is truly united to all humanity. Be it even on the thief's cross, he experiences the mystery of contact with Christ. The sacramental significance, and thus the justification, of suffering resides in the fact that the victim, without knowing that he does so, suffers not only for himself, but also for others; that he not only himself experiences salvation through suffering, but also, whether he knows it or not, is saving others.

Even "the human louse"—as Raskolnikov calls the old female moneylender—atones through her suffering for some part of humanity's common sin. But he is none the less an evil-doer, that madman who conceives himself to be an instrument of the justice that he cannot comprehend: he does not alleviate, but only adds to the world's sorrow. The murder of the old woman becomes, in a manner unforeseen by Raskolnikov, also the murder of the simple, innocent Elizaveta. She who brings salvation to the murderer, the teacher of repentance, the meek-hearted Sonia, who becomes a prostitute in order to save her parents, brothers and sisters from starvation, is also a victim for the sins of others. In contrast to Elizaveta, however, Sonia is at the same time herself a great sinner; for, albeit to save others, she deliberately and over-weeningly takes upon herself not only suffering, but also the curse of another's deed, by making it her own. In the sinner who expiates his sin by suffering, there is an antinomy of curse and salvation—unless it happens that love has not been extinguished within him; unless, like Svidrigaylov, he has not become incapable of loving. For inability to love is Hell itself, as Zosima teaches; and he who is incapable of loving breaks away entirely from the partnership of all men in both sin and salvation.

The act of suffering finds a recognition appropriate to its dignity in Raskolnikov's prostration of himself before Sonia, and in the obeisance made by Father Zosima before Dimitri. This respect for suffering is the reason, according to Dostoevsky, why the Russian people adopt an attitude of deferential compassion towards "the unfortunate", as Russians call the criminal who is paying a just penalty.

The new theories of the irresponsibility of the criminal are to Dostoevsky objects of loathing: for they take from man his freedom and nobility, his divine dignity. No, the criminal must, and wants to, accept retribution for the act that expresses the metaphysical self-determination of his free will. It is unjust to deny to the criminal that responsibility that raises him above the beasts, and also to deny him the punishment that purifies him and gives him new being. Only the death-penalty, which forcibly curtails his Calvary of expiation, is to be condemned, since it is both hateful to God and also inhuman.

Nevertheless, every crime is not only a sin of the criminal, but also a sin of the community and of society: nobody has a right to say that he has no share in the guilt of the guilty. This opinion of Dostoevsky has its roots in the deepest and oldest strata of the national soul.

Whereas Raskolnikov's confession before all the people recalls the Orestes of Aeschylus, Dostoevsky's attitude towards the question of irresponsibility recalls the assessment of the guilt of Oedipus made in the tragedy by Sophocles. Oedipus—although unanimously acquitted by the latest researches into this perplexing and still not finally unriddled work—condemns himself. Why does he do so? He faces this dilemma: either he must regard himself as an automaton, a blind tool of fate—and therefore, in that he is unfree and irresponsible, also innocent; or else, disregarding the consequences and the apparent inconsistency, he must assert his freedom and responsibility, and thereby pass judgment upon himself.

There is an incomparable moral grandeur in the fact that Oedipus, who has solved the riddle of the Sphinx, and broken its spell, with the word "man", now condemns himself, the unwitting and unwilling criminal, in the name of man. This irrational solution of the problem, which has been set by the irrational beings who guide man's destiny, turns the blind beggar, who on behalf of all mankind has given through his expiation a positive answer to the question of mankind's divinity, into a divine being and, in truth, a friend of the Eumenides.

It is not Oedipus, in Dostoevsky's view, who is the criminal; yet he remains essentially the scapegoat of the Old Testament, the scapegoat that carries the sins of the people, the φαρμακὸs of the ancient Greeks. Similarly, in the case of Raskolnikov, the will of the many, which is directed towards the elimination of the repulsive old woman, finds a fulcrum in the free consent of this sick man, who is sick because he is in revolt against Heaven and Earth.

In *The Brothers Karamazov*, Dostoevsky, with Mephistophelian acumen, stresses the fact that the inhabitants of the little town, who were so enraged by the murder of old Karamazov, secretly hoped that the murderer would prove to be his son.

These indications given us by Dostoevsky help us to understand the dark meaning of Raskolnikov's terrible dream, and to recognize its significance within the plan of the novel. Raskolnikov dreams of a pitiful old nag that is being tortured to death by a jeering, wild and drunken mob. Who bears the guilt of this disgusting act of cruelty? Obviously not only the wildly excited owner of the unfortunate animal, who is swaggeringly eager to amuse the company, but also every individual of those who in sheer wantonness add to a load that is already beyond the animal's strength.

Which, then, of the characters in the novel resembles this obscure victim? Sonia alone? No, also her father and mother—and Elizaveta. And not only they: also the murdered old moneylender, and above all the murderer himself, who has been condemned, or has condemned himself, to accomplish that which the collective will demanded.

Already in *Crime and Punishment* Dostoevsky discovers, to his horror, the truth which he later on expresses as a dogma: the truth of the guilt of all men, for all men and for everything. This dreadful discovery opens before him still another abyss, both terrifying and illuminating: he begins to apprehend that all humanity is—one man. *Omnes unum.* (*St. John* xiv, 20.)

# MAURICE BEEBE

## The Three Motives of Raskolnikov: A Reinterpretation of *Crime and Punishment*†

The wide appeal of *Crime and Punishment*, probably the most teachable of Dostoevsky's novels, seems to depend primarily on its

† From *College English*, XVII (December, 1955), pp. 151–158. Reprinted by permission of the National Council of Teachers of English and Maurice L. Beebe.

subject matter. Students of varied backgrounds and interests are attracted to and held by this story of a young man who brutally murders two women and pays the price of his crime. After reading it, students are likely to find the latest Mickey Spillane novel or last night's TV drama pale and thin in comparison. It is only when they ask themselves how and why it is better than the modern psychological thrillers they have seen or heard or read that they begin to realize that the value of this novel, like all works of art, depends more on its manner than on its matter.

If we approach *Crime and Punishment* with a knowledge of Dostoevsky's character and his method of writing, we are likely to be surprised at the disciplined skill the structure of the novel reveals. Dostoevsky was a man who could not control the events of his own life, a neurotic who dissipated and wasted his energies in several directions at once, yet who managed somehow not merely to control the imagined life in his novel, but to order it with an almost Jamesian economy. *Crime and Punishment* meets the test of unity in action: all the parts contribute to the whole, and the parts may be fully understood only when the whole is known. Joseph Warren Beach has demonstrated that this unity may be attributed in part to what he calls the technique of the "dramatic present"—Dostoevsky's careful restriction of time, place, and center of interest (*The Twentieth Century Novel*, 1932, pp. 155–163).

We may recognize Dostoevsky's adherence to the dramatic unities, yet fail to see that the ideological content of the novel is as carefully unified as the narrative structure. For instance, some critics regret the Epilogue. To them, Raskolnikov's regeneration appears to be insufficiently motivated, and they see no necessary connection between the crime and its ultimate result: as Ernest J. Simmons has put it, "The Epilogue is manifestly the weakest section of the novel, and the regeneration of Raskolnikov under the influence of the Christian humility and love of Sonia is neither artistically palatable nor psychologically sound." I shall try to show that, on the contrary, the ending is artistically and psychologically inevitable because the basic motive of regeneration is the same as the underlying motive for the crime. The spiritual principle of the novel, represented in part by Sonia, is equated with the passive will-to-suffering that impelled Raskolnikov to punish himself by murdering Alyona Ivanovna and her sister. Without the Epilogue much that precedes would seem confused and contradictory.

Theme and technique overlap. One of the ways in which Dostoevsky unifies his novel is through his technique of "doubles." The dual nature of his heroes is, of course, a commonplace of criticism. Because his protagonists are usually split personalities, the psychological and philosophical drama in a Dostoevsky novel is expressed in terms of a conflict between opposite poles of sensibility and intelligence, spirit and mind, passiveness and aggressiveness, self-sacrifice and self-assertion, God-man and Man-god, or, sometimes, "good" and "bad." To dramatize this conflict, Dostoevsky often gives his characters several alter egos or doubles, each projecting one of the extremes of the split personality. Even when the hero is not present in the scene, he may remain the center of interest because the characters present are likely to represent different facets of his personality. According to most interpretations of *Crime and Punishment*, the struggle within Raskolnikov becomes physical, eternal action as he wavers between Svidrigaylov, epitome of self-willed evil, and Sonia, epitome of self-sacrifice and spiritual goodness.

When we apply this thesis of doubles to the novel, we meet difficulties. The doubles are themselves complex personalities. Self-effacing Sonia, who became a prostitute to support her family, refuses to give up a pretty ribbon. She reads not only the New Testament, but also "books of romantic tendency" and, "with great interest," George Lewes's *Physiology*. Svidrigaylov, whom critics describe as "a man who has chosen to be above the moral law, merely to satisfy his appetites and greed" (Slonim), "a kind of obscene double or shadow" (Beach), "the entirely loathsome Svidrigaylov" (Woodhouse), "the incarnation of the evil will" (Murry), "the monster" (Lloyd), and "unredeemed scoundrel" (Roe), is, I think, a somewhat attractive and genial villain, an allegedly self-willed man who, ghost- or conscience-ridden, has trouble deciding just what to will and who ends by doing good. The conclusion suggests that Raskolnikov's problem was solved when, quite suddenly, "He was simply feeling. Life had stepped into the place of theory." For Dostoevsky, here at any rate, the intellect is evil, the senses good. What, then, are we to say about Svidrigailov, who lives by senses and feeling alone, all of whose sins are sins of passion?

Perhaps the ambiguity results from a failure to recognize that man is not split into two parts, but divided into three: Mind, Body, and Spirit. The conflict in the tripartite Raskolnikov is a struggle between the intellectual, sensual, and spiritual parts of his nature. Each of these three parts corresponds to a reason or motive for his crime, and for each part, each motive, there is a separate alter ego: Luzhin, who stands for the intellect; Svidrigaylov, who represents the senses; and Sonia, who is a symbol of spirit. If we read the novel in terms of "triples" rather than "doubles," we may not only do justice to Svidrigaylov, but also discover that the novel is unified thematically as well as dramatically.

Dr. Fredric Wertham, in his *The Show of Violence* (1944, p

168), makes a useful distinction between *reason* and *motive:* "*Reason* is the conscious explanation a man makes for himself or an outsider before, during, and after a deed. *Motive* is the real driving force which is at least partly unconscious and which can be understood only as part of a continuing and developing process." Using this distinction, we may say that within Raskolnikov there are three motives which during the course of the narrative rise to the surface of his consciousness and become reasons for his crime. The first of these, his wish to rob and murder the old pawnbroker that he may administer justice by distributing her ill-gotten riches to the more deserving poor or, more probably, that he may finance the education that is to make him a benefactor of mankind, is *motive* only in that it is rooted in Raskolnikov's dominating characteristic, the egoistic pride that makes him want to play God. Pride combined with intelligence and unencumbered with spiritual or ethical feeling leads to the doctrine of expedient self-interest, which is the intellectual justification of the crime. Because this motive supplies the idea for the crime, it becomes a reason almost immediately—and almost as immediately it is repudiated as the real cause.

The final dismissal of "thinking" in the last few pages of the novel should come as no surprise, for throughout the book the intelligence is presented as essentially an evil power. "Compassion is forbidden nowadays by science itself," says Marmeladov. He quotes Lebeziatnikov, the young progressive, who is supposed to have said in regard to Sonia, "How can a highly educated man like me live in the same rooms with a girl like that" After Raskolnikov has given almost the last of his coppers to the destitute family of Marmeladov, he reproaches himself with the significant words, "What a stupid thing I've done." Intelligence without feeling is indicated often in the following pages of the novel, most memorably in the mention of the Paris scientists who were conducting experiments "as to the possibility of curing the insane, simply by logical argument" and in Raskolnikov's dream of the intelligent microbes. The "progressive" Lebeziatnikov can do good only because he "really was rather stupid" and had "attached himself to the cause of progress and 'our younger generation' from enthusiasm."

Luzhin, on the other hand, adopts "many of the convictions of 'our most rising generation'" because he finds them useful; they help him to get ahead. Attempting to make an impression upon the students Raskolnikov and Razumihin, he defends the "progress" that has been made "in the name of science and economic truth":

> Hitherto, for instance, if I were told, "love thy neighbour," what came of it? . . . It came to my tearing my coat in half to share

with my neighbour and we both were left half-naked. . . .
Science now tells us, love yourself before all men, for everything
in the world rests on self-interest. You love yourself and manage
your own affairs properly and your coat remains whole. Economic
truth adds that the better private affairs are managed in society
—the more whole coats, so to say—the firmer are its foundations
and the better is the common welfare organised too. Therefore,
in acquiring wealth solely and exclusively for myself, I am acquiring, so to speak, for all, and helping to bring to pass my
neighbour's getting a little more than a torn coat; and that not
from private, personal liberality, but as a consequence of the
general advance. The idea is simple, but unhappily it has been
a long time reaching us, being hindered by idealism and sentimentality. (II:5)

This theory stated badly by a man whom Raskolnikov detests
strikes close to home, and the young murderer retorts, "Why,
carry out logically the theory you were advocating just now, and
it follows that people may be killed."

For this is precisely what has happened. The link between the
first of Raskolnikov's motives and the theory represented by
Luzhin is made explicit through the word *prejudice*. Luzhin is
"an opponent of all prejudices," pleased that "many injurious
prejudices have been rooted up and turned into ridicule." The
young man whose conversation overheard in a restaurant first gave
Raskolnikov the idea for the murder said, "We have to correct
and direct nature, and, but for that, we should drown in an ocean
of prejudice."

To refuse to give away half a coat is one thing; to steal a coat
is another. But as long as man is not alone, self-interest begins
in the passive refusal to help others and leads almost inevitably
to the aggressive use of others. Luzhin thinks of Dounia as a
potential business and social assets, of sex solely in terms of possession: "This creature," he thinks, "would be slavishly grateful
all her life for his heroic condescension, and would humble herself
in the dust before him, and he would have absolute, unbounded
power over her!" The most unfeeling, cold-blooded, and self-
willed crime in the novel is not Raskolnikov's murder of the old
pawnbroker nor Svidrigaylov's attempted seduction of Dounia,
but Luzhin's false accusation of Sonia on the day of her father's
funeral. In fact, if we look for the real symbolic antithesis of Sonia,
we are much more likely to find it in Luzhin, the enemy who
attempts to use her for his own selfish interests, than in Svidrigaylov,
the benefactor who makes a disinterested offering before her. If
Luzhin appears to be an unlikely representative of the principle
of intelligence, so do the Paris scientists and the microbes. The
paradox results from Dostoevsky's conception of intelligence, which

he consistently associates with the "western" and "progressive" doctrines of expediency and utilitarianism. Because self-interest cannot be disinterested, it is not even particularly intelligent in an objective sense, but it is the only kind of intelligence presented *as intelligence* in *Crime and Punishment.*

Raskolnikov's first reason, his rational one, is dismissed even before Luzhin appears to make it look ridiculous. Raskolnikov knows that there is a deeper motivation for his crime. "If it all has really been done deliberately and not idiotically," he asks himself, "if I really had a certain and definite object, how is it I did not even glance into the purse and don't know what I had there, for which I have undergone these agonies and have deliberately undertaken this base, filthy degrading business?" (II:2)

Raskolnikov's second motive also appears to him first in the form of a rational theory: his much-discussed notion of the "extraordinary" man who, above good and evil, may transgress any law that stands in the way of his uttering a "new word." "If such a man," he says, "is forced for the sake of his idea to step over a corpse or wade through blood, he can, I maintain, find within himself, in his conscience, a sanction for wading through blood." (III:5) The second theory or reason is only a refinement upon the first, but the distinction is an important one. It is not the "idea" that sanctions the bloodshed, but the "conscience" of the doer. It is this aspect of the theory which shocks Razumihin: " 'Well, brother, if you are really serious . . . You are right, of course, in saying that it's not new, that it's like what we've read and heard a thousand times already; but what is really *original* in all this, and is exclusively your own, to my horror, is that you sanction bloodshed *in the name of conscience,* and, excuse my saying so, with such fanaticism. . . . That, I take it, is the point of your article. But that sanction of bloodshed *by conscience* is to my mind . . . more terrible than the official, legal sanction of bloodshed.' " (III:5)

Raskolnikov commits a murder not that he may *be* an "extraordinary" man but that he may *see* if he is one. "I wanted to find out then and quickly whether I was a louse like everybody else or a man," he tells Sonia, "whether I can step over barriers or not, whether I dare stoop to pick up or not, whether I am a trembling creature or whether I have the *right* . . ." (V:4) And he adds, "Listen: When I went then to the old woman's I only went to *try.* . . . You may be sure of that." The real "extraordinary" man, he has already admitted, does not have to test himself: "No, those men are not made so. The real *Master* to whom all is permitted storms Toulin, makes a massacre in Paris, forgets an army in Egypt, *wastes* half a million men in the Moscow expedition and gets off with a jest at Vilna. . . . Napoleon, the pyramids, Waterloo, and a wretched skinny old woman, a pawnbroker with a red trunk under her bed. . . . 'A Napoleon creep under an old woman's bed! Ugh, how loathsome!' " (III:6)

The real motive behind this second reason is suggested when Raskolnikov admits to himself that he knew *before the murder* that he would be shaken and horrified by it, that he would be unable to withstand the test. "And how dared I," he asks himself, "knowing myself, knowing how I should be, take up an axe and shed blood! I ought to have known before hand. . . . Ah, but I did know!" (III:6) He has, in a sense, committed a murder for the thrill of it, because of his fascination with the horror of the very idea; and the murder is, in part, an act of aggressive lust.

This motive is revealed symbolically in Raskolnikov's dream of the horse beaten by drunken peasants. Just before he has this dream, Raskolnikov encounters a drunken girl, apparently seduced and abandoned by one gentleman and now pursued by another. He tries to help her by giving a policeman money to see her home, but no sooner has he performed this act of disinterested charity than he is overcome by revulsion. "Let them be!" he calls to the astonished policeman. "What is it to do with you? Let her go! Let him amuse himself." (I:4) The girl, who has mumbled, "Oh shameful wretches, they won't let me alone!" and who has placed both Raskolnikov and the policeman in the same category of wretches, is the association which brings on the dream. The girl becomes the unfortunate horse, and the "shameful wretches" are now the peasants who brutally beat the horse with sticks and *finally an axe* until it is dead. Significantly, when Raskolnikov awakens, he immediately exclaims, "Can it be, can it be, that I shall really take an axe, that I shall strike her on the head, split her skull open . . . ?" (I:5) The progression from seduced girl to beaten horse to murdered pawnbroker tells us much about the strain of aggressive sensuality that lies within Raskolnikov, a taint which he denies himself on the conscious level. After the murder he continues to associate the drunken girl with his victims: "But when he reached the K—— Boulevard where two days before he had come upon that girl, his laughter suddenly ceased. Other ideas crept into his mind." (II:2)

The introvert Raskolnikov is, however, more masochistic than sadistic. The passive will-to-suffering is stronger within him than the aggressive will to make others suffer. Dostoevsky does little more than suggest the sadistic side of Raskolnikov in order that he may place more emphasis on the will-to-suffering which is finally revealed as the basic, underlying motive of his crime. The greatest advantage of Dostoevsky's technique of alter egos is that it permits him to write with greater economy and clarity than would otherwise be possible. Once he has established the link between the hero and his symbolic "double" or "triple," he can show both sides at once. Thus Svidrigaylov not only stands for the sensualist in Raskolnikov but also represents the outer-directed form of the sensuality which in Raskolnikov is primarily inner-directed. For Dostoevsky, who wrote that "experience *pro* and *contra*" is essential for "life's calling and consciousness" (Simmons, p. 150), each thing requires its opposite—indeed, includes its opposite.

Svidrigaylov is usually described as self-willed. He is self-willed in the sense that he recognizes no spiritual force outside of himself—even the ghosts that plague him rise, he insists, from his own illness—but if *self-willed* implies that he controls his existence, then the designation is a misleading one. He is the victim of instincts within himself that he has not summoned into existence, but which are simply there. When he finally appears in person, he seems to have difficulty living up to the reputation that has preceded him, and he proves as capable of doing good as proficient in doing evil. His references to a certain "journey" indicate that he considers suicide from the time he first appears in Raskolnikov's. room, and at that time there is no reason why we should not accept his assertion that his offer of money to Dounia is made "with no ulterior motive." What he does for Sonia and the Marmeladov orphans appears to be disinterested. As for his pursuit of Dounia, "you've only to assume," he tells Raskolnikov, "that I, too, am a man *et nihil humanum* . . . in a word, that I am capable of being attracted and falling in love (which does not depend on our will), then everything can be explained in the most natural manner. The question is, am I a monster or am I myself a victim?" (IV:1)

Although Svidrigaylov appears to be a victim of the lust within him, he tries to rationalize his sensuality. Defending his passion for women, he says: "In this vice at least there is something permanent, founded indeed upon nature and not dependent on fantasy, something present in the blood like an ever-burning ember, forever setting one on fire and maybe not to be quickly extinguished, even with years." (VI:3) Because he has seen no evidence of anything else more noble or permanent than this natural instinct, his only purpose in life is to seek out new thrills.

Svidrigaylov's view rests, of course, upon an unfavorable impression of human nature. And nothing ever happens to him that would disprove his theory that man is a brute. It is significant that all of his victims appear to be willing and that he, when the chance arises, is incapable of rape. When he struck his wife with a switch, she was, he suggests, "very likely pleased at my, so to say, warmth," for "human beings in general, indeed, greatly love to be insulted."

(IV:1) The young girl to whom he is engaged, who sometimes throws him a glance that "positively scorches"; the five-year-old in the dream who with a look of shameless depravity invites his embrace; even Dounia, who once was "softened in the heat of propaganda" (VI:5) and who, when there is no turning back, discovers that she would rather submit than kill the man who would rather be killed than denied—these are typical of Svidrigaylov's victims, victims not of Svidrigaylov but of what they share in common with Svidrigaylov.

For Raskolnikov, Svidrigaylov is as embarrassing a personification of his second theory as Luzhin was of his first theory. "My own conscience is quite at rest on that score." (IV:1) Svidrigaylov's reply to Raskolnikov's accusation that he has murdered his wife is undoubtedly as disquieting as Luzhin's talk of overcoming "prejudice." The second theory, like the first, is repudiated both subjectively and objectively. Raskolnikov sees in Svidrigaylov that his theory does not work, for Svidrigaylov proves that it is impossible to live by instinct or "conscience" alone. When he has a chance to take Dounia by force, he finds that he cannot do so. Haunted by his victims, overcome by revulsion, he can only commit suicide, and his suicide, a repudiation of all that he has done earlier, is probably his first and only entirely self-willed act.

The third and most important of Raskolnikov's three motives is his will to suffer. The motive becomes a conscious reason when he says to himself, "And what shows that I am utterly a louse . . . is that I am perhaps viler and more loathsome than the louse I killed, and I *felt beforehand* that I should tell myself so *after* killing her. Can anything be compared with the horror of that! The vulgarity! The abjectness!" (III:6) He is like Marmeladov, who said, "I drink that I may suffer twice as much!" (I:2) And when he confesses to Sonia, she is horrified not by the deed itself nor by the fate of the slain women, but by the effect that Raskolnikov's crime has had upon him: "What have you done—what have you done to yourself!" (V:4)

Only if we recognize this masochistic motive in Raskolnikov can we understand much of his conduct both before and after the murder. *Motive*, "a continuing and developing process," determines Raskolnikov's actions after the *reasons* are rejected. The absence of remorse may be explained not only by his sense of the chain of fate that led to the murder but also by his overwhelming conviction that he is the principal victim of his crime. To protect his mother and sister, he tries to cling desperately to the theories or reasons that he thinks can justify the crime, but he is also driven by the urge to confess and take his punishment, a private form of which he has already begun to inflict upon himself in his semi-confessions and in his return to the scene of the crime. When finally he does confess, it is not because he has been trapped by Porfiry Petrovich—he could, after all, take Svidrigaylov's way out—nor because he has yet submitted to Sonia's "humanity," but because the desire to accept suffering has been the underlying motive of his life.

We are told on the first page of the novel that Raskolnikov "had become so completely absorbed in himself, and isolated from his fellows that he dreaded meeting . . . any one at all." This sense of alienation is not the product of his obsession with the idea of murder, but something that appears to be deeply rooted in his nature. It revealed itself long before he thought of the murder. We know very little of his childhood, but the dream episode of the beaten horse tells us that he was extremely sensitive, and we may conjecture that perhaps from that moment—or some such moment—he began to withdraw, denying in himself what he held in common with the human brutes. At the university, "he kept aloof from every one, went to see no one, and did not welcome any one who came to see him, and indeed every one soon gave him up. . . . He seemed to some of his comrades to look down upon them as all children, as though their beliefs and interests were beneath him." (I:4) We know too that he was once engaged to his landlady's daughter. "She was an ugly little thing," he tells his mother and sister, "I really don't know what drew me to her then—I think it was because she was always ill. If she had been lame or hunchback, I believe I should have liked her better still." (III:3) No doubt he felt compassion for the girl, but in the relish with which he describes her ugliness there is something of that masochism which made Stavrogin of *The Possessed* marry a simple-minded cleaning woman and to confess "anything more monstrous it was impossible to imagine." There is pride, too, and a sense of God-like superiority, not unrelated to Luzhin's comment on the advantage of marrying a penniless woman, and what in retrospect appears to have been a rather desperate attempt to escape aloneness, to participate at any cost. If the girl had lived, Raskolnikov would probably not have committed a crime.

In Dostoevsky's first outline of the plot of the novel, preserved in a letter to the editor Katkov, he wrote, "The feeling of separation and dissociation from humanity which he [Raskolnikov] experiences at once after he has committed the crime, is something he cannot bear." But the alienation is cause as well as temporary result of the crime. When, after the murder, he tells Sonia, "Did I murder the old woman? I murdered myself, not her!" (V:4) he means, I take it, that he has destroyed his separateness. For a time, his action has seemed to alienate him more than ever from his fellow men, but by the end of the novel he has identified his particular suffering with the suffering that is the natural lot of humanity: making this discovery, he joins society. What, intellectually rationalized, was to have proven his superiority and right to detachment from lesser men only reveals to him what he has in common with mankind.

Porfiry Petrovich tells Raskolnikov of a prisoner he once knew who "seized a brick and flung it at the governor . . . and 'took his suffering.' " The incident is described in greater detail in *The House of the Dead*, Dostoevsky's reminiscences of his experiences in a Siberian prison:

> There was a convict in the prison who . . . was distinguished for his mild behaviour. . . . He hardly ever spoke to anyone. He was looked upon as a bit queer in the religious way. . . . He was continually reading the Bible. . . . One day he went up and told the sergeant that he would not go to work. It [159] was reported to the major; he flew into a rage. . . . The convict threw himself upon him with a brick he had got ready beforehand, but he missed his aim. He was seized, tried and punished. . . . Three days later . . . As he lay dying he said that he meant no harm to anyone, but was only seeking suffering.

Here is, in gist, the subject of *Crime and Punishment*: a man who "hardly ever spoke to anyone," who was in comparison with his fellows an intellectual, determines to attack or kill an expendable person (the major in *The House of the Dead* is as despicable as the old pawnbroker) in order that he may attain suffering, which is somehow related to religion.

Porfiry mentions the incident in relation to Nikolay, who has inexplicably confessed to a crime he did not commit, and who, like the prisoner, is deeply religious: "And do you know he is an Old Believer, or rather a dissenter? There have been Wanderers in his family, and he was for two years in a village under the spiritual guidance of a certain elder. . . . And what's more, he wanted to run into the wilderness! . . . Do you know, Rodion Romanovitch, the force of the word 'suffering' among some of these people! It's not a question of suffering for some one's benefit, but simply, 'one must suffer.' " (VI:2) Raskolnikov, the young intellectual, has denied religion, but he has been deeply attracted to the religious sufferers: to the landlady's daughter; to Marmeladov, who drank that he might "suffer twice as much" and who enjoyed being beaten by his wife; and to Sonia, whom he defended, he told her, "because of your great suffering." For this aspect of his character, Raskolnikov has not one, but three alter egos: Sonia, her father, and Nikolay.

The Western reader—and certainly the average student—may have difficulty understanding this association of suffering with religion. But suffering is a matter of feeling, and feeling may be either sensual or spiritual. As long as Raskolnikov seeks in suffering a masochistic pleasure demanded by his particular psychological make-up, his aloneness, the second motive remains dominant; when he recognizes in suffering a force greater than himself outside of himself, his motivation becomes spiritual and, in time, a conscious reason by which to live. The God in Whom Raskolnikov comes to believe, Sonia's God, "does everything." He is more like the amoral God of the Book of Job than like the benevolent God of conventional belief, and He is superior to human reason. "Dostoevsky's heroes inherit the Kingdom of God," said André Gide (*Dostoevsky*, 1926, p. 98), "only by the denial of mind and will and the surrender of personality."

Raskolnikov never repented of his crime because he did not hold himself responsible for the murder. He had fancied that he could plan and carry out the deed, but when the time came to act, it was as if he were impelled by forces over which he had no control, by "some decree of blind fate." Man must suffer, he decides, because man, his intellect a delusion and its power demonic, trapped by his instinctive brutality and the conspiracy of his victims, does not will his destiny. "Not on earth, but up yonder," Marmeladov has cried out, "they grieve over men, they weep, but they don't blame them, they don't blame them! But it hurts more when they don't blame!" (I:2) The aloneness of man is offended by the gods' refusal to blame what they cannot blame, but once suffering, man's bondage, is accepted, man feels a part of something beyond aloneness, feels no longer that he can be a god but that he is a part of the God that is "everything." The revelation that comes to Raskolnikov through love and humility "in prison, *in freedom*," is inevitable because it is the obverse side, the *pro*, of the will-to-suffering, the *contra*, that has been throughout the entire novel his primary motivation.

# KAREN HORNEY

## [Raskolnikov's Self-Destructive "Should"]†

* * * the inner dictates constitute a coercive system, a tyranny * * * people may respond with shock and panic when failing to fulfill them. We are in the position now to understand more fully

† From *Neurosis and Human Growth* by Karen Horney, M.D., pp. 118–120. Copyright © 1950 by W. W. Norton & Company, Inc. Used by permission of W. W.

Norton & Company, Inc.
1. Published in the *American Journal of Psychoanalysis*, Vol. IX, 1949.

what accounts for the coerciveness, what renders the attempts to comply with the dictates so frantic, and why the responses to "failure" are so profound. The shoulds are as much determined by self-hate as by pride, and the furies of self-hate are unleashed when they are not fulfilled. They can be compared to a holdup in which a gunman points a revolver at a person, saying: "Either you give me all you have, *or else* I'll shoot you." The gunman's holdup is likely to be the more humane of the two. It is possible for the threatened person to save himself by complying, while the shoulds cannot be appeased. And also, being shot, for all the finality of death, seems less cruel than a lifelong suffering under self-hate. To quote from the letter of a patient:[1] "His real self is stifled by the neurosis, the Frankenstein monster originally designed for his protection. And it makes little difference whether you live in a totalitarian country or a private neurosis, either way you are apt to end up in a concentration camp where the whole point is to destroy the self as painfully as possible."

The shoulds are in fact self-destructive in their very nature. But as yet we have seen only one aspect of their destructiveness: that they put a person into a straight jacket and deprive him of inner freedom. Even if he manages to mold himself into a behavioristic perfection, he can do so only at the expense of his spontaneity and the authenticity of his feelings and beliefs. The shoulds aim in fact, like any political tyranny, at the extinction of individuality. They create an atmosphere similar to that in the seminary described by Stendhal in *The Red and the Black* (or George Orwell in *Nineteen Eighty-Four*), in which any individual thinking and feeling are suspect. They require an unquestioning obedience, which is not even felt as obedience.

Besides, many shoulds show their self-destructive character in their very contents. As an illustration I should like to refer to three shoulds, all of which operate in the condition of morbid dependency and which will be elaborated in that context. I should be big enough to mind absolutely nothing that is done to me; I should be able to make her love me; and I should sacrifice absolutely everything for "love"! The combination of these three shoulds is indeed bound to perpetuate the tortures of a morbid dependency. Another frequent should demands of a person that he assume full responsibility for his relatives, friends, pupils, employees, etc. He should be able to solve everyone's problem to everyone's instant satisfaction. This implies that *anything* that goes wrong is his fault. If a friend or relative is upset for any reason, complains, criticizes, is discontented, or wants something, such a person is forced to be the helpless victim who must feel guilty and set everything right. He is, to quote a patient, like the harassed manager of a summer hotel: the guests are always right. Whether or not any of the mishaps are actually his fault does not matter.

This process is well described in a recent French book, *The Witness*.[2] The main character and his brother are out boating; the boat leaks, a storm comes up, and they are capsized. Since the brother has a badly injured leg, he is not able to swim in the violent water. He is doomed to drown. The hero tries to swim ashore, supporting his brother, but soon realizes that he cannot do it. The alternatives are that both drown or that the hero save himself alone. Clearly realizing this, he decides to save himself. But he feels as if he were a murderer, and this is so real to him that he is convinced everybody else will regard him as a murderer. His reason is of no avail, and cannot be effective, as long as he operates on the premise that he *should* be responsible in *any* case. To be sure, this is an extreme situation. But the hero's emotional response illustrates exactly what people do feel when driven by this particular should.

An individual can also impose tasks upon himself which are detrimental to his whole being. A classic example of this kind of should is to be found in Dostoevski's *Crime and Punishment*. Raskolnikov, in order to prove to his satisfaction his Napoleonic qualities, felt that he *should* be able to kill a human being. As Dostoevski shows us in unmistakable terms, despite Raskolnikov's manifold resentments against the world, nothing was more distasteful to his sensitive soul than to kill. He had to beat himself into doing it. What he actually felt is expressed in a dream in which he sees a scrawny, underfed little mare forced by drunken peasants to try to pull an impossibly heavy cartload. It is brutally and mercilessly whipped and finally beaten to death. Raskolnikov himself rushes to the mare in an upsurge of deep compassion.

This dream appeared at a time when Raskolnikov was engaged in a violent inner struggle. He felt both that he *should* be able to kill and that it was so utterly distasteful that he simply could not do it. In the dream he realized the senseless cruelty with which he was beating himself into doing something that was as impossible for him as it was for the mare to pull the heavy cartload. And from the depth of his being emerged a profound compassion for himself over what he was doing to himself. Having thus experienced his true feelings, he felt more at one with himself after the dream and decided against the killing. But his Napoleonic self soon afterward again got the upper hand, because at that time his real self was as helpless against it as the underfed mare was against the brutal peasants.

2. Jean Bloch-Michel, *The Witness*, Pantheon Press, 1949.

# RALPH E. MATLAW

## Recurrent Imagery in *Crime and Punishment*†

\* \* \*

The clearest proof of a fundamental kinship among Dostoevskij's demonically dissolute characters is found in the fact that each is associated with the image of a spider. More generally, the mention of lower forms of animal life, of insects, flies, beetles, cockroaches, and reptiles, extends the image of the spider and is used to indicate a particular concept or series of concepts. This complex of images is central to, and recurrent in, Dostoevskij's work, but, like the rest of his imagery, has passed almost without comment. Svidrigailov's famous description of eternity as "one little room, like a bath-house in the country, blackened by smoke, with spiders in the corners," is crucial to the structure of *Crime and Punishment*, and has indeed so been noted. \* \* \* A writer and critic who is probably more fair to Tolstoj than Dostoevskij notes the existence of this image [of insects] eloquently if not altogether accurately:

> Dostoevskij's heroes are practically never in contact with higher animals. On the other hand, an unbelievable number of every kind of lower animal, of snakes and reptiles, appear before them —the most disharmonious creatures, inspiring man with the greatest horror and disgust. Tarantulas, scorpions, phalanges and spiders, spiders without end. They continually appear in dreams, and appear to almost all Dostoevskij's heroes without exception. Like the cold, gloom, and fog of lifeless nature, these monsters of animal life crawl into man's soul in order to separate and cut him off from the world of light and life.[1]

\* \* \*

The very fact that almost all Dostoevskij's important works are set in the confinement of man-made cities affects his use of insect imagery. From this point of view, the choice of "louse" as a symbol for Raskol'nikov's "idea" is particularly felicitous. For the louse, unlike the insect or fly, specifically requires human or animal blood for its nourishment. Indeed, in the last wavering before his confession, Raskol'nikov asks: "Crime? What crime . . . vile, nox-

---

† From *Harvard Slavic Studies*, H. G. Lunt, Managing Editor. Vol. III, Cambridge, Mass.: Harvard University Press. 1957. Pp. 202, 209–212. Reprinted by permission of Harvard University Press.

1. V. V. Veresaev, *Sochinenija* (Moscow, 1947), II, 434.
2. V. Rozanov, *Legenda o velikom in-kvizitore F. M. Dostoevskogo* (SPb., 1906), p. 57.

ious louse, she was sucking life out of people." The word "louse" is used in all fifteen times: thirteen times by Raskol'nikov, in meditating on his theory, and once by Sonja, when she points out the error of his idea. For Raskol'nikov's crime, Rozanov pointed out (as Sonja had), consists in considering a human being as a louse.[2] In his confession to Sonja, there is the following exchange:

> ". . . Well, of course in killing the old woman I did wrong . . ."
> "Oh, that's not it, that's not it," Sonja cried in distress. "How could one—no, that's not right, not right" . . .
> "I've only killed a louse, Sonja, a useless, loathsome, harmful creature."
> "A human being—a louse!"
> "I too know it wasn't a louse," he answered, looking strangely at her . . .

Raskol'nikov's rejection of his theory follows Porfirij's point of view rather than Sonja's. The very consideration of a division of humanity into "men" and "lice" carries the seed of its own doubt, for one may be in either category. Raskol'nikov questions himself frequently: "If I asked myself whether a human being is a louse"; "I wanted to find out then and quickly whether I was a louse like everybody else or a man . . . because I am such a louse as the rest . . . If I were not a louse I should not have come to you . . . Perhaps I've been unfair to myself. Perhaps I am a man and not a louse."

The louse has different attributes at different times, for it depends on the rest of the novel's ideological problems. Raskol'nikov first maintains that the pawnbroker's life "is no more than the life of a louse, of a cockroach." On the way to Porfirij, he turns the image on himself, when he calls himself an " 'aesthetic louse and nothing more. Yes, I am certainly a louse,' he went on, clutching at the idea, gloating over it and playing with it with vindictive pleasure . . . 'Of all the lice I picked the most useless one to kill . . . and what shows that I am utterly a louse . . . is that I am perhaps viler and more loathsome than the louse I killed, and *I felt beforehand* that I should tell myself so after killing her.' " When Raskol'nikov ascribes loathsomeness and vileness to the louse, we recognize the same emotional and ethical connotations ascribed to the insect by the underground man, as well as those of the spider imagery. Indeed, Raskol'nikov describes the pawnbroker as a blood-sucking louse, but in confessing his crime to Sonja, he attributes the same wasteful, socially harmful, ethically evil character to himself: "I sat in my room like a spider . . . whether I became a benefactor to others, or spent my life like a spider catching men in my web and sucking the life out of them, I couldn't have cared at that moment." This passage assumes particular importance not only because it equates Raskol'nikov in part with the pawnbroker, but also because it comes after Svidrigaylov's famous description of a spidery eternity. Raskol'nikov's use of the spider image, then, indicates again, and justifies Svidrigaylov's claim, that "there is something in common between us." Another imagistic connection between the two lies in Svidrigaylov's revelation to Raskol'nikov that he has overheard his confession. When Raskol'nikov imputes Svidrigaylov's moties for giving money to Marmeladov's children, Svidrigaylov asks, "Won't you admit that it's simply done from humanity? She wasn't a 'louse,' you know, was she, like some old pawnbroker?"

Two more similar images round out the complex in *Crime and Punishment.* The first is that of the butterfly, which, like all life in the city, assumes a different character from what it has in the country; particularly since Porfirij laments his own lack of exercise and fresh air and also advises Raskol'nikov to partake of nature. On his way to the preliminary investigation, Raskol'nikov suddenly thinks of himself as a "butterfly flying to the light." Porfirij, the brilliant criminal psychologist, uses exactly the same image to indicate to Raskol'nikov that the murderer is psychologically unable to escape him. Finally, there is the image of the fly. After the first examination, Raskol'nikov reassures himself that he was unobserved—"A fly flew by and saw it. Is it possible?" Raskol'nikov shortly thereafter has a dream that summarizes many problems of *Crime and Punishment.* The dream in part symbolizes unconscious processes in Raskol'nikov as indicated by the substitution of the "huge, round, copper-red moon [that] looked in at the windows. 'It's the moon that makes it so still, weaving some mystery,' " for the setting sun, with its slanting rays, at the beginning of the book, when Raskol'nikov first embarks on his crime. A fly buzzes against the window just before he dreams the murder,[3] and clearly does take the role of the witness:

> He drew a deep breath—but his dream seemed strangely to persist. His door was flung open and a man whom he had never seen stood in his doorway watching him intently. . . . Ten minutes passed. It was still light but beginning to get dusky. There was complete silence in the room. Not a sound came from the stairs. Only a big fly buzzed and fluttered into the window-pane. It was unbearable at last. Raskolnikov suddenly got up and sat down on the sofa.
> 'Come, tell me what you want.'
> 'I knew you were not asleep, but only pretending,' the stranger

3. Bem, *O Dostoevskom,* pp. 45 ff., *Queen of Spades.* notes the existence of this fly in the

answered oddly, laughing calmly. 'Allow me to introduce myself, Arkadij Ivanovich Svidrigaylov.'

Svidrigaylov, shortly before his suicide, has a sordid dream of mice, rats, and corruption. When he awakes, and realizes his own depravity, he begins to think:

> The revolver and the notebook lay beside him. Some flies woke up and settled on the untouched veal, which was still on the table. He stared at them and at last with his free hand began trying to catch one. He tried till he was tired, but could not catch it. At last, realizing that he was engaged in this interesting pursuit, he started, got up, and walked resolutely out of the room.

In the Epilogue, the cataclysmic plague that destroys humanity is induced by microbes, "but microbes endowed with intelligence and will."

\* \* \*

## A. BEM

## [The Problem of Guilt in Dostoevsky's Fiction]†

Dostoevsky's tragic novels aim at a "catastrophic" central event which is usually linked to a crime. Most important to Dostoevsky is not the crime itself, but the guilt connected with it. According to a very convincing interpretation by Viacheslav Ivanov, a crime can become a catastrophic event only if guilt is present; only thus can it form the unifying factor for almost all of Dostoevsky's novels. The conception of guilt plays a significant role even in the early works of Dostoevsky where crime does not yet have the function of supplying the coherence of plot.

Raskolnikov killed the old pawnbroker under the spell of an idea. All of *Crime and Punishment* is based on a peculiar discord in the soul of its hero: his spiritual life, separated from the emotional life within him, stagnates. Instead of spiritual unity, when all parts of the soul find themselves in harmony, a disturbance can sometimes occur, when one side of the soul takes the upper hand in darkening and overshadowing all the others. Withdrawn into the unconscious, the other parts stay active and influence all

† From A. Bem, "Das Schuldproblem bei Dostojevskij," *Zeitschrift für Slavische Philologie* (Leipzig, 1935), XII, 251 and 273–77; reprinted by permission of the publisher, Otto Harrassowitz, and H. Petzolt. Translated by Irene Verhovskoy. Bem was a Russian émigré scholar who published extensively in Czechoslovakia and Germany. One of his special interests was the application of modern psychological theories to the works of Dostoevsky.

actions from there in a peculiar manner. Hence the possibility, which in itself seems paradoxical, that one of the actions, which is criminal in character, nevertheless retains its inner generosity and decency. One such internal discord in Raskolnikov's soul forms the subject of *Crime and Punishment*.

The crime is presented here as a firmly given fact, in the formal as well as in the moral sense. This fact does not penetrate Raskolnikov's soul and conscious mind, but conceals itself in his subconscious as a potential force of his conscience. His intellect feels no repentance until the very end; even after being sentenced to compulsory labor Raskolnikov is still under the spell of the idea which justified the murder. Yet his whole being, his moral structure, is shaken by the moral aspect of the murder. It was Dostoevsky's intention to describe those moral processes which are hidden in our subconscious, conspicuously "crying out in us," but unknown to us. Raskolnikov feels them and asks himself questions about the nature of these unclear experiences appearing in our semiconscious actions. "Is there a law of nature," he asks himself in Dostoevsky's notebook, "which we do not know and which cries out in us?"

Sonia follows him always like a shadow and guides him on the way to his repentance. This symbolic role of Sonia in the novel is described by Dostoevsky with astonishing force. When Raskolnikov begins to waver in his resolution to turn himself in, she is with him as the embodiment of his conscience. He sees her in the distance as he leaves the police station: "Here, in the yard, not far from the exit, stood Sonia, pale and numb, and looked at him. He remained standing. Something painful and tormenting appeared on his face. A distorted forlorn laugh wandered over his mouth. He remained standing, smiled and turned toward the police station. His fate was sealed." Even this decision to take the expiating step, however, was arrived at not because of Raskolnikov's realization of his guilt, but under the pressure of the law of nature crying out within him. In his consciousness this step appeared as an expression of weakness rather than moral strength. The whole novel shows us the strong moral laws anchored in us which are not overcome by our conscious mind. Here we have to do with a rare case where, because of the failure of tne feeling of guilt to become conscious, the subconscious not only is present but determines the outcome of the spiritual drama. Hence Dostoevsky is right when he also suggests Raskolnikov's coming spiritual resurrection, that is, when he foresees the rebirth of his spiritual unity: Though this rebirth starts formally at the moment his repentance begins—immediately after the event treated in the novel takes place—a spiritual shock connected with the crime is necessary for its realization. Otherwise the hidden moral forces could not have come to the surface. It is this that makes Dostoevsky's note to the novel understandable: "At the moment of crime his moral evolution also begins. Now questions which did not exist before became possible."

The personality split resulting from isolation, self-containment, and retirement from the world of internal experiences is remarkably presented, and it does not contradict the "humanitarian" coloring of the Raskolnikov's logic which led him to the murder. This humanitarianism, the wish to free his mother and sister from suffering, to secure their future, is only the point of departure in his train of thought. These reflections will soon be superseded by the theory of conquest and domination of others. The tyrannical trait in Raskolnikov finds a particularly appropriate expression in Dostoevsky's notes for this novel: "His character in the novel stands for the idea of immoderate pride, presumptuousness, and contempt of society. His idea: to conquer society in order to do it good. Despotism is his trait of character . . . he will dominate and knows no limits. To seize power as soon as possible and to become rich. The idea of murder comes easy to him."

The constant idea of transgressing the laws of nature by personal exertion of will and blind accidents plays an unusual role in Dostoevsky's philosophy. The meeting with Marmeladov and his family means the return from the world of phantoms and phantasies into the real world of human suffering. Here Dostoevsky tried to combine organically his planned novel, *The Drunkards*, with the ideological subject of the "Story of a Crime."

Only by taking part in the suffering of this world is the return from unbelief to belief in Christ possible. Again we can see here Dostoevsky's intention of showing the deep meaning of his conception of "true life," as opposed to the world of phantasy and phantoms. Marmeladov in the notebooks speaks the significant words: "Every human being, though he may be stuck in dirt up to his neck, is really living only when he suffers and consequently needs Christ, and consequently there will be Christ. . . . Only those do not believe in Christ who are truly not alive and whose soul is similar to an inorganic stone." These words contain a deep meaning and seem to express the philosophy of Dostoevsky himself. It should be noted that here the way of finding God is the same as in the memorable "Confession" of Tolstoy: "God exists because he is necessary, because he who is truly alive, that is who lives in the world of suffering, cannot live without his faith in God—this is the way of a return to faith." The participation in human suffering is also of greatest significance. Only he who is "truly alive" suffers. Outside life there is no suffering, there is only seduction and imprisonment of the soul by dark forces, by demons, by doubles, or, as the last stage, petrification of the spirit, the soul's coming to resemble "inorganic stone." Unbelief is only an external expression of this falling away from the living tree of life. In order to be able to return to Christ, man must first return to life with its suffering and afflictions. Hence, it is the "compassion," the appreciative sharing of other people's suffering which is the most important sign of the possibility of spiritual resurrection—the restoration of a spiritual equilibrium. The turning away from the true life by Versilov and Stavrogin meant that they gave up this most important possession of the human soul, the feeling of common suffering. Raskolnikov found himself half way toward such final estrangement from true life. But his dream, like that of Dimitri Karamazov, revealed that the flow of life in him was not yet dead, that he was still capable of reacting to the suffering of others and that for him the road to rebirth was still open. The terrible crime into which he was pushed by his seclusion from life was the stone which lifted the still living moral forces from the depth of his soul and carried them to the surface. "Inscrutable are the ways of God by which he finds the man"; so Dostoevsky wanted to end this novel, and these last words in the novel also reveal its inner meaning to us.

# SIMON KARLINSKY

## Dostoevsky as Rorschach Test†

The plain fact of it is that Fyodor Dostoevsky was a novelist, a literary artist who wrote works of imaginative fiction. To say this is not to belabor the obvious: much of what one gets to read and to hear on the subject of Dostoevsky could very easily lead one to believe, if one didn't know better, that he was a theologian, a political analyst, an existentialist philosopher or some sort of revolutionary. Back in 1940, Ernest J. Simmons, in one of the earliest American books on this writer, had to remind his readers that whatever other dimensions Dostoevsky's books may possess, they are, after all, novels. That reminder is still as timely as ever.

No other novelist's work has been so widely drawn upon by fields and disciplines that do not normally draw on fiction for their sources. Cesare Lombroso and other turn-of-the-century criminologists used *Crime and Punishment, The Idiot* and *The Brothers Karamazov* as textbooks in courses on the role of heredity in criminal behavior. The idealistic philosopher Vladimir Soloviov based his theological concept of Godmanhood on these same novels, while

† From *The New York Times*, June 13, 1971. Copyright © 1971 by the New York Times Company. Reprinted by permission.

Sigmund Freud saw in them the key to explaining the impulse to parricide.

The impact Dostoevsky produces on some readers at times verges on the apocalyptic. I knew a young Yugoslav Catholic who gave up his intention of entering holy orders when he decided that *The Brothers Karamazov* was written, as he put it, "by a greater prophet of Christ than any of the four Evangelists." "It has often been said that it is lucky his Karamazovs were not finished," wrote Hermann Hesse in all apparent seriousness, "otherwise not merely Russian literature, but all Russia and all mankind might explode and vanish into the air."

All accepted standards of literary criticism and textual analysis tend to break down, to fade or to mutate when applied to Dostoevsky. His prose has always been a magnet for the kind of reader (and commentator) who does not give a hoot about the art of literature, who mistrusts sober observation of reality, and who primarily looks for a reflection of his own self and for a possible vehicle of self-expression in every book he reads.

While there exists a considerable body of meaningful and admirable Dostoevsky criticism in the West, many Western commentators are attracted to him mainly as a pretext for airing their own views, prejudices, concepts or moods. The Hermann Hesse essay on *The Brothers Karamazov* quoted above is a good example. Ostensibly analyzing the novel, Hesse actually describes the spiritual climate of German intellectual life at the end of World War I. Hesse does this quite honestly and openly: "One should not believe that all the thoughts and ideas which I express about this book were uttered consciously by Dostoevsky. On the contrary: no great prophet and poet has the power fully to interpret his own vision."

The numerous French admirers of Dostoevsky, who have been twisting and distorting his thought in recent decades in order to turn him into a Kierkegaard or a Sartre, on the other hand are not nearly so honest. The notion that Dostoevsky has not fully succeeded in expressing his own ideas in his novels and that somebody else had better bring them out and dot all the i's is exemplified by John Middleton Murray's book of 1916. Since that time, a number of other critics have constructed their own systems of supposedly Dostoevskian thought (often unwarranted by the texts of the novels or the known views of the novelist) and then proceeded, as Hugh McLean put it, to bend the knee before their own creations in worshipful wonder.

Dostoevsky is universally venerated, but just how much he is read or understood remains a puzzle. The author of the recent Broadway adaptation of *The Idiot* changed the heroine's name from Nastasya (a colloquial form of Anastasia) to Natasha (an endearment for Natalie and quite impossible with the patronymic Philippovna), but not a single drama critic who wrote of this widely reviewed production noticed the change.

An article on Leningrad in the *New York Times* travel section casually mentions the old prisons—"dark cells where Dostoevsky and others who criticized the czarist regime were confined." Such a simplistic image of Dostoevsky as a leading dissident of his time and a revolutionary martyr can be frequently encountered in the American press, both Establishment and underground, and this can only mean that neither his biography nor his general views are familiar to those who modishly bandy his name about. Someone ought to translate the set of disgustingly chauvinistic, jingoist and anti-Semitic poems (yes, poems) which Dostoevsky wrote in the late 1850's, urging that Russia conquer other countries, calling down God's blessings on Russian conquests and denouncing the Jews as leeches who torture Russia; copies of these poems should be handed out to all the starry-eyed champions of the progressive, revolutionary Dostoevsky. Of course, a simple reading of *The Possessed* and of *The Diary of a Writer* might also help.

Those who wish to enhance their grasp and understanding of Dostoevsky (as opposed to "relating to him" or "getting high on him") have at their service a whole little library of biographical and critical studies in English, some of which, in their informed and balanced presentation of the material, are superior to anything published on Dostoevsky in other languages, including Russian. The three excellent surveys of the writer's life and work are those by Ernest J. Simmons (in my opinion, the finest achievement of this veteran American Slavicist), Edward Wasiolek's *Dostoevsky: The Major Fiction* and the book by the émigré scholar Konstantin Mochulsky, now available in translation. Mochulsky's book is particularly important for its numerous quotations from the many as yet untranslated Russian studies of Dostoevsky. Donald Fanger's *Dostoevsky and Romantic Realism* is an absorbing demonstration of the origins of Dostoevsky's literary art and of his debt to his immediate predecessors Gogol, Dickens and Balzac. And of course those who would like to get deeper into Dostoevsky criticism can turn to the books and articles by Robert Louis Jackson, Joseph Frank, R. P. Blackmur, George Gibian, Ralph E. Matlaw, Vladimir Seduro, Philip Rahv (his essay on *The Possessed* is more timely today than it was 20 years ago) and many, many others.

Crowning all these riches, we now have the English translations of Dostoevsky's sketches and notebooks for his last five novels, very ably edited by Edward Wasiolek. It should be endlessly fascinating for the Dostoevsky buff who knows the novels thoroughly but cannot read Russian to be able to enter Dostoevsky's laboratory and to follow the various transformations the character of Stavrogin went through or to observe the gradual emergence of the father in *A Raw Youth* as the central and most important figure in the book.

The translation and the presentation of these notebooks are quite admirable, particularly impressive are Edward Wasiolek's highly intelligent and sensible introductory essays, especially the one to the notebooks for *The Brothers Karamazov.*

A possible effect of the publication of these notebooks might be an increase of objectivity in American Dostoevsky criticism, the appearance of a more level-headed, matter-of-fact approach. All too often, the only acceptable tone is that of hushed reverence. A few polite kicks at the awesome pedestal might be healthy. There somehow has to be room for a more balanced appraisal that takes into full cognizance Dostoevsky's obscurantist, reactionary ideology, the excessively nagging and hysterical tone of his narrators, the cheap and flashy effects with which he stages some of his dramatic confrontations and the occasional but undeniable sloppiness of his plots and of his Russian style (translators almost inevitably find it expedient to tidy Dostoevsky up and to tone down some of his stylistic extravagances). Dostoevsky's stature is much too secure to be endangered by any of these facts; but their open recognition could lead to a deeper, more genuine understanding of his art.

One of the best kept secrets in Western criticism is that Dostoevsky does not happen to be everyone's cup of tea. Many intelligent, compassionate, sensitive people find his overheated universe of stormy passions, gratuitous cruelty, tormented children and hysterical women definitely uncongenial. The strangeness of the Dostoevskian universe, so well conveyed by Virginia Woolf ("We open the door and find ourselves in a room full of Russian generals, the tutors of Russian generals, their stepdaughters and cousins and crowds of miscellaneous people who are all talking at the tops of their voices about their most private affairs"), which foreigners tend to ascribe to some peculiarities of the Russian national character, is just as strongly felt and often resented by Russians themselves.

Russian dictionaries list a common noun, derived from the writer's name, *dostoevshchina*, which is a derogatory term describing an undesirable mode of behavior. A person guilty of *dostoevshchina* is being deliberately difficult, hysterical or perverse. Another possible meaning of this word is excessive and morbid preoccupation with one's own psychological processes. The word is a part of the normal Russian vocabulary, incidentally.

Thus, while no Western critic or literate person would dare to admit publicly that he dislikes certain aspects of Dostoevsky or is bored by them, Russians themselves have never felt any such compunctions. In fact some of the most important Russian literary figures who came after Dostoevsky's time have shown themselves wholly unreceptive to his magic.

Leo Tolstoy, the greatest of Dostoevsky's contemporaries, made no attempt to meet him while he was alive. He bitterly regretted the omission after Dostoevsky died, although a meeting could have easily been arranged through numerous mutual friends, had either side been really interested. Of all the novels by Dostoevsky, Tolstoy valued only *Notes From the House of the Dead* for the universal accessibility of its condemnation of inhumanity, which he compared to *Uncle Tom's Cabin* and George Eliot's *Adam Bede*. *The Insulted and the Injured* is known to have touched Tolstoy—but there is no reason to think that he saw any worth in Dostoevsky's other novels. Tolstoy tried to reread *The Brothers Karamazov* in 1910, the year of his death. "I've started reading it," he wrote to one of his correspondents, "but I cannot conquer my revulsion for its lack of artistic quality, its frivolity, posturings and wrong-headed attitude toward important matters."

Anton Chekhov was 29 years old and a recognized writer when he first sat down to read his way through Dostoevsky. "I've purchased Dostoevsky in your store and now I am reading him," he wrote to the publisher Suvorin. "It's all right, but much too long and lacking in modesty. Too pretentious." In Chekhov's stories and personal letters, the name of Dostoevsky usually occurs in passages condemning some high-strung or hysterical or hypocritical female. Since Chekhov, with his gentle humanity, relativistic moral outlook and reliance on precise and unbiased observation of everyday life, is Dostoevsky's exact antipode in the Russian literary tradition (and for this reason is usually disliked by ardent Dostoevskians), the lack of affinity is both expected and understandable.

Maxim Gorky, who valued Dostoevsky's literary achievement very highly, nevertheless considered popularization of Dostoevsky's work detrimental to the cause of progress and revolution in Russia. On the eve of World War I, Gorky became embroiled in a major controversy when he made vehement protests against the stagings of dramatized versions of *Crime and Punishment* and *The Possessed* by the Moscow Art Theater and several other Russian theaters on the grounds that these productions would further the cause of political reaction. A number of prominent writers and intellectuals of the day wrote letters to editors, condemning Gorky's attack on Dostoevsky, but he received strong support from Lenin (whose most memorable comment on the subject of Dostoevsky came when he referred to a mediocre writer as "the ultra-bad imitator of the ultra-bad Dostoevsky").

While Gorky was careful to qualify his ideologically motivated denunciations of Dostoevsky with admiring statements about Dostoevsky's enormous literary talent, Gorky's one-time close associate (and later, after the Revolution, his sworn enemy) the Nobel Prize winner Ivan Bunin, refused to grant Dostoevsky any literary talent or stature whatsoever. The published diaries of Galina Kuznetsova, who was a member of Bunin's household during his residence in the south of France in the 1920's and 1930's, contain a wonderfully vivid description of a clash on the subject, complete with screaming and slamming of doors, between Bunin, who tried rereading *The Possessed* and found it totally worthless, and his wife, secretary and other members of his staff, all of whom were warm admirers of Dostoevsky. Bunin's conclusion was that the universal admiration for this, in his opinion, irritatingly inept writer must be the result of mass hypnosis.

Then there is Marina Tsvetaeva, one of the most important Russian poets of the 20th century, for whom Dostoevsky was a totally unnecessary writer. In a letter to a friend, Tsvetaeva compared Dostoevsky to her favorite Russian novelist, Leskov, and to the novels by Sigrid Undset and confessed that she could love their books the way she could not possibly love Dostoevsky. For Tsvetaeva, the world of Dostoevsky was "a dream-world, without colors, untinted, all in the even, artificial light of a photographic film that shows only the contours." A character in a novel by Nabokov, we might note, compared Dostoevsky's world to a room in which an electric bulb is gratuitously burning in broad daylight.

This is not to suggest for a moment that the majority of Russian writers were indifferent to Dostoevsky or rejected his influence. Almost all of Russian Symbolist poetry, all of Russian non-Marxist philosophy and much of the best in the Soviet prose of the 1920's can testify to the pervasiveness and the depth of Dostoevsky's impact on Russian culture.

The constant presence of Dostoevsky in the writings of Vladimir Mayakovsky (in his powerful, if flawed, masterpiece of autobiographical poetry *About This* as well as in his plays and many of his shorter lyrics) is as evident as it is unexpected. Paradoxically, it is to the theological aspects of Dostoevsky—the concepts of Redemption and the Redeemer, the dream of the Golden Age, the heavy reliance on Old and New Testament imagery—that the militant atheist Mayakovsky responded most frequently and profoundly. Only the schizophrenic attitude of the Soviet literary Establishment toward Dostoevsky and their insistence on a simplistically dogmatic treatment of Mayakovsky have prevented this fascinating and important problem in literary scholarship from getting the extensive treatment it deserves in the vast area of Soviet Mayakovsky studies.

The negative views of Dostoevsky held by the important Russian writers cited above might help Western readers to place in their proper perspective the numerous and well-publicized potshots that Vladimir Nabokov has been aiming at his illustrious compatriot. Reactions to Nabokov's qualifications of Dostoevsky as "a cheap sensationalist, clumsy and vulgar," "a prophet, a claptrap journalist, and a slapdash comedian" or "a much overrated sentimental and Gothic novelist" have ranged from puzzlement and stupefaction to rage. However, Nabokov's attitude to Dostoevsky, motivated in all probability by the same set of factors as the attitudes of Chekhov and Bunin, must have acquired its additional polemical bite from the author's decades of residence in the West, where the blind adulation of Dostoevsky can be as irritating as it is universal.

Nabokov, observing American motels and colleges and then reproducing their very fabric and climate in *Lolita*, and Dostoevsky, traveling through Paris and London and then reducing these cities to the private nightmares of his own anti-Western, sexually obsessed subconscious in *Winter Notes on Summer Impressions*; Nabokov, reading Pushkin's *Eugene Onegin* and then trying to reconstruct to the best of his ability every nuance of Pushkin's meaning in his voluminous commentary to his translation of that novel, and Dostoevsky, savagely distorting the characters, the plot and the very text of Pushkin's masterpiece in order to make it all conform to his nationalistic, Slavophile ideology in his famous Pushkin speech of 1880—these are only two of the many contrasts that illustrate the irreconcilable differences in the two writers' view of life and in their conception of the art of literature.

Yet, for all this repulsion. there remains the unanswered question of Nabokov's repeated utilization of themes and subjects that had earlier been treated by Dostoevsky. A character that functions as the hero's double (a topic that admittedly bores Nabokov) recurrently appears in various novels by these two writers. Some of the basic themes of *Crime and Punishment* are present, possibly parodistically, in Nabokov's *Despair*, while the narrators of both *The Eye* and *Pale Fire* are in many ways comparable to the narrator of *Notes From the Underground*. And it was none other than Nabokov who in *Lolita* gave the world a full-scale treatment of a subject around which Dostoevsky circled like a cat around a saucer of hot milk in novel after novel only to recoil from it in horror. But while these parallels are certainly present, the uses to which the two writers have put these similar themes are of course vastly different—as different, say, as a setting of the same melody by Moussorgsky and by Stravinsky would be.

Dostoevsky's prophetic gifts, which even Nabokov seems to admit grudgingly, are considerable. *Notes From the Underground* (the more correct translation of the Russian title would be *Diary Written in a Basement*) remains, whatever else it might be, a great prophecy of 20th-century irrationality and anti-intellectualism. A recent radio broadcast of a discussion between Herbert Marcuse and some black and white militants about the ways and means of making the contented American working classes dissatisfied with their lot and ready for revolution sounded uncannily like a replay of one of the key scenes in Dostoevsky's *The Possessed*.

When later on, during the same broadcast, Professor Marcuse, who had insisted that he loved and understood America, was pressed to specify which aspects of American life he found particularly attractive, he fumbled for an answer, said he loved the hippies, with their long hair, and after some more fumbling, mentioned the beautiful American scenery, threatened by pollution. Despite an obvious effort, he could think of no other items. It was a quintessentially Dostoevskian spectacle of a man brilliantly at home in the world of abstractions, generalizations and political theories, but hopelessly blind to the actual details of human existence, to the texture of life as it is experienced on this planet at this juncture of history.

In a novel by Richard Brautigan an incidental character compiles a book called *The Culinary Dostoevsky*. He claims that he eats quite well by reproducing various recipes he has found in Dostoevsky's novels. Brautigan's fancy is delightful, but in actual fact his character would end up very poorly nourished. Gogol, Tolstoy and Chekhov, among Russian writers, have written lovingly and at length about various foods eaten by their characters. But Dostoevsky, who can be so magnificent in his own realm of irrational passions and spiritual insights, had very little interest in the physical basis of human life or in man's natural surroundings. The only kinds of food that it would occur to him to use for literary purposes are a crust of dry bread someone denies to a starving little boy or a pineapple compote that a neurotic young girl dreams she would eat if she were witnessing the crucifixion of a child.

For the flavor and the feel of actual life as it was lived in Russia, reproduced with all the fidelity and subtlety that literary art is capable of, we have to turn to writers who were interested in such things: to the Turgenevs, the Pisemskys, the Chekhovs and the Bunins.

# ALBERTO MORAVIA

## The Marx-Dostoevsky Duel†

\* \* \*

The Russians deny, though weakly and with much hesitancy, that Dostoevsky was outlawed under Stalin. The truth was that

† From *Encounter*, November, 1956, pp. 3–5. Reprinted by permission of *Encounter* and the author, Alberto Moravia, a leading Italian novelist, is the author of *The Time of Indifference, Two Adolescents, The Woman of Rome*, and many other works.

Dostoevsky was not being re-published, old editions of his work passed from hand to hand among his faithful readers, getting dirtier and more tattered, and the literary periodicals didn't mention him. Dostoevsky, in short, as Fadeyev told me some years ago in Rome, was of course a Russian writer, indeed someone whom one could not and must not forget, yet he was also a reactionary, a supporter of Czarism and Orthodoxy, a psychological, decadent, individualistic, and introspective writer. But was this evaluation completely true? I believe that the Stalinists were partly right in regarding Dostoevsky as their adversary (just think of his novel, *The Devils*), but in large part they were wrong.

Let us take, for example, the best and most famous of Dostoevsky's novels: *Crime and Punishment*. This masterpiece will for a long time remain an indispensable key to understanding what has happened in Russia and Europe during the last fifty years. Who is Raskolnikov? He is the intellectual before the advent of Marxism, indignant against the social injustice and abject misery of Czarist Russia, and resolved to carry out a demonstrative, symbolic action against these conditions. Raskolnikov had not read Marx and he admired Napoleon, the model for the entire 19th century of the superman; yet it is symptomatic that, contrary to the Stendhalian Julian Sorel, another admirer of Napoleon, Raskolnikov does not dream of greatness, but rather of justice. And further, that his hate centres on a usurer, that is, on the extreme instance, according to the Marxist formula, of the exploitation of man by man. But who then is the usurer? He is the European bourgeoisie that speculates on the stock exchange with industrial stocks, the fruit of the working-class's surplus value, lives on the income furnished by the national and colonial proletariat, and does this all unawares and with a tranquil conscience. He is a symbol, in sum, fundamentally not very different from the conventional banker-figure of anti-bourgeois satire, with his pendulous fat and high silk hat, and the financier, his huge paunch wrapped in a white waistcoat and his hands loaded with rings that scatter glittering rays.

Although he had not read Marx and regarded himself as a superman beyond good and evil, Raskolnikov was already, in embryo, a people's commissar; and, in fact, the first people's commissars came out of that same class of the intelligentsia to which Raskolnikov belonged, and possessed his identical ideas—the same thirst for social justice, the same terrible ideological consistency, the same inflexibility in action. And Raskolnikov's dilemma is the very same one that confronts the people's commissars and Stalin: "Is it right for the good of humanity to kill the old usurer (read: liquidate the bourgeoisie)?" So why should the Communists have such an aversion to Dostoevsky?

The reason is quite simple. Raskolnikov's hatred of the usurer has a Christian origin. In reality, this hate is the hate of the medieval Christian for commerce and profit-making, the irreconcilability of the Bible's teachings with banking and interest rates. This hate, this irreconcilability placed banking and commerce for centuries in the hands of the Jews until the day when the Christian peoples of Europe (and first among them the Italians) realised that they could be bankers or merchants and at the same time upright folk fearful of God, at peace with themselves and their religion. But Raskolnikov belonged, as did the people's commissars and Stalin, to a medieval country where banking and commerce were controlled by restricted racial and social groups, a backward peasant country attached to a still primitive and mystical Christianity. Thus for Raskolnikov banking and commerce are usury and the European and Russian bourgeoisie which practises usury becomes the old usurer; one must therefore kill the old usurer, that is, liquidate the bourgeoisie.

But at this point the until-then united roads of Dostoevsky and Marxism divide and branch off. The Marxists, who are not Christians, say: "Let us eliminate the usurers and go forward. After the death of the usurer we shall inaugurate a new society without classes and without usury. The creation of this society fully justifies the murder of the usurer." On the other hand Dostoevsky, who has remained a Christian, after having led us step by step through all the stages of a crime that he had doubtlessly meditated, fondled, and approved a thousand times in his heart, suddenly, with an unexpected *volte-face*, puts Raskolnikov in the wrong, that is, the Marxists and Stalin, and declares: "No, it is not right to kill, even if it be for the good of mankind. Christ has said: You must not kill." And in fact Raskolnikov repents, and reads the Bible together with Sonia. Dostoevsky swathes the end of his novel in a mystical aura: "But here begins a new story, the story of the gradual rebirth of a man, the story of his gradual regeneration, of his gradual passing from one world to another, of his advance towards a new and hitherto unknown reality." The Marxists, however, would have ended it thus: "But here begins the revolution."

This divergence between Dostoevsky and Marxism is the result of different evaluations of what constitutes evil. For the Marxists evil is the usurer, that is, the bourgeoisie; Dostoevsky, however, after having at first accepted this thesis, rejects it and comes to the Christian conclusion that the evil is not so much the usurer as the means adopted by Raskolnikov to eliminate the usurer, namely, violence. In the novel this evil as seen by Dostoevsky is not only represented by the violent death of the usurer, but also and above all by that of the innocent and pious Lizabeta, the usurer's sister, whom Raskolnikov murders so as to get rid of a witness to his crime. In short, for the Marxists evil does not really exist, since it is solely a matter of a social evil which can be eliminated by the revolution. But for Dostoevsky evil exists as an individual fact, in each man's heart, and expresses itself precisely in the violent means used by the revolution. With their historic and social justifications the Marxists can wash clean even the blackest of consciences. Dostoevsky rejects this sort of cleansing and affirms the ineradicable existence of evil.

So, for the last ninety years, we have witnessed in Russia a kind of match between Dostoevsky and Marx. The first round was won by Dostoevsky, since he had written a masterpiece; the second round went to Marx, since his theories produced a revolution; yet the third round seems to have been won by Dostoevsky: the evil thrown out the window by Marxism has returned in torrents through the door of Stalinism, that is, through the means adopted by the revolution to establish and maintain itself. And what is this evil? Khrushchev has already told us in his speech; I will touch on it more briefly: The evil in the U.S.S.R. is represented by the innumerable Lizabetas, the innumerable innocents tortured, imprisoned, murdered in the name of the revolution, who are now being rehabilitated but to whom can never be given back what was taken from them. In short, the evil is the pain, the immense quantity of pain which has submerged Russia during the last fifty years. This pain, in turn, is the blow of Raskolnikov's axe, justified by the good of humanity. Unfortunately the axe blow, at least in reality, weighs much more than the good of humanity. On the scales, the good of humanity leaps up in the air, light, high, very high; while the axe blow pushes down the other plate, low, low, very low. Therefore: Dostoevsky's victory, at least for the time being. It is true that the Marxists will still insist on saying that the evil does not exist, that the evil is really, or rather objectively, capitalism. But is it possible to maintain, be it only "objectively," that Stalin and Beria were capitalists?

\* \* \*

# V. PEREVERZEV

## [A Marxist Summing-Up of Dostoevsky]†

F. M. Dostoevsky is a brilliant representative of the literary style created by the city bourgeoisie under the conditions of the destruction of the serf class system and the birth of capitalism. He was born in Moscow in the family of a doctor, Michael Andreevich Dostoevsky, who was of priesthood origin. It was the patriarchally bourgeois family of a member of the pre-Revolutionary intelligentsia. * * * The Petersburg of those days differed sharply from Moscow, where the childhood of Dostoevsky had been spent. Moscow still preserved its patriarchal way of life, to which the Dostoevsky family clung tenaciously. Petersburg was a real capitalistic city, the scene of acute class conflict which destroyed the barriers between classes and excited men's minds by the temptations of career and fortune. * * * The social basis of Dostoevsky's works is the bourgeoisie disintegrating under capitalistic development. The character of that social group is imprinted in the distinguishing features of Dostoevsky's style. On Dostoevsky's style there lies the stamp of a dark tragedy. The reason for this is that the bourgeoisie which gave birth to that style found itself in a truly tragic position. As capitalism developed, the bourgeoisie was placed under a double pressure. On one hand, it was being squeezed by the pressure of class disenfranchisement (the pressure of belonging to a socially low caste). On the other hand it was being squeezed by the pressure of capitalism which transformed the bourgeoisie into a petty bourgeoisie, an economically extremely unstable grouping, poised between the finance bourgeoisie and the urban depths. * * * The feelings of injury, of insult, of humiliation seethe in the hearts of the dissolving bourgeoisie and are resolved in a hysterical fight for honor which in view of evident hopelessness of the struggle assumes sickly, pathological forms, and most frequently of all ends in catastrophe. It is this sense of catastrophe which gives the tragic imprint to all Dostoevsky's works and makes them so tormented, so dark, and makes his talent into "a cruel talent."

A hysterical struggle for the honor of the bourgeois humiliated in his human dignity, a struggle which ends darkly, is Dostoevsky's

† From Vol. III of *Literaturnaya Entsyklopedia*, Moscow, 1930; translated by George Gibian. Pereverzev's encyclopedia article represents a Marxist attempt at relating Dostoevsky, in what later came to be called "vulgar sociologizing," to the social conditions of his day. Only a little later, in the 1930's and 1940's, official Soviet opinion turned against Dostoevsky, mainly because of his religious and other "reactionary" convictions.

constant theme. The motifs of his works are composed of manifold manifestations of a pathological struggle for honor. This struggle assumes wild, absurd forms. In order to feel he is a real, whole man whom nobody is allowed to injure, Dostoevsky's hero must himself dare to injure someone else. If I can and if I dare injure, insult, torment someone, then I am a man. If I do not dare to do it, I am not a man but a nothing. * * * In his works Dostoevsky created all the different manners in which it was possible for the falling bourgeois to react to a reality hostile to him. He tried to point out one manner of reacting after another as the true one which would successfully solve the life's task. But none of them really prove to be such.

* * * The chaotic dynamism which marks the composition of his works is characteristic also of his style. The language of the narrators and heroes is hurried, feverishly bustling, the words pile up hastily, forming a disorderly flood of sentences or falling into brief, fragmented phrases. In Dostoevsky's bustling syntax, one feels the hysterical language of a man who mixes up words, is torn apart by life, whose nerves are on edge, a man of the urban underworld. The disturbed, pathological mood created by such a bustling syntax is reinforced by the semantics. Dostoevsky finds ʻhe contents for his epithets, metaphors, and similes in the gloomv, inhospitable world of city back alleys.

* * * Dostoevsky's world, deeply democratic in form and content, saturated with social protest, embued by deep understanding and deep compassion for the socially declassed and injured man, bears a strong charge of socially progressive energy.

# U.S.S.R. MINISTRY OF CULTURE

## [The 1953 Outline for the Study of Dostoevsky in Soviet Universities]†

Dostoevsky's works as an expression of reactionary bourgeois-individualistic ideology. V. I. Lenin on Dostoevsky. Dostoevsky's literary career from the Forties to the Eighties as a journey away from progressive, democratic ideas of the "Natural School" and

† From *Programma po istorii russkoi literatury*, part III, pp. 35–36, Moscow University Press, 1953; translated by George Gibian. This outline, the governing syllabus for Soviet universities, was edited by A. M. Egolin, one of the most outspoken supporters of the strict Communist Party line in literary criticism and scholarship. Printed in the fall of 1953, after Stalin's death but before de-Stalinization, it represents the official Soviet anti-Dostoevskian case at its clearest.

towards reactionary, religious, protective ideas. The problems of Dostoevsky's works in the Forties and their connection with the "Natural School." Belinsky abouι the humanism of *The Poor Folk*, about the *Double*, and *The Landlady*. Dostoevsky's split with Belinsky. The depiction of tsarist prison in *The House of the Dead*. The critical realism of *The House of the Dead*. Pisarev[1] about Dostoevsky. Dostoevsky's works in the Sixties and Seventies. The reflection of the countradictions of reactionary bourgeois consciousness in the period of the sharp breaking up of social relations of post-Reform Russia.[2] The struggle of Dostovesky with the revolutionary democratic ideas of Chernyshevsky and Shchedrin under the conditions of the revolutionary situation in the Sixties. The reactionary criticism of materialism, Utopian Socialism, and revolutionary enlightenment in the *Notes from the Underground*.

The character of Dostoevsky's realism in the novels of the Sixties and Seventies. The reflection of contradictions of exploitative society in *Crime and Punishment*, *The Raw Youth*, and *The Idiot*. The representation of human sufferings and the affirmation of the cult of suffering and endurance. The problem of the rebellion of meekness in Dostoevsky. The images of "the hardened" and the "gentle" (Raskolnikov and Sonya Marmeladova, Nastasya Filipovna and Myshkin,[3] Ivan and Alyosha Karamazov). Dobrolyubov[4] about the harmfulness of Dostoevsky's heroes. *The Possessed* as a reactionary political novel. The novel *Brothers Karamazov* as a synthesis of the principal ideas of Dostoevsky's works. The social and psychological meaning of Karamazovism. Dostoevsky's struggle against materialism and atheism in the novel. The antihumanistic nature of Ivan Karamazov's rebellion. The reactionary political program of Dostoevsky embodied in the images of Alyosha and the Elder Zosima.

Dostoevsky's artistic method. The idealistic aesthetics of the writer and their connection with his method of psychological analysis. The psychology of the *Double*. The subjectivism, the publicistic nature, and the complicated plotting of the novels of Dostoevsky.

The negative opinion of Dostoevsky in Russian democratic criticism. The struggle of Gorky against Dostoevsky and manifestations of Dostoevskyism, in Russian and foreign literature. The political meaning of the cult of Dostoevsky in reactionary circles of Western Europe and the USA.

The unmasking by Soviet literary scholarship of the reactionary philosophical and political essence of Dostoevsky's views.

1. A nineteenth-century radical political and literary critic. He wrote a pronouncedly sociological-poiitical study of Dostoevsky [*Editor*].
2. Russia after the 1861 emancipation of serfs and other social and political reforms of that decade [*Editor*].
3. Characters in *The Idiot* [*Editor*].
4. Another nineteenth-century radical writer who wrote on social and literary themes [*Editor*].

# [The 1955 Outline for the Study of Dostoevsky in Soviet Universities]†

The works of Dostoevsky are a critical reflection of the deep inner contradictions which were corroding the Russian aristocratic-bourgeois society in the second stage of the liberating movement. The connections of the young Dostoevsky with the progressive ideological movement (the circle of Petrashevsky) and the "Natural School." Belinsky's high opinion of *The Poor Folk*, which contains the contradictory combination of the pride in work of "the down-trodden" with their individualistic reflections. The strengthening of the latter of these tendencies in other stories by Dostoevsky. Further development of the same contradictions in the stories and novels of the end of the Fifties and beginning of the Sixties. *The House of the Dead. The Insulted and Injured.* Realistic and anti-realistic tendencies in these works. Dobrolyubov and Pisarev about Dostoevsky.

Dostoevsky's switch to reactionary, anti-democratic positions in the period of the revolutionary situation. His struggle with the ideology of the Revolutionary Democracy from the standpoint of "Cult of the Earth"[1] in the *Notes from the Underground.* The magazines *Vremya, Epokha,* and *Notes of a Writer.* Dostoevsky's series of problematically-psychological novels containing on one hand deeply realistic exposure of antisocial, individualistic tendencies in the life of the bourgeois-*raznochinets,*[2] aristocratic, and bourgeois strata of Russian society, and of the dissolution of their ideology and way of life, and on the other hand, the reactionary and tendentious proclaiming of the ideals of religious meekness and love for one's neighbor, ideals intended to conceal and bypass the deepest contradictions of the existing system. *Crime and Punishment, The Idiot.* Dostoevsky's reflection of the crisis of bourgeois individualistic consciousness. The growing hostility of the writer on one hand to the ideas of materialism and socialism and the revolutionary movement (*The Possessed*), and on the other hand to the decaying aristocratic class (satirical images of Svidrigaylov, Stavrogin;[3] the novel *The Brothers Karamazov*). Dostoevsky's for-

† From *Programma po istorii russkoi literatury,* part III, pp. 31–32, Moscow University Press, 1955; translated by George Gibian. This syllabus was published in the fall of 1955, after the de-Stalinization speeches at the Twentieth Party Congress, and in the full swing of "The Thaw." Its editor is no longer Egolin, but A. N. Sokolov. A close comparison with the 1953 version will reveal many significant differences in this important guide line to Soviet teachers and students—the effort to defend and praise Dostoevsky; to stress those "progressive" sides of his thought which could be favorably viewed by a Soviet ideologist and to pay less attention to the unacceptable; to find more to praise in Dostoevsky as an artist; to omit various negative comments made in the 1953 syllabus.
1. "*Pochvennichestvo*"—an idealization of native, "earth" qualities of Russian life (especially rural, peasant, native features).
2. Intellectuals not belonging to the nobility [*Editor*].
3. In *The Possessed* [*Editor*].

mulation of a reactionary-Utopian social doctrine (*The Brothers Karamazov*).

The realism of Dostoevsky's novels, springing from the strong critical side of his opinions. Predominant attention paid by the writer to the moral world of his heroes, to the deep contradictions and pathological sides of their psyches. The psychological and plot hyperbolism in the image system of the novels; the complicatedness of the composition; the tenseness of the intonations of his language; his leaning towards the principles of parody; the image of the narrator—the focal point of all these stylistic devices. The objective significance of Dostoevsky's realism in the struggle of Russian democracy against the survivals of serfdom. The negative role of his reactionary doctrines and the extremeness of his psychologism. Gorky about Dostoevsky. The appraisal of Dostoevsky in contemporary Soviet literary scholarship.

# U.S.S.R. MINISTRY OF CULTURE

# [The 1984 Outline for the Study of Dostoevsky in Soviet Universities]†

Young Dostoevsky's connections with the progressive ideological movement (the Petrashevsky Circle), with the "Natural School." Belinsky's high opinion of the novel *Poor Folk*. The expression in this novel of the contradictory combination of plebeian pride with the individualistic reactions in the "downtrodden people." The intensification of this in other works by Dostoevsky. Further deepening of these contradictions in the stories and novels of the end of the 1850s and the beginning of the 1860s. *The Notes from the House of the Dead, The Insulted and the Injured*. Dobrolyubov and Pisarev on Dostoevsky.

Dostoevsky's struggle against the ideology of the revolutionary democrats, from the standpoint of the "cult of the soil," in the *Notes from the House of the Dead*. The magazines *Time* and *Epoch*. The positive and the critical in Dostoevsky's legacy.

Dostoevsky's novels. Realistic refutation of antisocial, individualistic tendencies in the life of petty burghers, those outside the class system, the nobility, and the bourgeoisie, of the moral disintegration of these

† In 1984, the Ministry of Higher Education issued a revised syllabus, which was still in force at the time of the preparation of the present edition, in the summer of 1988, that is, after three years of Gorbachev's *glasnost* and *perestroika*. It departed slightly from the earlier syllabus, in the direction of still greater acceptance of Dostoevsky's work. This latest version attempts to balance an increased attention to the artistic side of Dostoevsky's works and greater un-derstanding for his ideological positions with continued rejection of his religious outlook.

A close comparison of the three sets of Ministry guidelines to the study of Dostoevsky in Soviet universities is an interesting exercise in noting omissions, changes in formulation, and additions, resulting in subtle differences in the degree of acceptance of the Russian classic.

strata of Russian society. The preaching of the erroneous principle of moral rebirth, from a religious position, in an attempt to solve the deepest contradictions of the society of his day.

*Crime and Punishment, The Idiot.* The representation by Dostoevsky of the crisis of bourgeois individualistic consciousness. The writer's increasing hostility on the one hand towards materialistic ideas, "political" socialism, and the revolutionary movement (*The Possessed*); and on the other hand towards the disintegrating substratum of the nobility (images of Svidrigailov, Stavrogin). The novel *The Brothers Karamazov.* Its ideas and images. The journalistic and the artistic in *The Writer's Diary,* the story *The Dream of the Ridiculous Man.*

The special quality of the critical realism of Dostoevsky's novels. The writer's attention to the moral world of his heroes, to the deep contradictions in their psychology. Hyperbole in psychology and plot, in the system of images of the novels, their complicated composition; the tension in the intonations of the poetic language; the tendency towards the principles of parody; the image of the narrator, the use of the narrator as the focal point of all stylistic devices. The objective significance of Dostoevsky's realism for the struggle against the landed gentry-bourgeoisie system. Gorky and Lunacharsky on Dostoevsky. The world significance of Dostoevsky. The most important conceptions of Dostoevsky's creation in contemporary literary scholarship.

# LEONID P. GROSSMAN

## [The Construction of the Novel]†

*Crime and Punishment* firmly establishes Dostoevsky's characteristic form. This is his first philosophical novel on a criminal basis. It is also at the same time a typical psychological novel, partly even a psychopathological one, with rather noticeable traces of the police novel-feuilleton and the "black" or morbid-adventure novel of the English school (Dostoevsky was captivated by examples of all these genres in his youth). But it is, above all—like Dostoevsky's first work[1]—a social novel, which places in the thick

---

† "Dostoevsky-khudozhnik" in *Tvorchestvo F. M. Dostoevskogo* (Moscow, 1959), pp. 387–89, 390–92. Translated by Natalie Bienstock. L. P. Grossman is one of Soviet Russia's leading Dostoevsky scholars. The author of numerous articles and books about Dostoevsky before World War II, he came under a cloud when it became unfashionable in the U.S.S.R. to investigate Dostoevsky's connections with Western literary trends (a subject of Grossman's several studies) as well as the artistic, formal sides of Dostoevsky's works. The volume *Tvorchestvo F. M. Dostoevskogo,* a large anthology published by the Soviet Academy of Sciences, containing many articles by leading critics and scholars, was a landmark in the de-Stalinization period. Its general tone and approach towards Dostoevsky were favorable, and it contained studies of artistic aspects of his work, such as those of Evnin and Grossman. in this volume.

1. *The Poor Folk* [*Editor*].

of action and under dialectic fire the large, painful themes of the contemporary political moment in all the intensity of the battle of ideas and social forces.

Dostoevsky cast *The Poor Folk*, his first short social novel of 1845, in the traditional epistolary form. His first large social novel, *Crime and Punishment*, he carefully constructed twenty years later as an original problematic "inner monologue" of the hero, crisscrossed by philosophical dialogues placed against the background of a detective plot. The lengthy and deep self-analysis of Raskolnikov, his disputes with Porfiry, Svidrigaylov, Sonia amidst the incessant play of the murderer with the police and investigative forces—such is the fabric of *Crime and Punishment*.

The great artistry of the novelist is revealed in the organic fusion of this basis with the sharpest topics of contemporary journalism, which transformed a criminal-reflective novel into a grandiose social epic.

*Crime and Punishment* is first of all a novel of a big city in the nineteenth century. A widely developed background of a capitalistic capital determines here the character of the conflicts and dramas. Saloons, taverns, houses of prostitution, slum hotels, police stations, the attic of a student and the apartment of a money-lender, streets, alleys, courtyards and back yards, Haymarket Square and the "canal"—all of this produces the criminal scheme of Raskolnikov and marks the stages of his complex inner struggle.

Depicting this specifically Petersburgian "landscape and genre," in the tradition of the early "Natural School,"[2] Dostoevsky makes concrete the abstract idea of his composition. With inimitable talent and striking sharpness, he etches the urban struggles which he unfolds with that living palpability which evokes in the reader the feeling of full life and irresistible authenticity.

\* \* \*

The principle of how to present this "account of a certain crime" was not immediately found. Dostoevsky had jotted down three basic forms for his novel: (1) narrative in the first person or a confession of the hero himself, (2) the ordinary form of narration from the author's point of view, and (3) a mixed form ("the narration ends and the diary begins"). The first form (*i.e.*, the "I-narrative") in turn presumed two versions: recollection of an old crime (eight years ago) and the testimony during the trial. Such a public confession particularly attracted Dostoevsky and for a long time was predominant: "I am on trial and will tell every-

---

2. The "Natural School," a vague grouping in Russian literature of the 1840's, associated with prose works of Grigorovich, Gogol, and other writers, marked by the effort to render simply and with "scientific" accuracy the everyday habits and circumstances of life of working-class people and peasants [*Editor*].

thing. I will write down everything. I am writing for myself, but let others read it too, and all my judges, if they want to. This is a full confession. I will hide nothing," etc. . . .

This form was probably suggested to Dostoevsky by Victor Hugo's *The Last Day of a Condemned Man*. In the introduction to *The Gentle Spirit* he calls this work the French writer's *chef d'oeuvre*. Evidently at first the story about Raskolnikov was conceived along the lines of Hugo's story, the compressed confession of a condemned criminal, with the stunning opening: "I am sentenced to death" (*cf.* Dostoevsky's "I am on trial").

A variant to such a courtroom monologue appeared in the plan of the story—in the form of a memoir of a criminal about an old crime which took place eight years before the opening of the story: "A new plan. The tale of the criminal. . . . This happened exactly eight years ago and I want to tell everything in order. I began by going to her to pawn my watch" and so forth. It was difficult to exploit all the potentialities of the story in a first-person narrative. Inevitably, all episodes in which the narrator himself did not take part would have to be eliminated. Thus Dostoevsky was compelled to have second thoughts about this method.

He sketched a new plan in which the exposition was now carried on by the author, but was concentrated on the main hero (retaining in this manner a trace of the original exposition in the first person): "Another plan. Narrative by the author, as if he were an invisible, but all knowing creature, but not leaving him, Raskolnikov, for a minute even with the words: and all of this came about so haphazardly." This plan, as is known, soon did prevail with the only difference that the central hero, who really is almost constantly within the reader's field of vision, is excluded from several episodes (an insignificant number in the novel as a whole) of Svidrigaylov's story.

But the principle of narration in the author's person worked out in the process of these artistic searchings, a narration which as much as possible stays with the main hero, gave to *Crime and Punishment* that tightness, unity, and concentration of action which make this novel in terms of composition the best of Dostoevsky's works. The relating of events almost always from the subjective position of the main hero (a vestige, in the final version, of the original first-person narration) transforms the entire novel into a peculiar internal monologue of Raskolnikov, which gives the whole history of his crime an exceptional wholeness, tenseness, and fascination.

The concentration of a big novel on one topic which extends throughout all its action is accomplished here by Dostoevsky with rare mastery and persistence. Everything is connected to the center and circumscribed by a single circle. From the very first paragraphs of the novel the reader learns that a murder is being planned. For the duration of six chapters he is entirely in the grip of ideological motives for the crime and the material methods of its preparation. Immediately after the murder, Dostoevsky presents Raskolnikov's inner struggle, complicated most by its psychological drama—his plan, his theory, his conscience, as well as his outer struggle with authority in the person of the strongest of opponents, Porfiry Petrovich, and partly in the person of the police clerk Zametov. All who surround him are pulled into the murderer's drama. He either reveals his secret himself (to Razumikhin, Sonia, Dunia), or he is unable to hide it from them (Zametov, Svidrigaylov, Porfiry Petrovich). The three conversations with the inspector are a masterpiece of intellectual single combat. The precise "psychological" ring, which Raskolnikov's irresistible rival in dialectics begins to draw around Raskolnikov invisibly and surely from the first days after the murder, closes surely and precisely on the stormy night of their last talk, so calm at its outset. Raskolnikov can only submit to Porfiry's logical influence and to Sonia's moral influence —he goes out on the square and confesses his guilt in the police station.

The drama's line of development is interrupted nowhere. It is not broken by side episodes. Everything serves a single action, shading and deepening it. The tragedy of the Marmeladov family is the strongest argument for Raskolnikov's theory and action, as is the Svidrigaylov motif in his sister's fate arising out of his mother's letter, which rapidly receives a full and deep development in the novel. Svidrigaylov's character does not function at all as an independent, parenthetical episode. He illuminates Raskolnikov's fate and personality marvellously.

# [Dostoevsky's Descriptions: The Characters and the City]

The portraiture in the novel is distinguished by an exceptional compression and expressiveness. The heroes' exteriors are shown with a particular concentrated expression, recalling later famous portrayals, for example Stavrogin or Grushenka,[3] but not yet requiring large canvases and a background of deep perspective.

In *Crime and Punishment* Dostoevsky is, according to Pushkin's favorite epithet, a "fast" painter. A few immediate strokes take the place of the usual pages of broad descriptions. In the six lines

---

3. Characters in *The Possessed* and *The Brothers Karamazov*, respectively [*Editor*].

of the old woman's portrait there is a forceful concentration of typical features, giving an image of such amazing lifelikeness that much of what is unexpected in Raskolnikov's deed is made clear to the reader by this externally repulsive appearance of the revolting money-lender: "This was a tiny, dried up little old lady of about sixty with sharp and evil little eyes, with a small sharp nose and a bare head. Her light, slightly grey hair was greasily smeared with oil. Around her skinny, long neck, which looked like a chicken leg, was wrapped some sort of flannel rag and on her shoulders, in spite of the heat, there dangled a mussed and yellowed fur jacket."

In *The Raw Youth* and in *The Brothers Karamazov*, we no longer find that exhaustive brevity of the portraits of 1866, like the sketch of the main hero Raskolnikov ("he was amazingly handsome, with beautiful dark eyes, dark chestnut hair, above average height, thin and slender"), or the sketch of Svidrigailov ("this was somehow a strange face, resembling a mask: white, rosy, with rosy red lips . . . the eyes were somehow too blue, and their expression was somehow too heavy and immobile; there was something terribly unpleasant in this handsome face overly youthful for his years"). Or the brief snapshot of Lebeziatnikov ("a dried out, scrofulous man, of small stature, blond to the point of strangeness, with chop-shaped sideburns of which he was very proud"). Just as compressed and significant are the sketches of Sonia, Dunia, Luzhin, Marmeladov, Porfiry Petrovich ("the unforgettable white eyelashes on his womanish face"), the girls on the boulevards, the nice-looking Duklida and her pockmarked friend, Agafiushka, the drowned woman, Lizaveta Ivanovna, lieutenant Porokh, Zametov, Mikolka, the burgher, the Jewish soldier.

Dostoevsky's philosophical novel gives a rich collection of Petersburg types, resembling the albums or "panorama" of the outstanding illustrators of the period of the 1840's–60's. In the sharp, synthesizing images of *Crime and Punishment*, which are so characteristic and lifelike, even in spite of the occasional presence of a grotesque style ("he linked up with these little clerks for the very reason that both of them had crooked noses: the nose of one was crooked to the right, and the other's to the left"), Dostoevsky appears as an original and piercing draughtsman from nature. Not without reason did he value Gavarni, mentioned by him in *The Insulted and Injured*, and in his youth he was ecstatic over Agin, the illustrator of *Dead Souls*, and over the caricatures of Nevakhovich.[4] In the Petersburg sketches and the line drawings in *Crime and*

4. Gavarni was a French etcher and lithographer; Agin and Nevakhovich were Russian painters and illustrators. All three were active during the first half of the nineteenth century [*Editor*].

*Punishment* there is something of the original genre of the graphic artists of the middle of the century, who with their fine needles enlivened the sketches about everyday life in the various "physiologies"[5] of the capital.

The persons are characterized not only by their external appearances, but also by their speech peculiarities. [One critic] correctly notes the stylistic "office jargon" of Luzhin, the ironic carelessness of Svidrigaylov, and the ecstatic ornamentality of Razumikhin. It is also not difficult to catch the sarcastic businesslike way of talking of the legal scholar Porfiry and the affected politeness of Marmeladov's civil servant's speech, lavishly supported with Church Slavisms for the expressive painting of the shattering story of his falls and sufferings. In addition to their diction, the "verbal gestures" and the intonational systems of the heroes are apparent in the novel with ineffaceable variety.

Along with examples of portraiture and genre, the novel gives masterpieces of city description of "middling streets" of the capital with their stench and dust, laborer and craftsman population, saloons and various other low-grade "establishments." ". . . Melancholy, unsavory and stinking Petersburg in the summer"— stated Dostoevsky at the height of his work on *Crime and Punishment*—"corresponds to my mood and could even give me a somewhat false inspiration for the novel . . ." The preparatory studies for such city descriptions were realized by the artist in earlier works. The picture of Petersburg in *Crime and Punishment* is the culmination of a whole series of Dostoevsky's sketches in his earlier novellas as well as in his first novel, written after his imprisonment —*The Insulted and Injured*.

But the real studies toward the future city black-and-whites of *Crime and Punishment* were young Dostoevsky's newspaper sketches, which abounded in characteristic descriptions of summer Petersburg, enveloped in a "fine white dust." As early as the 1840's the novice author was struck by the social contrasts of the capital. In one of his anonymous articles he attempts to capture the composite image of Petersburg "with its glitter and luxury, thunder and rumble, with its infinite types, with its infinite activity, heartfelt yearnings, with its gentlemen and rabble—mountains of filth, as Derzhavin says, gilded and not gilded, with its swindlers, booksellers, money-lenders, hypnotists, crooks, muzhiks, and all kinds of riff-raff . . ."

---

5. Anthologies and sketches devoted to descriptions of "types" and "occupations," such as beggars, farmers, tailors, etc., or of streets and towns. This genre proliferated in the 1840's in Russia and was connected with the rise of the "Natural School" in Russian literature, referred to above in footnote 2, p. 619 [*Editor*].

In the novel of 1866, the glimmering strokes of these early sketches were fully developed, and the brief sketches were broadened into a wide panorama. The squalid and repulsive pictures of Haymarket Square and Meschanskiye Streets are offset by the contrasting view of St. Isaac's Cathedral and the embankments, of the palaces and the boulevards. The streets and squares, alleyways and canals not only serve as a background to the action, but enter with their outlines into the thoughts and actions of the heroes. The city constantly dominates the people and hangs over their fates.

In *Crime and Punishment* the internal drama is in a peculiar manner carried out into the crowded streets and squares of Petersburg. The action is constantly transferred out of narrow and low rooms into the noise of the capital's streets. It is in the street that Sonia sacrifices herself, it is here that Marmeladov falls dead, Katerina Ivanovna bleeds to death on the pavement, Svidrigaylov shoots himself on the avenue before a watch-tower, Raskolnikov attempts to confess publicly on Haymarket Square. Many-storied houses, narrow alleyways, dusty squares and hump-backed bridges —the entire structure of a big city of the mid-century looms as a heavy and merciless hulk above the dreamer of limitless rights and possibilities of the lone intellect. Petersburg is inseparable from the personal drama of Raskolnikov: it is that fabric upon which his cruel dialectic draws its designs. The Czar's capital sucks him into its saloons, police stations, taverns, hotels. Over this scum and foam of life with its drunkards, debauchers of minors, prostitutes, usurers, detectives, tuberculosis, venereal diseases, murderers, madmen, there looms, with the strict design of its architectural lines, the city of famous architects and sculptors, luxuriantly sprawling its "magnificent panorama" and hopelessly breathing out a "spirit deaf and dumb."

In view of the complexity of the inner scheme, the unity and fullness of its basic tone of narration is amazing. It is as if it absorbs all the intonations and shadings of the individual scenes and images (such varied motifs as those of Sonia, Svidrigaylov, Raskolinkov, Marmeladov, and the old woman) in order to merge them into one whole. The constant returning to these dominating and alternating themes imparts to the novel the symphonic sound of contemporary Petersburg, merging the enormity of its many voices, its weeping, its screams, into the unified, powerful whole of Raskolnikov's tragedy.

# F. I. EVNIN†

## [Plot Structure and Raskolnikov's Oscillations]

*Crime and Punishment* is the best constructed of Dostoevsky's later novels. The individual lines of action of the novel are unified by the socio-philosophical problem; the various sides of the problem ("the ideas") of Raskolnikov and the various means of its resolution are embodied in these lines of action. "Existence in a yard of space," which serves as the taking-off point for Raskolnikov's whole theory, is written all over the misfortunes of the Marmeladov family, on whose undeserved human suffering Raskolnikov tormentedly meditates. The plot of Svidrigaylov demonstrates that he who was able to transgress the taboos of morality (Raskolnikov was not able) is not a "superman" but a half-man, unworthy of life and rejecting it. In opposition to this, the plot of Sonia Marmeladov must, according to the author's plan, point out the true solution of Raskolnikov's "problem": selfless love of people and service to them. The central plot, that of Raskolnikov, is summoned forth to discredit directly his misanthropic "theory." Finally, the episodes connected with Luzhin discredit this "theory" indirectly by means of directing it towards an ordinary, everyday level. The unscrupulous, bourgeois Luzhin puts into practice in trifles the very same idea of the right to commit crime. One could say that the novel tells not one crime, but several, and their corresponding punishments: the unsuccessful attempt of the would-be "Napoleon" to step over blood; the monstrous, bestial crimes of the cynic Svidrigaylov, who is forced to execute the death sentence upon himself; the self-sacrificing crime of Sonia; Luzhin's revolting, everyday swindling crimes.

Thus the central problem of the novel subordinates to itself all the lines and links of a broadly branched-out subject.

The novel's perfect composition is also the result of the presence of a single core subject, a center. The chief incident (in which the "idea" of the main hero finds expression), the murder of the money-lender, ties the work into a unified whole. As far as plot alone goes, all the chief peripeteias of *Crime and Punishment* either prepare for this incident or are a result of it, in one way or another being interrelated with it. (Almost all of the characters are

---

† *Tvorchestvo Dostoevskogo* (Moscow, 1948), pp. 165–72; translated by Natalie Bienstock. Evnin is a Soviet academic scholar particularly interested in Dostoevsky. His essay illustrates the revival of Soviet publication of studies of Dostoevsky's literary art. For an account of the book in which Evnin's article appeared, see introductory footnote to L. P. Grossman's article.

involved in the struggle brought forth by the murder and in the search for its perpetrator.)

\* \* \*

In a letter to N. Strakhov, Dostoevsky writes: "I have my own peculiar view of reality in art and that which the majority calls almost fantastic and exceptional, is sometimes for me the very essence of reality. The commonplaceness of events and a standard view of them in my opinion is not yet realism, but even the opposite. . . . In every newspaper you run across accounts of the most real and most ingenious facts. To our writers they are fantastic and they do not even bother with them; yet they are reality, because they are *facts*. Who then will notice them, explain them and write them down? They are frequent and everyday, not *exceptional*."

Efforts to make the tale interesting played an outstanding role in the creative plans of the author of *Crime and Punishment*. In September of 1865, when Dostoevsky offered his novel to Katkov, he wrote: "As for interest, I guarantee it, but I can not take upon myself to judge its artistic execution." However, interest in Dostoevsky's eyes never became an aim in itself, something important or definitive; in the just quoted utterance, "interest" is even separated from "artistic execution" as from something much more essential. We have already tried to show how inseparably the entire plot pattern of *Crime and Punishment* is connected with the ideological contents of the novel. However, the ability of Dostoevsky to express this contents in a vivid and exciting plot in no way should be discounted: it attests to his exceptional skill in handling plots.

A peculiar dynamism of plot development in *Crime and Punishment* (which sets it so far apart from the novels of Turgenev and Goncharov) is immediately brought to our attention. The plot of the novel is reminiscent of a kaleidoscope: it is some sort of a whirlwind of events uninterruptedly piling up one on top of the other. But each one individually and all of them together are fully motivated both by the inner logic of the emotions of the characters and by the external connection of everything that is occurring. Dostoevsky knows how to find ever new "pushes," to put into action ever new springs of action, and he does not weaken the tension of the action for a minute.

After the murder is committed and the loose ends are tied up, nothing, it would seem, could lead to the unmasking of the criminal. It would seem that the action ought to slow down. But an "accidental" call to the police station (already prepared for several chapters before "Praskovia Ivanovna wants to complain to the police about you"), and then an "accidental" talk with Zametov and the "accidental" appearance of the criminal at the apartment of the murdered woman (both naturally resulting from his emotional state) create a chain of circumstantial evidence and draw Raskolnikov into a struggle with the investigators.

On the other hand, a series of dramatic episodes arises in connection with the arrival of the mother and sister (also fully motivated by the entire chain of events). The encounters of the hero with Luzhin, Sonia, and Svidrigaylov also serve as a powerful impetus to the action. As a result, a turmoil of events fills the novel right up to the epilogue.

The exceptional dynamism of the plot is particularly evidenced by the fact that the incidents of the novel are extremely concentrated in time. According to the interesting calculations of A. G. Tseitlin, the entire complex kaleidoscope of events which are directly related in *Crime and Punishment* is placed within 9½ days. At that, the events of the first part of the novel are confined to 2½ days, of the second part in two, and of the fifth and sixth in one day.

A. G. Tseitlin's true observation, that "between Sadovaya Street and Haymarket Square, Dostoevsky's heroes live through that which ordinary people do not manage to live through over a period of years, even a lifetime," can be applied first of all to Raskolnikov. The tenseness and dynamism of the plot also find expression in another manner: in the unexpected, sharp turns of the action, in the masterful "backward moves," which suddenly alter the entire situation. Let us recall, for instance, the story of Raskolnikov's rescue after the murder of the money-lender. Maximally intense situations succeed one another as if on the blade of a knife. Each thematic peripeteia cancels out the previous one. Dostoevsky keeps opening the way to escape for the murderer but then convinces the reader that the capture of the criminal is inevitable.

The same alternation of tense situations exists in the episode of Svidrigaylov's attempt upon Dunia. At the moment when his true intentions are revealed, it seems as if Dunia's fate were predestined. The revolver which she suddenly pulls out of her pocket drastically changes the balance of power. But then the revolver misfires and jams, and Dunia throws it away. Svidrigaylov approaches her, but at the last moment Dunia unexpectedly succeeds in her plea, and he lets her go.

Similar turn-abouts in action—completely credible, having none of the fantastic in them—are one of the manifestations of Dostoevsky's inventiveness in the plot. The alternation of contrasting situations is the law of development of the plot in *Crime and Punishment*, as it is in a number of his other works.

The fog of mystery which enwraps Raskolnikov also adds to the excitement of the novel and sharpness of plot. He is immediately presented to the reader as an "enigmatic hero." In the first chapter his "trial run" is described. Trial of what? One can only guess at this in the beginning. Even after it becomes clear that the matter concerns the proposed murder of an old woman and the murder itself is committed, his motives remain insufficiently clear to the reader. Raskolnikov's "theory" is completely revealed only in his confession to Sonia Marmeladova in the fifth part of the novel, which is the next to last part.

That the creation of an aura of mystery around the main heroes of his novels of the '60–'70's was a direct part of the creative intentions of the author is witnessed by comments in notebooks relating to Myshkin, Versilov, Peter Verkhovensky, Stavrogin.[1] Raskolnikov is the same type of "enigmatic hero."

In order to introduce Raskolnikov as a mysterious stranger Dostoevsky does not give any exposition in *Crime and Punishment*, nor does he inform the reader of his hero's past. Only step by step, parallel to the development of the plot, do the most important parts of his past become known (his relations with his family, with his friends; the episode with the bride; the episode of the article). It is noteworthy that two incidents from Raskolnikov's past which are essential to the understanding of his character (aid to his sick friend; saving the children during a fire) are found out by the reader only in the epilogue. Raskolnikov's inner struggle (the scene in the tavern, the talk between the student and officer) is related to the reader as late as possible: directly before the recounting of the old woman's murder.

However, in order for the aura of mystery really to surround Raskolnikov, it was not enough to keep silent concerning his "past": a particular tone and manner in the narration of his "present," engulfed by the novel's plot, was necessary. Dostoevsky therefore used a suitable narrative method in *Crime and Punishment*, as he does in the other big novels of the 1860–70's, in the center of which also stand enigmatic heroes. When he speaks in the person of the author he fulfills, as a rule, only a "protocol-informational" function: he tells of incidents, but does not completely reveal their inner meanings; he fixes emotions, actions, thoughts, the hero's internal monologues, but never fully explains them. Nothing is more alien to Dostoevsky than the role of an all-evaluating and all-explaining author, the position which Tolstoy assumes as a rule, weighing on the scales of analysis and scrupulous ethical evaluation the most most miniscule emotions of Pierre Bezukhov and Nikolai Rostov, or the feelings of Andrei Bolkon-

1. Characters in *The Idiot, The Raw Youth,* and *The Possessed* [Editor].

sky and Nikolai Levin on their deathbeds.[2] In Dostoevsky's notebooks to his novels one often finds comments of the following nature: "A shorter narration; a special tone and a special manner. A brief narrative special tone without explanations." "Write more briefly; just facts; without discussion and without descriptions of feelings." And in the third notebook to *Crime and Punishment* he comments: "only facts, without discussions."

As is known, Dostoevsky had at first planned the form of first-person narration for *Crime and Punishment* the diary of a criminal or his confessions of the murder, but later he rejected this form and preferred an author's narration. What is the explanation for this change of plan? The answer is contained in the first notebook to the novel: "Narrative in my person and not his. If it is a confession then everything, to the last extreme, must be clarified. So that everything at each moment of the story would be clear."

Evidently this necessity to clarify everything in a narration in the person of the main hero stopped Dostoevsky. He preferred another manner—an author's narration "without discussions," which permitted him to surround Raskolnikov with an aura of mystery.

The exceptional dynamism, "plottedness," of the novel is in the first place conditioned by the exceptional dynamism of the main hero. *Crime and Punishment* is almost wholly the story of Raskolnikov's violent oscillations. But the peculiar dynamism of Raskolnikov, like that of other major characters of Dostoevsky (S. Zweig[3] even contrasted them on this level with Balzac's characters) is deeply original and distinctive.

The novels of Dostoevsky, as a rule, do not tell of changes in the hero, but of his incessant, more and more intense oscillations between the same polar extremes which coexist in him—which are the result of his "idea-emotion."

The transfiguration of the hero as a result of his clash with life is the most characteristic and constant theme of the nineteenth-century novel—both Russian and Western European. In Dostoevsky's novels, however, constructed in this respect along dramatic rules, we mainly deal only with the incessant building up of the inner and outer collision of the hero, culminating in a tragic denouement. True, sometimes it culminates in his enlightenment (Raskolnikov's resurrection, Versilov's renewal). But this enlightenment, almost always relegated to the epilogue, is in essence a poorly convincing external attachment to the plot history of the

2. Characters in *War and Peace* and *Anna Karenina* [*Editor*].
3. Stefan Zweig, an Austrian author and biographer, who died in Brazil as an émigré in 1942. He published a book called *Three Masters* (1930) in which he discussed Dostoevsky, Balzac, and Dickens [*Editor*].

hero. Pierre Bezukhov and Alexander Aduiev, Bolkonsky, and Lavretsky, just as Wilhelm Meister, Emma Bovary, Rastignac[4] undergo a "change of soul" during the novel, sometimes more than once (not going, of course, beyond the limits of the unified complex of inner characteristics that each is endowed with). One cannot say this about the majority of Dostoevsky's central characters. At their appearance on the scene they already carry within themselves that basic collision, the revelation of which and the deepening of which is their entire further history. In this respect they stand next to such tragic heroes as Boris Godunov, Macbeth, and Hamlet. Their progression in the novel is not in a straight line, but in a spiral. Raskolnikov's oscillations in *Crime and Punishment* could be the best illustration for the aforementioned. His entire progression in the novel is an uninterrupted, tortured "change of phases" of his internal struggle.

At the beginning of the novel, the reader finds Raskolnikov in a state of uncertainty. As is made known later, he has been tortured by the thought of murdering the money-lender for a month and a half, but is incapable of coming to a decision. The first link of the plot, the "trial run," leads to the rejection of the planned crime (". . . no, this is nonsense, this is absurd . . ."). But already the second link—the meeting of Marmeladov and the visit to the Marmeladovs'—signals a reversal in motion in the direction of the "idea." Raskolnikov again relives that inner process which had formerly brought him to the thought of killing the old woman. What he sees and hears at the Marmeladov's as it were confirms the correctness of his theory (the amorality of existing relationships by which people live at the expense of the "sufferings of Sonias"; the right of the strong to "transgress" moral taboos).

The third peripeteia—(Raskolnikov's receiving the letter from his mother)—increases the tension and brings him face to face with decision ("whatever happens, I must decide . . ."). He feels responsible for the fact that his sister's fate will be partly similar to Sonia's, because Dunia is marrying a man whom she does not love in order to help Raskolnikov ("Sonechka, Sonechka Marmeladova, the eternal Sonia, since the world began! . . . And what are you doing now? You take from them.").

The fourth peripeteia (meeting the drunken girl on the boulevard) forces Raskolnikov to make a decision. In his mind he sees his sister in her place. However, after this there is a last convulsive repulsion away from the evil undertaking. The fifth peripeteia (the dream about the horse being beaten) cancels the decision made. It is as if Raskolnikov casts off a spell. But it is the turn of the sixth, decisive peripeteia—the accidental encounter with Lizaveta

4. Characters in novels by Goncharov, Tolstoy, and Turgenev in Russia; Goethe in Germany, and Flaubert and Balzac in France [*Editor*].

on Haymarket Square. This puts an end to the oscillations and forces Raskolnikov to take up the axe.

This ends the first round of the internal struggle. It is followed by the second, in which the instinct of self-preservation struggles with the instinctive urge of the criminal to cast off from himself the heavy burden—to make a confession. Intercourse with people close to him becomes impossible for the murderer. Further, the same inner collision leads to the waverings of the hero between Sonia Marmeladova (the epitome of his "good half") and Svidrigaylov (the epitome of his "evil half"). The inner waverings of the hero are accompanied by an external struggle, until finally he confesses to the crime committed. Characteristically even this last peripeteia is preceded by a "back-tracking." Having already come to the police station to admit his guilt, Raskolnikov at first declines to confess and leaves. Only upon returning does he find within himself the strength to utter the fateful words: "I killed."

Thus the "changes of phases" of Raskolnikov's inner struggle passes through the entire novel. The collision resulting from the hero's "idea" is revealed through the principle of dramatic build-up —ever increasing in depth, sharpness, and width.

The repetition of inner action sometimes calls forth the repetition of more or less analogous plot situations or scenes. With each one of these subsequent situations, however, comes a deepening and dramatic sharpening of the former situation (Raskolnikov's two talks with Sonia, his two talks with Svidrigaylov). On this point, the poetics of Dostoevsky's novel are linked with the poetics of drama. In the plot of a drama, the repetition of more or less analogous situations with an increased depth of the conflict is an important, frequently used artistic technique.

In spite of the repetitive actions and scenes, Dostoevsky actually does not repeat himself in his novel. Through the prism of the same internal collision, Dostoevsky knows how to refract newer and newer depths of the human soul—the most varied and complex feelings, experiences, and emotions. In illustrating the tortured emotional discord, the tragic struggles of the hero confronted by fate with problems which are insoluble for him (insoluble, because they reflect the contradictions of an entire social structure), Dostoevsky's great psychological mastery was revealed.

A wonderful artistic technique in Dostoevsky's hands is the contrasting "Rembrandt" light in which he shows the squalid rooms of the capital's poor and their faces distorted by suffering.

This is an important element of the background against which Dostoevsky exhibits his tragic heroes. This sort of light—the light of a candle stub in a room, the light of a gas lamp in the street at night—as though impotently struggling with the darkness, unable to dispel it, is the light that shades the terrible world in which the author's characters live. Dostoevsky later revealed the secret of his beloved light in *The Dream of a Ridiculous Man* through the words of the novella's hero: "It seemed to me that if the gas lamps went out everywhere, then it would become gayer, and that with the gas lamps on, the heart is heavier, because they illuminate all this [the sad Petersburg landscape]." By the dim, unsure light of a candle stub, Raskolnikov becomes acquainted with the Marmeladov residence and its inhabitants: "The candle-stub illuminated the shabbiest of rooms . . . that tubercular and excited face [Katerina Ivanovna's] made a painful impression by the last light of the burned down stub which flickered on her face." When the reading of the legend of Lazarus comes to an end in Sonia's room, Dostoevsky considers it necessary to comment: "The candle had started to go out a long time ago in its crooked holder, faintly illuminating in this impoverished room the murderer and the harlot, who had strangely come together to read the eternal book." It is not accidental that Raskolnikov's confession of the murder of the old woman to Razumikhin takes place in a dark corridor by a lamp. The lamp casts reflections on the "painfully distorted face" of the criminal.

\* \* \*

The religio-idealistic conceptions of Dostoevsky shrouded in a mystical cover the process of initial capitalistic aggrandizement of the 1860's. "Pessimism, pacifism, invocations to the 'Spirit' are the ideology which unavoidably is expressed 'in such an era when the entire old order has 'turned over.' "[5] Completely "earthly" socio-ethical collisions, resulting from the development of capitalism, under the writer's pen took on the characteristic of a Christian mystery of the Fall and Redemption.

Animosity against the revolutionary democrats in many respects narrowed Dostoevsky's scope of perception and brought forth several "mysterious marionettes, as though struggling in their sleep, made by hands trembling with rage"[6] and left an imprint on the image of the main hero.

But towards the middle of the '60's the better sides of Dostoevsky's brilliant talent, highly evaluated by Belinsky, achieved a full development. In a review written shortly before his death on a separate edition of *Poor Folk*, the great critic expressed rapture over the "striking truth of the portrayal of reality," the "deep understanding and artistic creation in the full meaning of the word, of

5. A quotation from Vladimir I. Lenin [*Editor*].
6. A quotation from the nineteenth-
century Russian satirist Michael Saltykov Shchedrin [*Editor*].

the tragic side of life," perceiving that in this lies "the main strength of Dostoevsky's talent and his originality."

Thanks to this chief strength of Dostoevsky's talent, the core of *Crime and Punishment* nevertheless consisted of a great truth, although it did receive a peculiar refraction: the truth about life "on a yard of space," about the monstrous distortions of man's psyche, the dehumanization of man under the conditions of a bourgeois society. This great truth, clothed in vivid artistic form, determines the permanent significance of *Crime and Punishment* in Russian and world literature.

# MIKHAIL BAKHTIN

## *From* Problems of Dostoevsky's Poetics†

### *The Idea in Dostoevsky*

\* \* \*

All of Dostoevsky's major characters, as people of an idea, are absolutely unselfish, insofar as the idea has really taken control of the deepest core of their personality. This unselfishness is neither a trait of their objectivized character nor an external definition of their acts—unselfishness expresses their real life in the realm of the idea (they "don't need millions, they just need to get a thought straight"); idea-ness and unselfishness are, as it were, synonyms. In this sense even Raskolnikov, who killed and robbed the old pawnbroker, is absolutely unselfish, as is the prostitute Sonya, as is Ivan the accomplice in his father's murder; absolutely unselfish also is the *idea* of the Adolescent to become a Rothschild. We repeat again: what is important is not the ordinary qualifications of a person's character or actions, but rather the index of a person's devotion to an idea in the deepest recesses of his personality.

The second condition for creating an image of the idea in Dostoevsky is his profound understanding of the dialogic nature of human thought, the dialogic nature of the idea. Dostoevsky knew how to reveal, to see, to show the true realm of the life of an idea. The idea *lives* not in one

† Mikhail Bakhtin (1895–1975) was a Russian literary critic, scholar, and theoretician, whose works were being published in the 1920's (some apparently under other scholars' names) but who was later forced to withdraw from literary life. His works were rediscovered by young scholars late in his lifetime. He is now widely known in the West as well as admired by a smaller circle of Soviet men of letters and semioticians. The passages about *Crime and Punishment* printed here are from his *Problems of Dostoevsky's Poetics*, trans. and ed. Caryl Emerson (Minneapolis: U of Minnesota P, 1984) 87–91, 166–70, 237–40, 285–86. Unless otherwise indicated, notes are by the translator.

person's *isolated* individual consciousness—if it remains there only, it degenerates and dies. The idea begins to live, that is, to take shape, to develop, to find and renew its verbal expression, to give birth to new ideas, only when it enters into genuine dialogic relationships with other ideas, with the ideas of *others*. Human thought becomes genuine thought, that is, an idea, only under conditions of living contact with another and alien thought, a thought embodied in someone else's voice, that is, in someone else's consciousness expressed in discourse. At that point of contact between voice-consciousnesses the idea is born and lives.

The idea—as it was *seen* by Dostoevsky the artist—is not a subjective individual-psychological formation with "permanent resident rights" in a person's head; no, the idea is inter-individual and inter-subjective— the realm of its existence is not individual consciousness but dialogic communion *between* consciousnesses. The idea is a *live event*, played out at the point of dialogic meeting between two or several consciousnesses. In this sense the idea is similar to the *word*, with which it is dialogically united. Like the word, the idea wants to be heard, understood, and "answered" by other voices from other positions. Like the word, the idea is by nature dialogic, and monologue is merely the conventional compositional form of its expression, a form that emerged out of the ideological monologism of modern times characterized by us above.

It is precisely as such a live event, playing itself out between consciousness-voices, that Dostoevsky saw and artistically represented the *idea*. It is this artistic discovery of the dialogic nature of the idea of consciousness, of every human life illuminated by consciousness (and therefore to some minimal degree concerned with ideas) that made Dostoevsky a great artist of the idea.

Dostoevsky never expounds prepared ideas in monologic form, but neither does he show their *psychological* evolution within a *single* individual consciousness. In either case, ideas would cease to be living images.

We remember, for example, Raskolnikov's first interior monologue * * * [portions of which we quoted in the preceding chapter]. That was not a psychological evolution of an idea within a single self-enclosed consciousness. On the contrary, the consciousness of the solitary Raskolnikov becomes a field of battle for others' voices; the events of recent days (his mother's letter, the meeting with Marmeladov), reflected in his consciousness, take on the form of a most intense dialogue with absentee participants (his sister, his mother, Sonya, and others), and in this dialogue he tries to "get his thoughts straight."

Before the action of the novel begins, Raskolnikov has published a newspaper article expounding the theoretical bases of his idea. Nowhere does Dostoevsky give us this article in its monologic form. We first become acquainted with its content and consequently with Raskolnikov's basic idea in the intense and, for Raskolnikov, terrible dialogue with Porfiry (Razumikhin and Zametov participate in this dialogue as well). Porfiry is the first to give an account of the article, and he does so in a deliberately exaggerated and provocative form. This internally dialogized account is constantly interrupted by questions addressed to Raskolnikov, and by the latter's replies. Then Raskolnikov himself gives an account of the article, and he is constantly interrupted by Porfiry's provocative questions and comments. And Raskolnikov's account is itself shot through with interior polemic, from the point of view of Porfiry and his like. Razumikhin too puts in his replies. As a result, Raskolnikov's idea appears before us in an inter-individual zone of intense struggle among several individual consciousnesses, while the theoretical side of the idea is inseparably linked with the ultimate positions on life taken by the participants in the dialogue.

In the course of this dialogue Raskolnikov's idea reveals its various facets, nuances, possibilities, it enters into various relationships with other life-positions. As it loses its monologic, abstractly theoretical finalized quality, a quality sufficient to a *single* consciousness, it acquires the contradictory complexity and living multi-facedness of an idea-force, being born, living and acting in the great dialogue of the epoch and calling back and forth to kindred ideas of other epochs. Before us rises up an *image of the idea*.

Raskolnikov's very same idea appears before us again in his dialogues with Sonya, no less intense; here it already sounds in a different tonality, it enters into dialogic contact with another very strong and integral life-position, Sonya's, and thus reveals new facets and possibilities inherent in it. Next we hear this idea in Svidrigailov's dialogized exposition of it in his dialogue with Dounia. But here, in the voice of Svidrigailov, who is one of Raskolnikov's parodic doubles, the idea has a completely different sound and turns toward us another of its sides. And finally, Raskolnikov's idea comes into contact with various manifestations of life throughout the entire novel; it is tested, verified, confirmed or repudiated by them. * * *

* * * The reflections of other ideas fall, similar to what happens in painting when a distinct tone, thanks to the reflections of surrounding tones, loses its abstract purity, and only then begins to live an authentic "painterly" life. If one were to extract these ideas from the dialogic realm of their life and give them a monologically finished theoretical form, what withered and easily refuted ideological constructs would result!

As an artist, Dostoevsky did not create his ideas in the same way philosophers or scholars create theirs—he created images of ideas found, heard, sometimes divined by him *in reality itself*, that is, ideas already living or entering life as idea-forces. Dostoevsky possessed an extraordinary gift for hearing the dialogue of his epoch, or, more precisely, for hearing his epoch as a great dialogue, for detecting in it not only individual voices, but precisely and predominantly the *dialogic relationship* among voices, their dialogic *interaction*. He heard both the loud, recognized, reigning voices of the epoch, that is, the reigning dominant ideas (official and unofficial), as well as voices still weak, ideas not yet fully emerged, latent ideas heard as yet by no one but himself, and ideas that were just beginning to ripen, embryos of future worldviews. "Reality in its entirety," Dostoevsky himself wrote, "is not to be exhausted by what is immediately at hand, for an overwhelming part of this reality is contained in the form of a still *latent, unuttered future Word*."[1]

In the dialogue of his time Dostoevsky also heard resonances of the voice-ideas of the past—both the most recent past (the '30s and '40s) and the more remote. Also, as we have just said, he attempted to hear the voice-ideas of the future, trying to divine them, so to speak, from the place prepared for them in the dialogue of the present, just as it is possible to divine a future, as yet unuttered response in an already unfolded dialogue. Thus on the plane of the present there came together and quarreled past, present, and future.

We repeat: Dostoevsky never created his idea-images out of nothing, he never "made them up" any more than a visual artist makes up the people he represents—he was able to hear or divine them in the reality at hand. And thus for the idea-images in Dostoevsky's novels, as well as for the images of his heroes, it is possible to locate and indicate specific *prototypes*. Thus the prototypes for Raskolnikov's ideas, for example, were the ideas of Max Stirner[2] as expounded by him in his treatise *Der Einzige und sein Eigentum*, and the ideas of Napoleon III as developed by him in *Histoire de Jules César* (1865);[3] one of the prototypes for Pyotr Verkhovensky's ideas was *The Catechism of a Revolutionary*; the prototypes of Versilov's ideas (*The Adolescent*) were the ideas of Chaadaev[4] and Herzen.[5] By no means have all prototypes for Dostoevsky's idea-images been discovered and clarified. We must emphasize that we are not talking of Dostoevsky's "sources" (that term would be inappropriate here), but precisely about the *prototypes* for his idea-images.

Dostoevsky neither copied nor expounded these prototypes in any way; rather he freely and creatively reworked them into living artistic images of ideas, exactly as an artist approaches his human prototypes. Above all he destroyed the self-enclosed monologic form of idea-prototypes and incorporated them into the great dialogue of his novels, where they began living a new and eventful artistic life.

1. Bakhtin is quoting from Dostoevsky's Notebooks. (The context of Dostoevsky's note is interesting. It is on Shakespeare and the paragraph continues: "From time to time prophets appear who divine and utter this integral word. Shakespeare was a prophet sent by God to proclaim to us on the mysteries of man and the human soul."

2. Max Stirner (1806–56), German individualist philosopher. His defense of philosophical egotism is reflected in Raskolnikov.

3. This book, published while Dostoevsky was working on *Crime and Punishment*,

found great resonance in Russia [Bakhtin's note].

4. Pyotr Chaadaev (1794–1856), Russian philosopher and social critic, author of a series of "Philosophical Letters," who lamented Russia's isolation from Europe, but saw in that isolation a hope for salvation and a divine mission.

5. Alexander Herzen (1812–79), Russian publicist, essayist, journalist, who emigrated to England. His philosophical and dialogic prose was a profound influence on Dostoevsky from 1862 to the novelist's death.

As an artist, Dostoevsky uncovered in the image of a given idea not only the historically actual features available in the prototype (in Napoleon III's *Histoire de Jules César*, for example), but also its *potentialities*, and precisely this potential is of the utmost importance for the artistic image. As an artist Dostoevsky often divined how a given idea would develop and function under certain changed conditions, what unexpected directions it would take in its further development and transformation. To this end, Dostoevsky placed the idea on the borderline of dialogically intersecting consciousnesses. He brought together ideas and worldviews, which in real life were absolutely estranged and deaf to one another, and forced them to quarrel. He extended, as it were, these distantly separated ideas by means of a dotted line to the point of their dialogic intersection. In so doing he anticipated future dialogic encounters between ideas which in his time were still dissociated. He foresaw new linkages of ideas, the emergence of new voice-ideas and changes in the arrangement of all the voice-ideas in the worldwide dialogue. And thus the Russian, and worldwide, dialogue that resounds in Dostoevsky's novels with voice-ideas already living and just being born, voice-ideas open-ended and fraught with new possibilities, continues to draw into its lofty and tragic game the minds and voices of Dostoevsky's readers, up to the present day.

In such a way, without losing any of their full and essential semantic validity, the idea-prototypes used in Dostoevsky's novels change the form of their existence: they become thoroughly dialogized images of ideas not finalized monologically; that is, they enter into what is for them a new realm of existence, *artistic* existence.

Dostoevsky was not only an artist who wrote novels and stories; he was also a journalist and a thinker who published articles in *Time, Epoch, The Citizen,* and *Diary of a Writer.* In these articles he expressed definite philosophical, religious-philosophical, and sociopolitical *ideas*; he expressed them there (that is, in the articles) as *his own confirmed* ideas in a *systemically monologic* or rhetorically monologic (*in fact, journalistic*) form. \* \* \*

\* \* \*

### Characteristics of Genre

\* \* \*

Carnivalization[6] is not an external and immobile schema which is imposed upon ready-made content; it is, rather, an extraordinarily flexible form of artistic visualization, a peculiar sort of heuristic principle

6. Carnivalization is an important concept in Bakhtin's writings. He popularized it through his emphasis on it in his book on Rabelais. Bakhtin regarded carnival (seen as a general idea) as a reaction against the official culture of its time. By breaking free from, and often turning upside down, the values and the symbolic systems of official culture, carnivalization overcomes social hierarchies and liberates culture, with humor and grotesque imagery [*Editor*].

making possible the discovery of new and as yet unseen things. By *relativizing* all that was externally stable, set and ready-made, carnivalization with its pathos of change and renewal permitted Dostoevsky to penetrate into the deepest layers of man and human relationships. It proved remarkably productive as a means for capturing in art the developing relationships under capitalism, at a time when previous forms of life, moral principles and beliefs were being turned into "rotten cords" and the previously concealed, ambivalent, and unfinalized nature of man and human *thought* was being nakedly exposed. Not only people and their actions but even *ideas* had broken out of their self-enclosed hierarchical nesting places and had begun to collide in the familiar contact of "absolute" (that is, completely unlimited) dialogue. Capitalism, similar to that "pander" Socrates on the market square of Athens, brings together people and ideas. In all of Dostoevsky's novels, beginning with *Crime and Punishment*, there is a consistent *carnivalization* of dialogue.

We find other instances of carnivalization in *Crime and Punishment*. Everything in this novel—the fates of people, their experiences and ideas—is pushed to its boundaries, everything is prepared, as it were, to pass over into its opposite (but not, of course, in the abstractly dialectical sense), everything is taken to the extreme, to its outermost limit. There is nothing in the novel that could become stabilized, nothing that could justifiably relax within itself, enter the ordinary flow of biographical time and develop in it (the possibility of such a development for Razumikhin and Dounia is only indicated by Dostoevsky at the end of the novel, but of course he does not show it: such life lies outside his artistic world). Everything requires change and rebirth. Everything is shown in a moment of unfinalized transition.

It is characteristic that the very setting for the action of the novel—Petersburg (its role in the novel is enormous)—is on the borderline between existence and nonexistence, reality and phantasmagoria, always on the verge of dissipating like the fog and vanishing. Petersburg too is devoid, as it were, of any internal grounds for justifiable stabilization; it too is on the threshold.

The sources of carnivalization for *Crime and Punishment* are no longer provided by Gogol. We feel here in part a Balzacian type of carnivalization, and in part elements of the social-adventure novel (Soulié and Sue). But perhaps the most vital and profound source of carnivalization for this novel was Pushkin's "Queen of Spades."

We shall pause for analysis on only one small episode of the novel, which will permit us to investigate several important characteristics of carnivalization in Dostoevsky, and at the same time clarify our claim concerning Pushkin's influence.

After the first meeting with Porfiry and the appearance of the mysterious artisan with his one word, "Murderer!", Raskolnikov has a *dream* in which he *again* commits the murder of the old woman. We quote the end of this dream:

He stood over her. "She is afraid," he thought. He stealthily took the axe from the noose and struck her one blow, then another on the skull. But strange to say she did not stir, as though she were made of wood. He was frightened, bent down nearer and tried to look at her; but she, too, bent her head lower. He bent right down to the ground and peeped up into her face from below, he peeped and turned cold with horror; the old woman was sitting and *laughing, shaking with noiseless laughter*, doing her utmost that he should not hear it. Suddenly he fancied that the door from the bedroom was opened a little and that there was *laughter* and whispering within. He was overcome with frenzy and he began hitting the old woman on the head with all his force, but at every blow of the axe the *laughter* and whispering from the bedroom *grew louder* and the old woman was simply shaking with mirth. He was rushing away, but the *passage was full of people, the doors* of the flats stood open and *on the landing, on the stairs* and everywhere below there were people, rows of heads, *all looking*, but huddled together in silence and expectation. Something gripped his heart, his legs were rooted to the spot, they would not move. . . . He tried to scream and woke up. [Part III, ch. 6]

Several points are of interest here.

1. The first is already familiar to us: the fantastic logic of dreams employed here by Dostoevsky. We recall his words: ". . . you *leap over* space and time, *over all laws of life and reason*, and only pause where your *heart's desire* bids you pause" ("Dream of a Ridiculous Man"). This same dream logic made it possible to create here the image of a *laughing murdered old woman, to combine laughter with death and murder*. But this is also made possible by the ambivalent logic of carnival. Before us is a typical carnival combination.

The image of the laughing old woman in Dostoevsky echoes Pushkin's image of the old Countess winking from the coffin, and the winking Queen of Spades on the card (the Queen of Spades is, incidentally, a *carnival double* of the old Countess). We have here a *fundamental* resonance between two images and not a chance external similarity, for it occurs against the background of a general resonance between these two works ("The Queen of Spades" and *Crime and Punishment*). This is a resonance both in the atmosphere of images and in the basic content of ideas: "Napoleonism" on the specific terrain of early Russian capitalism. In both works this concretely historical phenomenon receives a second *carnivalistic plane*, one which recedes into infinite semantic space. The motivation for these two echoing images (the laughing dead woman) is also similar: in Pushkin it is *insanity*, in Dostoevsky, the *delirious dream*.

2. In Raskolnikov's dream it is not only the murdered woman who laughs (in the dream, to be sure, it proves impossible to murder her). Other people are also laughing, elsewhere in the apartment, in the bedroom, and they laugh louder and louder. Then a crowd appears, a multitude of people on the *stairway* and *down below* as well, and in relation to this crowd passing *below*, Raskolnikov is located at the *top*

*of the stairs*. Before us is the image of communal ridicule on the public square decrowning a carnival king-pretender. The public square is a symbol of the communal performance, and at the end of the novel, Raskolnikov, before going to give himself up at the police station, comes out on the square and bows low to the earth before the whole people. This communal decrowning, which "came to Raskolnikov's heart" in a dream, has no *direct* echo in the "The Queen of Spades," but a distant echo is nevertheless there: Hermann's fainting spell in the presence of the people at the Countess' grave. A fuller echo of Raskolnikov's dream can be found in another of Pushkin's works, *Boris Godunov*. We have in mind the thrice-recurring prophetic *dream* of the Pretender (the scene in the cell of Chudovo Monastery):

> I dreamed I climbed a *crooked stair* that led
> Up to a tower, and there upon that *height*
> I stood, where Moscow like an ant hill lay
> *Under* my feet, and in the *marketplace*
> The *people* stared and pointed at me *laughing*;
> *I felt ashamed*, *a trembling overcame me*,
> I fell headfirst, and in that fall I woke.[7]

Here is the same carnival logic of self-appointed *elevation*, the communal act of comic *decrowning on the public square*, and a falling *downward*.

3. In Raskolnikov's dream, *space* assumes additional significance in the overall symbol-system of carnival. *Up*, *down*, the *stairway*, the *threshold*, the *foyer*, the *landing* take on the meaning of a "point" where *crisis*, radical change, an unexpected turn of fate takes place, where decisions are made, where the forbidden line is overstepped, where one is renewed or perishes.

Action in Dostoevsky's works occurs primarily at these "points." The interior spaces of a house or of rooms, spaces distant from the boundaries, that is from the threshold, are almost never used by Dostoevsky, except of course for scenes of scandals and decrownings, when interior space (the drawing room or the hall) becomes a substitute for the public square. Dostoevsky "leaps over" all that is comfortably habitable, well-arranged and stable, all that is far from the threshold, because the life that he portrays does not take place in that sort of space. Dostoevsky was least of all an estate-home-room-apartment-family writer. In comfortably habitable interior space, far from the threshold, people live a biographical life in biographical time: they are born, they pass through childhood and youth, they marry, give birth to children, die. This biographical time Dostoevsky also "leaps over." On the threshold and on the square the only time possible is *crisis time*, in which a *moment* is equal to years,

7. Translation by Paul Schmidt in his *Meyerhold at Work* (Austin: U of Texas P, 1980) 85.

decades, even to a "billion years" (as in "The Dream of a Ridiculous Man").

If we now turn from Raskolnikov's *dream* to what happens in the waking life of the novel, we will be persuaded that the threshold and its substitutes are the fundamental "points" of action in the novel.

First of all, Raskolnikov lives, in essence, on a threshold: his narrow room, a "coffin" (a carnival symbol here) opens directly onto the *landing of the staircase*, and he never locks his door, even when he goes out (that is, his room is unenclosed interior space). In this "coffin" it is impossible to live a biographical life—here one can experience only crisis, make ultimate decisions, die or be reborn (as in the coffins of "Bobok"[8] or the coffin of the Ridiculous Man). Marmeladov's family lives on the threshold as well, in a walk-through room leading directly onto a staircase (here, on the threshold, while bringing home the drunken Marmeladov, Raskolnikov meets the members of the family for the first time). Raskolnikov experiences terrible moments at the threshold of the murdered pawnbroker's when, on the other side of the door, on the stairway landing, her visitors stand and tug at the bell. It is to this place that he returns and himself rings the bell, in order to relive those moments. The scene of his half-confession to Razumikhin takes place on the threshold in the corridor by a lamp, without words, only in glances. On the threshold, near the doors leading to a neighboring apartment, his conversations with Sonya occur (with Svidrigailov eavesdropping on the other side of the door). There is certainly no need to enumerate further all the "acts" that take place on the threshold, near the threshold, or that are permeated with the living sensation of threshold in this novel.

The threshold, the foyer, the corridor, the landing, the stairway, its steps, doors opening onto the stairway, gates to front and back yards, and beyond these, the city: squares, streets, façades, taverns, dens, bridges, gutters. This is the space of the novel. And in fact absolutely nothing here ever loses touch with the threshold, there is no interior of drawing rooms, dining rooms, halls, studios, bedrooms where biographical life unfolds and where events take place in the novels of writers such as Turgenev, Tolstoy, and Goncharov. Of course, we can uncover just such an organization of space in Dostoevsky's other works as well.

\* \* \*

---

8. A bizarre short story by Dostoevsky, published in 1873, in which the narrator reports hearing weird conversations among the dead buried in a cemetery [*Editor*].

*The Hero's Discourse and Narrative Discourse in Dostoevsky*

\* \* \*

What strikes us especially about Raskolnikov's monologic discourse is its extreme internal dialogization and the vivid personal address it makes to everything he thinks and speaks about. For Raskolnikov as well, to conceive of an object means to address it. He does not think about phenomena, he speaks with them.

In this way also does he address himself (often in the second person singular, as if to another person), he tries to persuade himself, he taunts, exposes, ridicules himself and so forth. Here is an example of one such dialogue with himself:

> "It shall not be? But what are you going to do to prevent it? You'll forbid it? And what right have you? What can you promise them on your side to give you such a right? Your whole life, your whole future, you will devote to them *when you have finished your studies and obtained a post?* Yes, we have heard all that before, and that's all *words*, but now? Now something must be done, now, do you understand that? And what are you doing now? You are living upon them. They borrow on their hundred roubles pension. They borrow from the Svidrigaïlovs. How are you going to save them from the Svidrigaïlovs, from Afanasy Ivanovich Vahrushin, oh future millionaire Zeus who would arrange their lives for them? In another ten years? In another ten years, mother will be blind with knitting shawls, maybe with weeping too. She will be worn to a shadow with fasting; and my sister? Imagine for a moment what may have become of your sister in ten years? What may happen to her during those ten years? Can you fancy?"
>
> So he tortured himself, fretting himself with such questions, and finding a kind of enjoyment in it. [Part I, ch. 4]

Such is the dialogue he conducts with himself throughout the entire novel. To be sure, the questions change, the tone changes, but the structure remains the same. Characteristically, his inner speech is filled with other people's words that he has just recently heard or read: from his mother's letter, from things Luzhin, Dunechka, Svidrigailov had said that were quoted in the letter, from Marmeladov's speech which he had just heard, from Sonechka's words which he heard from Marmeladov, etc. He inundates his own inner speech with these words of others, complicating them with his own accents or directly reaccenting them, entering into a passionate polemic with them. Consequently his inner speech is constructed like a succession of living and impassioned replies to all the words of others he has heard or has been touched by, words gathered by him from his experience of the immediately preceding days. He addresses everyone with whom he polemicizes in the second singular "you," and to almost all of them he returns their own words, with altered tone and accent. Thus every individual, every new person immediately becomes for him a symbol, and their names become common nouns: the Svidrigailovs, the Luzhins, the Sonechkas, and so forth. "Hey! You Svidrigailov! What do you want here?" he shouts to the dandy who is trying to proposition the drunken girl. Sonechka, whom he knows from Marmeladov's stories, constantly figures in his inner speech as a symbol of unnecessary and senseless sacrifice. Likewise, but with a different nuance, Dounia also figures, and the symbol of Luzhin has its own special meaning too.

Each individual, however, enters Raskolnikov's inner speech not as a character or a type, not as a personage in the plot of his life (sister, sister's fiancé, etc.), but as a symbol of a certain orientation to life and an ideological position, the symbol of a specific real-life solution to those same ideological questions that torment him. It is enough for a person to appear in his field of vision to become for him instantly an embodied solution to his own personal question, a solution different from the one at which he himself had arrived; therefore every person touches a sore spot in him and assumes a firm role in his inner speech. He relates all these persons to one another, juxtaposes or counterposes them, forces them to answer one another, to echo each other's words or to expose one another. As a result his inner speech unfolds like a philosophical drama, where the *dramatis personae* are embodied points of view on life and on the world, realized in living situations.

All the voices that Raskolnikov introduces into his inner speech come into a peculiar sort of contact, one that would be impossible among voices in an actual dialogue. Because they all sound within a single consciousness, they become, as it were, reciprocally permeable. They are brought close to one another, made to overlap; they partially intersect one another, creating the corresponding interruptions in areas of intersection.

We have already noted above that Dostoevsky's work contains no evolution of thought, not even within the boundaries of the consciousness of individual heroes (with very rare exceptions). Semantic material is always given to the hero's consciousness all at once and in its entirety, and given not as individual thoughts and propositions but as the semantic orientations of whole human beings, as voices; it remains only to make a choice among them. That internal ideological struggle which the hero wages is a struggle for a choice among already available semantic possibilities, whose quantity remains almost unchanged throughout the entire novel. The motifs "I didn't know that," "I didn't see that," "that was revealed to me only later," are absent from Dostoevsky's world. His hero knows and sees everything from the very beginning. This is why it is so common for heroes (or for a narrator speaking about a hero) to announce, after a catastrophe, that they had known and foreseen everything in advance. "Our hero shrieked and clutched at his head. Alas! That was what he had known for a long time would happen!" Thus ends *The Double*. The Underground Man is constantly emphasizing that he knew everything and foresaw everything. "I saw everything myself, all my despair was as clear as day!" exclaims the hero of "A Meek One." It is true, as we shall soon see, that the hero very often hides from himself what he knows, and pretends to himself that he does not see what in fact is constantly before his very eyes. But in such cases this characteristic trait stands out all the more sharply.

Almost no evolution of thought takes place under the influence of new material, new points of view. All that matters is the choice, the resolution of the question "Who am I?" and "With whom am I?" To find one's own voice and to orient it among other voices, to combine it with some and to oppose it to others, to separate one's voice from another voice with which it has inseparably merged—these are the tasks that the heroes solve in the course of the novel. And this determines the hero's discourse. It must find itself, reveal itself among other words, within an intense field of interorientations. And all these discourses are usually given in their entirety at the very start. Throughout the entire internal and external action of the novel they are merely distributed in various ways in relation to one another, they enter into various combinations, but their quantity, given from the very start, remains unchanged. We could put it this way: from the very beginning a certain stable semantic multiplicity exists, with unchanging content, and all that occurs within it is a rearrangement of accents. Even before the murder Raskolnikov recognizes Sonya's voice from Marmeladov's stories, and immediately decides to go to her. From the very beginning her voice and her world enter Raskolnikov's field of vision, and are attached to his interior dialogue.

"Then, Sonya," [Raskolnikov says after his final confession to her] "when I used to lie there in the dark and all this became clear to me, was it a temptation of the devil, eh?"

"Hush, don't laugh, blasphemer! You don't understand, you don't understand! Oh God! He won't understand!"

"Hush, Sonya! I am not laughing. I know myself that it was the devil leading me. Hush, Sonya, hush!" he repeated with gloomy insistence. "I know it all, *I have thought it all over and over and whispered it all over to myself, lying there in the dark.* . . . *I've argued it all over with myself, every point of it and I know it all, all!* And how sick, how sick I was then of going over it all! I kept wanting to forget it and make a new beginning, Sonya, and leave off thinking. . . . I wanted to find out something else: it was something else led me on. *I wanted to find out then and quickly whether I was a louse like everybody else or a man.* Whether I can step over barriers or not, whether I dare stoop to pick up or not, whether I am a trembling creature or whether I have the *right* . . . I want to prove one thing only, that *the devil led me on then and he has shown me since that I had not the right to take that path, because I am just such a louse as all the rest.* He was mocking me and here I've come to you now! Welcome your guest! If I were not a louse, should I have come to you? Listen: when I went then to the old woman's I only went to *try.* . . . you may be sure of that!" [Part V, ch. 4]

In these whisperings of Raskolnikov, as he lay alone in the darkness, all the voices were already reverberating—and Sonya's voice as well. Among them he was searching for himself (and the crime was a breaking-through to himself), he was orienting his own accents. Now their re-orientation is taking place; that dialogue, from which we quoted an excerpt above, occurs at a moment of transition in this process of rear-ranging accents. The voices in Raskolnikov's soul have already shifted, and now they intersect one another in a different way. But the inter-ruption-free voice of the hero will not be heard by us within the bounds of the novel; its possibility is only hinted at in the Epilogue.

\* \* \*

### *"Towards a Reworking of the Dostoevsky Book"*[9]

\* \* \* Dostoevsky destroys the flatness of the earlier artistic depiction of the world. Depiction becomes for the first time multidimensional.

After my book (but independently of it) the ideas of polyphony, dia-logue, unfinalizability, etc., were very widely developed. This is ex-plained by the growing influence of Dostoevsky, but above all, of course, by those changes in reality itself which Dostoevsky (in this sense proph-etically) succeeded in revealing earlier than the others.

Surmounting monologism. What monologism is, in the highest sense. A denial of the equal rights of consciousnesses vis-à-vis truth (understood abstractly and systemically). God can get along without man, but man cannot get along without Him. The teacher and the disciple (Socratic dialogue).

Our point of view in no way assumes a passivity on the part of the author, who would then merely assemble others' points of view, others' truths, completely denying his own point of view, his own truth. This is not the case at all; the case is rather a completely new and special interrelationship between the author's and the other's truth. The author is profoundly *active*, but his activity is of a special *dialogic* sort. It is one thing to be active in relation to a dead thing, to voiceless material that can be molded and formed as one wishes, and another thing to be active *in relation to someone else's living, autonomous consciousness*. This is a questioning, provoking, answering, agreeing, objecting activity; that is, it is dialogic activity no less active than the activity that finalizes, ma-terializes, explains, and kills causally, that drowns out the other's voice with nonsemantic arguments. Dostoevsky frequently interrupts, but he never drowns out the other's voice, never finishes it off "from himself," that is, out of his own and alien consciousness. This is, so to speak, the

9. In 1961 and 1962, Bakhtin planned a new, revised version of his book on Dos-toevsky. The passage that follows is trans-lated by Caryl Emerson from notes by Bakhtin that were published posthumously in the Soviet Union, in 1976, in a collection of scholarly articles called *Kontekst*, and re-printed since then in the USSR [*Editor*].

activity of God in His relation to man, a relation allowing man to reveal himself utterly (in his immanent development), to judge himself, to refute himself. This is activity of a higher quality. It surmounts not the resistance of dead material, but the resistance of another's consciousness, another's truth. In other writers too we encounter dialogic activity in relation to those heroes who exert some internal resistance (for example, in Turgenev with regard to Bazarov).[1] But there this dialogism is a dramatic game, completely eliminated in the work as a whole.

\* \* \*

# MICHAEL HOLQUIST

## Puzzle and Mystery, the Narrative Poles of Knowing: *Crime and Punishment*†

The best way to see the biographical dilemma in *Crime and Punishment* is to focus on the distinctive plot of that novel. At first glance it would seem to be the least complex of all Dostoevskian narratives (which is no doubt why *Crime and Punishment* is so frequently called Dostoevsky's "best-made" novel). It is divided into six parts (or books) and an epilogue. In the first part Raskolnikov murders two women; then, in the next five parts, everyone (including Raskolnikov) tries to figure out the crime; in the sixth part Raskolnikov confesses, is tried, and sent to Siberia. In the epilogue he repents of the crime (but only in the second part of the epilogue) and has a mystical experience; the novel ends with the narrator's assertion that "here begins a new story." The murder in the first book, and its consequences in the next five books, constitute *one* kind of time, a pattern made up of one kind of privileged moment and the sequence that flows from it. The conversion in the epilogue and the "new story" it results in constitute *another* kind of temporality, another moment-sequence design.

Dostoevsky stresses that Raskolnikov discovers "another reality" in the concluding pages of *Crime and Punishment*. The argument of this chapter is that the difference between this reality and that other which dominates in the rest of the novel can best be grasped as the difference between two patterns of moment-sequence: that are dramatized as two different and opposing types of plot and the two different kinds of time, two different ways of understanding, two different modes of interpre-

1. One of the main characters in Turgenev's novel *Fathers and Sons* [*Editor*].
† From *Dostoevsky and the Novel* (Princeton: Princeton UP, 1977) 75–101, with some deletions, by permission of Princeton University Press.

tation that their traditions presuppose. The uniqueness of *Crime and Punishment* consists in the dialectical (or in Bakhtin's sense of the word, the dialogic) structure Dostoevsky has created out of these oppositions.

It has often enough been pointed out that the essential trait of Dostoevskian characters is their duality, the synthesis of extremes present in all of them, which results in dialogic or polyphonic relationships of enormous complexity.[1] As John Bayley has recently said, "[Dostoevsky's] characters . . . [are] all involved in a dream, in a dramatic relation with their own self-awareness . . . [they are both] the insulted and the proud, the hated and the hater. In Dostoevsky the contract is dissolved: its partners become one flesh."[2] There is a sense in which all his characters are "doubles." But behind the psychological unity he creates out of his metaphysically split *characters* is the structural unity of his *plots*, which are also made up of elements that, in the hands of a more conventional novelist, would be clashing, disparate, even mutually exclusive.

As Leonid Grossman long ago pointed out: "The book of Job, the Revelation of St. John, Gospel texts, the Epistle of Peter in the New Testament . . . are . . . combined in a manner peculiar to [Dostoevsky], with the newspaper, the anecdote, the parody, the street scene, the grotesque or even the lampoon. He daringly throws into his melting pot more and more new elements . . . the sensations of cheap thrillers and the pages of God-inspired holy books. . . ."[3] In another article, one devoted exclusively to Dostoevsky's frequent use of material from the Gothic (Radcliffe, Maturin) and adventure novel (Soulié, Sue), Grossman further documents his author's traffic with such questionable genres: "How did it happen that the lowest genre of [artistic prose] turned out to be the most convenient expression for the creative ideas of an artistic philosopher who was a genius?"[4] In Dostoevsky's novels you get material "ranging from philosophical doctrines to puppet show effects out of the folk theater . . . philosophical dialogue expanded into an epic of adventure; it is the *Phaedo* put at the center of *Mysteries of Paris*, a mixture of Plato and Eugene Sue."[5] We can, in the case of *Crime and Punishment*, be more specific about the terms of the plot contrasts Dostoevsky uses: what Grossman identifies as the Eugene Sue tendency is present in the six books that constitute the body of the novel as a detective story; the Platonic element is present as a wisdom tale in the epilogue.

1. The masterwork on this—as so many other topics in Dostoevskian criticism—is, of course, Mikhail Bakhtin, *Problems of Dostoevsky's Poetics* [see pp. 633–46 above—*Editor*].
2. "Character and Consciousness," *New Literary History*, Vol. v, No. 2 (Winter 1974), pp. 234–235.
3. As translated in: Vladimir Seduro, *Dostoevsky in Russian Literary Criticism*

*1846–1956* (New York, Octagon Books, 1969), p. 206. The original is in "Put' Dostoevskogo," *Tvorcestvo Dostoevskogo* (Odessa, Vseukrainskoe Izdatel'stvo, 1921), p. 84.
4. "Composition in Dostoevsky's Novels," *Balzac and Dostoevsky*, tr. Lena Karpov (Ann Arbor, Michigan, Ardis, 1973), p. 93.
5. *Ibid.*, pp. 94–95.

I

E. M. Forster once said that "in a novel there is always a clock,"[6] by which he meant, of course, that just as clocks organize time outside of texts, so does plot within them. Forster later goes on to discuss various kinds of plot, among them one most easily apparent in the detective story:[7] "It occurs through a suspension of the time-sequence; a mystery is a pocket in time . . . half-explained gestures and words, the true meaning of which only dawns pages ahead."[8] The first six books of *Crime and Punishment* constitute a very complicated variant of this narrative type. In order to get at its complexity, some basic considerations about detective plots should be kept in mind.

We may, first, extend Forster's metaphor by recognizing that the distinctiveness of such structures consists in their having not one but *two* clocks. There is a clock for the crime and another for the solution; one time for the criminal, another for the detective; and the action of the tale consists in the synchronization of the two clocks.

\* \* \*

The detective novel then may be said to have two clocks, *but they both tell the same time*. When the detective solves the crime he makes a past event present again, a situation that could be represented as 1, 2, 3, 4, 1′ in which 1 stands for crime, 2, 3, 4, for the detective's attempts to solve it, and 1′ as the crime reconstructed. For the reader, the end (as conclusion) is already present in the beginning; but the end (in the sense of *telos*) is in the *middle* of a detective novel for readers: its whole charm and purpose consist in the process of establishing the correct time (that is why there is usually so much "business" about timetables and diagrams in them). The question is whodunit, but the method is who-was-where-when. The time both of crime and solution, as well as process, in the detective novel, is all cause-and-effect, sequential.

Parallels between the deductive reasoning of detectives and physical scientists have often been noted: both use historical method in the sense that in order to reach conclusions of the sort each desires, they "must treat the past as continuous with the present, and interpret the traces left by earlier events in terms of the same laws and principles as apply in the present. . . ."[9] As Toulmin and Goodfield have pointed out, in

6. *Aspects of the Novel* (New York, Harcourt Brace and World [Harvest Book], n.d. [1st pub. 1927]), p. 29
7. Although he hesitates to use so lowly an example, taking instead *The Egoist*, rather than "Conan Doyle (whom my priggishness prevents me from enjoying)." *Aspects*, p. 92. For those who may find something anachronous in my suggestion that Dostoevsky uses detective-story techniques, I add an historical note: The first modern detective story, the one that immediately established all the conventions that have since become so familiar—the eccentric but brilliant detective, the admiring foil, the well-intentioned floundering of the police, etc.—was Edgar Allan Poe's "The Murders in the

Rue Morgue," which appeared in *Graham's Magazine* of April, 1841. Dostoevsky knew many of Poe's tales, and in his journal *Time* (*Vremja*) he actually published translations. He alludes to both of Poe's Dupin detective stories: "The same power of imagination . . . characterizes his satires of *The Purloined Letter*, of the murder committed by an orangutan . . . and so on." *Vremja*, 1, p. 230 (1861). Thus Dostoevsky would have been familiar—*before* he wrote *Crime and Punishment*—with the form of the classic detective story.
8. *Aspects*, p. 87.
9. Stephen Toulmin, June Goodfriend, *The Discovery of Time* (New York, 1966), p. 244.

order to "solve" the origin of species or of other natural phenomena, the procedure was the same: "In each case, men grasped the structure of the past only when they took a genuinely historical view; which meant interpreting the present states of Nature and humanity as temporary products of a continuing process developing through time."[1] In other words, the detective, like the scientist, assumes a homogenous time that is as characteristic for the *object* of his study as it is for the *method* of his study; what you get is a temporal democracy in which the past explains the present, which in its turn will one day in the future have the explanatory power of the past. This is a linear or horizontal conception of time and it stands over against another view of temporality that might, by contrast, be called hierarchical or vertical time.

If detective stories are the most elementary expression of horizontal time—horizontal, that is, in the sense that all events occur on the same level of reality—wisdom tales are the most basic index of a time that may be called vertical insofar as it presupposes a split-level ontology, a hierarchy of realities that are distinguished by the degree of stasis that attaches to each. Wisdom tales are understood here as a subdivision within the "simple forms" catalogued by André Jolles,[2] who identifies nine such forms, including proverbs, legends, riddles, etc., as well as the tale (*das Märchen*). Jolles stresses that the tale in its most basic expression is characterized by a strong ethical thrust: the world of which it tells is different from, better than, our own: "In the tale we are dealing with a form in which what happens, the course of events, is ordered in such a way that it entirely corresponds to the exigencies of naive or unreflexive morality; that is, events are good and just according to the absolute judgment of our feeling. As such the tale puts such events into the most pointed opposition to what we are accustomed to observe—to what, in fact, happens in the world."[3]

Wisdom tales—Midrash, koans, parables from the Bible, Hassidic stories—set themselves off from tales as such in their emphasis on hermeneutics: the distance between the two worlds is affirmed in a structure of conflicting interpretations about what that distance means: the final, "correct" interpretation is superior to the others insofar as it insists on the degree of the cut-off between the two worlds. It is very close to what Jolles calls *Antimärchen*. Whether it is understood as the Augustinian distinction between the Logos of God as opposed to the mere words of men, or the aboriginal neo-Platonism that distinguishes between the Dream Time and everyday flux, such a view assumes that what is most real does not change. All that does change—all that is historical—is meaningful or real only in the degree to which it can be referred back to the privileging stasis. Thus interpretative tales that spring from such

1. *Discovery of Time*, p. 246.
2. *Einfache Formen* (Halle, Max Niemeyer Verlag, 1930), pp. 218–46. In Russian tales the role of the other world (*inoe carstvo*) has been charted by Maria-Gabriele Wosien, *The Russian Folk-Tale: Some Structural and Thematic Aspects* (Slavistische Beitrage No. 41) (München, Verlag Otto Sagner, 1969), esp. pp. 107–44, which is a study of the quest motif in the miraculous tale (Aarne-Andreyev, pp. 300–749).
3. Jolles, p. 241.

a world view tend to have structural affinities with detective stories in that they, too, are characterized by plots that have their end in their beginning. However, when beginning and end are conceived as a non-historical alpha and omega, the interest is no longer in the process, the middle. The solution to a detective story exhausts the meaning of what it sets out to understand because its defining act of interpretation is grounded in a temporality that is unitary; criminal and detective act in the same historical reality, and thus logic is the tool of both. That is why so much ingenuity is expended in such tales to establish the equivalence of both, the endless search for an adequate antagonist, a "Napoleon of crime" to test the titan of deduction.

But the wisdom tale, while it frequently has the problem-false-answer-followed-by-correct-solution pattern of detective stories, does *not* treat "the past as continuous with the present and interpret the traces left by earlier events in terms of the same laws and principles as apply in the present."[4] It seeks not to demonstrate a gradual progress unfolding in horizontal time, but to remind men again of the cut-off between vertical levels of temporality, man's change and the Gods' stasis.

\* \* \*

\* \* \* Two attitudes toward interpretation, the two temporalities they presuppose, and the two narrative structures \* \* \* are the determining features, constitute the terms of, the moment-sequence *dominanta* in *Crime and Punishment*. That is to say, if I may recapitulate, that the plot of *Crime and Punishment* is arranged around two moments, each of which is privileged in a different way, and each of which results in a different sequence. The first is the moment of Raskolnikov's crime that occurs in Book One, and the sequence of punishment that flows from it in the following five books. The second is the moment of Raskolnikov's conversion in the epilogue, and the sequence of the "new story" with which the novel ends. The first has the formal properties of a detective story, the second of a wisdom tale.

II

The two clocks of a detective story are represented by two characters, the criminal and the detective. Now to the list of oppositions that is usually invoked to capture the duality of a typical Dostoevskian character (sinner-saint, proud-humiliated, etc.), we must in the case of Raskolnikov add another: he is both hunter and hunted. As happens in such twentieth-century metaphysical detective stories as Robbe-Grillet's *The Erasers*, Borges' "Death and the Compass," or Witold Gombrowicz' "Premeditated Crime," there is a mysterious collusion between detective and murderer; but in each of these examples what is essentially a subject-object dilemma is still neatly divided between two characters. In *Crime and Punishment* the split is internalized in the consciousness of a single protagonist, Rodion Raskolnikov.

4. *Discovery of Time*, p. 244.

He is the criminal, so much is obvious. But he is also victim: on the way to commit the murder he compares himself to a man on his way to execution (I,v); and as he confesses to Sonya later (v.iv), "I killed myself, not the old woman." What he means by this is that the man who murdered the pawnbroker *in that act* got rid of the self Raskolnikov conceived himself to be before the act of murder. Raskolnikov's identity is felt by him not to be continuous with itself before and after the crime: after discovering that the role of murderer made his old self a victim, in the first book, Raskolnikov is forced to take up a new role, that of detective of his old self's motive, in order to create a new identity, a new life for himself. If he can understand *why* his old self committed the crime he will know the self whodunit; and insofar as he understands whodunit, he will know who he is.

The crime itself is performed in a fog of uncertainty; everything happens by chance. Raskolnikov acts as if in a delirium; he is constantly surprised to find himself in this or that place, holding the axe, running away. His dream-like state is dramatized by the narrator's subtle but insistent emphasis on the cut-off between Raskolnikov's hallucinatory uncertainties and the precise chronology of all his movements, which are charted from moment to moment: "Suddenly he heard a clock strike. . . . It seemed to him strange and monstrous that he could have slept in such forgetfulness from the previous day and had done nothing, had prepared nothing yet. . . . And meanwhile . . . it had struck six" (I,vi). As he dazedly makes his preparations he hears someone in the yard say, "It struck six long ago," and he says, "Long ago, My God," and rushes out. As he walks to the pawnbroker's apartment, "he saw that it was ten minutes past seven." And then, as he gets there: "here was the house, here was the gate. Suddenly a clock somewhere struck once! What! Can it be half-past seven? Impossible, it must be fast!" After he murders the second woman, Lizabeta, "a sort of blankness, even dreaminess, had begun by degree to take possession of him; at moments he forgot himself. . . ." As Raskolnikov later says (III,iii): "I remember everything down to the smallest detail, and yet if you were to ask me why I did something, or went somewhere, or said something, I don't think I could give a clear explanation."

The confusion of the crime itself is contrasted in the rest of the novel with Raskolnikov's acute attempts to analyze it. He isolates three different motives, each of which becomes the iconic attribute of a self who is presented as a subject, only to be cleared in favor of one of the other motive-defined selves. In chapter iv of book v he reviews them all for Sonya. The first is robbery: "It was to rob her." He wanted the money for food, to save his mother from poverty, his sister from being sold to Luzhin. But he quickly dismisses this; he admits he buried the purse he stole without even looking into it: "if I'd killed simply because I was hungry . . . then I should be happy now."

The second motive is one that is much more deeply explored in the novel: "I wanted to make myself a Napoleon, and that is why I killed her. . . ." Earlier (III,v) we learn that Raskolnikov's old, pre-murder self had written an article; in it Raskolnikov "developed the idea that all the . . . law-givers and regulators of human society, beginning with the most ancient, and going on to Lycurgus, Solon, Mahomet, Napoleon and so on, were without exception transgressors, by the very fact that in making a new law they *ipso facto* broke an old one, handed down from their fathers and held sacred by society." While such ideas have obvious parallels in Nietzsche's essay on "The Uses and Abuses of History," Philip Rahv was surely right to point to the greater fruitfulness of a comparison with Hegel's conception of the world historical individual: "Dostoevsky gives us a parody-version of Hegel's theory of two types of men [the superior hero and the inferior mass he is to lead] by abstracting [the theory] from its historical logic."[5] Raskolnikov's conception of the murder as a world-historical act is absurd, as he becomes painfully aware. He does so under the shadow of yet another brutalized aspect of Hegel's philosophy of history, an aspect often expressed in Schiller's line, *Weltgeschichte ist Weltgericht*, "world history is the world court." That is, Raskolnikov not only advances as his most programmatically complete reason for *committing* the murder a motive derived from Hegel; he also *judges* his act by appealing to a debased Hegelian principle of interpretation: what succeeds is correct, what fails is wrong. As he says to his sister Dunia (VI,vii):

"I shed blood, which flows and has always flowed on this earth in torrents, which is poured out like champagne, and for which men are crowned in the Capitol and afterwards called benefactors of mankind. . . . I myself wanted to benefit men, and I would have done hundreds, thousands, of good deeds, to make up for that one piece of stupidity— not even stupidity, but simple clumsiness, since the whole idea was not nearly as stupid as it seems now when it has failed (failure makes anything seem stupid) . . . if I had succeeded I should have been crowned, but now I shall fall into the trap."

Let us recapitulate for a moment: it may be, as G. K. Chesterton had one of his characters say (in "The Blue Cross"), that, "The criminal is the creative artist; the detective only a critic." But even, as in Raskolnikov's case, when—or especially when—artist and critic are one man, a general ground for any specific interpretation is necessary. Raskolnikov committed the murder as in a trance, it is like a dream he must interpret. It is precisely for him the problem as Freud posed it: "The dream as a nocturnal spectacle is unknown to us; it is accessible only through the account of waking hours. The analyst interprets this account, substituting for it another text which is, in his eyes, the thought-content of desire, i.e., what desire would say could it speak without constraint." Raskolnikov, dreamer and analyst, turns for the ground of his interpretation

5. "Dostoevsky in *Crime and Punishment*," p. 612. Much that Martin P. Rice has to say about the underground man's "Hegelianism" would apply with equal or greater force to Raskolnikov. See: Martin P. Rice, "Dostoevsky's *Notes from the Underground* and Hegel's Master and Slave," *Canadian-American Slavic Studies*, 8, iii (1974), pp. 359–69.

to history: the causes can be known only in their effects. There is nothing higher than history; there is no transcendent, so the truth can be known only retrospectively, in events, as a judgment of historical trial by combat. The shape of events will explain them. As Hegel said, " It was for a while the fashion to admire God's wisdom in animals, plants, and individual lives. If it is conceded that Providence manifests itself in such objects and materials, why not also in world history? . . . Our intellectual striving aims at recognizing that what eternal wisdom *intended*, it has actually *accomplished*. . . ."[6]

Raskolnikov's historicism is important to any understanding not only of his own motives, the thematics of the novel if you will, but also to its morphology. Since Raskolnikov uses historical method in his search for self, he inevitably acts like a detective, interpreting "the traces left by earlier events in terms of the same laws and principles as apply in the present." Since all that is real is rational, and all that is rational real, in Hegel's oft-misunderstood formulation, reason will suffice unto a solution. It is reason that tells Raskolnikov he has failed in his intention to transcend morality; therefore at the end of the novel he turns himself in—he has finally discovered that he is no more than a criminal. The true self has been found, and like the detective story whose temporality it shares, the novel thus can close.

## III

But of course there is still the epilogue. In it, as Raskolnikov finds a new conception of time and selfhood, we discover that his Hegelian motive and its consequences are a false solution. Already in the novel proper Raskolnikov had hinted at a reason for his crime other than robbery or a secularized messianism. The murder was simply an extreme situation he sought to exploit in order to find out who he really *was*; as he says—in one of those terrifying Dostoevskian immediacies—"I longed to kill without casuistry, to kill for my own benefit and for that alone! I would not lie about it even to myself! I did not commit murder in order to use the profits and power gained to make myself a benefactor to humanity. Rubbish! I simply murdered; I murdered for myself, for myself alone . . . it was only to *test myself* . . ." (v,iv). But of course— given his historical bias—he can only conclude he failed the test. As late as the second chapter of the epilogue Raskolnikov "could find no particularly terrible guilt in his past except a simple blunder . . . he was ashamed he had perished so blindly and hopelessly, with such mute stupidity, by some decree of blind fate and must humble himself and submit to the 'absurdity' of that decree . . . the first steps of [the benefactors of mankind] were successfully carried out, and therefore *they were right*, while mine failed, which means I had the right to permit myself that step." Accepting history as the ultimate source of meaning,

6. *Reason in History*, tr. Robert S. Hartman (Indianapolis, Indiana, New York, Bobbs-Merrill Co., 1953), p. 18.

he can find no way to appeal its verdict, there is no extra-temporal supreme court; the sequence the moment of his crime has condemned him to is final: "An objectless and undirected anxiety in the present, and endless sacrifice, by which nothing would be gained in the future, was all the world held for him." Raskolnikov had sought to give himself definitive knowledge of his self in the murder; it was an attempt to create a secular *kairos*, a moment that would insure the validity of all his other moments. Among his other dualities, he thus has taken on the roles of both Christ and Lazarus, seeking to gain a new identity by his *own* actions, to bestow a new life through his own mediation. But instead of raising a new self, his old identity is executed in the murder. At the end of the novel, then, he is in the dilemma Hans Meyerhoff has described in connection with Oedipus:

"He is 'in fact,' that is, in terms of his own experience, two different persons—though in terms of the objective 'facts' of Nature and history he is one and the same. We say that Oedipus didn't know who he was, which is correct in that he failed to experience his life under the aspect of temporal continuity . . . the tragedy of Oedipus may still be seen in the light . . . of the fact that the break between his two 'pasts' was so severe and the consequences of this split in his personality were so disastrous that it was impossible to mend the broken pieces of the self."[7]

As Maurice Beebe has said, "Raskolnikov commits a murder not that he may be an 'extraordinary' man, but that he *may see* if he is one,"[8] and the novel up to its last three pages chronicles the failure of Raskolnikov's gamble in the lottery of selfhood. In those last three pages, however, he is granted another moment, another sequence, as he becomes a character in the wisdom tale with which the epilogue concludes.

It is Easter, time for rebirth. Raskolnikov has just come out of the hospital, where, in his illness, he has had one of those great Dostoevskian programmatic dreams that recapitulates in symbols the meaning of his novelistic actions. He sits by the bank of "the wide, solitary river. From the high bank a broad landscape was revealed. From the other bank far away, was faintly borne the sound of singing. There in the immensity of the steppe . . . it seemed as though . . . *time had stood still*, and the age of Abraham and his flocks was still the present" [emphasis added]. Sonya appears and "how it happened he himself did not know, but suddenly he seemed to be seized and cast at her feet . . . *now at last the moment had come*" [emphasis added]. What has happened here, of course, is that Raskolnikov has undergone a conversion experience, and even in its small details it is strikingly similar to the source of this and many another example of the *topos*, the famous scene in the garden at the end of Chapter VIII in Augustine's *Confessions*: tears, distant voices, being thrown onto the ground, and inability to speak, this last trait

7. *Time in Literature* (Berkeley and Los Angeles, U of California P, 1960 [originally published 1955]), pp. 42–43.

8. "The Three Motives of Raskolnikov," p. 582 in this edition.

especially significant in the conversion experience because it dramatizes the condition of infancy (*in-fari, infans*, he who does not speak) that is part and parcel of the rebirth that conversion symbolically makes possible.

But in order to be reborn, the old self must die. We are here touching on the main theme of *Crime and Punishment*, as Dostoevsky himself indicated in his notebooks to the novel: under the heading "The Main Idea" (followed by "Eureka!"), he writes: Raskolnikov sees in Sonya "perspectives for a new life and love . . . he finally comes to himself, victorious. From one point of view life has ended, from another, it is beginning."[9] This radical break in identity is present in almost all accounts of conversion (even when they are "secondary conversion") experiences: Augustine, the rhetor, dies, as the future Bishop of Hippo is born; Thomas Aquinas, after his experience, on the Feast of St. Nicholas in 1273, dies as a scholar: "All that I have written seems like straw to me . . ."; and he never wrote another line. In Raskolnikov's case this mystical suppression of self, the death of his old identity ("Love had raised [him] from the dead"), is just as decisive as was the death of an even earlier self, the one that died in the act of murder. Raskolnikov is a completely different person as the epilogue closes: "And what were all, *all* the torments of the past? Everything, even his crime, even his sentence and his exile seemed to him *now* . . . to be something external and strange, as if it had not happened to him at all."

And just as in the confessional mode of autobiography there is a break in the sequence of the self after the *kairotic* moment, so is there a change in the sequence of the telling. Augustine, again, provides a convenient example: to the moment of conversion, the tale of his life advances more or less chronologically, as an autobiography; but after the crucial moment in the Roman garden is recounted (and its immediate after-effects), the historical progression ceases, we are given no more biographical details for the fourteen years intervening between the mystical experience in Rome and the written account of it in the *Confessions*. Instead, the concluding chapters are devoted to a meditation on time and memory, and it closes with a reading of the book of Genesis. It, too, *ends* with an interpretation of a text that is about ultimate beginnings. After conversion, all else is felt to be anticlimactic, the ensuing series of discreet moments is already foreshadowed in that one moment. Augustine's first four books cover twenty-eight years, but the next five books treat only *four* years, climaxing in his conversion. The last four books abandon chronology altogether. What is significant is precisely the rupture between old and new identity, the meaning of the self in its discontinuity: "It is the internal transformation—which furnishes a subject for a

9. *Prestuplenie i Nakazanie: rukopisnye re-daktsii*, ed. V. V. Vinogradov, *Polnoe* (Leningrad, Nauka, 1973), Vol. 7, p. 138. It should be added, in all fairness, that Dostoevsky often gets carried away like this in his notebooks, which are peppered with "*samoe glavnoe's*" (the most important thing) even when this turns out to be far from the case in his final draft.

666 · *Michael Holquist*

narrative discourse in which 'I' is both subject and object. . . . It is because past 'I' is different from the present 'I' that the latter may really be confirmed in all his prerogatives. The narrator describes not only what happened to him at a different time in his life, but above all how he became—out of what he was—what he presently is . . . the deviation, which establishes the autobiographical reflection, is thus double: it is at once a deviation of time and of identity."[1]

This deviation in *Crime and Punishment* is experienced as a felt discontinuity between the narrative mode of the novel, on the one hand, and its epilogue, on the other. All readers of the book have sensed this disjunction, many objecting to the forced or tacked-on quality of the ending, usually because they assume Dostoevsky was striving for a conventional narrative homogeneity. But if we assume on the contrary that he seeks to accentuate, to dramatize, the differences between the two parts of the book, the shape of the text assumes another kind of unity.

The whole novel is an account of Raskolnikov's various attempts to forge an identity for himself with which he can live. From the very beginning of the novel he has sought a means to justify his existence or, in the language of the text, to find a faith. Porfiry Petrovich underscores this thirst for validity: the investigator says: "Do you know how I regard you? As one of those who would allow themselves to be disembowelled, and stand and face their torturers with a smile—if they had found a faith . . ." (VI,ii). All Raskolnikov's actions—his article on new law givers (who found a new faith), the murder itself, and his attempts to understand it—are probes toward a moment that will give lasting meaning to the rest of his life.

He is like the underground man in that he seeks a plot in which to become a character, a shape that will endow each of his discreet actions with an end. But *unlike* the underground man he attempts to ground his identity, not in fictive plots, but rather in historical narratives. The six parts of the novel tell how Raskolnikov, who feels he is existentially out of place in the historical context of nineteenth-century Russian society, tries to create a *new* historical sequence, as had Solon, Mahomet, etc. Like a tragic Baron Munchhausen, he seeks to pull himself out of the swamp of time by his own metaphysical pigtail. But he discovers that he is not a world historical individual; he is not a character in *that kind* of a history. It is only in the epilogue that he discovers the kind of narrative that is properly his own to live: it is not a secular history to which he belongs, but a wisdom tale.

Dostoevsky treats Raskolnikov as Steven Marcus has suggested Freud dealt with his patients: "Freud is implying that a coherent story is in some manner connected with mental health . . . and this in turn implies assumptions of the broadest and deepest kind about the nature of coherence and the form and structure of human life. . . . At the end—

1. Jean Starobinski, "The Style of Autobiography," in *Literary Style: A Sympos-* *ium*, ed. Seymour Chatman (London, New York, Oxford UP, 1974), pp. 289–90.

at the successful end—one has come into possession of his own story. It is a final act of self-appropriation, the appropriation by oneself of one's own history."[2]

As narrator, Dostoevsky assigns values to the various characters according to the degree they are successful in merging their character with a plot that is adequate to it. Thus Lebezyatnikov is a gentle, naive person, a utopian socialist nevertheless who seeks to live out a scenario of tough-minded nihilism that results in such absurdities as his assumption that Sonya has become a prostitute as a protest against society. Marmeladov's drunkenness, his wife's insanity, are the consequences of biographical failures of employment: he cannot live the role of philosopher; she cannot live that of a grande dame. Svidrigailov is a gambler, possibly a double murderer (of his manservant and his wife), and a sensualist who violates young girls. Yet the story into which he wishes to insert himself, a parody of the golden-hearted prostitute cliché, is one in which, by forcing Dunia to marry him (at gun point), he will be saved, can settle down to a quiet life of domestic bliss. The consequences of failing to arrive at a workable assimilation of character and plot are severe—Svidrigailov cannot make his *happy* ending work, so is (self) condemned to death—the "correct" ending for the character he has played all his life. He has lived the role of villain in a realistic novel, and because he cannot become the hero of a sentimental story, he dies.

Over against these failures stand those figures who have come to know themselves—or, in the terms we have been using, come to know the story to which their character corresponds. Porfiry Petrovich is able to sum up his whole life with conviction and modesty: "Who am I? I am a man who has developed as far as he is capable, that is all." He goes on to make the distinction between himself and Raskolnikov: "But you—that's another matter . . ." and suggests that Raskolnikov will "pass into a different category of men" (v,ii). It is the same distinction Raskolnikov will make in connection with Sonya: "You too have stepped over the barrier . . . you were able to do it. You laid hands on yourself, you destroyed a life . . . *your own* . . ." (iv,iv).[3] He recognizes that she has risen again, lives as a character in the Lazarus story she reads to him—even before he has been able to enter that same story himself, because he still sees himself in the light of historical narrative at this point in the novel. But after his conversion, the Lazarus plot will be his as well.

The deviation between "normal" lives and the one led by Raskolnikov is marked not only in a thematic distinction between his own old self and the new one he discovers, but in the difference between the formal properties of the detective story plot he lives in the novel and the formal

2. Steven Marcus, "Freud and Dora: Story, History, Case History," *Partisan Review* 41 (1974).

3. The theme of stepping over bounds is a central Dostoevskian concern, of course. For a sensitive analysis of the relationship between transgression (*perestupanie*) and

crime (*prestuplenie*) in *Crime and Punishment* see: Vadim Kozhinov, "The First Sentence in *Crime and Punishment*," in *Twentieth-Century Interpretations* of Crime and Punishment, ed. Robert Louis Jackson (Englewood Cliffs, N.J., Prentice Hall, Inc., 1974), pp. 17–25.

properties of the wisdom tale, in which he becomes a character in the novel's epilogue. Thematically *Crime and Punishment* is the account of Raskolnikov's search for a story that will endow his life with validity. He first seeks such a narrative structure in a theory of history that is recognizably Hegelian and unquestionably secular. He kills in order to test whether he is, or is not, an instrument of historical change: since there is nothing higher than history itself, you can know its judgments only after having acted. Having committed the murder, he discovers he is in fact not a character in the drama of historicism. In order, then, to establish a continuity in his identities, to reassemble the shattered "I" destroyed in the outcome of the crime, he seeks the existential glue of another kind of story. But since historicism is the source of the murder—and of the confusion following upon it until Raskolnikov turns himself in—this part of the narrative is told in a way that employs many of the features of a detective story, since, as R. G. Collingwood has pointed out:

"There is nothing other than historical thought itself, by appeal to which its conclusions may be verified. The hero of a detective novel is thinking exactly like an historian when, from indications of the most varied kinds, he constructs an imaginary picture of how a crime was committed, and by whom. At first this is a mere theory awaiting verification, which must come to it from without. Happily for the detective, the conventions of that literary form dictate that when his construction is complete, it shall be neatly pegged down by a confession from the criminal, given in such circumstances that its genuineness is beyond question."[4]

Since an authentic self is the object of Raskolnikov's various attempts to explain why he committed the murder (if he understands *why*-dunit, he'll know *who*-dunit), it is clear that his first public confession—which ends the novel proper—is an unsatisfactory solution. A self-construction has *not* been "neatly pegged down by a confession from the criminal." Raskolnikov exhausts the detective story formula without achieving its benefit—a complete resolution of the mystery that sets the story going. If we invoke the metaphor with which we began, the two clocks of the plot fail to synchronize. Thus, after his trial, it is said of Raskolnikov (now in Siberia): "An objectless and undirected anxiety in the present, and endless sacrifice, by which nothing would be gained, in the future—that was all the world held for him" (epilogue, II).

Raskolnikov has failed to find a self in the detective story into which his attempt to enter historical narrative has devolved; but another plot is vouchsafed to him, as we saw, in the epilogue's last pages—another time is broached. The last pages of the novel are not only *about* another time; they are told in a different time: the movement from the dream

4. R. G. Collingwood, *The Idea of History* (New York, Oxford UP, 1956), p. 243. For an extended treatment of the analogy between detective and historian, see the anthology: Robin W. Winks, *The Historian as Detective* (New York, Harper and Row, 1969).

to the final word of the text is constituted in a manner that sets it off from the body of the novel insofar as it tells of years in sentences, while in the body of the text minutes are told in pages. This has disturbed such readers as Ernest J. Simmons: "Following the line of least resistence, [Dostoevsky] often ignored the time-sequence. In one of the notebooks he boldly declares 'What is time? Time does not exist; time is a cipher; time is the relation of being to unbeing.' "[5] Exactly—and that is why, far from "following the line of least resistance," Dostoevsky is at great pains to emphasize the difference between the time of the novel, whose hundreds of pages tell of only two weeks (the crucial part I tells of only three days), while the last paragraph of the epilogue covers the rest of Raskolnikov's life. Since Raskolnikov has found his self, he has entered what Dostoevsky always called "living life" (*Živaja' žizn*'): the relation between mere flux—unbeing—and the non-changing significance of the being he discovers in the moment of his conversion results in a diminished significance for chronology. This is not the historical or even psychological time of the Bergsonian *durée* variety—it is time understood precisely as "the relation of being to unbeing."

## IV

If, as we have suggested, there is a disjunction between the temporal structure of the novel proper and its epilogue, does this mean—as many readers have felt—that there is a break in the unity of *Crime and Punishment*? The suggestion of this chapter has been, rather, that there is a bond between the parts, a bond that derives from the direction of time in the two story types that define the novel, on the one hand, and the epilogue, on the other. The detective story properties shaping Raskolnikov's search for identity in the novel tend toward a conclusion that will resolve all the mysteries.

But it does not, because in the course of his investigation Raskolnikov has, in his obsessive honesty, raised the question of evil, and, as H. R. Niebuhr has said, "the mystery of good and evil in human life and in the world cannot be completely comprehended as stated in perfectly logical terms."[6] What the theologian here states is the ancient message of the wisdom tale: "Knowest thou the ordinance of heaven? Canst thou set the dominion thereof in the earth?" The movement of the epilogue is analogous to the wisdom tale in that it points back to the inadequacy of answers that precede its concluding insistence on *another* realm, *another* time: the "correct" answer is not a solution, but the reminder of another and greater mystery. Thus the historical movement of the novel is a necessary step toward the debunking of its assumptions in the epilogue. The underground man, who never found a plot, is therefore condemned to a dreary life of "bad infinity," and endless succession of empty moments. Thus the formal conclusion of the Dostoevskian plot

5. "The Art of *Crime and Punishment*," p. 516 in this edition.
6. "The Truth in Myths," in *The Nature of Religious Experience* (Douglas Clyde MacIntosh Festschrift), eds. Bewkes et al. (New York, Harper and Bros., 1937), pp. 124–25.

that contains him is a note from the editor who says "the 'notes' of this paradoxalist do not end here. . . ." Whereas *Crime and Punishment* may conclude with a "new tale"—Raskolnikov has found a role for himself in the detective-story-become-wisdom-tale that defines the Dostoevskian plot containing him.

# CZESLAW MILOSZ

## Dostoevsky and Western Intellectuals†

Probably, after all, I will not write a book on Dostoevsky, but there is no reason why I shouldn't tell what that book would be about. I would not compete with the multitude of essential monographs and penetrating analyses of particular works, rather I would assume a certain familiarity with Dostoevsky on the part of my reader, and would try to indicate the writer's position in world literature in a manner slightly different from the generally accepted one. It is possible that precisely this different interpretation is what inclines me to believe that to write a book on him would be a dangerous and thankless task.

While studying Dostoevsky and lecturing about him to American students, I could not help but notice that this writer changes according to who speaks about him. This is not readily admitted by Dostoevskians of various nationalities, as they aspire to scholarly objectivity in spite of the fact that their *Weltanschauung* and their sympathies and antipathies do not fail to influence their method of research and their argument. The history of Dostoevsky's critical reception in the course of the hundred years which have elapsed since his death exemplifies intellectual fashions succeeding each other and the influence exerted by various philosophies upon the minds of the scholars. Leaving aside for the moment the Russian critics, we may distinguish a few phases in the reception of Dostoevsky in the West, beginning with *Crime and Punishment*, which was read in translation already in the nineteenth century. Though this novel was greeted with acclaim by Nietzsche, in general the so-called "âme slave" of which Dostoevsky seemed to be representative was treated with a bit of irony. French critics, in particular, shrugged at Sonia Marmeladov, a saintly prostitute taken alive, as it were, from a French sentimental novel. The victorious march of Dostoevsky's works through Western countries in the first decades of the twentieth century is directly connected with the discovery of a new dimension in man, the subcon-

† Czeslaw Milosz (1911– ) is a Polish poet, novelist, and scholar, who has been living and teaching at the University of California, Berkeley. In 1980 he was awarded the Nobel Prize for Poetry. The essay printed here was commissioned by the Tocqueville Forum of Wake Forest University for a program, "Politics and the Arts." A book with this title is forthcoming (University Press of America). Milosz's article is being republished here from *Cross Currents: A Yearbook of Central European Culture* 5 (1986): 493–505, by permission of the author and *Cross Currents*.

scious, and with the cult of Dionysiac elemental forces merging Eros with Thanatos. Nevertheless, the resistance to the growing impact of the Russian writer, presented by such writers as Middleton Murry and D. H. Lawrence, deserves attention. According to D. H. Lawrence, "The amazing perspicacity is mixed in [Dostoevsky] with ugly perversity. Nothing is pure. His wild love of Jesus is mixed with perverse and poisonous hate of Jesus: his moral hostility to the devil is mixed with secret worship of the devil."

These voices of objection soon were superseded by general admiration, and the fame of Dostoevsky grew parallel with that of Sigmund Freud. It is true that Freud, who for obvious reasons considered a novel on parricide, *The Brothers Karamazov*, as the greatest novel ever written, based his paper on the causes of Dostoevsky's epilepsy upon incorrect factual data. As subsequently proved by Professor Joseph Frank in his biography of the writer, Dostoevsky's epileptic attacks began in Siberia and not in his tender age, as Freud believed. For several decades Freudianism powerfully influenced research on Dostoevsky constituting a period of criticism which we may well call "psychological." A phase which was relatively short and difficult to delineate was that in which existentialism colored the analyses of Dostoevskian scholars. Next, they abandoned tracking down the author's thought as voiced by his characters in order to concentrate upon the artistic structure of Dostoevsky's extraordinary novels. Indeed, these novels are so extraordinary that the question justifiably arises whether they do not signify the end of the novel as a literary genre.

My students proved to be very receptive when I dealt with the psychology of his characters or when I tried to show how much of the author's intention is revealed by the method of structural analysis. They learned with amusement, as young people usually do in such cases, of the discrepancies between the *oeuvre* and its smelly kitchen, namely, the personality of this man of genius. However, their comprehension came to an end when they encountered certain facts. For instance, they had difficulty in understanding why Dostoevsky loved the autocratic tsarist government, and not just following his return from Siberia, when he became a conservative both in his journalism and in his fiction. Sentenced to death together with his twenty-one colleagues, placed before a firing squad, which was a comedy devised by the will of the Tsar, spared at the last moment, he writes three patriotic odes during his enforced stay in Siberia. In one of these, written in 1854 during the Crimean War, he directs threats at France and England; in the second, written after the death of Nicholas I, the Tsar who allowed him to experience what presumably were his final moments before the firing squad, he compares the emperor to the sun and humbly confesses that he is not worthy to pronounce the emperor's name; the third, written on the occasion of Alexander II's coronation, is a eulogy of the new tsar. The poems are very bad, and the desire to better his fate cannot be excluded as a motive, but they agree with what we know from other sources about the views of the author.

This biographical detail, and others of a similar nature, belong to an area in which the road of the majority of Dostoevsky scholars ceases to be my road, that is, our attention turns to different things. For me, Dostoevsky is most interesting as a man who in his life had only one serious affair, with Russia, and who chose Russia as the true heroine of his works. It may seem that the psychology of his characters and his discoveries in the domain of the structure of the novel make him a truly international writer, while his nationalism, his worship of the throne and of the altar, his chauvinistic hatred of Catholics and Jews, his jeering at Poles and Frenchmen enclose him within the boundaries of one country only. In my opinion, this is not the case; on the contrary, the more Russian Dostoevsky is, the more he succumbs to his phobias and obsessions out of his love for Russia, the greater his role is as a witness for the whole intellectual history of the last two centuries. Why two centuries? He himself said: "Everything depends upon the next century"—and we cannot deny his gift of prophecy.

In the Dostoevsky family, one of the basic readings was *The History of the Russian State* by Karamzin, and the future writer was familiar with it from childhood. This work sees the source and the pledge of Russia's greatness in the unlimited, autocratic rule of the monarchs. During his imprisonment in the Petropavlovsk fortress, Dostoevsky wrote a deposition, in which he presented his views on the monarchy, and he sounds so sincere that the mere desire to save his skin could not have dictated such words. According to him, revolution was necessary in France, while in Russia no one in his right mind would think of a republican form of government. The history of the Novgorodian republic alone—inglorious in Dostoevsky's eyes—should be warning enough. As for Muscovy, it found itself under the Tatar yoke when the authority of its princes had weakened, and it was saved when that authority was strengthened again—just as, later on, Russia was given strength by "the great pilot," Peter the Great.

How could a Socialist, a Fourierist, write in this manner? We may invoke a duality typical of Dostoevskianism, yet we would probably be closer to the truth if we assumed that these two tendencies, socialist and autocratic, always coexisted in Dostoevsky, and it was only the emphasis that changed. His colleague from the Petrashevsky circle, Nicholas Danilevsky, underwent a similar evolution. However, even though he glorified the Tsardom and proclaimed the victorious march of the Slavs in his work, *Russia and Europe,* Danilevsky did not renounce the socialist dreams of his youth; he simply was making them a part of his totalitarian doctrine.

Dostoevsky reasoned like a statesman. In his conversations with his fellow prisoners in the penal colony of Omsk, he considered the conquest of Constantinople the most important task facing Russia. The *oeuvre* of his mature age, beginning with his first trip to Western Europe in 1862, differs from his previous works in that, whereas before he was an artist, now the artist and the statesman in him worked together. His books describe the spiritual situation of the Russian intelligentsia, and form a chronicle of its spiritual transformations from decade to decade, and even almost from year to year. And they pose an essential question: What do those transformations mean for the future of Russia, in what are they a threat to her existence and vocation? Without fear of exaggerating, we may say that these books are a kind of police investigation conducted by a very intelligent public prosecutor who knows what he is looking for, as he himself is simultaneously the investigator and the subject.

The Russian intelligentsia in Dostoevsky's novels discusses the basic problems of human existence, which were by no means alien to characters of the Western novel, either in its eighteenth-century version or in its Romantic version, as, for instance, in George Sand. Nowhere else, however, do the participants in the discussion present the matter in such a sharp light, and draw such radical conclusions. They live through in dramatic fashion what Friedrich Nietzsche, a contemporary of Raskol'nikov, called "the death of God." Yet, in Russia atheism is by no means a private affair of the individual, it is of the highest concern to the authorities, for an atheist, as a rule, becomes a revolutionary, thus confirming the road taken by that forerunner of the Russian intelligentsia's generations, Vissarion Belinsky. In *Crime and Punishment*, the crime of Raskol'nikov is, in fact, a kind of substitution. In reality, he dreams of a great revolutionary deed, to which history would provide the justification. In his views and aspirations, he is completely alone: on one side, he is opposed by the authorities, represented by a police officer, Porfiry, on the other side, by the Russian people. When he is in Siberia, his fellow prisoners, simple peasants, want to kill him, as they guess him to be an atheist. Thus, already in *Crime and Punishment*, we discover a formula valid for all the mature work of Dostoevsky: the rampart and the foundation of Russia are the authorities of the State and the devoutly religious—as Dostoevsky believed—Russian people, while the intelligentsia constitutes a threat. *What* sort of threat, is demonstrated in the novel, *The Possessed*. Among the amazingly perspicacious diagnoses in this novel, perhaps the profoundest is expressed by an old military man, who, while listening to a conversation on the nonexistence of God, exclaims: "If there is no God, what sort of a captain am I?" That man grasped a link between religion and the sources of authority. Let us not forget that the Russian intelligentsia nourished itself on Voltaire's philosophy and on memories of the French revolution. The beheading of Louis XVI today seems only one of the sensational events abounding in the course of history, neither more nor less important than any other. In reality, it meant the end of an order based upon the conviction that the king rules because he is divinely ordained, while those below him rule by his dispensation. But now, other sources of authority were to be looked for—for instance, in a conspiracy directed by one man, Piotr Verkhovensky, as in *The Possessed*. The novel that the author intended to be the crowning work of his *oeuvre*, *The Brothers Karamazov*, has for its subject the rebellion of the sons against the father, and a parricide. The question arises, whether the weakness and immorality of the father do not abolish his authority. Ivan Karamazov answers yes to this question—and chooses his answer as the basis for his rebellion against both his father and God the Father. *The Brothers Karamazov* is, in its essence, a treatise on the Russian intelligentsia's act of abolishing the authority of God, of the Tsar, and the father of a family at the same time.

Western intellectuals, when writing on Dostoevsky, constantly wonder at a strange disparity, namely, that a man who penetrated so deeply into the psyche of his characters could have such reactionary views. They try to eliminate those views from their field of vision, in which they are helped by the hypothesis of the "polyphonic" structure of his novels. Yet they are unaware of the differences separating them from the Russian novelist. Not one of them, either in his theoretical writings or in his novels, places the interests of the State at the center of his concerns. On the contrary, they are emotionally on the side of those characters who want to abolish the existing order. For Dostoevsky, however, Russia as a state did not mean only a territory inhabited by the Russians. The future of the world depended on Russia, on whether she would become contaminated by the ideas of atheism and socialism imported from the West, just as her intelligentsia had become contaminated, or would be saved by the Tsardom and the pious Russian people and thus would be able to fulfill her vocation of rescuing all humanity. Aliosha Karamazov, in subsequent volumes of the unfinished novel, was to represent a new type of activist working in harmony with the faith of the people.

In his Slavophile idealization of the Russian people, Dostoevsky was mistaken. Yet he could not find any other reason for hope, and so, clearly there was a dilemma: if "Holy Russia" proves unable to present an effective resistance, the intelligentsia would do to her what the heroes of *The Possessed* started to accomplish on the scale of one provincial town. In the long history of Dostoevsky's critical reception in various countries, the highest place, as far as the understanding of his intentions is concerned, should be assigned to a group of Russian philosophers active at the beginning of the twentieth century, particularly to their pronouncements in a volume of essays, *Viekhi* [Landmarks, 1908], and *Iz glubiny* [*De Profundis*, 1918]. According to them, the prophecies of Dostoevsky were already being fulfilled. Perhaps this should not surprise us, as these philosophers were unsympathetic towards the Revolution. However, the opinion that the Revolution fulfilled Dostoevsky's prophecies was also widespread among the revolutionaries of 1917. One of the greatest admirers of Dostoevsky was the first Commissar of Education after the October Revolution, Lunacharsky. As late as 1920, *The Possessed* was extolled in the official press as a novel which had become a reality.

"It is impossible not to see in Dostoevsky a prophet of the Russian revolution"—wrote Nicholas Berdyaev in 1918. "The Russian revolution is imbued with those principles which were foreseen by Dostoevsky and which received in his works the sharp definition of genius. It was given to Dostoevsky to penetrate the dialectics of Russian revolutionary thought and to draw extreme conclusions from it. He did not remain on the surface of social and political ideas and constructs, he plunged into the depths and revealed that the Russian revolution is a metaphysical and religious phenomenon, not a political and social phenomenon. In such a way, through religion, he grasped the nature of Russian socialism."

The Russians understood Dostoevsky's political worries, for they, just as he himself, thought in terms of statesmanship, i.e., they attached importance to the consequences of a given idea for the existence of the State, whether it would be counter-revolutionary or revolutionary. Their Western colleagues were concerned with the individual, not with France, England or America. It is true, though, that during the twentieth century an opinion has taken root among them, according to which a self-respecting man treats the existing, capitalist system as something transitory, and quietly waits for its end. An astonishing similarity between the attitudes of the Russian intelligentsia, as described by Dostoevsky, and the attitudes of Western intellectuals a hundred years later leads us to conclude that his anxiety about the future of Russia enabled him to describe a phenomenon of immense dimensions, both in space and in time.

The term "Western intellectuals" is undoubtedly too general, and by using it we risk misunderstandings. Yet if we choose a figure who focuses the traits that we usually associate with this term, we will place ourselves on firmer ground. Such a figure exists: it is Jean-Paul Sartre, sometimes called the Voltaire of the twentieth century. What is striking in him is his extraordinary *intensity* in discussing ideas, an intensity similar to that of his Russian predecessors. The European intellectual upheaval which began in the sixteenth century reached Russia after a considerable delay, and educated Russians had to assimilate in a few decades ideas that, in Western Europe, had matured gradually during several centuries. Hence, perhaps, arises the exceptional force and virulence with which these ideas were taken up in Russia. Moreover, they were not confronted there by a well-developed, diversified social organism. For reasons which deserve a more thorough analysis than I can give here, a peculiar vacuum appeared, in turn, in the countries of the West in the twentieth century, a kind of nowhere inhabited by the intellectual, who thus, for decades, has been spinning out his concepts beyond any control by ordinary bread-eaters, just as in Dostoevsky. Raskol'nikov and Ivan Karamazov live alone with their reasoning. It is not only his intensity, but also the *abstractness* of his thought that brings Jean-Paul Sartre close to these characters.

Is it not strange that in free-thinking France, in a country which has seen much and has been inclined to shrug at quarrels over principles, suddenly "the death of God" becomes a crucial question, such as it once was, long ago, for young Russians talking about principles over vodka? Undoubtedly, for French existentialism, and above all for Sartre, it was a fundamental premise—and starting from it (again an analogy with Russia), one progressed to the obligation to be active in order to transform the world, as man, by dethroning God, himself becomes a god and must demonstrate his responsibility through action.

A chapter on Sartre as a Dostoevskian character would undoubtedly open interesting vistas. In such a chapter, it would also be possible to touch upon certain similarities between Sartre's philosophy and that of Dostoevsky. I have in mind here, first of all, Sartre's famous dictum: "Hell is the others," that is, the problem of the relations between a subject and other people, who are also subjects. The individual aspires to wield power over others and to change them into objects, but since he perceives, in the eyes of others, the same desire to change him into an object, the others become his hell. This is precisely the problem of pride-humiliation in Dostoevsky. At the time Sartre was writing his *Being and Nothingness*, a book published in 1943, he could not have known of the book by Bakhtin on Dostoevsky's poetics, in which that matter is thoroughly investigated. And yet, the "existential psychoanalysis" in Sartre's book agrees with the conclusions of Bakhtin, though Sartre seems to be unaware of such a kinship between himself and the Russian novelist.

Certain features of Russian life in the nineteenth century may contribute to a difficulty we encounter anytime we try to view the problems which preoccupied the Russian intelligentsia as still valid for our time. And yet Sartre, in his search for freedom, follows in the footsteps of Dostoevsky's Underground Man, a character who inaugurated a series of great philosophical monologists. In addition, Hegel's philosophy (introduced into France in the nineteen thirties by Alexandre Kojève, i.e. Kozhevnikov) proved to be decisive for Sartre's intellectual development. Likewise, it can already be distinguished in the background of Raskol'-nikov's article on great men who are exonerated by History if they have committed crimes while acting in its service. Raskol'nikov, a latent revolutionary, in his walks about St. Petersburg deliberately avoided the square where the unsuccessful rebellion of December 1825 took place. Certainly, he would have done better to give himself to the cause of revolution rather than senselessly murder a pawnbroker, but in the 1860's when the action of the novel occurs, the time is not ripe for political acts, and we must wait until the 1870's for the character of Nechaev—Piotr Verkhovensky, from *The Possessed*. Ivan Karamazov, in turn, engages in a most fundamental quarrel with God's immorality in the name of the Promethean obligations of man, and this is precisely the very core of Sartre's thought and his attempts to act.

*What is to be done?* While the title of Chernyshevsky's novel indicates the preoccupations of the Russian intelligentsia of the nineteenth century, it could serve, as well, as the motto for the whole, indefatigable activity of Sartre. He was constantly looking for *une cause* to which he could offer his abilities. All of these causes were connected with the hope of abolishing the existing political system and replacing it with another, but with what sort—on this point Sartre continually changed his mind. He pinned his hopes on a succession of countries, and his disappointments were both comic and pathetic at the same time. First the Soviet Union, then Yugoslavia, next Cuba and, finally, China were, for him, the lands of the future, but he ended his career distributing leaflets in the street, together with young Maoist leftists. In his need to provide ever new answers to the question, *what is to be done?* Sartre was by no means an exception, on the contrary, he exemplified the similar anxiety in thousands of intellectuals and semi-intellectuals.

Such a longing for causes engendered by actuality may merely indicate an inner void which must be filled with something meaningful, with a disinterested striving toward a noble goal. Similarly, Dostoevsky's characters are torn from the fabric of everyday life, which secures that internal peace of limited concerns and limited achievements for their not-so-bright fellow men. Dostoevsky's characters are bound neither by religion nor by the liturgical calendar, and they reject traditional morality. They also regard the accumulation of wealth as loathsome; after all, money can be gotten through crime, mere chance, inheritance, a game of roulette, usury, but never by work. Rural Russia is subject to a certain rhythm of customary activities, while a member of the intelligentsia is enclosed in the magic circle of his mind and daydreams about his exceptional role as a potential savior of mankind. He suffers from a lack of reasons to live, and Dostoevsky tries to define this *taedium vitae*, particularly by creating strong characters who are summoned to a commitment but who are unable to commit themselves because of excessive introspection, such as Svidrigailov or Stavrogin.

This illness, which has acquired vast scope in our century proportional to the progress of literacy, has perhaps not received, heretofore, a precise diagnosis. Possibly, its origin can be traced to a weakening in the perception of *being*, or to a perception of being as something absurd. Behind the nightmares visiting Svidrigailov and Stavrogin, we could perhaps see *La Nausée*, as Sartre entitled his novel written prior to his revolutionary commitments. *L'Entre-en-Soi*, or the whole world outside of man, does not provoke in Sartre any feelings of piety or amazement, as it did long ago, for instance, in Goethe; on the contrary, it presses upon him with its lack of meaning and forces him to escape into the realm of human action. Thus, it is a metaphysical question. Many Christians would be surprised to hear that "the Voltaire of the twentieth century" was not only representative of intellectuals unsympathetic towards religion, but also of many clerics and believers as well. For if the church has been, for some time, seeking noble social causes to embrace, it is perhaps because there is a feeling abroad that the metaphysical side of Christianity has evaporated, leaving behind only a set of moral precepts about how people should live with one another.

In Dostoevsky, the representatives of the intelligentsia either live in the underground or openly oppose society. Raskol'nikov does not consider himself guilty because he killed the pawnbroker and her sister, but because he is weak and defeated by society. After the first, sentimental phase of his work, when his heroes are "poor folk," Dostoevsky introduces a distinction between those who are aware and others who are on a lower level of awareness, and he is fascinated by the former alone. To his horror, this fascination leads him almost to identify with Ivan Karamazov and his parable of the Grand Inquisitor. It should be noted that such a distinction, of the initiated and the rest, is quite typical of those who, in our time, follow the example of the Russian intelligentsia. Perhaps it was unwise of Simone de Beauvoir, Sartre's companion, to name her novel about their milieu, *The Mandarins*. To belong to the chosen ones is comforting, and the chosen ones are those who grasp the secret of the historical process, so that they know the future. Then they are united not by a common faith, but by their shared knowledge. It is a peculiar gnosis which authorizes them to pronounce judgments deduced from presumably unshakable premises, without paying attention to tangible, but too down-to-earth reality.

What is the meaning of this transmutation of Dostoevsky's characters, whose traits are recognizable in a different society and a different epoch? If the Russian intelligentsia became a forerunner of the European and American intelligentsia, according to what rule did it happen? Why did the import—for everything which nourished educated Russia, including the literary models for Dostoevsky, was an import from Germany, France or England—why did the import result in the construction of such a mirror? We are accustomed to believing that societies, if they resemble each other in their economic, political and social structures, also find similar means of expression in their philosophy, literature and art. This assumption seems to belong to that part of the Marxist heritage that has become common property. But in what could tsarist Russia, with its division of the population into castes officially registered by the State, with its extreme centralization of power, and with its immense, illiterate peasant mass, resemble the developed countries of the West in the second half of the twentieth century? But is it indeed true, as I have hinted, that up to the present time the West has had no intelligentsia, i.e., a specific social layer separated from the common bread-earners, suffering because of that separation and assigning to itself a Promethean role? Or should we simply recognize that ideas lead an autonomous life and that they are more important than economic or political differences? Assuming this, it is possible to maintain that, though the metaphysical foundation of both ethics and authority crumbled in the West owing to what Nietzsche called "the death of God," the very complex praxis of economic growth obscured such problems. At a certain time, they appeared on the surface, and this coincided with the crisis of the parliamentary systems.

The activity of terrorist groups in the sixties and seventies of our century, such as the Weathermen or the Symbionese Liberaton Army in the United States or the Red Brigades in Italy, etc., means—as in *The Possessed*—that the legitimacy of the authorities has been called into question. In Russia, the Nechaev group, whose trial provided Dostoevsky with material for the novel, rejected the legitimacy of the monarchic authority and of the whole system founded upon the sacred. In the West, it is the turn of the authority founded upon elections. Of course, the revolutionaries know what makes "the true" will of the people, as distinguished from the apparent one, unaware of itself, and they act in the name of that "true" will.

Modern novelists, with the possible exception of V. S. Naipaul, do not explore the fascinating kinship between the motivations of these groups in the West and the motivations that we find in *The Possessed*—or the considerable differences, in view of the role of the mass media today. This proves, perhaps, that the novel as a genre no longer reacts to events of public life, plunging instead into subjectivity. There is, however, another explanation for this lack of interest on the part of literature in events of, after all, great importance. Dostoevsky reflected on the future of Russia and on the changes threatening her; his thought was that of a defender of the existing order, for instance, a district attorney. Upon its appearance, *The Possessed* enraged the progressive intelligentsia, who took it as a libel on the whole revolutionary movement. The sympathies of enlightened public opinion turned towards young rebels of various orientations, who were surrounded by a halo of heroism and martyrdom and whose trials put the authories themselves on trial. A novelist who dared, today, to choose as his subject the hostile analysis of a terrorist group's way of thought and behavior would expose himself to the reproach of being a defender of the existing order, which is considered an unforgivable offense by people of a certain intellectual level. It should be kept in mind that terrorist activity has drawn its justification from the writings of philosophers, Jean-Paul Sartre, Herbert Marcuse and others—both terrorist activity on a small scale, practiced by underground networks, and that on a large scale, such as the genocide introduced into Cambodia by former students of the Sorbonne. Since so many people of the intellect openly or tacitly sympathize with terror, it would be difficult to expect from them its portrayal, multilayered but negative, such as in *The Possessed* by Dostoevsky. Moreover, Dostoevsky, in his own time, had to free himself from the literary canons which were binding for the intelligentsia. We would look in vain for similar cross-sections from the pen of writers of the Chernyshevsky type. Thus, it would be proper to reject the widely held opinion that genius took hold of Dostoevsky in spite of his reactionary views. A quite opposite affirmation seems valid: he was a great writer because he was endowed with the gift of clairvoyance, and he owed this gift to his being a reactionary.

Nicholas Berdyaev, whom I have already quoted, noticed in Dostoevsky a capacity for understanding processes that go deeper than social conditions and politics. "Dostoevsky was a great master in unveiling *ontological* consequences of false ideas"—he says. "Dostoevsky foresaw that a revolution in Russia would be joyless, cruel and murky, that it would not bring any rebirth of the people. He knew that a considerable role would be played by Fedka the criminal and that victory would belong to Shigalov." Of course, we cannot but ask ourselves today whether Dostoevsky's diagnosis, conceived out of his fears for the fate of Russia, is also not rich in predictions for the fate of the West. It is easy to accept the premise—prepared, moreover, by evolutionism, which is taught at school and in the university—that there exist immutable laws of historical development. The similarities between the attitudes of the Russian intelligentsia and those of the intelligentsia in the West today may, in fact, be a confirmation of those laws, which led, over there, to the fall of the Tsardom, and which will lead, here, to the fall of a system based on free elections. In the pronouncements of Dostoevsky's characters there was no place for democracy. Raskol'nikov believed in the dictatorial rule of great, exceptional individuals; Shigalov, logical in his defense of universal slavery, becomes a theoretician of a revolutionary group in *The Possessed*; while a powerful philosophical mind, Ivan Karamazov, chooses the Grand Inquisitor to be the guardian of people who do not merit anything better, for they are arrogant children and, left to themselves, would not know how to govern themselves. "*La volonté générale*" of Rousseau remains beyond the mental horizons of these dreamers. In their loathing of democracy, which for them is synonymous with bourgeois mediocrity, they embody the views of Dostoevsky himself. In *The Possessed*, he identified the suicide of Stavrogin with the Swiss canton of Uri, and, in *Crime and Punishment*, makes a voyage to America a metaphor for the suicide of Svidrigailov.

The nineteenth century in the West swore allegiance to a new idea, that of the people as the source of authority, for after the beheading of Louis XVI that other source of authority, divine investiture, was lacking. Anti-monarchism became a part of libertarian rhetoric. In the United States, which emerged from a rebellion against the authority of the King of England, a contemporary of Dostoevsky, Walt Whitman, wrote poetry such as never existed before, a poetry of the citizen, equal among equals. What is astounding is the speed with which this current swelled and then subsided, and was followed, in the next century, by venomous mockeries directed at free elections and legislative chambers, as well as at the independent judiciary. By choosing Jean-Paul Sartre as a model, we may trace the passage to another kind of rhetoric, that of revolution. Such a rhetoric completely bypasses the question of the sources of authority, which in practice leads to a dictatorship of a few "knowledgeable" leaders presumably acting in the name of the people, and deprives people of the protection provided by the independent judiciary.

Thus, democracy has been abandoned by its most representative intellectuals, just as the Tsardom was once abandoned by the Russian intelligentsia. It is tempting to draw conclusions as to the future, but we may easily fall victim to illusory analogies. The Russian intelligentsia was isolated in the midst of the illiterate peasant masses, which drove it to despair as a force of inertia incarnate. A certain misadventure which occurred in the milieu known to Dostoevsky in his youth has more than merely anecdotal significance. Petrashevsky, the founder of a famous political circle which counted Dostoevsky among its members, somewhat earlier founded a model phalanstery for his peasants, according to Fourier's recipe. The peasants promptly burned down the buildings.

The isolation of the intellectual in the twentieth century is of a different nature. Jean-Paul Sartre's review, *Les Temps Modernes*, encountered a public able but unwilling to read it, as it preferred illustrated magazines, comics and TV. The universal rush to consumption, the progress of medicine and the "permissiveness" of society introduced completely new factors into the equation by creating a kind of soft social tissue, a target for intellectuals' pens and terrorists' bombs. Possible analogies notwithstanding, the differences between Dostoevsky's Russia and the contemporary West are, indeed, too serious to be neglected. Also, the historical past was different in different geographical areas, and we know that the past is always present behind the scene, shaping everyday life. In Russia, the function of the written word as a medium for expressing ideas has been different from that in the West. The complexity of the western social organism enables it to absorb and resorb various poisons; that complexity still exists in the West and takes on new forms which are less and less ideological.

The revival, in the twentieth century, of the "accursed problems" which once tormented the characters of a novelist from backward Russia mocks everything we know about the "laws" of history. Thus, in looking for signs of the future in such an unexpected phenomenon, we would be multiplying a paradox by a paradox. Nevertheless, there is nowhere else to be found a more faithful description of the tensions and conflicts proper to the twentieth century than in the legend of the Grand Inquisitor of Dostoevsky. Russian admirers of the writer very early recognized in this text a strength matched only in the Gospels and the Revelation of St. John, and predicted that it would never lose significance, as it reached to the core of the human condition. Yet, its apocalyptic features could shock only in the century in which it was written, a century not only non-apocalyptic, but imbued with faith in Progress. What to its first readers might have seemed only a terrifying and unclear fantasy, for us has acquired the distinctness of tangible things. For the Grand Inquisitor in this parable appears as someone who knows that man does not know how to be free, that he is a worshipper of gods, and that, if he has no gods, he bows to idols in whose name he is capable of the worst cruelties. Man wants to feel an authority above him and is afraid of free choice: "He is weak and base. What does it matter if he does rebel against our authority everywhere now and is proud of his rebellion? It is the pride of a child and of a schoolboy. They are little children rioting in class and driving out their teacher. But an end will come to the transports of the children, too. They will pay dearly for it. They will tear down the temples and drench the earth with blood. But they will realize at last, the foolish children, that although they are rebels, they are impotent rebels who are unable to keep up with their rebellion."

This formulation is so full of content that the text resists almost all attempts to unravel it completely. The Dostoevsky who was a partisan of the autocratic power of the tsar and an enemy of the revolutionaries imperceptibly changes into the Dostoevsky who bears a grudge against Christ for his failure to bring about the Kingdom of God on earth. In its crucial conclusion, the legend affirms that men are too weak to rise above the laws of Nature. Since Nature, in other words, reality, is under the control of the devil, whosoever would rule effectively over men must make the same decision as the Grand Inquisitor: to collaborate with the "terrible and wise spirit of Non-being."

# RICHARD WEISBERG

## The Brilliant Reactor: The Inquisitor in *Crime and Punishment*†

The tortured law student, Raskolnikov, has committed two murders to test his theory that an individual can "step across" the ordinary legal limits and say "a new word." Burning with fever and guilt, caught up in the seamy yet inspiring world of the second most artificial city in Europe (St. Petersburg being to Dostoevski what Venice was to Schiller and Mann) the troubled intellectual maintains a tenuous grip on reality and on his own theoretical superiority. But this begins to disintegrate rapidly the moment he meets the inquisitor assigned to investigate the murders. To an informed reader, the dynamic between inquisitor and suspect in *Crime and Punishment* surpasses even the perennially fasci-

† From *The Failure of the Word: The Protagonist as Lawyer in Modern Fiction.* New Haven: Yale UP, 1984, pp. 48–54. Reprinted by permission of Yale University Press, and the author.

nating relationship between the police officer and Jean Valjean in Hugo's *Les Misérables*.

As Dostoevski's attention to detail might lead us to expect, the investigation in *Crime and Punishment* parallels the criminal procedure in the Alexandrine Russia of the 1860s. After the typically brief role of the police in serious crimes,[1] the inquisitor Porfiry Petrovich is called in to commence formally the "preliminary inquiry" (*predvaritel'noe proizvodstvo*); a few days later, his first meeting with Raskolnikov occurs, almost halfway into the novel. Prior to this meeting, Raskolnikov has had only tangential brushes with two police officials, Zametov and Nikodim Fomich. While the student's behavior and remarks have inspired some suspicion on those occasions, Porfiry alone sufficiently grasps Raskolnikov's subtle mind to consider him a possible murderer of the old pawnbroker and her sister, Lizaveta.

Porfiry is inaccurately called the *zdešni pristav sledstvennikh del'* (the local police investigator of the case), first by Razumikhin, Raskolnikov's friend and Porfiry's distant cousin (part 2, chapter 4) and again later by Raskolnikov; Porfiry, however, calls himself either the *sledovatel' kotoromu poručeno delo* (the investigator charged with the case) or, more simply, the *sledovatel'*. The lay misapprehension that Porfiry is a police official, instead of a lawyer and officer of the court, is representative of the public confusion about criminal procedure in general, which contributed to the reforms that Porfiry specifically mentions to Raskolnikov later—"inquisitors are all at any rate to be called something different soon." Here as elsewhere in his works, Dostoevski demonstrates through these variations on the inquisitor's title both interest and competence in procedural law. Indeed, the Code of 1864 denominates the position *sudebni sledovatel'* (literally, "judicial investigator"), a clearer title which Dostoevski uses only for the inquisitor in *The Brothers Karamazov*, published fifteen years later.[2]

As soon as he enters the case, Porfiry enjoys predominance over both Police Chief Fomich[3] and the procurator, who is his hierarchical superior but must cede power to the inquisitor until the dossier is given over to him.[4] In such a case, an actual inquisitor would have had no trouble assuming Porfiry's broad powers. He would have had only to show that a crime of sufficient seriousness to engage his office had been committed, a fact already established during the police inquiry. The

1. Until recently, Continental police inquiry into serious crimes rarely extended beyond the first twenty-four hours, after which an inquisitor was called in.

2. I have made some alterations in the Jessie Coulson translation to suit the information provided here about technical legal terms. On the subject of public ignorance of, and displeasure with, prereform czarist legal procedures, see Samuel Kucherov, *Courts, Lawyers and Trials under the Last Three Tsars*, New York: Praeger, 1953, esp.

pp. 38–54. For Dostoevsky's specific association of Porfiry with the reformers, see also *The Notebooks for* Crime and Punishment, trans. and ed. Edward Wasiolek, Chicago: U of Chicago P, 1967, p. 167.

3. Articles 261 and 270 of the Code of Criminal Procedures of 1864.

4. For the parallel French provisions dealing with the relationship between inquisitor and procurator, see *Code de procedure penale*, 1968, articles 72, 82, and 120.

absence of an immediate suspect would not have prevented the inquisitor from interviewing anyone even vaguely connected with the incident. Hence, Porfiry can and does examine character witnesses in regard to Raskolnikov, legitimately probing into incidents which are totally unrelated to the crime;[5] he searches Raskolnikov's rooms in the latter's absence and without even the permission of the landlady. Continental inquisitors to this day may legally emulate Porfiry's techniques (many of them unconstitutional under American law) wherever such procedures will serve "the truth," and without prior judicial intervention.

Summarizing the virtually unparalleled powers of the Continental inquisitor, a Russian jurist of Dostoevski's time observes:

> All such functions demonstrate that our legislation entrusts to the inquisitor not only the responsibility to adjudicate fairly, but also the responsibility inherent in the function of criminal investigator and uncoveror of proof of guilt and innocence.[6]

But it may be precisely the need to be impartial (Article 265 of the Code of 1864 orders that the inquisitor must "*without prejudice* investigate all the favorable circumstances regarding the accused, as well as the unfavorable ones"), and the absence of the American prosecutor's political zeal to "get a conviction," that leads Porfiry to establish the ambivalent tone toward Raskolnikov which provides the operative tension behind their relationship.

Indeed, *Crime and Punishment* dissects the subtle nature of what might be called the inquisitor's pragmatic befriending of the protagonist. In contrast to the general absence of specific motive in other friendships, the attraction of inquisitor to suspect combines genuine human interest with the desire to elicit a confession. The inquisitor rarely hesitates to bring his great investigative powers to bear, occasionally assuming a virtually omniscient dominance over his increasingly befuddled "friend." Yet Porfiry's genuine interest in the criminal personality, which from time to time appears as envy of a man who can "step across" externally imposed social boundaries, lends an equality to the relationship and renders it both artistically compelling and immensely significant to our discussion. Throughout the second half of the novel, Porfiry engages in a battle of wits with Raskolnikov. Their verbal joust consists of three distinct "passes," culminating in the inquisitor's two-pronged victory: a confession of guilt and a thorough comprehension of the accused. As we shall see, Porfiry's subsequent willingness to conceal from his legal superiors parts of what he has learned both saves Raskolnikov's life and (somewhat precariously and artificially) preserves Dostoevski's Christian world view.

In part 3, chapter 5, Raskolnikov deliberately sets a tone of games-

---

5. The interviewing of persons who might shed light on the general personalities of all possible suspects was considered the most important function of the inquisitor. See the czarist code, articles 265, 269, 377; see the French code, articles 101–21.

6. Slučevski, *Učebnik Russkovo*, p. 635; translation Weisberg's.

manship in the relationship, by staging an entrance into Porfiry's apartment in which he light-heartedly banters with Razumikhin. Raskolnikov, whose every meeting with and ultimate confession to Porfiry are legally (though not psychologically) voluntary, wishes immediately to give an impression of total insouciance regarding the criminal investigation. While the inquisitor joins in the cordiality, nonetheless he "did not once take his eyes from the guest." Porfiry may have the caricatured physical appearance of a Dickensian lawyer, with his "fat, round, rather snub-nosed, dark-skinned face which had an unhealthy yellowish pallor, and a cheerful, mocking expression," but he possesses the subtle and careful mind essential to his profession.

In addition, he works hard. By the time Raskolnikov visits, the lawyer has already interviewed Zametov and other witnesses to Raskolnikov's strange behavior at the police station a few days earlier. He has also taken the time to read the suspect's recent article, "Concerning Crime." By reiterating at the interview Raskolnikov's argument in the article, Porfiry cleverly insinuates his suspicion that his guest may well have effectuated his "extraordinary man" theory by murdering the two women.

> It is this . . . really, I hardly know how best to express it . . . it is a very trifling little idea . . . Psychological . . . Well, this is it: when you were composing your article—surely it could not be, he, he, that you did not consider yourself . . . just a tiny bit . . . to be also an "extraordinary" man, one who was saying a *new word*—in your sense, that is . . . Surely, that is so?

Such maneuvers torture Raskolnikov, and by the end of the scene his feigned cheerfulness has changed to evident disequilibration. Tactically naive, he even blurts out, "Do you wish to interrogate me officially, with all the formalities?" failing to recognize that the unique procedural role of the inquisitor renders an overt accusation "quite unnecessary for the present," in Porfiry's own words. An arrested suspect is far less likely to confess than a confused man left free to implicate himself further.

Becoming gradually addicted to the game he is already losing (like Kafka's Joseph K. before the mysterious "court" of his undoing), Raskolnikov demonstrates the efficacy of Porfiry's strategy. He voluntarily returns for a second meeting the very next morning, this time at the inquisitor's office. Unlike his earlier entrance, Raskolnikov's second appearance displays fear, outrage, and even hatred toward his "friend." Porfiry continues his verbal undermining of Raskolnikov by establishing a tone of familiarity, even referring to him as *batjuška* (old boy). The unclear nature of his situation forces Raskolnikov to stifle all outward expression of his growing resentment (*zlost'*):

> "I think you said yesterday that you wished to question me . . . officially . . . about my acquaintance with the . . . murdered woman," began Raskolnikov again. "Why did I put in that *I think?*" flashed through

his mind. "And why am I so worried at having put it in?" came in another flash. Suddenly he felt that, simply because he was in Porfiry's presence, and had exchanged a couple of glances and a couple of words with him, his uneasiness had instantly increased to gigantic proportions . . . and that this was terribly dangerous: his nerves were tense, his emotion was increasing. "This is disastrous! . . . I shall say too much again."[7]

As for Porfiry, a growing certainty of Raskolnikov's guilt, together with a continuing sense that arresting such a suspect will only forestall confession, move him to prolong the contest. But it is something beyond these factors, something beyond even Porfiry's obvious delight in the game itself, which inspires him to broaden the inquiry. For the lawyer, too, begins to experience a personal, reactive fascination with his adversary. Indeed, suspect and lawyer create, in this novel, the poignant duality which has marked much of recent literature's perplexing stance on criminality. As Porfiry's investigation closes in on Raskolnikov's guilt, the lawyer grows spiritually closer to the transgressor. The two unite in what Raskolnikov recognizes as their uncommon mutual brilliance:

> "Do you know," he said suddenly, looking almost insolently at Porfiry Petrovich, and delighting in his own insolence, "there must exist, I believe, a lawyer's procedure, a legal method, applying to all sorts of investigations, by which they begin with trivial matters, far removed from the real subject, or even with something serious, so long as it is quite irrelevant, so as to encourage the person being interrogated, or rather to distract his attention and lull his mistrust, and then suddenly and unexpectedly stun him by hitting him on the crown of his head with the most dangerous and fatal question. Am I right? Isn't the principle enshrined in all the rules and precepts to this day?"

Porfiry's own explanation of the inquisitor's ultimate success is "double-edged." "The criminal's nature comes to the rescue of the poor investigator"; but only the inquisitor's wit discerns that nature and re-creates it verbally in a legal context. Like the perceptive novelist, Porfiry ferrets out the individual subject's deepest meanings, then uses his verbal skills to formulate a portrait which will further his own subjective goals. If the end of justice is to apply codified legal wisdom fairly in each particular case, the inquisitor's aim is to make of every case a generalized portrait.

As their fascinating relationship progresses toward Porfiry's inevitable victory, Raskolnikov's internalized resentment grows to a level matched in Dostoevski only by the Underground Man and by Ivan Karamazov when he is faced with the insidious Smerdyakov during the comparable three interviews of that final novel. In the last of their dialogues (part 6, chapter 2), Porfiry displays an almost genuine fondness for the de-

---

7. Raskolnikov only seems to react this way to *lawyers*, however, unlike the universal resentments (indicated by the same Russian word) of the Underground Man and Ivan Karamazov. In his earlier scenes with Dounia's suitor (the lawyer Luzhin), Raskolnikov also experiences resentful rage, but largely for different reasons.

bilitated suspect, occasionally patting his knee or shoulder, and alternating his self-styled giggling "clownishness" with a seeming melancholy at the imminent termination of the game. It was "as if he now scorned to use his earlier tricks and stratagems"; but his sincerity, while not entirely feigned, also serves his strategic purposes.

After "confessing" his own technique as a lawyer, during a lengthy statement about the immense power of the inquisitor, Porfiry can quite naturally proceed to articulate Raskolnikov's actions as a murderer. Porfiry admits to secret violations of Raskolnikov's existence: covert searches and seizures, interviews with his closest friends, spreading rumors to confuse the suspect, staging spurious confessions, and subtle verbal manipulation of people and events. From a theoretical point of view, Porfiry's decision to lay bare his own amoral or excessive, though legal, procedures in investigating the guilt of Raskolnikov is fascinating. Drawing close to the desired confession, Porfiry decides that he owes the tortured intellectual suspect a "statement of his own transgressions." In acknowledging these excesses, Porfiry accomplishes at least two things. First, he boasts of a "stepping across" which Raskolnikov thought could be accomplished only through crime. Lawyers, too, he seems to say, act on a moral level quite different from that of the ordinary bourgeois. But second, Porfiry associates himself with the novelist who has created him; for his "laying bare" of professional techniques duplicates the self-conscious use of narrative techniques within the novel. This may be why the interviews culminate in Porfiry's lengthy third-person narration of Raskolnikov's homicidal actions. The inquisitor's recapitulation of the crime embellishes upon the original account in part 1, but remains essentially truthful to it.

As the more perfect evocation of the legal theme in *The Brothers Karamazov* exemplifies, the association in *Crime and Punishment* of lawyer with criminal on the one hand and with author on the other raises questions which the earlier novel does not fully answer. Since Porfiry's account of the crime and the criminal during this final interview achieves essential accuracy, it would appear that Dostoevski was not yet fully ready to face the self-critical implications of legalistic ratiocination. This task was left to his last masterpiece. However, he plants the seeds of that recognition during the extremely brief trial scene at the end of *Crime and Punishment*.

Fittingly placed in the epilogue, which contains several aesthetically weak reversals, the description of Raskolnikov's trial emphasizes the creative falsehood of the inquisitor. The defendant (with Porfiry's tacit consent) pleads poverty and even emotional instability as the reasons for the double homicide. While these lies definitively bar Raskolnikov from the superhuman status he vainly sought, they also indicate the way in which legal recreation of events sometimes serves more to fulfill the psychological and artistic goals of the lawyer than to achieve justice in the individual case. Porfiry, having totally dominated Raskolnikov in the pretrial interviews, has no enduring personal need to see the defendant pay the supreme penalty for what was, after all, at least one premeditated murder. The inquisitor therefore deletes from his dossier (and hence keeps from the procurator) his firm insight into the utterly intellectualized nature of the crime. At the trial, Raskolnikov is presented as just another starving student, and thus deserving of a sharply mitigated sentence in exile.

Foreshadowing the theme fully expressed in his final work, and in Camus' novels about the law, Dostoevski indicates that the process of legal investigation contains the potential for imaginative artistry. Porfiry, fascinated by the criminal mind, perhaps even envious of it, plays a game of life and death within the context of a perfectly respectable professional position. The lines between lawyer and criminal start to blur; the lines between lawyer and novelist begin to appear. But since Porfiry's artifice at the end of *Crime and Punishment* allows the reader to take from his experience the satisfaction that a protagonist for whom he has oddly sensed tremendous sympathy despite two brutal murders emerges from the novel a free and changed man, Dostoevski perhaps saw no reason, for the moment, to explore those lines of identity. Fifteen years later, having added greatly to his store of legal knowledge and artistic experience, Dostoevski was again ready to grapple with the crucial significance of imaginative legal investigation.

# MICHAEL T. KAUFMAN

## Polish Director Finds Haunting Relevance in Dostoyevsky†

WARSAW

The thing that most impressed Andrzej Wajda as he adapted "Crime and Punishment" for the stage was how accurately prophetic Dostoyevsky's great novel had been in projecting what the Polish director terms our contemporary era of theoretical crimes.

"When Raskolnikov killed the old woman money lender, it was a murder in the style of our century, a murder to justify a theory," said the 60-year-old film and theater director as he sat in the garden of his Warsaw home discussing the production which his theater, the Stary, or old, Theater of Cracow will present starting Friday at the Pepsico Summerfare festival at Purchase, in New York's Westchester County.

Mr. Wajda explained how the protagonist Raskolnikov's defense of justifiable murder, in an article that the impoverished St. Petersburg

† *New York Times*, July 6, 1986. Reprinted by permission of the *New York Times*.

student writes before committing the actual crime, struck him as a contemporary idea, whose tragic realization has come in our time. "Who can kill and who cannot," said Mr. Wajda. "How familiar I find the argument. From Hitler's extermination camps to the newest political murders, behind all of them is the same argument of authorized, permissible spilling of blood."

At one point in the book Porfiry Petrovitch, the prosecutor to whom Raskolnikov gradually justifies his killings, ironically expresses thanks that the student's theory was relatively modest. Mr. Wajda quoted the line, "It's a good thing that you, sir, murdered only the old woman, because if you had thought up some worse theory, well . . ." The director paused a second to shed the character and on his own added: "Unfortunately, significantly worse theories have been invented and enacted."

"It seems to me that the particular cry of Dostoyevsky," Mr. Wajda continued, "was to warn us of a time that was coming—a time that is now here—when it is not only a bizarre student who kills the two old ladies to realize a point, but terrorists in almost every city who are ready to kill anyone. They believe they are honest men and they defend their acts by citing a now general view that killing is justified by theory."

Mr. Wajda, who is best known in the West for his direction of such recent films as "Man of Iron," "Man of Marble," "Danton" and "Love in Germany," has over the last 26 years alternated between film work and directing the Stary Theater. The two activities, he says, are as fundamentally distinct as sculpture and painting. "When I am in the theater, I forget that I ever directed a film, and when I am directing a film, there is nothing that I bring to it from my theater experience."

The theater production of "Crime and Punishment," which was first staged in 1984, is a case in point. Mr. Wajda cut back on the action, which he says he would have stressed more in a film, and gave free rein to the long speeches of the student and prosecutor.

"Theater is for words, for beautiful, complicated words and thoughts," said Mr. Wajda. "For a long time people have been saying that film, or television would kill theater, but it has not happened and it will not happen. People will always go to the theater to hear words, dialogue, speeches and ideas, which are the basis of Western theatrical traditions."

In rereading the novel—the third Dostoyevsky work after "The Possessed" and "The Idiot" that he has adapted for the stage, Mr. Wajda determined that its heart lay not in the action of the murders but in the remarkable long dialogues between Raskolnikov, the student (played by Jerzy Radziwilowicz who starred in "Man of Marble" and "Man of Iron"), and Porfiry Petrovitch, the prosecutor (played by Jerzy Stuhr). "At the outset, the reader knows that Raskolnikov is the murderer and for that reason, 'Crime and Punishment' does not ask who killed, but rather it seeks the answer of what was the motivation."

According to Mr. Wajda, the killing is no gratuitous act stemming from the perverse psychology of some aberrant being. "It was a crime that Dostoyevsky knew presaged other crimes to come and through those long exchanges he was telling us that we must look closely and learn about sin, guilt and redemption and religious ideas."

Essentially, the play consists of three long exchanges between the prosecutor and the student and three other scenes in which Raskolnikov confides his secrets to Sonia. "Here I am much more intrigued by the punishment than by the crime," said Mr. Wajda.

# A Chronology

# of Dostoevsky's Life

1819  Dostoevsky's father, Michael Dostoevsky, marries Marie Ne-
      chaeva.
1820  First son, Michael, born.
1821  Father becomes doctor in Hospital for the Poor, Moscow.
      *Oct.* 30 Fyodor Mikhailovich born.
1837  *Jan.* 29 Poet Pushkin killed in a duel.
      *Feb.* 27 Dostoevsky's mother dies.
      *May* The two brothers move to Petersburg.
      *July* The father retires and moves to the country with the two
          youngest daughters.
1839  *Jan.* Dostoevsky enters military Engineering School.
      *June* Dostoevsky's father is murdered by his serf peasants be-
          cause of his cruelty and strictness.
1842  *Aug.* Dostoevsky commissioned Second Lieutenant.
1844  *Aug.* He leaves the military service, begins literary career. Starts
          writing *The Poor Folk.*
1845  *Summer* *The Poor Folk* is a great success with literary leaders.
1846  *Spring* Dostoevsky meets Petrashevsky. Begins to suffer epileptic
          seizures. Publishes *The Double.*
1848  Participates more and more in political discussions of Petrashev-
          sky's circle.
1849  *Apr.* 23 Dostoevsky arrested. Later sentenced to death. Re-
          prieved at last minute, on execution scaffold in Petersburg
          square.
1850–54  Spends four years as convict in Siberia, in Omsk.
1854–59  Serves as common soldier in Siberia, in Semipalatinsk.
1857  *Feb.* Marries Maria Isaeva.
1859  Is permitted to live in Tver, later, in St. Petersburg. Resumes
          writing. Two of his stories are published.
1860  Publishes *The House of the Dead* about his Siberian experiences.
          A two-volume edition of his works appears.
1861  Emancipation of Serfs Proclamation. *The Insulted and The
          Injured* published.
1862  Visit to France and England.
1862–63  Liaison with Apollinaria Suslova.
1860–63  Writes for and edits magazine *Time* (*Vremya*).
1863  *May* *Time* stopped by the government.
      *Aug.–Oct.* Stays in France and Italy.
1864  *Jan.* Permitted to publish new magazine, *Epoch* (*Epokha*).
      *Apr.* His wife dies.
      *June* *Epoch* stops because of lack of funds.
      *July* His brother Michael dies.
      Visits Germany. Sees Suslova. Works on *Crime and Punish-
          ment.* Two-vol. edition of his works published by Stellovsky.

1866 Works on *Crime and Punishment*. Proposes to and is accepted by Anna Grigorievna Snitkina. Further volumes of his works published.

1867 Stays in Germany; gambles. Works on *The Idiot*.

1868–69 Lives abroad—in Germany and Switzerland.

1871 Returns to Petersburg. Works on *The Possessed*. *The Possessed* published in *The Russian Messenger*.

1873–76 Dostoevsky collaborates on magazine *The Citizen*. Writes *The Raw Youth*. Lives in Staraya Russa and visits Germany three times.

1875 *The Raw Youth* published.

1876–77 Publishes magazine *Writer's Diary*

1876 Nov. Writes story *The Gentle Spirit*.

1878 May Dostoevsky's three-year-old son Alexey dies of epilepsy. Dostoevsky and the philosopher Vladimir Solovyov visit together the Optina monastery. Begins work on *The Brothers Karamazov*.

1879 *The Brothers Karamazov* begins to appear.

1880 June 8 Dostoevsky delivers widely acclaimed speech at dedication of Pushkin's statue. Concludes work on *The Brothers Karamazov*.

1881 Jan. 28 Dostoevsky dies after three days of illness, of lung hemorrhages.

## Dates of Publication of *Crime and Punishment* in Dostoevsky's Lifetime

1. In 1866 *Russian Messenger* (*Russki Vestnik*)
   Jan., No. 61: Part I, chapters 1–7
   Feb.: chapters 8–13 [in final version, chapters 1–7 of Part II]
   Apr., No. 62: Part II, chapters 1–6 [in final version, chapters 1–6 of Part III]
   June, No. 63: chapters 7–9 [in final version, chapters 1–4 of Part IV]
   July, No. 64: chapters 10–13 [in final version, chapters 5–6 of Part IV and chapters 1–3 of Part V]
   Aug., No. 65: chapters 14–15 [in final version, chapters 4–5 of Part V]
   Nov., No. 66: chapters 1–6 of Part III [in final version, chapters 1–6 of Part VI]
   Dec.: chapters 7–8 and Epilogue [in final version, chapters 7–8 of Part VI and Epilogue]

2. In two volumes, St. Petersburg, 1867 (somewhat shortened in comparison with magazine version; some stylistic changes).

3. As Volume IV of *Collected Works of F. M. Dostoevsky*, St. Petersburg, 1870 (same version as the 1867).

4. In two volumes, St. Petersburg, dated Dec., 1876; published in 1877, the same as the 1870 version except that Dostoevsky himself seems to have read the proofs for this edition and made several dozen corrections. It is this text which is usually reprinted and translated.

# Selected Bibliography

Works included in this volume are omitted from the bibliography.

## General Works on Dostoevsky

Berdyaev, Nicholas. *Dostoevsky*. New York, 1974.
Carr, Edward Hallett. *Dostoevsky, 1821–1881: A New Biography*. London, 1949.
Chapple, Richard L. *A Dostoevsky Dictionary*. Ann Arbor, 1983.
Coulson, Jessie. *Dostoevsky: A Self-Portrait*. London, 1962.
Cox, Gary. *The Tyrant and the Victim in Dostoevsky*. Columbus, 1984.
Dostoevsky, Anna G. *Dostoevsky: Reminiscences*. Ed. and trans. Beatrice Stillman. New York, 1975.
Fanger, Donald. *Dostoevsky and Romantic Realism*. Cambridge, 1965.
Frank, Joseph. *Dostoevsky, The Seeds of Revolt, 1821–1849; Dostoevsky: The Years of Ordeal, 1850–1859; Dostoevsky: The Stir of Liberation, 1860–1865*. Princeton, 1983–86. The first three of a five-volume biography.
Fülop-Miller, Rene. *Fyodor Dostoevsky*. New York, 1950.
Gide, Andre. *Dostoevsky*. New York, 1926.
Gifford, Henry. *The Hero in His Time: A Theme in Russian Literature*. London, 1950.
Grossman, L. P. *Dostoevsky: A Biography*. Trans. M. Mackler. London, 1974.
Hingley, Ronald. *The Undiscovered Dostoevsky*. London, 1962.
Ivanov, Vyacheslav. *Freedom and the Tragic Life: A Study in Dostoevsky*. New York, 1952.
Jackson, Robert Louis. *The Art of Dostoevsky*. Princeton, 1981.
Jackson, Robert L. *Dostoevsky's Quest for Forms: A Study of His Philosophy of Art*. New Haven, 1966.
Jones, John. *Dostoevsky*. Oxford, 1983.
Krieger, Murray. *The Tragic Vision*. New York, 1960.
Lord, Robert. *Dostoevsky: Essays and Perspectives*. Berkeley, 1970.
Magarshack, David. *Dostoevsky*. New York, 1963.
Merezhkovsky, Dmitri. *Tolstoy as Man and Artist, with an Essay on Dostoevsky*. New York, 1952.
Miller, Robin Feuer. *Critical Essays on Dostoevsky*. Critical Essays on World Literature. Ed. Robert Lecker. Boston, 1986.
Mirsky, Dmitri. *History of Russian Literature*. New York, 1974.
Mochulsky, Konstantin. *Dostoevsky: His Life and Works*. Princeton, 1967.
*Modern Fiction Studies* (Dostoevsky number) 4.3 (Autumn 1958). Contains articles and bibliography.
Muchnic, Helen. *Dostoevsky's English Reputation (Smith College Studies in Modern Language* 20.3–4). Northampton, 1939.

Pachmuss, Temira. *F. M. Dostoevsky: Dualism and Synthesis of the Human Soul.* Carbondale, 1963.

Peace, Richard. *Dostoevsky: An Examination of the Major Novels.* Cambridge, 1971.

Poggioli, Renato. *The Phoenix and the Spider.* Cambridge, 1957.

Rosen, Nathan. "Chaos and Dostoevsky's Women." *Kenyon Review* 20:257–77.

Seduro, V. *Dostoevsky in Russian Literary Criticism.* New York, 1957.

Seeley, F. F. "Dostoevsky's Women." *Slavic and East European Review* (London) June 1961.

Simmons, Ernest J. *Dostoevsky: The Making of a Novelist.* London, 1950.

Steiner, George. *Tolstoy or Dostoevsky.* New York, 1959.

Terras, Victor. *F. M. Dostoevsky: Life, Works, and Criticism.* Fredericton, 1984.

Vivas, Eliseo. *Creation and Discovery.* New York, 1955.

Wasiolek, Edward. *Dostoyevsky.* Cambridge, 1964.

Wellek, Rene, ed. *Dostoevsky: A Collection of Critical Essays.* New York, 1962.

Yarmolinsky, Avraham. *Dostoevsky: Works and Days.* New York, 1971.

Zander, L. A. *Dostoevsky.* London, 1948.

## Works on Crime and Punishment

Blackmur, R. P. "Crime and Punishment: A Study of Dostoevsky." *Chimera* 1943; and in Ray B. West, ed. *Essays in Modern Literary Criticism.* New York, 1952.

Jackson, Robert Louis, ed. *Twentieth-Century Interpretations of* Crime and Punishment. Englewood Cliffs, 1974.

Johnson, Leslie. *The Experience of Time in* Crime and Punishment. Columbus, 1985.

Lindenmeyr, Adele. "Raskolnikov's City and the Napoleonic Plan." *Slavic Review* 35 (1976): 37–47.

Reeve, Frank D. "In the Stinking City: Dostoevskij's *Crime and Punishment.*" *Slavic and East European Journal* 4:127–36; and in Reeve, F. D. *The Russian Novel.* New York, 1966: 159–204.

Snodgrass, W. D. "Crime for Punishment: The Tenor of Part One." *Hudson Review* 13: 202–53.

Wasiolek, Edward, ed. Crime and Punishment *and the Critics.* San Francisco, 1961. A collection of articles about the novel.

———, ed. and trans. *The Notebooks for* Crime and Punishment. Chicago, 1967.

———. "On the Structure of *Crime and Punishment.*" *PMLA* March 1959.